CORPORATE PUBLIC AFFAIRS

Interacting With Interest Groups, Media, and Government

LEA's COMMUNICATION SERIES
Jennings Bryant/Dolf Zillmann, General Editors

For a complete list of titles in LEA's Communication Series, please contact Lawrence Erlbaum Associates, Publishers, at www.erlbaum.com

CORPORATE PUBLIC AFFAIRS

Interacting With Interest Groups, Media, and Government

Otto Lerbinger

Boston University

Routledge
Taylor & Francis Group
New York   London

First published by Lawrence Erlbaum Associates, Inc., Publishers
10 Industrial Avenue
Mahwah, New Jersey 07430

Reprinted 2008 by Routledge
Routledge
Taylor & Francis Group
270 Madison Avenue
New York, NY 10016

Routledge
Taylor & Francis Group
2 Park Square
Milton Park, Abingdon
Oxon OX14 4RN

Transferred to Digital Printing 2007

Cover design by Tomai Maridou

Library of Congress Cataloging-in-Publication Data

Lerbinger, Otto.
Corporate public affairs : interacting with interest groups,
    media, and government / Otto Lerbinger.
        p.   cm. — (LEA's communication series)
    Includes bibliographical references and index.
    ISBN 0-8058-5642-0 (cloth : alk. paper)
    ISBN 0-8058-5643-9 (pbk. : alk. paper)
    1. Corporations—Public relations. 2. Corporations—Politi-
    cal activity. 3. Social responsibility of business. I. Title.
    II. Series.
HD59.L47   2005
659.2'85—dc22   2005045462
                                                        CIP

Contents in Brief

v

Contents

II: Interest Group Strategies

III: Media Strategies

V: Dominance Versus Competition

Preface

A corporation's sociopolitical environment can affect its profitability, growth, and, in extreme cases, its very survival. Not surprisingly, corporations have established a public affairs function—often an extension of existing public relations—to deal with that environment. In recognition of this function, business schools have added courses to their business and society curriculum. The professionals who specialize in dealing with the external environment are called corporation public affairs vice-presidents and directors.

Public affairs professionals are given responsibility for many activities, such as government relations, direct and grassroots lobbying, issues management, and media relations. All of these activities, discussed in the book, focus on the generation and application of political power. In a sense, the professional's task is to convert a corporation's economic resources into various forms of political power.

Practically everybody wants to deal with others advantageously in our dynamic society, where success depends not only on marketplace strength but also political shrewdness. The powerful flourish; the weak wither. Within organizations, all managers are aware of power: who has authority over others and who has access to needed resources. The same is true externally, where an organization may be confronted by labor unions, environmental and other social action groups, the media (including the pervasive Internet), and all three branches of government: executive, legislative, and judicial.

Strategies and their supporting tactics, however, cannot effectively be applied unless professionals understand their underlying theory and dynamics. Each chapter is therefore interlaced with management and communication concepts—some from professionals and some from academicians. Such knowledge helps prevent the blind application of campaigns that worked elsewhere but might not be appropriate for a current situation. In part, therefore, this book serves as a manual of corporate public affairs strategies and tactics

Readers can view each part of the book from several angles: as dynamic forces in a corporation's sociopolitical environment, as stages in a public affairs campaign, and as major modes of communication: opinion leader communication, public communication, legislative communication, and litigation communication. Following the life cycle concept of issues management (discussed in chap. 1), a professional can decide which stage is appropriate for a particular situation (e.g., an emerging issue or one already on the legislative agenda). The strategies and techniques associated with a particular stage can then be examined and applied.

The book frequently refers to the model of a political marketplace: the stage on which the players interact. The demand side is represented by corporations and interest groups, as well as the public; that is, citizens with their "voting power"—a parallel to consumers' "purchasing power." The supply side is represented by legislative and regulatory bodies that "sell" public policies and a variety of favors, such as tax benefits, subsidies, and tariff protection to the buyers. Using the metaphor of the political marketplace has several advantages. One is a reminder to management that success in this marketplace is often of equal importance to success in the marketplace for goods and services. As corporations, following their markets, become more global, they also subject themselves to the laws and agreements of other governments and international bodies.

A second advantage of the political marketplace metaphor is that it reminds us of the need to be competitive and to use marketing tools while considering the long-term requirement of maintaining a competitive system. Profit maximization guides business behavior in the competitive marketplace; similarly, the quest to attain preeminent power is the motivation behind a corporation's dealings with others. However, just as some corporations temper profit maximization with concerns of social responsibility, their penchant to win in the political marketplace shows concern for continuing corporate legitimacy and survival of the free enterprise system. Public affairs professionals must take responsibility for this concern, or they will unwittingly erode corporate reputation and jeopardize public confidence in business.

Part I of the book, consisting of chapter 1, provides an overview of the corporate public affairs function. Of special importance is a review of activities engaged in by public affairs professionals and an inventory of available political resources. The chapter also summarizes the tool of issues management and one of its key concepts, the life cycle of an issue, which involves four stages: when an issue first emerges, when the public becomes involved, when lawmakers and regulators ponder and initiate legislation, and when lawyers and judges adjudicate disputes. Subsequent parts of the book are organized according to these stages: interest group strategies, media strategies, legislative strategies, and litigation strategies.

Part II—on interest group strategies—deals with the myriad interest groups in the United States, such as labor unions and environmental, consumer, women's, and human rights groups, that compose a powerful force. They promote their agendas, make demands on corporations, and insist on the inclusion of their interests in a firm's profit-making calculations. Confrontations between interest groups and corporations contribute to media exposure and sometimes involve lawsuits that seek compliance and punishment. Chapter 2 discusses such contrasting strategies as containment and engagement, as well as various "opinion leader communication" techniques to deal with interest groups. Chapter 3 shows how environmental groups and others use the process of public participation and the increasingly used strategies of conflict resolution to reconcile their differences with others and to achieve mutual benefit.

Part III—on media strategies—recognizes the media's increasing coverage of business events, especially negative ones, that have tremendous power both to undermine corporate credibility and to support public policy positions. Serving as society's watchdog, they draw attention to product flaws, management misconduct, environmental damage, and other criticisms of business. Corporate reputations, so important in attracting investors, recruiting workers, and selling products, can be tarnished and permanently ruined. The media also promote or criticize the policies and views of all contending actors in the political marketplace: government, corporations, and interest groups. Five chapters deal with media strategies—the first three with gaining greater control over what the media say, and the next two with desired long-term structural changes in the media and how corporations communicate directly with its stakeholders and the public.

Part IV—governmental strategies—deals with all three branches of government: legislative, executive and judicial. Government is the most powerful force in a corporation's sociopolitical environment because it holds ultimate power and resources. In terms of power, it can restructure the marketplace, ban a product or demand a recall, impose environmental and occupational health and safety requirements, and restrict exportation. In terms of resources, government can grant licenses and loan guarantees, provide subsidies, and help promote the sale of products overseas. Three major ways of influencing lawmakers and regulators—direct and grassroots lobbying as well as electoral activities—are presented in chapters 9, 10, and 11. Chapter 12, "Litigation Communication," extends governmental communication to the judicial branch. Recognizing that ours is a litigious society, the chapter examines efforts to influence judges and juries. The outcome of lawsuits can undermine profits and seriously damage corporate reputation and viability.

Part V—"Dominance Versus Competition"—raises the question of how corporate power strategies have affected the political marketplace. Chapter 13, "Ascendancy of Corporate Power," assesses how well U.S. corporations have achieved their public affairs goals and whether some of the strategies and techniques used are harmful to themselves and society in the long run. Chapter 14 prescribes reforms required in corporate policies and behavior, as well as in the role of government, to achieve the norm of a competitive political system. Chapter 15 asserts that corporations must heed the public interest by recognizing the double bottom line of profits and social responsibility. After reviewing five levels of corporate social responsibility, the importance of engaging in constructive stakeholder relationships and incorporating the public interest in corporate governance is discussed. It also recognizes another scoreboard: corporate reputation, which is largely determined by the CEO's reputation. Using the marketplace metaphor, the book recommends that the healthiest state of affairs is continued competition among all legitimate contenders of power.

ACKNOWLEDGMENTS

Many professionals, colleagues, alumni, and students have contributed to this book. Kenneth Kansas, Frank LeBart, James Morakis, and Mary Ann Pires have shared their knowledge with me and my Corporate Public Affairs classes. Wes Pederson and his colleagues at the Public Affairs Council have generously provided reports on the latest developments in their field. Members of the Corporate Section and Public Affairs and Government Section of the Public Relations Society of America have contributed information about their programs and campaigns. Several graduate assistants—Lauren Knebel, Lillian Oben, MinJung Sung, and Sara Kemp—have helped with research and editorial improvements. I thank my colleague, Joyce Marcario, who applied her graphic design skills to the book's figures. My wife, Beth, has endured my unavailability for many events and served as my social conscience.

—*Otto Lerbinger*

I

Introduction

Part I sets the stage for exploring specific public affairs strategies for attaining power. A corporation's external environment must be mapped out in a manner that selects its most important aspects and simplifies them. Just as accountants observe money transactions and engineers and scientists concentrate on technological changes, public affairs professionals focus on the public issues, trends, and public policies that can affect a corporation. Like public relations people, they are mainly concerned with an organization's sociopolitical environment.

Public affairs professionals monitor the environment for issues and trends that affect their organizations. In a process called *issues management*, described in chapter 1, they then analyze issues and trends for the purpose of participating in a corporation's and society's public policy process. Once a corporation—or any other organization—formulates its policy position, it plans and executes campaigns and programs to influence government and other participants. The main purpose of this book is to help professionals choose the most effective influence strategies and techniques to accomplish those tasks within ethical limits and with a consideration for maintaining existing relationships.

Figure I.1 lists the functions involved in this public affairs process together with their interrelationships. The functions are arranged on three occupational levels: executive, professional, and technical. The executive level is where responsibility is lodged; the professional, where knowledge resides; and the technical, where skills predominate. The public affairs professional, centered in the middle professional level, serves as a counselor to management and a public affairs manager of the technical staff, in addition to exercising professional judgment on the two functions. Two loops connect the sociopolitical environment (shown on the bottom) with the corporation (shown on the top). The upward loop (on the left) describes the preliminary steps of issues management, which is a major tool discussed in chapter 1; the downward loop (on the right) completes the issues management process, showing how a public policy formulation is communicated and promoted to others. The public affairs campaign (Function 5) is a major organizing tool.

Public relations professionals will recognize that Fig. I.1 is a specialized application of functions that apply to the practice of their field. The upward loop is essentially the same but the downward loop would ap-

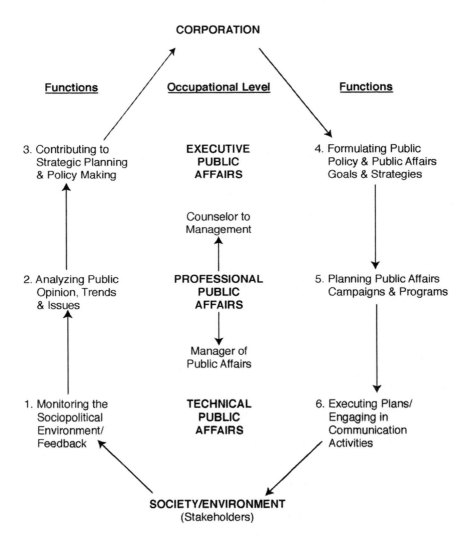

FIG. I.1.   Public affairs functions and levels.

ply to programs in investor relations, employee relations, community relations, customer relations, and relations with all publics that affect the corporation or that the corporation affects. Government and the variety of interest groups (e.g., environmental, consumer, women's, and human rights groups) that participate in the public policy process are simply seen as additional publics.

This view is in keeping with definitions of public relations. In its briefest form, public relations is the "management of communication between an organization and its publics."[1] Thus, as the seminal book, *Excellence in Public Relations and Communication Management* points out, the term *public affairs* "applies to fewer communication activities than does public relations/communication management. Public affairs applies to communication with government officials and other actors in the public policy arena."[2] Earlier definitions of public relations, which tended to be longer and more comprehensive, include the well-known definition by *Public Relations News*: "Public relations is the management function which evaluates public attitudes, identifies the policies and procedures of an individual or an organization with the public interest, and plans and executes a program of action to earn public understanding and acceptance."[3]

As shown in chapter 1, most listings of public affairs activities include more public relations activities than activities of any other type. Besides government relations, they include, among others, community relations, media relations, employee communications, and stockholder relations. The emphasis in these programs would, of course, relate to public policy issues.

The other public relations contribution to public affairs is its emphasis on establishing and maintaining long-term relationships between an organization and its publics. Thus the general orientation of public relations is not to get the upper hand over opponents and "to win," but to seek solutions that are mutually beneficial. Some of the more aggressive public affairs strategies, such as proactive media relations and fierce lobbying, would be replaced with collaborative efforts, such as those discussed in chapter 3.

The central role of communication in public affairs is fully reflected in chapter 1, and each of the succeeding parts of the book treats a predominant type of communication. Thus part II on interest groups highlights opinion leadership; part III on media relations highlights various forms of public communication; and part IV on government discusses lobbying, involvement in the electoral process, and the growing role of litigation communication.

For readers who are not sufficiently familiar with the modern public affairs department, chapter 1 also provides an overview of this function: its objectives, major activities associated with it, and political resources that support it. The chapters of this volume explain how these resources can be generated and applied.

ENDNOTES

1. James E. Grunig, editor, *Excellence in Public Relations and Communication Management* (Hillsdale, N.J.: Lawrence Erlbaum Associates, 1992), p. 4.
2. Ibid., pp. 5–6.
3. One source of this definition is in the popular textbook, Scott M. Cutlip, Allen H. Center, and Glen M. Broom, *Effective Public Relations*, 6th edition (Englewood Cliffs, N.J.: Prentice-Hall, 1985), p. 4.

Chapter 1

An Overview
of Corporate Public Affairs

The purpose of corporate public affairs is to attain sufficient power to enable an organization to achieve preferred outcomes in the political arena and to forge and maintain a sociopolitical environment favorable to it. To achieve this goal, public affairs professionals identify and analyze the environmental forces in the political arena and engage in political activities and various forms of communication to craft public policies. Political scientists, too, recognize the importance of the constant flow of messages among participants who initiate and influence what policies, laws, and regulations will govern society.[1] The process can aptly be called *strategic communication*, which seeks to manage the behavior of people and organizations to enhance the chances of achieving a desired outcome. As described by Jarol B. Manheim of George Washington University, it is "a term of art that refers to the use of sophisticated knowledge of such attributes of human behavior as attitude and preference structures, cultural tendencies, and media-use patterns, as well as knowledge of such relevant organizational behaviors as how news organizations make decisions regarding news content and how legislatures and government agencies form their agenda, to shape and target messages so as to maximize their desired impact while minimizing collateral damage."[2]

The three most important participant groups—interest groups, news media, and government—comprise the major forces in a corporation's sociopolitical environment. All three relate to the foundation of public opinion. As stated in Bernard C. Hennessy's classic book *Public Opinion*, "The measurement of public opinion is as important in a society as is the extent to which the support of the masses is necessary, or is thought to be necessary, for the legitimating or the operation of government."[3] In a democracy, public opinion links individuals with society's governing bodies, which on the widest level is government and on the narrowest level, a company's board of directors and management. Developing this idea more broadly, Harold Brayman, a pioneer corporate public relations director, said, "Because public opinion has learned nearly everywhere how to dominate governments, or influence them strongly, it has become the dominant force in our late 20th-century world; and it imposes upon institutions, our enterprises, and our philosophies a new demand for effective communication so that the decisions of the people will be wise and in the long-term interest of a civilized society."[4]

The growth and importance of public relations and the specialized function of public affairs is closely linked to public opinion. This connection was recognized by John W. Hill, one of the founders of the giant public relations firm of Hill & Knowlton. His book, *The Making of a Public Relations Man*, states, "as long as we live in a society where freedom of speech prevails and public opinion is the ultimate power, public relations will be an essential and important force."[5] Public relations professionals are concerned not only with opinions of the general public but with those of specific groups of people with common concerns, which they call *publics*. Hennessy's definition of public opinion reflects this focus: "for any given issue, public opinion is the collection of views, measurable or inferable, held by persons who have an interest in that issue."[6]

Instead of speaking of publics, this book uses the term *stakeholders*, which refers to any group that can affect an organization or be affected by it. The same definition applies to publics, but sometimes a distinction is drawn. James E. Grunig, editor of *Excellence in Public Relations and Communication Management*, says that publics become stakeholders when they become more aware and active. He describes stakeholders as "people who are linked to an organization because they and the organization have consequences on each other—they cause problems for each other.[7]

Communication means more than the creation of messages to inform and persuade. The aim in public affairs is to participate in the public policy process with government, interest groups, and the public with the aim of producing reasonable laws, regulations, and other understandings that enable a company to function at an optimal level. Although efforts are always undertaken to win others over to our own way of thinking, we must also be willing to listen to the views of others and modify our policies to achieve the best and most workable solutions. The goal is not necessarily to win a battle in the short run but to establish sound relationships with one's stakeholders and thereby achieve sustainable long-term growth and profitability. Public affairs professionals continually face the dilemma of seeking to get the upper hand in short-term contests without sacrificing existing relationships with opponents and the public good will necessary in the long term.

MODERN FUNCTION OF PUBLIC AFFAIRS

Simply defined, *public affairs* is an organization's concern for its sociopolitical environment. A fuller and more formal definition, used in a Foundation for Public Affairs survey, is "the management function responsible for interpreting the corporation's non-commercial environment and managing the corporation's responses to that environment."[8] Douglas G. Pinkham, president of the Public Affairs Council, further explains public affairs as "the management function that interprets and works to strengthen a corporation's business environment."[9] Public affairs refers to a company's political strategy, which John F. Mahon, an academician, defines as "those activities taken by organizations to acquire, develop, and use power to obtain an advantage (a particular allocation of resources) in a situation of conflict."[10]

Although emphasizing the social and political factors, this environment indirectly includes economic factors, which, however, are already adequately represented by the duties and responsibilities of operating managers. Sometimes public affairs is called *external relations* because of its emphasis on the environment surrounding a corporation. Schools of business and management now recognize the importance of a business's sociopolitical environment through books and courses such as *Business and Society*,[11] *Business Environment and Public Policy*,[12] and *Business, Government, and Society*.[13]

What happens in the public affairs arena can have an impact on the bottom line as great as, or even greater than, financial, marketing, and manufacturing decisions. Success in achieving deregulation, for example, has helped energy and telecommunication companies expand and develop new markets. Corporate executives used to fret over the question of whether it was proper for business to become active in the political arena. The clarion call for a change in attitude was reflected in a 1959 book, *The Businessman's Guide to Practical Politics*, in which J. J. Wuerthner, Jr., the author, proclaimed:

> The handwriting on the wall is perfectly clear for all to read. Businessmen must either set aside their traditional aversion and timidity regarding political action and accept the responsibility for the free enterprise system that is their privilege to bear or else stand silently by, content to see others— who realize that the game of politics and government are one and the same thing—destroy not only American business but also the United States as we have known it.[14]

The business community gradually decided that when corporate profitability, growth, and survival are affected by what government, innumerable interest groups, and the media do, they must not merely react but become proactive. Strengthening the corporate public affairs function, therefore, has been a top priority of corporations. Furthermore, public affairs is seen not just as a staff function. Chief executive officers (CEOs) and other top-line managers have become personally involved and all line managers are expected to assume some responsibility.

In the academic world, corporate political activity was recognized by Edwin Epstein in his 1969 book, *The Corporation in American Politics*.[15] He refers to John Kenneth Galbraith's *The New Industrial State*,[16] in which the author not only perceived a symbiotic relationship between the "industrial system" and the state but predicted that the "previously sacrosanct line between publicness and privateness" would become less and less distinct.[17]

Mapping the Sociopolitical Environment

Public relations professionals have long found it practical to view the relationship of their company to society by listing the publics who are in some way connected with the corporation. A minimum list includes investors, employees, customers, community citizens and groups, and government, as shown in the "wheel" diagram in Fig. 1.1.

A useful way of visualizing the public affairs function is to map a company's sociopolitical environment by recognizing the specific persons and stakeholders that relate to the company. Indirectly, this mapping recognizes the major "forces" that exert pressure on the corporation. This essential information enables a public affairs professional to analyze a situation, problem, or crisis faced by a corporation. For public affairs purposes, the stakeholders shown in Fig. 1.2 can be listed in a column and next to each additional columns can show the following

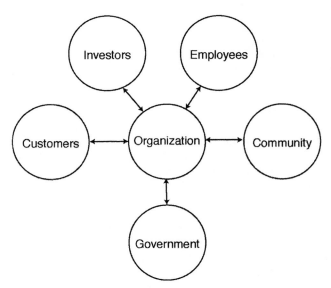

FIG. 1.1.   The corporation and its publics.

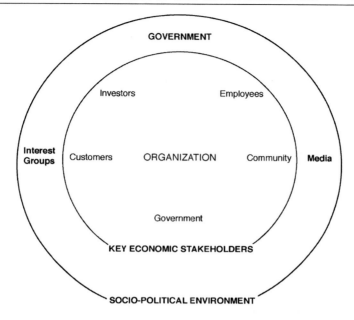

FIG. 1.2.   Key economic stakeholders and forces in sociopolitical environment.

information: (a) the basis of the relationship (e.g., investors provide capital); (b) attitude toward the company, whether cooperative, antagonistic, or neutral; (c) issues important to it; (d) its stand on each issue; and (e) the kind and amount of power possessed by it.

A more complete list of publics appears in a management book, *Organization Theory and Design*, by Richard L. Daft. He refers to "sectors":

• Financial resources.
• Market.
• Technology.
• Economic.
• Government.
• Sociocultural.
• International.
• Industry (e.g., competitors).
• Raw Materials (e.g., suppliers).
• Human resources.[18]

In addition to maintaining a core list of stakeholders, a company can add supplementary items to the list for specific situations or campaigns. For example, in dealing with a crisis, a list might include all the public officials and other stakeholders who should be notified when a crisis occurs; in a lobbying campaign in support of a trade agreement, another list might include those groups for or against it.

A more sophisticated and practical representation of an organization's stakeholders—this term, rather than publics, is favored in almost all management literature—and sociopolitical environment is John F. Mahon's *extended organizational chart*. It depicts three circles around a corporation:

- Resource base: Investors, shareowners and lenders; customers and users; employees.
- Industry structure: Regulatory authorities; joint venture partners and alliances; supply chain associates.
- Social political arena: Governments, local communities and citizens; unions; private organizations.[19]

Figure 1.2 is a simplified depiction of McMahon's extended organizational chart. The inner circle is like Mahon's resource base except that it includes the community. From an economics viewpoint, which refers to capital, labor, and land as the three basic factors of production, the community represents land and the accompanying infrastructure (roads, utilities, etc.). In addition, the inner circle includes customers because they provide the revenue needed to pay for the factors of production and provide the incentive for entrepreneurs. Omitting the middle circle of industry structure, the outer circle shows the three forces discussed in this chapter: government, interest groups (including labor unions), and, not shown in other diagrams, the media. It should be noted that whereas management can exercise authority of its employees, it cannot do so with its extended stakeholders; it must rely on persuasion.

Generating Political Power

The basic function of public affairs is to help an organization generate political power and use it effectively to influence public policy. Political power is the external equivalent of authority within an organization, namely, the capacity to get things done in a desired way, rather than be "pushed around" by government, labor, public interest groups, and the media. A manager typically craves maximum autonomy in affecting outcomes—to operate with the least constraints on decision making and actions. Public affairs extends the concept of formal authority to influential relationships with stakeholders in the company's external environment, thus affording managers greater discretion and wider freedom of action to make the kinds of business decisions that are efficient and profitable.

The purpose of this and following chapters is to help public affairs managers recognize the types of power they possess and to apply these resources effectively and efficiently. Box 1.1 lists the political resources developed by Microsoft to influence government when its president Bill Gates belatedly realized that it had to enter the political arena.

Converting Economic Resources Into Political Power.

Because corporations, especially large ones, have more economic resources than other groups in society, a core public affairs function is to convert economic resources into political power, for example, using money to purchase media space and time, sponsor surveys, and hire well-connected and expert lobbyists.

The corporations' economic role enables them to gain political clout through *patronage*, which Edwin Epstein defines as the dependency of other businesses and social groups on the activities of the corporation, such as providing jobs. Furthermore, financial and other economic resources enable a company to make political contributions that help it to gain access, if not outright influence (see chap. 11). Corporate philanthropic contributions, rather than being purely altruistic, may also be intended to influence nonprofit organizations and social action groups. As Richard Eells has convincingly stated in his *Corporate Giving in a Free Society*, corporations may engage in a "philanthropic design" that seeks to strengthen and preserve the many nonprofits in the private sector of society, thereby lessening the potential growth of the government sector.[24] His rationale is consistent with the modern approach of strategic corporate philanthropy, which is discussed in chapter 15.

Human and Other Relational Resources.

A corporation's human resources and relationships with various stakeholders are a further source of political strength. Employees constitute a talented technostructure with expertise in such politically significant areas as public relations, lobbying, and law. When a company, or coalition of companies, imbues employees with a common sense of purpose, it can mobilize them to write letters and engage in other forms of grassroots lobbying. The impact is enhanced when a company employs large numbers of employees who are geographically distributed in many congressional districts. When employees are willing to do volunteer work in community and political organizations, a company's reputation for public service is strengthened, and this may be translated into political gain. Companies can extend and fortify their relationships with other stakeholders: investors, community citizens, customers, suppliers, dealers, and others.

The high organizational and social status of the CEO and other top managers is a special human resource because it provides easier access to political figures and possible influence. Prominent executives may be on newspaper advisory boards and even on boards of directors. Furthermore, because of the wide acceptance of marketplace economics and the free enterprise system, corporations enjoy considerable legitimacy as long as they produce valued products and services. Legitimacy might be

Box 1.1 Political Resources Used by Microsoft to Influence Government[21]

- Political campaign contributions: Gave $1.5 million to candidates in both parties, plus soft money gifts of over $860,000 and $1 million to help underwrite the two political conventions in the summer of 2000.
- Legal talent: Engaged blue-chip law firms and legal experts, constraining major firms from working for Microsoft's competitors.
- Lobbyists: Built an in-house lobby shop of 14, from zero in 1995, and spent $4.6 million on lobbying in 1999. One of the lobbyists hired is Ralph Reed, who is George W. Bush's top adviser.[22]
- Direct lobbying: Chairman Bill Gates and CEO Steve Ballmer visited Washington, DC, immediately after Judge Jackson's April 3 ruling that Microsoft violated antitrust laws. Gates participated in a technology summit set up by President Clinton and then visited congressional leaders in four meetings on Capitol Hill.
- Grassroots pressure: Organized a website called the Freedom to Innovate Network. Shareholders received a letter, dated April 4, that defends its antitrust position and lets them "know where we stand and what you can do to help." The letter states Microsoft created the network "to provide an effective method for you and other concerned citizens to communicate directly with government officials."
- Public relations: After Judge Jackson's April 3 ruling that Microsoft had stifled innovations, Microsoft spent millions on television ads featuring Bill Gates talking about Microsoft's innovations. And after Jackson's April 30 proposal to break the company into two units, Microsoft placed a full-page ad, signed by Chairman Bill Gates and President and CEO Steve Ballmer, that appeared in the May 1 editions of major newspapers.
- Charitable giving: A multimillion dollar effort by the Gates Foundation, including $10 million to the U.S. Capitol Visitors Center.
- Think tanks: Wrote six-digit checks to those that supported its position, and withdrew support from those that didn't (e.g., the American Enterprise Institute, because of Robert H. Bork, a former federal judge and one of the institute's senior fellows).
- Opinion polls: Funded and distributed to the media polls that showed lack of public interest in the Department of Justice case.[23]
- Television image advertising: Put a friendly face on its name instead of hawking its products in trade publications. In three new television commercials, one depicted the company's technology as a positive force in society; a second showed a mischievous son trying to tap into a website his mother warned him not to go to, but is stopped by safeguards installed on his computer; a third showed a dyslexic girl in her bedroom using a computer program to help her learn how to read.[24]

reflected in public goodwill stemming from a favorable corporate image, which would be lost, at least temporarily, by public outrage against questionable or outright unethical and illegal behavior by a corporation. A company's legitimacy is further reinforced when it has an impressive history and a corporate culture that commands respect and when it espouses policies that win public support.

Public Affairs Activities

Public affairs managers face the formidable task of mobilizing corporate political resources for the purpose of influencing other participants in the public policy process. This is achieved by engaging in an ever-enlarging variety of public affairs activities. The core activity has long been government relations. In fact, before the term *public affairs* was more widely used, the list of activities would simply refer to the three levels of government relations: federal, state, and local.

Today, however, public affairs is more than government relations, as is evident in the 1999–2000 survey of 1,087 companies by the Foundation for Public Affairs.[25] Based on 223 companies that had a formalized government relations program, the report listed 25 functions within a public affairs department. Only three specifically refer to government relations; another two—grassroots/grasstops lobbying and regulatory affairs—might be embraced by the term. The complete list is as follows:

Federal government relations (87%)
Business/trade association memberships (84%)
Issues management (83%)
State government relations (83%)
Grassroots/grasstops lobbying (81%)
Local government relations (79%)
Political action committee (75%)
Direct corporate contributions (73%)
Public policy group relations (70%)
Community relations (61%)
Public interest group relations (58%)
Regulatory affairs (55%)
Public relations (54%)
Media relations (54%)
Employee communications (49%)
International public affairs (43%)
Employee volunteer programs (40%)
Internet (38%)
Corporate foundation (35%)
Educational relations (35%)
Advertising (28%)
Environmental affairs (22%)
Stockholder relations (18%)

Institutional investor relations (13%)

Consumer affairs (13%)

Besides government, the list recognizes two other forces in the political arena: media relations and public policy group relations (i.e., public interest groups). The fourth, underlying force—the general public (expressed through public opinion)—is not explicitly listed, but is represented by reference to public relations and practically every stakeholder group associated with public relations: community relations, employee communications, educational relations, stockholder relations, institutional investor relations, and consumer affairs. Moreover, some activities associated with public relations are also included: direct corporate contributions, corporate foundations, employee volunteer programs, and advertising (presumably institutional and issues advertising). Public relations activities are obviously an integral part of public affairs.

The broad scope of public affairs beyond government relations and public relations is further reflected in the inclusion of several specialized activities: business/trade association membership, issues management, public policy group relations, political action committee, international public affairs, and the Internet. Of these, issues management, moved from seventh to third place since 1996, because, as stated in the Foundation's survey, it "has matured into a core public affairs function" and is a responsibility whose implementation is shared with staff and line executives elsewhere in a company (116 companies out of 213 report the regular involvement of non-public-affairs personnel in issues management).[26] As discussed throughout this volume, issues management serves as a major frame of reference for public affairs planning. Three other activities—business/trade association membership, public policy group relations, and political action committees—enable a corporation to leverage its political influence.

Inclusion of international public affairs recognizes the global arena in which corporations now operate. Although this book concentrates on the U.S. scene, most of the strategies and techniques are applicable, albeit with some modifications, in other countries. Furthermore, globalization is itself an issue, as well as the many specific issues relating to it (e.g., free trade, overseas codes of conduct, global warming, and protection of intellectual property rights).

The Public Policy Process

Public affairs extends beyond government relations because it entails a role in the public policy process larger than that of influencing legislative and regulatory decisions. It refers to all of the various ways public policy is made in our society to address the concerns of society. Thus a corporation may decide to work out its own public policy solution with stakeholders by voluntarily changing its corporate policies and behavior or by negotiating with stakeholders to arrive at a mutually acceptable solution. These solutions can be seen as an alternative public policy process to that of government and may occur at any of the three stages in the life cycle of an issue. There is an advantage to engaging in the process in the early stages of an issue's life cycle, when it emerges and when it involves the public. During these earlier stages, a company has a better chance to influence the outcome of an issue than after the process has proceeded to the public involvement or legislative stage.

When the Chemical Manufacturers Association (now called the American Chemical Society) adopted its Responsible Care program with guidelines that exceeded governmental requirements, this trade association engaged in public policy making. So did apparel makers such as Nike, Reebok, and Liz Claiborne when they formed a task force to develop a code to reassure the public that their products were not made in sweatshops.[27] Similarly, when one chain saw manufacturer decided to add a safety lock to its chain saws, despite opposition by its own trade association, the company engaged in policy making. Thus, the public policy process refers to all the various methods by which public policy is made by a diversity of organizations and groups in our society.[28]

One reason a company engages in a private public policy process is to preempt government action. An example is the Trojan Nuclear Plant of Portland General Electric, which hired the consulting firm of Kearns & West to engage in what was called collaborative planning. The aim was to find a win–win solution on the vital public policy issue of what to do with an ailing nuclear power plant beset with technical problems and one of the worst performance ratings in the nation. Portland General Electric was targeted by antinuclear groups, including the Coalition for Safe Power, Don't Waste Oregon, and Physicians for Social Responsibility. One of the groups, Don't Waste Oregon, sponsored a referendum on the November 1990 ballot to shut down the plant. Rather than face this possibility, the utility chose its own public policy process. Using a variety of research tools—focus group meetings, surveys, and dialogue sessions—a solution was agreed on by all concerned parties: The plant would be allowed to keep operating 2 more years without extensive retrofitting. (See chap. 3 for further details about this case.)

Openness With Stakeholders

A corporation commits itself to operating as an open system when it embraces public relations and public affairs. An open organization is permeable; it interacts with its environment at many points along its boundary with society. It is ready to listen to stakeholders, include their concerns in decision making, and sometimes involve them in coalitions and collaborative decision making. In contrast, a closed system is like a fortress, recognizing its interactions with society only through the economic marketplaces for necessary inputs (e.g., factors of production) and outputs (of its products and services).

Viewing an organization as an open system greatly influences how a corporation conducts its public affairs activities. First, by shunning a reactive approach, it favors a proactive or interactive approach. It seeks to shape the environment in which it operates and to work with groups in society rather than impose its own view on them.

These virtues of an open system are seen in sharp contrast to organizations that operate as closed systems. The latter are defensive, often deny criticism, and are often aggressive toward outside agitators and "antis" who stir up trouble. Indeed, some social activists are avowed protesters and "serial demanders" who are unwilling to consider arguments contrary to their stated positions. Business should not be similarly rigid and refuse to acknowledge the possible validity of social grievances and demands made by stakeholders. Furthermore, they shun direct confrontation with attackers in the hope of warding off unfavorable publicity. They will rely on legal approaches to "keep the hounds at bay," if not to defang or exterminate the opposition. Believing that conflicts are caused by public misunderstanding or ignorance, if not outright malice, they ask their public relations staff to "straighten people out" by creating public understanding, building favorable public opinion, and educating employees and the public on the "American way."

A second way in which operating as an open corporation influences public affairs activities is by accepting the concept of mutual benefit; that is, that both the corporation and its stakeholders can benefit. A corporation's responsibilities to society go beyond producing goods and services at a profit. While recognizing the primacy of operating in the interests of its stockholders, a corporation acknowledges that the interests of customers, employees, and the local community, as well as concern for the physical environment, must be factored into decision making. Managers seek stakeholder symmetry. Finally, a corporation honors a wider range of human values than solely economic ones.

Several public affairs arguments support the recognition of social responsibility. First, if a significant gap exists between public expectations and a corporation's social performance, the ensuing social tension leads to loss of public confidence in business and a demand for government intervention. This consequence defeats the corporate public affairs objective of maintaining a balance of power with government. Closely related to this objective is a second argument, that a company may wisely choose to resolve a grievance or demand by dealing directly with the stakeholder(s) involved. This option is not as available to companies that ignore stakeholders and their interests.

A third argument says that a public affairs campaign often requires grassroots support, which can more easily be achieved through sound relationships with a company's stakeholders and the support of public opinion.

THREE CHARACTERISTICS
OF PUBLIC AFFAIRS COMMUNICATION

Public affairs communication supports the public affairs function as practiced by large corporations, government, and public interest groups. Some basic knowledge of public affairs—including the related concepts of public policy process and issues management—is helpful in understanding the role of communication. Readers who already possess this knowledge can quickly scan this overview; others may want to study this background more carefully.

Public affairs communication possesses three characteristics: (a) It follows the steps of strategic campaign management; (b) it uses the process of issues management; and (c) it chooses media appropriate to the life cycle stage of an issue.

Strategic Campaign Management

Public affairs communication is part of strategic campaign management, which, in turn, relates to the broader concept of strategic planning or management. It is considered a critical characteristic of excellent public relations departments.[29] The basic idea is that everything an organization does must in some way relate to its goals. Thus, Richard Daft defines strategy as a "current set of plans, decisions, and objectives that have been adopted to achieve the organization's goals."[30] The relationship between goals and strategy is that goals define where an organization wants to go; strategy defines how it will get there. As Robert Dilenschneider, a public relations consultant, states, the central question in strategic thinking is, "Why are we doing this?"[31] In other words, goals must be considered, as well as their relationship to the organization's stated mission, or its basic purpose.

Besides reference to goals, strategic planning recognizes the growing significance of environmental impacts on an organization. Environmental scanning and monitoring not only identifies issues but also analyzes an organization's strengths and weaknesses in meeting the opportunities and threats in the environment—this is called SWOT analysis. This information helps public affairs professionals to find or correct the fit between external opportunities and internal strengths.

Communication activities are a major part of strategic campaign management. The relationship of communication messages and channels to other elements of an overall campaign must therefore be understood. The central focus of a campaign is its objectives, best defined as expected results. In public affairs, results pertain to the quality and agreeableness of public policies that are formulated. These policies appear in the form of government legislation and regulation or in agreements and understandings with a company's stakeholders—investors, employees, customers, suppliers, dealers, community citizens, and any other group that affects the success or failure of the company. In general terms, public affairs is effective when it enhances a company's power to shape events and the environment in which it must operate.

Strategic campaign management is implemented by designing a campaign, which uses some type of problem-solving process. In public relations, John E. Marston's RACE formula—which includes the stages of research, action, communication, and evaluation—continues to be one of the better known problem-solving processes.[32] Another version is that of Scott M. Cutlip, Allen H. Center, and Glen M. Broom, which lists four basic steps to solving problems: (a) defining the problem, (b) planning and programming, (c) taking action and communicating, and (d) evaluating the program.[33] A public affairs campaign implements the problem-solving process, which, like other communication campaigns, includes the following minimum components:[34]

1. Statement and analysis of the situation.
2. Objectives.
3. Strategy.
4. Target audiences.
5. Message.
6. Media/channels.
7. Timing.
8. Budget.
9. Evaluation.

The strategy component is especially important in public affairs because it establishes fundamental orientations. One element is how to view other participants in the public policy process: whether to play it alone or form coalitions, and whether to fight opponents or try to negotiate. Another is what organizational resources to employ, for example, whether to rely exclusively on expert lobbyists or to use other tools, such as grassroots lobbying and advocacy advertising.

Most other components refer to elements of a communication model: who says what (message), to whom (target audiences), through what channels (media/channels), and with what effects (evaluation). Timing and budget are additional variables.

Process of Issues Management

Public affairs communication uses the process of issues management, which is a powerful tool used by public affairs professionals to identify and evaluate governmental and societal issues that could significantly impact their organization.[35]

Issue Life Cycle.   A major framework of issues management is the categorization of an issue by its life cycle stage. Although different models are used to define the life cycle stages, a simplified one is the following (shown in Fig. 2.1 in chap. 2):

1. *Emerging issue stage.* An issue appears when a thought leader conceives it and attempts to gain support from interest group opinion leaders and their supporters. These issue initiators use media suitable for reaching small audiences.
2. *Public involvement stage.* If opinion leaders and the interest groups are successful in their publicity efforts, the mass media will report on the issue and thereby make the public aware of it.
3. *Legislative stage.* Legislators become aware of the issue from the media, from public opinion surveys, and directly from their constituents; then they proceed with the legislative process.
4. *Regulation/litigation stage.* Because laws are complex, government agencies interpret and implement them by formulating regulations. The ensuing regulations are often controversial, thus those affected by them file lawsuits to challenge them or defend themselves against suits brought by government and aggrieved groups to force compliance.

Issues in the life cycle stage of facing litigation or immediate legislative action usually receive urgent attention, whereas emerging issues are simply monitored. However, once an issue is on the public agenda (the media and the public talk about it), communication efforts must be undertaken, paying attention to active political participants. Public opinion surveys help determine how involved the general public or special publics are and what their leanings are. An examination of the media—perhaps using formal content analysis procedures—shows the amount and kind of media coverage the issue receives. Finally, any legal or regulatory aspects of an issue must be considered; for example, do antitrust laws or environmental laws apply, as well as possible constitutional considerations (e.g., free speech).

Issues Management Process.   Issues management is a problem-solving process that follows five steps: issue identification, issue prioritization, issue analysis, strategy formulation, and implementation.

1. *Issue identification.* By scanning and monitoring the sociopolitical environment, an organization lists the issues of immediate or potential concern to an organization. Scanning is a broader, less focused way of looking for issues, events, and trends relevant to an organization's strategic goals; monitoring focuses on the previously identified variables. The typical method of identifying issues is to talk with key executives and experts within one's company, other companies in an

industry, and trade associations. Another is to scan the literature relevant to one's industry, sometimes using the research technique of content analysis.

A further useful technique is scenario planning, especially relevant when one's environment is highly volatile and looking into the future is important. As two authorities on scenario writing said, "You can't predict the future, but you can put together a process that takes a pretty good shot at it in an uncertain world."[36] Scenarios are described by the Global Business Network as "tools for ordering one's perceptions about alternative future environments in which today's decisions might be played out."[37]

Scenario planning is different from forecasting because instead of extrapolating current trends from the present, scenarios present alternative images, some of which may be sharply discontinuous from known ones. The basic technique is to create a set of stories, written or spoken, built around carefully constructed plots. These stories can express multiple perspectives and give meaning to the complex events that stories present. Although there is no single standard for scenario writing, one approach is to present stylized narratives, much in the manner of a screenplay or novel. Each has a plot and contains a sequence of plausible, interrelated, connected events. More than one scenario is typically written; they usually come in sets of three, showing a trend progressing from the present to the future.

2. *Issue prioritization*. This process is used to select the top issues for attention. After compiling a list of 50 issues, for example, one company selected 10 for attention during the following year. Three criteria apply:

- Imminence of action: Concentrate on issues that have the highest chance of occurring, particularly in the near future.
- Impact on the organization: Focus on issues that have strategic importance and the greatest impact on the company activities in terms of profits, costs, and reputation.
- Actionability: Choose issues that you can do something about—either alone or with allies.

3. *Issue analysis*. Once an issue has been identified and assigned a high priority by a company, it is analyzed so that an effective strategy can be formulated. A blend of professional judgment, practical experience, and research competence is needed for a clear understanding of an issue and the appropriate response to it. Analysis requires an examination of 5 aspects of an issue: the nature of an issue; its life cycle stage; identification of political participants; importance of public opinion; amount and kind of media coverage; and its legal, regulatory, and constitutional context.

Regarding the nature of an issue, one of the most useful classifications was developed by Peter F. Bartha, research and analysis manager in the corporate affairs department of Imperial Oil.[38] He identified four types of issues:

- Universal—Affect the general public in a direct, personal manner (e.g., unemployment, inflation, energy crisis). Government is expected to deal with it in a relatively simple manner.
- Advocacy—Groups claiming to represent broad public interests, such as environmental and consumer groups, initiate an issue that is a potential rather than actual problem for most of the public. The typical solution is the belief that "somebody (not necessarily government) ought to do something about it."
- Selective—Matters of concern to special interest groups based on demographic, geographic, occupational, sectoral, or other similar criteria (e.g., tariff protection for the steel industry). Involved groups are likely to concentrate their efforts on building up their own constituency rather than on broad grassroots support, unless they feel they can relate their special interest with the public interest.
- Technical—Matters the public is willing to leave to experts (e.g., regulatory issues). These issues are negotiated by specialists in interest groups and government bureaucracy on the basis of well-reasoned and well-documented arguments.

4. *Strategy formulation.* An organization decides on the position it will take on an issue and how it will respond to it. Issue analysis will suggest whether a company should contain or resolve an emerging issue or become proactive and influence public opinion before others do—following the reasoning that once opinions are crystalized, they are difficult to change. Thus, if an emerging issue gains momentum and the public is likely to become aware of it, a company's strategy is to act quickly to shape opinions. Should legislators become interested in an issue, it can escalate to legislative action or a crisis.

Several types of common strategy decisions must be considered: choosing the appropriate "mode"—whether to be reactive (which is seldom advised), proactive, or interactive; whether to undertake voluntary public policy changes; or whether to act alone or form a coalition with others.

In addition, one of three sets of strategies formalized by John F. Mahon should be selected—containing, shaping, and coping—all of which relate to different life cycle positions of an issue. Containment applies to an emerging issue that individuals or groups espouse and for which they seek to attract broader public attention. The strategy is to prevent an issue from receiving media and pubic support. Thus a company may decide to deal with the issue directly or with those who are promoting it. A variety of tactics apply: setting up a special committee to look into the issue, attacking or undermining the advocacy group, or attempting to frame an issue in a manner favorable to oneself. Shaping strategies apply to issues already on the public agenda and involve such tactics as total resistance, bargaining, or capitulating. With coping strategies, a company decides to take substantive action to change its behavior.[39]

5. *Implementation.* The overall plan is designed and executed, following the outline of strategic campaign management described earlier. This outline includes evaluation as an essential component. The actual results of a public affairs campaign or ongoing activities are checked against stated objectives.

Aside from the strategic question of whether to pursue activities alone or with a coalition of other corporations or associations, a further implementation decision is whether to use internal corporate resources or contract out to specialized intermediaries such as lobbyists, public affairs and relations offices, pollsters, law firms, and so forth. As companies expanded beyond government relations to full-fledged public affairs, they realized that a larger array of activities would be required beyond old-fashioned lobbying and campaign contributions. Firms realized that they could not perform many activities themselves or that it would be more efficient to have them performed by others (i.e., agents).[40] This realization led scholars like Barry M. Mitnick to view the central problem of politics as "agency," saying he saw democracy itself as "a system of competition over whose agents will govern, and which goals of which principals those agents will seek to advance."[41]

Public Affairs Campaign Based on an Issue's Life Cycle

The practical value of analyzing an issue in terms of its stage in the life cycle is that it allows public affairs strategists to select the most appropriate and effective media for a public affairs campaign. Parts II through IV of this book are organized by the major stages of an issue life cycle: opinion leader communication (dealing with interest groups), public communication (dealing with media), legislative communication and political action (dealing with government), and litigation communication (dealing with judicial aspects of the government).

Each of these life cycle stages is characterized by specific communication media and strategies and activities:

Stage 1: Opinion Leader Communication. These are mostly interpersonal media—one-on-one communication, small group meetings, and speeches to reach individuals and small audiences—and such small-audience vehicles already familiar with it and not inadvertently to help the opposition by disseminating the issue to larger audiences, which would tend to promote it to the next life cycle stage of public involvement. The reasoning is this: Why help the opposition move the issue to the next stage by attracting public media attention?

The range of media used includes:

- Face-to-face communication.
- Small group meetings and forums.
- Dialogue communication.
- Speechmaking.
- Newsletters, small publications, and the Internet.
- Mediation and negotiation.

Stage 2: Public Communication. Now the public is aware of an issue, understands it in various degrees, and may be aroused to take political action. Public opinion surveys, if taken, would indicate the degree of public involvement. Because by definition, the issue is deemed to be on the public agenda, the mass media cover the issue. A content analysis of the media would confirm this status. At this point public affairs managers engage in strategic media relations and, if necessary, employ the tool of advocacy advertising. The mass media—newspapers, magazines, trade publications, television, and radio—are used to reach larger audiences. Increasingly the Internet is being used to reach individuals in a wide variety of social settings.

Activities include:

- Proactive media relations.
- Broadcast appearances.
- Advocacy advertising.
- Holding the media accountable.
- Bypassing the mass media.

Stage 3: Legislative Communication and Political Action. When lawmakers become aware of an issue and consider legislation, companies that are affected must engage in efforts to influence the outcome. The means include:

- Direct lobbying.
- Indirect (grassroots) lobbying.
- Electoral activities (fund raising and a variety of political activities).

Stage 4: Litigation Communication. After laws are passed, companies may decide to challenge them in court or defend themselves against lawsuits filed by government, public interest groups, and others. Part of the contest is in the court of public opinion, which companies attempt to influence through media relations and other communication.

Although specific media are listed at specific stages, some are sufficiently versatile in application to be used at other stages. Speeches can be directed not only at a specific small audience, but also at larger audiences. For example, excerpts and copies of the speech can be used to achieve greater news coverage. Speeches can also be distributed to law-makers, regulators, and opinion leaders.

In supporting various life cycle stages, public affairs strategists choose from the entire range of media—not just the mass media but also interpersonal media and computer technology (e.g., the Internet). Furthermore, supplementary strategies and activities are employed, such as mediation and negotiation in Stage 1, holding the media accountable and bypassing the mass media in Stage 2, electoral activities in Stage 3, and campaigning against junk science in Stage 4.

CONCLUSIONS

This overview of corporate public affairs explains how corporations have responded to the increasing complexity and turbulence of the sociopolitical environment in which they do business. They have created new public affairs departments (sometimes from existing public relations departments) and given them the assignment of making this environment more manageable—trying to control it to preserve maximum management autonomy.

To control the major forces in their external environment, public affairs devises strategies and tactics that draw on the enormous political resources possessed by their corporations. Resultant communication campaigns center around controversial issues that arise among contending forces. This is the reason why the management tool of issues management has made such a major contribution to public affairs. The four stages of a life cycle used to analyze issues are also used in this volume as the basis of selecting the audiences and communication strategies and tactics most appropriate to each stage: (a) opinion leaders of interest groups, (b) media reporters and editors, (c) government lawmakers and administrators, and (d) judicial bodies.

ENDNOTES

1. See Roger W. Cobb and Charles D. Elder, "Communication and Public Policy," in *Handbook of Political Communication*, ed. Dan D. Nimmo and Keith R. Sanders (Beverly Hills, Calif.: Sage, 1981), pp. 391–416.
2. Jarol B. Manheim, *The Death of a Thousand Cuts: Corporate Campaigns and the Attack on the Corporation* (Mahwah, N.J.: Lawrence Erlbaum Associates, 2001), p. 17.
3. Bernard C. Hennessy, *Public Opinion* (Belmont, Calif.: Wadsworth, 1965), p. 25.
4. Harold Brayman, speech on "The Importance and Impact of Communications in Our Modern Society," October 13, 1964.
5. John W. Hill, *The Making of a Public Relations Man* (New York: David McKay & Co., 1963), p. 264.
6. Ibid., p. 20.
7. James E. Grunig, *Excellence in Public Relations and Communication Management* (Hillsdale, N.J.: Lawrence Erlbaum Associates, 1992), pp. 125–126.

8. Foundation for Public Affairs, *Corporate Public Affairs: The State of Corporate Public Affairs Survey Final Report 1999–2000* (Washington, D.C.: Public Affairs Council, 1999), p. 3.

9. Douglas G. Pinkham, "Today's Key Task for Public Affairs," in *Public Affairs Council 45! Sapphire Anniversary Report* (Washington, D.C.: Public Affairs Council, 1999), p. 6.

10. John F. Mahon, "Shaping Issues/Manufacturing Agents: Corporate Political Sculpting," in *Corporate Political Agency: The Construction of Competition in Public Affairs*, ed. Barry M. Mitnick (Newbury Park, Calif.: Sage, 1993), p. 196.

11. See James E. Post, et al., *Business and Society: Corporate Strategy, Public Policy, Ethics*, 10th edition (New York: McGraw-Hill, 2002).

12. See Rogene A. Buchholz, *Business Environment and Public Policy: Implications for Management*, 5th edition (Englewood Cliffs, N.J.: Prentice-Hall, 1995).

13. See George A. Steiner and John F. Steiner, *Business, Government, and Society: A Managerial Perspective* (New York: McGraw-Hill, 1997).

14. J. J. Wuerthner, Jr., *The Businessman's Guide to Practical Politics* (Chicago: Regnery, 1959), p. xiii.

15. E. M. Epstein, *The Corporation in American Politics* (Englewood Cliffs, N.J.: Prentice-Hall, 1969).

16. John Kenneth Galbraith, *The New Industrial State* (Boston: Houghton Mifflin, 1967).

17. Epstein, op. cit., p. 2.

18. Richard L. Daft, *Organization Theory and Design*, 3rd edition (New York: West Publishing, 1989), p. 46.

19. John F. Mahon, "Managing the Extended Enterprise: The New Stakeholder View," *California Management Review*, Vol. 45, Fall 2002, p. 10.

20. Richard Eells, *Corporate Giving in a Free Society* (New York: Harper & Brothers, 1956), p. 6. He says, "Business enterprise has a direct interest in promoting the strength of private sectors because it is itself a private sector. For this reason, business must maintain the barriers against progressive absorption of these sectors into state-controlled areas. Corporate philanthropy can and should aid the weak and private sectors in maintaining their autonomy" (pp. 103–104).

21. Dan Carney, with Amy Borrus and Jay Greene, "Microsoft's All-Out Counterattack," *BusinessWeek*, May 15, 2000, pp. 103–106. Also most of the resources listed are from ibid., pp. 103–106. Also Stanley Holmes, "Microsoft Ad Aims to Boost Image," *Los Angeles Times*, April 29, 2000, p. C-2.

22. Mike France, "Commentary: The Unseemly Campaign of Mr. Microsoft," *Business Week*, April 24, 2000, p. 53.

23. A survey conducted by Harris Interactive for the *Wall Street Journal*, based on 3,830 computer-using respondents found the following::
    - Nearly half said they disagreed with the government's proposal for breaking up Microsoft; about 605 said Microsoft should remain one company.
    - More than half agreed that Gates is a positive role model.
    - Only 29% believed the government is being fair in its treatment of Microsoft.
    - 42% agreed that the company is a monopolist.
    - Only 23% said it treats its competitors fairly.
    Rececca Buckman, "Looking Through Microsoft's Window," *Wall Street Journal*, May 1, 2000, p. B1.

24. Stuein L. Hwang, "A 'Predatory' Monopolist Tries the Old Soft Sell," *Wall Street Journal*, April 21, 2000, p. B1.

25. Foundation for Public Affairs, op. cit. The previous survey was James E. Post and Jennifer J. Griffin, *1996 Survey: The State of Corporate Public Affairs* (Washington, D.C.: Foundation for Public Affairs, 1997).

26. Foundation for Public Affairs, op. cit., pp. 15–16.

27. Steven Greenhouse, "Accord to Combat Sweatshop Labor Faces Obstacles," *New York Times*, April 13, 1997, p. A1.

28. For further discussion of the concept see Buchholz, op. cit., "The Public Policy Process," pp. 119–149.

29. Grunig, op. cit., pp. 17, 81.

30. Daft, op. cit., p. 491.

31. Robert L. Dilenschneider, editor, *Dartnell's Public Relations Handbook* (Chicago: The Dartnell Corporation, 1996), p. 339.

32. See John E. Marston, *Modern Public Relations* (New York: McGraw-Hill, 1979), pp. 185–203.

33. Scott M. Cutlip, Allen H. Center and Glen M. Broom, *Effective Public Relations*, 6th edition (Englewood Cliffs, N.J.: Prentice-Hall, 1985), pp. 199–201.

34. Two excellent books describing campaign strategies and management are Robert Kendall, *Public Relations Campaign Strategies; Planning for Implementation*, 2nd edition (New York: HarperCollins College, 1996); and Robert E. Simmons, *Communication Campaign Management: A Systems Approach* (New York: Longman, 1990).

35. For an overview of issues management, see Rogene A. Buchholz, "Public Issues Management," in *Essentials of Public Policy for Management*, 2nd edition (Englewood Cliffs, N.J.: Prentice-Hall, 1990), pp. 180–215. For a comprehensive review see R. L. Heath and Associates, *Strategic Issues Management: How Organizations Influence and Respond to Public Interests and Policies* (San Francisco: Jossey-Bass, 1988).

36. Steven Schnaars and Paschalina Ziamou, "The Essentials of Scenario Writing," *Business Horizons*, Vol. 44, July–August 2001, pp. 25–32.

37. See http://www.gbn.org/public/gbnstory/scenarios.

38. Peter F. Bartha, "Managing Corporate External Issues: An Analytical Framework," *Business Quarterly*, Vol. 47, October 1982, pp. 78–90.

39. See John F. Mahon, "Corporate Political Strategy," *Business in the Contemporary World*, Vol. 2, Autumn 1989, pp. 50–62.

40. Allen M. Kaufman, Ernest J. Englander, and Alfred A. Marcus, "Selecting an Organizational Structure for Implementing Issues Management," in Mitnick, op. cit., p. 153.

41. Mitnick, op. cit., p. 1.

II

Interest Group Strategies

Interest groups constitute one of the three major forces in a corporation's sociopolitical environment, and they are the starting point for public affairs communication. In his *The Interest Group Society*, first published in 1989, Jeffrey M. Berry states that we are truly an interest group society and that the role of interest groups in the policymaking process has expanded. They are an enduring part of American political life and "today have more resources, represent more constituencies, and do more lobbying than ever before."[1] On the simplest level, says Barry, "when we speak of an interest group we are referring to an organization that tries to influence government."[2] They serve several functions: (a) as "a primary link between citizens and their government, forming a channel of access through which members voice their opinions to those who govern them"; (b) as an opportunity for people to participate in the political process; (c) as a means of educating the American public about political issues; (d) bringing an issue to light and agenda building; and (e) program monitoring.[3]

Many issues that later appear in the news media or on legislative agendas begin their life cycle when interest groups champion them. Corporations are among these groups, but most often they resist disturbing the status quo rather than initiating issues, such as deregulation. The opportunity to do so, however, remains an important corporate public affairs strategy. In this book the term *interest group* is restricted to nonbusiness groups unless otherwise indicated. Part II, therefore, discusses how thought leaders originate issues or how interest group leaders respond to social tensions created when the expectations and demands of discontented people are not met. Some social tensions and resultant issues are traceable to the gap between these public expectations and corporate performance.

The two prominent issues that gave rise to public affairs—consumerism and environmentalism—resulted from public dissatisfactions in the marketplace and with corporate environmental performance. Ralph Nader popularized the consumerism movement with his book *Unsafe at Any Speed*, and Rachel Carson inaugurated the environmental movement with her *Silent Spring*. Other social movements followed: women's rights, gay and lesbian rights, animal rights groups, and a host of others. Their variety is reflected in *Public Interest Profiles*, a manual of the Foundation of Public Affairs, which classifies 250 of the most influential public interest groups in such areas as civil and human rights, community improvements, consumer and health, corporate and governmental accountability, the economic system, energy and environment, and public policy.[4]

These movements—and the not-to-be-forgotten civil rights movement—were preceded by the labor movement, which is represented by hundreds of labor unions, most of which fall under the umbrella of the American Federation of Labor and Congress of Industrial Organizations (AFL-CIO). Although union membership has fallen sharply over the last decade, the AFL-CIO's president, John Sweeney, has mobilized union-organizing drives to win more members and launched lobbying and electoral campaigns to advance legislative interests.[5] He has also supported new strategies, notably the "corporate campaign," which adds to the traditional union tactics of strikes, pickets, and boycotts.[6]

Interest groups play a vital role in society. "The labor movement and community organizing are indispensable to a democracy," says Mike Miller, editor of *Social Policy*. "They are 'civil society,' 'mediating institutions,' or 'intermediate structure' that stand between the individual and government and corporations.... They defend communities and individuals against corporate or government excess." They also serve as incubators for new ideas about how we should live together in society.[7] Viewed collectively, interest groups, along with the news media, serve as society's watchdogs; they initiate issues of concern to a variety of constituents; and they apply pressure on corporations, as well as government, to consider the needs of society in their decision making.

Each decade the number of interest groups grows, as reflected in the number of entries in the *Encyclopedia of Associations*. (See Box II.1 for categories of such interest groups.) In the mid-1950s, it listed just under 5,000 associations. By 1990, the number was 22,000, and, although growth slowed, the number reached 23,000 in 1997. Estimates of the number of nongovernmental organizations (NGOs), from the smallest neighborhood association to huge international relief agencies such as CARE, suggest that the United States alone has about 2 million NGOs. Growth in recent decades has been enormous, as 70% of them are less than 30 years old. Growth in membership of environmental groups has been especially vigorous: The Sierra Club now has 572,000 members, up from 181,000 in 1980; and the Worldwide Fund for Nature has

---

Box II.1   Categories of Public Interest Groups (With Examples)

Business/economic: The Business Roundtable, Citizens for a Sound Economy, U.S. Chamber of Commerce

Civil/constitutional rights: American Civil Liberties Union, Amnesty International USA

Community/grassroots: Mothers Against Drunk Driving, Nuclear Free America, People for the Ethical Treatment of Animals

Consumer/health: American Medical Association, Consumer Federation of America, National Consumers League

Corporate accountability/responsibility: Center for Business Ethics, Committee for Economic Development, INFACT

Environmental: Friends of the Earth, Greenpeace, National Wildlife Federation, Sierra Club

International affairs: Foreign Policy Association, Union of Concerned Scientists

Media: Accuracy in Media, Action for Children's Television

Political/governmental process: Center for Responsive Politics, Common Cause, The Conservative Caucus.

Public interest law: Center for Law in the Public Interest

Religious: Anti-Defamation League of B'nai B'rith, Interfaith Center on Corporate Responsibility

Think tanks: The Heritage Foundation, Investor Responsibility Research Center, The Urban Institute, Worldwatch Institute

---

around 5 million members, up from 570,000 in 1980.[8] The Natural Resources Defense Council now has 550,000 members.[9]

THE THIRD SECTOR

Among interest groups of greatest concern to corporations is the large category of social action groups—the myriad activist groups that represent individuals with grievances or espoused causes. They are part of what Theodore Levitt called the "third sector," whose traditional role has been to care for the casualties of society that are neglected by government and business sectors. Even these traditional nonprofit organizations that primarily provide client services increasingly engage in advocacy activities to promote their mission. The social action groups described by Levitt are best known for actively, and sometimes very aggressively, advocating and pursuing social reforms. In addition to persuasion and pull, they believe in publicity and push. "Its tools are loud, insistent, assertive, impatient, and sometimes violent."[10] In the 1980s and 1990s, these third-sector activists preferred to take direct action against corporations rather than wait for government to act.[11]

NGOs

The term *NGO* is widely used in the international sphere, where these organizations deal with governments and speak out on many high-profile issues. Among the top five issues are environment, conservation and ecology, labor conditions and human rights, trade policies, and wages and working conditions. They are recognized by the United Nations (U.N.) at certain important international meetings and the U.N. uses them for such purposes as dispensing aid. Since "The Battle of Seattle," which targeted the World Trade Organization, NGOs have gained more media coverage. Some, such as Amnesty International and Greenpeace, have become "superbrands."

NGOs are highly effective because they: (a) play the offensive all the time, (b) know how to simplify complex issues, (c) form unusual coalitions (e.g., with labor unions and youth groups), (d) have a clear agenda, (e) move at Internet speed, and (f) know how to feed on the media. They hit where it works: a company's customers, legislators and regulators, the media, and, now becoming more important, financial markets and institutions (e.g., the World Bank and the International Monetary Fund).[12]

The entire nonprofit sector of society accounts for a formidable part of the economy. It represented 5.9% of all organizations in the United States in 1998 and had a 6.7% share of national income. The Independent Sector reports that it employs 10.9 million workers and that 74% of adult volunteers worked in nonprofit sector organizations. As the demand for their services increased, the number of charitable organizations increased at an annual rate of 5.1% between 1987 and 1997—more than double the growth rate of the business sector.[13]

Advantages Possessed by Noncorporate Groups

It takes a professional staff and an adequate budget to apply the sophisticated media relations strategies and techniques that are available to every group in society. Besides corporations, some large nonprofits, such as the Sierra Club, can also afford professional media relations staffs. Although less wealthy activist groups often resign themselves to their relative weakness in media relations and thus shun the mass media, many are beginning to change their attitude. Instead of relying only on the strength of their own communication channels with members, they realize the importance of enlisting the support of public opinion and of "democratizing" the media. This is the view of Charlotte Ryan in *Prime Time Activism*: "Our society is heavily media-dependent and if we ignore mainstream media, we abandon audiences with little or no access to alternative and opposition media."[14]

Media Power.   More important, activist groups have some advantages over business. One is they are able to attract media attention when they confront visible corporations. Such events become newsworthy because conflict and crises play into the media's definition of news. Newsworthiness is further enhanced because social action groups can use a wider repertoire of tactics than business. They can engage in colorful and action-filled demonstrations, rallies, and events—chaining themselves to trees, lying in front of bulldozers, and occupying a building. It is mostly the tactics of activists, not the underlying issues, however, that tend to gain prominent media attention. Even when issues are mentioned, they are usually not analyzed in depth. In a labor dispute, strike actions, not the reasons underlying the strike, dominate the news. Social injustice and grievances are covered lightly because the mainstream news media are basically conservative.

People Power.   Noncorporate interest groups have the great advantage of people power relative to corporations, even though the latter have relationships with many stakeholder groups, such as employees and stockholders. The pluralistic feature of American democracy is that it includes tens of thousands of public interest and other social groups. Even Carl Boggs, a critic of corporate America who believes "the corporate stranglehold over social and political life shows no signs of weakening," acknowledges that "civil society in the United States does remain surprisingly fluid and resilient—witness the capacity of thousands of local organizations and movements to sustain a grassroots presence that, while now scattered and largely impotent, could provide the basis of a more unified oppositional politics."[15]

Social groups' focus of power is the local level, where community groups can mobilize people power to counteract corporate money power, says Pennsylvania State University sociologist Ed Walsh, author of *Don't Burn It Here: Grassroots Challengers to Trash Incinerators.*[16] He states, "Ordinary people increasingly confront large bureaucracies over which they feel they have little or no control. Our evidence shows, however, that corporate power is more fragile than many citizens imagine."[17] He urges people to organize and to draw support from outside by mobilizing politically; for example, by going door to door to place issues on a referendum or to elect certain legislators.[18] People will do this only, however, when an issue becomes important enough to engage their interest and involvement.

It is this strong identification by citizens with the causes and visions of specific public interest groups that gives them an advantage over corporate relationships with their stakeholders. These groups have the great ideological advantage that their members are motivated by broad ideals of social justice, human rights, and environmental preservation—ideals that resonate with the general public. Furthermore, some groups are headed by strong popular leaders, such as Ralph Nader and Jesse Jackson, and their causes are often endorsed by celebrities, as with Meryl Streep's support of the Alar campaign.[19] In contrast, business is weakened by a lack of the kinds of core values that can win the minds and hearts of Americans. Business is typically perceived as concentrating too heavily on the bottom line and on increasing shareholder value at the expense of the public interest.

Occasionally, the strong motivations that exist on the local level also appear on the national level when specific issues, such as the environment, are at stake. However, on a national level, public interest groups are usually so diversified in their interests and causes they fail to present a common political front. They also compete with one another in obtaining government and private funding.

Internet Power.   Added to the arsenal of activist groups is the power of the Internet. It boosts the effectiveness of activist groups because it enables them to mobilize their members and sympathizers much more efficiently than they could in the days before websites and e-mail. "For very, very little cost, you can have amazing effect, if you have real grassroots power out there," says Margaret Conway, managing director of the Human Rights Campaign, the largest U.S. political organization for gays and lesbians.[20] Andrew Kohut, director of the Pew Research Center for the People & the Press, notes, "People are now bonded together in communities that were very loosely knit or did not exist at all 10 years ago."[21]

Activists are supported by numerous websites. On Protest Net, Evan Henshaw-Plath posts information about hundreds of protests, meetings, and conferences, most of which are left-leaning in their politics. Another site, E-The People, gives viewers hundreds of petitions to choose from and 170,000 e-mail addresses of government officials. To learn how to contact officials at the national, state, and local levels, people can consult the Electronic Activist site.[22]

BusinessWeek concludes that "in the Internet Age, it's possible for a handful of Web-savvy activists to exert pressure on policymakers working out of their homes. The result may be a fundamental transformation of the nature of politics."[23] The Internet enables activist groups to recruit members and volunteers, raise money, inform their members about the organization's position on issues, organize protests and rallies, and lobby lawmakers. Greenpeace is credited with having an e-mail list of 5,000 activists "who join protests over everything from polyvinyl chloride in Japanese toys to plutonium shipments in Britain."[24] Corporate public affairs professionals recognize that the Internet has increased the power of activist groups, making money a less important factor in the political marketplace.

Credibility Power. NGOs, such as Greenpeace and Amnesty International, are generally more trusted and respected than governments, media, and corporations. This contention was supported by a survey of 500 respondents aged 34 to 64 in several countries (United States, France, Germany, Australia, and the United Kingdom) conducted by the Strategy One unit of Edelman PR Worldwide. Steve Lombardo, president of Strategy One, said, "These [respondents] are two to three times more likely to trust an NGO to do what is right compared to a large company because they are seen as being motivated by morals rather than just profit." Overall, 64% said the influence of NGOs has increased significantly over the decade, with 80% saying Greenpeace is highly effective and 78% saying the same of Amnesty International. Only 11% saw governments or corporations making the world a better place. In the United Kingdom, 65% of respondents rated the World Wildlife Fund favorably, as did 50% for Greenpeace, 29% for British Airways, and 13% for Exxon-Esso.[25]

Tactics Used by Social Action Groups

Over a quarter of Americans belong to "cause organizations," according to the Times Mirror Center for People and the Press.[26] The actions taken by these members vary widely. Some engage in traditional lobbying efforts, whereas others take direct action through the use of protests, boycotts, and shareholder resolutions. A 1994 Gallup poll reveals some relatively conservative political actions by Americans: 25% have "worn a campaign button or displayed a campaign poster," 25% have "asked someone to vote for your candidate," 22% have "gone to a political meeting to hear a candidate speak," and 14% have "worked for a political party or candidate."[27]

An international study classified political activist groups into five types: inactive, conformists, reformists, activists, and protesters. The repertory of direct actions taken by them increases with each type. Inactives might do no more than glance at political news and sign a petition if asked; reformists might engage in "moderate" levels of protest, such as lawful demonstrations and boycotts; and protesters would shun any conventional involvement in favor of aggressive protest methods, including violence.[28]

Philip Lesly, a public relations consultant, devised an equally useful range of categories for opposition groups along with strategies to deal with each:

- Advocates: Propose something they believe in; for example, business proposes lower taxes to help the economy. Use the strategy of reason.
- Dissidents: Against something, or many things, because it's their character to be sour on things as they are. They use logic and selected emotions.

- Activists: Want to get something done or changed: "Don't just stand in the picket line—do something." May push legislation, stop construction of highway, or urge an amendment forbidding abortion. They use logic and strategic actions.
- Zealots: Distinguished by overriding single-mindedness, absorbed with one issue such as stopping a power plant or liberating a geographic area of social groups. Egocentric, must run the show, consider moderates to be enemies. They use the strategy of creating climate of opinion and understanding among the public, which isolates zealots and may wither their zeal.[29]

An extreme example of zealots are members of the Earth Liberation Front (ELF), a furtive ecoterrorist group. To stop forest development, they have claimed responsibility for burning two Vail, Colorado, lodges and torching homes under construction in California. More recently they set fire to three auto dealerships in the Los Angeles suburb of Duarte, charring or damaging more than 40 SUVs, mostly gas-guzzling Hummer H2s. The ELF website contains how-to manuals for setting fires and tips on evading police. Attackers have evaded police because "It's such a shadowy, loose-knit collection of cells that it's hard to find them."[30]

Many business crises have been triggered by social action groups because one of their favorite strategies is to target large, visible corporations whose concern for their reputations makes them vulnerable. By threatening to seek government intervention or further regulation, the numerous social action groups have succeeded in pressuring corporations to accede to their demands. By classifying a specific group according to this typology, a corporation can better decide how to deal with it (e.g., whether to agree to a meeting).

ENDNOTES

1. Jeffrey M. Berry, *The Interest Group Society*, 3rd Edition (New York: Longman, 1997), p. xi.
2. Ibid., p. 4.
3. Ibid., pp. 6–8.
4. See table of contents in Foundation for Public Affairs, *Public Interest Profiles, 1992–1993* (Washington, DC: Congressional Quarterly, 1992).
5. See Robert L. Rose, "New AFL-CIO President Seeks to Revitalize Old Federation," *Wall Street Journal*, October 29, 1996, p. B1.
6. These are discussed in Jarol B. Manheim, *The Death of a Thousand Cuts: Corporate Campaigns and the Attack on the Corporation* (Mahwah, NJ: Lawrence Erlbaum Associates, 2001).
7. "Social Policy Themes," *Social Policy*, Vol. 32, Winter 2001/2002, p. 2.
8. "After Seattle—Citizens' Groups: The Non-governmental Order," *Economist*, December 11, 1999, p. 21.
9. *Nature's Voice*, September/October 2004, p. 1.
10. Theodore Levitt, *The Third Sector: New Tactics for a Responsive Society* (New York: AMACOM, 1973), p. 73.

11. John M. Holcomb, "Citizen Groups, Public Policy, and Corporate Responses," in *Practical Public Affairs in an Era of Change: A Communications Guide for Business, Government, and College,* ed. Lloyd B. Dennis. (Lanham, Md.: University Press of America, 1996), p. 209.

12. Based on comment by Michael McDermott and Jonathan Wootliff in a session on "Building Relationships with Non-Government Organizations," at Public Relations Society of America Conference in Atlanta, Georgia, October 2001; also see *pr reporter,* November 5, 2001.

13. Yvonne Lo, editor, *A Public Relations Guide to Nonprofits* (Exeter, NH: PR Publishing Company, 2003), p. vii.

14. Charlotte Ryan, *Prime Time Activism: Media Strategies for Grassroots Organizing* (Boston, Mass.: South End Press, 1991), p. 29. Another source of information about the media practices of nonprofits and activists is Jason Salzman, *Making the News: A Guide for Nonprofits and Activists* (Boulder, CO: Westview Press, 1998). This handbook is based on interviews with media-savvy activists and 25 professional journalists.

15. Carl Boggs, *The End of Politics: Corporate Power and the Decline of the Public Sphere* (New York: Guilford, 2000), p. 258.

16. Groups with large geographically dispersed memberships, however, can duplicate and multiply the power of community groups. Members can strongly identify with the often single-cause political and social goals of their chosen organizations, especially in times of conflict with corporations or government.

17. Doug Nurse, "Professor Fertilizes Grassroots; Sociologist Has studied Community Activism for a Quarter of a Century," *Atlanta Journal,* November 27, 1997, p. 22E.

18. Activist groups devote a lot of their efforts to organizing their members. In his recent book, *Corporations Are Gonna Get Your Mama* (Monroe, Maine: Common Courage Press, 1996), Kevin Danaher, an activist, proclaims, "Demystify the system and teach ourselves how to organize alternatives" (p. 199). He cites several training sources that provide help, among which are the Center for Third World Organizing, ACORN (Association of Community Organizations for Reform Now), and the Industrial Areas Foundation (IAF).

   Stating the goal of developing ways to control the behavior of corporations, Danaher says that "Government and citizens' movements have been pushing on many fronts to codify rules on how corporations can treat their workers, customers, and the environment. Extending his reach internationally, he credits the National Labor Committee in New York for succeeding in forcing The Gap to improve working conditions in its El Salvador factories. NLC had generated widespread publicity about dismal working conditions of girls as young as 13 "who toil in Central American sweatshops up to seventy hours a week earning less than 60 cents an hour." The Gap signed an agreement with (NLC) on December 15, 1995, that establishes new standards for health and safety and protection of human rights, subject to independent monitoring of its contractors. Gayle Liles, "The U.S.-Salvador Gap," op. cit., p. 177.

19. See "How a PR Firm Executed the Alar Scare," *Wall Street Journal,* October 3, 1989, p. A22.

20. Ibid., p. 9.

21. Ibid., p. 11.

22. Edward Harris, "Web Becomes a Cybertool for Political Activists," *Wall Street Journal,* August 5, 1999, p. B11.

23. Pete Engardio, "Activists Without Borders," *BusinessWeek*, October 4, 1999, p. 144.
24. Ibid., p. 150.
25. *O'Dwyer's PR Service Report*, February 2001, pp. 1, 26.
26. Holcomb, op. cit., p. 211.
27. "Election Preview," *American Enterprise*, Vol. 7, January/February 1996, p. 88.
28. Alan Marsh, "The New Matrix of Political Action," *Futures*, Vol. 11, April 1979, p. 98.
29. Philip Lesly, *Managing the Human Climate*, May–June 1978.
30. Ronald Grover, "Burning to Save the Planet," *BusinessWeek*, September 8, 2003, p. 41.

Chapter 2

Interest Group Strategies and Forms of Opinion Leader Communication

Societal issues are rooted in people's dissatisfaction with their experience as consumers, employees, members of cause organizations, or victims of dislocation or crises. In addition, some people in the activist third-sector groups have deeper resentments and want to change the status quo. In both cases, people in these groups form interest groups, or, alternatively, existing groups may take up their dissatisfactions. Societal issues also arise from the initiative of so-called public interest groups whose thought leaders and opinion leaders conceive and develop issues for which they seek public support. In both situations, the life cycle of an issue begins with an emerging issue.

As with all ideas and issues, months and usually years are needed for them to become widely accepted and adopted. Furthermore, when ideas concern public policy, they are, because of their controversial nature, contested by a variety of political participants. Thus, the proponents of an issue face an uphill struggle to build up enough "social energy"—enough highly motivated people—to convince the public that their issue deserves priority.[1] An emerging issue goes through several life cycle stages, as shown in Fig. 2.1.

Corporations practicing modern public affairs begin the issues management process by constantly monitoring their external environments for early warning signals of emerging issues initiated by interest groups that might affect them. They thus begin the issues management process. After identifying, prioritizing, and analyzing an issue, a company engages in strategy formulation to decide what actions to take or not take.

37

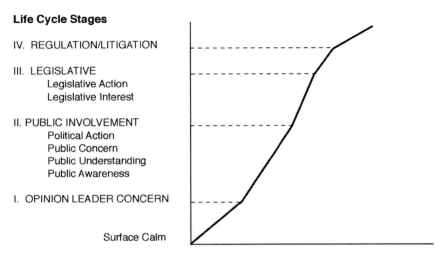

Life Cycle Stages

IV. REGULATION/LITIGATION

III. LEGISLATIVE
        Legislative Action
        Legislative Interest

II. PUBLIC INVOLVEMENT
        Political Action
        Public Concern
        Public Understanding
        Public Awareness

I. OPINION LEADER CONCERN

Surface Calm

FIG. 2.1.   Build-up of social energy: four stages in life cycle of an issue.

As part of their political strategies, corporations can also be the initiators of issues of concern to them. Regulations that deal with price, entry, and trade practices have often been sought by business because they provide industry with such benefits as stability and protection against competitors. Much uncertainty, disliked by business, is thus reduced.[2] Therefore some companies may seek new laws and regulations or a change in existing ones; for example, Enron Corporation lobbied hard for deregulation in the energy industry. For many years the federal regulation of transportation through the Interstate Commerce Commission (ICC) was actively supported by the regulated industries. There was no stronger protector of the ICC against threats of deregulation than the trucking industry.[3] Support or opposition to regulations is one way a public affairs strategy contributes to a firm's marketing strategy. The main thrust of this chapter, however, is to examine the strategies used by corporations in response to initiatives taken by nonbusiness interest groups.

INTEREST GROUPS DEVELOP CAMPAIGNS TARGETING CORPORATIONS

In recent decades, nonbusiness interest groups have developed sophisticated strategies and tactics to confront corporations. Borrowing some ideas from the Far Left (e.g., from Saul Alinsky's *Rules for Radicals*[4]) and several social movements, labor unions developed the strategy of the corporate campaign. In his *The Death of a Thousand Cuts*, Jarol B.

Manheim of George Washington University defines and describes it as "an assault on the reputation of a company that has somehow offended a union or some other interest."[5] Manheim points out that although organized labor became the principal initiator of corporate campaigns from the mid-1970s, other groups—notably environmentalists, human and civil rights advocates, and feminists—have also employed the strategy. Some of these other groups often have a much stronger anticorporate ideological basis than the typical labor campaign by relying for their motivation and approach on philosophical opposition to the corporation per se. Manheim calls their efforts "anticorporate campaigns." In contrast, unions have a more obvious self-interest-based economic motivation and should not be viewed as anticorporate.[6]

Union Faces Off With Farah and J. P. Stevens

The union corporate campaign strategy was launched when the Amalgamated Clothing Workers of America (ACWA) sought to unionize workers in Farah Manufacturing Company's new plant in El Paso in 1972. Seeing that the usual tactic of a strike was ineffective—largely because so many Mexican replacement workers were available—the ACWA launched a nationwide boycott, which was the first time a labor organization had used that tactic to organize a workforce. Mass picketing became a natural for TV news coverage. On December 11, 1972, called "Don't Buy Farah Day," 175,000 pickets marched nationwide.[7]

An important feature of a corporate campaign is the link between labor and other interest groups. Because most of ACWA's members were Catholics, support was easily obtained not only from the pastor of El Paso's largest parish, but from the Most Reverend Sidney M. Metzger, bishop of El Paso. A letter addressed by him "to all Catholic Bishops in the United States," which recommended the boycott of Farah slacks, was part of a full-page ad placed by ACWA in newspapers in the 13 largest advertising markets to call attention to what it called unfair labor practices at Farah. Cardinal Mederios of Boston reflected the views of many religious leaders when he said, "the internal affairs of business become the concern of religious leadership when violations of social justice and human dignity are at stake."[8] Farah capitulated on February 24, 1974, by ratifying an agreement with the union. The use of prominent leaders and placement of ads in support of the national boycott were instrumental in the union's success.

Union corporate campaign tactics were soon extended in the union's conflict with J. P. Stevens, a diversified corporation, primarily concentrated in the textile industry with the majority of its plants located in North and South Carolina. The main issue was the company's refusal to bargain collectively with plants where workers had accepted a union—even after condemnation by the National Labor Relations Board and a federal appeals court, which stated that "never has there been such an example of such classic, albeit crude, unlawful labor practices."[9] Besides declaring a national boycott on a scale greater than that ever undertaken by the American labor movement, the union began the campaign in earnest in 1976 by employing the strategy of embarrassing the officers of the company or of the banks it did business with—as well as using the economic power of pension funds.[10]

The campaign was partly designed and organized with the help of Roy Rogers, a new type of consultant who takes credit for developing the concept of the corporate campaign. "In effect, Rogers began by identifying all of the key stakeholder relationships of the target company, assessing the strengths and weaknesses of each, and devising ways to exploit the weaknesses."[11] For example, one tactic was to force the resignation of some of J. P. Stevens's directors. Among them were James Finley, Stevens's chairman, who resigned from the board of New York Life, and the chairman of Avon Products, who resigned from both the Manufacturers Hanover board and the board of Stevens. Another tactic was the use of shareholder resolutions and demonstrating at Stevens's annual meeting.

Anticorporate Campaigns

Labor unions were not the only adversaries of corporations. As Manheim documents, nonlabor entities launched 29 anticorporate campaigns between 1989 and 1999. Some better known ones are these:

- BP Amoco: Greenpeace seeks to halt offshore oil development on Alaska's North Slope.
- Conoco: Rainforest Action Network pressured the company to cease operations in the Amazon region.
- DuPont: Greenpeace wanted the company to stop using ozone-destroying chemicals.
- Freeport-McMoRan: Rainforest Action Network and Project Underground launched an effort to force the company to stop operations said to threaten indigenous Indonesian tribes.
- Hoechst/Rhone Poulenc: Fund for the Feminist Majority sought to speed U.S. availability of RU-486, the day-after birth control pill.
- Monsanto: Greenpeace attempted to dissuade the company from engaging in genetic engineering.
- Shell: Targeted by Project Underground for doing business in Nigeria.
- Siemens: Global 2000 and Friends of the Earth aimed to force the company to cease upgrading and operating nuclear power facilities in Russia, Eastern Europe, and elsewhere.[12]

This list can be vastly extended when a broader range of confrontations between social action groups and corporations are considered. A chapter on confrontation crises refers to the more than 200 national boycotts held in 1990 alone and reviews such confrontations as the Natural Resources Defense Council's crusade against McDonald's use of hard-to-recycle plastic foam food containers and the long-lasting boycott of South Africa during the apartheid era. Case studies include the PUSH (People United to Save Humanity) boycott of Nike for not doing more to help the African American community and the classic demand from FIGHT (Freedom, Integration, God, Honor—Today) of Eastman Kodak to train and hire more African Americans.[13]

When a corporation is targeted by a labor union or social action group, it has two major choices: (a) seek to contain the issue, which is the traditional approach; and (b) seek to engage the challenging group, an option that is gaining in acceptance.

CONTAINMENT STRATEGIES

The most compelling strategy for a company facing an emerging issue is to contain it—to prevent it from building up social energy and progressing to the next life cycle stage where it receives media and public support. To contain or resolve an issue, a company limits its target to individuals and groups that present or promote an idea, or air a grievance and press demands. To use mass communication media would be counterproductive because the public would become aware of the issue in question and support for it would thereby grow. If this were to occur, the issue would have reached the second stage of the life cycle—the stage of public involvement—and be on the public agenda.

This containment strategy is analogous to the handling of a rumor. Assuming that a rumor is not widespread, efforts to counter it are restricted to people who presumably already have heard it. To hold a news conference, send out news releases, or place an advocacy ad would simply spread the rumor further and do even more damage. Thus, when McDonald's heard a rumor that it ground red worms into its hamburger meat, the company limited its response to the store where the rumor started. It took out an ad in the local paper, saying only that McDonald's hamburgers are made of 100% beef, implying that worms could not possibly be part of that 100% beef product.[14]

In a rumor situation, the mass media should be avoided entirely. This may not be possible, however, if a local newspaper or broadcast station has reported the rumor. In such an eventuality, factual information should be supplied only to those specific media. Management runs the risk, of course, that the wire services or alert national media may pick up the story. A prudent organization will, therefore, prepare a news release for such a contingency but not send the news release or hold a news conference. The case study in Box 2.1 adapted from the *Harvard Business Review* illustrates the factors that must be considered in such a situation.

Both judgment and research are required to determine whether a containment strategy will succeed. Reporters and editors, as well as public re-

Box 2.1 Case: Naturewise Deliberates Its Media Relations Policy[15]

Dana Osborne, founder and CEO of Naturewise Apparel, makers of chemical-free natural-fiber children's wear, suddenly faced a potential crisis. A local TV news station and a local paper in Chicago carried a story that the company condoned the bombing of an abortion clinic in Joliet, Illinois, by a group called TermRights. The only actual connection with Naturewise was that a division of the company contributed to the nonprofit organization called CHICARE. TermRights, a radically pro-life group, was only one of 140 social service organizations in Chicago and the Midwest supported by CHICARE.

The company's contribution policy was as follows: It had recently decided that its $400,000 annual donation to charities, formerly administered by corporate headquarters, would now be allocated by each regional division as a way of paying back the various communities that supported it.

Facing Osborne was the immediate problem of whether to answer a call from a reporter of the *Chicago Daily Bulletin*. In the case study, five experts present their analysis of the situation and recommendations. They gave their reactions to the headquarters communication director's advice: "We're going to need to make some kind of statement to the press."

One expert, Mike Woods, senior editor of Los Angeles-based *Investor's Business Daily*, said he wanted to be ready for the possibility of regional and national media coverage by assembling three relevant facts: (1) a list of all the charities Naturewise has supported and of other companies that have given to the same charities; (2) information from CHICARE about how long it has been in business and which other companies have supported it; and, (3) whether this type of incident has ever happened before. As the experts commented, these questions should have been asked before making the contribution.

Another expert, Madge Kaplan, Boston bureau chief for *Marketplace*, Public Radio International's program on business and finance, favored calling the reporter to announce a press conference for 1 p.m. Pacific time at company headquarters.

Stephen Greyser, a marketing professor at the Harvard Business School, made a different recommendation: that Osborne take the call from the Chicago reporter, even if only to arrange a callback. He saw the possibility of the *Chicago Daily Bulletin* reaching a large audience, some of it through syndication pickup. Greyser was explicit about what the reporter at the Chicago paper and other media should be told:

- Reiterate the company's well-known corporate giving policy and its rationale of "we do it because it's the right thing to do."
- Admit that Naturewise's Midwest division did give money to CHICARE, "as do many companies in the area, adding that while CHICARE is involved with so many worthy causes," the company should have checked into all of the agency's associated groups.
- Deplore the bombing.

lations professionals, know whether a story is of great public or media interest. A content analysis of the print and broadcast media—even an informal scanning—indicates whether an issue or story appears on the public agenda. Survey findings, even a quick, overnight telephone survey, would confirm whether the public has become aware of an issue.

If there is evidence an issue has broken the bounds of containment and stands a good chance of reaching the second life cycle stage, the strategy of preemptive communication must quickly be employed. An organization is then in a race to try to shape public thinking before the opposition does. Reaching the public mind first is like checking into a room at an overcrowded hotel before other guests do. The sign over the door leading to a particular "issue room" then reads "occupied," making it difficult and awkward for someone else to enter. This is known as the *law of primacy* in learning theory: What is learned first tends to remain in memory better than that which is learned later. For those entering an issue discussion late, the challenge is to find attention-getting ways of invoking the opposite *law of recency* that what is heard last is better remembered.

A company can choose one, or a combination, of three containment strategy variations: (a) oppose an interest group, (b) weaken antagonists, and (c) foster offsetting interest groups.

Oppose an Interest Group

Most issues are initiated by interest groups or government, and many are targeted at business. Understandably, therefore, companies feel attacked and become defensive. A typical expression of defensiveness is to counterattack and weaken the "enemy."

SLAPP Suits. A legal tactic used by some companies to discourage or stop activists from attacking them is to threaten, or actually take, civil law action, alleging that injury has been caused by the party. Such legal action has been labeled *strategic lawsuits against public participation* (SLAPPS.)[16] Industry groups, such as land developers, typically file these suits. Their targets are generally not radicals, such as extreme environmentalists, but ordinary, middle-class citizens concerned about their local environment or other problems. What started as a tactic against small targets, however, has expanded to national groups, according to Al Meyerhoff, a senior attorney with the Natural Resources Defense Council.[17]

Each year thousands of Americans are sued for speaking out against governments and corporations, states Sharon Beder, who wrote a chapter on SLAPP suits.[18] Individuals and groups are sued for such acts as "circulating petitions, writing to public officials, speaking at, or even just attending, public meetings, organizing a boycott and engaging in peaceful demonstrations."[19] These actions are all legal and protected by First Amendment rights. Nevertheless, plaintiffs who file suits claim that such injuries constitute defamation, invasion of privacy, conspiracy, nuisance, and interference with business.

SLAPP suits typically have the intended effect of silencing opponents. Defendants must often spend years entangled in the court system. Lawsuits distract antagonists from the main controversy by using up their time, energy, and money in the courtroom. Although most of the suits are eventually dismissed or dropped, they nevertheless have a chilling effect, making antagonists and their supporters cautious in speaking out. That was the intention of McDonald's when it filed a libel suit against two unemployed members of London Green Peace (no connection with Greenpeace International) who engaged in a smear campaign against the company (see Box 2.2).

Weaken Antagonists

A corporation can weaken the power base of an opposition group in at least two ways: (a) remove funding sources and (b) create obstacles to membership drives.

Remove Funding.   When a utility publication ran an article called "Where Do the Antis Get Their Money?" it pointed to Carter administration programs that were creating, training, and funding so-called public interest groups critical of business.[20] Government funding started in 1977 when the director of the independent federal agency ACTION started granting millions of tax dollars to groups such as the Association of Community Organizations for Reform Now (ACORN), which, according to its preamble, sought to gain "neighborhood control of the private sector ... by including workers on all corporate boards."[21] This practice was continued by former Nader associate Michael Pertschuk after he became chairman of the Federal Trade Commission. He granted more than $150,000 to various Nader and other antinuclear groups, such as the Union of Concerned Sci-

Box 2.2   McDonald's SLAPP Suit

McDonald's UK became aware that activist groups were distributing leaflets containing such appellations as McDeath, McDestruction, McProfits, and Big MacNasty. A pamphlet, "What's Wrong with McDonald's," blamed McDonald's for being cruel to animals, destroying the rainforest for cattle raising, having poor employment practices, and being an "aggressive capitalist."[22]

Eddie Bensilum, McDonald's spokeswoman, said, "This leaflet first came to our attention in 1984 and we wrote then asking London Green Peace to stop defaming McDonald's. We wrote repeatedly but never got a reply, and we were concerned many people would think the leaflet came from Greenpeace International."[23] With the approval of McDonald's headquarters, McDonald's UK started investigating the group by attending meetings and collecting printed materials. In 1990, writs were served on five group members. Three backed down; two, David Morris and Helen Steel, decided to fight it out. They received financial support from an international "McLibel Support Campaign."[24]

Selecting to represent themselves, the two activists contrasted sharply in the courtroom with McDonald's senior trial lawyer, a barrister who wears the traditional black gown and white wig. Steel, a former gardener, wore a striped T-shirt and slacks, and Morris, a former postman, wore sandals and socks. Some of McDonald's witnesses appeared foolish. On cross-examination, McDonald's senior vice president Edward Oakley said McDonald's menu items are nutritious because they include "nutrients." And a U.S. vice president for marketing said the Coca-Cola drink served is nutritious because it contains water "and this is part of a balanced diet."[25]

Throughout the years of court proceedings, the trial served to broadcast the group's message to millions. The trial became Britain's longest libel suit ever and turned into a public relations disaster for McDonald's, demonstrating the risk of a SLAPP suit. Legally, McDonald's eventually won the case in February 1997 when the trial judge found some claims untrue. On the other hand, he considered the claims true that hamburgers have poor dietary value, employees were underpaid, children were exploited through advertising, and cruel animal practices were employed in producing the meat for the hamburgers.[26] But "besides spending $16 million to get a $98,000 settlement (which the defendants couldn't pay), the company brought international attention to the activists' allegations, and set itself up as a corporate bully for going after them in court."[27]

entists, Friends of the Earth, the Sierra Club, the Environmental Defense Fund, and the National Resources Defense Council.

Some businesspeople have accused their brethren of financing the "antis." David Packard, a cofounder of Hewlett-Packard, stated that it was foolish to support institutions, such as Harvard University, that produce so many anti-business proponents. His view found expression when Central Michigan University came under fire from Dow Chemical following an antibusiness speech given by Jane Fonda. Central Michigan University received about $70,000 a year in direct cash grants from nearby Dow.[28] Although the announced title of the talk was "Politics in Film" and she was expected to speak on women's issues, Fonda lambasted multinational corporations and criticized the lack of economic freedom in America. She specifically mentioned Dow Chemical by quoting from the chairman's book *Global Reach*: "I have long dreamed of buying an island owned by no nation, and of establishing the World Headquarters of the Dow Company on the truly neutral ground of such an island beholden to no nation or society."[29]

Angered by Fonda's speech, Dow Chemical threatened to suspend its support for the university. In a letter to the university president, Dow Chemical's president wrote,

> While inviting Ms. Fonda to your campus is your prerogative, I consider it our prerogative and obligation to make certain our funds are never again used to support people intent upon destruction of freedom. Therefore, effective immediately, support of any kind from the Dow Chemical Company to Central Michigan University has been stopped, and will not [be] resumed until we are convinced our dollars are not expended to supporting those who would destroy us.[30]

Philip H. Knight, CEO of athletic shoe and apparel maker Nike, Inc., followed the same reasoning as Dow when on April 24, 2000, he announced that he would no longer donate money to the University of Oregon, his alma mater. The reason: A few days earlier, the university announced that it would join the Worker Rights Consortium, supported by students and several U.S.-based labor unions, to fight for higher wages and better working conditions in Nike's overseas manufacturing operations. Knight preferred that the university choose the less threatening Fair Labor Association, which had grown out of President Clinton's Apparel Industry Partnership initiative and was vigorously backed by Nike. Knight broke off tentative plans to make the company's biggest donation ever to renovate the football stadium. He said, "For me personally, there will be no further donations of any kind to the University of Oregon. At this time, this is not a situation that can be resolved. The bonds of trust, which allowed me to give at a high level, have been shredded."[31]

Another example of undermining an opposition group's source of funding is the campaign by business to prevent unions from using dues for political purposes. After the AFL-CIO spent $35 million in the 1996 elections, business introduced H.R. 1625 on the federal level; it would prohibit unions from using dues for lobbying, issue advocacy, election-related contributions and expenditures, and communications to union members on political topics.[32] Similar legislation was introduced in 25 states and the right-wing Americans for Tax Reform will eventually seek it in all 50 states. California's Proposition 226, introduced in June 1998 and supported by Republican governor Pete Wilson, "would force un-ions to get annual written permission from members before donating money to political campaigns."[33] The further effect of this measure is that labor would be forced to siphon off millions of dollars from its congressional campaign, which did actually help secure the Republican victory.

Create Obstacles to Membership Drives.   The opposition can be weakened by creating obstacles to their membership drives. Companies have established union avoidance programs when confronted by labor unions seeking to organize their employees. Using labor laws to its ad-vantage, a company announces that no union solicitation may take place on its premises. It openly tells employees that it opposes unioniza-tion, and states its reasons. It is allowed to do so under section 8(c) of the Taft-Hartley Act, provided that neither a promise nor a threat is made or implied. It cautions its supervisors not to intimidate any subordinates.

One likely reason why union membership has been declining is the greater use of antiunion tactics, which was *BusinessWeek's* answer to the enigma of "What's behind labor's poor showing lately?" Otherwise, ac-cording to a survey by Peter D. Hart Research Associates, some of the 43% of employees surveyed nationally who say that they would vote for a union at their workplace might just do that.[34]

Richard Bensinger, the former head of the AFL-CIO's organizing de-partment who was ousted by its president John J. Sweeney, criticizes business leaders for deterring unionization through a range of unethical tactics. He characterized labor laws as "a joke," and that "the right to or-ganize isn't respected by most companies.... There's not a free and open debate in a union election. Instead, there's coercion by management, which has total access to and control over the electorate. And there's no real punishment if they violate the law." When asked how CEOs should behave toward their employees who want a union, he answered: "Un-ions and companies should be adversaries, not enemies, which is how most executives treat us. We're the price business must pay to keep America a democracy. There is no example on earth of a democracy without unions. Unless CEOs respect their employees' wishes about whether to form a union or not, America can't really be called a demo-cratic country."[35]

Wal-Mart, the country's largest employer—it had 1.3 million work-ers as of June 2004 who earned an average of $9.76 an hour[36]—has been expert in keeping out unions, as its record of having won all but one of seven union votes in the United States proves. Coleman Peterson, executive vice president of the company's People Division, reflects the company's attitude: "Where associates [which is how Wal-Mart designates employees] feel free to communicate openly with their management, why would they need a third party to represent them?"[37] To discourage unionization, employers, like Wal-Mart, play hardball in these ways, as summarized by *BusinessWeek*:

- Hold mandatory antiunion meetings with workers (92%).
- Direct supervisors to meet one-on-one with workers (78%).
- Hire an antiunion consultant (75%).
- Mail antiunion letters to workers at home (70%).
- Fire union activists (25%).[38]

Foster Offsetting Interest Groups

Instead of weakening opposition groups, a corporation can offset them by fostering probusiness groups and forming coalitions with existing interest groups on specific issues. Why leave the designation of a public interest group only to others? Some probusiness interest groups already exist. Citizens for a Sound Economy, for example, seeks "to return decision-making to citizens by reducing government interference in the economy."[39] Many think tanks that support business or its ideology receive corporate financial support.

Ethical lines are sometimes crossed when business establishes a "front organization" that reflects its interests. A company may create or use the name of an organization that has the ring of an independent and unbiased group while serving the undisclosed interests of the company organizing and funding its activities. For example, a company may establish a "citizens' task force" for the purpose of opposing an environmental bill that negatively affects the company.[40] Instead of looking for outside supporters, corporations have extraordinary opportunities to develop true, formidable grassroots support by mobilizing stakeholders who share economic interests with them—investors, employees, local communities, and sometimes customers. The opportunity is greatest with employees, who are a company's largest natural constituency. A company can use its own channels of organizational communication to reach employees. If a unity of interest exists between company and employee interests, the likelihood of employee support is high. Chances are further enhanced when companies have excellent human resources policies that build employee cohesiveness, a feeling of belonging, and dedication to the corporate culture. This approach merges with engagement strategies.

ENGAGEMENT STRATEGIES

In contrast to containment strategies, a company can deal with interest groups by recognizing their legitimacy and working with them in a mutually beneficial manner. Engagement means developing relationships with interest groups and the stakeholders they represent. Although aspects of power and influence, as in containment strategies, are involved, the usual goal is to understand the concerns of an interest group and the more ambitious goal is to involve it in the decision-making process.

Unilateral Strategies

With engagement strategies, monitoring activities associated with issues management are focused on the concerns and demands of specific interest groups. Through formal opinion research, focus groups, and informal contact, an organization seeks to understand the perceptions of a target group: what aspects of organizational policy and actions it criticizes, what reasons underlie this evaluation, and what it plans to do to change the organization's behavior. This information enables an organization to determine whether a group's perceptions are accurate in terms of the reality of corporate performance. A company can go a step further and also consider its goal of how it wants to be seen by the public.

These three reference points—the perception, the actual facts, and the organization's ideal self-image—are summarized in so-called gap analysis as illustrated in Fig. 2.2.[41]

This diagram of how an organization relates to a target audience suggests two strategies, used singly or in combination: (a) a communication strategy to address the perception gap, and (b) a performance strategy to reduce the gap between current performance and that sought by the organization. These strategies are often confused with engagement strategies, but they shouldn't be because they do not require involvement with a target audience. Unilateral action is not collaboration. Nevertheless, they are discussed here because they are often a precursor to engagement.

Current Situation Point Scale:

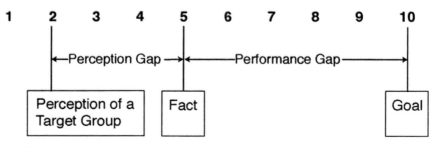

FIG. 2.2.   Gap analysis.

Communication Strategy to Manage Perceptions.   Conflict with an interest group arises when corporate performance does not measure up to its expectations, as reflected in the perception of the target group. A large gap between the two reference points triggers interest group action and indicates the rise of an emerging issue. In response, a company can close the perception gap through various communication actions, such as publicity, advocacy ads, speeches, seminars, and publications. Box 2.3 illustrates a McDonald's communication effort to address criticisms of protest groups.

Sometimes an organization's management may see the perception problem not as giving a target audience correct and adequate information but as changing the expectations of the group. Corporations have used this strategy with its employees; for example, telling them

---

Box 2.3   McDonald's Attempts to Set the Record Straight

McDonald's has increasingly been the target of protest groups abroad. In France, a variety of incidents received wide media coverage. Among them are the destruction of a restaurant under construction in the central French city of Millau in August 1999 by a left-leaning farm organization and the bombing of an outlet in the western region of Brittany in mid-2000, killing a young manager. McDonald's risked losing more customers as unions accused it of exploiting its workforce of 35,000, composed largely of youth and ethnic minorities.

McDonald's France decided on a communication strategy to provide its critics and customers with more information about its operations. It decided to acknowledge what its critics had been saying and to answer them by publishing a book, *McDonald's Se Met a Table* (McDonald's Turns the Tables). By doing so, the company challenged the precept that communicating one's troubles to the public is not always a sound strategy—a precept based on the notion that public awareness of the criticisms and actions taken by some protesters leads to further dissemination of negative messages.

McDonald's France president Denis Hennequin and his two managing directors, Jean-Pierre Petit and Philippe Labbe, authored the book for the purpose of setting the record straight. They sought to explain why consumers flock to the chain while French opponents of globalization roast it over the coals. In their 110-page book, they defended the quality of its food, the company's role as a major player in the French economy, and its commitment to good employee relations. The time has come to say enough is enough, the trio said. They stated, "Like any company, we are exposed to the problems of society, to the problems of change, to the problems of employment. And so it is in this context that we should know how to make our brand liked, beyond prejudice, rancor and partisan interests."

that the old social contract of providing lifetime jobs is no longer fea-sible. Changing people's expectations is a difficult task that requires much long-term effort. When a crisis occurs, however, such as the prospect of job loss, the task is easier because people's frame of refer-ence is different.

Performance Strategy.   The performance strategy is an alternative suggested by gap analysis. If a company decides that its actual perfor-mance—the fact—is truly short of meeting its desired goal or the legiti-mate interest groups' expectations, it can narrow the performance gap by taking concrete actions, such as removing human rights violations, reducing pollution, or improving employee and community safety.

In "Engagement with Integrity," Michael A. Santoro discusses public criticism of the human rights violations of multinational corpora-tions.[42] He states that most business executives believe they have no par-ticular responsibility for human rights. However, public attention to the issue has led some business groups to issue statements. On the interna-tional scene, the American Chamber of Commerce in Hong Kong (AmCham) made a strong and direct pledge to "refuse to do business with firms which employ forced labor, or treat their workers in inhu-mane or unsafe ways."[43] It subscribed to the author's fair share theory, which states that business bears some but not all responsibility to un-dertake the burden of advancing human rights. It proposed that a corporation has these responsibilities:

- Maintain acceptable working conditions in its own operations and uphold the rights of its employees to freedom of expression.
- Take responsibility for the actions of its business partners in such matters as employment practices, wages and benefits, working hours, use of child labor, use of prison labor or forced labor, dis-crimination, and disciplinary practices.
- Resist pressure from the Chinese government to use the multina-tional corporation as a vehicle to abuse human rights, for example, by not hiring (or rehiring) employees who are punished by with-holding jobs from them.[44]

Nike, mentioned earlier, has been targeted by student activists and others for paying low wages and ignoring human rights violations in its Asian plants. The company received much negative publicity in the me-dia. Two stories were particularly damaging. *Life* magazine documented the use of child labor in Pakistan to produce soccer balls for Nike and other companies, showing photographs of small children sitting in a dirty environment stitching together the panels of a soccer ball. The sec-ond was a CBS News *48 Hours* broadcast in October 1996 that focused on low wage rates, extensive overtime, and physical abuse of workers in Nike's factories in Vietnam.[45]

A marketing research study of Nike among young people aged 13 to 25 reported that their top three perceptions were (a) athletics, (b) cool, and (c) bad labor practices. The company decided to do something about the third perception. In 1992 it drafted its first Code of Conduct, which applied to subcontractors and suppliers; in 1994 it hired Ernst & Young, the accounting firm, to monitor alleged worker abuses in its Indonesian factories; in 1996 it hired GoodWorks International, headed by former civil rights leader Andrew Young, to investigate conditions in overseas factories; and in 1998 it formed a Corporate Responsibility Division. Later that year CEO Philip H. Knight gave a speech at which he announced several initiatives; for example, to raise the minimum age for employment in the company's shoe factories to 18.[46]

Social Audits.   Nike, McDonald's, and others have accompanied changes in performance with adopting various forms of social audits, which attempt to measure a company's social performance. Nike hired Ernst & Young for this purpose. Even more extensive has been the trend toward social reporting, which is a way of keeping interest groups, the media, and others informed about the results of social audits and, more generally, such areas of social responsibility as employee benefits, environmental improvements, and corporate philanthropy.

McDonald's ventured into this method of communicating in April 2002 when, being sensitive to its status as an international symbol of American capitalism and globalization, it published its first worldwide social responsibility report. Its 46 pages address many criticisms hurled at the company, as reflected in the report's four headings: community, environment, people, and wider marketplace, including animal welfare and labor practices at McDonald's suppliers. For example, it describes its new "U.S. standards" for the way chickens are housed, which are being followed by other leading retailers. The company also points out other accomplishments: its long-standing policy not to buy beef from rainforest lands and its testing of new packaging materials such as EarthShell (made mostly from calcium carbonate and recycled potato starch rather than paper or plastic).

Both strategies—communications and performance—can be taken unilaterally by management without the involvement of interest groups. The communications strategy might be called a one-way, asymmetrical approach, in the language of public relations.[47] Their tone is that interest groups and their members are ignorant or misinformed about a company and that the antidote is to give them the facts—to "educate them." This traditional approach is increasingly considered inadequate and condescending by target groups. The unilateral performance improvement strategy also has a failing because it may not consider the specific grievances of a target group; that is, the type of performances that the group thinks should be changed. Neither strategy, therefore, constitutes an engagement strategy.

Public Participation Strategies

Engagement means working with interest groups and their stakeholders. It is a two-way, symmetrical process that involves the groups that have targeted, or might target, an organization.

Efforts are therefore undertaken to listen to the concerns of people, not only through opinion surveys but through personal contact with them. These concerns are integrated into the decision making of an organization and efforts are undertaken to measure the outcome of subsequent actions taken. Good examples of the application of public participation have been government agencies and, in the private sector, various types of community involvement programs.

Citizen Participation in Government.   Government programs generally use the term *public participation* for federally assisted programs that require or recommend the involvement of citizens. The introduction to a booklet by the Community Services Administration published in 1978, when the concept began to become highly accepted, provides this explanation:

> The decade and a half preceding our Bicentennial celebration of the establishment of representative democracy in this country witnessed the emergence of participatory democracy, referred to as "citizen participation." Today virtually all programs in which Federally appropriated funds are used require citizen access to the decision-making process. With respect to these programs, citizens are defined as those persons whose membership in a population served or affected by a specific Federal program entitles them to assist variously in designing, operating, and evaluating the program. The nature of such participation is varied and is established by statute to administrative regulation.[48]

Government organizations have continued to promote public participation. This process was discussed in a landmark Public Participation Benchmarking Conference, held in October 1997 and organized by Gary Pitchford, director of Communications of the Argonne National Laboratory's Chicago Operations Office.[49] Martha Crosland, Acting Director of the Department of Energy's (DOE) Office of Intergovernmental and Public Accountability, described public participation as "open, ongoing, two-way communication, both formal and informal" between stakeholders and the DEO.[50] She stated that DOE's three major goals were:

1. To actively seek and consider public input, and incorporate or respond to stakeholder views in making DOE decisions.
2. To provide a public involvement process where the public is informed in a timely manner about, and empowered to participate in, the decision-making process.

3. To incorporate credible, effective public participation into the department's programs, planning, and decisions.[51]

The DOE discovered that access to information is an important factor affecting public trust and confidence, which is crucial to accomplishment of its mission. Donald Beck, senior project director of the Gallup Organization, stated that trust in government leads to a more ready public acceptance of decisions, especially difficult ones involving risk estimates and hazard policies.[52] Giving the public access to information is highly important in creating such trust.

Public participation involves a shift away from *wholesale* to *retail*, said Jim Creighton, president of Creighton & Creighton, Inc. Instead of a tendency to invite everyone to every issue, the retail approach moves toward targeting the most interested groups and individuals. Creighton advises organizations to avoid large public forums for issues in which risk is a significant factor, because such public meetings "tend to exaggerate the differences among different positions and generally won't bear the process of consensus building."[53] Furthermore, he draws a distinction between consensus-seeking public participation and dispute resolution and negotiation, which is discussed in the next chapter.

Community Involvement Programs. The private sector has applied the principles of public participation to community relations, often using the term *community involvement*. This approach is fostered because of the proximity of local interest groups to a specific organization. Business has learned that it can gain greater freedom in finding ways to cut pollution by engaging in dialogue with government officials and environmental groups. The President's Council on Sustainable Development (PCSD), consisting of top executives from Dow Chemical and Chevron, government officials from the Environmental Protection Agency (EPA) and DOE, and heads of organizations like the Sierra Club and the National Wildlife Federation, recommended greater use of dialogue to resolve problems. The PCSD report further states: "For their part, businesses need to build the practice and skills of dialogue with communities and citizens, participating in community decision-making and opening their own values, strategies and performance to their community and society." David Guzzelli, vice president and corporate director at Dow Chemical, stated: "We believe that consensus will move America forward both faster and further than confrontation."[54]

Community involvement programs have often been developed in response to crises. After the gas leakage in Union Carbide's Bhopal, India, plant in 1984, which killed more than 2,500 people, Congress passed Title III, the Emergency Planning and Community Right-to-Know Act. The act gave the EPA authority to mandate the formation of local emergency planning committees across the nation. Although they were primarily intended to plan for emergencies, they were also designed to serve as forums where citizens could request information and voice concerns.[55] One example of this process is that in the early 1990s, the Chemical Manufacturers Association (now the American Chemistry Council) advised members to form community advisory panels (CAPs) as part of its Responsible Care program. CAPs were intended to "serve as forums for public dialogue over risk identification, assessment, and reduction."

Public participation is facilitated by a variety of mechanisms: advisory councils consisting of community leaders, ambassador and envoy programs that allow an organization's members to listen to and involve community members, and a variety of outreach programs that attract community citizens to an organization's activities. Box 2.4 describes the experience of Brookhaven National Laboratory and the programs it developed to regain public trust and confidence through its public participation program. Key features are its Community Advisory Council and its envoy program. The latter serve as the eyes and ears for the lab. At one time 45 envoys were actively engaged, "reaching out" to external organizations and bringing back feedback. Box 2.5 lists suggestions from the International Association for Public Participation to facilitate the practice of public participation.

Public Participation Beyond the Community—The World Bank.   As the next chapter describes, public participation has been a means of conflict resolution with environmental groups, used by corporations as well as government (e.g., the EPA). It has also been used by international institutions. After facing protests at its meetings, the World Bank learned that it is better to deal with "civil society" by shifting from confrontation to engagement.

Instead of treating criticism as a matter of wrong perceptions, the bank introduced forms of collaboration and a more open information policy with protest groups. This approach was started when James Wolfensohn became the bank's president in 1995. The five strands in the bank's new strategy were described as follows by John Clark, the bank's principal social-development specialist:

- Expand collaboration in operations, emphasizing early involvement by civil society in project design.
- Engage civil society by discussing strategies within each country.
- Adopt a new disclosure policy of making a wider array of information public.
- Establish a regular dialogue on big policy issues, such as environment and debt relief, replacing more informal consultations.
- Use the bank's influence over governments that borrow from the bank to encourage greater tolerance of civil groups.[56]

The purpose of the World Bank is compatible with the process of public participation in dealing with civil society, including interest groups that have demonstrated against it. The bank, which is one of the world's

Box 2.4 Brookhaven National Lab Demonstrates Value of Public Participation

When a policy, decision, or behavior by an organization affects the vital interests of a stakeholder group, that group has an expectation that it be included in the decision-making process. Serious confrontations and consequences can occur if that expectation is not met. One of the policymaking roles of a public relations or public affairs director is to advise top management when such public involvement is desirable—or absolutely necessary.

Brookhaven National Laboratory, a U.S. DOE laboratory founded in 1947, was named Organization of the Year by the International Association for Public Participation (IAP2) last May for making the right policy decisions. "Brookhaven not only actively seeks out and facilitates the involvement of those potentially affected by lab decisions, but also effectively provides the public with information that allows them to participate in a meaningful way," IAP2 said. A new management group, installed after the DOE fired the former managers, recognized the importance of such public affairs measures in creating a community action plan and forming a community advisory council. Dr. John Marburger, the lab's director since 1998, recognized that science could not be put ahead of safety, which his predecessor had done. He said, "It pays to have the community understand what we do … and try to operate in harmony with the community instead of fighting with them."

One member of the Lab's Community Advisory Council said, "Brookhaven's public participation initiatives are remarkably effective. I think the Lab has put forward an exceptional effort and has made a significant, honest effort to listen and respond to issues raised by the community. I am quite impressed with the major strides the Lab has made in being open and responsive to the issues that we and other community groups raise."

Recognizing the importance of public affairs, one of Marburger's first actions was to bring the communications, community involvement, and government affairs functions under one manager who sits at the policymaking table and who reports directly to him. Marge Lynch was appointed to that position and given the title of assistant laboratory director. Most responsible for public participation programs is Kathleen Geiger, manager of the community involvement office.

Brookhaven's public participation program has several components: (a) the Community Advisory Council consisting of representatives from more than 30 local civic, health, environmental, and business organizations; (b) a 15-person Stakeholder Relations Team that had face-to-face interviews with 60 Long Island opinion leaders and covered 20 issues; (c) Ambassador program, which involves employees in community activities; (d) the Envoy program that builds on relationships employees already have with community organizations; (e) outreach and community programs, such as Summer Sunday; and (f) a speakers bureau.

The lab sought community participation to deal with a difficult environmental crisis: Plumes of volatile organic compounds were discovered off site in 1996 and in 1997 an on-site plume of groundwater contaminated with radioactive tritium was discovered. After receiving extensive community input, the DOE and Brookhaven are reviewing alternative options for cleaning up contaminated sediment in the site and neighboring communities' Peconic River. Says a community activist, "Their interest and willingness in getting involved in public participation is still new. The journey is hardly over." Brookhaven National Laboratory would agree, realizing that relationship building is an ongoing process and not just a way to deal with crises.

largest sources of development assistance, works with government agencies, NGOs, and the private sector to formulate assistance strategies. Its country offices worldwide deliver the Bank's program in countries, liaise with government and civil society, and work to increase understanding of development issues.

Because members of specific interest groups are difficult to reach directly, the World Bank and other large organizations have learned the value of the two-step flow of communication and consequently reach their audiences through their opinion leaders. The following section of

---

Box 2.5   Core Values and Practices That Promote Public Participation

Core values

- The public should have a say in decisions about actions that affect their lives.
- Public participation includes the promise that the public's contribution will influence decisions.

Facilitating processes

- Communicate the interests, and meet the process needs of all participants.
- Involve participants in defining how they participate.
- Communicate to participants how their input affected the decision.
- Provide participants with the information needed to participate in a meaningful way.

this chapter deals with various forms of opinion leader communication intended to change the perceptions and attitudes of interest group leaders. The next chapter extends communication to include conflict resolution through mediation and negotiation. When an issue is resolved at the emerging-issues stage, its life cycle is aborted; the issue no longer threatens a company by moving to the stage of public involvement and, later, to the legislative stage.

OPINION LEADER COMMUNICATION

The most practical way to communicate with interest groups is through their thought and opinion leaders because they are the thinkers, writers, disseminators, and activists who originate ideas and synthesize issues. These individuals, sometimes with the help of accompanying events and crises, create the emerging issues that begin the life cycle of an issue. Furthermore, opinion leaders may form public interest groups to propagandize and promote these emerging issues, or existing groups may adopt their issues.

Communication theory provides an audience perspective of opinion leaders. Individuals seek out opinion leaders to obtain information and opinions about questions of concern to them. The subject matter ranges from new products and technology to political questions about candidates and issues. Researchers identify opinion leaders by asking people various forms of the question "Who do you ask when you want to know about ...?" Early political studies assumed that these leaders would be sought from among those with a higher socioeconomic status than the inquirers, but subsequent studies have proven that opinion leader status can be on any level, depending on the subject matter.

What distinguishes opinion leaders from others is that they know more about a subject than ordinary people, or are so perceived. In the two-step flow of mass communication, opinion leaders are more avid consumers of newspapers, magazines, television, and radio and can therefore relay messages to others as well as add opinions of their own. Another theory, the diffusion of innovation, depicts opinion leaders as the first to become aware of and adopt a new idea. They are likely to be cosmopolitans who are more concerned with national political issues and more likely to be exposed to national magazines and public affairs broadcasts than local leaders. In the language of communication networks, the locals are oriented to a single network of interpersonal relations whereas cosmopolitans are oriented to several networks, particularly outside ones, which might include a professional society.

Viewed from a political perspective, opinion leaders are an important target audience for corporations because they provide links with members of interest groups and the general public. Interest groups, mostly the activist type, are important entities in modern societies because they represent individuals with shared attitudes who make claims on other groups in society.[57] In theory, individual citizens function primarily through these interest groups, which promote group goals when appropriate and necessary. A fundamental characteristic of the public policy process is that these groups select and formulate goals as well as initiate specific actions. If all groups engage in this process, policymakers would ultimately recognize all individual interests.[58]

A corporation engages in opinion leader communication as a way of gaining some control over the political process. It does so by targeting specific individuals and small groups that introduce new ideas, some of which become emerging issues. By getting involved at an early stage, corporations have the greatest chance of influencing the outcome of an issue.

One way a corporation can directly affect an issue's outcome is to arrest its development by resolving the issue with the leaders of the relevant interest group or groups before it becomes a full-blown legislative matter. Determining when it is practical to do this and how conflicts can be resolved before they proceed to the public involvement and legislative stages are issues discussed in chapter 3.

Interpersonal communication skills are essential to opinion leader communication. One rule in such endeavors is that communication must be two-way. A company must be willing to listen to those who seek change, and be prepared to amend its own thinking and action. As communication theorists point out, such responsiveness is particularly necessary when dealing with people who espouse strong views on an issue or who may not consider messages from an opposing organization to be credible. Also, whenever an organization deals with an unfriendly or opposing audience, both sides of an issue should be presented. Preferably, the audience's views should be mentioned first before presenting one's own.

Saying that communication should be two-way, however, does not adequately describe the willingness to allow audience members to participate in decision making. Increasingly people demand a voice in decisions that affect them. Forms of public participation—sometimes required by law—and collaborative planning go far beyond the simple model of two-way communication. The views of participants become integrated into the decision making of an organization. A corporation's quest to have its way may be restrained at this stage in return for an issue's resolution.

Overall, therefore, the objectives of opinion leader communication are several: (a) open a communication link with persons who hold differing views and values, (b) provide new information for their consideration, (c) attempt to enlarge their perspective, (d) change their perceptions, and (e) bring about a meeting of minds.

Interpersonal media dominate opinion leader communication. These range from face-to-face communication between two persons or a small group to speeches made to larger audiences. With smaller numbers, it is possible to engage in a dialogue in which information and views are exchanged with the aim of discovering areas of agreement as well as disagreement. A dialogue is often the prelude to resolution of an issue. When resolved, the issue exits from the life cycle chart.

Face-to-Face Communication and Other Forms of Personal Communication

One of society's basic building blocks is the relationship between two persons. This is exemplified by spontaneous conversations, interviews, and various encounters, such as between husband and wife, parent and child, doctor and patient, teacher and pupil, and other dyads.

Close, face-to-face contact allows for the conveyance of maximum information. Besides the spoken message, the appearance, clothes, and body language of someone may suggest certain attitudes and personality traits. For example, a carefully groomed man wearing a pin-striped dark blue suit would appear to want to hold conventional attitudes and fit in with the business community. Face-to-face contact permits immediate feedback, thus allowing for flexibility in presenting an argument. If something is known about another person, the conversation may incorporate his or her interests and thereby enhance receptivity.

Personal communication, especially face to face, requires people to develop their listening skills. But "from talk shows to offices, everybody is jabbering but few are listening" in today's society.[59] In our fast-paced world, says Kathy Thompson, a conversation teacher at Alverno College in Milwaukee, "we're always in a hurry. Mentally we're saying, get to the point, we don't have time to hear the whole story.... Good listening takes time."[60] Furthermore, says Wicke Chambers, a partner in Speechworks, an Atlanta communications-training firm, "People think listening is boring; it's more fun to talk."[61] Talking is perceived as active and dominant, listening as passive and deferential.

Basic face-to-face personal communications are supplemented by other forms that contain decreasing amounts of information: telephone conversations, letters, and e-mail. Telephone voice quality may reflect mood, a handwritten letter may still convey personality through handwriting style, and e-mail may reflect limited personality attributes.

The shortcomings of other forms of personal communication are revealed in a study of the e-mail system at a southeastern university. One finding is that senders overly concentrate on the technological process while ignoring the message's impact on the receiver. Because inhibitions seem to drop, a more aggressive stance is taken because "you're not face-to-face," said full-time faculty and administrators. Cues obtained from a person's eyes, gestures, posture, and facial expressions are absent and therefore do not affect the message. Words carry the entire meaning in e-mail, so more phrases that convey the intent of a message, such as "I'm asking for clarification, not admonishing you," or "This is a very difficult question and I'm feeling uncomfortable asking you" should be used.[62]

Small-Group Meetings, Forums, and Dialogue Communications

Many of the features of a conversation are extended into small-group meetings, which can take a variety of forms: corporate guest speakers in college classrooms or at community meetings, an open house where small groups gather to listen to an executive or guide, or a panel discussion at a professional meeting. The presentation of papers at a professional meeting may be in the form of a small-group meeting or, if the number of people is large and prohibits much interaction, in the form of a speech or lecture.

Dialogue communications are conversational meetings of a small group of people who share their concerns, exchange information, and seek solutions to problems. These meetings can take place informally in an office when a manager meets with representatives of a group to address an issue. Or meetings can be more formal, held in a conference room with a larger group of people to discuss problems of mutual concern. These meetings can be one-time, occasional, or regular.

Dialogue Versus Discussion.   The distinct meaning of a dialogue becomes clearer by comparing it with a discussion, a necessary counterpart of dialogue.[63] In a discussion, different views are presented and defended; in dialogue, different views are presented "gently" as a means of discovering a new view. Participants in a dialogue are willing to suspend assumptions and enter into genuine "thinking together." In a sense, participants become observers of their own thinking. Such dialogue is divergent, however, as complex issues are explored and a richer grasp of them is obtained. When the goal is to converge on a conclusion or course of action, a discussion is necessary. Alternative views need to be weighed and a preferred view selected. Thus, movement back and forth between dialogue and discussion is needed.

Members of an organization who plan to meet with members of outside groups are advised to engage in a dialogue among themselves before and during meetings with others. The purpose, as explained in Peter M. Senge's *The Fifth Discipline*, is that team members understand their own views better, both individually and collectively—unlike the discussion format, which seeks to have one's own view accepted by the group.[64] In a dialogue we are not trying to win but to go beyond the understanding of any one individual. New insights are gained, based on the full depth of people's experience and thought.

For dialogue to occur, three conditions must be met:

1. All participants must suspend their assumptions, which in itself requires an awareness that each view is based on assumptions rather than incontrovertible fact.
2. All participants must regard one another as colleagues in a mutual quest for deeper insight and clarity. Differences in hierarchical status must be set aside.

3. A facilitator should be present who keeps the dialogue flowing and knows how to balance discussion with dialogue.[65]

Many social and political problems are caused by misunderstandings among different groups. They hold stereotyped views of one another and operate on the basis of partial and inaccurate information. As a community participant said to management representatives at a consumer roundtable held by a utility company: "I used to believe that capitalists are people who don't have feelings … that they run money-making machines. Now I know you have feelings."[66] At these same roundtables, the utility was asked about affirmative action criteria in hiring. The participants were uninformed of the facts because the local media had not reported such information. Through the dialogue of the consumer roundtables, the human resources manager was able to explain the utility's policy and the extent to which minority group persons (e.g., of Hispanic and Chinese descent) had been hired. The utility was also able to point out that union contracts made it impossible for it to move faster in meeting affirmative action goals.

Creating a Neutral Zone. Carlton Spitzer, a public relations counselor who is a leading proponent of dialogue communications, explains that some kind of "neutral zone" must be discovered or invented. It is needed "to give us time to consider, to relate, to sort out the trade-offs, to articulate national and local priorities in a democratic but nonthreatening atmosphere."[67] Although his frame of reference was the turbulent era of the 1960s and 1970s, which wrought riots, demonstrations, and confrontations in the nation, his ideas apply to any time or situation when an organization faces new issues and demands. The neutral zone, says Spitzer, is in the mind: "It is the willingness of people having different interests to come together to draw a montage on the wall; to identify gaps and misconceptions; to compromise in order to gain consensus toward the achievement of larger purposes in which all people have a stake."[68] Spitzer maintains that the nation needs brokers and matchmakers who will bring adversaries together on common ground.

In dialogue communications, however, the adversarial mind-set must be put aside so that people with different interests can come together and achieve a "candid exchange of ideas, the cooling of tempers, and the resolution of basic misunderstanding."[69] One of Spitzer's examples is the rumor disseminated by the media that during the Iranian revolution, ARCO and other oil companies had tankers, loaded with oil, sitting offshore to create an oil shortage and a corresponding jump in prices. To correct this media inaccuracy, Anthony Hatch, then ARCO's manager of corporate media relations, took a group of oil executives on the road to meet with reporters and editors in on-the-record informal discussions.

As to the structure of dialogue meetings, Spitzer says that they "must maximize freedom, assure nonattribution, and demand nothing in terms of official statements or decisions or actions."[70] In describing meetings between business leaders and government officials, he notes these characteristics:

- There was just plain talk in plain surroundings.
- No agenda was printed.
- Everyone was able to speak candidly with his or her counterparts without fear of attribution.
- No secrets were leaked or confidential data disclosed.
- No one was allowed to make a speech about any special problem or to plead for a favor.

Spitzer emphasizes that dialogue must begin long before issues develop into legislative or legal battles: "It is never enough to do the right things; industry must also convince others whose support and understanding it needs that it is, in fact, doing the right thing."[71]

Constituency Relations. Another example of dialogue communications is the constituency relations program established at Texaco by Mary Ann Pires, former manager of planning and constituency relations and now president of The Pires Group. She met regularly with a variety of national consumer and public interest groups. Pires's mandate was to "systematically open lines of communication with influential third-party groups; in short, to develop the interaction necessary for proactive public relations/public affairs."[72] Her objectives were "to become familiar with each organization, its goals and needs, and to enable the group to put a 'face' to Texaco—to actually meet and talk with someone from a 'Big Oil Company.'"[73] Texaco's program illustrates that public relations practitioners are "facilitators of communication in a complex society, brokers between competing interests."[74]

Pires followed these principles in dealing with Texaco's constituent groups:

- Develop long-term relations. Too many companies, she was told by consumer and public interest groups, would meet with them once and never return. Texaco became convinced, says Pires, it could not expect people to have any interest in the company and its issues if the only time it approached them was when it wanted something.
- Don't promise anything you can't deliver. But when you say you'll do something, do it.
- Don't develop a "checkbook relationship." Texaco's policy is not to make contributions in situations where it cannot work with the organization on a mutual objective.

Speechmaking: Supplementing Interpersonal Communication

Speechmaking is a useful tool in various life cycle stages of issues management. In Stage 1, speeches provide an opportunity to reach opinion leaders and activist groups; in Stage 2, speeches provide an opportunity to send reprints to media; and in Stage 3, speeches allow a company to present its views at public hearings.

The important advantages of speeches in Stage 1 communications are:

- They can be given to audiences of various sizes: to small, select groups that are identified with specific issues, or to larger groups with a common interest.
- They can be delivered by the most credible spokesperson: an executive, scientist, or other specialist who is most knowledgeable about an issue or has authority in relationship to it.
- They can provide immediate feedback, and thus, to a smaller extent, emulate face-to-face communication (a blank look on someone in the audience might indicate lack of interest, and raised eyebrows might signify doubt or hostility).
- They demonstrate the organization's openness—its respect for others and willingness to deal with them.
- They help humanize an organization.

Make Strategic Use of Speeches.   Corporate executives make the mistake of addressing essentially the same audiences year after year on just about the same subjects, observed Robert S. Mason in a 10-year review of speeches.[75] Although some ritual speaking is obligatory and unavoidable, speeches should be designed with specific objectives in mind. Mason said they should "be part of a speaking program expressing and furthering the company's public relations policies, which in turn support overall company strategy."[76] He points out that an innovative speaking program "creates the opportunity for dialogue between top management and the groups representing the full range of interests and aspirations stirring in the social environment."[77]

One way to assure the strategic use of speeches is to employ a management-by-objectives (MBO) approach. As with other activities, MBO allows management to focus on achievable goals and to make the most efficient use of its resources. It is a systematic and organized approach involving the following steps:

1. Set objectives.
2. Define the audience—Treat it like a market niche.
3. Allocate resources—personnel, money, executive time—to support the program.
4. Determine the content of the speech.
5. Plan the further dissemination of the speech through reprints and publicity.

Further dissemination of speeches can support government relations objectives, states a booklet by the North American Precis Syndicate, a media relations agency that distributes hundreds of editorials, cartoons, and feature stories for use by small papers. It lists these advantages:

- "You reach suburban women and senior citizens who hate inflation and write to legislators.
- You reach the legislative aides who keep track of what the newspapers back home are printing about the issue.
- You reach hometown political leaders and contributors to whom legislators turn for guidance and support."[78]

Make News as Well as Speeches.   A speech can be viewed as a newsworthy special event, rather than empty rhetoric that is unrelated to the philosophy, policies, and actions of a company. Speeches are opportunities to enunciate policy for the benefit of specific groups, including the company's own employees.

Speeches by CEOs have newsworthy potential because leaders of organizations have the power to institute policy changes. Sometimes it is the speechwriter, however, who serves as a catalyst for policy changes. Aram Bakahian, a speechwriter for former president Richard Nixon, notes that when existing policy is vague, speechwriters play an important role in clarifying stands as well as creating new policies.[79] Although this example applies to Stage 2 communications, speeches to select groups in Stage 1 communication can serve the purpose of announcing a change in organizational policy that accommodates the needs of the group.

CEO speeches are prepared in various ways. One survey of the nation's top 1,000 companies showed that just over one third of CEOs say they write their own speeches, either a draft or a final version; about a quarter tell their public relations directors what to write, and seldom change their drafts; and about another quarter ask for drafts from a number of executives.[80] Although busy executives can use help, there are good arguments why they should write major speeches themselves: Their thoughts and beliefs are clarified by the discipline of choosing the right words for clarity of expression; delivery is apt to be more natural, direct, and convincing; and valuable practice is obtained in talking extemporaneously. In an article titled "Corporate Speechmaking: It's Not Like Selling Soap," Norman Wasserman, a former Ruder-Finn vice president, insisted that "Speeches by corporate officers should bear their own imprimaturs and convey their own personal, incisive corporate viewpoints."[81]

For purposes of opinion leader communication, news dissemination of speeches should be contained within membership groups or within a community. Weekly newspapers in communities are particularly receptive to speeches about local issues. For Stage 2 communication, however, speeches could be used as a basis for a national news release to support company goals.

Apply Techniques of Persuasion in Speeches. Because public affairs speeches are intended to persuade an audience to adopt a certain point of view, they must contain a variety of types of evidence. Mary Jane Genova, a communications consultant for Fortune 500 executives, lists these: statistics (from research studies and opinion surveys); scientific evidence and statements by experts; history, case histories, and organizational histories; personal experience, anecdotes, and visuals.[82] She suggests that at the conclusion to the speech, the speaker should ask the audience to do something: think a certain way about a problem, write a letter to a representative, and take personal action.

Communication theorists suggest applying some of the following principles of persuasion in a speech before a group of people who are likely to disagree with a corporate position:

1. Build a bridge of common values. Try to overcome the difference in outlook by referring to common values and goals.
2. Use a two-sided approach. Start by demonstrating your understanding of their position and indicate where you are in agreement. Then talk about other points of view, including your own. In this way you are again establishing a bridge between you and them.
3. Allow for a Q & A session, but make sure you are prepared in at least two ways: (a) Know what your corporate policies are (these should be thought out very carefully), and (b) anticipate questions that will be asked, and have prepared answers.

Newsletters, Small Publications, and the Internet

Like speeches, newsletters and small publications can reach small groups of people who initiate change. They bear similarities to small-group communications when people know one another. However, if circulation is large and members do not know one another, newsletters are more like a newspaper reaching a mass audience. Most intellectual and political movements communicate with their members through newsletters. Their editors may be open to letters and reports from outsiders if the material is of interest to their members. The academic journals of professional groups are another vehicle through which ideas and studies can be disseminated.

The Internet provides another means of interacting with a variety of groups, as discussed in the introduction to part II. Activist groups and nonprofit organizations may benefit the most from the Web by using its two-way communication potential to engage in dialogue and build relationships with its publics. These interest groups have embraced the technical aspects of website design that enable them to be effectively used during the early stages of relationship building, but they fall down in creating a dialogue. "Dialogic loops" and feedback or "generating return visits" are necessary to build relationships. Visitors have to be offered reasons to return to sites. A study of how activist organizations use the Internet to build relationships lists important features of a site that encourage dialogue: ease of interface (e.g., a site map), usefulness of information to media publics and volunteer publics, conservation of visitor (e.g., making important information available on the first page), return visits (e.g., calendar of events and links to other Websites), and dialogic loop (e.g., opportunity for user response and voting on issues).[83]

Interest groups are not, however, getting high scores in incorporating enough of these two-way communication features in their sites. Although 94% of organizations in one survey provided places for users to "respond," only 44% allowed visitors to show how they felt about issues and only 16% on whether they agreed with the activist organization's position. Also, only 54% of the organizations update their "calendars of events" within 30 days of a visit.[84] To realize the potential of websites, organizations must engage in better relationship-building practices.

CONCLUSIONS

Corporations must learn to deal with interest groups because they represent a major force in a corporation's sociopolitical environment and initiate many issues. Strategies to contain the efforts of these groups have predominated, but a newer approach is to seek engagement in an effort to resolve issues for mutual benefit. Although some unilateral action may be taken in response to demands, corporations are also applying public participation strategies, often on a community level.

Various forms of opinion leader communication are used to either to contain an issue or resolve it. Containment strategies seem appropriate for an emerging issue that is not widely recognized and is unlikely to gain support. If the interest groups supporting an issue appear successful in gaining recognition and support for the championed issue, corporations must immediately prepare for the next life cycle stage of public involvement. Before an issue becomes full blown, they can attempt to gain understanding for their perspective on the issue through one-on-one meetings and group discussion and give dialogue a chance to clear mutual misunderstandings. At this point winning is not the goal. The quest for dominance is restrained in favor of removing a contentious issue and reaching a mutual accommodation. An appraisal of these efforts will determine whether a resolution is possible (as discussed in chap. 3) or whether proactive public affairs programs must be undertaken to win public support.

ENDNOTES

1. For a chart on the "Build-up of Social Energy in Response to an Emerging Public Issue" see Hazel Henderson, *Creating Alternative Futures: The End of Economics* (New York: Berkley Publishing, 1978), p. 231.

2. On this point, see Barry M. Nitnick, editor, "The Strategic Uses of Regulation—and Deregulation," *Corporate Political Agency: The Construction of Competition in Public Affairs* (Newbury Park, Calif.: Sage, 1993), p. 73.

3. Ibid., p. 74. Also see pp. 75–76 for other examples.

4. Saul D. Alinsky, *Rules for Radicals: A Practical Primer for Realistic Radicals* (New York: Vintage Books, 1971).

5. Jarol B. Manheim, *The Death of a Thousand Cuts* (Mahwah, N.J.: Lawrence Erlbaum Associates, 2001), p. vii.

6. Ibid., pp. 91–92.

7. The "Farah Manufacturing Company" case is included in Frederick D. Sturdivant and Larry M. Robinson, *The Corporate Social Challenge: Cases and Commentaries* (Homewood, Illinois: Richard D. Irwin, 1977), pp. 71–81.

8. Ibid., p. 79.

9. James E. Stacey and Frederick S. Sturdivant, "J. P. Stevens & Co., Inc.," *The Corporate Social Challenge: Cases and Commentaries* (Boston, Mass.: Irwin, 1994), p. 294.

10. Manheim, op. cit., p. 55.

11. Ibid., p. 54.

12. Ibid. See Appendix B, pp. 341–346.

13. Otto Lerbinger, *The Crisis Manager: Facing Risk and Responsibility* (Mahwah, N.J.: Lawrence Erlbaum Associates, 1997), pp. 112–143.

14. Ibid., pp. 147, 170.

15. See Sandi Sonnenfeld, "Media Policy—What Media Policy," *Harvard Business Review*, Vol. 72, July/August 1994, pp. 18–32.

16. Penelope Canan and George W. Pring, "Strategic Lawsuits Against Public Participation," *Social Problems*, Vol. 35, No. 5, pp. 506–519.

17. Catherine Dodd, "SLAPP Back," *Buzzworm: The Environmental Journal*, Vol. 4, No. 4, p. 36.

18. See an excellent review of SLAPPS in Sharon Beder, "Lawsuits Against Public Participation," in *Global Spin: The Corporate Assault on Environmentalism* (White River Junction, Vt.: Chelsea Green Publishing, 1997), pp. 63–74.

19. Ibid., p. 63.

20. H. A. Cavanaugh, "The Management Report: Where Do the Antis Get Their Money? Parts 1 and 2," *Electrical World*, April 15, 1980, pp. 51–54; May 1, 1980, pp. 25–29.

21. Ibid., April 15, 1980, p. 53. Stopping such blatant support of what was perceived as anticorporate groups was one of the goals of Dr. H. Peter Metzger, manager of public affairs planning at Public Service Co. of Colorado, in a speech given at the 47th Annual Conference of the Southeastern Electric Exchange.

22. Emma Wilkins, "McDonald's Turned Private Investigators on Fastfood Critics," *Times*, June 29, 1994, Home News section. Also see Jackie Kemp, "McDonald's Suffers From Court Grilling," *Scotland on Sunday*, June 25, 1995, p. 4.

23. James Erlichman, "'McLibel 2' Bite Into Court Fight With Burger Chain," *The Guardian*, March 15, 1994, Home Page, p. 7.

24. Beder, op. cit., p. 68.

25. Beth Karlin, "McDonald's Has Big Beef With Vegetarian Critics; Burger Giant Suing Unemployed Pair for Libel in London," *Rocky Mountain News*, August 14, 1995, p. 43A.

26. Ibid.

27. George A. Steiner and John F. Steiner, *Casebook for Business, Government, and Society* (New York: Random House, 1980), pp. 27–37.

28. Ibid.
29. Ibid., p. 29.
30. Ibid., p. 31.
31. See case study: "Nike's Dispute With the University of Oregon," in James E. Post, Anne T. Lawrence, and James Weber, *Business and Society: Corporate Strategy, Public Policy, Ethics*, 10th edition (New York: McGraw-Hill Irwin, 2002), pp. 570–580.
32. Orrin Baird, "Labor's Right to Speak Under Attack," *Legal Times*, May 18, 1998, p. S34.
33. Aaron Bernstein and Steven V. Brull, "Labor and the GOP: A Shootout in California," *BusinessWeek*, February 16, 1998, p. 44.
34. Aaron Bernstein, "Commentary: All's Not Fair in Labor Wars," *BusinessWeek*, July 19, 1999, p. 43.
35. "Tough Love for Labor," *BusinessWeek*, October 16, 2000, p. 120.
36. Ann Zimmerman, "Wal-Mart Plans Changes to Wages, Labor Practices," *Wall Street Journal*, June 7, 2004, p. B3.
37. Wendy Zellner, "How Wal-Mart Keeps Unions at Bay," *BusinessWeek*, October 28, 2002, p. 94.
38. Ibid., p. 96.
39. Foundation for Public Affairs, *Public Interest Profiles 1998–1989* (Washington, D.C.: Congressional Quarterly, 1988), p. 58.
40. This example and explanation appears as an ethical dilemma in Dennis L. Wilcox, Phillip H. Ault, and Warren K. Agee, *Public Relations Strategies and Tactics*, 3rd edition (New York: HarperCollins Publishers, 1992), p. 120. Reference is also made to the Public Relations Society of America's Code of Professional Standards for the Practice of Public Relations, Paragraph 8, which states: "A member shall not use any individual or organization professing to serve or represent an announced cause, or professing to be independent or unbiased but actually serving another of undisclosed interest" (p. 122).
41. Adapted from Andrew B. Gollner, *Social Change and Corporate Strategy* (Issue Action Publications, 1984), p. 153; also *Corporate Public Issues*, Vol. 16, September 1, 1991, p. 103.
42. Michael A. Santoro, "Engagement with Integrity: What We Should Expect Multinational Firms to Do About Human Rights in China," *Business & the Contemporary World*, Vol. 10, No. 1, 1998, pp. 25–54.
43. Ibid., p. 30.
44. Ibid., summarized in Appendix A.
45. Post et al., op. cit., p. 575.
46. Ibid., pp. 575–576.
47. James Grunig is credited for developing four models of public relations: (a) press agentry/publicity, (b) public information, (c) two-way asymmetric, and (d) two-way symmetric. See James E. Grunig and Todd Hunt, *Managing Public Relations* (New York: Holt, Rinehart and Winston, 1984), pp. 21–43. Also see James E. Grunig and Larissa A. Grunig, "Models of Public Relations and Communication," in James Grunig, editor, *Excellence in Public Relations and Communication Management* (Mahwah, NJ: Lawrence Erlbaum Associates, 1992), pp. 285–325.
48. *Citizen Participation* (Washington, D.C.: The Community Services Administration, 1978).
49. Argonne National Laboratory, *Final Report: Public Participation Benchmarking Conference*, October 23, 1997.
50. Ibid., p. 11.

51. Ibid., p. 12.
52. Ibid., p. 13.
53. Ibid., p. 12.
54. "A New Tune for Protecting the Environment, in Harmony," *Chemecology*, March/April 1996, pp. 2–3.
55. Robert L. Heath, Julie Bradshaw, and Jaesub Lee, "Community Relationship Building: Local Leadership in the Risk Communication Infrastructure," *Journal of Public Relations Research*, Vol. 14, No. 4, 2002, p. 318.
56. "Lessons From the World Bank," *pr reporter*, February 4, 2002, pp. 2–3.
57. The full definition of an interest group is given by David B. Truman in *The Governmental Process: Political Interests and Public Opinion* (New York: Knopf, 1951), p. 33: "As used here 'interest group' refers to any group that, on the basis of one or more shared attitudes, makes certain claims upon other groups in the society for the establishment, maintenance, or enhancement of forms of behavior that are implied by the shared attitudes."
58. For a brief overview of interest group theory, see Jay M. Shafritz, *The Dorsey Dictionary of American Government and Politics* (Chicago: Dorsey Press, 1988), pp. 286–288.
59. Cynthia Crossen, "Blah, Blah, Blah: The Crucial Question for These Noisy Times May Just Be: 'Hugh?'" *Wall Street Journal*, p. A1
60. Ibid.
61. Ibid.
62. Llyle Sussman, Peggy Golden, and Renee Beauclair, "Training for E-Mail," *Training and Development Journal*, Vol. 45, March 1991, pp. 70–73.
63. This explanation is based on Peter M. Senge, *The Fifth Discipline: The Art and Practice of the Learning Organization* (New York: Currency Doubleday, 1990), pp. 238–249.
64. Ibid., p. 240.
65. Ibid., pp. 243–247.
66. From a roundtable meeting with a utility company at which the author was the moderator.
67. Carlton E. Spitzer, *Raising the Bottom Line: Business Leadership in a Changing Society* (New York: Longman, 1982), p. 7.
68. Ibid., p. 8.
69. Ibid., p. 138.
70. Ibid., p. 8.
71. Ibid., p.200.
72. Many Ann Pires, "Working With Public Interest Groups," *Public Relations Journal*, Vol. 39, April 1983, p. 16.
73. Ibid., p. 17.
74. Ibid., p. 19.
75. Robert S. Mason, "SMR Forum: Is Anybody Listening? A Fresh Look at the Art of Management Speechmaking," *Sloan Management Review*, Vol. 18, Spring 1977, p. 79.
76. Ibid., p. 89.
77. Ibid., p. 88.
78. North American Precis Syndicate, "Do Your Officers Make Speeches That Are Worth Quoting," n.d.
79. Gage W. Chapel, "Speechwriting in the Nixon Administration," *Journal of Communication*, Vol. 26, Spring 1976, pp. 58–72.
80. Otto Lerbinger and Nathaniel H. Sperber, *Key to the Executive Head* (Reading, Mass.: Addison-Wesley, 1975), pp. 45, 141.

81. Norman Wasserman, "Corporate Speechmaking: It's Not Like Selling Soap," *Management Review*, Vol. 68, November 1979, pp. 25–28.
82. Mary Jane Genova, "Speechwriting" in *Dartnell's Public Relations Handbook*, ed. Robert L. Dilenschneider (Chicago: Dartnell, 1996), pp. 256–259.
83. Maureen Taylor, Michael L. Kent, and William J. White, "How Activist Organizations Are using the Internet to Build Relationships," *Public Relations Review*, Vol. 27, Fall 2001, p. 273.
84. Ibid., p. 279.

Chapter 3

Conflict Resolution:
Mediation and Negotiation

Mediation and negotiation extend dialogue communications into the public policy realm of conflict resolution and consensus building. The objective is to resolve an issue with its protagonists and thereby discourage, and perhaps preempt, public and government involvement. Resolution is based on the premise that the parties involved need each other and can mutually benefit by arriving at a win–win agreement.

A sign of the importance of negotiation and negotiating skills for managers is the continuing popularity of seminars for executives offered by the Program on Negotiation at the Harvard Law School. The program was the outcome of a consortium of Harvard University, Massachusetts Institute of Technology, and Tufts University experts in business management, mediation and dispute resolution, economics, government, law, psychology, and strategic planning. A brochure tells senior executives that negotiation techniques have "proven especially effective as a tool for achieving better business relationships, resolving complicated corporate disputes, untangling complex litigation, defusing threatening international crises, repairing intra- and intergovernmental conflicts, and addressing critical labor-management issues."[1]

Public relations professionals, who must often deal with confrontations, have also recognized the importance of negotiation skills.[2] In a monthly newsletter, the Public Relations Society of America (PRSA) announced a pilot program on how to negotiate. It said that it "will teach participants basic negotiating skills and give them the chance to use those skills in actual case study situations involving, for example, irate community groups, tensions between two organizations that have just merged, or media aggressively covering a strike."[3] Seminars on conflict resolution and negotiation are now routinely offered by PRSA.

A further confirmation of wide interest in conflict resolution methods is the spectacular success of the book *Getting to Yes: Negotiating Agreement Without Giving In* by Roger Fisher and William Ury, who have been associated with the Program on Negotiation.[4] The book has sold more than 3 million copies worldwide and has been translated into several languages.

APPLICATIONS OF CONFLICT RESOLUTION METHODS

As suggested by brochures and literature on conflict resolution, many types of problems and situations are amenable to the processes of mediation and negotiation and the associated processes of consensus building and collaborative planning. Several are discussed here: alternative dispute resolution in contractual relationships, resolving environmental disputes, engaging in collaborative planning in a nuclear power dispute, and resolving differences between Hydro-Quebec and native populations.

Alternative Dispute Resolution

As an alternative to litigation, businesses have turned to conflict resolution methods. The increasing use of alternative dispute resolution (ADR) demonstrates an effort to avoid costly litigation and crowded court dockets. ADR's general purpose is to link disputants with a neutral third party experienced in using these methods. More than 500 corporations have signed ADR corporate policy statements, according to Catherine Cronin-Harris, vice president of research and publications at the Center for Public Resources. Among the companies are Bank of America, Abbott Laboratories, Cigna, and Bristol-Myers Squibb. These corporations pledge to try ADR in disputes with companies that have made the same pledge.[5] One company, General Mills, goes a step further by refusing to sign a contract with another company unless it agrees that disputes will be settled through ADR.

The Internet is helping the ADR movement by changing the art of legal negotiating. Cybersettle.com, formed in 1998, is the world's top claim settlement site. It facilitates high-speed, confidential claim settlements by matching offers and demands through a blind-bidding, patented, secure website. It is the official and exclusive online settlement tool of the Association of Trial Lawyers and the Canadian Bar Association. Both the plaintiff and the defendant, who get confidential passwords, enter bids over encrypted software. If an insurer wants to settle, it enters three confidential offers. Cybersettle.com then contacts the plaintiff's lawyer and asks for three offers that will be acceptable. The computer compares them and automatically settles the case if they fall within $5,000 or 30% of each other. As of June 2003, Cybersettle has processed approximately 75,000 claims. The smallest claim ever settled was $500, but most settlements fall within the range of $5,000 to

$50,000. In June 2003, it announced its largest "cyber-settlement" ever: $12.5 million.[6]

ADR is also recommended in labor disputes by the Commission on the Future of Worker-Management Relations, the so-called Dunlop Commission, formed in 1993. These disputes are about dismissals under the employment-at-will doctrine, equal employment opportunity, and other regulatory matters.[7]

Resolving Environmental Disputes

Conflict resolution methods—mediation and negotiation, as well as dialogue—have been especially successful in resolving environmental disputes. These methods were started in the mid-1970s as one answer to the age of confrontation. One of the earliest successes came in 1974. Two mediators helped settle a flood-control dam dispute between the Army Corps of Engineers and local conservationists on the Snoqualmie River near Seattle. By early 1983, about 40 environmental wars were settled through mediation and another 40 were cooled off. The Conservation Foundation actively encouraged the use of mediation.[8]

Vermont's Deer River Reservoir. New England Electric System used stakeholder negotiations to solve a decade-long dispute on how water from the huge Deerfield River reservoir in Vermont should be shared by contending parties—the power company, rafting and canoeing companies, fishermen, and local communities. Key to the successful agreement was the skillful negotiating role of Kenneth O. Kimball, director of research for the Appalachian Mountain Club. A *Wall Street Journal* article commented, "The surprise is that this one [dispute] is ending amicably, with environmentalists and power-company executives praising each others' sensitivities."[9]

As in many other mediation and negotiation situations, certain pressures in the sociopolitical environment prodded the parties into action. In this case the incentive for the power company to negotiate was the expiration in 1993 of its federal license to operate the Deerfield Project's eight dams. Furthermore, the Electric Consumer Power Act of 1986 requires the Federal Energy Regulatory Commission to balance electric-power generation with the concerns of other stakeholders, including fish and wildlife, recreation, environmental quality, and energy conservation.

Corps of Engineers Misstep. The result of another community conflict, with the Corps of Engineers, was quite different because no effort was made to listen to community citizens and learn what was on their minds. The Corps of Engineers decided to build a second dam in rural North Dakota to cure the area of flooding. Believing it had the support of opinion leaders, the Corps drew up a plan and prepared to present it at a public hearing.

After spending large sums to complete the plan, the Corps of Engineers learned strong local opposition could be expected. Nevertheless, it decided to go ahead on the "decide, announce, defend" principle. Had the engineers visited the dam site to gain local feedback on the problem's real cause, or even to observe for themselves, they would have learned what the community really wanted: not a new dam, but managing the old one differently so that the river below the dam would not freeze solid, causing floods in the spring. The well-organized local opposition eventually killed the new dam project.[10]

McDonald's Packaging Decision.   Another highly publicized use of consensus building was the McDonald's decision to phase out foam packaging in its then more than 8,500 restaurants, which was hailed as an "environmental touchdown."[11] Actually, it demonstrates both the triumph of consensus building and some hazards.

McDonald's formed an alliance with the Environmental Defense Fund in the summer of 1990 in a joint task force to study ways to deal with the solid waste generated by the restaurant chain. The outcome was the replacement of the foam "clamshell" with a paper-based wrapper, which has the advantage of coming from a renewable resource.

Although a confrontation was avoided and McDonald's can call itself "green," the decision was based on public perception, not science, Ed Rensi, president of McDonald's USA admits: "Although some scientific studies indicate that foam packaging is environmentally sound, our customers just don't feel good about it. So we're changing."[12] Obviously the manufacturer of the clamshells thinks the decision was faulty. Thomas Kornegay, western regional director for the issues management department at Amoco Foam Products, says, "We firmly believe that polystyrene is the most environmentally-friendly packing material." He conceded, however, "McDonald's is in the business of selling hamburgers, not packaging."[13] A decision should be scientifically sound as well as agreeable to its stakeholders. What went wrong is that somebody failed to educate the public about the relative merits of polystyrene and paper. Consensus building requires an aware and educated public and participants.

Collaborative Planning

Citizen groups are increasingly invited to participate in corporate planning or decision making. The public relations model of two-way communication is expanded in that the input of citizens or stakeholders is an integral part of the decision-making process. Often this occurs in the absence of conflict, such as in consumer advisory panels (CAPs), issue councils, and product panels. However, as mentioned by two professionals, Kenneth D. Kearns and Anna L. West, collaborative planning can be used to "develop public policy recommendations; make siting decisions; develop facility operational plans; develop strategic plans; develop community actions plans; and lots more."[14]

Collaborative planning, however, is more like short-circuiting the often lengthy public policy process by taking private initiative. It "helps parties, often with divergent views, solve problems, reach goals, resolve differences, satisfy needs, or complete tasks to the mutual benefit of the participants."[15] Bringing together all interested and affected parties improves the quality of final decisions, in addition to building support for them. Kearns and West therefore view collaborative planning as dispute avoidance and distinguish it from mediation and arbitration, which are used to resolve existing disputes.

Companies engage in collaborative planning when other methods of coping with a problem are unsuccessful. Portland General Electric, whose Trojan nuclear power plant faced technical problems and social opposition, realized this fact after exhausting traditional approaches. Although licensed to operate until the year 2011, the plant had been beset with technical problems since its opening. Its performance was among the worst in the nation. It soon was targeted by antinuclear groups, including the Coalition for Safe Power, Don't Waste Oregon, and Physicians for Social Responsibility.

One of the groups, Don't Waste Oregon, sponsored a referendum on the November 1990 ballot to shut down the plant. A representative of the group said, "Everybody wins if this measure passes. Nobody gets killed, nobody lives in fear. Nobody raises their child in the shadow of a cooling tower."

Were the referendum to pass, Northwest power customers would have paid an additional $800 million to $2.2 billion over the ensuing 20 years, so Portland General Electric conducted a fierce campaign, spending $3.5 million to defeat the measure. The vote was 40.6% in favor and 59.4% against the shutdown, even though early polls indicated about 65% of voters favored the initiative. A similar attempt failed in 1986.[16]

Despite the utility's victory, the plant had to be closed in March 1991 when cracks and other defects were discovered inside the pressurized tubes that carry superheated water to the plant's generators. Repairs had to be made, and the utility faced the alternative of replacing—not just repairing—four defective steam generators within 10 years at a cost of between $125 million and $200 million.[17]

Preferring neither the option of mothballing the plant nor that of spending up to $200 million on replacement parts, the utility was receptive to the concept of collaborative planning. The question then became whether some third alternative could be found.

Kearns and West undertook collaborative planning efforts, as described in the following:

1. Identify stakeholders: Discover who has an interest in the outcome and, after obtaining balanced representation, conduct research to learn about their history, issues, and concerns.

2. Assess context: Following the pattern of issue analysis, ask: (a) What are top issues for the organization and stakeholders? (b) What is the history of the organization's relationships with stakeholders? (c) What are the social, demographic, and geographic qualities of the community? (d) What is the nature of media coverage?

3. Develop, test, and refine the collaborative process: (a) Enter into dialogue—conduct a stakeholders meeting with an organization or industry to explore options for mutual gain. (b) Conduct further communication and research. Public relations research was used to the maximum (see Box 3.1).

4. Implement the collaborative process: Invite participants to the first meeting where ground rules and the scope of effort are reviewed; conduct "offline" contacts with one-on-one and small-group discussions; use documentation to reflect group discussion and direction; continue meetings, communications, and research.

5. Communicate outcomes and build understanding and support for decisions: Use media briefings or announcements, white papers, newsletters, employee briefings, and so on, to share results and build interest in outcomes.[18]

As a result of this collaborative planning, stakeholders agreed on the compromise to phase out the Trojan nuclear plant in 5 years. Portland

---

Box 3.1   Portland General Electric Trojan Nuclear Power Plant: How Public Relations Research Methods Were Used

- Survey research was used as follows: Seventy personal interviews were conducted with key stakeholders to determine their underlying interests, their recommendations for how to conduct the public involvement process, and their recommendations on who should be involved in the process. Stakeholders included state officials (including the attorney general, public utility commissions and staff, and representatives from the governor's office and the Oregon Department of Energy); environmental leaders from the state and region; industrial, commercial, and residential customers; members of the financial community; other leaders important to these issues, including the activist community; and company officials.

- Focus groups were held with some stakeholder groups, primarily residential customers.

- Other meetings would not formally fall under the heading of survey research. These groups ranged between 5 to 30 people and were classified as:

   Technical advisory groups

   Public policy groups

   Demand-side management subgroups

General Electric would not have to invest in an expensive replacement program and antinuclear groups had a guarantee the plant would be closed in a reasonable amount of time.

Resolving Public Disputes: The Mutual Gains Approach

The broadest application of mediation and negotiation is in resolving public issues. This application is the subject of Lawrence Susskind and Patrick Field's book, *Dealing With an Angry Public: The Mutual Gains Approach to Resolving Disputes*, which reflects the ideas and approach of the MIT-Harvard Public Disputes Program.[19] The book's aim is to help business and government leaders negotiate, rather than fight, with their critics. The core method is the mutual gains approach, the gist of which is "to think of the interaction with the public as a multiparty, multi-issue negotiation."[20]

This approach is based on six key principles:

1. Look at the needs and concerns of the other side instead of demonizing or ridiculing others. Don't get stuck in a zero-sum bargaining game.
2. Open the doors wide and engage in fact finding together. Remember that your "best possible" information may not be convincing to others.
3. If you promise that something will not happen, be ready to promise a contingent offer of compensation.
4. Accept responsibility but admit mistakes when made, and be willing to share power with others who have a stake.
5. Act in a trustworthy fashion at all times. Don't conceal intentions, sugarcoat the truth, or spin the story to make it sound better.
6. Focus on building long-term relationships if you care about your reputation and credibility.[21]

Susskind and Field comment, "In one respect, this book is about public relations. How to interact with the public in a way that will minimize harm to and maximize gain for [government] agencies and organizations."[22] This idealized version of public relations, however, is not always realized. Thus, they add another aspect to the book: It "is about honesty, accountability, reputation, and integrity.... It is about qualities we value above and beyond their ability to generate profits or votes."[23] These values, which are attributes of leaders, are exposed during controversies that typically require quick thinking and rapid response.

Susskind and Field apply the mutual gains approach to three major categories: accidents (the Exxon *Valdez* oil spill and the Three-Mile Island nuclear accident), risks (the breast implant controversy and the New Bedford Harbor Superfund Forum), and value conflicts (the clashing cultures of Hydro-Quebec and the Cree, and the animal rights dispute). Of these three, value conflicts are the most difficult because values are not the same as interests, which are central to most negotiations. Different positions or "packages" can be invented to accommodate a variety of interests. However, with values, which are strongly held beliefs, a dispute translates into who we are, our very identity and, perhaps, existence.[24]

The Hydro-Quebec dispute with native peoples over the flooding of ancestral lands in northern Quebec for the purpose of creating more hydroelectric power dramatically illustrates the consequences of not using a mutual gains approach (see appendix).

HOW MEDIATION AND NEGOTIATION WORK

In mediation, a neutral party intervenes between conflicting parties to promote reconciliation, settlement, or compromise. He or she listens to evidence and helps negotiate a settlement but does not have the power to make a binding decision. Gerald W. Cormick, executive director of the Institute for Environmental Mediation in Seattle, Washington, sees mediation as a device for facilitating the negotiation process. He defines mediation as "a voluntary process in which those involved in a dispute jointly explore and reconcile their differences." He adds: "The mediator has no authority to impose a settlement. His or her strength lies in the ability to assist the parties in settling their own differences. The mediated dispute is settled when the parties themselves reach what they consider a workable solution."[25]

Cormick distinguishes mediation, which is used in conflict resolution, from dialogue and consensus building. Policy dialogues, he says, "are intended to identify joint positions which can be advocated in the public policy arena by interest groups that are normally opposed to one another." Consensus building "emphasizes the common interests of disputants in jointly defining and solving problems."[26] An outside mediator facilitates such discussions.

In negotiation, however, contending parties confer with one another directly in an effort to reach an agreement. Negotiation depends on communication and persuasion in which each party seeks to gain something that requires the cooperation of the other party. Both sides engage in a sequential process whereby each alternately presents demands or proposals, and offers counterproposals.[27] As stated by Gerard I. Nierenberg in *The Complete Negotiator*, "Whenever people exchange ideas with the intention of changing relationships, whenever they confer for agreement, they are negotiating."[28] Each party has to feel it has won something, however. As Nierenberg reminds us, "The objective should be to achieve agreement, not total victory."[29]

Negotiation is a very common and important process, not only in settling disputes but also in handling all kinds of exchanges between different persons and organizations when neither has formal power or authority over the other. Certain conditions must be present, however, for negotiation to work. Furthermore, there are limits to what negotiation can accomplish.

The limits to negotiation listed in Box 3.2 are recognized by Lawrence Susskind and Alan Weinstein in environmental disputes where sophisticated scientific and technical evidence clashes with social and political arguments. They recognize that when contending parties hold extreme ideological views and do not acknowledge the legitimacy of one another's concerns, mediation and negotiation are not possible.[30]

Cormick also recognizes that mediators are better off if they're not technical experts because of the danger of "leading" the parties. But they must be conversant with the issues in dispute and understand the legislative, legal, and organizational environment in which they occur.

Some Useful Competencies

Negotiation has become a specialized field requiring considerable training. Several skills are commonly recognized as important in all kinds of negotiations: understanding human needs, knowing what information to reveal or not reveal, and learning to be creative and flexible.

Understanding Human Needs.   A negotiator must understand the interests and needs of the other party. Roger Fisher and William Ury list four features of successful negotiations: (a) the separation of people from problems; (b) a focus on interests, not positions; (c) the invention of options for mutual gain; and (d) the use of objective criteria.[31]

Their second feature is particularly important because too often negotiations focus on the position taken by the other, without realizing that for every interest there are several positions that could satisfy it.[32] Asking the other person why a certain position is taken is a way to explore the interests behind it.[33] Negotiators who have an understanding of human needs may obtain additional insight. This is the reason books on negotiation pay a lot of attention to lists of human needs.[34]

Revealing the Right Kind of Information.   For negotiations to progress, both parties must have information about each other's aims, expectations, and acceptable solutions. Just how much to reveal about oneself is a tactical matter. Ideally, each party seeks to uncover three kinds of information about the other, which define the *utility schedule:*

- Resistance point, beyond which no bargaining will take place. For example, a seller is willing to sell at a price no lower than $100,000 and a buyer is willing to pay no more than $150,000. The bargaining range lies between these two figures.
- Status quo point, which leaves conditions unchanged.

Box 3.2   Necessary Conditions and Limits

Negotiation involves two or more distinct parties with differing interests with respect to one or more issues. But the parties at least share an interest in reaching agreement (and often have other common interests as well). They recognize that more is gained through accommodation than confrontation and that the payoffs of negotiations will exceed their costs. They also recognize their interdependence, that is, that each needs something that the other has or controls. This involves the voluntary sharing or exchange of one or more specific resources or the resolution of an intangible issue or issues. Furthermore, both sides have respect for each other. They recognize their mutual legitimacy and right to survive, and they are aware of the power each possesses.[35]

The application of these general conditions for negotiations to environmental disputes has shown that the following nine conditions must be present:

1. All parties with a stake in the outcome are identified.

2. Involved groups are appropriately represented.

3. Differences among the values and assumptions of contending parties are discussed and narrowed to fit a workable agenda.

4. A sufficient number of alternatives and options are raised. Disputes cannot be narrowed to a yes or no decision.

5. Parties agree on the scope of the dispute and the length of time needed for the appearance of negative environmental effects.

6. Relative values of costs and benefits are agreed on.

7. The worth of compensating actions is established.

8. Bargains are implemented.

9. Parties are held to their commitments.[36]

In contrast to these enabling conditions, Cormick points out what mediation and negotiation cannot do:

• Resolve basic differences that separate parties in a conflict. Mediation helps them make accommodations that enable them to coexist.

• Avert conflict. Quite the opposite: There is no basis for negotiations until conflict emerges. The inadequacy of unilateral solutions must first be recognized.

• Remove the adversarial nature of the relationship. Parties must remain mindful of their conflicting self-interests. A viable bargain is one that can stand up to the pressure of implementation and possible repudiation by constituents.

• Offer an absolute alternative to litigation. Actual or threatened litigation often helps bring parties to the table to seek mediation.

• Teach negotiators to like, trust, and agree with one another. Although sufficient public trust among parties is needed to negotiate in good faith, too much cooperation may be seen as a sell-out by constituents.[37]

- A level of aspiration, which is the agreement each prefers; for example, the buyer to obtain a sales price of $100,000 and the seller to obtain $150,000.[38]

The strategy of negotiating lies between the poles of cooperating and fighting. Hence a negotiator is faced with such questions as "Am I pressing too hard?" or "Was my concession too early or too big?"

Although each party wants to withhold information for fear of having to make concessions, too much reticence renders effective negotiation impossible. Negotiating skill requires careful handling of what Willem F. G. Mastenbroek calls the information dilemma—a skill that consists of carefully bringing about a step-by-step exchange of information that gradually gives shape to realistic expectations on both sides.[39]

Mastenbroek warns of two related dilemmas. One is credibility. This reminds a negotiator that, at one extreme, trusting the opponent without reservation results in a bad deal, whereas mistrusting might seriously undermine the likelihood of an agreement. If, for example, a negotiator is caught lying, his or her credibility is lost and the relationship between the parties is seriously worsened. The second dilemma is self-presentation—the identity or image the bargainers present to their adversaries. They must appear tough but also be flexible and fair. They must attempt to be conciliatory but not transmit the image of an appeaser. Their concern about losing credibility is one reason they restrain themselves from bluffing or using deceit or coercion to gain their objectives.

Being Creative. Negotiation is a problem-solving situation where the goal is to find solutions that solve not only your own problem, but also that of the other side. To do this, flexibility and creativity are required. Fisher accordingly advises negotiators to avoid (a) premature judgment, (b) looking for the single best answer, (c) assuming there is a "fixed pie," and (d) thinking that solving the other side's problem is their problem (and not also yours).[40]

Media Usage During the Consensus-Building Process

The Hydro-Quebec case described in the Appendix, as well as others, requires that a delicate balance be maintained between keeping the affected public informed about ongoing dialogue and not, through such public communication, undermining that dialogue. Susskind and Field present two common ground rules and a third that is sometimes added. Participants must agree on the following:

1. Statements may be made to the press about one's own concerns and reactions to meetings, but no statements or views should be attributed to other participants.

2. A participant should immediately inform the group if remarks made to the media have been misrepresented or misinterpreted.
3. No derogatory or personally demeaning statements about others in the process should be made.

These rules are a test of whether participants can come to an agreement about their own conduct. If they can, the chances increase they can also agree on substantive matters. Another advantage of these rules is that they enable participants to present their arguments and positions to the press and thereby to influence the thinking of other participants. Most experts on negotiations believe the process works best when the parties dispute matters among themselves without appeals for media intervention and, perhaps, support. However, the temptation to do so is strong, especially in the face of a likely impasse. By following the media rules, the parties at least minimize damage to the negotiation process.

Dialogue participants need not rely on the mass media to keep stakeholders informed. Summaries of meetings can be mailed directly to participants, the media, and interested citizens. If a community has a local public-access cable station, videotapes of meetings can be sent so that they can be broadcast at regularly scheduled dates and times. Citizen groups can publish their own newsletters or hold public forums. The growing use of computers allows further communications through e-mail, home pages, and various electronic bulletin boards.

Sometimes a local newspaper is willing to develop special inserts about a meeting. The *Boston Globe* did this when it sponsored, along with Harvard University and MIT, a 3-day conference, stretched over 2 months, on transportation planning in the metropolitan Boston area. Called "Shaping the Accessible Region," the special 16-page insert included nine recommendations issued by a jury selected to hear arguments.[41]

CONCLUSIONS

Mediation and negotiation—and their many expressions in consensus building and collaborative planning—show enormous promise as a way to resolve issues among contending parties before they escalate into broader public or legislative issues. Many managers are now trained in conflict resolution, even in the international sphere, as stated by Joseph Duffy, director of the U.S. Information Agency: "The new information technologies are transforming international relations, opening up new possibilities for conflict prevention, management and resolution."[42]

However, the use of conflict resolution has to be based on more than a hopeful assumption that because harmony among human beings is more natural than conflict, all we have to do is make the parties in conflict talk with one another. One might expect, however, that as the level of mistrust declines and mutual understanding increases, the conflict will diminish.

APPENDIX
CASE STUDY: HYDRO-QUEBEC DISPUTE
WITH NATIVE PEOPLES

Hydro-Quebec, a giant hydroelectric complex owned and operated by the Quebec government, was embroiled in controversy over its plans to build more dams. Having completed Phase I of the Hydroelectric Project begun in 1973, the utility was ready for Phase II, which included plans to dam eight more rivers north of the LaGrande River, including the Great Whale River. Thus called the Great Whale project, plans required the flooding of thousands of acres of land in the James Bay region of the Canadian sub-Arctic.

Environmentalists were concerned about the devastation of the wilderness and possible extinction of local seals. Native Cree, Inuit, and Naskap Indians, who have lived in this huge wilderness for thousands of years, feared the loss of their traditional homeland and native way of life. Their livelihood has largely been based on hunting, fishing, and trapping. Furthermore, the upheaval caused by the project had already released mercury into the rivers and flooded waters of the area, making the fish inedible.

To help stop or limit the size of the project, the Cree Indians hired Hill & Knowlton of Toronto, Canada. As stated by the *Ottawa Citizen* newspaper:
The Cree strategy was simple:

1. Fight the billion-dollar project on the international stage.
2. Quietly use public relations consultants while maintaining a very visible grassroots campaign.
3. Identify Hydro-Quebec's markets in the United States and convince them to say no to cheap electricity.
4. Push an alternative energy policy.
5. Attract sympathetic celebrities like Robert Kennedy Jr. to the cause.
6. Run high-impact ads. Target the utility's investors, especially U.S. colleges such as Dartmouth.[43]

One objective was to convince the legislature of New York State and Governor Mario M. Cuomo not to proceed with a $17 billion deal to purchase electric power from Hydro-Quebec. The Indians were encouraged by Maine's cancellation of a $4 billion deal. Without this and the markets of Massachusetts, Rhode Island, and Vermont, the Great Whale project could not be financed.

To help put the Great Whale project back on track, Hydro-Quebec hired PR giant Burson-Marsteller. The key objective was to counter Hydro's bad image in the United States and to convince the legislatures of New York and the New England states to stick with their plans to buy power from Hydro-Quebec. One of the Cree claims Hydro wanted to discredit was the statement that the Great Whale project would destroy a wilderness the size of France. (Cree leaders said they meant to say an ecosystem approximately the size of France would be affected by both the Great Whale and the already built Grande River project.)

In April 1990 the Cree and Inuit Indians achieved a publicity success by paddling a native vessel called an *odeyak*, half-canoe and half-kayak, down the Hudson River to New York City where the 50 paddlers arrived just in time for Earth Day celebrations at Times Square. Furthermore, Greenpeace, the Sierra Club, and the National Audubon Society sponsored a full page in the *New York Times* that showed pictures of dead caribou in an area previously flooded by Hydro, questioning Hydro's contract with New York State.

Ultimately Hydro-Quebec postponed the project indefinitely, demonstrating that the utility's traditional ways of resolving confrontations were outmoded. Susskind and Field point out several errors in the behavior of Hydro and the Province of Quebec. One is that they stonewalled over the disclosure of a secret sweetheart deal with multinational aluminum-smelting plants whereby power costing 2.4 cents per kilowatt-hour to produce was sold at 1.5 cents.[44] The company convinced the provincial government to support it by forbidding the Quebec press to make mention of this deal.

Another error is that by ignoring or belittling the opposition, the utility created misunderstanding, polarized opinion, and increased criticism.[45] For example, responding to the opposition's ad, Robert Bourassa, then the Quebec provincial leader, asked, "How can you seriously consider those ads in the *New York Times*?" He also commented, "Seven million Quebecois can't be wrong"; this was seen as an insult to the Cree nation.[46] Hydro should have considered the evidence the Cree had submitted, by following this prescription: "Keep an open mind, be open to reason, and consider carefully that you might be wrong."[47]

Hydro also refused to listen to other critics. When a New York legislative committee met to review the state's $17 billion contract with Hydro-Quebec, the company refused to attend the meeting, with one company spokesperson saying, "The contention that Canada can't conduct its own economic review is not only insulting, but it has no basis in fact."[48]

The impact of the project on indigenous peoples was not given enough weight. Massive damming of their hunting and fishing territories and disturbance of their way of life deteriorated their health. Cases of obesity, heart disease, and diabetes, previously almost unknown, increased. Various social problems also rose dramatically: alcohol and drug abuse, spouse abuse, unemployment, and teenage suicide. Typifying Hydro's attitude was that when the native population complained that high mercury levels put their eating of fish at risk, the general secretary of the utility said, "All they have to do is change some of their fishing habits for a while."[49]

To sum up, perhaps Mercredi, the chief of the First Nations Assembly, said it best: "The problem with this province [and presumably Hydro-Quebec] is that there is no debate, there is no dialogue."[50] As Susskind and Field emphasize, the mutual gains approach asks that one talk with, not at, the other. One of the prescriptions they advocate in this approach is: "Search for shared or overarching principles on which to base a continuing dialogue."[51] When a package is agreed on by the stakeholder negotiators, the entire community should have a final say by means of a vote, referendum, or similar means of approval.[52] Everyone must, however, be informed about the voting process and the arguments for and against the package.

ENDNOTES

1. Program on Negotiation at the Harvard Law School, "Dealing with an Angry Public," 1987. The 1997 brochure refers to strategies for resolving conflicts and disputes with dissatisfied customers, potential litigants, and concerned interest groups.
2. For example, in 1972, David Finn, chairman of Ruder & Finn, explained that his job was to get people in disagreement to "talk together constructively, as never before, to find the solutions which will enable us to save our society." Speaking about the role of the public relations counselor, Finn said, "He is no longer primarily a communicator: he is a sort of moderator whose job it is to try to prevent the crisis from getting out of hand." From a monograph, "Modifying Opinions in the New Human Climate."
3. "Pilot Program Teaches How to Negotiate," *PRSA News*, May 1989, p. 1.
4. Roger Fisher and William Ury, with Bruce Patton, editor, *Getting to Yes: Negotiating Agreement Without Giving in* (Boston: Houghton Mifflin, 1981).
5. Deborah L. Jacobs, "Controlling Litigation Costs With a Neutral Third Party," *New York Times*, September 23, 1990, p. F12. Several organizations provide ADR. services. A partial list is issued each year by the Bureau of National Affairs. The following qualifications should be considered before retaining an ADR provider:
   1. Number of cases it has handled, and percentage of cases resolved through ADR. Ask for a client list.
   2. Ability to offer neutral parties nationwide.
   3. Ability to provide ADR training for managers.
   4. Provides a fee structure. (The American Arbitration Association bases its fee on the amount at issue and charges between one tenth of 1% and 3% of that sum, depending on the size of the case.)
6. Ann Davis, "For Dueling Lawyers, the Internet Is Unlikely Referee," *Wall Street Journal*, May 12, 1999, p. B1. Also see Cybersettle's press release, June 20, 2003 on its website, Cybersettle.com.
7. Walter J. Gershenfeld, "Presidential Address: Future Industrial Relations: Guide for the Perplexed," in *Industrial Relations Research Association Series, Proceedings of the Forty-Eighth Annual Meeting*, ed. Paula B. Voos, January 5–7, 1996 (Madison, Wis.: University of Wisconsin, Industrial Relations Research Association), pp. 4–5.
8. Lawrence Mosher, "EPA, Looking for Better Way to Settle Rules Disputes, Tries Some Mediation," *National Journal*, March 5, 1983, p. 504. The mediators were financed by a Ford Foundation grant.
9. Neil Ulman, "Unlikely Allies: Pact for River's Use Unites Conservationists and a Power Company," *Wall Street Journal*, May 20, 1996, p. A9.

10. "Public Participation Requires 2-Way Communication as Demonstrated in Environmental Issues," *tips & tactics* (a supplement to *pr reporter*), Vol. 34, July 15, 1996, p. 2.
11. "Public Pressure, Not Science Behind McDonald's Decision," *Chemecology,* February 1991, p. 6.
12. Ibid.
13. Ibid.
14. Kenneth D. Kearns and Anna L. West, "Innovations in Public Affairs Programming: Collaborative Planning and Beyond," in *Practical Public Affairs in an Era of Change: A Communications Guide for Business, Government, and College,* ed. Lloyd B. Dennis (Lanham, Md.: University Press of America, 1996), p. 358.
15. Ibid., pp. 356–357.
16. "Oregon Voters Reject Measure to Close Trojan Nuclear Unit," *Electric Utility Week,* November 12, 1990, p. 3.
17. Marla Williams, "Nuke-Plant Troubles Could Lead to Closure—Idle Facility May Bring Rate Boosts, Blackout," *Seattle Times,* November 14, 1991, p. C1.
18. Kearns and West, op. cit., pp. 359–363.
19. Lawrence Susskind and Patrick Field, *Dealing With an Angry Public: The Mutual Gains Approach to Resolving Disputes* (New York: Free Press, 1996).
20. Ibid., p. 13.
21. Ibid. Principles are summarized from pp. 13, 36–42.
22. Ibid., p. 223.
23. Ibid., pp. 223–224.
24. Ibid., see pp. 154–155.
25. Gerald W. Cormick, "The Myth, the Reality, and the Future of Environmental Mediation," *Environment,* Vol. 24, September 1982, p. 16.
26. Ibid.
27. James P. Ware, "Bargaining Strategies: Collaborative Versus Competitive Approaches," Harvard Business School (HBS Case Services, No. 9-480-055), April 1980.
28. Gerard I. Nierenberg, *The Complete Negotiator* (New York: Nierenberg & Zeif, 1986), p. 16.
29. Ibid., p. 34.
30. Lawrence Susskind and Alan Weinstein, "How to Resolve Environmental Disputes Out of Court," *Technology Review,* Vol. 85, January 1982, p. 40.
31. Fisher and Ury, op. cit., pp. 10–11.
32. Ibid., p. 42.
33. Ibid., p. 45.
34. Nierenberg, for example, devotes a whole chapter to "How to Recognize Needs," op. cit., 145–153. Fisher and Ury also provide a list of human needs.
35. These conditions are discussed in Ware, op. cit.
36. Susskind and Weinstein, op. cit., pp. 41, 46–47.
37. Cormick, op. cit., pp. 17, 37–38.
38. James T. Tedeschi and Paul Rosenfeld, "Communication in Bargaining and Negotiation," in *Persuasion: New Directions in Theory and Research,* eds. Michael E. Roloff and Gerald R. Miller (Beverly Hills, Calif.: Sage, 1980), pp. 227–228.
39. Willem F. G. Mastenbroek, "Negotiating: A Conceptual Model," *Group and Organization Studies,* Vol. 3, September 1980, p. 329.
40. Fisher and Ury, op. cit., pp. 57–58.
41. Susskind and Field, op. cit., p. 218.

42. Irving Kristol, "Conflicts That Can't Be Resolved," *Wall Street Journal*, September 5, 1997, p. A12.
43. Jack Aubry, "The Beaching of a Whale: The Crees Spent $8.2 Million to Fight the Great Whale Project on Environmental Grounds. This Week Their Determination Paid Off When Quebec Harpooned the Project," *The Ottawa Citizen*, November 26, 1994, p. B3.
44. Susskind and Field, op. cit., p. 163.
45. Ibid., p. 177.
46. Ibid., pp. 162–163.
47. Ibid., p. 168.
48. Ibid., p. 163.
49. Ibid., p. 161.
50. Ibid., p. 164.
51. Ibid., p. 166.
52. Ibid., p. 174.

III

Media Strategies

When an emerging issue progresses to the public involvement stage, the mass media play a critical role. By drawing attention to an issue and possibly influencing the way people think about it, the media set the agenda of what people talk about. Managers know that once public opinion is crystallized, it is more difficult to change. Thus, if an issue is important to a company it quickly endeavors to shape public discussion in its favor. If an unwelcome issue is initiated by government or an interest group and there are indications that the issue cannot be contained, a corporation or industry group would try to jump the gun and move to the public involvement stage as quickly as possible.

The news media are a major force in the business environment because of their reputed power to reach most people and sometimes influence attitudes and behavior. A 2004 annual report on American journalism reports that by a 55% to 29% margin, most Americans say the media's influence is growing, a view held consistently since the mid-1980s.[1] Public relations practitioners are heavily engaged in media relations because they generally believe that the news media are the most powerful outside force in the life of a business executive. As investigative journalists Bob Woodward and Carl Bernstein demonstrated in Nixon's Watergate scandal and incessant media coverage of the Clinton–Lewinsky sex scandal dramatized, even the president of the United States could be unseated. Thus, could not the heads of major corporations face a similar fate?

The answer came with the bankruptcy of Enron Corporation in December 2001 and the subsequent media concentration on corporate violations of the "full and timely disclosure" requirements of the Securities and Exchange Act. Many CEOs were subsequently unseated: Imclone's Samuel Waksal, Adelphia Communications' John Rigas, Tyco International's Dennis Kozlowski, and WorldCom's Scott Sullivan.[2] Furthermore, with continuing media coverage of corporate deception and wrongdoing, public attitudes toward business soured and led to greater government intervention in business affairs, as symbolized by passage of the Sarbanes-Oxley Act (see chap. 14). These events proved that the news media play a major role in influencing public opinion and stimulating government action, even though they faltered in their watchdog function of exposing business wrongdoing. There is no doubt that business reinforced the reality that the media are one of the major forces in their sociopolitical environments.

Business news has been the fastest growing editorial segment in newspapers, both among metropolitan giants and hometown dailies.[3] Business news has also become a staple of mainstream television, said a cover story in *USA Today* during the first month of the new millennium. It reported that in the last 3 months of 1999, the financial news cable network CNBC attracted more viewers than general news network CNN on weekdays from 5:00 a.m. to 7:30 a.m. This trend prompted CNN to boost its weekday business news programs to 5.5 hours a day from 2.5. A further indication of rising interest in business news is that, even on the three American evening network news programs (NBC, ABC, and CBS), the number of business stories rose 19% in 1999 to 1,175 from 989 in 1998, according to the Center for Media and Public Affairs. Its president, Robert Lichter, declared, "The genre of financial journalism isn't just a beat. It's a whole industry of its own."[4]

Several reasons account for the growth in business news: the long economic boom of the 1990s, especially the rise of the Internet economy; the proportion of Americans owning stock, which grew to 80% in 2002; and the spread of globalization.[5] Furthermore, according to the results of the 2003 Middleberg/Ross Survey of Media, reports of unethical or illegal behavior by corporations or individual executives have focused journalists' attention on the critical topic of corporate credibility. Among journalists who regularly cover business and technology issues, 86% say disclosures of unethical behavior on the part of a corporation's ruling body sometimes or always affect financial coverage, and 72% say they sometimes or always affect product coverage.[6]

POWER OF THE MASS MEDIA

News media in the United States are especially powerful because they are protected by the First Amendment. They represent the fourth estate—after the legislative, executive, and judicial branches of government. Business might question to whom the media are accountable; but when business or government has sought to interfere with the media, the courts have defended them by opposing prior restraint of news stories and allowing the press to keep its sources confidential.

The basic function of the news media is to direct public attention to selected events, provide important information, and offer analysis and comments. In the United States, as well as in all democratic societies, the media serve the surveillance function of warning the public of dangers, malfunctions, and social transgressions. Stephan Lesher's *Media Unbound* describes how modern journalism "for three hundred years the people's gadfly, gossip, town crier, court jester, and sometimes champion—had assimilated sinister power."[7] Lesher states, "America has become media-minded, believing and acting on journalistic information more than any other source or institution."[8]

Most public relations campaigns and other public communication campaigns rely heavily on the mass media, on the assumption that they are effective in reaching the general public. This reliance was demonstrated when the PRSA announced the 1994 winners of the prestigious Silver Anvil Awards. The awards chairman, Jim Roop, observed that "central to almost all the programs was extensive media coverage and support, belying the criticism that public relations is media soft."[9] Elaborating on this statement, he said, "There has been some criticism that the industry is moving away from its traditional roots in publicity and going with more controlled media. The fact that so many of the Silver Anvil programs were based on publicity campaigns suggests it's not a correct assessment."[10] That statement remains valid a decade later. For example, in awarding the 2004 Bronze Anvil Awards for "outstanding achievement in public relations tactics," the public relations firm of Jackson Spalding was praised for its effort in generating more than 16.5 million media impressions, with more than 2,200 positive stories and coverage on major television affiliates throughout the United States for its client's consumer campaign.[11] Bacon's MediaSource, as well as other publicity reference services, remain an essential part of most public relations offices.

In believing that the mass media continue to be highly effective, Roop referred to the Silver Anvil entry on Pepsi's syringe crisis in which some customers complained that they found syringes and needles in Pepsi cans.[12] He commented, "Through mass media Pepsi alleviated fears," bringing people back to buy its product. In a second reference, to CARE's Somalia effort, he said, "People contributed as a result of CARE's effort to raise awareness about the problems in that country and the need for food and clothing there."[13]

Roop, however, does not limit the media's power to crisis situations that are fanned by the media in the first place. By saying that the mass media can be effective in raising people's awareness of tragedies in the world and prompting them to be generous, he implies that the mass media can be effective in motivating people's behavior. He thus believes that the media are effective on all four levels of the hierarchy of effects: raising awareness, increasing understanding, changing attitudes, and influencing behavior. This success is rarely achieved.

Interest Groups Use the Mass Media Too

Besides corporations and government, labor unions and social action groups recognize the importance of the news media. Although questioning the impartiality of the media and therefore relying on their own communication channels with members, these groups realize it is important to enlist the support of public opinion and to "democratize" the media. Charlotte Ryan supports this view in *Prime Time Activism:* "But our society is heavily media-dependent and if we ignore mainstream media, we abandon audiences with little or no access to alternative and opposition media."[14] She helps "challengers" understand how to make their causes and activities "newsworthy." She describes how Local 26, in seeking a new master contract with 14 large Boston hotels, at first despaired of not being able to get media coverage for its cause, but learned how to play the game.[15]

AGENDA SETTING

In serving their watchdog function, the news media also set the agenda for society. As described by Donald L. Shaw and Maxwell E. McCombs, "The mass media may not be successful in telling us what to think, but they are stunningly successful in telling us what to think about."[16] However, the media's effectiveness goes beyond this modest function of agenda setting. There is mounting evidence that the modern mass media shape how people think about an event or issue.

Framing

The media influence how people think about a topic by *framing* it: drawing attention to certain features of an issue while minimizing attention to others. As described by Joseph N. Cappella and Kathleen Hall Jamieson, "The act of framing determines what is included and excluded, what is salient and what is unimportant. It focuses the viewer's attention on its subjects in specific ways."[17] The act of framing thus shifts the focus from what is said to how it is said.

This process is illustrated by an analysis of U.S. newspaper coverage of the merger of the automobile manufacturers Daimler-Benz and Chrysler in 1998. A major public relations effort created the mythic frames of "marriage"—establishing an equilibrium of two partners—and "birth." In this way the global relevance of the merger and the oligopolistic tendencies of the car industry, as well as other divisive issues, were avoided. "The PR departments were successful mythmakers who established the overall frame of reference for the coverage. Unlike the familiar agenda-setting dictum, public relations told the journalists what to think about and how to think about it."[18]

In addition to framing, journalists engage in *priming*, which refers to the frequency with which they refer to a story. When a political issue receives more news attention than other issues, people assign greater weight to that issue when judging politicians who had some direct responsibility for it.[19] Priming thereby serves to establish criteria for judgment.

Framing techniques are routinely used by television news commentators and newspaper reporters, as described in *Dirty Politics* by Kathleen Hall Jamieson.[20] By using a script or story form schema, reporters condition audiences to see a political campaign as a "game" or "war" between a "front runner" and an "underdog" in which each candidate's goal is winning.[21] She adds, "Schemas influence how we perceive new information, how we remember old information, and how we relate the old and new."[22] By using a horse race analogy, reporters in effect define policy issues, or substance, as lying outside the orbit of real news.

Because framing labels events and issues, corporate public affairs professionals must pay attention to its impact. For example, public perceptions are more severe when an accidental spill of toxic chemicals into a river is called an environmental disaster rather than an incident. Framing also judges events: Does the collapse of scaffolding at a construction site indicate criminal negligence by a construction company? Is a payment to a foreign political figure a sign that a company is corrupt?

How words influence choices is illustrated in an experiment in which audiences were asked about the desirability of military intervention by the United States in defending a hypothetical foreign country from invasion by one of its neighbors. The first scenario reminded readers of the Vietnam War by mentioning "chinook helicopters" and briefings taking place in "Dean Rusk Hall." A second scenario, which indirectly cued memories of World War II, used phrases such as "blitzkrieg invasion" and briefings in "Winston Churchill Hall." The second scenario resulted in greater support for intervention than did the first. As the example suggests, the words used invoke different inferences and arouse "well-established knowledge structures."[23]

Arbiter Function of the Media

Louis Banks, a respected journalist whose editorial career with Time, Inc., spanned nearly 30 years, summarized this expanded role of the media. He said the media are not only conveyers of news, but arbiters of its content as well: "The news industry—television, radio, magazines, newspaper—stands as the principal arbiter of social attitudes toward business (and all institutions)." His view was, "Broadly speaking, mass media news selection and interpretation feeds the public's suspicions about corporate practice ... and interprets corporate affairs with a negative bias."[24]

Because of the power of the media, Banks advises that a business's basic media relations strategy must be to compete in the marketplace of ideas. Warning against merely being reactive to media inquiries, he urges business to systematically, factually, and carefully engage in intellectual debates such as those that were previously lost by default. His thesis is that "not only is an 'issues' campaign the soundest long-range strategy for business-media relationships, but also that the effort involved is intricately connected with the future of the freedom of large corporations to operate as centers of independent managerial decision making."[25]

Banks reminds businesspeople that although the news industry stands as the principal arbiter of social attitudes toward business, "today the thoughtful elements of the media are willing to listen to corporate arguments on specific issues—if they are rational, and shown to be in the public interest."[26] He says what a corporation or an industry can offer the media is its technical know-how, its experience or point of view on a particular issue. Business, in other words, possesses valuable information that the media need.

Despite this advantage, business executives have been hesitant to follow Banks's advice to engage in the marketplace of ideas, because of fear of media hostility. Having seen what damage the media can inflict on companies such as Exxon and Dow Corning, some companies simply prefer to avoid talking to journalists.[27]

BUSINESS DEVELOPS A MULTIPRONGED STRATEGY

When businesses recognized the shortcomings of the news media and growing public hostility toward them, they and other organizations developed a multipronged strategy to guide their media relations. They have also, as discussed in chapter 8, become defensive and feel that the best strategy is to operate "under-the-radar of media attention" and go directly to their audiences.[28]

Figure III.1 depicts the major public communication strategies that businesses use. The horizontal boxes show the central role of the news media as the intermediary between an organization and the general public. The news media are the main channels through which information and views are disseminated.

The circles in the diagram indicate the three major ways an organization deals with the news media: (a) proactive media relations, (b) broadcast appearances, and (c) advocacy advertising. It should be noted that the arrows stemming from the circles have different penetration distances. These reflect the degree of control the organization can exercise over the media. The proactive media relations circle merely touches the news media box, and the broken line below the box indicates that the message may or may not reach the general public; if it does, it may appear in a distorted form. In this type of situation the media are classified as uncontrolled. Chapter 4 examines proactive media relations as a means of seizing the initiative and exerting countervailing pressure on the media.

The arrow from the broadcast appearances circle penetrates halfway through the news media box, indicating semicontrol over the media. Chapter 5 examines this special opportunity. When spokespersons rep-

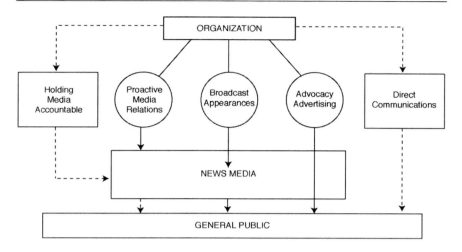

FIG. III.1.   Public communication strategies.

resenting an organization appear on a television talk show, for example, they have no control over the questions that will be asked, but they do have control over their answers. Media training helps spokespersons develop skills that enable them to exercise considerable control; thus, the arrow may have even greater penetration than the halfway point shown in the diagram.

When a company wants complete control over a message disseminated through the news media, it can buy advertising space or time. When ideas rather than products are featured, such advertising is called either advocacy advertising or issues advertising. As discussed in chapter 6, a corporation determines exactly how the message will appear in a print medium: It chooses all the words, their size, their position in the ad, the date the ad will appear, and sometimes, as with op-ed ads, the place in a newspaper or magazine where it will appear. An advocacy ad, therefore, is a controlled medium.

Besides deciding on these three options in dealing with the news media, business can decide on two more extreme strategies: (a) to hold the media accountable and, if necessary, to sue, and (b) to bypass the news media entirely. The broken line on the left of Fig. III.1 shows an aggressive strategy that business employs to put pressure on the news media. As discussed in chapter 7, it seeks to hold the media accountable for the stories they disseminate by reminding them of their reciprocal obligation to their First Amendment rights. Media accountability is achieved primarily through such means as media analysis centers and news councils and, if these ways are ineffective, by suing them for libel or fraud. The intended message to the media is "You're being watched, be careful about what you say."

As depicted by the broken line on the right of the figure, a corporation may decide to bypass the news media and communicate directly with relevant segments of the general public. Several traditional means of bypassing the media are available, such as direct mail and the use of private media in various constituency communications to employees, shareholders, customers, and other groups. The new medium of the Internet increasingly provides another vehicle to reach audiences. In 2001 more than 475 million people worldwide had Internet access at home. In the United States, 55% of American households (174 million) had an Internet connection, of which about 60% were "active" users each month. Internet users spent an average of 17 hours a month online in December 2001.[29]

ENDNOTES

1. "Strong Opposition to Media Cross-Ownership Emerges," *The State of the News Media 2004*, Pew Research Center for People & the Press, http://people-press.org/reports/display.
2. Robert Frank et al., "Scandal Scoreboard," *Wall Street Journal*, October 3, 2003, p. B1.
3. Lewis M. Simons, "Follow the Money," *American Journalism Review*, Vol. 21, November 1999, p. 55.
4. David Lieberman, "TV's New Look: All Business, All the Time," *USA Today*, January 14, 2000, pp. 1A, 2A.
5. Elfriede Fursich, "Nation, Capitalism, Myth: Covering News of Economic Globalization," *Journalism & Mass Communication Quarterly*, Vol. 70, Summer 2002, p. 356.
6. "Business Coverage Impacted by Reports of Corporate Scandal," *Public Relations Tactics*, January 2003, p. 7.
7. Stephan Lesher, *Media Unbound: The Impact of Television Journalism on the Public* (Boston: Houghton Mifflin, 1982), p. 4.
8. Ibid., p. 6.
9. "PRSA Cmte Chair Asks, `Is Public Relations 'Media Soft,'" *pr reporter*, Vol. 37, May 16, 1994, p. 3.
10. Ibid.
11. From June 11, 2004 news release of pr newswire. See http://www.prnewswire.com.
12. For more information, see Otto Lerbinger, *The Crisis Manager: Facing Risk and Responsibility* (Mahwah, NJ: Lawrence Erlbaum Associates, 1997), pp. 153–154.
13. Ibid.
14. Charlotte Ryan, *Prime Time Activism: Media Strategies for Grassroots Organizing* (Boston, Mass.: South End Press, 1991), p. 29.
15. Ibid. The local union bought ads in four consecutive issues of the *Sunday Boston Globe Magazine*, each centering on a single employee, who described his or her job and economic plight; took out an ad on WBZ radio; organized several union members to call local radio talk shows; and obtained television coverage through a "chance encounter with a TV reporter." It also held a union rally that filled Boston's historic Arlington Street Church to over-

flowing (which made for good TV coverage). Local leaders and national figures such as Cesar Chavez led the crowd in songs, one of which was expressly written for the union by a local musician, reiterating social justice themes: "We're Boston's hotel workers and we're fighting for our rights. We want justice, we want dignity, and we want respect" (p. 39).

Ryan alerts the reader to the typical biases of the news media once the obstacle of being considered unnewsworthy is overcome. One is their tendency to lump all labor issues together as "unrest," blaming unions for disrupting orderly life (a value strongly held by the media). Typically the main union activities that get coverage are picket lines, sit-ins, and large events with good visuals. The theme of social injustice tends to be ignored (p. 44).

16. Donald L. Shaw and Maxwell E. McCombs, "The Agenda-Setting Function of Mass Media," *Public Opinion Quarterly*, Vol. 36, Summer 1972, pp. 176–187.
17. Joseph N. Cappella and Kathleen Hall Jamieson, *Spiral of Cynicism: The Press and the Public Good* (New York: Oxford University Press, 1997), pp. 38, 45–46.
18. Fursich, op. cit., p. 367.
19. Ibid., p. 52.
20. Kathleen Hall Jamieson, *Dirty Politics: Deception, Distraction, and Democracy* (New York: Oxford University Press, 1992).
21. Ibid., pp. 163–164.
22. Ibid., p. 166.
23. Ibid., pp. 42–43.
24. Louis Banks, "Taking on the Hostile Media," *Harvard Business Review*, Vol. 56, March–April 1978, pp. 123–130.
25. Ibid.
26. Ibid., p. 129.
27. Brian Moskal, "Why Companies Avoid the Limelight," *Industry Week*, Vol. 206, July 21, 1980, p. 56.
28. "Even Media Pros Now Question Validity of Current 'News'; Another Reason to Go Under-the-Radar Directly to Publics," *pr reporter*, Vol. 37, March 21, 1994, p. 1.
29. Leslie Miller, "Web Growth Slows, But Time Online Rises," *USA Today*, March 28, 2002, p. 3D.

Chapter 4

Proactive Media Relations

When a company engages in proactive media relations, it not only responds to media inquiries but also seizes the initiative to convey its messages to the public. The goal of proactive media relations is to gain maximum control over the media so that organizational objectives, such as promoting its public issues agenda, can be achieved. Proactive media relations requires a company to take an aggressive, high-profile approach in dealing with the media. However, such a strategy often conflicts with a corporation's deeply held preference to maintain a low profile with the media and with the public: It does not hold news conferences or send out news releases; instead it limits its activity to warily responding to telephone calls by journalists.

Disney follows this low-profile approach, says Steve Crescenzo, a writer who tried to get the company to respond to criticism about various controversies, such as boycotts by different religious groups, animated movies that offend some groups, and the proposed theme park 4 miles from the Manassas National Battlefield and near Bull Run. Disney "communication personnel" wouldn't answer any questions; nor would several Disney beat reporters at major California outlets who were afraid they would jeopardize their access to the company. Said one anonymous agency person, "They feel that because they're so big, and nobody else does what they do, that they can ignore all the bad press and just keep churning out this positive image of the company." When one of the two people in charge of corporate public relations did return a call to Crescenzo, he was bluntly told that answering his questions—he had submitted a list of them—"isn't something we do.... We just don't talk about what we do. Sorry." "Click" went the phone.[1] Disney was using a high-profile approach for its entertainment news but a low one on other company matters.

The usual rule is that a low-profile approach works if there is little public interest in a company. This is ordinarily not an option for a large or visible organization, especially a consumer goods company, because both the media and the public want to know what is going on. In either case, however, a low profile is a deficit when a crisis occurs because there is little or no good will with the media or public to fall back on. Opportunities to win favorable mention and to build a positive corporate image are forfeited. Disney had to retreat from its plan to build a theme park near Civil War battlefields in Virginia because its soft-and-fuzzy image was portrayed as mean, arrogant, and insensitive.[2] CEO Michael Eisner found himself "besieged on all sides: from the courts, from former directors (including Walt's nephew, Roy Disney) and even from supposedly sleepy shareholders," said *The Economist*.[3] Robert L. Dilenschneider, a veteran public relations consultant, states, "A good image—one that's well made and well cared for—can survive everything, including the test of time. Scandal. Change. Bad earnings."[4]

The greater loss incurred by a low profile is the lost opportunity to advance company views on public issues. Most companies affected by government action have therefore rejected the low-profile strategy in favor of proactive media relations. They use several approaches: (a) intervene in the news creation process, (b) take a tough media stance, (c) make their corporate news "irresistible," and (d) take advantage of the enlarged media menu.

INTERVENE IN THE NEWS CREATION PROCESS

To be proactive means to take action before something happens. Media relations professionals must intervene in the news creation process. They can do this in four ways: "jump start" the news, engage in preemptive communication, "correct" the news—take out the impurities (inaccuracies) and add desirable ingredients (positive statements)—and influence reporting (e.g., by hiring media people with connections).

"Jump Start" News

The White House does not wait for news to happen. It knows that as a major newsmaker it can serve as the gatekeeper for major news from all federal departments and agencies. In a well-established procedure, all agencies submit important news stories to the White House daily, so that the president's communications staff can select the "story line of the day."[5] As Michael Deaver, President Reagan's chief of staff, explained, the president "must figure out a strategy and game plan" to maintain the upper hand with the media.[6]

Attempting to emulate the success of the White House, public relations professionals in other organizations try to "make news happen." In "Is the Press Any Match for Powerhouse PR?" Alicia Mundy, a contributing editor to *Washingtonian Magazine*, discusses the "new aggressiveness" in media relations, saying public relations firms have learned new tricks in "media manipulation."[7] A key technique is to jump start news by arranging to have outside third parties—an expert or other credible source—speak up on an issue of concern to one's organization, in the expectation that the news media will report on his or her comments. Care must be taken, however, not to violate ethical norms.

A much publicized incident occurred after Iraq seized Kuwait and the United States was deciding whether to intervene. Television networks showed a 15-year-old girl telling the American people she saw Iraqi soldiers pull tubes from babies' incubators, leaving them to die. What was not said, however, were three facts: The public relations firm of Hill & Knowlton arranged this interview, the girl was the daughter of the Kuwaiti ambassador to the United States, and she did not actually witness the act. News was indeed generated, but in this case manipulation of the press backfired when the identity of the girl and the truth of the situation were exposed.[8]

In an attempt to gain news coverage by keeping self-interested sources of information secret, a related practice is to use credible persons to author articles that are actually ghostwritten by someone else. To suit client interests, some public relations firms have purportedly paid prominent doctors to sign their names to ghostwritten scholarly reviews about new drugs for publication in medical journals. In an extreme case, a journal editor, who attempted to speak with the so-called senior author of an article, discovered the person had no idea of what had been written.[9] (See Box 4.1 for the argument that funding source should be disclosed.)

Box 4.1   Disclosure of Funding Sources

Dr. Troyen A. Brennan of the Harvard School of Public Health urges researchers who write articles to disclose the source of funds. He argues that monetary motivation skews the integrity of the scientific process, even if the views expressed are truly the author's. He told the *New England Journal of Medicine* that he was offered $2,500 by a prominent public relations firm to write an editorial on liability issues that might arise from prescribing drugs with sedative side effects, such as antihistamines.[10]

As medical journals extend their coverage to social and political issues, public affairs professionals may join marketers in exploiting the use of these journals. For example, in spring 1990 the *Journal of the American Medical Association* published a special issue on the uninsured and underinsured in health coverage. Its editor, Dr. George Lundberg, frankly stated that he wanted to have an impact on politicians and hoped "to create an aura of inevitability that this problem will be solved." In the same issue the influential former editor of the *New England Journal of Medicine*, Dr. Arnold Relman, attacked for-profit health care.[11]

Engage in Preemptive Communications

When an organization knows or suspects that a critical source is about to announce disturbing or controversial news in an upcoming news-release or news conference, a targeted organization can preempt the release by publicizing its version of the story first. It engages in preemptive communications by holding a news conference, distributing news releases, arranging to appear on broadcast talk shows, taking out advocacy ads, and using direct communications to each audience. The advantage of taking the initiative is that the news can be placed in a fuller and more favorable perspective. Subsequent stories by others then lack news value. President Clinton often did this in connection with questionable political fund raising. Madeline Albright also did this when the media were about to reveal that one of her parents was Jewish, a fact that might suggest she could not be unbiased in negotiations between Israel and Palestine.

Metabolife.   Michael Ellis, CEO of Metabolife International, decided on a formidable and expensive preemptive strike after he was interviewed by Arnold Diaz, a reporter for the ABC television news magazine program *20/20* on September 9, 1999. Diaz was preparing a segment on the reported dangerous side effects of the company's popular diet pill, Metabolife 356. Ellis said the interview "felt more like a deposition." After learning the reporter ran a website, "Schemes, Scams and Savin' a Buck," and one of the critics cited in the story was on the board of a competing company, Ellis expected the program to be unfair.[12] He took the advice of his publicist Michael Sitrick, known for his aggressive damage control on behalf of Food Lion supermarkets, and launched a preemptive attack.

Using an Internet site (www.newsinterview.com), Metabolife posted Diaz's complete, unedited 70-minute videotaped interview of Ellis and Randy Smith, the company's medical director. Before the segment was aired, Ellis also spent $1.5 million on full-page newspaper ads, which appeared on October 6, and radio programs to publicize the site and the company's concerns that ABC would broadcast an unfair report on the medical risks of its dietary supplement. ABC News spokeswoman Eileen Murphy considered the posting "a not very subtle attempt at intimidation."[13]

After the Metabolife segment appeared on *20/20* on October 15, Ellis, however, judged it as "not terribly unfair." He said, "I think they did the best job of doing a balanced 'unbalanced' story that they could do." But he credited the $2 million publicity campaign as "effective in holding '20/20's feet to the fire to some degree."[14] Diaz, however, maintains, "I don't think they were successful in neutralizing our report. I don't think our report would have been any different, as far as the thrust of it, had they not done this.... If their intent was to get more people to watch the story, they were successful in doing that."[15] The broadcast was in fact the highest rated that night among women ages 18 to 49. Furthermore, the website attracted more than 1 million users in its first 15 hours, according to publicist Sitrick.[16]

Metabolife's preemptive attack undoubtedly attracted widespread media and public attention. Ellis's side of the story was better known through the website, and despite its denials, ABC perhaps took greater care to make the segment balanced and fair. However, Ellis faced two risks: More people would know of the possible side effects of the diet pill, and embarrassing personal information would be revealed, namely, that in 1988 he was charged with illegally making methamphetamine, or speed. Now the "dynamite idea," as Ellis called it, of drawing millions of visitors so that people can make up their own mind would be tested. His lucrative business, which claims to sell 225,000 of its diet capsules an hour and was expected to yield revenues of $900 million in 1999, was at stake.[17]

EMFs. Preemptive communication can also be employed when a company expects an emerging issue to escalate and move to the next stage of public communication. Regular monitoring of an issue, including the use of public opinion surveys that track changes over time, is required to determine when an issue progresses in its life cycle.

The survey approach was used by the Edison Electric Institute when it learned from a 1993 Cambridge Reports/Research International survey that the percentage of people who were aware of electric and magnetic fields (EMFs) suddenly jumped 18 percentage points to a 63% awareness level. Previously the increase had averaged about 4 or 5 percentage points a year.[18] For some utilities, that jump was a signal to begin a public communication program. Although most utilities preferred to communicate with only their own stakeholders, others sent news releases to the media in an attempt to interest them in the EMF issue. Their strategy was to preempt the issue by publicizing their side of the story before opposition groups presented their own side.

Similar jumps in news coverage can be monitored through another method: computer tracking of issues and sources of news. Brent Baker, former dean of Boston University's College of Communication, illustrates how a system, which he calls *frame mapping*, works.[19] By analyzing the frequency of stories (about animal rights) appearing in three sources—print media, television, and the Internet—he was able to plot frequency distribution curves for each. He discovered that the Internet curve peaked several days before the curves of the print and television media. This information can thus serve as a leading indicator that allows an organization affected by an issue to take proactive measures. Because an increasing number of journalists visit websites, one of these measures could be to participate in newsgroups covering the issue. A 1996 survey by Successful Marketing Strategists (Berkeley, California) lends support to this approach because it found that 51% of journalists believed that Web pages today offer more news value than in past years.[20]

Correct the News

In an ideal business world, a company could review stories prior to publication or broadcast. Thus, if a story is judged false or distorted, it can attempt to correct it. With the advent of computer monitoring of wire service stories and stories written in foreign countries before they reach the United States, the possibility of "refining" inaccurate stories is greatly enhanced.[21]

As more newspapers first publish online versions of a story before hard-copy ones, some companies assign staff members in a 24-hour cycle to monitor stories about them. When inaccuracies, half-truths, and misinformation are spotted, specific reporters and editors are immediately sent fact sheets, corrected quotes, and counterstories on the Internet.

Monitor and Respond to Internet Attacks. Recognizing the potential danger of negative stories on the Web, companies are monitoring what people do or say on the Web and respond. Middleberg Interactive Communications in New York launched a computer monitoring service, called M-3 (the 3 stands for monitoring, analysis, and response), that scans the Internet daily for online complaints about its clients' products.[22] As stated by Steve Ulfelder: "The downside [of the Internet] is that anyone can run a smear campaign full of libelous information that reaches millions of people in seconds. There are no editors or safeguards ensuring that 'net information is fair and factual."[23]

Another monitoring service is Cybersleuth, a product from Dallas-based eWatch sold through the Edelman Interactive Solutions public relations agency and PR Newswire. "We can neutralize the information appearing online, identifying the perpetrators behind uncomplimentary postings and rogue websites," says the company's online promo material. Its objective: "To stop the spread of incorrect information and to ensure that what has already spread is eliminated," eWatch says. For example, if someone is spreading phony tips about XYZ stock on an online financial forum, XYZ could "work with" an Internet service provider to erase the comments from the site.[24] Northwest Airlines Corp. used this service to help it identify employees who organized a "sickout" that nearly halted flights over a Christmas holiday (see Box 4.2).

The danger in such a tough approach is that people will fear saying anything critical about a company online, whether factual or not. An employee could no longer share his or her opinion about a company online without worrying that the company would find out about it. Even if no legal action is taken, a person may become the target of a company "reeducation" campaign (e.g., an e-mail trying to change the employee's mind). Free speech is endangered.

Box 4.2   Northwest Airlines Uses Monitoring Service to Combat Strike

When the flight attendants' union and several others staged an illegal strike, Northwest Airlines resorted to Cybersleuth to strike back by suing the unions. The service helped it identify employees who organized a "sickout." Obtaining a court order, Northwest forced a veteran flight attendant, Kevin M. Griffin, who had hosted the message board, to turn over his computer so it could copy his hard drive. It also subpoenaed the company that hosted Griffin's website for the Internet addresses of the people who posted prosickout messages. Sometimes an offended company files a John Doe suit to obtain a sender's Internet protocol address from the Internet provider and then files a second subpoena "for any and all records" related to the person who had anonymously criticized the company. In one case, the provider disclosed not only the name of the person but also his credit-card numbers, the location of his checking account, and a list of some of the books and software he had purchased online. Although the provider says it no longer gives out this information, the law requires providers to honor court subpoenas.

Companies must decide how to respond to Internet-monitoring reports about customers as well as employees. The Ford Motor Company is one company that failed to respond to Internet smearing. After watching his Ford Ranger pickup burn on his driveway, Ed Goldgehn of Marietta, Georgia, and his wife opened a website they named www.flamingfords.com. The *New York Times* and CNN credited the Web page as one of the catalysts for a recall, which eventually added up to 8.7 million vehicles estimated to have cost Ford $200 million to $300 million. Ford never went online to combat the website. Ford spokeswoman Joy Wolfe explained, "Anything we'd do on our own [corporate] site would validate what these people are saying"; this reflects the rather old-fashioned attitude of not recognizing an opponent.[25]

In contrast to Ford, the Tommy Hilfiger Corporation, a publicly traded clothing manufacturer, took action when it fell victim to a rumor that spread like wildfire. The rumor asserted Hilfiger, a designer, appeared on *The Oprah Winfrey Show* and made racist comments about several groups, after which he was tossed off the set by Winfrey. After the rumor was a year old, it hit Usenet in the spring of 1997 and consequently spread so rapidly and generated so much controversy among customers and potential customers that the company responded. Company spokeswoman Ruth Pachman said, "As soon as the misinformation was brought to our attention," the company posted a statement to the appropriate newsgroups denying the allegations, a step that produced "immediate results."[26]

Companies are advised to familiarize themselves with newsgroups, mailing lists, chat rooms, and websites. When misinformation is found, these rules should be followed:

1. Go to the source of the attack and try to establish a dialogue, making sure to document everything. For example, Shell International bought banner advertising on the *Mother Jones* website after the magazine repeatedly ran articles on its website critical of the company's environmental and human rights policies. The ads led readers of the magazine to Shell's site, which included a forum area where users were invited to engage in a dialogue with the company about the issues the magazine had raised.[27]
2. Try to avoid the phone because it may seem like a "ham-fisted threat and will be immediately described and mocked on the 'net.'"
3. Prepare a contingency website that provides information that reinforces your position.
4. Muzzle your lawyers; they should be used as a last resort. "Nothing raises the hackles of the 'net faster than a legal threat."[28]

Influence Reporting

Some individuals and organizations establish working relationships with reporters who cover them on their beat, thereby lessening the reporters' independence. In one example, President Lyndon Johnson hired Robert E. Kintner, former NBC News president, as a White House special assistant in communications. Kintner revealed in a memorandum to the president he was willing to use his former connections. He stated he would "do some work" with the news chiefs of ABC, NBC, and CBS with reference to the "Civil Rights portion of your State of the Union address."[29] In another example, Ronald Reagan hired columnist George Will to coach him in preparation for his debates with incumbent Jimmy Carter in 1980. After one of the debates, Will went on television and, exercising his role as a journalist, commented favorably on Reagan's performance.[30] This practice raises the ethical question of a conflict of interest.

Speaker's fees may be paid to journalists as another way of influencing reporting. The National Speakers Forum, representing about 50 print and electronic journalists, says fees range from $3,000 to $30,000. ABC's Sam Donaldson reportedly receives the top sum of $30,000 for a speech. When David Gergen was editor-at-large at *U.S. News & World Report*, he earned $466,625 for giving 121 speeches in 1992.[31] Cokie Roberts accepted a $35,000 fee to speak at a Junior League-sponsored function, with the money coming from a large Florida Toyota distributor.[32] Although the giver of an honorarium may have the intention of influencing news stories, a reporter may not even know the source of his or her honorarium.

If a company is fortunate enough to hear of an upcoming news conference by an adversary, it can attempt to present its side of an issue at the same time. For example, someone at the *Washington Post* tipped off Chrysler that Consumers Union (CU) was planning a press conference in New York City to announce findings that Chrysler's subcompact cars, Dodge Omni and Plymouth Horizon, were unsafe. Chrysler immediately asked to attend, a request supported by friendly media representatives, but CU refused. As an alternative, Chrysler held a news conference at its Chelsea proving grounds on the same day—attended by Detroit and network television and radio reporters—and declared there was no relation between CU's test and a real driving situation.[33]

TAKE A TOUGH MEDIA STANCE

Proactive media relations can often go beyond taking the initiative and become confrontational and aggressive. A recent book by *Washington Post's* media critic Howard Kurtz, *Spin Cycle—Inside the Clinton Propaganda Machine*, demonstrates the White House's tactics and its use of this approach. In response to press corps hostility, the White House denies accusations, releases as little information as possible, attacks the accuser's motives, focuses on any inconsistencies, describes the allegations as part of a right-wing conspiracy, and changes the subject to the economy or some administrative initiative.[34]

As applied to the corporate world, Herb Schmertz's *Good-Bye to the Low Profile* introduces executives to his fundamental operating principle of "creative confrontation"—the willingness and ability to challenge your opponents and critics head-on, with imagination and flair.[35] "Don't try to make friends with reporters," he warns, "but do try to establish a real relationship."[36] Public relations professionals may have overdone this advice, however. When 32 South Florida broadcast and print journalists were asked what these professionals do right, only 3 said "build a relationship." The pros don't know the publication or the reporter, said 61% of the journalists.[37]

Part of that relationship is a mutual recognition that business and other news sources have as much power as the reporter: "Because the reporter needs your participation to do the story, you are in a position to set up conditions that are favorable to you as the price for your participation and cooperation."[38] If a story involves delicate issues or technical information, tell the reporter you'd prefer to take down questions and give your answers in writing.

Schmertz rejects the fourth-estate status of the news media, their insistence on "viewing themselves as surrogates for the American public." If they are, he asks, "Who appointed them?"[39] He apparently rejects the notion that the American public has accepted the special status of the news media.

Following the clarion call by Schmertz, many companies have taken a tough media stance in several ways: demanding rebuttal time, setting conditions for cooperation, boycotting the news media or imposing a "freeze-out," rating reporters, threatening to withdraw advertising, requiring advance notice of upcoming articles, and mounting a preemptive strike.

Demand Rebuttal Time

When media relations professionals are dissatisfied with how their organizations are treated by the news media, they have traditionally written or called the appropriate reporter, columnist, editor, or producer. Heeding the advice of veteran political consultant Bob Gray of Hill & Knowlton, some companies have now decided to "go after the little lies in a big way" so that the media would be less likely to fight them on the major facts.[40] (Three of the big ways—disclosing errors in an advocacy ad, referring such instances to media accountability groups, or suing the media—are so important that they are discussed in chaps. 6 and 7.) A method of challenging the media, specifically the broadcast media, is to demand rebuttal time.[41] How Kaiser Aluminum succeeded in this effort is described next.

Kaiser Aluminum.   When Kaiser Aluminum was accused on *20/20*, ABC's news magazine, of intentionally selling unsafe house wiring and hiding information about its dangers, the company immediately went on the offensive with an advertising, publicity, and political campaign against what it termed "trial by television."[42] The company's advocacy ad asserted: "When a TV production team does an unbalanced investigative report, the production team becomes the accuser, the judge, and the jury of people or institutions. By controlling the editing of pre-taped interviews, they even control what the accused can say on his own behalf."[43]

Ron Rhody, then Kaiser's vice president for advertising and public relations, further explained, "Since the producer edits the tape or film, all the taped or filmed interview does is put the producer (that is, the accuser) in full control of deciding what portions, and how much of the accused's defense the public will be allowed to see. The viewing public is led to believe that what it's seeing represents the accused's best arguments."[44]

Kaiser demanded rebuttal time, at first, and ABC offered an unprecedented 4 minutes of unedited rebuttal, but then it reneged. Kaiser filed a formal complaint with the Federal Communication Commission demanding that ABC be ordered to give 10 minutes of response time. The suit was later dropped after ABC promised to accommodate Kaiser in a new program, called *Viewpoint*. It was designed to "deal with broad subjects affecting broadcast journalism generally, and at the same time provide a forum for a discussion of complaints about accuracy or fairness."

Kaiser's rebuttal was aired on the premiere of the new show.[45] However, Geraldo Rivera, ABC's correspondent on *20/20*, was on hand to respond to the rebuttal. In answer to Kaiser's objection to Rivera's final words, Rivera said it would have destroyed "the responsibility of responsible journalists."[46] Besides demanding and receiving rebuttal time, Ron Rhody assembled arguments to show that adversarial interviews and one-sided reporting are damaging to the concept of a free press.[47]

Set Conditions for Cooperation

During the Reagan administration, officials harnessed the broadcast media by setting their own terms for appearances. Lesley Stahl said she could not get Secretary of State George Schultz on CBS's *Face the Nation* unless she guaranteed him two thirds of the airtime and promised that no unfriendly foreign spokesman would appear.[48]

Companies have also set the conditions for cooperation. Former Celanese (now Hoechst) vice president of corporate communications, Dorothy Gregg, said she would not permit television interviews unless the station agreed to show the company the final edited film in advance. When asked about possible press antagonism to these rules, she replied, "New York media think you're a dummy unless you take these precautions."[49] She did not, however, demand to see final copies of print media articles, even to check for factual accuracy.

Set Strict Guidelines.   Following this pattern, Johns-Manville (now called the Manville Corporation) established some strict press guidelines when, as the leading producer of asbestos in the United States, it had to defend itself against charges that it knew about the link between asbestos and cancer. The company's "Reserved Cooperative Approach" in working with the media stated:

1. *If a reporter calls and deadline is too short* to lay out company's case effectively, [respond with] no comment or "uncooperate." Do not help legitimize story as objective.
2. If a PR person detects by reporter's questions that *story is already written*, refuse to cooperate. Chastise reporter for lack of objectivity and fairness.
3. *For TV programs*, learn about the number of people to be on show, and who they are, before committing to appear. J-M will not participate if more than 3 people [are present] because there won't be enough time to present company's story. Medium is surfacy anyway.
4. When a medium runs a *story which is totally unbalanced and unfair*, respond to it promptly with letter or phone call.
5. *Sales force and other non-media sources* act as early warning system, alert corporate relations to local media questions. PR responds by initiating call to press instead of waiting to see what develops.

6. Corporate relations *covers all key events* on subject—whether trials, government testimony, science conference, OSHA hearings. Goal is to learn—and work with media.
7. J-M has installed *direct phone line* to Denver HQ for Washington media—with 7 digits—to help meet their deadlines.
8. Materials are kept not only at HQ but in D.C. office and at NYC PR firm. If media calls from NYC or D.C. and has a day to do story, company has *package of position papers delivered immediately.*
9. PR gives *AP, L.A. Times, N.Y. Times special attention.* "Their coverage has been most fair and balanced" although "company hasn't always agreed."
10. PR *responds to every phone call* immediately and promptly.[50]

Through these guidelines, Johns-Manville seized the initiative in dealing with the media and rewarded those who played the game right. Curtis Linke, then the company's senior director of corporate relations, defended the guidelines by saying the press is generally uninformed on health and science topics and doesn't show a willingness to give the couple of hours needed to hear facts on a complex issue. He said the company's media relations would "continue to be one of mutual advocacy. I respect the power of the media, but I do not believe any of us can condone or permit unfair, biased treatment to go unchallenged."[51]

Insist on Accompanying Filming.   When a demand is unlikely to be met, some companies prepare rebuttal material that enables them to reach important audiences through other media. Illinois Power was an early user of this counterattack technique.[52] In October 1979, *60 Minutes* approached Illinois Power and, according to company spokesman Howard Rowe, said that "CBS was going to produce a balanced, factual presentation of the economics of building nuclear power plants."[53]

Illinois Power decided to cooperate because CBS, intent on doing the story, had alternative sources of information, mainly from hearings by the Illinois Commerce Committee. The company saw cooperation as "the only opportunity to get the truth told and straighten out some of the misinformation.... Refusing to cooperate could only lead to the shot through the plant gate with a statement that we had refused to talk, carrying its 'guilty as charged' insinuation."[54] As a precaution, however, Illinois Power added one critical stipulation in its agreement to cooperate: Whatever CBS filmed on its property, a camera crew hired by the company would also film. How Illinois Power used their film is described in Box 4.3.

Companies that are approached by *60 Minutes* should heed the advice of Robert Chandler, CBS's vice president in charge of the program and other public affairs programming: "Get the best representative available ... somebody who doesn't 'ramble.' " He elaborated:

You could be contacted by a researcher just beginning to explore a story, a producer or correspondent. The "60 Minutes" representative might want background material, an off-camera chat, or he might want to film the site to interview someone in authority. If they do want to talk to someone in authority, "60 Minutes'" representatives may not tell you much about the subject matter.[55]

Box 4.3   Prepare to Counterattack—Illinois Power Raps
60 Minutes

When company officials saw the *60 Minutes* broadcast, they were appalled. So were many shareholders. By the end of Monday following the Sunday broadcast, three times as many shares had been traded as ever before in a single day, and the stock, which had been selling in the low 20s, closed the day off a full point. A few weeks later, the stock fell to $15 a share.[56] Employee morale was also suffering badly, and hate letters soon began arriving at company headquarters. Compounding its problems, the company knew that CBS had timed the segment to air just 3 days prior to a decision by the Illinois Commerce Commission on the company's rate case.[57]

Illinois Power had to act quickly to defuse the *60 Minutes* program and get the facts of the case to its employees, the press, the financial community, stockholders, and the public. The company's trump card was its own filming of what *60 Minutes* filmed. Working speedily, the company prepared a 45-minute rebuttal tape within a week of the broadcast. It was first reviewed by company officers, then released for showing to employees, their families, and retirees, and finally shown to the local media.

Response was favorable. Harold Deakins, Illinois Power's media representative, reported, "Many of our employees sat down to write their congressmen that very night."[58] Numerous media articles written about the event opened the door to a much wider audience. The company suddenly found itself busy with requests for showings before business clubs, church groups, suppliers, and high school and college classes. The company reported that 3,000 cassette videotapes of its film *60 Minutes/Our Reply* were in circulation.[59]

Interestingly, CBS threatened to sue, on the basis of copyright violation, if the Public Broadcasting System or independent stations presented the company video. Furthermore, CBS defended its actions. In answering the complaint that the CEO of Illinois Power was interviewed for one and a half hours, but only 3 minutes appeared on television, Robert Chandler, CBS's vice president in charge of *60 Minutes* and other public affairs programming, said, "We're paid to synthesize material. We're reporters. We're not common carriers." He added, "Corporate decisions affect a wide number of people, and it's our job to go after those stories."[60]

In conclusion, Chandler said, "You'll know what it is about." Be prepared for hard questions, he advised, and you better have answers. "If you don't know, we're going to show it."[61]

The Behavior Research Institute followed the example of Illinois Power when CBS asked for its cooperation with *Eye to Eye with Connie Chung*. Its experience is described in Box 4.4.

Impose a News Boycott or "Freeze-Out"

Imposing a news boycott is an extreme response to perceived unfair treatment by the media. When the Electric Boat Division of General

---

Box 4.4   Behavior Research Institute Does Not See "Eye to Eye With Connie Chung"[62]

The Behavior Research Institute (BRI) reluctantly decided to allow an investigation of its services by CBS's *Eye to Eye With Connie Chung*. The Providence, Rhode Island, institute feared that Connie Chung was already predisposed to accept allegations against it and to discredit it. The institute felt that its residential treatment center was vulnerable because it treats mentally retarded and autistic individuals with extreme behavior disorders, some of whom have been classified as "hopeless." Some individuals are prone to self-abuse to the point of gouging out their own eyes, ripping out pieces of their throats, or banging their heads on the floor. Therapy is consequently severe and can take the form of an electric shock applied to a patient's arm or leg.

So the institute faced a difficult challenge: "How does an organization defend itself against false accusations from the press?" Its decision was to take on *Eye to Eye* and CBS by telling others in the press—convincing them that the show was a "one-sided, prefabricated story meant to do little more than win ratings points."

BRI took several actions. First, the institute invited more than 40 parents (who volunteered to be interviewed and insisted on being present during the show's filming) to participate in the videotaping. Next, BRI declined to allow videotaping of patients receiving therapy on the grounds of protecting patients' privacy, but offered its own tape of treatments instead. CBS responded by hiring a "plant" who filmed the treatments with a hidden camera. The institute also wisely declined CBS's request that BRI's legal counsel be seated next to Matthew Israel, BRI's executive director, while he was being interviewed. BRI knew the attorney's presence would imply guilt on the part of the executive director. BRI took two final steps. It hired its own video crew to tape the interview so that it would have a complete and accurate record of what was said prior to the March 3, 1994, broadcast, and it sent copies of these tapes to 300 media critics across the country.

Dynamics was angered by what it considered biased and unbalanced reporting by the *Day*, the local newspaper, the company cut off the news flow to the paper, even though its 18,500 Groton, Connecticut, employees read the *Day*. General Dynamics excluded the paper from access to any information about its activities (except the launching of submarines because U.S. Navy regulations required such notification), refused to send news releases that were sent to other papers and broadcasters, shut it out of news conferences open to other publications, and refused to return phone calls or answer questions posed by *Day* reporters.[63]

Mobil is another company that imposed a news boycott. Angered by a story that the chairman's son-in-law would benefit financially from the company's construction of a tower in Chicago, Mobil announced it would no longer "have anything to do with the *Wall Street Journal*."[64] It would no longer answer any of its reporters' questions or give them any information.[65]

In the field of investor relations, the freeze-out is a version of a news boycott imposed by a company when analysts have written something negative about it (see Box 4.5). "Basically, it's management's way of punishing an analyst who is not part of the cheering squad," says Jullianne C. Iwerson-Niemann, senior vice president of equity research and portfolio management at Huntleigh Securities. "What happens is your phone calls are not returned. You're relegated to junior people. You're the last on the fax list. You basically become Zachary Zilch, the last person in the phonebook to get the message on anything. And sometimes you have to resort to talking to other people to find out what's going on."[66] Christopher McFadden, a Goldman Sachs Group analyst, experienced the same "big chill"after he downgraded some stocks, such as Cardinal Health and McKesson. He claims that the companies' executives pointedly didn't take questions from him during conference calls. Larry Kurtz, head of investor relations for McKesson, denies this treatment, saying, "We talk to everyone who calls us, regardless. That's our ethic here."[67]

The risk of freeze-outs and news boycotts is that analysts and reporters have "a long memory for things like that" and will seek to punish the company. It's the worst thing to do, says Eugene P. Beard, vice chairman of finance and operations at Interpublic Group of Companies, an advertising conglomerate. "Companies that do that will find it coming back to haunt them."[68]

"Get tough" tactics, such as a boycott or freeze-out, should be used prudently not only because some violate journalistic tradition but also because they can backfire. For example, when the *Day* complained to the National News Council about General Dynamics' boycott, the council sided with the newspaper, saying, "When public funds and the public interest are involved to such an extent in a company that employs a quarter of all the workers in southeastern Connecticut, the community is ill-served by an arbitrary decision on the company's part to withhold all information from the chief newspaper directly serving the region."[69]

Box 4.5   Freeze-Out of Financial Reporters

Bonnie Wittenburg, a food and agriculture analyst at the Minneapolis securities firm of Dain, Bosworth & Co. and a former reporter at the *Des Moines Register,* suffered a freeze-out. For years she had recommended that investors buy Archer Daniels Midland Co. (ADM) stock. One of her reports, 40 pages long, so pleased the company that it mailed copies to its 34,000 shareholders. However, because of a price-fixing investigation into the company and the resignation of Howard G. Buffett, a director and company spokesman, she put out a "sell" recommendation on what she called her "flagship stock." This act caused her stress, but it was compounded when officials at ADM failed to return her phone calls and, in fact, refused to have anything to do with her.[70]

Another analyst, Christopher McFadden of the Goldman Sachs Group, suffered a similar fate. After downgrading some pharmaceutical company stocks, he was put on hold during company conference calls and the companies' executives pointedly didn't take questions from him. The companies disputed McFadden's notion, saying that they were coping with numerous participants and more questions than they could accommodate. Larry Kurtz, head of investor relations for McKesson, said, "We talk to everyone who calls us, regardless. That's our ethic here."[71]

Rate Reporters

Rating reporters is a common, informal practice. It helps a company select which reporters to avoid and which to favor. To rate reporters, a media relations person typically reads some articles written by a reporter or calls colleagues for their opinions. Several actions might then be taken: Send news releases to favorably rated reporters and not to others, select cities for a media tour where reporters in local media are friendly toward your company and industry, or meet with low-rated reporters to provide them with more information and, hopefully, make their stories more balanced. Despite the acceptance of this practice, however, government agencies must exercise caution. The U.S. DOE took some heat in 1995 when the *Wall Street Journal* disclosed that the agency spent $43,500 to hire a firm that ranked reporters on how favorably they wrote about it.[72]

The growth of electronic databases containing reporters' stories and the emergence of an entrepreneurial group of former journalists willing to report on their ex-colleagues has fostered a new media evaluation industry. The giant is Carma International (Computer-Aided Research & Media Analysis) in Washington, DC, which charges $500 to $15,000 for 1 month's analysis, depending on the number of reporters and variables involved. Chuck Werle of Chicago-based Werle+Brimm Ltd. judges journalists on a scale of 1 to10 on accuracy, verification, interview skills, industry knowledge, balanced reporting, writing ability, integrity, and personality.[73]

The beef industry used another measure. It investigated whether reporters ate steak, which might persuade them to portray beef more favorably, or whether they were vegetarians and therefore would not do the industry much good. When the National Cattlemen's Association saw Tom Kenworthy, a *Washington Post* reporter, at the bottom of Carma's charts, its public affairs director arranged to discuss matters with him and introduce him to some live cattlemen. The result: "We're a little bit happier with his reporting."[74]

Some of information about reporters can be obtained from online media directories such as MediaMap's Media Manager. It not only lists reporter contacts by phone number, fax, and e-mail, but also provides information on reporters' background, what areas they report on, what stories they are working on, deadlines they must meet, and how they prefer to be contacted. Users can also obtain information on editorial calendars, access the archive section, and read past stories written by particular reporters that give a sense of their interests, subjects, and writing styles. Information about most subjects can also be found on the Internet's huge database.[75]

Threaten to Drop Advertising

Another way to discipline a news medium is to threaten to drop advertising, thereby undermining the news organization's commercial viability. All media organizations are commercial to the extent they must contend with the economic reality of remaining solvent. This reality has been intensified by the current era of media concentration, which demands that media be profitable investments. Advertising generates the largest revenue source of almost all media (exceptions are premium cable services and the film industry). To advertisers, the media are simply an audience delivery system.[76]

With the advent of wider alternatives to newspaper advertising, advertisers wield more bargaining power. In Detroit, car dealers who were angry at negative news stories printed their own tabloid advertisements rather than advertise in local papers. Even large newspapers respond to advertiser pressure. Car dealers in Hartford pulled their ads from the *Hartford Courant* after a story was run that warned consumers about high-pressure sales tactics. The editor of the paper was forced to apologize to the dealers to woo them and their advertising dollars back to the paper.[77]

Even public television is not immune, for businesses see it as a means of enhancing corporate images and thereby creating a favorable climate for marketing. For this reason, various drug companies have supported shows on health care (being careful to avoid controversial health issues); and Boeing Corporation funded a PBS program on the president's plane, *Air Force One*, Boeing's own product.[78]

Companies can indirectly threaten to drop advertising through their advertising agencies. According to *Hollywood Reporter*, an entertainment industry paper, General Motors warned its advertising agencies to avoid two episodes of the syndicated *Donahue* talk show that dealt with the movie *Roger & Me*. The film was critical of General Motors and its chairman, Roger B. Smith.[79]

Require Advance Notice of Upcoming Articles

Some advertisers and retail chains demand advance notice about upcoming articles. In January 1996, Chrysler's advertising agency sent a letter to more than 100 magazines saying, "In an effort to avoid potential conflicts, it is required that Chrysler Corporation be alerted in advance of any and all editorial content that encompasses sexual, political, social issues or any editorial that might be construed as provocative or offensive."[80] In response, the Magazine Publishers of America and American Society of Magazine Editors accused the company of practicing a form of censorship. They issued a strong statement urging magazines not to "submit tables of contents, text or photos from upcoming issues to advertisers for prior review." In October 1997, Chrysler, which is the nation's fifth-largest magazine advertiser, dropped its controversial policy; but it also said, "In the end, we reserve the right to decide where and when to place advertising."[81]

Some big retail stores, such as Winn-Dixie supermarkets and Wal-Mart Stores, regularly demand advance copies of publications suspected of containing material that might be objectionable to many of its customers. The concerns involve nudity or lewd language and such controversial subjects as abortion, homosexuality, and religion. "We serve a broad spectrum of customers, and we don't want to offend them," explains G. E. Clerc, Jr., a spokesman for Winn-Dixie, based in Jacksonville, Florida.[82] For example, a possible objection to *Cosmopolitan's* March 1997 issue was that its cover headline included the words "His & Her Orgasms."

Supermarket and big discount chains have enormous power over magazines because they control 55% of single-copy sales of U.S. magazines. Wal-Mart is the biggest seller, with about 9% of single-copy sales. If an outlet judges an issue to be offensive, it might simply not carry a specific issue or, as Dana Sacher, circulation director of *Vibe*, warns, "If you don't let them know in advance, they will delist the title and never carry it again."[83]

Frank Lalli, president of the American Society of Magazine Editors, believes publishers should not give previews to retailers. "When you give them a look, there is the potential that people outside the magazine will say, 'I have a solution. Drop that cover. Change the story.'" He says editors are "deeply concerned" about this trend, and "worries that some advertisers may mistake an early warning" from a magazine "as an open invitation to pressure the publisher or editor to alter, or even kill, the article in question." Norman Pearlstine, *Time*'s editor-in-chief, warns of establishing a dangerous precedent: "When you start giving advance looks to either advertisers or retailers you are creating opportunities for censorship."[84]

Exercise Restraint: Procter & Gamble's Excessive Zeal

Several other kinds of "get tough" tactics are not discussed here because they are blatantly unethical or unwise. For example, Procter & Gamble's (P&G's) effort to hunt down the source of a leak to the *Wall Street Journal*[85] earned the company one of *Fortune*'s "10 Biggest Business Goofs" mentions.[86] Several articles had appeared that revealed possible changes in top management and some troubles with its food-and-beverage division. Saying its own internal investigation failed to identify the leak, P&G asked Cincinnati's fraud division to look into what was regarded as a violation of a state criminal law that bars anyone from giving away "articles representing trade secrets."[87] Using subpoena powers, the court ordered Cincinnati Bell to identify "all 513 area code numbers that dialed the office or home phone number of *Wall Street Journal* reporter Alecia Swasy [the author of the articles] between March 1 and June 1, 1991." The privacy of some 655,297 home and business telephone lines was violated as at least 35 million toll calls made in that period were searched.[88] To the press, this was an indirect way of seeking to identify a news source, which in Ohio and many other states is illegal. P&G's CEO Edwin L. Artzt finally conceded, "We made an error in judgment ... we regret it ... we were just plain wrong."[89] But veteran columnist William Safire observes that while Artzt admitted to a public relations blunder, he still did not understand the ethical violation of people's rights to privacy.

MAKING NEWS IRRESISTIBLE

News can be made so attractive to journalists and editors that they can't resist. Two basic ways of getting a story published are: (a) making a story newsworthy, and (b) subsidizing the media.

Create Newsworthy Stories

News is timely information of interest to many people.[90] Perhaps the essence of news is contained in the comment by a former *New York Sun* editor who said, "When a dog bites a man, that's not news. But if a man bites a dog, that is news."[91] From a media relations viewpoint, news is what a reporter and editor will accept. Unfortunately, too many corporate executives have a house organ mentality, thinking a story written for employees would also be interesting to outsiders. Thus, as a survey of *Fortune* 500 companies shows, business would like journalists to be more interested in stories about the following topics:

- Corporate social responsibility programs.
- Environmental achievements and the need for trade-offs.
- Human side of corporate life and personal glimpses of management.
- Research, technical achievements, and innovations.
- Positions on legislative or regulatory matters.
- Employee recognition.[92]

Some of these in-house themes may, indeed, be of interest to journalists if implications for the broader community and society are drawn. A company should tap its information resources, including insights of corporate executives and other employees. A good media relations professional tries to keep an inventory of the special facts and perspectives that a company is able to provide and thus become known as a valuable source of industry information. Of course, she or he knows that the story must be well written, meaning the five Ws—what, where, when, who, and why—are covered and that the style and level of difficulty meet the readability requirements of the intended audience.[93]

Subsidize the Media

Subsidies to the media help make a submitted story irresistible. In *Beyond Agenda Setting*, Oscar H. Gandy, Jr. explained that the idea behind a media subsidy is to reduce the "costs of access to self-serving information."[94] On a very basic level, a well-written news release or feature story is in itself a subsidy to a newspaper, magazine, or broadcast station because the story would otherwise have to be produced with the medium's personnel and other resources. Without the public relations departments of thousands of organizations, the news media would have to increase their staffs drastically. However, Gandy gives media subsidies a sinister twist by saying it is most often the public relations specialist who delivers the "undercover subsidy, where the source and the source's self-interest is skillfully hidden from view."[95] Also revealing, he feels, is that press releases follow the advice of publicists to interpret the significance of a story in case the editors and writers miss it.

Public relations professionals have used the following imaginative ways to subsidize the media: (a) distributing voluminous press kits, (b) using media distribution service companies, (c) providing video news releases, (d) sponsoring and citing public policy polls, and (e) creating a website on the Internet.

Distribute Press Kits.   Press kits, often enclosed in a folder or portfolio, are collections of background materials that aid a journalist in writing a story. This information is now typically provided on an organization's website. The usual materials include photographs (of company facilities, personnel, and products), biographies of persons mentioned in a news release, speeches by executives, the annual report, and other organizational data. Box 4.6 describes some of the advantages in distributing press kits.

Use Media Distribution Services.   North American Precis Syndicate, Inc. (NAPS) provides releases to 1,500 dailies and 10,000 newspapers in all. NAPS CDs allow top dailies, Sunday, and feature editors to fill whole pages and special sections. The radio release goes on CDs with scripts to NAPS contacts at 6,500 stations. A Video Feature Release provides broadcasters with 1-minute features.[96] Gandy describes how the Business Roundtable hired this syndicate to distribute hundreds of editorials, cartoons, and feature stories to help defeat the establishment of the Consumer Product Safety Commission.[97] According to Gandy, the syndicate guarantees a 10% success rate for each mailing.[98]

Box 4.6   Advantage in Distributing Press Kits

A study about news coverage of the environment by two journalism professors shows that press kits and news conferences result in greater acceptance of the source's angle.[99] (They also studied whether news selection and bias were caused by the nature of a report titled "Toxic Clusters: Patterns of Pollution in the Midwest," prepared by the New York-based nonprofit environmental research group Inform, Inc. The report was based on information provided by the EPA on the amount of hazardous chemicals manufacturers have released into the environment. Manufacturers annually report this information to the EPA, as required by the 1986 Superfund Amendments and Reauthorization Act.

A week prior to holding a news conference, Inform sent press kits to about 200 media outlets in the seven-state region of the Midwest. These kits served as an "information subsidy" to the media and encouraged coverage of the story. The kit also persuaded newspapers with larger staffs to assign reporters to the story.

The use of press kits is justified by the finding that those media receiving press kits were fairer to business in their treatment of the pollution data than were those that did not receive them. Of 373 daily Midwestern newspapers analyzed, the papers tended either not to cover the story—even though coverage was most likely in communities where manufacturing was at least of medium importance in their economies—or to give more lenient headline treatment.[100] Furthermore, little was said about the health risks resulting from local toxic releases.

NAPS also provides "public policy publicity" when an issue prominently appears in the mass media. Some techniques suggested by Ronald N. Levy, the syndicate's president, are:

- Canned editorial: Enables you to editorialize in a way that would not be acceptable in a feature. However, editorials get less readership than features, and many papers will not run canned editorials.
- "Believe It or Not" type of cartoon: Works if you can make your point in few words. Gains the attention of people who might not read a text release on the subject.
- Stories based on speeches: Allow writing of releases, especially for suburban newspapers, based on senior executive speeches that have already been carefully researched, the ideas carefully thought out, and the materials cleared with company legal staff.
- "Economic reality" stories: When a person's own money is involved, he or she becomes interested. If a solution to an issue raises the cost of producing a product of your company or industry, point out how it's going to cost the average person money.
- Other techniques: Use signed columns, perhaps in a Q & A format. Quote government experts who agree with you. Write several stories when each key point warrants a story.[101]

Provide VNRs. Local television stations welcome video news releases (VNRs) from reliable sources. By resembling television news reports, the intention of these releases is to capture maximum exposure on television news to promote company viewpoints and other news. "What we do by definition is advocacy. It's not journalism," says Doug Simon, president and CEO of the production and event company DS Simon Production. To create a good VNR that confusion must be clarified up front. Medialink CEO Larry Moskowitz advises PR pros to disclose more than they even think necessary when sending out a VNR.[102]

This norm was violated when PR professional Karen Ryan signed off her voice-over on a Department of Health and Human Services VNR by saying she was "reporting" from Washington, DC, thus implying a journalist's impartiality. To make doubly sure that its client stations know a VNR's source, CNN Newsource, one of the distributors of the controversial VNR, will now add a fourth label in addition to "clearly" identifying a VNR in the script and in the window that displays the source.[103]

A Nielsen Media Research Survey of 130 TV news directors showed 75% found VNRs helpful in preparing their daily newscasts.[104] A later poll found that 78% of editors used edited VNR material at least once a week.[105] Box 4.7 provides details of a specific case of VNR use.

In 1992 more than 4,000 VNRs were produced; Medialink, the largest distributor, alone sent out 2,000. The company has a news wire that in 1991 reached nearly 700 television newsrooms coast to coast. It describes its Medialink/AP Express Newswire as "a comprehensive, pow-

---

Box 4.7   TV News Directors' Use of a VNR on "America Responds to AIDS"

A VNR, "America Responds to AIDS (ARTA)," produced by the government's Centers for Disease Control (CDC), suggests the extent to which television news directors use VNRs. Findings are based on a survey and content analysis of 47 "air checks" of television news stories from 42 television news organizations (39 local broadcasters, *ABC World News Tonight*, *Cable News Network*, and *USA Today*). The key findings were:

- No station used the entire VNR package.
- 85% of the air checks contained only half or less of the packaged video; the same held true for the script.
- Of seven key story elements, an average of 21% appeared in the air checks.
- Sound bites from officials were used infrequently. Celebrity James Mason's sound bite from the Washington press conference was mentioned the most (by 25%), and one by Louis Sullivan (10%).
- The source, CDC, was mentioned in only 8% of the stories. Instead, stations cited such general sources as "the federal government."
- 75% of the stories focused on the *AIDS Prevention Guide*. In this context, the CDC was mentioned in 17 of the 35 stories focusing on the guide; 22 mentioned Health and Human Services.[106]

---

erful and high-speed electronic service that delivers critical information right to the desks of TV editors throughout the U.S."[107] Medialink president Laurence Moskowitz claims that "overall, VNR results continue to rise, and the performance of the most successful projects continues to be stunning."[108] To illustrate, Burson–Marsteller, a leading U.S. public relations firm, prepared a videotape for a client after the Food and Drug Administration ruled that a client's product was the only safe one of its kind. The tape appeared in the form of a news report and was distributed to 100 television stations.

The most dramatic VNR, according to Medialink's 1993 list of the "Top Ten" organizations using VNRs, was Pepsi-Cola's response to the Diet Pepsi syringe hoax in June 1993. The VNRs attained a record-breaking 500 million aggregate viewership on 3,170 stations airing over a period of several days in June. (The previous most aired VNR was the speech by the president of Colombia imploring Americans to stop snorting cocaine, a broadcast that reached an audience of 80 million.) Following Pepsi-Cola on the Top Ten list were Princeton University's "Fusion Energy" with an audience of 56,900,000 and 197 airings, and Time-Warner's "Venture with US West" with 49 million viewers.[109] On average, a VNR will get a median of 18 usages from a possible 700 outlets, says Nick Peters, Medialink's vice president of operations.[110]

Corporate use of VNRs has the advantage of making a message more memorable to a news audience, largely because of the credibility assigned to television news programming.[111] No claim can be made, however, that attitudes are influenced, at least not by a single exposure.

To increase the acceptance of VNRs, public relations practitioners are advised to send the traditional pitch letter with story angles, accompanied by press conference footage, sound bites, and raw footage. Sending some printed materials in advance of a story is not only more cost effective but also helps journalists view the public relations practitioner as more of a partner and less of a manipulator in the news process.[112]

Media relations practitioners should also avoid making some mistakes that discourage TV stations from airing VNRs. *Media Relations Inside*, a newsletter, gives this advice:

- Approach the story like a reporter. Douglas Simon, president and CEO of New York's D.S. Simon Productions, said to focus on what's news to the public, not to your own organization. *USA Today*, he says, does this by covering stories of interest to people nationwide and writing to the lay person. Try to make the VNR fit the style of a local newscast, which can be achieved by hiring producers and crews with broadcast news backgrounds who understand the need to tell a good story with creative visuals and no industry jargon.
- Don't go over 90 seconds.
- Use highly credentialed experts with broad knowledge. Sally Jewett, president of Los Angeles-based On the Scene Productions, advises securing independent endorsements from credible spokespeople who are willing to appear on the video.
- Understand the distribution format your contacts want. Sending out a VNR by satellite might be a good idea for time-sensitive videos. Some outlets, however, like CNN, only accept videos on tapes. The Internet has become another outlet for VNRs.[113]

Many TV stations prefer to use the background materials of a VNR but not the supplied commentary. It is advisable, therefore, to send a B-roll, the supplementary or backup material. It generally follows the primary material on the same cassette in which alternate scenes are arranged on two reels, an A-roll and a B-roll, and then assembled.[114]

Sponsor and Cite Public Policy Polls.   Newspapers, magazines, and broadcasters seem eager to use poll findings. In 1990, after the first in-house poll of the *Detroit Free Press* in the mid-1960s, 82% of national newspapers (with circulation of 100,000 and over) and about half of the television stations were engaged in polling, according to a study conducted by the Roper Center.[115] The *New York Times* has been among the first media organizations to do in-house research and their own polls, often in collaboration with a major survey company. The caliber of the *New York Times*—and CBS News—polls is often comparable to that of academic surveys.

Problems arise, however, with polls conducted by smaller local news outlets or made available by external organizations. Some of these are Internet polls, which "are not real polls and the results mean nothing," according to Lori Robertson in an article on "Poll Crazy."[116] Low-budget press operations are nevertheless tempted to use these polls. The *New York Times*, however, discourages the use of a poll conducted by an external organization if the organization won't describe its methods or claims proprietary methods. As polls have become ubiquitous, the danger is that poor practices can lead to an overall decline in the credibility of survey research in general.[117]

Mervin D. Field, chairman of Field Research, explains why polls are so popular with the media. The media realized, he said, that the public puts an inordinate value on impeccable arithmetic: "If something adds up to 100 percent, this fact conveys an aura of something perfect and possessed of values that often do not exist."[118] Actually, news commentators unwillingly give survey results a precision they do not possess. For example, when Walter Cronkite announced that 65% of Americans supported the Supreme Court decision on abortion and that this percentage had a tolerance of 4 percentage points plus or minus, he implied, at worst the percentage might be a low of 61% or a high of 69%. Actually, however, the figures might be further off because of sources of more serious errors.

Supporting the view that reporters understandably find a number of superficial advantages of polls difficult to resist, Warren Miofsky and Martin Plissner state:

> For starters, a good many polls can legitimately be called scientific. The statisticians who do the work often hold degrees entitling them to be known as "Doctor." The poll very likely bears the trademark of a firm called something like Research Analysis, Inc., of Princeton, Arkansas. Unlike anything else in journalism, the scientific poll also does not flinch at the notion of error. It boldly proclaims it—telling you, in percentage points, how wrong it is going to allow itself to be. This is the scientific way of doing things. You don't fight error; you measure it.[119]

Mervin Field feared the trend of using public policy polls would result in confusion, suspicion, and a negative image of survey research methods. What's wrong is not their use, he said, but how polls are conducted and publicized (see Box 4.8). Any organization has the right to sponsor an opinion survey to demonstrate to politicians and the public that public opinion is on their side—especially when the contrary is claimed by the media or opponents. In a democracy public opinion is supposed to count.

Box 4.8   Hill & Knowlton's Questionable Publicity of Survey Results

Journalistic ignorance of polling techniques and ethics further increases reporters' vulnerability. For example, in 1980 Hill & Knowlton, then the largest public relations firm in the United States, arranged simultaneous press conferences in five cities to publicize the results of a poll favorable to its client, the American Trucking Association. It referred to survey results that indicated there was "virtually no public support for the move in Congress to deregulate the nation's trucking industry," a finding that was subsequently cited by wire services and a number of regional papers. [120] What Hill & Knowlton did not state was that the survey firm, Group Attitudes, was its subsidiary and that the publicized finding was based on slender data. Only about 3% of a sample of 405 respondents—or only 12 persons—mentioned that the industry should be deregulated, hardly enough to warrant a major announcement at a press conference. [121]

When reporting on a poll, writers should consider how reporters treat such information. They need to interpret the data and to make a story out of it, instead of just citing numbers. Warren Miofsky says, "When they cite numbers they put the burden on the reader to draw the conclusions. The numbers are boring. The conclusions based on those numbers are not." To do this, poll reporters' main tasks are: "1) knowing how sampling works so they can interpret the data properly including understanding the limits to a survey's precision, and 2) providing necessary context—trend data, news events, etc.—that give the numbers meaning." Miofsky also suggests that reporters borrow from social sciences by starting with a hypothesis and see if the data support it or not. The surprise of a knocked-down hypothesis can wind up being the big news. An example for the ages is "Clinton Job Approval Despite Lewinsky." [122]

The media must also do their part by not blindly swallowing every statistic that is handed out to them. They should follow the advice of Philip Meyer in *Precision Journalism*, who lists minimum information that should be presented with every published survey:

1. Identity of the sponsor of the survey.
2. Exact wording of the key questions asked.
3. Description of the population sampled.
4. Sample size and, when relevant, response rate.
5. Some indication of the allowance that should be made for sampling error.

6. How interviews were collected: in person in homes, by phone, and so on.
7. When the interviews were collected.[123]

A longer list based on the guidelines of the American Association for Public Opinion Research also lists: (a) who conducted the survey; (b) a description of the sample selection procedure, including whether the respondents were self-selected; (c) precision of the findings; (d) location of data collection; and (e) if applicable, an indication of the results that are based on parts of the sample rather than the whole sample.[124]

Reach Journalists Through the Internet

Making news available to reporters online is an increasingly important way to make corporate news more attractive and accessible to the media. It is transforming the way journalists work, allowing them to do their jobs "faster, better, and cheaper."[125] Reporters use the Internet as a daily source of story ideas, background, and facts about fast-breaking events. According to the seventh annual study in 2000, *The Middleberg/ Ross Survey of Media in the Wired World*, nearly all (98%) of the 4,000 print and broadcast journalists participating in the survey reported going online at last daily to check e-mail. They spend about 15 hours each week reading and sending e-mail. Net usage by journalists is at an all-time high in each of the following categories:

- Article research and to retrieve reference material (86%).
- Obtain press releases online (72%).
- Find new sources and experts to interview and quote (71%).
- Read publications online (70%).
- Accept story ideas and pitches (54%).
- Download still images or video for use in their work (46%).[126]

Although reporters prefer a live source for a breaking story, reporters use company websites as their second most important source. Especially in a crisis situation, reporters will supplement information from live spokespeople by going online to enrich and expand their stories. After business hours when sources are unavailable, the importance of websites increases significantly.

Corporate websites.   Because reporter use of online resources is now common practice and with the advent of real-time news cycles and online scoops, corporations are advised to open websites and keep them as accurate and up-to-date as possible. According to a 2001 study of *Fortune* 500 company websites, only a little over a third of them (195) provide clearly labeled press room site areas focused on assisting journalists. The most commonly used label was "News Room" (60 companies), followed by "Press Room" (40 companies). Companies ranking higher on the *Fortune* 500 are more likely to have press rooms than companies ranking lower. The study also suggested that press rooms be linked from the home page, which nearly two thirds of sites with press rooms included as a key public.[127]

To be of value, press rooms must contain relevant content. The most extensive press room contained 16 items, but the average number was only 6.5.[128] The 12 items most frequently included in all company websites were as follows:

- Press/news releases: 96.9%% of companies.
- Executive bios/profiles: 51.3% of companies.
- Executive photographs: 48.7% of companies.
- Company fact sheets: 35.4% of companies.
- Annual reports—financial: 33.8% of companies.
- Company history: 31.8% of companies.
- News alert service for media: 30.8% of companies.
- Company staff speeches and presentations: 29.7% of companies.
- Product or company-in-action photos: 28.2% of companies.
- Press release search engine: 25.6% of companies.
- Company logos for use in publication: 22.6% of companies.
- Media kits: 21.0% of companies.[129]

Ideally, according to *Los Angeles Times* Syndicate columnist Larry Migid, what is really wanted is one-stop shopping for an array of media materials.[130] Also desirable is the listing of a practitioner by name as a media contact, which more than half of all press rooms did. Corporations should also endeavor to be listed prominently with the major search engines because journalists first turn to them and directories such as Yahoo! and Alta Vista to locate information.

Corporate sources are warned, however, that the credibility of their information is not assured. Business sources face greater resistance because findings show that 59% of journalists are likely to use free online information from nonprofits versus 50% from business.[131]

TAKE ADVANTAGE OF THE ENLARGED MEDIA MENU

Public affairs communicators looking for outlets for their messages are no longer limited to the traditional news media of local television news, network television news, newspapers, radio news, and news magazines. As the *Economist* reported in 1998: "Until two years ago, Americans had three evening news shows, one cable news network and a couple of weekly news-magazine programmes. Now it has three evening news programmes, ten weekly hour-long news-magazine shows, three cable news networks, three cable business news networks, two sports news networks and three new websites furnished with video."[132]

Communicators could take advantage of an enlarged media menu. They are advised to do so, because as Herb B. Berkowitz and Edwin J. Feulner, Jr. observed, "a handful of elite news organizations no longer controls the agenda and defines the terms of the debate."[133]

Changes in Regular Viewership and Readership

CNN was heralded as the major entry into the news media a decade ago. While serving as the Navy's chief of information, Rear Admiral Brent Baker said, "I believe CNN is the dominant factor in the news media today. Clearly we must all understand that in the 1990s CNN has arrived with the technological and editorial ability to reach out instantaneously and globally."[134] Baker later envisioned that "tomorrow's crisis will be covered by a new group of international multimedia giants—such as the Microsoft–NBC cable television and cyberspace network and the new Global Fox News Channel."[135] Its reporters would be computer savvy and multimedia trained. They would be less dependent on government news releases because they could go directly into government records with computer-assisted research methods.[136] They would be better equipped with new lightweight digital satellite and multimedia cyberspace gear and therefore less dependent on government communications gear or blessing.[137] He warns all players—government leaders, military leaders, journalists, and media owners—had better realize no one is in control of information as they were in the good old days of the early 1990s.[138]

By 2001, CNN, the original 24-hour cable news network, which was started in 1980, became a division of media giant AOL Time Warner and faced competition from Fox and MSNBC. The number of viewers watching CNN dropped 2% in 2000 as Fox News grew by 62% and MSNBC by 25%. CNN's rescue plan called for greater efficiency by cutting 400 CNN staff from its 42 foreign bureaus and 1,000 overseas staff. It also sought to make shows more "dynamic," and to this end it hired Andrea Thompson, an actress from *NYPD Blue*, a cop series, as one of its *Headline News* anchors.[139]

By the beginning of 2002, cable was the top overall source of news for Americans. Kohut states, "The public has come to believe that if you want national news you go to cable." The audience for network news dropped by 50% in the last 10 years. Their coverage has also dropped as they got rid of expensive foreign bureaus and switched to cheaper lifestyle and celebrity news, says Tom Rosenstiel, director of the Project for Excellence in Journalism. CNN spokeswoman Christa Robinson listed the following size audiences for the three top cable news channels: CNN, 86 million homes; Fox News, 77 million; MSNBC, 73 million.[140]

The Pew Research Center's biennial news survey, conducted among slightly more than 3,000 adults shows that viewership of nightly network news has declined sharply, from 60% in 1993 to 32% in 2002, as shown in Box 4.9. In April 2000, however, viewership was only 30%, indicating that the steady erosion of this audience may have abated. Newspaper readership continues to inch downward, with a large portion of this decline occurring in the 35- to 49-year-old age category. Less time per day is spent reading a newspaper, down from 19 minutes a day in 1994 to 15 minutes in 2002.

"Alternative Media"

The traditional media of newspapers, network news, and local TV news have been joined by cable TV news, TV news magazines, network morning news, call-in radio shows, and online news. Some loosely call these newer media and formats the "alternative media." To this category are added such grocery store tabloids as the *National Enquirer*, niche magazines, and a variety of program formats.

Audiences can now turn to mainstream talk radio, cable and direct-satellite television, new computer technologies, and alternative newspapers and periodicals. Radio talk shows have multiplied and increased their impact, as have television magazine programs such as *911*, *A Current Affair*, and *Hard Copy*.[141] Use of computer media, such as the Internet and online services, is also expected to grow.[142]

Searching for alternative media for its political messages, the Bush administration recently used niche magazines: President Bush appeared in *Runner's World*, a magazine he has been a fan of; White House lobbyist Nicholas E. Calio appeared in *Wine Spectator*; national security advisor Condoleezza Rice appeared in *Vogue*; and White House Spokesman Ari Fleischer was on the cover of the alumni magazine of his alma mater. The advantages of these niche magazines are several:

Box 4.9 Trends in Regular News Consumption			
	May 1993	April 1998	April 2002
Local TV news	77%	64	57%
Cable TV news	—	—	33
Nightly network news	60	38	32
Network TV magazines	52	37	24
Network morning news	—	23	22
Radio	47	49	41
Call-in radio shows	23	13	17
National Public Radio	15	15	16
Newspaper	58	48	41
Online news	—	13	25[143]

- They don't cover troublesome topics, such as Iraq, the economy, or corporate malfeasance, and offer a "feel-good" tone for the White House.
- They reach far more people than newspapers. *Wine Spectator*'s circulation is 325,000; *Runner's World* is 520,000, and *Vogue*'s is 1.2 million. The demographics of these audiences is what the White House seeks to expand its political base: "They're trying to pick off people who are open and independent," said Michael K. Deaver, Ronald Reagan's public relations advisor. "If they get a portion of those over the years by building up that regular guy impression, yeah, I think it gets votes."[144]

One way to view the alternative media is to distinguish between the reportorial media and the access media. As exemplified by network television news, reportorial media are closed, controlling, and judgmental. In contrast, access media are open, revelatory, direct-to-audience entertaining media. They include television host and call-in shows, radio talk shows, public affairs panels, advertorials in print media, television advertorials, and radiomercials. Carol Mashe, executive director of the National Association of Radio Talk Show Hosts, not surprisingly believes, that of all the media, talk show hosts are the most powerful because they are the most personal.[145] Chapter 8 gives further examples of how Bill Clinton and other politicians used alternative media. The next chapter, on broadcast appearances, illustrates the powerful effects of radio talk show.

CONCLUSIONS

Taking the initiative is a prerequisite to gaining greater control over the media. Media relations specialists who formerly worked as journalists find it easy to become a part of the news creation process by writing news releases that promote their company's viewpoint. They also encourage high-credibility sources with like-minded views to submit stories. Going one step further, corporate news staffs may create events that serve as the basis of newsworthy stories. They can use alternative media to disseminate their stories.

Corporate communicators are increasingly willing to apply various forms of pressure to obtain at least fair, if not favorable, treatment. These pressures range from threatening to withdraw advertising to demanding corrections or rebuttal time when company news is distorted or seen as unfair. Because company news is a valuable resource, corporate communicators can also set conditions for cooperation. Furthermore, through media subsidies such as supplying VNRs, results of commissioned surveys, and various other background materials, companies are learning how to make their stories appealing to the news media. The chances of conveying their messages in a favorable manner to the public have been greatly enhanced.

ENDNOTES

1. Steve Crescenzo, "Disney's Cheesey Public Relations," *The Strategist*, Vol. 3, Fall 1987, pp. 17–21.
2. Richard Turner, "Disney Hopes Retreat Is Better Part of Public Relations," *Wall Street Journal*, September 30, 1994, p. B4. Also see background: Linda Feldmann, "Disney Theme Park Sparks New Civil War in Virginia," *Christian Science Monitor*, June 28, 1994, p. 10; and Katharine Q. Seelye, "A New Battle of Manassas Is Under Way in the Senate," *New York Times*, June 22, 1994, p. A16.
3. "Hunting Disney," *Economist*, February 14, 2004, p. 9.
4. Robert L. Dilenschneider, "Forming a Distinctive Company Image," in *Dartnell's Public Relations Handbook* (Chicago: The Dartnell Corporation, 1996), p. 376.
5. Hedrick Smith, *The Power Game: How Washington Works* (New York: Ballantine, 1988), p. 401.
6. Ibid., pp. 402–409.
7. Alicia Mundy, "Is the Press Any Match for Powerhouse PR?" *Business and Society Review*, Vol. 87, Fall 1993, p. 34.
8. Ibid.
9. Lawrence K. Altman, "The Doctor's World; Some Authors in Medical Journals May Be Paid by 'Spin Doctors,'" *New York Times*, October 4, 1994, p. C3.
10. Ibid.
11. Emily Friedman, *Medical World News*, May 1991, pp. 16-18, as reported by *pr reporter*, October 11, 1991.
12. Bill Carter, "Anxious Pill Maker Puts ABC Interview of Its Chief on the Web," *New York Times*, October 7, 1999, p. A23.
13. Ibid.
14. Howard Kurtz, "Over-the-Counter Strategy; Preemptive Interview a Coup for Metabolife," *Washington Post*, October 25, 1999, p. C1.
15. Ibid.
16. Ibid.
17. Jamie Reno and John Leland, with Anne Underwood and Ana Figueroa, "Heavy Meddling," *Newsweek*, October 18, 1999, p. 56.
18. Otto Lerbinger, *The Crisis Manager: Facing Risk and Responsibility* (Mahwah, N.J.: Lawrence Erlbaum Associates, 1997), p. 325.
19. Dean Brent Baker, interview by author, December 19, 1996.
20. "Reporters Rate Web Pages," *Public Relations Tactics*, Vol. 3, August 1996, p. 19.
21. Melvin J. Thompson of Clarke & Company, a major Boston public relations firm, gives the example of a story about a client filed with the wire services by a *Boston Globe* writer. The firm's computerized "real time news monitoring," which it calls "InfoAdvantage," spotted the story, and an immediate critical review of it showed that it contained inaccuracies that were damaging to the client. There was time to call the writer and ask him to make a correction, which he was willing to do. Thompson explains that the firm's InfoAdvantage system works well for clients who receive much news coverage. When a client is facing a crisis, the computer printout is checked at least every hour. One of the firm's computers is dedicated to this service. Searches are made for stories about both organizations and subject matter. Melvin J. Thompson, vice president for interactive communication, telephone conversation with author on December 20, 1996.
22. Beth Snyder, "Bad Rap: Companies Patrol Internet for Online Abuse," The Freedom Forum Online, June 22, 1998.

23. Steve Ulfelder, "Lies, Damn Lies, and the Internet" *Computerworld*, July 14, 1998, p. 75. Among the companies that have been targeted are Sears, Roebuck and Co., General Electric (the message was, "Beware of GE Microwaves"), AT&T ("Deceptive Practices—Know the Facts!"), MCI Communications, Kmart, and Wal-Mart Stores ("Best Buy is Consumer Unfriendly! and Wal-Mart too!").

24. Marcia Stepanek, "You Called Our Widget a What?" *Business Week*, September 25, 2000, p. 188.

25. Ibid.

26. Ibid.

27. Shel Holtz, *Public Relations on the Net*, 2nd edition (New York: AMACOM, 2002), pp. 286–287.

28. Ibid.

29. Gary C. Woodward, *Perspectives on American Political Media* (Boston: Allyn & Bacon, 1997), p. 40.

30. Ibid., p. 41. Woodward quotes Jack W. Germond and Jules Witcover, *Whose Broad Stripes and Bright Stars? The Trivial Pursuit of the Presidency, 1988* (New York: Warner, 1989), p. 428.

31. Alicia C. Shepard, "Talk Is Expensive," *American Journalism Review*, Vol. 16, May 1994, pp. 20–27.

32. See Alicia Shepard, "Take the Money and Talk," *American Journalism Review*, Vol. 17, June 1995, pp. 18–25.

33. Allen H. Center and Frank E. Walsh, "Chrysler/Consumers Union Square Off," in *Public Relations Practices: Managerial Case Studies and Problems*, 3rd edition (Englewood Cliffs, N.J.: Prentice-Hall, 1985), pp. 234–241.

34. Richard S. Dunham, book review by Howard Kurtz, *Spin Cycle—Inside the Clinton Propaganda Machine* (New York: Free Press, 1998), *Business Week*, March 30, 1998, p. 17.

35. Herb Schmertz with William Novak, *Good-Bye to the Low Profile: The Art of Creative Confrontation* (Boston: Little, Brown, 1986), p. 8.

36. Ibid.

37. The study was conducted by Florida International University (Miami) public relations students. See *pr reporter*, December 3, 2001, p. 4.

38. Ibid., p. 102.

39. Ibid., p. 79.

40. Mundy, op. cit., p. 34.

41. See "Watchdog Watch," *American Journalism Review*, Vol. 15, April 1993, pp. 32–34; Andrew Randolph, "An Expensive Rebuttal," *Editor & Publisher*, March 30, 1985, p. 13, in connection with Three Mile Island, showing a double page ad by General Public Utilities in the *Philadelphia Inquirer* to protest the newspaper's stories on the company's safety procedures in cleaning up the reactor.

42. The case is described in "Taking the Offensive Against 'Trial by Television' …," *pr reporter*, Vol. 25, February 23, 1981, p. 1.

43. The ad, titled "Good News," is from a Kaiser Aluminum press kit.

44. "Taking the Offensive Against 'Trial by Television,'" op. cit.

45. "Kaiser at Last Gets Equal Time," *pr reporter*, Vol. 24, August 17, 1981, p. 2.

46. Stephan Lesher, *Media Unbound* (Boston: Houghton-Mifflin, 1982), p. 163.

47. "Taking the Offensive Against 'Trial by Television,'" op. cit.

48. Smith, op. cit., p. 425.

49. "Celanese's Hard-Line Media Strategy," *pr reporter*, Vol. 22, November 19, 1979, p. 3.

50. "Trend: Another Company Refuses to Talk to Reporters Who Don't Have Time to Listen," *pr reporter*, Vol. 22, October 29, 1979, pp. 1–2.

51. Ibid. Curtis Linke further explained that Johns-Manville was initially very co-operative with the media in line with its policy of openness and candor. When management discovered, however, that it was consistently treated unfairly, it entered the second stage of becoming combative, taking a tough media stance. "We argued with the media, and we were uncooperative. This did not work, so we became aggressive. We threatened to sue, and we published in our annual report accounts of biased reporting." The next stage [fourth] for us was being selective. "We simply refused to work with a reporter if he or she did not under-stand the issue and was not willing to take the time to try and understand this very complex issue. If we were called 20 minutes before deadline on a story that had been in the works for days or weeks, we simply explained how unfair we thought that was and hung up without providing any comment to legitimize the story." This selectivity stage lasted the longest—from 1980 to 1982. Then in August of last year we declared bankruptcy and the tables turned. "We be-came the injured party, the aggrieved entity—and the media wrote more posi-tive things about the situation in the next few days than they had in the prior 4 years." Today, we are more tolerant of the media, "which is another way of saying we did not expect much on the asbestos issue, but we do try to work with them, judiciously applying selectivity."

52. The case is described in "Trend: Business Takes Hard Line Media Stance; 60 Minutes Is Latest Target," *pr reporter*, Vol. 23, February 18, 1980, pp. 3–4.

53. Lesher, op. cit., p. 169.

54. "60 Minutes/Our Reply," material from a press kit provided by Illinois Power Company, p. 1.

55. Ibid., p. 2.

56. Lesher, op. cit., p. 170.

57. Ibid., p. 177.

58. "Trend: Business Takes Hard Line Media Stance," op. cit., p. 4.

59. Lesher, op. cit., p. 171.

60. Ibid.

61. Ibid.

62. Based on Roderick L. MacLeish, Jr., "Eye to Eye With a Media Crisis: BCS Inc.'s 'Eye to Eye With Connie Chung' Television Program; Behavior Research Insti-tute, Inc." *Across the Board*, Vol. 31, November 1994.

63. "National News Council Report," *Columbia Journalism Review*, Vol. 18, Sep-tember–October 1979, pp. 85–87.

64. Schmertz and Novak, op. cit., pp. 71–72.

65. This approach was in sharp contrast to Kodak when the company was un-happy about what it felt was false analysis. *Forbes* did a tough piece about the company's problems and its management and Kodak decided to prove *Forbes* wrong with bottom line results in the months ahead. "Mobil Should Get the Picture from Kodak," editorial, *Forbes*, December 1984.

66. "IRQ Roundtable: Life With or Without IR," *IRQ (Investor Relations Quar-terly)*, Vol. 1, Summer 1997, p. 68.

67. Kate Kelly, "One Analyst Learns Candor Doesn't Pay," *Wall Street Journal*, February 5, 2003, p. C1.

68. "IRQ Roundtable," op. cit., p. 68.

69. "National News Council Report," op. cit.

70. Richard Gibson, "Analyst Takes Heat for 'Sell' Rating on Archer-Daniels," *Wall Street Journal*, August 31, 1995, p. C1.

71. Kate Kelly, "One Analyst Learns Candor Doesn't Pay," *Wall Street Journal*, February 5, 2003, p. C1.
72. Michael Moss, "Reverse Gocha: Companies Are Paying Big Fees to Get News About Beat Reporters," *Wall Street Journal*, November 10, 1995, p. A1.
73. Ibid, p. A4.
74. Ibid.
75. Tedd Rodman, "Technology in Public Relations Today," term paper (Corporate Public Affairs, Boston University, College of Communication, May 5, 1997).
76. Woodward, op. cit., p. 41.
77. Steve Singer, "Auto Dealers Muscle the Newsroom," *Washington Journalism Review*, Vol. 13, September 1991, pp. 24–28.
78. Ibid., p. 42.
79. Those who contend that this tactic is unwise can point to the fact that this threat made matters worse for GM because host Phil Donahue disclosed the attempt and publicized filmmaker Michael Moore's charge that big U.S. companies, and GM in particular, were selling out U.S. workers for profit. Joseph B. White, "GM Seeks to Keep Ads off Talk Show About 'Roger & Me,'" *Wall Street Journal*, February 1, 1990, p. A6.
80. Russ Baker, "The Squeeze," *Columbia Journalism Review*, 36, September–October 1997, p. 30. Also see G. Bruce Knecht, "Hard Copy: Magazine Advertisers Demand Prior Notice of 'Offensive' Articles," *Wall Street Journal*, April 30, 1997, p. A1.
81. Dave Phillips, "Chrysler Drops Censorship Policy," Detroit News, October 14, 1997, p. B1.
82. G. Bruce Knecht, "No Offense: Big Retail Chains Get Special Advance Looks at Magazine Contents," *Wall Street Journal*, October 22, 1997, p. A1.
83. Ibid.
84. Ibid., p. A13.
85. For an excellent summary of this case, see "P&G, News Leaks, and The Wall Street Journal, Parts (A) and (B)," in Raymond Simon and Frank Winston Wylie, *Cases in Public Relations Management* (Lincolnwood, Ill.: NTC Business Books, 1994), pp. 11–23.
86. Peter Foster, "Anticorporate Crusader," *Canadian Business*, January 1994, p. 76.
87. James S. Hirsch and Mil Geyelin, "P&G Says Inquiry on Leak to Journal Was Done Properly," *Wall Street Journal*, August 13, 1991, p. A3.
88. James S. Hirsch, "P&G Search for News Leak Led to Sweep of Phone System Wider Than Thought," *Wall Street Journal*, August 15, 1991, p. A3.
89. Simon and Wylie, op. cit., p. 22.
90. A simple definition in a high school text, Norman B. Moyes, *Journalism* (Lexington, Mass.: Ginn & Company, 1984), p. 5. He adds that news usually concerns events that have just occurred or are about to occur.
91. Carole M. Howard and Wilma K. Mathews, *On Deadline: Managing Media Relations*, 2nd edition (Prospect Heights, Ill.: Waveland Press, 1994), p. 15.
92. Bernard Rubin and Associates, *Big Business and the Mass Media* (Lexington, Mass.: Lexington Books, 1977), p. 77.
93. Technical formulas are used to measure readability. See Dennis L. Wilcox and Lawrence W. Nolte, *Public Relations Writing and Media Techniques* (New York: Harper & Row, 1990), p. 446.
94. Oscar H. Gandy, Jr., *Beyond Agenda Setting: Information Subsidies and Public Policy* (Norwood, N.J.: Ablex, 1982), p. ix.

95. Ibid., p. 64.

96. "Key Decisions of Great PR Teams," a full-page ad in *Public Relations Tactics*, September 2003, p. 2.

97. Gandy, op. cit., p. 67.

98. Gandy, op. cit., p. 69.

99. Robert J. Griffin and Sharon Dunwoody, "Impacts of Information Subsidies and Community Structure on Local Press Coverage of Environmental Contamination," *Journalism & Mass Communication Quarterly*, Vol. 72,. Summer 1995, pp. 271–284.

100. Whether the community had a pluralistic structure—a diversified population and economy and a greater number and variety of interest groups—had no significant influence on coverage.

101. Ronald N. Levy, "Public Policy Publicity: How to Do It," *Public Relations Journal*, Vol. 31, June 1975, pp. 19–21, 35–36. Telephone call on February 28, 2004 to New York City office confirmed that this service is still provided.

102. "Using VNRs Without Sparking Controversy," *PR Week*, May 17, 2004, p. 26.

103. "Labeling to Be Clarified; Newsource Will Name Funders of Video News Release, *Television Week*, March 22, 2004.

104. "Video News Releases: What Works and Why?" In *The Video News Release Handbook* (New York: Medialink Video Broadcasting, 1991), p. 8.

105. Glenn Cameron and David Blount, "VNRs and Air Checks: A Content Analysis of the Use of Video News Releases in Television Newscasts," *Journalism and Mass Communication Quarterly*, Vol. 73, Winter 1996, p. 891.

106. "The Television Version of the Printed Press Release," Medialink Worldwide, http://www.medialink.com/vnr.htm.

107. Steve Coe, "Mixed Blessings of Video News Releases," *Broadcasting and Cable*, Vol. 123, June 28, 1993, p. 17.

108. Ibid., pp. 896–900.

109. See "Medialink List of Top Ten VNRs for 1993 Breaks Viewership Record," *Business Wire*, February 15, 1994.

110. Coe, op. cit.

111. Anne R. Owen and James A. Karrh, "Video News Releases: Effects on Viewer Recall and Attitudes," *Public Relations Review*, Vol. 22, Winter 1996, pp. 369–378.

112. Cameron & Blount, op cit., p. 901.

113. "Score More Coverage by Avoiding These Leading VNR Distribution, Production Pitfalls," *Bull Dog Reporter's Media Relations Insider*, Sample Issue, 2001, p. 7.

114. Richard Weiner, *Webster's New World Dictionary of Media and Communications* (New York: Webster's New World, 1990).

115. Krisztina Marton and Lowndes F. Stephens, "The New York Times' Conformity to AAPOR Standards of Disclosure for the Reporting of Public Opinion Polls," *Journalism & Mass Communication Quarterly*, Vol. 78, Autumn 2001, p. 486.

116. Lori Robertson, "Poll Crazy," *American Journalism Review*, Vol. 25, January–February 2003, p. 40.

117. Marton and Stephens, op. cit., pp. 498–499.

118. Mervin D. Field, "Polls and Public Policy," *Journal of Advertising Research*, Vol. 19, October 1979, p. 14.

119. Warren Miofsky and Martin Plissner, "A Reporter's Guide to Published Polls," *Public Opinion*, Vol. 3, June–July 1980, p. 16.

120. Michael R. Gordon, "The Image Makers in Washington—PR Firms Have Found a Natural Home," *National Journal*, Vol. 12, May 31, 1980, p. 884.
121. Ibid. It should be noted that the press conference news release was not cleared with the vice president of Group Attitudes, who, as a member of the American Association of Public Opinion Research, would have been obligated by the association's Code of Professional Ethics and Practices to disclose the sponsorship of the survey. The code reads, "When we become aware of the appearance in public of serious distortions of our research we shall publicly disclose what is required to correct the distortion" (section II.A.2). The code also states, "We shall not knowingly make interpretations of research results, nor shall we tacitly permit interpretations, which are inconsistent with the data available" (article IX, section I.B.3). A Hill & Knowlton memorandum subsequently told the staff to clear release with Group Attitudes when its survey findings were reported.
122. From owneraapornet@usc.edu, January 3, 2002.
123. Philip Meyer, *Precision Journalism*, 2nd edition (Indiana University Press, 1979), pp. 185–186.
124. Marton and Stephens, op. cit., pp. 491–492.
125. John V. Pavlik, *New Media Technology: Cultural and Commercial Perspectives* (Boston: Allyn & Bacon, 1996), p. 141.
126. Holtz, op. cit., p. 159.
127. Coy Callison, "Media Relations and the Internet: How *Fortune* 500 Company Web Sites Assist Journalists in News Gathering," *Public Relations Review*, Vol. 29, March 2003, pp. 38–39.
128. Ibid., p. 39.
129. Ibid., p. 34.
130. Ibid., p. 39. Originally mentioned in Michael Lissauer, "Online Media Strategy: Reaching dot-com Newsrooms," *The Public Relations Strategist*, Vol. 6, No. 3, 2000, pp. 26–28.
131. "Survey: Media Are Becoming Wired," op. cit.
132. "The New Business—Stop Press," *Economist*, July 4, 1998, p. 17.
133. Herb B. Berkowitz and Edwin J. Feulner, Jr., "Impact of the Communications Revolution on Public Affairs: Pervasiveness of Public Affairs Messages Today," in *Practical Public Affairs in an Era of Change*, ed. Lloyd B. Dennis (Lanham, Md.: University Press of America, Inc., 1996), p. 51.
134. Brent Baker, "Decisions at the Speed of TV Satellites," *Vital Speeches of the Day*, Vol. 58, July 15, 1992, p. 581.
135. Brent Baker, "War & Peace in a Virtual World," *Proceedings*, April 1997, p. 37.
136. Ibid., p. 38.
137. Ibid., p. 39.
138. Ibid., p. 40. In the context of the Gulf War, Baker didn't like what he saw, namely, that the government and the military were falling behind the changes in the news media industry.
139. "CNN in the Doldrums: The Network's Not Working," *Economist*, August 2001, p. 54.
140. *ComNews*, a private newsletter distributed by former Dean Brent Baker, Boston University, College of Communication, January 30, 2002.
141. Stempel, op. cit., pp. 550–551.
142. Ibid., p. 552.

143. PEW Research Study on Nightly News Viewership, Spring 2002, www.people-press.org.

144. Elisabeth Bumiller, "White House Letter; It's Not Time or Newsweek, By Design," *New York Times*, September 30, 2002, Late Edition, p. A22.

145. "Of All Media, the Most Powerful Are Talk Show Hosts Because They're the Most Personal," *pr reporter*, Vol. 35, June 8, 1992, p. 3.

Chapter 5

Gaining Semicontrol Over the Media: Broadcast Appearances

Broadcast appearances by corporate executives and other spokespersons allow corporations to gain greater control over messages disseminated through the mass media. Messages are no longer delivered to newspapers, magazines, and broadcasters and left there for their gatekeepers to decide on whether or how to use the materials. With broadcast appearances, the "sender" delivers the messages directly to television and radio audiences. As someone who is interviewed on a broadcast medium or appears on a panel, he or she has wide latitude in deciding what to say. The interviewer or moderator, of course, sets the agenda and asks questions, but the interviewee or participant can carefully compose answers and skillfully interpose messages he or she wants to transmit.

The sender in the communication process thereby establishes semicontrol over the media, the degree depending largely on the communication skills of the spokesperson. Although these skills vary widely among corporate individuals, they can be enhanced through training programs and advice, such as this chapter provides.

Semicontrol, however, does involve risks. On television the camera reveals all and, in Ronald Reagan's words, "The camera doesn't lie."[1] Larry King, the well-known talk show host, elaborated on Reagan's statement: "People are transparent when you put them in front of the cameras, which is why we use lots of close-ups. No one, not the most disciplined performer, can control every gesture, every expression all the time—but those things all transmit important information to viewers."[2] As stated by Vice President Al Gore, "The television camera really is a kind of personality X-ray machine.... Over time the character of the individuals being judged by the American people will be more or less accurately assessed" through television.[3]

137

POLITICS ILLUSTRATES THE POWER OF TELEVISION

Of the two broadcast media, radio and television, television is usually the most effective and efficient means of communicating to large audiences. Local and network television is the source from which most Americans receive their news. Viewers actually watch television programs about 12 hours a week (although their TV sets are on between 22 and 28 hours a week).[4]

From a propaganda viewpoint, the major advantage of reaching audiences through television is people simply receive what is dished out to them through inadvertent exposure. They do so uncritically because their defense mechanisms are set at "low" or "off." Communication theorists call this behavior *information processing*, which is variously described as passive learning or learning without involvement, in contrast to "information seeking."[5]

Television has another attribute: viewing has become a habit similar to a drug. An addicted person spends a great deal of time using a substance, uses it more often than intended; makes repeated unsuccessful efforts to reduce use; gives up important social, family, or occupational activities to use it; and reports withdrawal symptoms when use is stopped. When researchers beeped into people who were watching TV, people reported feeling relaxed and passive. EEG studies similarly showed less mental stimulation during viewing than during reading. TV has such a hold on people because of their *orienting response*—the instinctive visual or auditory reaction to any sudden or novel stimulus. It's a built-in sensitivity to movement and potential predatory threats. People remember what they have seen when the program has many edits—a change from one camera angle to another in the same visual scene. However, there's a limit: If the number of cuts exceeds 10 in 2 minutes, recognition drops off sharply.[6]

The effectiveness of television is best illustrated by its widening use and success in political campaigns. Reflecting the properties of information processing, Kathleen Hall Jamieson, in her book *Dirty Politics: Deception, Distraction, and Democracy*, tells how television grants creators of campaign discourse "some Svengalian powers" that print and radio lack. The visual capacity of television enables politicians to "reconfigure 'reality' in ways that heighten the power of the visceral appeal" and "make the analytic processing of rapidly emerging claims all but impossible."[7]

Cognitive psychologists explain this effect by pointing out that visuals are processed peripherally "on the edges of consciousness, where critical acuity does not come into play."[8] The testing of evidence and evaluating of propositions does not occur in the absence of central processing. What counts, therefore, is not the quality of arguments but the presumed expertise or attractiveness of the communicator.[9]

This attribute of visual communication is exploited in negative political advertising. Jamieson describes the Bush campaign's famous Willie Horton ad, which dramatized the message that George Bush was tough on crime and Michael Dukakis was soft on crime. A bright picture of a smiling Bush says, "Bush supports the death penalty for first-degree murderers." A dark photo of Dukakis (in which his hair is unkempt) then appears and a voice says, "Dukakis not only opposes the death penalty, he allows first-degree murderers to have weekend passes from prison."[10] The emotional words "kidnapping," "stabbing," and "raping" appear on the screen with Horton's picture, and the announcer adds, "Horton fled, kidnaping a young couple, stabbing the man and repeatedly raping his girlfriend." Another "revolving door" ad sequence showed a bleak prison scene and "then cut to a procession of convicts circling through a revolving gate and marching toward the nation's living rooms."[11]

Argument, engagement, and accountability—Jamieson's criteria for judging political discourse—are absent in this political ad. An assertion made in a 30-second ad is not the same as argument, which is backed up by facts and logical reasoning intended to demonstrate the truth or legitimacy of a proposition. Argument takes more time than a sound bite allows.[12]

Gone, however, are the hour-long speeches typical of the 19th century, which allowed the advancement of the argument. In 1988, an average stump speech was under 17 minutes, answers in debates between 1 and 2 minutes, candidate sound bites on CBS, ABC, and NBC evening news programs 9.8 seconds, and presidential campaign ads 30 seconds.[13] Candidates have learned to speak in sound bites. Even low-key Walter Mondale, in a debate with Gary Hart in 1984, skewered his opponent by saying, "When I hear your new ideas, I'm reminded of that ad, 'Where's the beef?'"[14] Because political debates do not allow sufficient time for in-depth arguments, "beef" is in short supply. The criterion of engagement—"a process of comparison that enables audiences to determine which argument has the greater force"—was thus violated.[15] At least accountability was present because the audience heard words spoken by the actual candidates and not some faceless announcer as in the Willie Horton ads.

If corporations were allowed to present advocacy ads on television, the "marketplace of ideas" would be in jeopardy of deteriorating into the kind of abbreviated sound bites characteristic of political advertising. In broadcast appearances by corporate executives and other employees, however, accountability is at least assured, and depending on the professionalism of the interviewer, arguments may be demanded. On programs such as the *Lehrer News Hour*, where both sides of an issue are typically presented, engagement is also possible. However, as participants in broadcast appearances become increasingly sophisticated, the pressure to win an argument drives them to copy the methods of political campaigning, as a subsequent section on learning how to "speak TV" will demonstrate.

OPPORTUNITIES ABOUND FOR BROADCAST APPEARANCES

With increased opportunities to appear on radio and television talk shows, executives and spokespersons, such as scientists, are learning to take advantage of the semicontrol they can exercise through these access media. The challenges in dealing with these media are (a) to select those that best reach desired audiences and (b) to enlarge the semi-control aspect in your favor.

There is no lack of broadcast stations in the United States. As of September 2002, there were 1,714 television stations and 13,296 radio stations.[16] Network television talk shows include *Good Morning America, The Today Show, CBS This Morning, The Tonight Show With Jay Leno, Larry King Live, Late Show With David Letterman,* and *Sunday Today.* Syndicated shows include Geraldo, Oprah, Regis and Kelly, Maury Povich, Sally Jesse Raphael, and Jenny Jones.[17]

Talk radio has also flourished, as these facts show:

- The early 1990s witnessed an explosion of talk programs, reaching 1,168 stations in 1994 from 360 in 1990.[18]
- Fifty-six percent of carbound adults and 85% of all Americans aged 12 and older tune into the radio during morning driving time (6–10 a.m. weekdays).
- During afternoon driving time (3–7 p.m.), 60% of commuters and 80% of all Americans tune in.[19]
- The popular Rush Limbaugh show broadcasts on more than 650 stations, representing about 20 million listeners. His audience is 97% white, 60% male and middle-aged, and it generally dislikes the national press, according to the Times Mirror Center for People and the Press.[20]

The impact of radio talk shows is enormous. They are credited with the passage of California's Proposition 13 and the spreading of the idea of local tax limits across the nation. In Massachusetts, Jerry Williams, host of Boston's WRKO, singlehandedly forced repeal of his state's seatbelt law.[21] Talk shows were also credited for the November 1994 Republican election victory, partly because about 70% of the country's talk radio hosts call themselves conservative.[22] In the 2002 elections, the talk shows may have contributed to the Democratic election losses of the Senate majority and six House seats. These hosts are recipients of faxes and talking points from Republican leaders. Many brag about their new status as political power brokers.[23] Some of their methods, however, are often outrageous, as illustrated in Box 5.1.

Most talk shows are conservative, ranging from right to extreme right, says Joe Conason. Following Rush Limbaugh is Sean Hannity, with an audience of more than 10 million. Among the top 10 radio hosts there is not a single liberal.[24] Looking for ways to deliver their message to voters beyond the Beltway, Democrats were planning to launch a national talk show, *Democracy Radio*, in January 2004. Ed Schulz, a radio personality with a liberal bent. who hosts a radio program broadcast on seven stations in the Dakotas, has been signed on.[25]

Talk shows affect business as well as politics, partly because business coverage has grown in recent years. A well-known example is the appearance of a Florida man on CNN's *Larry King Live* who said his wife died of cancer because she used a cellular phone. Eight days later, the stock price of Motorola, the biggest maker of cellular phones, dropped 20%—despite the lack of scientific studies on the question.[26]

Some major corporate executives have also been treated like celebrities by the media—first built up by the media and then taken down. This happened to Robert C. Stempel of General Motors, John F. Akers of IBM, and James D. Robinson III of American Express. These executives are viewed as "shared talismans, points of reference in a fragmented society."[27]

INCREASED CORPORATE USE OF BROADCAST APPEARANCES

For over two decades, the corporate use of broadcast appearances has grown. One study of 1,300 *Fortune* corporations found that 62 % of 395

Box 5.1   Examples of Excesses of Some Talk Shows

1. Thomas S. Foley (D-Wash.), former Speaker of the House, lost his seat partly because he took round-the-clock hits from three radio stations. In one, Richard Clear of KGA-AM asked Mr. Foley, married to the same woman for 24 years, if he was a homosexual (something Clear picked up from one of the anti-Clinton broadsides faxed to hundreds of talk shows every week). Mike Fitzsimmon, another conservative host, was bothered by this and said, "The mean-spiritedness, the desire to create an us-versus-them, that bothers me."[28]

2. Bob Mohan of KFYI, in criticizing the wife of Jim Brady (President Ronald Reagan's former press secretary who was shot in an assassination attempt on the president), said, "You know, she ought to be put down. A humane shot at a veterinarian's would be an easy way to do it. Because of all her barking and complaining, she really needs to be put down."[29]

3. Don Baker of KVOR in Colorado Springs, Colorado, said of Attorney General Janet Reno, "We ought to slap Janet Reno across the face" and "send her back to Florida where she can live with her relatives—the gators."[30]

respondents said one or more senior executives in their company had participated in a broadcast news interview during the preceding 18 months.[31] Now the practice is so widespread that media training has become an accepted part of management training, reports *Retail Week*.[32]

Corporations typically choose spokespersons with high rank in the company—chairman, CEO, president, chief financial officer—or someone with expertise in a particular area. Corporate spokespersons say their executives are treated "'fairly' in almost all interviews," and two in five respondents likewise reported receiving fair treatment in every interview, which suggests that spokespersons feel they are in reasonable control of their performance. It is not that news organizations have mellowed, said John A. Higgins, public relations director of Brouillard. "Instead, we think more and more top corporate executives have learned what their rights are in a news interview situation and are using this information to their advantage."[33]

Media Training and Skills

For decades now, corporate executives have been flocking to a variety of media training programs that teach them to face a hostile newscaster, to become aware of nonverbal cues, and to respond correctly. These training programs have been offered by advertising agencies, public relations firms, universities, and specialized training organizations. For example, Rowan & Blewitt claims it is one of the largest media training companies in the United States, providing more than 500 training sessions a year to half of the top 50 *Fortune* 500 companies.[34] In typical training sessions, executives' performances are often taped so they can observe themselves and make any improvements.

PR Week reported in April 2000 that media training had become a hot market. As Virgil Scudder, CEO of Virgil Scudder & Associates, a New York City training firm states, "Few top executives go before the television cameras or face notebook-wielding reporters without spending time with a media trainer."[35] Because so many business executives deeply distrust the media, an understanding of how journalists work lessens their tendency to dodge reporters. Scudder believes that at a minimum, a training program should accomplish these objectives:

- Increase the skill and confidence of the executive(s) being trained.
- Test and refine your organization's message points.
- Identify the most difficult questions your company is likely to encounter and formulate answers for them.
- Give the executive a better understanding of how the media work.[36]

Burson-Marsteller reported in 2000 that it quadrupled its media training revenues in the previous 2 years, and The Heminway Media Group doubled its revenues. Burson-Marsteller charged $7,500 for a half-day session for up to three people or $9,500 for a full-day session for up to five people. The sessions cover a variety of situations—preparing for crisis situations as well as client presentations. Sessions also vary in topics included. Burson-Marsteller offers sessions in media training, presentation skills training, communication and leadership skills, specialized communication settings, and communicating difficult issues.[37]

The skills learned also vary. For example, the public relations firm Hill & Knowlton uses realistic methods such as putting trainees through "ambush interviews." When least expected, glaring lights and a television camera confront a trainee while the reporter tries to use shock tactics such as interrupting an answer to get a story. "A few words and some body language must convey everything," says George Glazer, senior vice president at Hill & Knowlton.[38]

Deciding Whether to Appear

Public relations professionals and others who are familiar with broadcast opportunities know the risks and benefits of various programs. PBS's *News Hour with Jim Lehrer* is a relatively low-risk venture with the benefit of reaching relatively highly informed viewers, including lawmakers and government officials. However, a television magazine program, such as *60 Minutes*, is a high risk, partly because it is more an entertainment than a news show. Some producers on these programs tend to be highly skeptical, if not downright hostile, toward corporations. The danger also exists that a company spokesperson might be sabotaged by previously undisclosed video footage or other deprecatory information.

This risk was apparent to Reebok's senior public relations director, Dave Fogelson, when his company was asked to provide a company spokesperson to go on camera for a live broadcast on CBS's *Eye to Eye With Connie Chung* on a story about child labor abuse in a Sialkot, Pakistan, factory where Reebok's soccer balls were produced. Fogelson adamantly declined the request but, not wanting to appear to be closing off or avoiding the media, agreed to provide a written statement of Reebok's perception of the incident and assurance that the proper steps would be taken to correct the situation.[39] The program, aired on April 6, 1995, showed films of children as young as 6 years old making soccer balls for Adidas or Reebok for a few dollars a day. It also said that as many as 25,000 children labored in Sialkot workshops. Reebok was spared further unfavorable mention; an Associated Press news story on the CBS show said Reebok, along with Adidas, first learned of the practice from CBS and was working to halt it.[40]

Herb Schmertz, former vice president of public affairs and a member of the board of directors for Mobil Oil, states the game is fixed in programs such as *60 Minutes*; it is they who are in control. However, there are ways to reduce uncertainty.[41]

- Schmertz recommends that, when first contacted by a show, you do some research before deciding to participate.
- Ask the producer such questions as, "Exactly what is the segment about? What is its thesis? Whom do you want to interview from our organization, and why?"
- Call a meeting of the top people in the organization to decide whether the person they want to interview is effective on TV, whether the segment could be done without your participation and what the consequences would be, and, finally, what your response will be. In the process, review the work of the producer and journalists who are working on the particular segment.
- Explore various requests and options with the producer. Ask for copies of documents and sources of any negative statements they plan to question you about. Say you want the interview unedited. Even though the request will be denied, it shows you're wise to their tricks, says Schmertz. Offer the possibility of an off-camera background briefing by your technical people if the subject is complex.

How to Handle the Interview

Your goal is not to compete with the stars—the program's network will never allow its stars to look bad—but to make the audience think well of you and your views. In preparation, try to avoid plowing through mountains of material.

Do the following:

- Take a clean sheet of paper and write down the essential points. Keep rewriting until they are crisp, clear, and colorful.
- Decide to make three points on the show regardless of what questions are asked.
- Rehearse your answers in at least two mock interviews with both inside and outside experts.
- Avoid the advice to "be yourself" on TV; try to be a bit of an actor.
- Use a makeup person, and on the day of the interview, go for a swim or long walk, take a nap, or get a massage or facial.
- Play your comments in the direction of a conversation because the listening audience sees itself as eavesdropping.
- Repeat your main points because only a small portion of the interview will actually be aired.[42]

Media coach Lori Robertson, who started her own consulting business in media training after 13 years as a radio and TV reporter, explains what reporters do and offers advice on how to respond to reporter questions:

- Speak in sound bites—10- to 12-second statements

- Be honest; don't lie.
- Never accept a false premise. The interview has the right to correct the record first.
- Stay on point with whatever message you try to convey.
- Avoid the "Paul Harvey trap." Matt Lundy, a former media coach, says, "Harvey often has long pauses, and in an interview people tend to rush into an answer rather than wallow in the silence. By doing so," Lundy says, "you're probably going to go down a road you don't want to go."

Another consideration: Reporters don't always like to deal with people who are coached—"they're not giving their real responses"; they're acting.[43]

Impressions Count

Marshall McLuhan wrote in his well-known book, *Understanding Media*, that television is a cool medium, meaning the viewing audience highly participates in forming a complete image of what is broadcast.[44] Intuitively, Ronald Reagan used television for both its impression-creating quality and intimacy. He demonstrated his skill in the famous debate with Jimmy Carter in which he successfully presented himself as a likeable and capable person who would not embroil the nation in war. When Carter turned on Reagan, the latter undercut Carter's image of personal decency—which was one of Carter's few remaining campaign assets—by turning to his opponent and saying, "There you go again," thereby reinforcing his own air of gentle reason. Reagan knew that impressions count.

Handling Trick Questions

Peter Hannaford in *Talking Back to the Media* gives many examples of how to identify and handle trick questions. How should Coors handle this question containing a loaded preface: "Your business is slipping, there's an effective national boycott against you, people say you're antiblack, antiwoman. How can you expect to survive?" The correct response, said Shirley Richard, former head of corporate communications for Coors, is, "I don't agree with your statements, but we will survive because we brew a unique quality beer."[45]

Here are some rules to follow in television interviews:

- Never repeat your accuser's allegations. Instead, be positive. Nixon's statement "I am not a crook" should have been "I'm honest."[46]
- Have a SOCO—a single overriding communications objective. (Hannaford quotes Anne Ready, a Los Angeles–based media consultant, who says the biggest mistake people make is "waiting for the

right questions and not remembering their objective." She suggests that once a question is asked, acknowledge it and then
"bridge" to the answer that furthers your objective.)[47]

- Focus on what you want to tell. Don't be afraid to cover something. Don't feel compelled to respond to every question if it's not
in your interest.[48]
- Remember the advice of Paul Bender, Boeing's public relations director: You can control any interview.

Learning How to "Speak TV"

Because television is a mass medium, many people who appear forget
that they're having a conversation, not making a speech or a statement, says Clarence Jones in *How to Speak TV*.[49] You have to think of
the TV audience as one or two people sitting in their living room
about 6 or 7 feet away. Talk to the camera, but if you're being interviewed, people expect you to look at the reporter who asked the question and not at them.

More than 10,000 people are interviewed each day for television
news, says Jones. If you are one of them, he offers these formulas for
improving your performance:

1. *Condense, condense, condense.* Dealing with electronic journalism requires a completely different mind-set than dealing with print
media. Time is the master. Most stories run 30 seconds or less and a
major story only 90 seconds. Story forms are dictated by findings
that the attention span of most adults is 20 to 30 seconds. One exercise, therefore, is to try to say in one sentence everything you feel or
know about a difficult subject. Then pad it out to make 20 or 30 seconds. One-liners are guaranteed to air!

2. *Apply the FACE formula. F is for feels.* When you're on camera,
reciting facts or figures is out. Tell it with graphs and charts instead.
Or use analogies such as "The money we spend treating this disease
would buy everybody in the state a new Cadillac this year." What
television is interested in is having you say how something feels. But
beware: Don't lose your temper on camera, particularly with a
young reporter or employee. People expect leaders to be patient.

A is for analysis. You're the expert, so give people your opinion on a
subject., but do it in short, simple sentences. Avoid parenthetical
thoughts and phrases (e.g., "As I said earlier") that make a sentence
too long for television.

*C is for revolving your story around one of six broad catego-
ries—the *compelling Cs*: catastrophe, crisis, conflict, crime, corruption, and color (the television term for human interest). For example,
a school board member might say at a budget hearing, "Looks to me
like the school superintendent has sold out [corruption] to the real-

tors who are fighting this tax increase [conflict]. If this tax is not approved, we may have to shut down some of our schools [crisis]."

E is for *energy*. You must project that you truly believe what you're saying.[50]

Keeping a message simple and attention getting is key. Hannaford tells us to avoid the jargon of your own business or profession. For example, don't, as an educator once did, use the term "primarily modular learning environment" when what is really meant is classroom.[51] In the preparation of statements for broadcast, Michael M. Klepper teaches how to rephrase statements into an abbreviated, attention-grabbing opening. Instead of saying, "George Ellis, chairman of the XYZ Plastics Corporation, has just returned from Europe where, he says, plastics are easily burned in clean, modern incinerators," he suggests saying, "Plastics! How can we dispose of them? Some say we can't. George Ellis says we can."[52]

Looking Your Best on TV

Hannaford and others give the following advice about looking your best on television:

- Wear blues, grays, and pastels. Avoid wearing anything black or white; bright reds may also be a problem. Other solids or clothing with small patterns are safest; herringbone patterns, plaids, checks, or stripes create a lot of visual activity in the scene.
- Wear socks that are long enough to reach under your pants.
- Women should wear simple, small pieces of jewelry and should avoid wearing sparkling, glittery jewelry or noisy bracelets. Also avoid dangling earrings that distract the audience. Men should avoid giant, glistening gold tie clasps.
- Men should use a little powder or natural base makeup to cover the blue outline of their beards. Women should use normal makeup but avoid dark reds or maroons because they are accented by the camera.
- When sitting in a chair in television appearances, sit in the front part of the chair and lean forward because this shows involvement and interest.
- Don't look too slick; audiences respond to someone they can relate to.
- Use hands to gesture, up to a point. Avoid such body language and habits as wriggling in your seat or putting hands in your pocket.
- Maintain eye contact with the interviewer; do not look at the camera. Looking at another guest who is speaking is permissible, but afterward look at the interviewer.
- Smile whenever possible, except when it would be considered insensitive.[53]

CONCLUSIONS

By observing the techniques of successful broadcast appearances, corporate executives can greatly enhance the amount of control they have in conveying their messages to radio and television audiences. Semi-control is an apt term for this process. There is never complete control, but a skilled communicator can operate somewhere in the range of 50% to 80% percent control.

ENDNOTES

1. Larry King, with Mark Stencel, *On the Line: The New Road to the White House* (New York: Harcourt Brace, 1993), p. 147.
2. Ibid., p. 96.
3. Ibid., p. 73.
4. John A. Bace, "Broadcast Media Relations," in *The Handbook of Strategic Public Relations & Integrated Communications*, ed. Clarke L. Caywood (New York: McGraw-Hill, 1977), p. 78.
5. James E. Grunig and Todd Hunt, *Managing Public Relations* (New York: Holt, Rinehart & Winston, 1984), p. 149. The authors credit Herbert E. Krugman for this concept. See "The Impact of Television Advertising: Learning Without Involvement," *Public Opinion Quarterly*, Vol. 29, 1965, pp. 349–345, and, with Eugene L. Hartley, "Passive Learning From Television," *Public Opinion Quarterly*, Vol. 34, 1970, pp. 184–190.
6. Robert Kubrey and Mihaly Csikszentmihalyi, "Television Addiction Is No Mere Metaphor," *Scientific American*, No. 286, February 2002, pp. 74–80.
7. Kathleen Hall Jamieson, *Dirty Politics: Deception, Distraction, and Democracy* (New York: Oxford University Press, 1992), pp. 9–10.
8. Ibid., p. 60.
9. Ibid., p. 53.
10. Ibid., p. 17.
11. Ibid., pp. 18–19.
12. Ibid., p. 216.
13. Ibid., p. 206.
14. Ibid., p. 209.
15. Ibid., p. 216.
16. Federal Communications Commission, News Media Information: "Broadcast Station Total as of September 30, 2002," November 6, 2002.
17. Rene A. Henry, Jr., *Marketing Public Relations: The Hows That Make It Work* (Ames: Iowa State University Press, 1995), p. 104.
18. Timothy Egan, "Triumph Leaves No Targets for Conservative Talk Shows," *New York Times*, January 1, 1995, p. 1.
19. Rebecca Pirto, "Why Radio Thrives," *American Demographics*, Vol. 16, May 1994, p. 42.
20. Egan, op. cit., p. 1.
21. "Of All Media, the Most Powerful Are Talk Show Hosts Because They're the Most Personal," *pr reporter*, Vol. 35, June 8, 1992, p. 3.
22. Egan, op. cit., p. 1.
23. Ibid., p. 22.

24. Joe Conason, *Big Lies: The Right-Wing Propaganda Machine and How It Distorts the Truth* (New York: St. Martin's, 2003), p. 47.
25. Mark Preston, "On the Air in '04: A Liberal Voice," *Roll Call*, October 27, 2003. Internet.
26. Howard Fineman, "The Power of Talk," *Newsweek*, February 8, 1993, p. 24.
27. Allen R. Myerson, "Are Fallen Barons Victims of Their Press Clippings?" *New York Times*, February, 7, 1993, p. F7.
28. Ibid.
29. Timothy Egan, "Talk Radio or Hate Radio? Critics Assail Some Hosts," *New York Times*, January 1, 1995, p. 22.
30. Ibid.
31. The study was conducted by Richard Manville, Inc., for Brouillard Communications, a division of J. Walter Thompson Company, 420 Lexington Ave., New York, NY 10017. See news release dated October 5, 1981. The very largest companies—those with $1 billion or more in annual sales—showed the highest rate (74%) of participation. Seventy-two percent favored using broadcast interviews to communicate company policy; only 15% were opposed. More than 60 companies moved to this proactive policy during the preceding 5 years.
32. "Retail People—Media Training," *Retail Week*, November 9, 2002, p. 43.
33. Ibid.
34. From an announcement of an April 11 and 12, 1994, event by the National Media Relations Forum, P.O. Box 2189, Berkely, Calif. 94702.
35. Virgil Scudder, "Media Training—Getting It Right," *Public Relations Tactics*, May 2003, p. 14.
36. Ibid.
37. "The Media Training Mavens," *PR Week*, April 5, 2000, p. 21.
38. Edith Terry and Bradley Hitchings, "Learning to Shine in the Limelight," *BusinessWeek*, July 18, 1986, p. 88.
39. Based on a report by Karen Carney in a crisis communication class at Boston University's College of Communication, October 5, 1999
40. Associated Press, "Pakistani Child Labor Used on UNICEF Tools, CBS Says," *Seattle Post-Intelligencer* [Online], April 6, 1995.
41. Herb Schmertz, with William Novak, *Good-Bye to the Low Profile: The Art of Creative Confrontation* (Boston: Little, Brown, 1986), pp. 102–117.
42. Herb Schmertz, "Talking Back to Mike Ambush and Harry Reasonable," *Across the Board*, Vol. 23, June 1986, pp. 60–66. Also see Edith Terry and Bradley Hitching, "Learning to Shine in the Limelight," *BusinessWeek*, July 7, 1986, pp. 88–89.
43. Lori Robertson, "The Art of Self-Defense," *American Journalism Review*, Vol. 24, April 2002, pp. 46–51.
44. Marshall McLuhan, "Media Hot and Cold," in *Understanding Media: The Extensions of Man* (New York: New American Library, 1964), pp. 36–45.
45. Peter Hannaford, *Talking Back to the Media* (New York: Facts on File, 1986), pp. 46–47.
46. Ibid., p. 59.
47. Ibid., p. 60.
48. "There Are Only 2 Reasons to Meet the Press," *pr reporter*, Vol. 32, January 23, 1989, p. 4.
49. Clarence Jones, *How to Speak TV* (Marathon, Fla.: Video Consultants, 1983), p. 22.
50. Ibid., pp. 23–25.

51. Hannaford, op. cit., p. 43.
52. Michael M. Klepper, *Getting Your Message Out: How to Get, Use, and Survive Radio and Television Air Time* (Englewood Cliffs, N.J.: Prentice-Hall, 1984), p. 70.
53. Hannaford, op. cit.; also "Survive the Interview," *PR Week*, June 18, 2004, p. 29.

Chapter 6

Gaining Complete Control Over the Media: Advocacy Advertising

It is important to have complete control over a message when it carries serious legal implications, when the media have distorted facts and your views, and when you want to be on record. Advocacy advertising—also known as issues advertising—allows almost total control over when and how a message reaches the public through the mass media.

With advocacy advertising, an organization can take its case to the people and decide on the exact wording of the message, its style, timing, frequency of appearance, and, on occasion, its position in a publication (e.g., on the op-ed page of a newspaper). Furthermore, says Marc Rosenberg, advocacy ads are an "unavoidable part of the information stream and can themselves make news.... And an ad campaign can keep your message in front of the public long after the novelty value of your news story has faded."[1]

As suggested by the term *advocacy*, an advocacy ad states one's views and position on a controversial matter. S. Prakash Sethi, author of *Advocacy Advertising and Large Corporations*, says advocacy advertising is "concerned with the propagation of ideas and elucidation of controversial social issues of public importance in a manner that supports the position and interests of the sponsor while expressly denying the accuracy of fact and downgrading the sponsor's opponents."[2]

Advocacy advertising falls under the larger heading of corporate advertising, which is defined by the Association of National Advertisers as "aimed at improving consumer and investor perceptions of a company rather than directly selling its products or services."[3] Included in corporate advertising is institutional advertising—also called image advertising—that portrays an organization in a favorable fashion so as to win

151

public goodwill and enhance its reputation. Product advertising is not included in corporate advertising.

Political issue advertising should be distinguished from advocacy advertising, although the line between them is not always clear. A clear but narrow definition of issue advertising in politics is that it supports the election of a candidate or political party. However, issue advertising may be used by business, labor, and other interest groups to influence public opinion positions that are espoused by particular candidates. For example, pharmaceutical giant Pfizer in 2001 broadcast its own issue advertisement on prescription drug affordability in seven congressional battleground states. It did so up front rather than working through various organizations.[4] Anytime an ongoing public policy issue, such as privatization of Social Security, becomes a campaign issue, the line between advocacy advertising and political issue advertising becomes muddied.

Another ambiguous advocacy advertising campaign was a 30-second advertisement, prepared by the Bush administration, assuring Medicare beneficiaries that the new Medicare prescription drug law passed in 2003 would not affect them in any way except to provide "more benefits." The government planned to spend $9.5 million to run the ad on national network and cable programs over 6 weeks. Democratic members of Congress and some liberal advocacy groups, however, complained, saying the ad amounted to a taxpayer-subsidized political commercial for the administration. CBS consequently stopped running the ads while the accuracy of the ad was investigated by Congress's General Accounting Office.[5]

When the tobacco industry runs an ad to oppose a congressional antismoking bill, that is an advocacy ad intended to influence congressional votes. However, when an antismoking bill ad appears in the context of political campaigning and, as occurred during the spring and summer of 1998, the ad shows a voter who pledges "to remember this fall what the politicians do this summer," the ad crosses over into a political ad. This and other ads were shown in five markets of choice, including Atlanta, Denver, and St. Louis, which happen to be markets where Republican senators who opposed the bill were up for election. Senator Mitch McConnell (R-Ky.) told his fellow Republican colleagues that the industry would advertise to support those who voted against the bill.[6] Issue advertising of this kind is no longer clear advocacy advertising but crosses the line to political issue advertising, a controversial subject discussed in chapter 11.

USE OF ADVOCACY ADS GROWS

In 2002 various organizations spent a total of $645 million on advocacy ads, up from $520 million the year before, according to TNS Media intelligence/CMR.[7] Much of this money is spent in the nation's capital.

The Annenberg School study, *Print and Television Legislative Issue Advertising in the Nation's Capital in 2001*, states that more than $45 million was spent by about 375 advocacy groups on ads designed to influence federal policymakers. About half of it was spent to purchase print or television issue ads in the Washington, DC, media market.[8] "This is certainly a growing niche," said Linda Dove, senior vice president at the Washington office of the American Association of Advertising Agencies. Many of the largest public relations firms maintain advocacy practices in the Washington, DC, area, as well as a slew of political shops that specialize in the practice. Among the large firms are WPP Group's Burson-Marsteller, Omnicom Group's Fleishman-Hillard and Porter Novelli, and independent Edelman.[9]

Corporations and business interest groups are the major sponsors of advocacy ads. Their superiority in economic resources gives them a relative advantage over nonbusiness interest groups in being able to afford such ads. Energy and power, education, telecommunications, and health care issues lead in the capital area, accounting for 61% of the total spending there. The top spender in 2001 was Balanced Energy Choices, which spent more than $5 million on ads promoting coal as "affordable, clean, efficient and reliable."[10]

As shown by the Annenberg study, of the $15.4 million spent on issues relating to national energy policy, about 94% ($14.5 million) came from energy and business interests; environmental interests accounted for a mere 6%. The largest spender promoting the president's policy was the Alliance for Energy and Economic Growth, whose members include the U.S. Chamber of Commerce, the American Gas Association, the American Petroleum Institute, BP, Chevron Texaco, and other energy firms and associations. In contrast to the $1 million spent by them, the environmental coalition Save Our Environment, the largest spender in opposition, spent only about $40,000. The spending pattern was reversed, however, on the issue of the Arctic National Wildlife Preserve with ads opposing its development beating out those in favor of drilling with 53% of total spending, led by the National Audubon Society.[11]

Although most interest groups find the cost of ads prohibitive and save their dollars for public relations activities, in a recent trend some interest groups are willing to budget for ads supporting their views because they recognize the effectiveness of advocacy advertising. People for the Ethical Treatment of Animals (PETA) was an early adopter of corporate advertising techniques. "Grassroots flavor and moral weight can no longer compete with the polished, engaging tone of consumer advertising," said Dan Mathews, PETA's vice president for campaigns. PETA learned over a decade ago in its antifur campaign that an ad showing models posing in the buff was much more effective than showing animals writhing in leg-hold traps. "Once upon a time, when hippies ruled the earth, you wanted to avoid looking too slick," said Mathews, "Nowadays, slick is the only thing that much of the masses understand."[12] Further impetus may have been given to interest group advertising by the success of MoveOn.org, an electronic advocacy organization that said it raised $250,000 in 18 hours to run an antiwar newspaper ad campaign in more than 111 cities in 50 states.[13]

Besides PETA, other interest groups have also used advocacy advertising in their campaigns:

- The Communications Workers of America broadcast a high-gloss commercial immediately after the September 11 attack that called on Verizon Communications, their employer, to abandon plans to lay off thousands of workers.
- The Evangelical Environmental Network created the "What Would Jesus Drive?" fuel-efficiency campaign, a lighthearted play on "What Would Jesus Do," a popular evangelical Christian slogan. It hoped to turn its $65,000 budget into a blizzard of media coverage in outlets like *Time* magazine, *NBC Nightly News*, *The Wall Street Journal*, and *The New York Times*.
- Survival International in London added focus to its advertising by linking diamond exploration by De Beers to the dislocation of native Bushmen in central Africa. Instead of television or the print media, it replaced a billboard, showing model Iman wearing a De Beers diamond, with a near-exact mock-up of a woman from the Bushmen group and parodied the De Beers slogan, "A diamond is forever," with the line, "The Bushmen aren't forever."[14]

Broadcast Networks Restrict Advocacy Advertising

Unlike political issue advertising where television dominates, newspapers and magazines have been the major outlets for advocacy advertising because broadcast networks have generally rejected such ads. Before 1987 broadcasters resisted these ads because the Fairness Doctrine forced them to provide free airtime for opposing viewpoints. Resistance to advocacy advertising lessened when this requirement was eliminated and more advertising time was available with which to earn extra revenue. For example, in September 1990, NBC dropped the ban and allowed its seven owned and operated stations to accept such spots.[15]

Despite the absence of legal restrictions, networks have imposed their own restrictions. CBS's policy is not to "sell time for the advocacy of viewpoints on controversial issues of public importance." Specifically, a commercial is considered unacceptable if it explicitly takes a position on such an issue, or without taking an explicit position, presents arguments parallel those made by one side or the other.[16] For example, CBS rejected MoveOn.org's ad "Child Play" for broadcast during the Super Bowl. Set to slow music, the 30-second spot features a montage of children working in menial adult jobs as janitors, dishwashers, and garbage collectors and asks, "Guess who's going to pay off President Bush's trillion-dollar deficit?"[17]

CNN follows a similar policy. It refused to air a pair of 30-second announcements from two Jewish groups, saying, "CNN does not take international advocacy ads concerning regions in conflict. This is the same policy we applied when turning down ads that dealt with Egypt, Qatar, UAE and Saudi Arabia." The ad read: "America is Israel's only real ally in the Middle East. Israel is a democracy that respects the rights of individuals and gives all citizens a right to vote.... All people—Christians, Muslims, and Jews—enjoy freedom of religion, press and speech." Disagreeing with CNN, The American Jewish Committee and Israel 21 said the TV spots stress common values between America and Israel and should not be classified as issue advocacy.[18]

Fortunately for users of advocacy advertising, these network policies have not been forced on local television stations, nor does cable television follow them. These outlets are often willing, and even eager, to accept advocacy ads. For example, only 3 of 14 television stations in Michigan rejected the Right to Life adoption reform ads. One reason broadcasters give for viewing advocacy advertising more positively is that it looks tame and is less likely to upset viewers compared with the trend toward below-the-belt political advertising.

Although a common explanation for rejection of ads is that controversial issues are best handled in regular news programs where balanced treatment can be provided, it is clear broadcasters accept or reject ads on the basis of a mixture of economic and political considerations. For example, when WNBC in 1990 rejected a 30-second ad from Neighbor to Neighbor, a national group that favors ending U.S. investments in El Salvador, David Vacheron, standards and license manager for WNBC, explained, "There was no proof for the ad's claim that American aid was used to murder four Jesuit priests and 40,000 other innocent civilians in El Salvador."[19] Another factor may have been the fear of offending Procter & Gamble. The network had good grounds for this fear: when WHDH in Boston ran a Neighbor to Neighbor spot in which consumers were urged to boycott P&G's Folgers coffee, the company canceled approximately $750,000 in annual advertising at the station.[20]

Print Media More Hospitable Toward Advocacy Ads

In contrast to television, free-speech protection allows the print media to accept all kinds of politically and socially controversial ads following the argument that pages are readily available, whereas broadcast frequencies are limited relative to the many who wish to use them. Nevertheless, because advocacy ads are attacked by those who feel offended, a newspaper may also restrict such advertising. For example, on Thanksgiving Day in 1991, Minneapolis' *Star Tribune* published an ad by the Citizens Committee to Stop the Northwest Airlines Loan, asking readers to voice their dissent regarding government loans. Northwest Airlines was outraged, but the newspaper pointed out it could not limit its ads to those with which the paper agrees.[21]

OBJECTIVES OF ADVOCACY ADVERTISING

Advocacy ads can achieve four objectives: (a) correct media errors and distortion, (b) attract public attention to, and support for, an issue neglected by the media, (c) stimulate news coverage, and (d) attract the attention of and inform the legislature.

Correct Media Errors and Distortion

As mentioned in chapter 4, advocacy advertising can be viewed as "counter advertising to counter the news."[22] It is a way to hold the media accountable. Advocacy ads allow a company to fight back when reporters, commentators, and editorial writers are perceived as misinforming the public. As stated by Herbert Schmertz, former Mobil Oil vice president of public affairs:

> The use of advertising in controversial situations is not designed to convince—to get people with different viewpoints to say, "I agree," (or "I believe"). It is designed to "give pause"—to arrest the process of easy assumptions, to establish that there *is* another point of view. This is a necessary preliminary stage to "open debate with open minds."[23]

Mobil initiated intensive communication efforts to set the record straight in the early 1970s. (See Box 6.1 for a celebrated example.) As stated by Rawleigh Warner, Jr., then Mobil's chairman, "People know that if they take a swipe at us, we will fight back."[24] At first Mobil simply joined other companies that believed in speaking out, but soon "the fact that we were different came out," says Warner. Mobil's aim, he said, is to educate people on the intricacies of the petroleum industry and the American economic system:

Box 6.1   Mobil's "Hatchet Job" Ad

Mobil's 1976 "hatchet job" ad headline was "What ever happened to fair play?"—referring to a miniseries titled "The Great Gasoline War," on New York City's nightly WNBC-TV news. In this show's five segments, adding up to 36 minutes, Liz Trotta set out to reveal the economics of the oil industry and why gasoline prices were high in the New York area. The implication was that the oil industry was engaged in a scheme to cheat consumers. Within a week, Mobil responded with ads in the *New York Times*, the *Daily News*, and the eastern edition of the *Wall Street Journal*. The ad charged, "WNBC-TV's recent series on gasoline prices was inaccurate, unfair, and a disservice to the people." The ad was festooned with 17 small hatchets to highlight each distortion of truth as seen by Mobil.[25]

In short, we wanted to speak our piece. If we didn't make sense, if we proved not credible over a long period of time, then we would take our lumps. But we wanted to broaden the spectrum of ideas, information and viewpoints, and we were willing to take our chances on the good sense of the people.[26]

Schmertz expanded on this strategy. He said Mobil's public affairs program was an integral part of the energy business—"not something extraneously designed to get our name in the paper, or make friends in high places, or persuade people to love us."[27] Great statesmen, he said, don't make decisions based on popularity polls. "They move ahead on the course that right and nation require."[28] Furthermore, Mobil intended to go beyond merely responding to the media. "We expect to continue in our attempts to influence events rather than act on them after the fact."[29]

Sometimes a film rather than a news story requires correction, as happened with *The Insider*, a docudrama about whistle blower Jeffrey Wigand, who exposed what Brown & Williamson knew about the relationship between smoking and cancer. The tobacco company, concerned about the film's allegation that it threatened Wigand and his family, used a full-page ad to tell readers otherwise. The ad, "A Letter to Disney Shareholders," signed by Nick Brookes, chairman & CEO of Brown & Williamson, states:

We are compelled to communicate with you in this fashion because we have no other recourse. Your company is defaming us in a movie and has refused our repeated attempts to set the record straight.... The film clearly suggests that Brown & Williamson threatened Wigand. We state here categorically that Brown & Williamson did *not* threaten Wigand or his family in any way.... Although Disney and Touchstone [the film's producer] try to absolve themselves of any responsibility for the many inaccuracies in the movie by saying, "certain events depicted in the film have been fictionalized for dramatic effect," such disclaimers are too little too late. No disclaimer can overcome the effect of such scenes on the audience, particularly where an actor of Al Pacino's stature asserts repeatedly, "he's telling the truth."[30]

Garner Public Attention and Support

One of the cornerstones of a proactive policy is to garner public attention and support and thereby shape the outcome of an issue. Schmertz sees advocacy ads as being in the pamphleteering tradition: "It's a feisty, frisky, free-swinging tradition that goes back at least to John Locke in 1689. We try to wear Tom Paine's hat when we're writing an advocacy message or producing one for TV." The ads are directed at "those who *make* news, who *write* the newspapers and *produce* the TV—and at all the other opinion-molders and thought-leaders who shape public discourse in this country."[31]

Mobil's advocacy campaign took four forms, as described by Donald S. Stroetzel, Mobil's manager of communications programs:

> *Op-eds*, begun in September 1974, have been the mainstay of Mobil's program. They appear every Thursday in the *New York Times* at the lower quarter-page opposite the editorial page. They also appear in eight other major newspapers and two news magazines. The ads are aimed at opinion leaders, primarily politicians in Washington and state government, commentators and editors on TV and radio, newspaper editors, educators, and senior business executives.
>
> *Observations*, a column targeted at a popular audience, published in Sunday supplements about every other week. The ad goes to about 500 newspapers, reaching about 40 million households. The column uses cartoons and woodcuts, and bold typeface to spark reader interest.
>
> *TV commercials*, a 60-second spot on the same themes as the op-ed ads, seen on evening news programs of 80 TV stations, reaching about 25 million households a month.
>
> *Special ads*, a full-page treatment, usually for fire-fighting situations.[32]

When a major issue arises, Mobil organizes "media blitzes" to have their executives appear on broadcast shows and to meet with local newspaper editors. In one of these, 21 executives were dispatched to 21 target cities, and within a day or two, they appeared on more than 100 talk shows, news broadcasts, and radio call-in programs.[33]

The nuclear industry wanted to activate public support, motivated by the fact that a number of plants were seeking 40-year license renewals. A flashy image campaign sponsored by the Nuclear Energy Institute (NEI) seeks to activate support from the "silent majority" of educated Americans. The NEI believes they back nuclear power but are afraid to go public because they are certain most Americans are rabid antinuclear activists. The ads carry the tag line, "Nuclear: More Than You Ever Imagined," and they position nuclear power as safe, efficient, and clean. "Influentials" are targets via full-page ads in publications such as *The New York Times*, *Washington Post*, the *Economist*, *New Republic*, and *Atlantic Monthly*.[34]

Stimulate News Coverage

Well-crafted advocacy ads not only draw public attention but, as the Harry and Louise ads during the health care reform debates in 1994 demonstrated, also provide a media event that engenders news stories, which, of course, attract more public attention.[35] Advocacy ads are useful, therefore, when proactive media relations efforts to obtain free media coverage are inadequate or ineffective.

Research conducted by Kathleen Hall Jamieson, Annenberg School's dean, concluded, "Several ad campaigns succeeded in generating news coverage worth many times the cost of the ad placements themselves."[36] One half-page ad, "Stop Teenage Addiction to Tobacco (STAT)," accused media CEOs of "taking blood money by helping to promote a product that the Surgeon General says is harmful and addictive."[37] The ad received widespread news coverage, partly because it was timed to appear the day before the Surgeon General's annual report on tobacco products was released. Even more publicity was generated by stories about the refusal of *The New York Times* and the *Los Angeles Times* to run the ad.

Another example of publicity generation is the California Poultry Industry Association's 1994 ad, drawing attention to the fact that the Agriculture Department's definition of "fresh chicken" included frozen birds—a definition to which the association objected. Three months after the ad appeared, *The New York Times*'s Living section featured a story entitled "If It Clucks Like a Bowling Ball."[38]

Influence Government Action

Advocacy advertising is also aimed at lawmakers and government officials to discourage legislation and regulation. Thus, as mentioned in Part IV of this book, advocacy advertising can extend into the legislative stage of an issue's life cycle. The aim is not only to influence lawmakers and officials directly—and thereby become an arm of direct lobbying—but also to influence public opinion that will enhance grassroots lobbying efforts. Some past and recent examples are:

• West Publishing used an advocacy ad to pressure the Justice Department into holding a meeting with it about a proposal that would allow the government to compete directly in case law publications. After West ran a series of ads featuring cartoons with a trick-or-treat theme, the Justice Department agreed to a meeting.[39]

• The health care industry used advocacy ads to influence government in the 1994 debate over the Clinton health plan. Besides the Harry and Louise ad by the Health Association of America, other threatened interests used advocacy ads. Delta, an insurance company, placed a low-key, relatively high-frequency ad in the *Washington Post*, showing the value of dental insurance and the danger of proposed changes. The ad also included image material, that Delta was the nation's oldest provider of group dental insurance. According to Delta, Majority Leader George Mitchell told Delta company lobbyists he was aware of this message from having read the ads.[40]

• The AFL-CIO launched a major advertising blitz in July 1998 for a sweeping managed-care overhaul bill; it warned congressional candidates they would pay a price in November if they did not back the measure. The ads were scheduled to run in 20 House districts and in five states where senators were targeted. The ads were part of a larger grassroots effort supporting Patients' Bill of Rights legislation and including the shipment of fliers on the issue to regional councils, to be distributed to workers at hundreds of work sites around the country.[41]

• The tobacco industry has engaged in the most extensive use of ads to arrest legislative action and to influence public opinion. On May 23, 1994, R. J. Reynolds Tobacco, a unit of RJR Nabisco Holdings, began a multimillion-dollar advertising campaign to present its views in the debate on smoking. The company announced that it planned to follow up on the theme of individual freedom, a theme that James W. Johnston was thought to have effectively communicated during the congressional hearings the previous month.[42] (See Box 6.2 for examples of tobacco company ads.)

• The probusiness group Arctic Power, Inc., led a $4 million advertising campaign to support President Bush's plan to open the Alaska National Wildlife Refuge to oil and gas exploration. The ads were timed to appear just as the Audubon Society planned to air its own commercial in the Washington, DC market reminding people of the rescue of oil-coated birds after the Exxon *Valdez* spill.

• The Tax Relief Coalition, a group with more than 400 member associations, planned to publish ads around the country in spring 2001 to promote Bush's tax plan. It was joined by the tax-cut advocacy group, Club for Growth, which had already started with its $1.5 million ad campaign. Illustrating the increasing use of advocacy ads in politics, a group of Republican political consultants planned to spend $5 million on ads bolstering Bush policies, starting with the tax cut. "We will run ads depending on where the debate is and where help is needed," said Bill Dal Col, director of the Issues Management Center, an activist public relations agency set up by conservatives.[43]

HOW EFFECTIVE ARE ADVOCACY ADS?

The assumption underlying advocacy ads is that they are effective. With reference to tobacco company ads, Jay Mathews, writing for the *Washington Post*, states, "Advertising experts say that advocacy campaigns can have a marked effect on the strength of voter support for more restrictions on smoking." He cites Tim Elliot, a partner in the firm that produced Reynolds's ads, saying such advocacy campaigns have been shown to change minds and ease political problems "if the point is a real one and you are prepared to commit to it over time."[44] Advertising executives who benefit from such advertising are, of course, inclined to exaggerate its effectiveness—claiming, in this case, the ability of issue ads to change attitudes.

A 1981 survey of business and media executives, which explored the basis of claims in support of issue advertising, was less confident about its effectiveness. These executives generally rated issue advertising average or very good as a vehicle for achieving exposure of the market audi-

Box 6.2 Tobacco Company Ads

The first ad, which appeared in the May 23, 1994, issues of *The New York Times,* the *Wall Street Journal, USA Today, Washington Post,* the *National Journal,* and *Roll Call,* carried the headline "Second-hand Smoke: How Much Are Non-smokers Exposed To?" It answered, "Very little," and buttressed it by presenting three calculations. One was, "In a month, a non-smoker living with a smoker would, on average, be exposed to second-hand smoke equivalent to smoking approximately 1½ cigarettes."[45] The ad said, "We believe that the solution to most smoking issues can be found in accommodation. There are ways for smokers and non-smokers to co-exist peacefully. And we encourage discussion that will help solve the issues without resorting to Government intervention."[46]

The ad indirectly addresses the EPA's 1993 announcement that exposure to second-hand smoke causes lung cancer. In a subsequent ad on May 26, 1994, R. J. Reynolds reprinted a *Wall Street Journal* editorial by Jacob Sullum called "Smoke & Mirrors: EPA Wages War on Cigarettes." It states, "The EPA twisted the evidence to arrive at a predetermined conclusion." The editorial becomes technical when it refers to the agency's *blatant trick* of using an unconventional definition of statistical significance. It refers to an article in *Science* stating that the EPA was able to claim only a weak association between "environmental tobacco smoke" (second-hand smoke) and lung cancer, even by using "fancy statistical footwork."[47]

Philip Morris also took out ads in a four-part series on second-hand smoke. The first was an article from *Forbes MediaCritic,* written by Jacob Sullum (identified as managing editor of *Reason* magazine).[48] Another ad headline echoes the theme of "Accommodation" and refers to a recent *USA Today*/CNN poll reporting that "nearly 7 out of 10 respondents said they think that rather than banning smoking in public places, smokers should be allowed to smoke in separate, designated areas. The ad then refers to a program that "helps owners of businesses, such as restaurants, bars and hotels, to accommodate the choices of both their smoking and nonsmoking customers by setting up designated smoking and nonsmoking areas." The ad ends, "We want you to know where we stand."[49]

R. J. Reynolds also used humor in some ads, for example, showing a suburban house surrounded by police cars with the caption, "We've got you surrounded. Come out with your cigarettes."[50] Joining the humor theme, an ad by Philip Morris poked fun at smoking restrictions by showing workers puffing cigarettes at desks floating outside their upper story office windows; the caption read, "Have you noticed finding a place to smoke is the hardest part of your job?"[51]

(continued)

Box 6.2   *(continued)*

Together, R. J. Reynolds and Philip Morris tried to sway public opinion by presenting three negative consequences of a smoke-free society: the loss of the contribution of tobacco tax to government budgets, a black market of tobacco products, and more unemployment. Referring to the previous prohibition of alcohol, an R. J. Reynolds ad says, "These most recent anti-smoking proposals represent nothing less than an attempt at tobacco prohibition, something that will have serious implications for Americans." This ad, like others, optimistically ends with the slogan "Together, we can work it out."[52]

---

ence to the desired message or messages.[53] However, they thought that effectiveness was limited because the public would perceive ads as being too self-serving.

Furthermore, business executives of *Fortune* 500 companies thought the use of the "good corporate citizen" copy focus had been overused "to the point it is now counter-productive in enhancing the image of an individual firm."[54] Several noted, "The often repeated symbolism of a company who sees no evil, does no evil, and speaks no evil gets very hard to swallow." What target groups want answered by ads is, "What have you done for me today and what will you do for me in the future?"[55] The real problem, some executives contended, is subject matter: "Substance is lacking and there is little or nothing to build the campaign around." The fundamental question is whether the types of problems, issues, and topics corporations now address in their corporate issue campaigns can really be dealt with through advertising.[56]

The effectiveness of advocacy advertising depends on many factors. One factor is whether the ads themselves become newsworthy. The famous Harry and Louise TV ads for the defeat of the Clinton administration's 1994 health care reform bill, which were targeted only in the home districts of key members of Congress and the Washington, DC market, were successful because they stimulated millions of dollars of free publicity on network news shows. Even more attention was inadvertently drawn to the ads when groups supporting the Clinton plan ran ads attacking Harry and Louise. Further awareness of the ads was created by a White House parody by President Clinton and his wife, Hillary, at a gridiron dinner.[57] Achieving public awareness, however, is only one of several levels of effectiveness.

Determine the Criteria for Effectiveness

The Harry and Louise ads attracted attention and stimulated news coverage, but is that enough? To be effective by themselves, the ads had to also influence attitudes toward health care reform and, ultimately, congressional voting behavior. As indicated in the well-known hierarchy of effects, effectiveness must be measured on at least four levels:

1. *Attracting attention or creating awareness.* Ads are highly likely to be effective in achieving this objective. An ad serves to place an issue on the public agenda. According to an Opinion Research Corporation (ORC) study, 90% of U.S. adults said they had read or heard an advocacy ad in the past 2 years.[58]

2. *Creating understanding and comprehension.* This result is less likely and depends on such factors as public interest in the issue, its complexity, and its emotional character. An ORC study reports that 58% of adults see the ads as at least "fairly believable," with 64% claiming they help them understand the issue under discussion. However, a survey of congressional and other government leaders by Yankelovich, Skelly, and White turned up less sanguine results. Although 90% said they read Mobil advocacy ads on the energy issue, 66% found them of little use in understanding energy deregulation issues; nor did the ads influence their opinion on any policy matter. Furthermore, the ads were found to be "abrasive," "unpersuasive," and "antagonistic."[59]

3. *Influencing attitudes.* Communication theorists contend information by itself rarely influences attitudes; it must be reinforced by other activities, such as interpersonal communication. However, this conclusion is tempered by the ORC study finding that 51% said the ads changed their minds. Furthermore, the Harry and Louise ads created "negative" attention to the health care reform measure.

4. *Influencing behavior.* This result is the least likely. It should be noted, however, that 25% in the ORC study said they took action by writing to a public official about an issue and 12% said they wrote a letter to an editor about it. Special situations, as described later, account for some successes.

The quality of an advocacy ad and its many attributes determine how effective it is in reaching one or more of these four levels. Although lessons from product advertising apply, a few specific studies of the effectiveness of advocacy advertising suggest some special factors. One study, which sought the reactions of a company's internal stakeholders, identified three criteria: professionalism, creativeness, and consistency. Professionalism meant that an ad was distinctive or unique, credible, up to date, recognizable, made a clear promise, addressed target audiences, was typical of the company, and was appealing to its own employees. Professionalism was necessary to educate stakeholders; that is, to create understanding.[60]

To change attitudes, creativeness was needed—exhibiting such attributes as being striking, authentic, original, surprising, unique, and humorous. To change behavior, consistency as well as professionalism were required. Consistency refers to being consequent and coherent, having a single concept and long-term focus. Judgment and skill are obviously required to translate these attributes into the design and composition of an ad.

Additional variables are described in an academic study conducted in a classroom. Students were asked to contact their congresspersons to help defeat impending legislation that would ban saccharin. The study found that students considered a message in an advocacy ad more interesting and informative, and hence more persuasive, than a news story. This finding refutes the general belief that a news story about a controversial subject is more effective than a similar message in a paid advertisement because the source of the latter is assumed to be biased. Furthermore, what can make an ad more effective is its superior format—layout, larger type size, and straightforward presentation. The study also refuted the premise that a corporate source has lower credibility. For example, ads by Pepsi were as effective in inducing written correspondence to congresspersons as ads attributed to the American Cancer Society.[61]

Two cases, those of Allstate Insurance and W. R. Grace & Company, suggest circumstances when advocacy advertising can affect behavior. Ray Ewing, former director of Allstate's issues management effort, reported that a 1971 ad headlined "New York State Supports Auto Thieves" influenced one key person at the time: Governor Nelson Rockefeller. Reporting on the ad to the governor, his staff interpreted it as implying the insurance industry might oppose his upcoming bid for reelection. After the ad was run, Rockefeller announced that although he would not include a title law in his legislative package, he would not oppose one either. The law was passed that session.[62]

In the second case, W. R. Grace's "Disincentivization of America" campaign, the then director of advertising, Stephen Elliott, concluded, "While many other factors were at work regarding this issue, Grace believes the campaign was an influential contributor to the congressional action which reduced the capital gains tax to 20 percent instead of the proposed increase to 52 percent."[63] What should be noted of this 4-month campaign is advocacy advertising was coordinated with press relations and with formal and informal contacts with congressmen and senators. Each ad was keyed to specific issues debated in Congress at the time. Readers were asked to write to their member of Congress on the capital gains tax issue. Direct mail, which included ad reprints and a 49-page report titled "The Disincentivization of America," supplemented the newspaper ads. The targets of direct mail were U.S. congressmen and senators, chief executives of *Fortune* 1000 companies, and editors of 665 U.S. newspapers. A by-product of the campaign was widespread publicity.[64]

Conditions That Enhance Effectiveness

A fair conclusion to the debate over the effectiveness of advocacy advertising is that it can be effective—even to the point of influencing attitudes and behavior—if carefully designed and under special conditions, such as the following:

1. The ad is part of a larger public affairs campaign and thus supplemented by such activities as proactive media relations, grassroots lobbying, and political action committee (PAC) contributions. As stated by Joseph Klapper in the early literature of communication theory, mass communication is "a contributory agent, but not the sole cause" in producing attitudinal and behavioral changes.[65]
2. The advertiser has high source credibility. Often this means the company has a history of public communication and does not try to reach the public only during a crisis. Recognizing they have to build credibility slowly, some companies begin by talking about things of interest to their audiences and with which they can agree.
3. The ad is based on facts and persuasive reasoning, not flag-waving, posturing, and preaching. One reason the Harry and Louise ads were so effective is that of the $15 million the Health Insurance Association of America (HIAA) spent on the campaign, between $300,000 and $400,000 went for survey research. The aim was to find message themes that bridged the concerns of HIAA with those of the public. Focus groups tested the wording of the message and the setting; for example, Harry and Louise were found to be more persuasive when seated at their kitchen table than on a sofa in their living room.[66]
4. The ad creates interest and involvement by talking in terms of the audience's own life and the things that are important to them.
5. Present both sides of an issue. Because the less attractive facts about your firm or industry are likely already known, critics can be defused by the ad's admitting these.[67]
6. Initiate layout innovations and develop a signature style.[68]
7. Use targeted messages and media whenever possible. For example, DuPont began running "Voice of the American Farm" ads on television, on radio, in major newspapers, and in farming publications that focus mainly on farm issues, problems, and solutions.[69]

A review of political campaign ads (see chap. 11) suggests other ways in which advocacy ads can be effective.

TRENDS IN CORPORATE ADVERTISING

Some trends in advocacy advertising also affect image advertising, which is a major part of overall corporate advertising. Image advertising is about the character of a corporation. Its objectives are to increase public familiarity with a company, improve attitudes toward it, and associate favorable personality traits with it. Image advertising supports advocacy advertising when favorable attitudes toward a company increase the credibility of its issue messages.

Image ads can also be used to influence regulatory decisions while not explicitly advocating legislation. In 1998 several utility companies with expiring licences to operate nuclear plants were seeking 40-year license renewals.[70] To help them, the Nuclear Energy Institute launched an image campaign that positioned nuclear power as a safe and environment- friendly energy source. Ads were targeted at influentials through publications such as *The New York Times, Washington Post*, the *Economist, New Republic*, and *Atlantic Monthly*. The ads' tagline is "Nuclear: More Than You Ever Imagined." The ads promote nuclear power as safe, efficient, and clean. Radio spots were also used on popular radio shows such as *Don Imus*.[71]

Corporate Branding

A fundamental change in the nature of corporate ads during the 1990s holds implications for both image and advocacy advertising. There is more "corporate branding" than "corporate image," says James R. Gregory, a consultant hired by the Association of National Advertisers. Corporate branding is "more marketing-oriented, much more aggressive, much more savvy." In contrast, image ads "are viewed as fluff and not really valuable, except for self-gratification.... That type of corporate advertising is eyewash and people don't pay attention to it." Furthermore, says Gregory, "corporate image ads are the chairman of the company and the 100th anniversary of the company; they're past tense.... What people are interested in is the future, the company's vision."[72]

Branding is also distinguished from identity, which is concerned with "defining and shaping the entity behind the brand." Identity concentrates on management and leadership as opposed to marketing. In other words, the difference between branding and identity, as in the corporate context, is "who is doing the talking as opposed to what they are talking about." With corporate identity, public image both inside and outside of an organization is of great importance as well. For instance, Philip Morris has yet to shake "Philip Morris, tobacco company." To remove this stigma placed on it by the public, Philip Morris has come up with a new name—Altria (meaning *higher* in Latin). The logo accompanying the new name is a mosaic—inspired by a "compartmented shelf in the Philip Morris corporate reception area that features packages sold by its several companies." The new symbol is both appropriate and fun, with its splashes of color representing the multiplicity and diversity of Altria.[73]

Schmertz says fundamental changes in the marketplace dictate a more compelling response than companies have been making; the public wants to know more about a company than just the quality of its goods and services. People want to know who the company is, what it stands for, and how it differs from the competition. They also want to know why the company is relevant to them.[74] A corporation must speak with a clear, coherent, and distinctive voice. It can spring from a powerful corporate voice of an inspired leader (e.g., Sony founder Akio Morita), or a strongly defined culture (e.g., McDonald's or Herman Miller's).

Because it is directed at issues, advocacy advertising should be more rational and less fluffy than image advertising. Schmertz stated in an interview with Bill Moyers on Public Broadcasting Service in 1993:

> I think corporate America should be dealing in hard aspects of the issues rather than in emotional kinds of appeals.... If you look at the Conoco ads with the penguins and seals clapping, you have an emotional appeal. That doesn't tell you anything about what they are doing or the consequences of what they are doing, or alternative policies.... Corporate America should create a dialogue and debate on important public-policy issues. These kinds of ads don't do that. The real issue in the debate ought to be on priorities. And the debate ought to be nonemotional.[75]

CONCLUSIONS

Advocacy advertising provides corporations with another way to gain control over the mass media—by buying space or time to disseminate chosen messages to the general public or a selective audience. Although most organizations have this privilege, only those who can pay can use it. Large corporations, with their considerable wealth, have a comparative advantage over others. Even if a corporation is willing to pay for an adversary's reply, as Mobil has done, it has the upper hand because it sets the agenda.

Although advocacy advertising's ability to influence attitudes and behavior on a particular issue is questionable, it does more than simply attract attention to an issue. Together with other forms of corporate advertising, such as image advertising, it keeps the public aware of the corporate presence in society. This awareness can serve the function of legitimizing an individual corporation, an industry, and the business system as a whole. Whether it succeeds depends on the public acceptability of its messages. Too often the public is told what the corporation is against but not for what the corporation stands.

ENDNOTES

1. Marc Rosenberg, "The Power of Advocacy Advertising in Newspapers," *Editor & Publisher*, February 11, 1995, p. 48.
2. S. Prakash Sethi, *Advocacy Advertising and Large Corporations: Social Conflict, Big business Image, the News Media, and Public Policy* (Lexington, Mass: Lexington Books, 1977), p. 7.
3. Stuart Elliott, "The Media Business: Advertising," *New York Times*, January 18, 1995, p. D5.
4. Jonathan Weisman, "Adopting Union Tactics, Firms Dive More Deeply Into Politics; Employees Targeted With Voter Guides, Turnout Efforts," *Washington Post*, October 24, 2002, p. A08.

5. Robert Pear, "CBS Pulls Advertisement on Medicare Prepared by Administration," *New York Times*, February 14, 2004, p. A20.
6. Jeffrey Taylor, "Is Tobacco Industry Playing Politics With Issue Ads?," *Wall Street Journal*, September 1, 1998, p. A20.
7. Lisa van der Pool, "Ad Units of PR Shops Seek More Advocacy Work, Marsteller Adds Specialist in D.C. to Chase Growing Niche," *Ad Week*, October 6, 2003, p. 9.
8. Peter Roff, "Study: $45m Spent on Issue Ads in D.C.," United Press International, January 7, 2003. The study was conducted by the Annenberg Center at the University of Pennsylvania. To be included in the study, the ads had to run in 2001 in the *Washington Times*, *Washington Post*, *The Hill*, *Congress Daily AM*, or *Roll Call*, all of which are Washington publications read by significant numbers of legislators, federal officials, and others who have an influence on public policy formulation.
9. Van der Pool, op. cit.
10. Roff, op. cit.
11. "Study Finds Energy Issues Account for Most Policy Advertising," *Oil Daily* [Online], June 19, 2003.
12. Ibid.
13. Lucia Moses, "Advocacy-Ad Dollars Flow," *Editor & Publisher Magazine*, March 3, 2003, p. 4.
14. Nat Ives, "The Media Business: Advertising; Unions and Advocacy Groups Are Putting a Madison Avenue Finesse on Their Protest Ads," *New York Times*, December 26, 2002, p. C3.
15. Joann S. Lublin, "TV Networks Gingerly Lift Prohibition on 'Issue Ads'," *Wall Street Journal*, January 15, 1990, p. B1.
16. Pear, op. cit. Also see "CBS Statement on Advocacy Advertising," *PR Newswire*, January 28, 2004.
17. "Anti-Bush Ads Rejected by CBS Are Slated to Air on CNN During Super Bowl," Knight Ridder Tribune Business News, January 30, 2004, p. 1. Also see Danna Harman, "Advertising or Advocating?," *Christian Science Monitor*, February 20, 2004, p. 11.
18. Jennifer Harper, "CNN Rejects Ads by Jewish Groups," *The Washington Times*, September 20, 2002, p. AO8.
19. Lublin, op. cit.
20. Ibid.
21. James A. Diazi and Carol VanOrnum, "Star Tribune Cannot Limit Ads to Those It Agrees With," *Star Tribune*, December 5, 1991, p. 25A.
22. Sethi, op. cit.
23. Herbert Schmertz, letter to editor of *pr reporter*, January 3, 1978.
24. Ibid.
25. Irwin Ross, "Public Relations Isn't Kid-Glove Stuff at Mobil," *Fortune*, September 1976, pp. 106–111, 196–202.
26. "Mobil … A Case History," Brochure, No. PR1102, prepared by *Time*, 1976.
27. "Top Line," *Madison Avenue*, Vol. 25, February 8, 1983, p. 32.
28. Ibid.
29. Ibid., p. 36.
30. *Wall Street Journal*, November 12, 1999, p. C24.
31. Ibid., p. 34.
32. Donald S. Stroetzel, "Why Mobil Uses Advocacy Advertising," *Public Affairs Review*, Vol. 3, 1982, pp. 32–33.
33. Ross, op. cit.
34. "Nuclear Industry Seeks to Activate 'Silent' Supporters," *O'Dwyer's Report*, Vol. 12, September 1998, pp. 1, 49.

35. Rosenberg, op. cit.
36. Ibid.
37. Ibid.
38. Ibid.
39. Ibid.
40. Ibid.
41. Laurie McGinley and Glenn Burkins, "AFL-CIO Ad Blitz on Revamp of Managed Care Has Warning on the Political Cost of Opposition," *Wall Street Journal*, July 15, 1998, p. A16.
42. Eben Shapiro, "R. J. Reynolds Fights Back in Campaign," *Wall Street Journal*, May 23, 1994, p. B5.
43. Tom Hamburger and Jim VandeHei, "Ads Backing Bush Proposals Proliferate as Advocacy Groups Become Permanent," *Wall Street Journal*, March 19, 2002, p. A4.
44. The ad that appeared in the *Wall Street Journal* on August 9, 1994, p. A11, showed four individuals, each with a quote, and the ad's headline was "We Have Never Smoked. But It Was Our Choice, Not the Government's."
45. See *Wall Street Journal*, May 23, 1994, p. A9.
46. Ibid.
47. The ad appeared in the *Wall Street Journal*, May 26, 1994, p. B3. The opinion editorial by Jacob Sullum appeared on March 24, 1994.
48. See *Wall Street Journal*, June 28, 1995, p. A5.
49. An ad appeared in the *Wall Street Journal*, November 3, 1994, p. B9.
50. Rosenberg, op. cit.
51. See Andrew Eolfson, "Embattled Companies Fight Back With Ads," *Courier-Journal*, May 27, 1994, p. 1A.
52. Eva Hoeffelman, "The Crisis of the Tobacco Industry," class paper in Managing Corporate Crises, Boston University, College of Communication, November 16, 1994, p. 18.
53. Barbara J. Coe, "The Effectiveness Challenge in Issue Advertising Campaigns," *Journal of Marketing*, Vol. 12, No. 4, 1983, p. 27.
54. Ibid., p. 29.
55. Ibid., p. 28.
56. Ibid., p. 32.
57. Rosenberg, op. cit.
58. A study of 1,010 persons in the United States conducted by ORC reported that 90% said they had read or heard an advocacy ad in the past 2 years. When asked about the source of the ad, 70% answered television. Unfortunately this raises doubt about the accuracy of respondents' impressions because television is the least likely source as networks have generally refused to accept advocacy ads. But Kenneth Schwartz of ORC explains that, "because of the predominance of television, this medium tends to be cited by the majority of people as the source of almost any kind of information about which they are questioned." Stephen A. Kliment, "Advocacy Advertising by U.S. Corporations—Can Money Buy Friends?" *Madison Avenue*, Vol. 23, February 1981, p. 40.
59. Lynn Adkins, "How Good Are Advocacy Ads?" *Dun's Review*, June 1978, p. 76.
60. Cess B. M. van Riel and Gerrit H. van Bruggen, "Impact: A Management Judgment Tool to Predict the Effectiveness of Corporate Advertising Campaigns," *Journal of Brand Management*, Vol. 11, September 2003, p. 22.

61. Charles T. Salmon, et al., "The Effectiveness of Advocacy Advertising Relative to News Coverage," *Communication Research*, Vol. 12, October 1985, pp. 546–567.

62. Raymond P. Ewing, "Advocacy Advertising: The Voice of Business in Public Policy Debate," *Public Affairs Review*, Vol. 3, 1982, pp. 35–39.

63. Ibid.

64. See S. Prakash Sethi, *W.R. Grace and Company, New York—A Short-Burst, High Intensity, Saturation Campaign in Advocacy Advertising*. (Center for Research in Business and Social Policy, School of Management and Administration, University of Texas at Dallas, 1980).

65. Joseph Klapper, "What We Know About the Effects of Mass Communication: The Brink of Hope," *Public Opinion Quarterly*, Vol. 21, Winter, 1957–58, pp. 453–474.

66. James A. Barnes, "Privatizing Politics," *National Journal*, Vol. 27, June 3, 1995, pp. 1330–1334.

67. Coe, op. cit., p. 33.

68. Ibid., pp. 33–34.

69. Debbie Coakley, "Ag Advocacy Advertising Alive and Well," *Agri Marketing*, *Skokie*, Vol. 35, April 1997, pp. 74–76.

70. Two of the companies whose plant licenses date back to the 1950s are Duke Power's Oconee plant in South Carolina and Baltimore Gas & Electric Co.'s Calverg Cliffs plant in Maryland. "Nuclear Industry Seeks to Active 'Silent' Supporters," *O'Dwyer's Report*, Vol. 12, September 1998, pp. 1, 49.

71. Ibid.

72. Elliott, op. cit.

73. Tony Spaeth, "The Name Game," *Across the Board*, Vol. 39, March–April 2002, pp. 27–31.

74. Alan Siegel, "Defining the Corporate Voice; Corporate Identity," *Across the Board*, Vol. 31, November 1994, p. 56.

75. Ibid.

Chapter 7

Holding the Media
Accountable and Suing

A long-term corporate strategy is gradually to change the behavior of journalists and news organizations by exerting various kinds of pressures on them, with the aim of reforming their policies and practices. This strategy extends the short-term options already discussed—taking full advantage of current media practices, outsmarting the media, and buying time and space in the media.

The new strategy is to hold the media accountable to their own journalistic standards and the same laws and standards of society the media expect others to uphold. Unfortunately, many reporters reflect the attitude attributed to them by William Greider at a seminar: "Are the news media responsible to their audience? Are they responsible for what their audience knows and understands? A dozen reporters and TV types ... said, 'Hell no, that's not what we do. We do news.'"[1]

Greider's cynical comment overlooks a major development in the past decade: a significant increase in "media reporting" and "media criticism." In *Media Ethics & Accountability Systems*,[2] Claude-Jean Bertrand considers these forms of self-regulation as part of larger "media accountability systems," which he defines as "any non-State means of making media responsibility towards the public."[3] Included among these systems are press councils, codes of ethics, journalism reviews, ombudsmen, and some nongovernmental institutions concerned with media issues. He urges media owners, media professionals, and media consumers to hold the news media accountable.

Some of these systems flourished in the late 1960s and early 1970s when social unrest grew. During this time and after, however, media criticism languished because the news media turned blind eyes on the failings of colleagues. That changed in the mid-1990s when there was

171

"an absolute explosion of the genre of media reporting and media criticism in the United States."[4] *The New York Times*, the *Washington Post*, the *Boston Globe*, and other leading newspapers now regularly report on media behavior. Magazines like *Time* and *The New Yorker* and broadcast media like CNN's *Reliable Sources* and National Public Radio's weekly *On the Media*. also engage in media criticism.[5] As stated by the *Washington Post*'s Howard Kurtz, the "essence" of his job was "to hold journalists and news organizations accountable."[6]

Media self-criticism has become more urgent as several major newspapers admitted that their reporters violated journalistic standards. To its great embarrassment, the prestigious *New York Times* faced a scandal over years of journalistic fraud committed by its reporter Jayson Blair. On May 11, 2003, the paper published a long article describing his "widespread fabrication and plagiarism" in at least 36 of 73 articles written since he started writing national news stories. These stories included the Washington-area sniper shootings and stories about the families of U.S. military personnel serving in Iraq. While he was in New York, his stories contained datelines from elsewhere. The management style of its top editors and the paper's internal processes were also at fault. Intent on pushing affirmative action, Howell Raines, the paper's executive editor, gave Blair, an African American, strong encouragement and support. A culture had evolved at the *New York Times* that failed to respond to reported suspicions by staff members about Blair's reporting. Taking responsibility, Raines and Gerald M. Boyd, the managing editor, resigned after 5 weeks of furor over the Blair affair. Raines gets credit, however, for the paper's winning of eight Pulitzer Prizes during the 2 years he was in charge of the newsroom.[7]

A similar problem of story fabrications occurred at *USA Today*, where one of the newspaper's star reporters, foreign correspondent Jack Kelley, was found to have dishonestly reported dozens of articles between 1991 and 2003 and having stolen at least 100 passages from other publications, some word for word. It was another case of the "'Golden Boy' syndrome: executives coddling a charming and charismatic star performer and ignoring repeated warnings about the reliability of his work from outsiders and insiders." The held perception in the newsroom was that Kelley was untouchable, partly because a "careerism culture" at the paper led some editors to put career concerns above the integrity of the news report.[8]

Other publications had also reported failures of journalistic ethics. Stephen Glass, who was associate editor at the *New Republic*, invented 27 of the 41 articles he wrote; Mike Barnicle, a veteran *Boston Globe* columnist, resigned after he was charged with plagiarism and fabrication; Patricia Smith, another *Boston Globe* columnist, was asked to resign after admitting she invented people and quotations; and CNN producers April Oliver and Jack Smith were fired after reporting an unsupportable two-part special accusing the Pentagon of using nerve gas against U.S. Army defectors in Laos in 1970.[9]

Finally, the vaunted CBS, once considered the nation's top broadcast news division, suffered an embarrassing lapse of professional journalism. In his September 8, 2004, report "For the Record," Dan Rather claimed on CBS's *60 Minutes* that memos proved that President Bush shirked his National Guard Service duty. The story had special significance because it was aired in the heat of the presidential election. Within hours of the broadcast, the CBS report was attacked, starting with conservative websites that pointed to suspect typography (suggesting that the "typing" was by a modern printer). Rather stood by the story and CBS "brushed aside criticism."[10] Finally, after 12 days, CBS said the use of the documents was "a mistake" and Dan Rather admitted that CBS could "no longer vouch" for the authenticity of the news. He apologized, "I want to say personally and directly, I'm sorry" for the story. The source of the documents, Bill Burkett, a retired and disgruntled National Guard lieutenant colonel, who confessed he misled the network about where he had obtained the documents but wouldn't say where they came from.[11]

A subsequent scathing 224-page report from an independent review panel held Mary Mapes, an award-winning producer, mainly responsible. It said that carelessness and "myopic zeal" tainted the CBS production. In her zeal to defend the story, the report said, she ignored or brushed aside legitimate concerns about the story regarding how thoroughly she personally vetted the documents and their source. Bob Steele of the Poynter Institute for Media Studies cited other failures: heavy reliance on Burkett, who had written scathing online commentaries about Bush, and failure to uphold its "ethical responsibility" to interview key people, such as the secretary of the supposed writer of the documents, before rushing to air.[12] After the report's release, CBS fired Mapes and asked three senior news executives to resign. Dan Rather escaped punitive action; he had previously announced plans to retire from the "Evening News" in March 2005. In blunt terms, the review panel outlines how the news division repeatedly failed to carry out "basic journalistic steps" to ensure accurate and fair reporting.

The business community is not wholly depending on media self-regulation to achieve accountability. They are also pursuing other strategies to protect themselves: (a) using media monitoring and oversight groups, (b) launching a media blitz against misrepresentation, (c) acquiring media ownership and membership on media boards of directors, (d) engaging in public journalism, and (e) suing news organizations that engage in libel or defamation or that use illegal means to obtain news.

USING MEDIA MONITORING AND OVERSIGHT GROUPS

Two major types of organizations monitor the treatment of news by the media and judge complaints made about them: media watchdogs and news councils.

Media Watchdogs

Corporations are helped by organizations that monitor and report on the performance of the news media. Although they reflect varying political persuasions, most are conservative. Among media watchdog organizations are Accuracy in Media, Center for Media and Public Affairs, Fairness & Accuracy in Reporting, the Institute for Media Analysis, and the Media Research Center.[13] The largest is the Media Research Center, launched in 1987 by L. Brent Bozell, III, with the mission of promoting balance in the "liberal media." In 1993 it had a staff of 24 who logged and indexed every network, CNN, and PBS newscast and talk show. It also reviewed 50 magazines, five major dailies, and the wire services. Its public reporting was conducted mainly through "Notable Quotables," a twice-monthly collection of quotes intended to reflect reporters' liberal biases, and a monthly newsletter, *MediaWatch*, with a circulation of 27,000. In 1990 it published a book, *And That's the Way It Isn't: A Reference Guide to Media Bias.*[14]

Dan Rather has become very aware of conservative media activists like the Media Research Center's Bozell, noting they are "all over your telephones, all over your e-mail, all over your mail," and it "creates an undertow in which you say to yourself 'you know, I think we're right on this story, I think we've got it in the right context, I think we've got it in the right perspective, but we better pick another day....'"[15] Peter Jennings expressed this apprehension by saying he sensed a degree of "anxiety in the newsroom, and I think it comes in part from the corporate suite."[16] And Tom Brokaw likened the pressures created by Bozell's "pressing a button" to a "kind of tsunami.... He's well organized, he's got a constituency, he's got a newsletter, he can hit a button and we'll hear from him."[17] Robert McNeil warns against pressure turning into a "culture of animosity" in which "motives are attacked, morals are attacked and even patriotism is questioned."[18]

Occasionally these watchdogs try to apply pressure on the media; e.g., Fairness & Accuracy in Reporting took out a quarter-page op-ed ad in the Sunday edition of the *New York Times* carrying the headline, "Is Bigotry a Disney Family Value?"[19] Addressed to Mr. Michael D. Eisner, chairman and CEO of The Walt Disney Co., the ad attacked the racist comments of host Bob Grant on New York City's WABC Radio. Because Disney owns WABC, the offending station, the ad asked Disney to make its policies clear.

Various publications review media performance. Jude Wanniski's *1991 Media Guide* illustrates how this is done.[20] It reviewed more than 700 journalists and 50 publications in North America, including a commentary on the year's major news stories, broadcast news, and the Canadian press. Its publishers say its primary purpose is to promote quality in journalism. The guide assigns half- to four-star ratings to a list of the 101 "highest rated journalists of 1991," followed by roughly half-page analyses of what each said. (See Box 7.1 for an example of contents.)

Box 7.1   Example Contents of Wanniski's Media Guide

These analyses of journalists cover six groups: (a) commentators; (b) financial reporters and columnists; (c) foreign correspondents; (d) national security/diplomatic correspondents; (e) science, health, and environment reporters (new this year); and (f) social/political reporters. About a sixth of the book is an overview of the print media and broadcast news, another fourth on publications, and the remainder on journalists and their stories. A useful index allows a company to discover who wrote what about the organization.

Exxon Corporation, for example, could find commentaries on six journalists and learn that Peter Nulty of *Fortune*'s board of editors earnestly covers the energy beat and "clearly has knowledge and industry contacts, but almost never uses them to get ahead of the curve." His article, "Exxon's Problem: Not What You Think," is described as an attempt "to psychoanalyze morale and the 'leadership crisis' at Exxon, employing the cutesy *Fortune* style that makes us wince: 'For now, at least, Exxon is as strong as the healthiest oil-rig roustabout.'"[21]

Wanniski's guide also includes overall assessments of various media. C-SPAN is *MediaGuide*'s choice for raw news, mainly on government. *Mother Jones*, it says, is "losing ideological ground to the politically serious *In These Times* and lacking the broad, eclectic spectrum of the *Utne Reader*." And kudos go to the *National Interest*, "this splendid quarterly foreign policy journal," and for Francis Fukuyama's farsighted, "The End of History" (Summer 1989), that shook the intelligentsia globally. It says: "The issue became a 'cause celebre' for analysts, commentators, and strategists everywhere."[22]

News Councils

News councils serve as informal juries to adjudicate complaints by aggrieved parties about distorted media coverage. These councils provide a public hearing without necessitating the cost and time required for legal suits.

National News Council.   A prototype is the former National News Council, an independent body set up in 1973 to review the performance of the national media and to judge specific complaints about news coverage.[23]

Both Shell Oil and Exxon used this council to complain about NBC-TV's unfair coverage of the oil industry during the Arab oil crisis, which was aired in a five-part nightly news series in the fall of 1979. Shell's complaint was leveled at the first broadcast, "Fly Now, Freeze Later," which contended some big oil companies were emphasizing the sale of jet fuel rather than home heating oil. The National News Council agreed with Shell and reported, "Contrary to the impression that the NBC report clearly intended to convey, Shell 'acted in a responsible and careful manner'" when it withdrew from the home heating oil market in the Northeast.[24]

Exxon took issue with the second segment, "Dirty Oil and Dirty Air," which linked the deterioration of air quality in southern Florida to the firm's decision to cut low-sulfur fuel shipments to Florida Power & Light. The council agreed with Exxon that the broadcast was marked by "factual error, the selective use of information, lack of perspective, and the building of effect through innuendo."[25]

The council closed its doors in April 1984 because it felt impotent. "The public doesn't seem to know we're here," lamented Richard Salant, former president of CBS News, who served as council president during its last 10 months. "And worse yet, the press just didn't think we were very useful." In fact, when the council dissolved itself, Creed Black, president of the American Society of Newspaper Editors, summed up the view held by his colleagues: "An editor is accountable to his readers, not some self-appointed group."[26] Despite this disappointment, Salant called the News Council "a valid idea whose time has not yet come, but will in the near future."[27]

As summarized in the *American Journalism Review*, newspaper publishers such as *The New York Times*, *Washington Post*, and the *Boston Globe* have opposed the very idea of news councils for these reasons: (a) they create another obstacle to hard-hitting stories, and some journalists opt not to write a story for fear they will be unfairly targeted; (b) they substitute the judgment of people who don't fully understand the field for the judgment of trained journalists; (c) they are the first step toward government regulation and perhaps censorship; and (c) one could not be sure to find impartial members who would be fair to the media.[28]

Mike Wallace unsuccessfully sought to rekindle the national news council discussion after the bitter experience of defending himself in a suit by General William C. Westmoreland against CBS for a *60 Minutes* segment. In it Wallace alleged the general deliberately deceived his superiors by underestimating enemy troop strength. Westmoreland sued, not because he wanted money, but because he wanted to vindicate himself.

Public hostility and cynicism toward the media have persuaded other media people to join Wallace in reconsidering the idea. He helped bring together NBC, CNN, CBS News, and the editors of the *Detroit News* and the *Louisville Courier-Journal*, as well as 10 other representatives of the media and foundations, at a Ford Foundation meeting on February 26, 1997, to discuss improving the media's credibility and the possibility of reviving a national news council. One of those attending, Charles Eisendrath, director of the Michigan Journalism Fellows program at the University of Michigan, however, favored calling it a "Committee on Professional Standards," not only to express how he perceived the problem, but also to avoid reviving past negative attitudes toward the old news council.[29]

Minnesota News Council.   Mike Wallace's support of some kind of national news council was favorably influenced by his observation of how the Minnesota News Council, one of the two existing state-level councils (the other is in Hawaii), handled the high-profile complaint brought by Northwest Airlines against WCCO-TV for a three-part series shown in spring 1996.

The Minnesota News Council consists of a balanced body of 12 journalists and 12 community representatives, with a state supreme court justice presiding over its public hearings. Its mission is to "exert a moral influence on media behavior."[30] As explained in its literature, "The News Council serves, most of all, an idea: Fairness. We do not describe ourselves, or function, as a watchdog. We are a facilitator. Because the power of the press is so great, we work to create a level playing field, by getting a news outlet to come to the table as an equal with a member of the public who wants to air a complaint."[31]

To qualify for a hearing, a complainant must agree not to sue regardless of the outcome. The council's decision carries no legal weight, but the verdict can embarrass the medium in question. Over its 25-year history, 2,000 complaints have been filed with the council. Of these, most were dropped or settled after council-initiated discussion. Of the 116 that went to hearings, close to half were decided in the media's favor. The case Mike Wallace heard, Northwest Airlines vs. WCCO-TV, is described in Box 7.2.

LAUNCH A MEDIA BLITZ AGAINST
MEDIA MISREPRESENTATION

When General Motors (GM) saw NBC's falsified "Waiting to Explode" segment on *Dateline NBC*, it was so enraged it outdid Herb Schmertz's advice to get confrontational with the media. The subsequent media blitz organized by GM against NBC's misrepresentation was so persistent and intense that it serves as a landmark example of how to hold the media accountable.

The producers of the program had deliberately used incendiary devices to explode the controversial side-mounted gasoline tank on GM pickup trucks manufactured between 1973 and 1987. Inaccuracies in the story were pointed out by GM in a letter to the show's producer, but no action had been taken. GM's good fortune in learning about the deception and in uncovering evidence allowed its general counsel, Harold J. Pearce, to convene a news conference in Detroit to hold NBC publicly accountable for its disreputable behavior. The repercussions were sufficiently severe to stop the practice of falsely staged events (see the full story in the Appendix).

Box 7.2   Northwest Airlines Versus WCCO-TV[32]

Northwest Airlines charged that WCCO-TV of Minneapolis distorted its investigative reporting of alleged safety and maintenance problems. In its three-part series in spring 1996, the station revealed new information on $7,825,000 in fines the Federal Aviation Administration had levied against Northwest for maintenance problems. Among the allegations made by anchor Don Shelby was that Northwest "violated national safety standards and endangered the lives of passengers." He also suggested that the airline pressured mechanics to skimp on maintenance to maintain its on-time record.

Northwest Airlines accused Shelby of relying on questionable sources and failing to put the airline's safety record in context with the records of other airlines. It also found fault with WCCO's promo, which showed a Northwest 747 flying across the screen and appearing to crash.[33]

The council met on October 18, 1996, to deliberate three questions: (a) Did WCCO-TV paint a distorted, untruthful picture of Northwest Airlines? (b) Should promotional announcements for news be held to the same standards as news? (c) If yes, did WCCO-TV's promotions paint a distorted, untruthful picture of Northwest Airlines? Each side was allowed a maximum of 10 minutes to make its case on each of the questions. Then the 24 council members engaged in a Q&A session lasting no more than 40 minutes. The session was open to the public, but total seating was limited to 150, including the news media.

The Council voted in favor of Northwest Airlines on all three questions: 19 to 2, with 1 abstention, on the first question; 14 to 5, with 2 abstentions, on the second question; and 18 to 1, with 3 abstentions, on the third question. As stated by University of Minnesota journalism professor Bill Babcock, director of the Silha Center for the Study of Media Ethics & Law, the Minnesota News Council was saying, "We have a new era here. We are not dealing with the standards of the industry. We are dealing with public standards, which no longer tolerate this kind of work."

Despite the rebuff to WCCO-TV and its presumed embarrassment, the following evening the station won an Emmy award for this investigative series. Editorial writer D. J. Tice of the *St. Paul Pioneer Press* notes that "the sensational expose, regardless of how inadequately the evidence offered supports the accusations made, remains a highly esteemed style in television news."

ACQUIRE MEDIA OWNERSHIP AND BOARD MEMBERSHIP

The ultimate way for corporations to hold the media accountable is to own them. Control over a wide range of media is made easier when ownership is concentrated in media giants that have been emerging through a dizzying procession of mergers and purchases. When the purchasers are in nonmedia industries, grave dangers are added to ownership control. Business values may intrude into, and conflict with, the values of journalism. When controlling companies are themselves the subject of news, they may pressure their news organizations—bluntly or gently—to interfere with newsgathering and reporting. Another way for a corporation to exert top-level influence over news policies is through membership on a newspaper's or network's board of directors.

Concentration of Ownership

Concentration of media ownership in the hands of a few conglomerates may sound appealing from the viewpoint of gaining greater control over the media, but it is dangerous to business because the media are more likely to control them. Six media conglomerates—AOL Time Warner, Disney, Viacom, News Corp, Vivendi, and Bertelsmann—control, to a significant degree, what the American people see, hear, and read. The Federal Communications Commission (FCC) would like to see further consolidation, as discussed in chapter 13. It argues that alternative media, such as the Internet, cable TV, and direct broadcast satellites have made existing limits on ownership less essential. However, even the FCC's own survey in September 2002 reported that people relied primarily on TV for their news and information, 23% on newspapers, 10% on radio, 7% on cable, and even less on the Internet. The danger of further consolidation is that it would lead to less access to diverse channels of communication by business as well as various interest groups.[34] It would also lead to an increase in advertising rates for business and higher cable and satellite prices for consumers.

Recent Consolidation. Two recent purchases indicate the pace and impact of consolidation. In March 2000 the Tribune Company announced it would acquire Times-Mirror, adding the *Los Angeles Times*, *Newsday* on Long Island, and the *Sun* in Baltimore. The Tribune Company would leap from regional to national status and "control enormous content and be in everything from newsprint to magazines to broadcasting and the Net," said *BusinessWeek*.[35] The new statistic was that less than 20% of U.S. dailies, only 264 papers, would be independent. With the sale, the 118-year ownership of the *Los Angeles Times* by the influential Chandler family ended. Although family owners care about making profits, they are not "the corporate behemoths obedient to the quarterly whip of Wall Street."[36] It was *The New York Times* and the *Washington Post*, both family newspapers, that had the courage to publish the Pentagon Papers. As the late Katharine Graham, former chairman of the executive committee of the Washington Post Company, stated, "family ownership provides the independence that is sometimes required to withstand governmental pressure and preserve freedom of the Press."[37]

The biggest acquisition was America Online's purchase of Time Warner in 2000 for $183 billion.[38] The world's biggest online company and the world's biggest media company were joined. Competitors and others expressed fear that the combined company would dominate content and delivery because AOL was the dominant online service and Time Warner the number two cable operator. Time Warner owns four of the most popular cable channels: CNN, TBS, TNT, and the Cartoon Network, as well as HBO, the leading premium cable network.[39] The Federal Trade Commission approved the merger, but took the rare step of appointing a "monitor trustee" to oversee the company for 5 years.[40] In writing about media concentration, Larry Grossman had earlier offered up Time Warner as an example of a corporation that owns major national magazines, is the second biggest operator of cable television systems, holds all or part of the most important cable program networks (including HBO and CNN), and owns a leading movie and television production company, several of the largest book-publishing companies, and the biggest recording companies.[41]

Implications of Media Concentration.   Larry Grossman was one of the early writers warning about the implications of media concentration. The danger he saw was that "the inordinate power of a rich and privileged few ... can dominate the debate, influence the views of the many, and manipulate public opinion."[42] From the perspective of strategic corporate media relations, this situation might have the positive benefit of reining in the power of the so-called liberal press and establishing newsroom awareness of certain limits. The danger, however, is that if the ideas of a particular industry or company are not deemed newsworthy by the conglomerates, or if they oppose them, they simply wouldn't appear. Furthermore, if the conglomerates are critical of some views, they could launch an attack against them. Disappointed in how the national media treated them, some companies in the past (e.g., Alcoa) have been able to send their news releases through local media. However, when the local media are also controlled by the conglomerates, that option vanishes.

Grossman worries about the impact on society, viewing "the shrinking oligopoly of powerful corporate interests" as a danger to democratic pluralism.[43] So do others. *BusinessWeek* warns, "One of the central pillars of America's democracy and market economy is an independent media with multiple voices."[44] The editors of *The New York Times* asked the FCC to take a "holistic approach to deregulation" and "to protect the public interest by managing deregulation in a way that preserves a diversity of news, opinion and entertainment."[45]

Another danger exists in the cross-industry ownership by conglomerates, as illustrated by anecdotal evidence that Time Warner in 1990 canceled publication of a book called *Connections: American Business and the Mob* by one of its book subsidiaries, Little, Brown. The publisher was already in its final round of prerelease publicity for this exposé that linked some U.S. corporations to organized crime. One of the companies named was *Time*. This reference, some believe, was the probable cause for the book's late rejection.[46]

General Electric's Ownership of NBC.

When industrial corporations extend their ownership empire to include media enterprises, the specter of corporate editorial interference with news operations is raised. After General Electric's (GE's) December 1995 deal to acquire RCA and, thereby, NBC, an editorial/opinion column in *The Arizona Republic* raised the question: "What happens if General Electric commits fraud on the Pentagon and NBC has to report it?" Morton Mintz claims that in 1989 "officials of NBC News deleted three sentences critical of GE from a segment of a five-part *Today* show series on the use of bogus and substandard materials in American industry."[47]

An article in the *Humanist* also suggests that the pattern of ownership affects how news and commentary are manufactured. The reference was not only to GE but also to major stockholders of other broadcast networks, such as Chase Manhattan, J. P. Morgan, and Citibank, and to Merrill Lynch as the prime stockholder of the Associated Press.[48] One illustration of possible corporate influence, says the article, is that the concerns of labor are regularly downplayed. A study analyzing all reports dealing with workers' issues—including child care and minimum wage—carried by the ABC, CBS, and NBC evening news broadcasts during 1989 found that coverage amounted to only 2.3% of the total coverage.[49]

Although no solid evidence exists that GE interferes with the news, several sources insist GE's bottom-line mentality permeates every cranny of NBC News. Grossman charges that GE's internal environment emphasizes profits over public service or community responsibility. He recalls that in one of GE Chairman Jack Welch's first meetings with NBC News, he asked why authors, book publishers, and movie companies are not charged for the interviews and feature time they receive on the *Today* show.[50] Most vociferous in his denunciation of the profit-making motive, Andrew Jay Schwartzman, executive director of the Media Access Project, said, "They don't think about the impact of the little cheap, sleazy incremental budget cutting they do."[51]

Disney's Ownership of ABC.

"What's happening to the world as we know it?" asked Bob Harper, Fox marketing president, when he was told by Walt Disney's ABC television network that it would not broadcast ads for Fox's holiday animated film *Anastasia* or any other animated movie during a 7 p.m. Sunday slot that featured a revival of the *Wonderful World of Disney* franchise.[52] This incident shows network ownership can get in the way of the kind of advertising it will carry. ABC's advertising sales representatives blamed higher-ups at Disney for the decision. Fox was told ads for live-action family films during the same time period would be considered only on a case-by-case basis.

From Disney's perspective, such control justifies its purchase of Capital Cities/ABC for $19 billion in 1995.[53] Executives say the company has in essence opted to make ABC part of Disney's film distribution chain. Plans are to air three or four of its recent animated theatrical releases on Sunday evenings, making them a part of the revival of *The Wonderful World of Disney* series.[54] The opportunity to cross-promote Disney and ABC brands was a key attraction of the merger, but some at ABC were surprised "at how blatant such promotions have been."[55] Furthermore, ABC managers were surprised at the level of Disney's scrutiny of their operations and the vastly different corporate cultures.

Yet, what Disney did to ABC is what Disney fears about AOL's acquisition of Time Warner. Disney worries that the television stations owned by Disney's ABC network on Time Warner Cable systems in several markets might be excluded. A number of other entertainment and media companies also expressed concern that the merger would squeeze them out of AOL's online distribution vehicles. For example, without equal access, consumers signing on to AOL could be directed to Warner Music artists. Although AOL's CEO Steve Case and Time Warner chairman Gerald Levin pledged that the merged companies would carry a diversity of content on their systems, they also stated that they would distribute Time Warner's own content as widely as possible.[56]

Interconnections among business and media organizations are another possible means of ownership influence. Mintz raises the question of whether CBS might go easy on the insurance company CNN in reporting the harmful effects of smoking, because Laurence Tisch not only is CBS's chairman but also heads the Loews Corporation, which, in turn, owns CNN and Lorillard, a major cigarette manufacturer.[57]

Even the Public Broadcast System (PBS) is underwritten by GE, GM, Metropolitan Life, Pepsico, Paine Webber, and, contributing more than 70%, four giant oil companies. An article insinuates that this sponsorship is one reason, according to a media watchdog, corporate representatives constitute 44% of the sources interviewed about the economy whereas activists accounted for only 3% and labor virtually none. Furthermore, most PBS documentaries are considered politically nondescript or centrist. *Deadly Deception*, an Academy Award-winning critique of GE and the nuclear arms industry, was, with a few local exceptions, denied broadcast rights on both commercial and public television.[58]

Board Membership

Many corporate heads are on the boards of newspapers, observes Mintz. On Katharine Graham's board at the *Washington Post* are James Burke, retired chairman and CEO of Johnson & Johnson; Nicholas Katzenback, who for many years was senior vice president and general counsel of IBM; and George Gillespie, a long-time partner in Cravath, Swaine & Moore, which Mintz considers to be the nation's premiere corporate law firm.[59]

Mintz suggests that this board membership pattern may be related to why the press failed to report on drug-related deaths revealed at congressional hearings or in court cases where pharmaceutical companies are sued by the victims or their relatives. For example, although three drug companies were convicted and fined for withholding information from the Food and Drug Administration on foreign deaths, press coverage was inadequate. The companies were Hoechst AG, a German-based multinational, on its drug Merital; Smith Kline on Selacryn; and Eli Lilly on Oraflex. Mintz considered the matter a "significant national and international story," deserving of full news status, but it drew only five paragraphs on page B3 of the *Wall Street Journal* and two paragraphs at the bottom of page D4 in *The New York Times*.[60]

ENGAGE IN PUBLIC JOURNALISM

Because media companies are becoming aware of public distrust of the media—through opinion surveys and reduced readership—some newspapers are themselves seeking reform through public journalism projects. The basic idea is to encourage newspeople to create discourse by convening public forums, seeking out the views of ordinary citizens, giving readers more voice in news and on editorial pages, and actively enlisting citizens in a search for solutions to society's problems.[61] Guido H. Stempel, III, author of several journalism articles, says, "The focus of civic journalism is on finding solutions rather than just pointing out problems."[62]

These efforts are called public journalism or civic journalism because their broader goal is to strengthen civic life in America by reengaging in public discourse people who have dropped out of public life. Readers are encouraged to participate in the political process and improve government institutions.[63] The Pew Charitable Trusts, with $3.8 billion in assets, since 1994 have helped to fund projects at 30 American newspapers. For example, in San Jose, California, citizens who are readers of the *Mercury News* drafted a "statement of accountability" and asked lawmakers and candidates to sign it.[64]

Jay Rosen, a New York University journalism professor who has been promoting the concept of public journalism, laments the lack of mature judgment by the public. He blames the media for "reporting too much of the process and minutiae in politics, with too many dueling experts." He sees public journalism as helping the community "come to public judgment." The journalist focuses on readers and viewers rather than on experts. The public is helped to "work through" a problem, which is done by providing information and helping people "understand that there are some choices to be made; that these choices involve tradeoffs; and that there are consequences to choosing."[65]

Although public journalism is now practiced by nearly 200 news organizations, critics fear journalism's traditional objectivity is sacrificed. *Washington Post* editor Leonard D. Downie Jr. reflected this view when he said, "No matter how strongly I feel about something that's going on out there, my job is not to try to influence the outcome."[66] Some journalists fear civic journalism will turn newspapers into advocates and discourage reporters from exposing wrongdoing and failures.[67]

Has public journalism increased public interest in elections and the political process? A 1997 study of the *Record*, a Hackensack, New Jersey, newspaper, that showed 9 weeks and 54 full pages of issues-based coverage in the 1996 New Jersey Senate race failed to interest readers and increase their knowledge of candidates or issues. Only one in five readers said they even noticed the special "Campaign Central" pages, which appeared every day but Saturday inside the paper's front section.

After listening to focus group discussions, editors "felt stunned and somewhat shaken." The study showed that "the frames through which respondents viewed the campaigns seemed to have been shaped mostly by the candidates' commercials." Indeed, 44% of the newspaper's readers said television was their most important source of campaign news.[68] The candidates had spent more than $17 million on television commercials.[69] The newspaper's "public-style" election coverage hardly made any impact on North Jersey voters. In addition, the effort cost the paper about $100,000 in additional newsprint and required almost a dozen reporters and editors to be shifted temporarily from their regular assignments.

One lesson learned applies to journalism in general: Journalists can't reconnect citizens with democratic institutions solely by altering the way they write their stories. Readers best remembered charts, such as a side-by-side grid comparing the environmental positions of the candidates. Charts were significantly easier than prose to understand, and they were more believable. Charts in the "Voter's Guide" were especially useful and noticed.

Another lesson is that newspapers have to back up their rhetoric about "public-style" election coverage with concrete activities of public involvement. The *Record* did conduct a poll to identify issues of public interest. It also conducted a series of "town hall" meetings—open to anyone who returned a coupon published on the page. However, these instruments of public empowerment may have been too weak. The only description of the public forums is that one session gave citizens the opportunity to discuss the issues they felt the campaigns should address (thus duplicating the purpose of the poll) and that other forums "featured debates between the congressional candidates, with citizens, rather than a panel of reporters, asking the questions. All the sessions were recorded for telecast on cable, and excerpts from transcripts were published in the newspaper."[70]

Finally, some obstacles may impede journalism's effectiveness: the public's disenchantment with politics, the lack of dynamic political leaders, and loss of public confidence in the press itself.

SUING THE MEDIA

An extreme way to hold the media accountable is to sue them. A growing number of people and organizations that feel they have been damaged or falsely accused by television news have been retaliating in court.[71] This approach was illustrated in November 1996 when a Miami, Florida, jury ordered ABC News and the producer of *20/20* to pay $10 million to Alan Levan, chairman of Florida Bank Atlantic, and his bank. A November 1991 program had accused him of bilking investors in a series of complex real estate deals. Levan was delighted by the verdict, saying, "We were seeking an apology and a change in the way broadcast journalism is conducted."[72]

1996 Becomes a Peak Libel Suit Year

As 1996 came to a close, the *Wall Street Journal* wrote, "A year of tough libel verdicts for the U.S. news media just got tougher."[73] The number of awards filed against journalists increased sharply during the year, and so did the award amounts. A preliminary study by the New York–based Libel Defense Resource Center stated the median libel jury verdict in 1996 before the ABC case was $2.4 million, more than double that in the previous 2-year period and more than 10 times the 2-year median of $175,000 in 1992 and 1993. ABC attorney Floyd Abrams explained, "The public for some years has tended to be angry at the mass media even as it watches it."[74]

More people and corporations have felt this way since television news executives and editors began ordering more investigative stories in the aftermath of Watergate. As seen by plaintiffs and their attorneys, reporters are "a bunch of hip-shooters ... who don't know what they're doing, and they ought to be taught a lesson."[75]

Another impetus to suing the press is the existence of new nonprofit organizations that provide necessary legal support. Reflecting their purpose and mood is the American Legal Foundation, which established the Libel Prosecution Resource Center. As stated by Michael P. McDonald, the foundation's general counsel, "We're going to throw open the doors of the center to people who feel that they have been assaulted by news organizations, who feel that they are media victims and would like to find information about how they can vindicate their rights in court."[76]

A final incentive is the Supreme Court's changing and seemingly antagonistic stance toward the media, which stems from the early 1980s.[77] There was further cause for alarm in 1993 when the Second U.S. Circuit Court of Appeals unanimously ruled reporters from four newspapers and two networks must relinquish their notes and videotape outtakes of interviews with a criminal-defense lawyer.[78]

Cases of Deceptive or Careless Newsgathering

Overzealous reporters sometimes use fraudulent means to obtain their news. In 1993 three CNN reporters piggybacked on a search warrant when they joined 18 Fish and Wildlife agents to search a Montana ranch where the owner, Paul Berger, was suspected of poisoning eagles preying on his sheep. The three reporters, dressed in the same clothes as the federal agents, hid their identities and were wearing wires feeding a CNN tape. The search warrant did not mention the inclusion of CNN reporters. Berger and his wife sued the federal government and CNN for violating their Fourth Amendment rights against unreasonable search and seizure.[79]

Major Cases of Deceptive News Practices.   A major case of deceptive newsgathering involved ABC News and Food Lion. At the end of November 1991, a federal jury ruled ABC News reporters committed fraud by posing as employees in the supermarket chain of Food Lion to produce a hidden-camera report on alleged unsanitary food-handling practices at the stores. Food Lion sued ABC, not on the usual grounds of libel but on the legality of its newsgathering techniques.[80] Box 7.3 describes the details. A second celebrated case of media deception is the invasion of the Chiquita Brands International computerized voice mail system by reporter Michael Gallagher of the *Cincinnati Enquirer*, which is reviewed in Box 7.4.

The Food Lion suit motivated participants in a seminar at the Poynter Institute for Media Studies to update the criteria the Society of Professional Journalists uses to determine when it is justifiable for journalists to use deception for a story. The following conditions must be met:

- When the information sought is of profound importance. It must be of vital public interest, such as the revelation of great "system failure" at top levels, or it must prevent profound harm to individuals.
- When all other alternatives to obtain the same information have been exhausted.
- When the journalists are willing to disclose fully and openly the nature of the deception and the reason for it to those involved and to the public.
- When journalists and their news organization apply excellence, through outstanding craftsmanship and the commitment of time and funding to the project, to fully pursue the story.
- When the harm prevented by the information revealed through deception outweighs any harm caused by the act of deception.
- When the journalists have followed a meaningful, collaborative, and deliberative decision-making procedure in which they weigh the following:
  - The consequences (short and long term) of the deception on those being deceived.
  - The impact on journalistic credibility.
  - The motivations for their actions.
  - The deceptive act in relation to their editorial mission.

Box 7.3   Food Lion Suit Against ABC

Food Lion's successful civil suit against ABC for fraudulent news-gathering techniques led Tom Smith, president and CEO of Food Lion, to say the jury "has told ABC that networks, producers and reporters, like everyone else in the country, are not above the law."[81] The case was encouraging to companies fighting damaging reports from television news organizations. The number of claims based on news-gathering issues had been rising, said Sandra Baron, executive director of the Libel Defense Resource Center. She noted, "It seems that what plaintiffs are hoping for is that the public at large is not going to like some of the tools of the trade, such as hidden cameras and hidden mikes."[82]

By not filing a libel suit, Food Lion never denied the truth of the November 1992 *PrimeTime Live* segment that it had "routinely foisted rotted and infected food on an unwitting public."[83] The story contained references to spoiled chicken, rotted fish, and rats in the cheese. However, the jurors never saw this program because this was not a libel case in which the truth of the matter counted; the case was about the methods used by ABC producers in an undercover investigation. Reporters obtained jobs at Food Lion by lying about their previous work experience and giving phony references. Once employed, they gathered data with cameras hidden in their hair and other equipment tucked into their bras. In the 2 years following the disclosures, however, Food Lion closed 84 stores and laid off thousands of employees, presumably because of loss of consumer confidence.[84]

When the jury decided on a $5.5 million verdict against ABC, its message was that media deception and misrepresentation had gone too far.[85] In the words of Marvin Kalb, a veteran broadcaster who is now director of Harvard University's Joan Shorenstein Center on the Press, Politics and Public Policy, lying became the rule when it should have been the exception: "The use of deception is so widespread and sophisticated it demeans journalism and damages badly the journalist and the public."[86]

- The legal implications of the action.
- The consistency of their reasoning and their action.[87]

This tightened code addresses the broader message of the Food Lion jury decision, which, according to Scott Andron, business reporter for the *News & Record* in Greensboro, North Carolina, is this: "The public does not like us, does not trust us and does not understand us. If we don't start explaining our work better to the public—and, where appropriate, cleaning up our ethical decision-making—we can expect more large punitive damage verdicts in the future."[88] In light of the new code,

---

Box 7.4   Cincinnati Enquirer *Invades Voice Mail of Chiquita.*

Another case of deceptive practices is the invasion of Chiquita Brands International computerized voice mail system by reporter Michael Gallagher of the *Cincinnati Enquirer* in violation of state wiretapping laws. With the help of a corporate insider, he wrote an 18-page report based on information obtained from 2,000 voice mail messages. The report charged Chiquita with union-busting, pesticide poisoning, and shady dealings in Central America, and included allegations of a Colombian bribery scheme.

Eight weeks after the articles were run, the *Enquirer* fired Gallagher, apologized, and paid Chiquita more than $10 million (some say the sum was closer to $15 million) in "one of the quickest and most expensive settlements in media history." The apology appeared on the front page and was signed by the *Enquirer*'s editor, Lawrence Beaupre, and publisher, Harry Whipple. They said they had become convinced "'representations, accusations and conclusions' about Chiquita in the series 'are untrue and created a false and misleading impression of Chiquita's business practices.'" In a memo to the newspaper's managers, the publisher said Gallagher "lied to us repeatedly over a period of nearly a year.... His deception was massive."

Daniel Schorr, senior news analyst for National Public Radio, labels this investigative story as one "that is accurate and may perform a real public service, but raises questions about how the information was obtained." The larger lesson is "businesses, feeling the pressure of stepped-up financial reporting over the last decade, are becoming bolder about attacking journalists publicly and with lawsuits." Gallagher was later sued separately by Chiquita.

---

it is also important to add that in its own defense, ABC commented, "We never engage in undercover activities lightly, but sometimes they are necessary to bring stories of real importance to the public's attention."[89]

As an epilogue to the case, U.S. District Judge N. Carlton Tilley, Jr. ruled the $5.5 million award to Food Lion was out of proportion to the actual harm suffered and was unconstitutional. He said Food Lion would have to accept a $315,000 award or he would order a new trial. The company accepted the reduced award, but ABC decided to appeal further.[90]

Judge Tilley's ruling was not based on support for the First Amendment rights of the press; rather it was based on the concept of considering the ratio of actual damages to punitive damages. This argument was used in a 1996 case in which the Supreme Court struck down a jury's $2 million award against a BMW dealer who was sued by a doctor because the dealer had failed to disclose the paint of the car he purchased had been scratched before it was sold to him. The court considered the ratio of 500 to 1 excessive. Likewise in the Food Lion case, the ratio of the $1,402 in actual damages to the $5.5 million in punitive damages is about 3,900 to 1.[91]

Careless News-Gathering.   Deception is sometimes mixed with carelessness in the news-gathering process. The following are some prominent cases.

- U.S. Army General William C. Westmoreland sued CBS and several individuals for more than $100 million because, in a January 1982 broadcast, "The Uncounted Enemy: A Vietnam Deception," he was accused of being part of a "conspiracy" to underestimate enemy strength in the Vietnam War. Litigation lasted more than two years, and legal costs were estimated at $113 million. He dropped his case, however, before it went to the jury. Many people agreed CBS was unfair in using the loaded word *conspiracy* and stacking the decks against the general.

- Israeli General Ariel Sharon sued Time, Inc., for $50 million, charging the magazine with "blood libel" for implying he had encouraged the massacre of Palestinians at the Sabra and Shatila Palestinian refugee camps in Beirut, Lebanon. The story claimed Sharon had discussed "revenge" with the Lebanese Phalangists just before the massacre. Although the jury agreed the story was false, he lost his case because the jury did not find *Time* guilty of the other two elements of a successful libel suit: that the story was defamatory and that it was written with actual malice. *Time* was embarrassed when testimony revealed that the cover story was based on a "damning paragraph" from an interoffice memorandum written by an Israeli reporter, David Halevy, in *Time*'s Jerusalem bureau. On cross-examination, Halevy admitted he had no basis for his accusation other than an inference "based on my 43 years of living in Israel."

- Paul Engler's beef against Oprah. Illustrating the trend to sue the media is the $6.7 million suit by cattleman Paul Engler against Oprah Winfrey and others because of losses incurred when, on her show in April 1996, she referred to England's recent mad-cow disease outbreak as "the biggest health crisis since Chernobyl." Worse yet, after her guest, a food safety activist, opined that mad cow posed a dire threat to America as well, Winfrey exclaimed, "It has just stopped me from eating another burger."[92]

Attesting to the power of some television shows, the prices of cattle and cattle futures plunged on the day of the television show, resulting in a loss of $6.7 million for Engler, who runs a big cattle-feeding operation and ranch. The legal basis for his suit is that Texas, where the suit was filed, is one of 12 states that has a False Disparagement of Perishable Food Products law—passed after the U.S. apple industry was pummeled by the Alar scare. The law states a critic of agricultural products can be held liable if the criticism isn't based on "reliable scientific inquiry, facts, or data."[93] With this law as his weapon, Engler sued not only Oprah Winfrey but also her production company, Harpo Productions, Inc.; the show's distributor, King World Production, Inc.; and beef critic Howard Lyman, who is a National Humane Society official. His fellow ranchers cheered him on. Said one, "Don't argue. Go over and blow the hell out of them." Another said, "The only Mad Cow in America is Oprah."[94]

After nearly 6 weeks, during which Winfrey moved her television show from Chicago to Amarillo, Texas, where the trial took place, the jury voted she and the other defendants did not hurt Amarillo ranching families and their cattle companies.[95]

Effects of Libel Suits: The Media Become More Careful, and Some Are Intimidated

After the Westmoreland and Sharon suits, Mike Wallace neatly summed up their effects: There is a need to "be damned careful.... Put it [the story] through your typewriter once again or put it through the screening process once again to make absolutely certain that it can withstand the kind of scrutiny that we give other people, other events—government, business." He added, "There should never have been a lawsuit and there wouldn't have been if all of us at CBS had been more intelligent in handling the reaction to that broadcast." For example, Westmoreland said he would have been satisfied earlier with the statement CBS made to have the suit dropped, namely, that it "never intended to assert, and does not believe, that General Westmoreland was unpatriotic or disloyal in performing his duties as he saw them."[96]

60 Minutes Temporarily Succumbs to Tobacco Industry.   Mike Wallace leveled some sharp criticism at CBS for succumbing to a threatened lawsuit by Brown & Williamson Tobacco when in November 1995 it canceled a segment of *60 Minutes* containing an interview with "Jeffrey Wigand, PhD, B&W's former vice president of research." The company accused CBS of inducing Wigand to break a confidentiality contract with it. In the interview, Wigand accused B&W's former chairman, Thomas Sandefut Jr., of lying before Congress when he and other industry executives maintained a solid front in declaring that they did not manipulate levels of nicotine in cigarettes. Wigand also said B&W enhanced the effect of nicotine through the use of various chemical carcinogens, including ammonia, through a process known as "impact boosting," which results in nicotine being absorbed into the lungs faster and affecting the central nervous system more quickly. On a personal note, he claimed in his *60 Minutes* interview that he received threatening phone calls, such as, "Leave tobacco alone, or else you'll find your kids hurt," and, "Don't mess with tobacco any more. How are your kids?"

The 1999 movie *The Insider* dramatizes the way the CBS program handled the report on the tobacco industry in 1995. Don Hewitt, executive producer of *60 Minutes*, criticized Lowell Bergman, who consulted on the film and was portrayed as a principled reporter who eventually quit his job over CBS's handling of the report. Mr. Hewitt was cast as more concerned with CBS's stock price than the truth. Hewitt said that by turning himself into a hero and portraying Hewitt as a toady, Bergman lied, destroying his credibility as a journalist.[97]

In a substitute program, *60 Minutes* reported on the lengths to which the tobacco industry has gone to muzzle its critics. In a personal note at the close of the program, Mike Wallace said the program's staff had been "dismayed that the management of CBS had seen fit to give in to perceived threats of legal action." He added, "We lost out—only to some degree—on this one, but we haven't the slightest doubt that we'll be able to continue the *60 Minutes* tradition of reporting such pieces in the future, without fear or favor."[98] On hearing Wallace's statement, Richard Campbell, author of a book on *60 Minutes*, quipped, "Unless it involves the tobacco industry." He added, "But I think the end result was pretty *weak-kneed*," and noted the program's failure to mention the management decision came as CBS stockholders were considering a merger with the Westinghouse Electric Company.[99] *The New York Times*'s comment on the cancellation of the original program was that "In so doing, in the eyes of some journalism analysts, the program risked its twenty-seven-year reputation for taking on any subject, no matter how large or powerful."[100] Said Marvin Kalb: "I think what happened here is proof of the primacy of lawyers over editors."[101]

Small dailies and weeklies particularly have felt the chilling effect the proliferation of libel suits has had on aggressive reporting. They lack the size, money, and resources to fight them and are often unduly influenced by social and financial pressures in their local communities. These factors, rather than the fear of losing libel cases, have caused editors to become more cautious in their approach to investigative stories and even routine but controversial reporting about public figures.[102]

The threat of suits has helped to improve journalistic accuracy. Reporters are more apt to double-check their facts rather than prove a preconceived story. Editors and publishers are also likely to be more responsible by checking for factual accuracy and moving away from the use of unnamed sources.

The media may also be learning better manners. A study by Gilbert Cranberg of the Iowa Libel Research Project found that unsatisfactory postpublication experiences with the press influenced most of the 164 interviewed libel plaintiffs to file libel suits.[103] They complained that when they called the newspaper, they were bounced from one person to another. When they did reach someone, they often received such discourteous responses as, "Well, that's just the way we do it, buddy! That's our policy," or even worse: "Fuck you, you're full of shit."[104] Instead of cooling them down, calls to the press made the aggrieved parties angrier, and they sued. Cranberg, whose goal is to develop nonlitigation methods to deal with libel complaints, gives the following advice to editors:

- Remind employees of the great power of the press to hurt people and of the need therefore to treat complainants courteously.
- Assign responsibility for dealing with complaints to a person who has good human relations skills and who is not also responsible for news coverage.
- Develop written policies and procedures for addressing complaints.
- Make sitting on serious complaints a firing offense.[105]

By following these rules, public attitudes toward the media are likely to be improved and serious grievances avoided.

CONCLUSIONS

On a day-to-day basis, a business that dislikes a news story about itself can call a medium's reporter and editor or producer and voice its displeasure. Corrective action may or may not follow, and the long-term impact of such calls may be minimal. New strategies are more powerful and are aimed at producing institutional changes in media structure and behavior. By supporting media-monitoring activities and news watchdogs, corporations can expose bad reporting and undermine public confidence in the media. The public journalism movement is one sign the media are sensitive to public opinion and want to involve the public more. However, the ultimate weapon of business is to sue news organizations—not only for libel but also for using illegal news-gathering techniques. Occasionally those sued are not the media but activists who allegedly make wrongful accusations that garner media attention.

APPENDIX
GM ONE-UPS NBC ON
"WAITING TO EXPLODE" PICKUP TRUCKS

On November 17, 1993, a 15-minute segment on *Dateline NBC* showed how a GM pickup truck with a side-mounted gasoline tank exploded and burst into flames when another vehicle struck the tank side of the truck. Viewers were led to believe what some motorists and the National Highway Traffic Safety Administration (NHTSA) were claiming, that the 10 million pickup trucks built between 1973 and 1987—4.7 million of which were still on the road—were unsafe.[106] GM had insisted the trucks were safe and posed no greater risk of postcollision fire than Ford and Dodge full-size pickups. NBC's "Waiting to Explode" show seemed to undermine GM's position.

Not only was GM's reputation at stake; it also faced 30 separate class action suits. In a major defeat in February 1993, GM was struck with a whopping $105.2 million verdict in an Atlanta court in the highly publicized case of 17-year-old Shannon Moseley, who, in 1989, was killed in a crash of a GM pickup truck.[107] Secretary Federico F. Pena of the NHTSA stated GM "appears to have made a decision favoring sales over safety," and asked for a recall of the trucks.[108] GM could have faced $1 billion in costs, plus lost sales.

Good luck, followed by careful investigation, exposed the fact that the NBC reporter had placed incendiary devices under the GM truck, overfilled the gas tank, and left the gas cap loose so the truck would explode and burst into flames. The break for GM came when the editor of *Popular Hot Rodding* magazine received a call from a reader telling him of a firefighter who was on the scene of the staged crash and videotaped the whole test, saying he thought the explosion had been rigged. After investigators checked 22 junkyards, they found the trucks used in the test and discovered a spent model rocket engine in the bed of one of the pickups. (It was later disclosed the rocket engines had been detonated by remote control.)[109]

Using this evidence, GM general counsel Harold J. Pearce held a news conference in Detroit and, after revealing the facts, called NBC's news program an "outrageous misrepresentation and conscious deception."[110] The two-hour news conference was telecast to GM offices, factories, and dealers throughout the country.[111]

Although in January GM had sent a letter outlining some of its findings to *Dateline* producer Robert Read, he did not inform NBC News president Michael Gartner. The latter learned about GM's letter only after a second letter, dated February 1, was copied and sent to him and to NBC president Robert Wright.[112] After NBC held its crisis meeting, Gartner sent a letter to GM asserting three separate times that the NBC story was entirely accurate: "NBC does not believe that any statements made … were either false or misleading…. The Dateline report … was and remains completely factual and accurate."[113] However, after NBC officials watched the GM news conference, they decided on a settlement. Jane Pauley, the anchor, apologized on the air the next day.[114]

Mounting criticism from the journalism establishment and concerns by NBC affiliate stations about withdrawal of advertising by GM dealerships helped convince NBC the settlement was desirable. Marvin Kalb, a former network news correspondent, commented that a television journalist would have been fired for pulling such a stunt in years past; he lamented, "But so radically have journalistic news standards changed over the last 20 to 30 years that a network can now do this kind of simulation—and then argue that it pursued a proper journalistic course. I find it rather astounding."[115] CBS's *60 Minutes* executive producer Don Hewitt stated, "There was no reason to do that. They had a pretty good story up to that point. You can't ever play fast and loose with the people who watch you, or you lose them."[116]

Gartner stated he would move with "deliberate speed" on an internal review of what went wrong, but in early March he decided to resign.[117]

ENDNOTES

1. Donald K. Baldwin, editor, *Making Sense of the News* (St. Petersburg, FL: Modern Media Institute, 1981), p. 6.
2. Claude-Jean Bertrand, *Media Ethics & Accountability Systems* (New Brunswick, NJ: Transaction, 2000), p. 149.
3. Susanne Fengler, "Holding the News Media Accountable: A Study of Media Reporters and Media Critics in the United States," *Journalism & Mass Communication Quarterly*, Vol. 80, Winter 2003, p. 818.
4. Ibid., p. 819. Refers to Bertrand, op. cit., p. 132.
5. Ibid., pp. 819–820.
6. Ibid., p. 826.
7. Editorial, "Leadership at The Times," *New York Times*, June 6, 2003, p. A32.
8. Jame Bandler, "Report Cites 'Virus of Fear' at USA Today," *Wall Street Journal*, April 23, 2004, p. B1.
9. See Jonathan Chait, "Bad Press," *The New Republic*, Vol. 229, November 10, 2003, pp. 20–23.
10. Brooks Barnes and Joe Flint, "Four to Leave CBS News in Wake of '60 Minutes' Probe," *Wall Street Journal*, January 11, 2005, p. B1. Also see James Rainey and Scott Gold, *Los Angeles Times*, January 16, 2005, p. A1.
11. Joe Flint and Greg Hitt, "Rather Retreats, Calling Report 'A Mistake,' " *Wall Street Journal*, September 21, 2004, p. B1.
12. Ibid., p. B4.
13. See Bob Davis, "Self-Styled Media Critic Dissects TV Coverage to Expose Perceived Liberal Bias at Networks," *Wall Street Journal*, August 15, 1996, p. A12.
14. "Watchdog Watch," *American Journalism Review*, Vol. 5, April 1993, pp. 32–34.
15. Eric Altman, "Anchors Aweigh: The Refs Are Working," *The Nation*, November 1, 2004, p. 12.
16. Ibid.
17. Ibid.
18. Said on "The Connection," a WBUR program in Boston, January 18, 2005.
19. Ad appeared March 31, 1996, p. E15.
20. Jude Wanniski, *1991 Media Guide*, 6th annual edition (Morristown, NJ: Polyconomics, 1991).
21. Charlene J. Brow, Trevor R. Brown, and William L. Rivers, *The Media and the People* (New York: Holt, Rinehart & Winston, 1978), pp. 395–396.
22. Ibid., p. 232.
23. Ibid., p. 172.
24. "Blowing the Whistle," *Industry Week*, July 21, 1980, p. 42.
25. Ibid.
26. William Rivers, *Backtalk: Press Councils in America* (San Francisco: Canfield Press, 1972), p. 115.
27. Thomas Griffith, "Watchdog Without a Bite," *Time*, April 9, 1984, p. 103.
28. Alicia C. Shepard, "Going Public," *American Journalism Review*, Vol. 19, April 1997, p. 29.
29. Ibid., p. 28.

30. "News Council Finds Coverage 'Untruthful,' But Wins Emmy," *pr reporter,* Vol. 39, November 11, 1996, pp. 1–2.
31. Ibid.
32. Ibid.; G. Bruce Knecht, "Media: Rare Breed: Media Watchdog With Some Bite," *Wall Street Journal,* November 20, 1996, p. B-1; Mike Wallace, "The Press Needs a National Monitor," *Wall Street Journal,* December 18, 1996, p. A20; and Shepard, op. cit., pp. 24–29.
33. Shepard, op. cit., pp. 28–29.
34. "Beware Media Consolidation," *BusinessWeek,* May 26, 2003, p. 126.
35. Joseph Weber, "This Old-Media Deal Has New-Media Promise," *BusinessWeek,* March 27, 2000, p. 46.
36. Susan E. Tifft, "American Journalism Loses Another Family," *Wall Street Journal,* March 14, 2000, p. A30.
37. Katharine Graham, "Journalistic Family Values," *BusinessWeek,* July 8, 2002, p. 118.
38. Martin Peers, Nick Wingfield, and Laura Landro, "Media Blitz: AOL, Time Warner Leap Borders to Plan a Mammoth Merger," *Wall Street Journal,* January 11, 2000, p. A1.
39. Catherine Yang, "A Real Test for Trustbusters," *BusinessWeek,* July 17, 2000, pp. 78, 81.
40. Dan Carney, "Who Will Watch AOL's Watchdog?" *BusinessWeek,* January 8, 2001, p. 39.
41. Lawrence K. Grossman, *The Electronic Republic: Reshaping Democracy in the Information Age* (New York: Viking, 1995), pp. 200–201.
42. Ibid., p. 173.
43. Ibid.
44. Editorial, *BusinessWeek,* July 8, 2002, p. 118.
45. Editorial, "Protecting Media Diversity," *New York Times,* February 23, 2002, p. A14.
46. Gary C. Woodward, *Perspectives on American Political Media* (Boston: Allyn & Bacon, 1997), p. 31.
47. Morton Mintz, "The Pro-corporate Tilt," *Nieman Reports,* Vol. 45, Fall 1999, p. 24. Mintz is a former reporter at the *Washington Post* and chair of the Fund for Investigative Journalism.
48. Michael Parenti, "The Myth of a Liberal Media," *The Humanist,* Vol. 55, January 1995, p. 7.
49. Ibid.
50. Grossman, op. cit., p. 175.
51. Tom Shales, "The Endangered NBC Peacock: How Owner GE Is Ravaging the Once-Proud Network," *Washington Post,* March 29, 1991, p. B1.
52. Bruce Orwall, "Disney's ABC Keeps Ad Hole Mouse-Friendly," *Wall Street Journal,* July 17, 1997, p. B1.
53. Elizabeth Jensen and Thomas R. King, "World of Disney Isn't So Wonderful for ABC," *Wall Street Journal,* July 12, 1996, p. B1.
54. Bruce Orwall, "Disney to Show Its Animated Film Hits on ABC," *Wall Street Journal,* January 6, 1997, p. B6.
55. Ibid.
56. Kathy Chen, "Disney Frets Over AOL Merger Plan," *Wall Street Journal,* March 23, 2000, p. A24.
57. Mintz, op. cit., p. 32.
58. Parenti, op. cit.
59. Mintz, op. cit., pp. 31–32.

60. Ibid., p. 25.
61. Christopher Conte, "Angels in the Newsroom," *Governing Magazine*, August 1996, p. 20.
62. Guido H. Stempel, III, *Media and Politics in America: A Reference Book* (Santa Barbara, Calif: ABC-CLIO, 2003), p. 52.
63. G. Bruce Knecht, "The Newsmakers: Why a Big Foundation Gives Newspapers Cash to Change Their Ways," *Wall Street Journal*, October 17, 1996, p. 1.
64. Ibid.
65. "Public Journalism: Possible Answer to What Ails the Press," in Julie Rovner, "Covering Health Care: Are Reporters Missing the Beat?" A Special Supplement to *Advances*, Issue 3, 1996, p. 2.
66. Ibid.
67. Knecht, op. cit., p. 1.
68. News release, "Public Journalism Can't Do It All," by the Pew Center for Civic Journalism, Washington, DC, May 21, 1997.
69. David Blomquist and Cliff Zukin, "Does Public Journalism Work?: The 'Campaign Central' Experience," Pew Center for Civic Journalism, Washington, DC, May 1997, p. 30.
70. Ibid., p. 6.
71. See William M. Carley, "Bad Reception: As Television News Reporting Gets More Aggressive, It Draws More Suits," *Wall Street Journal*, January 21, 1983, p. 1. For a scholarly compendium of the many recent lawsuits against the press, see Rodney A. Smolla, *Suing the Press: Libel, the Media, and Power* (New York: Oxford University Press, 1987).
72. Kyle Pope, "ABC Network Loses Libel Suit Over '20/20,'" *Wall Street Journal*, December 19, 1996, p. B1.
73. Ibid.
74. Ibid.
75. Carley, op. cit.
76. James E. Roper, "Who's Behind the Media Libel Suits," *Editor and Publisher*, March 2, 1985, pp. 9–10.
77. Carley, op. cit., pp 1, 15.
78. Milo Geyelin, "Limits on Shield for Reporters Alarm Media," *Wall Street Journal*, September 28, 1993, p. A5.
79. Kevin Helliker, "Feathers Fly: CNN Got Its Story About Poisoned Eagles but Rancher Cries Foul," *Wall Street Journal*, September 25, 1997, p. A1.
80. For background of this case, see Barry Meier and Bill Carter, "Undercover Tactics by Television Magazines Fall Under Attack," *New York Times*, December 23, 1996, p. A1.
81. Elizabeth Jensen, "ABC Reporters Committed Fraud in Undercover Report, Jury Rules," *Wall Street Journal*, December 23, 1996, p. B5. The year 2000 started with the announcement of the biggest merger of all: AOL's acquisition of Time Warner for $156.14 billion.
82. Elizabeth Jensen, "ABC Aggressively Contests Suit Over News Gathering," *Wall Street Journal*, August 29, 1995, p. B6.
83. Dorothy Rabinowitz, "ABC's Food Lion Mission," *Wall Street Journal*, February 11, 1997, p. A20.
84. Ibid.
85. Susan Paterno, "The Lying Game," *American Journalism Review*, Vol. 19, May 1997, p. 40.
86. Ibid., p. 43.

87. Ibid., p. 42, which refers to *Doing Ethics in Journalism*, a handbook by the Society of Professional Journalists.
88. Scott Andron, "Message to Journalists More About Trust than Law," *Quill*, Vol. 85, September 1997, p. 15.
89. Barry Meier, "ABC Held Liable for Fraud in Reporting on Store Chain," *New York Times*, December 21, 1996, p. 8.
90. Peter Johnson, "Walters: Viewers Don't Care About News Purity," *USA Today*, October 14, 1997, p. 3D.
91. Scott Andron, "Scratched Car Saves ABC," *Quill*, Vol. 85, September 1997, p. 14.
92. Laura Jereski, "Oprah Knocks Beef, and a Big Rancher in Texas Has a Cow," *Wall Street Journal*, June 3, 1997, p. A1.
93. Ibid.
94. Ibid., p. A8.
95. Sue Anne Pressley, "Oprah Winfrey Wins Case Filed by Cattlemen," *Washington Post*, February 27, 1998, p. A3.
96. Katherine Evans, "Declarations of Victory," *New York Times Book Review*, April 5, 1987, p. 13.
97. Alex Berenson, "'60 Minutes' Producer Aims Bitter Blast at Ex-Colleague," *New York Times*, June 4, 2000, p. NE26.
98. Ibid.
99. Ibid.
100. Bill Carter, "CBS Executives Killed Story, '60 Minutes' Broadcast Says," *New York Times*, November 13, 1995, p. B8.
101. Ibid.
102. In small towns, politicians and businesspeople often gang up on editors and bombard them with lawsuit threats. The size of awards, besides the expenses, intimidates editors. Even libel insurance does not help small papers because they may not be able to afford the deductible and insurance does not cover the time, energy, and loss of morale involved in lengthy court battles. Observers see a danger as small papers pull out of investigative reporting and leave large papers the responsibility to speak out. "Try to imagine a world in which the only available outlets for communication are the huge institutional media." A lawyer for the Libel Defense Resource Center in New York warns that "there are certain officials who don't accept the fact that there's supposed to be a give and take in public issues. They don't believe there should be criticism." David Zucchino, "Publish and Perish; Libel and the Little Publication," *Washington Journalism Review*, Vol. 7, July 1985, pp. 28–35.
103. Gilbert Cranberg, "The Libel Alternative," *Columbia Journalism Review*, Vol. 24, January–February 1986, p. 39.
104. Ibid., p. 40.
105. Ibid., pp. 39–41.
106. Douglas Lavin, "GM Plans a Public Relations Battle After Punitive Award in Pickup Trial," *Wall Street Journal*, February 8, 1993, p. A4.
107. Douglas Lavin, "GM Emerges Victorious as Court Overturns Truck-Safety Verdict," *Wall Street Journal*, June 14, 1994, p. B10.
108. Douglas Lavin and Daniel Pearl, "GM Trucks Had Fuel-Tank Flaw, Regulators Find," *Wall Street Journal*, October 18, 1994, p. A3.
109. Elizabeth Jensen, Douglas Lavin, and Neal Templin, "Tale of the Tape: How GM One-Upped an Embarrassed NBC on Staged News Event," *Wall Street Journal*, February 11, 1993, p. A1.

110. Douglas Lavin, "GM Accuses NBC of Rigging Test Crash of Pickup Truck on 'Dateline' Program," *Wall Street Journal*, February 9, 1993, p. A3.
111. Jensen, Lavin, and Templin, op. cit., p. A7.
112. Ibid.
113. Ibid.
114. James B. Treece et al., "Now, the Court of Public Opinion Has GM Worried," *BusinessWeek*, February 22, 1993, pp. 38–39.
115. Elizabeth Jensen, "Some Journalists Join GM in Criticizing NBC's Treatment of Truck-Crash Story," *Wall Street Journal*, February 10, 1993, p. B1.
116. Ibid.
117. Elizabeth Jensen, "Off the Air: NBC News President, Burned by Staged Fire and GM, Will Resign," *Wall Street Journal*, March 2, 1993, p. A1.

Chapter 8

Bypassing the News Media: Direct Communication

The most drastic way business can reduce the media's power is to break its monopoly as the sole deliverer of news to the public. Companies can bypass the mass media and reach target audiences directly. Traditionally, companies communicate with the public by sending news releases to the media—increasingly electronically by using Business Wire and other electronic news delivery services—and, if the news is sufficiently important, by holding a news conference. This process places the news at the mercy of reporters, editors, producers, and hosts of the mass media who serve as gatekeepers. They decide what stories or segments will be used and what slant each will be given.

This control by the media over what messages reach the public is analogous to labor union control over management communication with unionized employees in the 1940s, which was prescribed by the National Labor Relations Act of 1935. When the Taft-Hartley Act of 1947 finally broke this supposed monopoly of the unions, companies were again allowed to communicate directly with their employees. In the same spirit, companies now want to communicate with their important audiences directly through private or alternative channels, taking advantage of new communication technologies.

Some companies are also rebelling against what they see as the news media's perversion of the traditional reportorial role of objectivity and devotion to news values. Companies in trouble seek other options when they see themselves "being served up as the day's or week's entertainment for the masses by media desperately trying to survive and politicians desperately trying to divert attention from their wholesale failure," says *pr reporter*. The new corporate strategy is to "adopt a low profile, concentrate their energies directly on key stakeholders, avoid

199

controversy and even visibility, focus on your mission and growl at those who try to pull you off course."[1] Bypassing the news media and dealing with the public directly becomes an attractive alternative.

DISENCHANTMENT WITH THE NEWS MEDIA

Public opinion polls, panel discussions, and news stories about questionable behavior by journalists reflect the decline of trust in the news media by both business and the public. Business has some serious misgivings about the media's objectivity, fairness, and devotion to news values. If public cynicism about the media continues to grow, the media's effectiveness may erode to a point where corporate communicators must substitute other channels of communication and influence.

Illustrative of the many questionable journalistic practices that have added to public cynicism is Connie Chung's "Just Between You and Me" episode with Newt Gingrich's mother. Interviewing Gingrich's mother off-air, Chung implied she would keep her comments confidential. Not having had experience in dealing with reporters, Mrs. Gingrich took her promise at face value and gave an honest reply. Chung, however, publicly reported what was said, namely, that her son, Newt Gingrich, thought Hillary Clinton was a "bitch."[2] Trust in the media wanes as the public learns of these improprieties.

Polls Reveal Public Doubts About the Media

The "State of the News Media 2004," which is described as "An Annual Report on American Journalism," reports that public distrust of the news media has been declining over the last 18 years, except for the one up-tick in November 2001, after the 9/11 terrorist attacks. The report asks, "How long can the profession of journalism endure if people increasingly don't believe it?"[3] Some of the changes between 1985 and 2002 include: The number of Americans who think news organizations:

- Are highly professional declined from 72% to 49 %.
- Generally get the facts straight declined from 55% to 35%.
- Care about the people they report on declined from 41% to 30%
- Are politically biased rose from 45% to 59%.

The believability of most news organizations has declined. By August 2002, the percentage of Americans who rated their daily newspaper as highly believable fell from 80% to 59%. The believability ratings of national television networks also declined: ABC News fell from 83% to 65%, CBS from 84% to 64%, and NBC from 82% to 66%. Local news stations also lost believability, falling from 81% to 65%. Among the few who stand out for their relative stability are public broadcasting's *NewsHour* and *The Wall Street Journal.* Andrew Kohut of the Pew Research Center concludes that today the public considers the news media less professional, less accurate, less moral, less helpful to democracy, more sensational, more likely to cover up mistakes, and more biased. The larger problem, he says, is a disconnection between the public and the news media over motive: "Journalists believe they are working in the public interest and are trying to be fair and independent in that cause, but the public thinks these journalists are either lying or deluding themselves. The public believes that news organizations are operating largely to make money and that the journalists who work for these organizations are primarily motivated by professional ambition and self-interest."[4]

A 1996 survey of 3,000 respondents by the Center for Media and Public Affairs showed that a majority of Americans believe "special interests, such as corporate media owners and advertisers, as well as pressure for profits, improperly influence the way news is gathered and presented."[5] Perhaps for this reason, this survey also reports that 53% support licensing of journalists and 70% favor court-imposed fines for inaccurate or biased reporting.[6] Other findings reveal that the media have a negative impact on society:

- 73% of the American public blame the news media for making them dissatisfied with the way things are going in this country— with 43% saying they are dissatisfied "a lot" and 30% saying "somewhat."
- 48% believe that the media make things sound worse than they really are.
- 62% (another survey says 71%) feel the news media get in the way of solving the country's problems.[7]

Researchers and critics have interpreted these survey results in worrisome terms. Kohut says the 1996 survey amounts to a sweeping indictment by a public that appreciates the media's watchdog role but hates the way they practice their craft. He adds that most of the anger is directed at the mainstream media, especially television, which is seen as drifting toward a tabloid mentality that blurs the line between news and entertainment.[8] The late social critic Christopher Lasch worried about the steady decline in Americans' knowledge of public affairs even while they are drowning in information.

Concerns about the failings of journalism were voiced and elaborated on in a 2-day discussion by a panel of journalists and nonjournalists moderated by Hodding Carter III. The panel concluded that journalism has been corrupted and that there exists no mechanism of accountability that fosters trust in the media. Journalism is corrupt in several ways, said the panel: (a) journalistic arrogance, which is manifested when journalists spend more time talking with one another than with people in their communities; (b) too close identification of journalists with their sources to protect their celebrity status, and sacrificing the

ability to obtain truthful news; (c) insufficient understanding by journalists of the subjects they write about, or they "know the truth before
they get the facts"; and (d) "corporatization" of the media, which has replaced locally owned newspapers, a trend that allows profits to be
placed ahead of such goals as informing citizens and protecting their
freedoms. In some instances, community attitudes have become so negative that many communities consider newspapers irrelevant.

Because of these failings, business and conservatives see bias entering
the treatment of such economic issues as inflation by blaming wage and
price hikes on the private sector while government policies, such as creating too much money, are exonerated.[9] Their slant on many stories reflects their obsession with the need to write about conflict. Said another
critic, Adam Gopnik, the media can be faulted for its "tone of high-
minded moral indignation" which is intended to suggest the media's
superiority, for example, to a public figure under discussion.[10]

The view that the media have sacrificed their news values is widely
held by Americans, confirms James Fallows, Washington editor of the
Atlantic Monthly, in his book *Breaking the News:* "Americans believe that
the news media have become too arrogant, cynical, scandal-minded,
and destructive."[11] A *Harvard Business Review* article on books that tell
business managers how to think about the media extends the indictment. It charges that the U.S. media is corrupt. "It fails to do what it
claims to do, what it should do, and what society expects it to do," says
Peter Vanderwicken, the reviewer.[12]

Liberal Bias

A major cause of disenchantment with the news media among business
and conservative politicians has been the belief that the media harbors a
liberal bias. They point to a poll released in April 1996 by the Freedom
Forum Media Studies Center and the Roper Center for Opinion Research
that shows 89% of journalists voted for Bill Clinton in 1992, compared
with only 43% of the popular vote in the election.[13] Another continuing
study, *A Measure of Media Bias*, by Tim Groseclose of the University of
California and Jeff Milyo of the University of Chicago, finds that the liberal inclination is pronounced. The test was that liberal national media,
such as *Newsweek*, *The New York Times*, *Time* magazine, *the CBS Evening
News*, *USA Today*, and *NBC Nightly News* overwhelmingly cite left-leaning think tanks in their stories. Only *Fox News Special Report* cited conservative ones.[14]

These studies appear to confirm the findings of a major study, *The
Media Elite*, published in 1986. The study asserted that the typical leading journalists from major newspapers, magazines, and TV networks
have a liberal bias. They fantasize about the abuse of power and are
more likely than businessmen to uphold social underdogs and criticize
authorities (see Box 8.1 for more details).

> **Box 8.1   Studies and Surveys of Media Bias**
>
> A major study that supports the contention of a liberal media bias is *The Media Elite* by S. Robert Lichter, Stanley Rothman and Linda S. Lichter.[15] The typical leading journalist is described as "the very model of the modern eastern urbanite" and "politically liberal and alienated from traditional norms and institutions."[16] The authors based their findings on a sample of 238 men and women journalists at the *New York Times, Washington Post, Wall Street Journal, Time, Newsweek, U.S. News and World Report,* CBS, NBC, ABC, and PBS. These reporters, bureau chiefs, editors, producers, and executives are made up largely of white (95%) men in their 30s and 40s (79%), whose fathers are professionals or businessmen (80%), and who come from northeastern or north central cities (68%).[17]
>
> The authors say, "journalists are consistently more likely than businessmen to uphold social underdogs and criticize authorities."[18] Responding to pictures (using the Thematic Apperception Test), they fantasize about the abuse of power—whether by greedy businessmen, conniving politicians, intimidating policemen, or bullying military superiors. More than businesspeople, they are motivated by the need to be the center of attention and to feel important and influential. They seem fearful that others may gain control over them, therefore, and attack others who are perceived as powerful. Seeing the world as a struggle for power helps to explain why political campaigns are hyped as horse races and why many business stories are treated in terms of who will come out on top.
>
> Another expression of the current intellectual and emotional milieu of the national media is in news coverage of long-term social controversies. Several chapters in *The Media Elite* report on a content analysis of such issues as busing, nuclear safety, and the role of the oil industry in the energy crisis of the 1970s. The conclusion is not so much that today's leading journalists are biased but that they tend to see elements of social controversies in a way that corresponds with their own attitudes.[19]
>
> An essay in *BusinessWeek* by Bruce Nussbaum agrees with the viewpoint that media bias manifests itself in social issues. "Reporters and editors bring to their jobs a white-collar cultural bias" in that they are more likely to know people who are gay than those who are religious conservatives.[20] Nussbaum says this social bias is not political partisanship.

The reason for this concern is that the national media have unquestionably become a major force in American life, say the authors of *The Media Elite*. They have become a catalyst for political activists and social critics. The news media see themselves as surrogates for the public, a role sanctioned by society. Don Hewitt, executive producer of *60 Minutes*, says, "We have become America's ombudsman." Echoing the characterization of TV documentaries and news magazine shows as "show biz," he states, "Our purpose is to make information more palatable and to make reality competitive with make-believe."[21]

There is no such thing as an "objective" national news media, asserts the Media Research Center, a nonprofit educational foundation formed in 1987 to document liberal media bias and distribute this research to the public. Its book, *And That's the Way It Isn't*, provides ample evidence on a variety of topics that "media bias is real, that it is prevalent, and that it obscures the reality that the journalistic profession has sworn to report." The inference that journalists do have an ideological axe to grind suggests a deliberate attempt to slant the news, rather than the kinder view that "journalism is inherently subjective; a journalist's approach to a story invariably reflects his opinion."[22]

Intrusion of Commercial Values

The drive to maintain or increase newspaper and magazine circulation and, for broadcast stations, to receive high Nielsen ratings, is increasingly important as investors see the media as just one more industry in which to make a profit. Indeed, newspapers have been highly profitable. *Washington Post* ombudsman Geneva Overholser states, "The trouble is that newspapers have become so profitable—profitable beyond any normal retailers' dreams—that the pressure on corporate executives to run them with an emphasis on the short term as opposed to the long term is just enormous."[23]

The result has been a clear shift from the idea of news as information to the idea of news as a market commodity. The media have lost their distinctiveness in serving the public interest and instead are seen as just another business. Jay T. Harris, chairman and publisher of the San Jose *Mercury News*, was so chagrined over staffing cuts that he resigned. He told his corporate bosses that their bottom-line profit motive for the newspaper staff cuts risked "significant and lasting harm to the paper as a journalistic enterprise." He said he hoped his resignation would cause the corporate bosses "to closely examine the wisdom" of the 20% corporate profit targets.[24]

Like Bagdikian, Gary C. Woodward, in *Perspectives on American Political Media*, blames the rise of media conglomerates, and their treatment of news organizations as investments, for this shift in the treatment of news. The story is told that when Larry Tisch, the chief financier of Loews, became chairman of CBS after purchasing large blocks of its stock, one of his first acts was to downsize the news and entertainment division staffs. As stated by Woodward, "Tisch's reign over CBS generally had the effect of maintaining its short-term attractiveness as an investment, but weakened it as a media corporation with a unique history and identity."[25] Woodward also cites examples of how "financial interests may dictate not getting involved in reporting on issues affecting another business owned by the parent company, or avoiding negative comment and reporting on the actions of an important advertiser."[26]

Other sources of pressure may be political. In *Inside Congress*, Ronald Kessler tells how ABC officials, out of fear of Congress, allegedly shelved a story about allegations of sexual harassment against Representative Sonny Bono (R–Calif.) and of sexual activities by other unnamed lawmakers. ABC News producers spoke of a new conservatism under ABC News chairman Roone Arledge and ABC News president David Westin. As one producer rationalized, "Westin is a former corporate lawyer from Washington, and Disney, ABC's parent company, has regulatory issues pending before Congress.... There's fear here that this piece was killed because the network didn't want to take on Congress."[27] Although he realizes the mass media industries must remain profitable and attractive to their investors, Woodward fears their role as agents of social and political interaction is being weakened.

Disenchantment with the media also occurs when they run ads that are found to be blatantly false. The commercial need to increase advertising revenue seemingly overrides social responsibility concerns. Media outlets protest that they can't possibly have any level of responsibility for ads because it is unduly burdensome and impractical to require them to compare the products against claims made in advertising. Furthermore, First Amendment rights are threatened when the FTC asks the media to reject false ads. Says FTC Chairman Timothy Muris, "Reputable publications should be doing a better job screening them." When they don't, the FTC threatens enforcement action. For example, it settled a case with Blue Stuff Inc.'s advertisements on national cable TV for its emu–oil–based gel, priced at $60 for 8 ounces, which claims to relieve severe pain. Muris is pressing for self-regulation, however, because he realizes the First Amendment implications of FTC regulation. John Kimball, marketing director for the Newspaper Association of America, believes that "the ultimate decision on what appears in a newspaper rests with the publisher, not with any other entity." [28]

Although most journalists complain about pressures to cater to the commercial organizational demands, some are themselves driven by rewards in the form of prestige, popularity, and financial gain. Receiving special attention is the questionable practice by journalists of accepting speaker's fees. This raises questions about journalists' credibility and possible conflicts of interest, especially when they accept "honoraria" from the same organizations they criticize for trying to buy influence on Capitol Hill. Fueling further cynicism about the media is that many of these journalist speakers resist disclosure of their sources and the amounts of their lecture fees. Sixty–eight percent of readers of the *Washington Journalism Review* (renamed *American Journalism Review*) in a 1991 poll favored reform in this area. When Bernard Kalb, moderator of CNN's *Reliable Sources*, asked columnist Robert Novak to reveal his outside income, the latter answered, "It's none of the public's business. I'm a private citizen." If Kalb were asked the same question, his answer would probably be, "I don't listen to my own questions."

Entertainment Values and Tabloid Journalism Crowd Out News Values.
One consequence of the dominance of business values over news values is that the press is under mounting pressure to provide entertainment-oriented news.[29] National Public Radio host Scott Simon reflected this concern in his "Weekend Edition" essay: "Over the past few years, so much of the American news industry has invested so much effort to spotlight sensational superficialities and celebrity inanities, that by the time we wanted to throw light on something truly and tragically serious (genocide in Bosnia), our audience no longer took us seriously."[30] The same is true in the treatment of health news. James Fallows cites the example of *Newsweek* as preaching the journalism of "big ideas" by hyping Prozac one minute and playing it down the next, in a way that trivializes important issues.[31] He points out how a cynical and superficial press has shattered faith in public institutions.

Ben Bagdikian, author of *The Media Monopoly*, noted that as the marketplace, not journalistic values, sets the standards, the line between tabloid and mainstream media fades. All the media, from *The New York Times* to the evening news, are infected by the tabloid approach. *Los Angeles Times* TV critic Howard Rosenberg commented about the "incestuous media process" whereby a sleazy paper or program carries some scandalous item, then "the so-called respectable media fall in behind them—squandering themselves on relative minutia but also diverting the public's eye from the truly significant issues of the day."[32] The practice of "tabloid laundering" was dramatically illustrated by coverage of Princess Diana's death, as described in Box 8.2.

Tabloid journalism has also touched television news magazine shows. Don Hewitt, *60 Minutes* creator, devoted the inaugural William S. Paley Lecture at the Museum of TV & Radio to denouncing the network's compulsion to produce them:

> In the rush to put more [of them] on the air ... taste and integrity and all the intangibles that made [TV news] respected the world over get lost. American's television sets [get loaded] with the same garbage that weighs down supermarket checkout counters.... There's a line that separates the news business from show business ... and I think it's being crossed all the time now. The *Hard Copies*, *Current Affairs* and *Inside Editions* do all the things we would never even flirt with.[33]

Business Deal Between the Los Angeles Times and Staples. Another manifestation of how a leading newspaper succumbed to commercial values was the proposed profit-sharing deal between the highly regarded *Los Angeles Times* and the Staples Center. Journalistic traditions were neglected when Mark Willie, chairman of the parent

---

Box 8.2   News Coverage of Princess Diana's Death Illustrates "Tabloid Laundering"

When Princess Diana was killed in an automobile accident in a Paris tunnel on August 31, 1997, the three major networks devoted to it 197 minutes of their evening newscasts for the week—not as much time (255 minutes) as to the coup against Soviet leader Mikhail Gorbachev in 1991, but more than to stories about U.S. Marines arriving in Somalia (182 minutes), the Mississippi River floods (167 minutes), and Hurricane Andrew (151 minutes). Mother Teresa's death a few days later received only 16 minutes. Nielsen ratings showed that public attention to Diana's death was enormous. Television coverage of Diana's funeral was watched in more than 26 million U.S. households. *USA Today* 's total circulation was several hundred thousand above normal for the week after Diana's death and *Time*'s first issue about Diana's death had newsstand sales of about 850,000, which is 650,000 more than normal.

Commenting on tabloid journalism, Margaret Carlson, *Time* columnist, said, "We take what the tabloids do and write about it, and that way get what we wouldn't write about originally into the magazine. And then we run pictures of the pictures to show how terrible the pictures are." *Newsweek* did that on September 8 with a full-page spread about the media's celebrity obsession. It included a color picture of one cover of the British tabloid, *The Sun,* showing the now-famous photo of Diana with her swimsuit straps slipped down her arms on a boat with her companion Emsad Mohamed "Dodi" Al-Fayed.

Times Mirror Company, gave priority to business interests. This occurred when *Los Angeles Times* editor Michael Parks and publisher Kathryn Downing made an unwise decision to engage in a profit-sharing deal between the paper's magazine and its subject, the Staples Center sports arena, and not disclose it publicly until the issue came to light in other publications. The October 10 issue of the *Times* magazine had been entirely devoted to the Staples Center. Profits from the magazine issue were shared by the Times Mirror Company, which is a sponsor of the arena, and the arena's owners.

Embarrassed by disclosure of this agreement, the *Los Angeles Times* took the unusual step of investigating itself and publishing a 14-page special section, which called its arrangement "a tangled tale of ignorance and arrogance."[34] The section was written by longtime *Times* media reporter David Shaw and was not shown to Parks or Downing before publication. Shaw wrote, "*Times* journalists now fear that the very essence of their work—the bond of trust between them and their readers—has been jeopardized." The two senior news executives also apologized in Sunday's *Times*. Parks told Shaw, "Clearly, I underestimated the impact of the Staples arrangement on our credibility, on the journalistic ethos that we foster, on our standing in the community and in the profession."[35] As executive producer of the CBS *Evening News*, Erik Sorensen noted, the wall that has long separated the business from the editorial side of the paper is being breached.

METHODS OF ALTERNATIVE AND DIRECT COMMUNICATION

To avoid the gatekeeping function of the mass media, organizations have been addressing their target audiences directly by means of alternative media, private communication systems, database marketing that eliminates the filter of the mass media, and the Internet.

Use of Alternative Media by Politicians

Reference has already been made to structural changes in the media. Chapter 4 suggested that companies and politicians take advantage of the enlarged media menu beyond the traditional mass media. Lessons in using alternative media and direct methods of reaching desired audiences can be learned from politicians.

In the realm of politics, audiences as well as politicians have been seeking a way around the press, traditionally described as the "snide, frenzy-driven trivializers who were contributing to the erosion of their democracy."[36] Interactive shows such as *Larry King Live* have allowed viewers to serve as "remote-control reporters," in that they can interview newsmakers themselves by telephoning in and commenting on events as they watch them.[37] When presidential candidates appeared, the public felt it had direct access to political leaders. With the advent of C-SPAN, which allows the audience to see press conferences live, viewers became critical of national networks' reports, saying, "That's not what I saw today. Why are these guys saying this?"[38]

Politicians and others who consider using the "alternative media" must, however, be cautious and prudent in their selection. When Paul Tsongas was a presidential candidate, he was asked whether he would consider hosting *Saturday Night Live*, which was an opportunity to gain attention. He declined because he felt it was not in his best interest as a candidate. "I was trying to present myself as a serious truth teller," he said.[39] For similar reasons both Walter F. Mondale in 1984 and Michael S. Dukakis in 1988 declined invitations to appear on *Donahue*, even though they were trailing in the polls. Donahue's reaction was: "While it is true our program has always suffered from the daytime tabloid, we're-not-quite-the-news attitude, I thought this is an awful lot of pretense to be summoning to deny yourself this free television time."[40]

Candidate Bill Clinton welcomed the opportunity to appear on alternative media and accepted an invitation from the *Arsenio Hall Show*, where he played his saxophone. Many political consultants and reporters were fearful such an appearance would demean Clinton. Said Tom Wicker of *The New York Times*, "When two other candidates are making such a point of traditional family values, whatever they are, for a guy to appear on television playing jazz with dark shades on, on the *Arsenio Hall Show* after midnight, I don't think that enhances his standing on family values."[41] However, Clinton's media consultant, Mandy Grunwald, saw matters differently. She said it would "explain to people who Bill Clinton was, what his life was about, what he was about, what he was about in personal terms. We had a strategic mandate to do that."[42] Her strategy was to go to nontraditional news sources because they "were trying to convey biography and personality" and not news.[43] As election results showed, the appearance likely helped Clinton, especially among the young. Just under half of first-time voters—about 5.5 million—supported Clinton, which accounted for nearly all of Clinton's 5.8 million vote margin.[44]

Private Communication Systems

Private communication systems consist of two types: (a) constituency communications, such as an organization's communications with its stakeholders, and (b) privately financed cable channels. Communication with employees through newsletters, newspapers, magazines, and electronic communications is most common. The writers and editors of these internal media are represented by the International Association of Business Communicators with its more than 16,000 members. Besides reaching employees through these controlled channels, organizations have the opportunity to communicate with their employees through one-on-one communications with supervisors and through a variety of group meetings.

Motorola went directly to its employees with mass-media-related news with the aim of taking the sting out of impending bad press or other issue-related matters. One way was to place "sandwich boards" at exits, which alerted employees at the end of the workday to expect television coverage that evening and criticisms or investigations and headlines the following morning. The company also used its cleaning staff to distribute red alert messages so employees would immediately see them on their desks or workstations when they report to work. Message sheets carry a special logo to identify their urgency.[45] Private channels can also be used to target other stakeholders of an organization.

Public relations textbooks and handbooks are replete with examples of communication programs that can be used with an organization's multiple stakeholders, as illustrated by the following:

- Investors can be reached through annual reports, interim reports, and annual meetings (reports of which are sometimes made available in video format, on CDs, or on websites).

- Customers, dealers, and suppliers can be reached through newsletters, special bulletins, and other means.

The importance of going directly to key stakeholders, at least before going to the news media, was demonstrated when First Chicago invited banking reporters to a briefing at which senior bank officials explained the bank's new fee policy when customers go to a bank teller instead of an ATM. Of all the complex details discussed at the briefing (e.g., the circumstances when a teller may be seen without paying a fee), the reporters jumped on the story of a new $3 teller fee. The story was then amplified by grandstanding politicians and late-night comedians, as well as public relations critics. The main lesson learned, said bank officials, is "that getting information into customers' hands before they see it in the media is crucially important."[46] Officials already knew that employees must also be informed: Branch employees, the bank's first line of defense against irate customers, were provided communications materials beforehand. They supported the teller fee decisions and have done an excellent job of explaining the decision and telling customers about less costly banking options. Other stakeholders that should be informed, said officials, are government and community leaders, the minority community, and civic and political leaders.[47]

The second type of private communication system is the privately financed cable channels that are viewed by the general public but have their contents controlled by their owners. An example is Pat Robinson's cable television channel, which broadcast the August 1996 Republican National Convention in San Diego. The cost of the broadcast was defrayed by Amway, which contributed $1.3 million. Amway's president Richard M. "Dick" DeVos, Jr. said he viewed this contribution as a "public service."[48] Pat Robinson also bypassed the mass media by producing audiocassettes that are distributed free to targeted audiences.

Database Marketing

Database marketing can bypass the media entirely, or counter the media's influence. The application of database marketing allows communicators to reach audiences on a "personal," one-on-one basis. Tom Brennan of Brennan & Brennan, a public relations firm in Anchorage, Alaska, defines himself as a database user: "For years I've been using mass media only as supplementary communication channels. The important stuff goes direct to targeted audiences.... When we issue a press release we think through which people we would most like to have read the story if a newspaper used it in its original form. Then we send the press release to them. It's also a way of insuring the media doesn't garble the message."[49]

In writing his releases, Brennan includes "some things I know the media will leave out.... At the same time, you have to be careful you don't lose the interest of the news media."[50] Brennan gives the example of a hotel that decided to close its well-known restaurant and turn it into a private dining room. Fearing the local newspaper would interpret this announcement as a sign the hotel was in financial difficulty, which it wasn't, Brennan sent 5,000 "Dear Friends of the Restaurant" letters; he also reserved an ad in the paper to appear the next day. About a week later, the media wrote a story, but "by that time the story was well distributed and correctly perceived by the audience."[51]

When using a database marketing approach, communicators should consider its full meaning. As defined by Skip Andrew of the National Center for Database Marketing, database marketing involves

> managing a computerized relational database system, in real time, of comprehensive, up-to-date, relevant data on customers, inquiries, prospects, and suspects, to identify your most responsive customers for the purpose of developing a high-quality, long-standing relationship of repeat business, by developing predictive models which enable us to send desired messages at the right time in the right form to the right people—all with the result of pleasing our customers, increasing our response rate per marketing dollar, lowering our cost per order, building our business, and increasing our profits.[52]

In his book on the direct marketing of politics, *One Billion Dollars of Influence*, R. Kenneth Godwin reported more than 200 million direct mailings are typically sent each year to generate resources for political action.[53] Some examples are the following:

• The Center for Resource Economics, a public interest group that monitors corporations, used the Freedom of Information Act to identify and communicate with companies that threaten food supplies or the environment.[54]
• Philip Morris started a glossy new magazine in October 1996 called *Unlimited: Action, Adventure, Good Times* to reach close to 2 million male smokers between the ages of 21 and 29. Barred from broadcast advertising and facing possible new restrictions on billboards, sponsorships, and magazine advertising (requiring the use of black-and-white, text-only ads in any magazine with substantial youth readership), this private magazine intends to "reinforce loyalty to the brand and to provide added value," says a Philip Morris spokeswoman.[55] This is not the first magazine Philip Morris published for its smokers. In the mid-1980s, it published the *Philip Morris Magazine*, which dealt with such controversial subjects as smokers' rights. It reached a circulation of 12 million people six times a year but was discontinued in 1992.

Videos as well as direct mail print material can be used in direct marketing. When Oliver North, the ex-Marine colonel, ran for the Republican nomination for a Senate seat in Virginia, he sent party regulars an

11-minute videocassette containing a minibiography with commentary tailored to their concerns.[56]

Commenting on the use of videos, Tom Edmonds, a political consultant, reiterated the advantage of direct marketing: "You can bypass the mass media and target only the people you want to reach."[57] He says that for about $2 a cassette, he can send his clients' customized messages to thousands of demographically desirable television screens, thereby avoiding the need to buy expensive commercial time on a station or cable system.

The Internet

The Internet has become an essential part of public affairs campaigns. It and other modern online systems (e.g., e-mail, forums, bulletin boards, and newsgroups) allow persons and organizations to communicate their messages directly to their intended audiences without filtering or distortion by reporters, editors, producers, or hosts.[58] Online services, such as America Online, allow a sender to select audiences on the basis of topics of common interest, such as the environment or animal rights. An estimated 10,000 bulletin boards existed in 1996.[59]

The Web is a medium that works best when information is available for those who go looking for it, using the pull model of communications, says Shel Holtz, author of *Public Relations on the Net*.[60] A company can take advantage of user initiative by dedicating a site, or a clear section of a company home page, to an issue of special importance. When several companies share a view on an issue, a consortium can build a single website, such as the Camisea website on oil exploration in the Peruvian rainforest.[61] Trade associations can likewise centralize positions shared by the majority of their members. Holtz suggests that readers be invited to submit their thoughts in response to a website, but a company should then be ready to respond to each. websites can help support grassroots lobbying efforts. A company's intranet can reach employees, as Caterpillar did in spring of 2000 to convince Congress to grant China permanent normal trade relations.[62]

Among the converts to online systems are some members of Congress. In *The Hill on the Net*, Chris Casey tells how they have learned to post material to the Net and thereby "bypass traditional media and enhance their ability to deliver material directly to constituents."[63] Furthermore, says Casey, "reading the speeches and other statements of a member of Congress will tell you much more than you would get from the sound bite coverage (if any at all) that print or broadcast media gives to these types of events."[64]

Burson-Marsteller's research has identified *e-fluentials* among Internet users—a powerful group of online users who steer current cultural and consumer trends.[65] This emerging class of online elites participate in chat rooms, use e-mail frequently, utilize message boards and forward selected information to others. E-fluentials also yield clout offline as well as online: 77% vote, 55% sign petitions, 48% e-mail government agencies, 47% e-mail congressmen or senators, and 40% serve on committees of local organizations. Companies, as well as communities and special interest groups can tap the power of e-fluentials and enlist their support. Users of online services insist that messages are brief, simply stated, and contain essential information, because they have limited time, either because of restrictions or because they are billed for the time used. They want to browse rapidly and will reject a message that wastes their time.

E-Mail.　The clearest way to reach people directly, without mass media interference, is through e-mail. When the audience is one individual, this new channel simply imitates personal correspondence. Special conventions, called *netiquette* should, however, be observed in using e-mail. As recommended by Nadine Udall Fischer of NADIA, The Professional Speaking Company (Lawrenceville, NJ):

1. Use e-mail for urgent, time-sensitive matters.
2. Be brief, action-oriented, and direct. Make your point within 30 seconds of the reader's time.
3. Be sensitive. Avoid hiding behind e-mail to say something you would not want to say face-to-face. Write in upper- and lowercase letters because writing in all caps is the e-mail equivalent of hollering. Avoid slam-o-grams—negative, curt e-mail messages.[66]

The ability to send an e-mail message to a list of people, instead of just a single recipient, differentiates e-mail from personal correspondence and enhances e-mail's capability to bypass the mass media. When using such mass-distributed e-mail messages, several common elements should be included: the name of the individual or institution that sent the message, date, listing of the contents in the same order in which the items appear, information on how to contact the author of the message, and how to unsubscribe from the mailing list.[67]

Companies are neglecting the opportunity to respond to people who send e-mail to them. According to the consulting firm Customer Respect.com, 37% of the 100 largest corporations who were sent e-mail didn't respond at all, even with an automated form letter. Only after 3 or more days did an additional 22% answer. "It was as if they were saying 'Don't communicate with us. Ever.'" In grading companies on the speed and quality of responses, researchers who posed as customers found several companies most responsive: Freddie Mac, Costco Wholesale, DuPont, Allstate, Lowe's, Verizon Communications, Intel, Sears Roebuck, Hewlett-Packard, and IBM. Among the least responsive was Pepsi, appearing in 97th place. Said a Pepsi spokeswoman—and, hopefully, others on the least responsive list—"We are making changes as we speak."[68]

Discussion Groups and Blogs. The Internet allows users to get on-line with "communities" of like-minded people on specialized topics through forums, bulletin boards, and newsgroups. Listserv and electronic mailing lists are available that enable someone to subscribe to discussions covering a wide variety of topics.[69] "More than 53 million American adults have used the Internet to publish their thoughts, respond to others, post pictures, share files and otherwise contribute to the explosion of content available on line," according to a report from the Pew Internet & American Life project.[70] It also reports that somewhere between 2% and 7% of American Internet users have created blogs and about 11% of Internet users are blog readers.

Blogs, or Web logs, are becoming a public affairs tool of choice for associations and corporations to influence public policy, says Ken Deutsch, executive vice president of Issue Dynamics.[71] He outlines four techniques used by bloggers to allow people to process a growing amount of content:

1. Develop an audience and become the place to go on an issue with the most up-to-date information. Do this by sifting through all of the Internet's content and providing high-quality and usually short postings for a very specifically segmented audience.
2. Benefit from the ranking system of returns on Google, currently the dominant online search engine, which ranks sites and key words based on how many other Internet sites link to them. Make an effort, therefore to link to other sites and promote other sites through content reference within each blog entry.
3. Use the community-building approach by allowing site visitors to become participants.
4. Get your message heard by using "rich rite summary" or "really simple syndication," which are akin to a news feed.[72]

Companies can take advantage of discussion groups to reach participating individuals, including e-fluentials. If a company wants to submit information or views on discussion group sites, however, it must make sure the message conforms to the interests of the site. In some cases a "moderator" may serve as an intermediary. Certain Internet norms must be observed. Blatant advertising and self-promotion must be assiduously avoided, and messages must be of clear benefit to recipients.

Home websites. A major growth industry in public relations has been the establishment of home pages by companies and others. These company-sponsored sites make messages available to the public. The messages typically contain product information, press releases, company backgrounders, fact sheets, financial statements, and reviews of issues. Unlike a newspaper or television station that is routinely "processed" by readers and viewers, a company home page requires motivated audience members intent on "seeking" information. This is called the pull model of communication—that receivers go to those sites that they think contain the information they want when they need it. In other words, the sender must depend on audience initiative because a proactive information-seeking effort is required by the user to locate a site and utilize it. A certain amount of random navigating of the Internet is done by some computer users, but this audience is irrelevant. The use of company home pages was explored by Yi-Chun Regine Liu in a master's thesis, as described in Box 8.3.

Push Technology. Theoretically push technology—in contrast to pull technology"—enables organizations with home pages to "broad-

---

Box 8.3 Study of Some Corporate Websites

Yi-Chun Regine Liu examined the use of home pages in the top 10 companies in four industries—chemicals, airlines, commercial banks, and health care—to determine whether and how they used home pages. Even as early as 1996, when the research was conducted, 35 of the 40 companies carried home pages: all 10 airlines and all 9 banks (reduced to 9 because Chase Manhattan and Chemical Bank merged); 8 chemical and 7 health care companies. Home pages typically display a company logo and slogan; for example, DuPont's "Better things for better living," bears this explanation: "We're a science and technology based global company of people who make products that make a difference in everyday life."

Liu found that almost all of the information in these company home pages, such as annual reports and employee publications, duplicated material already existing in other media. But home pages had certain advantages. Aside from potentially reaching new audiences, two features of home pages make them a potentially powerful medium, says Liu. One is their multimedia capability—the ability to use audio and video materials, such as brief speeches by CEOs and pictures of products and services (thus imitating colorful high-quality magazines and reports). Another is their capability to provide audience interaction. "Visitors" can select the specific information sought, enhance it, and give feedback. For example, airlines provide interactive schedules that allow someone immediately interested in a certain destination to receive the departure and arrival schedule; some airlines go a step further by accepting online reservations.

The Internet has the further advantage of creating a one-on-one relationship between an organization and a person. As stated by Brian Johnson of Alexander Communications, an Atlanta-based public relations agency. "The Internet is about interactivity, a dialogue, and public relations is about interactivity, the give and take of ideas, ideals, and information. On the Internet, listening is as important as talking."

cast" messages to audiences without requiring their initiative. Instead of relying on Web users to "pull" news and ads from a variety of sites by browsing and searching, push technology places material on users' PC screens to receive their attention.[73] However, as Shel Holtz points out, such push technology cannot be relied on to get a message to a targeted audience. It is the user who configures the tool to receive only material in categories that are of interest.[74] The user specifies generic channels such as news, companies, industries, and sports, or branded channels from news organizations like *The New York Times* or CNN. Topics can then be chosen within these channels, but customization does not extend to refined levels.

These push technologies were pioneered in 1996 by two California firms: PointCast of Cupertino, and BackWeb Technologies of San Jose. PointCast software goes out to the Internet and retrieves the kinds of stories demanded. PointCast presents stories to the user in headline form via a screen saver, and BackWeb does so in the form of Info-Flashes— "little graphics that pop out of the edge of your screen or march along its borders in whatever program you're using."[75] By clicking a headline, the user displays the text. What is considered a complaint by a reviewer of this software is to the advantage of an organization. Walter S. Mossberg frets that "a significant proportion of the stuff in the generic channels isn't independently written news but one-sided company press releases."[76]

Spamming Endangers the Internet. Spamming has become the number one scourge of the Internet and threatens to undermine its value. Worldwide, 10.4 million spam e-mails are sent every minute. AOL says that every day it tags as spam and blocks 80% of the e-mail reaching it.[77] Spam accounts for 50% of all electronic mail in the United States[78] and costs U.S. businesses $10 billion annually in lost productivity and additional equipment and software.[79]

Spamming is defined as "an inappropriate attempt to use a mailing list, or Usenet or other networked communications facility as if it was a broadcast medium (which it is not) by sending the same message to a large number of people who didn't ask for it."[80] Efforts are underway to control spamming through antispam technology and legislation. One of the most popular technologies is the so-called white list, which accepts mail only from a list of approved contacts. EarthLink, the third largest Internet service provider, has been building such a system. Users are installing antispam software, the use of which is expected to reach $653 million in 2003. The "unfettered, open and chaotic" nature of the Internet is being replaced by an orderly and closed system. Mailing from work, friends, and e-tailers will be filed into separate mailboxes.[81]

After much debate in Congress, a sweeping antispam bill was passed, Can-Spam of 2003, which was signed by President Bush on December 10 and took effect January 1, 2004. The debate centered around marketers' First Amendment rights of commercial speech versus people's privacy rights. As the Supreme Court said in 1951 in response to solicitors of magazine subscriptions, the First Amendment didn't give companies free rein to invade "the living rights of others to privacy and repose."[82] Because 79.1% of spam messages are claimed to originate in North America, the European Union is asking for stronger measures, such as an "opt-in" system rather than the new law's "opt-out" provision. The powerful Direct Marketing Association has opposed a blanket opt-in rule and instead wants harsher penalties for the worst offenders.[83]

Use of Web Pages During a Crisis.[84]   The characteristics of speed and availability make the Internet an ideal tool for a company to provide the media and others with information about a crisis. In today's 24/7 environment, word of a crisis is quickly broadcast by the news media, even as the crisis unfolds and before details are available. To obtain balanced treatment from the media, a company can offer three types of websites: the company site; a special site dedicated to the crisis; and the sites of supporters, advocates, and allies.[85] The Internet can also take a company's message directly to stakeholders, such as vendors, franchisees, customers, and employees. Thus, a new role for public relations practitioners is that of content provider, a role that eliminates the "filter." The Internet's multimedia capability makes possible the exciting prospect of broadcasting visual images directly to a company's stakeholders. Box 8.4 describes how Odwalla effectively used a dedicated website when its apple juice was implicated in several cases of E. coli poisoning.

CONCLUSIONS

When customers dislike a product, they find a substitute. The same is true for corporations that have depended on the mass media to disseminate their messages. When trust in the news media is low, companies may bypass them entirely or supplement the media's version with their own through various forms of direct communication with their audiences. Trust has been undermined as evidence mounts that the media are failing in their mission of objective and fair reporting. Charges abound of a liberal media bias and commercial values that favor sensationalism and entertainment over journalistic values. Fortunately for business, alternatives to the traditional news media are growing—in the form of alternative media, private communication channels, direct marketing channels, and the Internet.

ENDNOTES

1. "Strategy '92 & Beyond ...," *pr reporter,* Vol. 35, March 2, 1992, pp. 1–2.

Box 8.4   Odwalla's Tainted Apple Juice Crisis

Late in the evening of October 30, 1996, health officials in Washington State notified the San Francisco juice maker Odwalla that its company's apple juice was implicated in several cases of E. coli poisoning. Sixty-one people eventually became sick and 1 child, a 16-month-old girl, died from the same type of bug that had contaminated Jack-in-the-Box hamburgers in 1993.

Within 20 minutes after receiving the news of contamination from state officials, Odwalla held a press conference to announce a recall of all products containing unpasteurized apple juice, which amounted to about 70% of its product line. It also shut down its production facility and carefully analyzed every point in the process.

During the recall, Edelman Public Relations Worldwide worked with Odwalla. Although the company did not have a corporate or promotional website, Edelman set up a crisis-related site within 72 hours. Edelman uses its domain name (www.enw.com) as a way to create a subdomain to host a client's site when crisis strikes.

Odwalla's site became an important part of the company's response. The website address in news releases led many reporters to refer to the site for updated information. Within 48 hours of its establishment, the site generated 19,000 hits. Odwalla had a chance to tell its story after the immediate crisis passed.

A feature of Odwalla's site appreciated by reporters was that it offered links to two government agencies most closely involved with the recall: the Food and Drug Administration and the Centers for Disease Control and Prevention.

Odwalla's swift action and communication are the likely reason an independent survey conducted by America Online found 96% of the respondents said they approved of the way the crisis was handled and 86% said they would continue to buy its products. The company survived, but its stock price, which was $28.70 a share before the crisis, is only slowly recovering from a 52-week low of $9.25 a share.

Based on its Odwalla experience, Edelman has prepared a "Crisis Preparation & Response" (CPR) product that "enables rapid, real-time Internet response" as well as updating and worldwide access. Within an hour, CPR can place an immediate text response online. In 12 hours it can add third-party influence statements, graphic sophistication, and digitized video footage, including interview segments a program such as *60 Minutes* might have left out (provided the company prepared its own film).

2. "In the News: Prepared Testimony of Dr. Jay Black Before the Senate Committee on the Judiciary," Federal News Service, December 19, 1996.
3. "The State of the News Media 2004," Pew Research Center for People & the Press. www.stateofthenewsmedia.org/narrative_overview_conclusions
4. Ibid.
5. Ibid.
6. Ibid.
7. From Roper Center, Public Opinion Online. Also see Rita Beamish, "Voters Rate the Coverage by News Media as Mediocre," *Los Angeles Times*, November 27, 1994, p. A-19; Reginald Stuart, "A Year of Sizzle Boosts Audiences, Arms Our Critics; Sensationalism in Journalism to Erode Public Confidence in Media," *Quill*, Vol. 82, November 1994, p. 56.
8. Steve Berg, "Gingrich Joins Chorus of Media Critics," *Star Tribune*, January 18, 1995, p. 6A.
9. Ibid.
10. Ibid.
11. James Fallows, *Breaking the News: How the Media Undermine American Democracy* (New York: Pantheon, 1996), p. 3.
12. Peter Vanderwicken, "Why the News Is Not the Truth," *Harvard Business Review*, Vol. 73, May–June 1995, pp. 144–152.
13. Bruce Nussbaum, "The Myth of the Liberal Media," *BusinessWeek*, November 11, 1996, p. 34. The poll, however, is criticized for including only 139 Washington journalists.
14. Robert J. Barro, "The Liberal Media: It's No Myth," *BusinessWeek*, June 14, 2004, p. 28
15. S. Robert Lichter, Stanley Rothman, and Linda S. Lichter, *The Media Elite: America's New Powerbrokers* (Bethesda, Md: Adler & Adler, 1986).
16. Ibid., p. 294.
17. Ibid., pp. 20–23.
18. Ibid., p. 86.
19. Ibid., pp. 294–295.
20. Nussbaum, op. cit., p. 35.
21. Lichter, Rothman and Lichter, op. cit., p. 150.
22. "Watchdog Watch," *American Journalism Review*, Vol. 5 , April 1993, pp. 32–34.
23. Lichter, Rothman, and Lichter, op. cit., pp. 294–295.
24. *New York Times*, March 20, 2001, pp. C1, C6.
25. Gary C. Woodward, *Perspectives on American Political Media* (Boston: Allyn & Bacon, 1997), p. 46. Also see p. 48.
26. Ibid., p. 49.
27. Jane Hall, "ABC Pulls Story on Misdeeds in Congress," *Los Angeles Times*, May 17, 1997, p. A15.
28. John R. Wilke, "FTC Asks Media to Reject False Ads," *Wall Street Journal*, November 20, 2002, p. A3.
29. Jacqueline Sharkey, "The Diana Aftermath," *American Journalism Review*, Vol. 19, November, 1997, p. 22.
30. "Even Media Pros Now Question Validity of Current 'News'; Another Reason to Go Under-the-Radar Directly to Publics," *pr reporter*, Vol. 37, March 21, 1994, p. 1.
31. Michael Elliott, "Blunt Arrows Miss the Mark," *Guardian*, April 8, 1996, p. T16.
32. Ed Siegel, "The Tabloid Approach Takes Hold; News Analysis," *Boston Globe*, December 23, 1993, p. 1.

33. "Television Newsmagazine Shows Called Trash—Yet Rate Highest; Watch for Local Television Reporting to Turn Uglier," *pr reporter*, Vol. 36, August 23, 1993, p. 3.

34. Lisa Bannon, "In Special Section, Los Angeles Times Raps Executives' Role in 'Tangled Tale,'" *Wall Street Journal*, December 21, 1999, p. B10.

35. Ibid.

36. Larry King, with Mark Stencel, *On the Line: The New Road to the White House* (New York: Harcourt Brace, 1993), p. 6.

37. Ibid., p. 60.

38. Ibid.

39. Ibid., p. 160.

40. Ibid., p. 16.

41. Ibid., p. 36.

42. Ibid., p. 161.

43. Ibid., p. 32.

44. Ibid., p. 155. He cites the *Congressional Quarterly Almanac, 102nd Session, 1992* (Washington, D.C.: Congressional Quarterly, 1993), p. 6-A.

45. "Natural Communications Methods Work Best; Some Examples," *pr reporter*, Vol. 38, June 26, 1995, p. 2.

46. "One More Reason for Going Around the Media to Publics," *pr reporter*, Vol. 38, June 5, 1995, pp. 2–3.

47. Ibid.

48. Bill Vlasic, Douglas Harbrecht, and Mary Beth Regan, "The GOP Way Is the Amway Way," *BusinessWeek*, August 12, 1996, pp. 28–29.

49. "Database PR: Opinion Leader List Overpowers Media List," *pr reporter*, Vol. 36, February 1, 1993, p. 1.

50. Ibid.

51. Ibid.

52. "Database Marketing Could Be Threat to PR, or an Ally," *pr reporter*, Vol. 36, January 18, 1993, p. 1.

53. R. Kenneth Godwin, *One Billion Dollars of Influence* (Chatham, N.J.: Chatham House, 1988), p. 1.

54. Eileen Gannon, "Solving Environmental Problems With Information Technology," *The CPSR Newsletter*, Vol. 13, Summer 1995, pp. 9–10.

55. Sally Goll Beatty, "Philip Morris Starts Lifestyle Magazine," *Wall Street Journal*, September 16, 1996, p. B1.

56. Andy Meisler, "From Your Mailbox to Your VCR: More Ads," *New York Times*, October 16, 1994, p. E6.

57. Ibid.

58. For an excellent review of the subject see Daniel S. Janal, "Public Relations: Influencing Editors and Your Target Market," in *Online Marketing Handbook* (New York: Van Nostrand Reinhold, 1955), pp. 287–333.

59. John V. Pavlik, *New Media Technology: Cultural and Commercial Perspectives* (Boston: Allyn & Bacon, 1996), p. 170.

60. Shel Holtz, *Public Relations on the Net*, 2nd edition (New York: AMACOM, 2002).

61. Ibid., p. 345.

62. Ibid., p. 225.

63. Chris Casey, *The Hill on the Net: Congress Enters the Information Age* (Boston: AP Professional, 1996), p. 84.

64. Ibid.

65. See www.efluentials.com.

66. "What's Proper & What's Not in the Use of E-Mail? *Channels* (monthly newsletter published by PR Publishing Co., Exeter, N.H.), p. 7.
67. Holtz, op. cit., p. 125.
68. "1-Way Patrol: E-Mail: Signed, Sealed, Deleted," *BusinessWeek*, November 11, 2002, p. 14.
69. Casey, op. cit., pp. 77–78.
70. "44 Percent of American Internet Users Have Contributed Their Thoughts, Digital Content to Online World," *Ascribe Newswire*, February 26, 2004.
71. Ken Deutsch, "Blogging Bids to Become the New Tool of Choice for Influencing Public Policy," *Impact*, May 2004, p. 1.
72. Ibid., pp. 1–3.
73. Walter S. Mossberg, "Personal Technology: 'Push' Technology Sometimes Pushes News You Can't Use," *Wall Street Journal*, March 27, 1997, p. B1.
74. Holtz, op. cit., p. 123.
75. Ibid. PointCast has been replaced by Entrypoint, owned by Launchpad Technologies. This service displays information in an on-screen toolbar that enables users to link to shopping, financial, and news sites of their own choice. Laurie J. Flynn, "Compressed Data; 'Push Technology' Returns in a Form That Is More Polite," *New York Times*, March 13, 2000, p. C4.
76. Ibid.
77. Stephen Baker, "The Taming of the Internet," *BusinessWeek*, December 15, 2003, pp. 78–81.
78. Stephen Baker, "From Open Doors to Gated Communities," *BusinessWeek*, September 8, 2003, p. 36.
79. Mentioned in a professional paper by Marinos Papadopoulos, who references the Direct Marketing Association (www.the-dma.org). An early infamous case is the "green card lawyer" who, in April 1994, sent an advertisement to more than 5,500 Usenet newsgroups without any regard for the groups' topic of discussion. The sender was consequently vilified across the Internet. The lawyers violated the rule, or netiquette, that messages should only be posted to newsgroups appropriate to the subject of the message. Casey, op. cit., p. 57.
80. Ibid., p. 55.
81. Baker, "The Taming of the Internet," op. cit.
82. Lorraine Woellert, "Commentary: Will the Right to Pester Hold Up?" *BusinessWeek*, November 10, 2003, p. 73.
83. Brandon Mitchener, "Europe Blames Weaker U.S. Law for Spam Surge," *Wall Street Journal*, February 3, 2004, p. B1.
84. The crisis story is based on a press kit by Edelman Public Relations Worldwide and the following: "Take Control," *PR's Magazine of Reputation Management*, November–December 1997, pp. 48–50; Richard Rapaport, "PR Finds a Cool New Tool," *Forbes ASAP*, October 6, 1997, pp. 101–108.
85. Suggested by Holtz, op. cit., p. 336.

IV

Governmental Strategies

Governmental strategies begin when an issue at the public involvement stage begins to interest lawmakers and regulators. If they place the issue on their agenda, the issue advances to the legislative stage. Here public affairs professionals seek to influence key persons in the legislative and executive branches of government through direct contact and indirectly through the mobilization of interest groups and citizens to put pressure on senators, members of Congress, and various government officials. The goal usually is to discourage unwanted government action or, if government does take action, to obtain as favorable an outcome as possible. When a corporation is interested in the enactment of certain legislation, however, it will use legislative strategies to promote its own views.

Most laws are embellished by regulations that are promulgated by various government agencies and many of them are later challenged in court. For this reason, the regulation and litigation stage has been added to the issue life cycle. Chapters 9 and 10 on lobbying encompass both legislatures and regulatory agencies; chapter 12 discusses the growing subject of litigation communication.

FORCES IN THE GOVERNMENT ARENA

Legislative communication and litigation communication are of vital importance because they address government, a major force in a corporation's sociopolitical environment. They also recognize the previously discussed influence of interest groups, as well as the fundamental role of public opinion.

Increasingly, legislative communication resembles political campaigning, as corporations realize that one-on-one contact with members of Congress is inadequate. Lawmakers must be assured their actions will not alienate their constituents. Therefore, corporations use public opinion polls to measure public acceptance, form coalitions with other interest groups, and attempt to gain media support for their position.

Government

Businesses operate within the parameters of what government allows. Government regulations can define what products or services are legal, as the banning of alcoholic beverages during the prohibition era demonstrates. Regulations can specify the distribution channels through which a product may be sold, as with the distribution of prescription drugs through licensed pharmacists. Regulations can also restrict how a product may be advertised, such as banning cigarette ads on television.

Not surprisingly, one of the favorite charts in business–government books shows the precipitous rise in the number of regulations during the 1960s and 1970s. Murray L. Weidenbaum's book, *Business, Government, and the Public*, shows a mildly rising curve in the number of federal consumer protection laws passed between 1890 and 1972. The curve rises sharply, however, in the mid-1960s and the author notes that legislation shows little sign of diminishing.[1] Furthermore, some of the newer regulations are across the board and apply to all industries (e.g., regulations on the environment, affirmative action, and occupational health and safety). Traditional regulations were industry specific and therefore relatively more acceptable because regulators might actually understand how a regulation would impact a particular industry.

Although corporations emphasize the onerous aspects of government regulations in their public statements, many are equally interested in these other functions of government:

- Promoter of business (e.g., tax credits, tariffs, subsidies).
- Guarantor of business (e.g., the Chrysler & Lockheed "bailouts").
- Buyers of goods and services from the private sector.
- Manager of the economy through monetary and fiscal policy.
- Owner of enterprises (e.g., the Tennessee Valley Authority).
- Planner of economic growth and prosperity.[2]

Some of these functions hold the promise of government contracts, subsidies, and loan guarantees. With a worldwide movement toward marketplace economies, public ownership of enterprises can be converted into business potential through the process of outsourcing and privatization. Besides maintaining a stable and growing economy, business and the public expect government to strengthen the country's infrastructure, which now focuses not only on better roads, but the building of an information infrastructure. The subject of what "public goods" the government should provide will always remain highly controversial.

Interest Groups

Interest groups exert enormous power in legislative and regulatory decision making because all of them are potential lobbyists. (Their role in originating and disseminating issues has already been discussed in the introduction to Part II.) Jonathan Rauch, national correspondent for the *National Journal*, believes the reason for the inability of Congress and the White House to achieve their sometimes lofty goals is that real control lies with these pivotal groups.[3]

As economist Mancur Olson wrote, the more parochial a lobby is, the more likely it is to form and thrive. Rauch further explains, "Lobbies exist to secure some favorable measures for themselves. Each group cares much more about keeping its little piece of the pie than anyone else cares about taking it away."[4] These lobbies can be beaten only by mobilizing broad public opinion against them, but that happens only in response to a crisis or when a bipartisan elite spends months or years seeking to do so. Sometimes, however, a corporation can form a coalition with some interest groups, recognizing that some normally opposed to business might join it in support of specific issues.

Public Opinion

Public opinion comprises what is on the minds of the general public, and a variety of writers have recognized its importance. Public relations counselor Edward L. Bernays wrote in his classic, *Crystallizing Public Opinion:*

> Perhaps the most significant social, political and industrial fact about the present century is the increased attention that is paid to public opinion, not only by individuals, groups or movements that are dependent on public support for their success, but also by men and organizations which until very recently stood aloof from the general public and were able to say, "The public be damned."[5]

Public opinion surveys serve several purposes related to public affairs: They are a useful way of monitoring what issues Americans are concerned about, what their stand is on specific issues, and what their mood is; for example, whether the country is on the right track. Many pertinent survey findings are reported in subsequent chapters.

Leo Bogart, former vice president of marketing planning and research at the Bureau of Advertising, said, in a *Harvard Business Review* article, the main purpose of opinion research is to "inform management on the general climate of opinion, to point out public relations issues with which the company may be faced."[6] And Robert O. Carlson, a former opinion researcher for the then Standard Oil Company of New Jersey, said large corporations wanted to "evaluate their place in the public's mind."[7]

Illustrating Carlson's concern about how big business is viewed by Americans, a 2000 Gallup poll found 65% of the American public thinks big government is the "biggest threat to the country in the future"; in contrast only 22% named big business and 7% named big labor as threats.[8] The American people appear not to have a lot of confidence in government. A Gallup poll in 2000 found that only 7% said they had a great deal of confidence and another 17% said they had quite a lot of confidence in Congress. Confidence in the presidency was somewhat higher, with 15% having a great deal of confidence and 27% quite a lot of confidence.[9]

Surveys also anticipate trends. The American Management Association's survey, "Business and Society: 1976–2000"—which was conducted during the early phase of growth of public affairs—found 68% of the respondents agreed with the statement: "We have reason to be concerned whether the corporation as we know it ... will survive into the next century.... The corporation itself must change, consciously evolving into an institution adapted to the new environment." The AMA report concluded: "There is a fundamental change coming in the relationships between American business and the society it serves."[10]

ACTIVITIES OF LEGISLATIVE COMMUNICATION

The first two chapters on governmental communication introduce lobbying techniques to the arsenal of communication tools used in the life cycle of an issue. Lobbying can be direct or indirect—the latter is now usually called grassroots lobbying. Direct lobbying, discussed in chapter 9, refers to communication with legislators or administrative officials who affect a pending vote or decision on public policy. Hedrick Smith calls this "old breed" or "retail" lobbying, characterized by one-on-one contact.[11]

In contrast, Smith characterizes grassroots lobbying, discussed in chapter 10, as the "new breed" or "wholesale" lobbying. Back-home pressure is built up by activating natural constituencies and state-level political networks. The idea is to build on a politician's motivation to get reelected by creating public opinion favorable to one's interests and motivating the "folks back home" to communicate with their legislators and other government officials.

Both types of lobbying can be reinforced with what political scientist Edwin Epstein calls electoral activities—activities that "center around the selection and support of candidates or of issues that come before the public."[12] The aim of these electoral activities, discussed in chapter 11, is to influence public voting behavior so political players favorable to one's position are elected.

Finally, strategies for dealing with the judicial branch of government must be considered. The life cycle of an issue no longer ends with legislation but extends to a fourth stage: litigation. After laws are passed, relevant government agencies promulgate and enforce regulations.[13] Chapter 12 reviews the increasingly important subject of litigation communication.

The first three chapters in Part IV draw heavily on interpersonal communication techniques, discussed in Part II in dealing with opinion leader communications. Because public support is required in most situations, techniques of strategic media relations and advocacy advertising discussed in Part III are also applied, usually as part of grassroots lobbying.

ENDNOTES

1. Murray L. Weidenbaum, *Business, Government, and the Public* (Englewood Cliffs, NJ: Prentice-Hall, 1977), pp. 33–35.
2. See Rogene A. Buchholz, *Business Environment and Public Policy: Implications for Management*, 5th edition (Englewood Cliffs, NJ: Prentice-Hall, 1995), pp. 142–157.
3. Jonathan Rauch, "Demosclerosis Returns," *Wall Street Journal*, April 14, 1998, p. A22.
4. Ibid.
5. Edward L. Bernays, *Crystallizing Public Opinion* (New York: Liveright, 1923), p. 34.
6. Leo Bogart, "Use of Opinion Research," *Harvard Business Review*, Vol. 29, No. 2, 1951, p. 121.
7. Robert O. Carlson, "The Use of Public Relations Research by Large Corporations," *Public Opinion Quarterly*, Vol. 21, No. 3, Fall 1957, p. 341.
8. Roper Center at University of Connecticut, Public Opinion Online, October 25, 2000, Accession Number 0374111, Question 015.
9. Guido H. Stempel, III, *Media and Politics in America: A Reference Handbook* (Santa Barbara, Calif.: ABC-Clio, 2003), p. 47.
10. John L. Paluszek, *Business & Society 1976–2000* (New York: AMACOM, 1976), p. 1.
11. Hedrick Smith, *The Power Game: How Washington Works* (New York: Ballantine, 1988), p. 230.
12. Edwin M. Epstein, *The Corporation in American Politics* (Englewood Cliffs, NJ: Prentice-Hall, 1969), p. 67.
13. Raymond P. Ewing recognizes this stage in "Issues Management: Managing Trends Through the Issues Life Cycle," in *The Handbook of Strategic Public Relations & Integrated Communications*, ed. Carke L. Caywood (New York: McGraw-Hill, 1997), p. 183.

Chapter 9

Direct Lobbying

The right to lobby is guaranteed by the First Amendment of the Constitution, which states, "Congress shall make no law ... abridging the freedom of speech or of the press; or the right of the people peaceably to assemble and to petition the government for redress of grievances." People can also make demands and advocate specific public policy. One-on-one contact with lawmakers or governmental officials is called direct lobbying and today is routinely conducted by paid professionals who represent corporations, trade associations, and other interest groups. Although lobbyists come in all political persuasions, many are lobbyists for hire by those who can afford them.

Millions of dollars in lobbying fees and political contributions were spent by industry and opposing groups in the summer of 2003 to influence the FCC's ruling to relax limits on media ownership. The Center for Responsive Politics reported that media companies spent more than $82 million on federal lobbying efforts between 1999 and 2002 and another $26 million on political contributions. The biggest spenders were the most famous names in broadcasting: AOL Time Warner spent $15.77 million on lobbying and $6.2 million in political contributions; Disney spent $16 million on lobbying and $2.8 million on contributions; the Hearst Corporation spent $394,000 on lobbying and contributed $180,000 to candidates and PACs. Lobbying intensified in the months leading up to the vote and Clear Channel, owner of more than 1,200 radio stations and 36 television stations, which barely had a presence in Washington 2 years earlier, hired four additional lobbying firms and set up its own Washington office.[1]

The use of professionals has evolved because of a highly specialized society that requires representation by interest groups as well as individual citizens. As the eminent political scientist V. O. Key, Jr. stated, "The study of politics must rest on an analysis of the objectives and

229

composition of the interest groups within a society."[2] Whether the influence of pressure groups has gone too far, however, is subject to much debate. Many believe we now live in an era of single interest groups that neglect the good of society as a whole.

THE LOBBYING BUSINESS

By all measures, the lobbying industry has been growing rapidly and is commensurate with the growing role of government in business affairs. Nearly $2 billion was spent for Washington lobbying in 2003. Health care issues accounted for the single biggest share, about $297 million, partly because Congress was considering Medicare prescription drug coverage. Finance and insurance lobbying was next, with at least $259 million spent; and lobbying on communications and technology issues third, with about $248 million.[3] *The New York Times* reported, "Lobbying has turned into a well-ordered global business, with the influence game taking on a decidedly corporate look."[4] As of March 2004, the number of registered lobbyists was about 25,000, up from the 14,946 registered on September 30, 1997.[5] In all there were more than 38 registered lobbyists and $2.7 million in lobbying expenditures for every member of Congress.[6]

Official figures include only those who register under the requirements of the law. Under the old Federal Regulation of Lobbying Act of 1946, anyone who solicited or accepted contributions for lobbying purposes had to keep accounts, present receipts and statements to the Clerk of the U.S. House of Representatives, and register with the Clerk of the House and the Secretary of the Senate. The new Lobbying Disclosure Act of 1995 law—and the Lobbying Disclosure Technical Amendments Act of 1997—provides more information about interest groups' activities and more accuracy in reporting their spending.[7] Grassroots lobbying groups, however, are not required to register.[8] Unofficially, the number of lobbyists is much higher than official figures because many fall outside the legal requirements or simply do not register. Ken Silverstein, in a blistering book on Beltway lobbying, *Washington on $10 Million a Day: How Lobbyists Plunder the Nation*, places the actual figure between 40,000 and 80,000, roughly 75 for each member of Congress, even at the lower figure.[9]

Washington correspondents Michael Kilian and Arnold Sawislak said that lobbying was the fourth largest DC industry—after government, printing, and tourism.[10] Because they play a large legislative role, lobbyists are often called the third House of Congress. They are also known as the fifth branch of government (after the media, which serves as the fourth).

Who Hires Lobbyists?

Industries most affected by government regulation, especially by impending legislation, are most likely to be active in lobbying. In 2000 the top five spenders by industry group were:

1. Finance, insurance, and real estate, $201 million.
2. Health, $209 million.
3. Communications and electronics, $201 million.
4. Energy and natural resources, $159 million.
5. Transportation, $138 million.[11]

Finance, insurance, and real estate lead (also the perennial leader in campaign contributions), because over the last 20 years lawmakers have debated dozens of proposals that would allow banks, securities firms, and insurers to enter each other's line of business. For example, banks, which were the leading proponents of the legislation, would be permitted to offer checking accounts, insurance, and stocks under one roof. Banking deregulation—named bank modernization to seem more appealing—finally succeeded in 1999, thanks to a bipartisan push for banking overhaul measures.[12]

The communications and electronics industry group was the third biggest spender. The motivations of this industry are clearly revealed by Microsoft's increasing presence on the lobbying scene (see Box 9.1) and increased campaign contributions. Its total soft money, PAC and individual contributions to federal parties and candidates, jumped between 1993 and 2000, as shown here:

- 1993–94, $109,134.
- 1995–96, $256,634.
- 1997–98, $1,407,271.
- 1993–87 (total), $1,773,039.
- 1999–00, $2,226,387.[13]

Who Are the Lobbyists?

Most lobbyists are ex-Hill people, ex-government workers, lawyers, and public relations practitioners. For example, in 2003 General Electric, Comcast, Citigroup, and many other *Fortune* 500 companies hired Bush administration officials and former Republican congressional advisers for top lobbying posts. A Republican National Committee official told a group of Republican lobbyists that 33 of 36 top-level Washington positions he was monitoring went to Republicans.[14]

The Center for Responsive Politics identified 138 former members of Congress who turned up as registered lobbyists during 1998. One of them, former representative Bill Paxon (R-N.Y.), who headed the National Republican Congressional Committee, joined the law firm Akin, Gump, Strauss, Hauer & Feld for $1 million a year.[15] Lobbyists are employed in the Washington offices of corporations, trade associations, national business groups, law firms, public relations firms, political consulting firms, research institutes, and think tanks. However, a handful of huge firms dominate Washington's lobbying business. These

Box 9.1   Microsoft's Entry Into the Beltway

Microsoft's belated presence in Washington, DC, illustrates the motives that prompt lobbying activities. Before opening an in-house lobbying office in 1995, the company shunned politics and barely acknowledged Washington existed. In low-key fashion, it relied on the DC law offices of Preston, Gates, Ellis & Rouvelas Meeds (Gates is the father of Bill Gates). By the second half of 1997, however, Microsoft extended its activities; it spent $1.2 million on lobbying, nearly double the $660,000 spent during the first 6 months.

Even before its antitrust troubles started with the Justice Department, Microsoft hired Grover Norquist, the head of Americans for Tax Reform and one of the best connected conservatives in Washington. He was able to help Microsoft in two ways. One was to fight changes in proposed immigration legislation in 1996 that would have jeopardized the status of numerous legal immigrants that Microsoft employs. Another way was to help secure passage of the Software Export Equity Act in 1997, which rewarded software exporters with a tax break worth an estimated $1.7 billion over the next 10 years. Although the law benefits almost 100 companies, Microsoft is the biggest beneficiary.

Microsoft was further spurred into action by an October 20, 1997, Justice Department suit seeking a $1 million-a-day fine from Microsoft for allegedly violating a 1995 antitrust consent decree. In question was Microsoft's requirement that PC makers who want to use its Windows operating system must load Microsoft's Internet Explorer Web browser on their machines. A week before November 4, 1997, when a Senate Judiciary Committee hearing was scheduled to discuss the matter, lobbyists implored members to tread softly on their client, and Microsoft's home state senators blitzed the members with "Dear Colleague" letters asking for fairness in questioning Bill Gates about his business practices.

Microsoft also countered Ralph Nader, who convened a conference on the software business in November 1997. Microsoft and Charles Kelly, president of the Worldwide Association of NT Users Groups, which represents 180,000 programmers, staged a counterconference that called for the government not to interfere in Microsoft's affairs. On November 25, Microsoft also released findings of a survey commissioned by it from political pollsters Peter D. Hart and Robert M. Teeter. By a margin of more than four to one, the survey supported Microsoft's contention that the market, not the government, should determine the contents of software products.

Among other actions, Gates invited Patrick J. Leahy of Vermont, the senior Democrat on the Senate Judiciary Committee, to corporate headquarters and his luxurious home. Another action was to appear on ABC's *Nightline* to argue his case.

Outside lobbying firms, mostly law firms, are the beneficiaries of lobbying expenditures. Microsoft hired a bipartisan group of prominent lobbyists, which included four former members of Congress and 32 former congressional staffers and government officials. Microsoft currently has 10 outside lobbying firms on retainer. Only one, Edelman PR Worldwide, is a public relations firm. Its assignment, according to a memo made public by the *Los Angeles Times,* was to place op-eds and letters to the editor in newspapers in states where Microsoft is under antitrust investigation.

firms offer a full range of services—"everything from public relations, traditional lobbying, research, polling, and direct-mail canvassing to specialists who deal in drumming up 'grass roots' support for issues."[16] According to a *Roll Call* review of lobbying reports for 2002, the revenues of the top 25 lobbying firms were $304.3 million—and the total lobbying fees for all firms from January 1 to June 20, 2002 exceeded $859.5 million.[17] (See Box 9.2 for list of Washington's top lobbying firms in 2001.)

Corporate DC Offices.   Corporate offices are primarily maintained by large corporations; smaller companies tend to rely entirely on their trade associations. Besides engaging in lobbying, these Washington offices perform the following functions:

1. Supply information to the home office by acting as a listening post and "early warning system" on current government policies and future plans and actions that might affect company operations.

Box 9.2   Washington's Top Lobbying Firms in 2001

Firm	Fees (in Millions)
Cassidy & Associates	$33.0
Patton, Boggs	23.5
Akin, Gump, Strauss, Hauer & Feld	19.2
Verner, Liipfert, Bernhard, McPherson & Hand	18.5
Greenberg Traurig	16.4
Van Scoyoc Associates	13.4
Barbour Griffith & Rogers	12.3
Washington Council Ernst & Young	12.0
Williams & Jensen	10.9
PricewaterhouseCoopers	10.8

2. Render service to visiting home office personnel.
3. Provide marketing assistance.
4. Provide legislative representation.
5. Supply analyses of government programs and policies.[18]

Trade Associations.   Well-heeled trade associations "are taking on a growing role ... as intermediaries between their industries and an increasing army of federal regulations."[19] The American Society of Association Executives reports 25,000 members for 2003, 30% of which are Washington-based trade associations.[20] At the end of the 1980s, the number was only about 3,000.[21] Many joined the migration to the capital during the 1960s and 1970s when federal regulation of business became rampant. This reaction suggests lobbying is a particularly strategic function. Other functions are marketing, education, employer–employee relations, research, standardization and simplification, and statistics.[22]

National Business Groups.   Corporate political activity often centers around supra-organizations that represent broad segments of business. Most important among these are the Business Roundtable (see Box 9.3), U.S. Chamber of Commerce, the National Association of Manufacturers, the American Business Conference, and the National Federation of Independent Business.

One feature that has accounted for the Business Roundtable's notable success is CEOs' engagement in direct lobbying with leaders of Congress, the executive branch, and high levels of the civil service. Previously, few CEOs had lobbied government officials, as the incident in Box 9.4 demonstrates. Another factor that has accounted for the Roundtable's effectiveness is the use of a pragmatic rather than an ideological approach: "Its basic rationale for survival is solid and still stands: economic strength in America's capitalist society cannot exist without the cooperation of the managers of the nation's largest corporations."[23]

However, the tide may have turned against the Business Roundtable's effectiveness. In recent years it has lost much of its influence because CEOs can no longer walk into a few key offices at the White House and Capitol and fix problems. With the demise of the old seniority system, each member of Congress now acts like an independent contractor. CEO members of the Business Roundtable simply cannot deliver the huge numbers of votes required to pass or defeat legislation. Furthermore, membership is so diverse that the group has difficulty arriving at a consensus.[24]

Another type of national business group has been spawned by the new high-tech industry and reflects its ever-shifting concerns. Called *adhocracy*, these are temporary virtual associations that reflect the industry's policy interests. Similar to coalitions, they serve as temporary umbrella groups to advocate interests ranging from privacy to taxation. One of them, Americans for Computer Privacy, was instrumental

Box 9.3   The Business Roundtable

The giant among the national business groups is the Business Roundtable, which consists of about 200 CEOs of big business in the industrial, financial, and services industries. The combined gross revenues of its members are equal to about half of the gross domestic product of the entire nation. The group was formed in 1972 after the Nixon administration began its unprecedented peacetime program of wage and price controls to combat high inflation, unemployment, and international exchange problems. As stated by Kim McQuaid, "Executives became increasingly aware that they needed stronger and better negotiating techniques at the federal level; the situation demanded up-to-date political acumen." Executives also recognized that new regulations, such as those of the EPA or Occupational Safety and Health Administration, cut across industry lines—unlike old-style regulations that pertained to particular industries.

The Roundtable employs modern managerial techniques to cope with the fragmented power structure of Congress. It is organized into issue-oriented task forces, it assigns responsibilities on the basis of expertise, researches legislative proposals, makes recommendations on bills, drafts its own proposals, and supports or opposes legislative proposals. The Roundtable has in recent decades spearheaded the political mobilization of business. It often forges alliances with other business lobbies, including organizations like the United States Chamber of Commerce, the National Association of Manufacturers, and the National Federation of Independent Businesses.

Box 9.4   Historic Meeting: DuPont's CEO Meets With the House Speaker

In 1961 Crawford H. Greenewalt, then president of DuPont, arranged a 1-hour meeting with House Speaker John W. McCormack of Massachusetts to talk about the divestiture of General Motors stock. Surprised, McCormack told a friend,

"You know, Clarence, I've just had a most refreshing experience with a businessman. He was the president of the DuPont Company, Crawford H. Greenewalt, and it was the first time in the 30-odd years that I've been a member of Congress that the head of one of the six or eight largest corporations in the United States came to my office to talk directly with me on a problem that gave him concern. It was about the recent decision of the Supreme Court in the General Motors case.

"He came straight to the point without beating around the bush, without talking about his maiden aunt who had gone to the same school with my mother, or anything of that sort. He was forthright, he knew the facts, and he explained them clearly."

in persuading the Clinton administration to reverse its long-standing policy on the export of encryption technology. Another, the Internet Tax Fairness Coalition, supports a simplified uniform sales tax for Internet commerce.[25]

Other Lobbying Groups: Law, Public Relations, and Accounting Firms. Washington, DC abounds with law firms, some of which are branches of the country's leading law firms. Of the nation's top 50 firms in 1981, 47 had offices there compared with 33 offices in 1978. Most attorneys in these offices are specialists in such governmental areas as regulatory and international law.[26]

There is no ballpark estimate of how many people work in public relations in Washington, according to Kilian and Sawislak, who say that these professionals do the job of keeping their clients informed about regulatory activities, "write speeches and testimony for congressional hearings and agency appearances, plan and run seminars and conventions, set up press conferences, lay on cocktail parties, and take clients and contacts to lunch and dinner."[27] Mainly, however, public relations firms enable corporations and interest groups to coordinate lobbying and public relations campaigns. On the basis of 1998 revenues, the top public relations firms in the Washington area are the following:

- Burson-Marsteller, $32.9 million.
- Hill & Knowlton, $27.0 million.
- Fleishman-Hilliard, $19.6 million.
- Ketchum, $18.9 million.
- Porter Novelli, $17.5 million.
- Ogilvy PR Worldwide, $16.2 million.
- Powell Tate, $15.7 million.
- GCI/APCO, $14.3 million.
- Shandwick Public Affairs, $13.0 million.
- Edelman PR Worldwide, $12.3 million.[28]

Public relations firms have been active in acquiring lobbying firms. In November 1999, Shandwick USA acquired the well-known Cassidy Companies; a decade ago, Hill & Knowlton acquired the lobbying firm of Gray & Company. Both public relations firms, in turn, are owned by larger advertising firms. Shandwick USA belongs to the Interpublic Group, and Hill & Knowlton belongs to the WPP Group, which also owns the advertising giants Ogilvy & Mather and J. Walter Thompson.[29]

Further consolidation has occurred. By early 2004, three publicly traded advertising and public relations companies—WPP Group PL, Omnicom Group, Inc., and Interpublic Group of Companies, Inc.— owned most of the influence industry's best known names. They control firms founded by former president Bill Clinton's pollster, former president Jimmy Carter's spokesman, and the current chairman and immediate past chairman of the Republican party. One impetus behind this consolidation is that these public affairs firms are more profitable than public relations.[30]

Corporations also hire accounting firm lobbyists, largely because tax laws are becoming increasingly complex. As stated by Jeffrey H. Birnbaum: "the hottest tactic in lobbying these days pits corporate technicians-for-hire, like those at Price Waterhouse, against the government's own technicians. And increasingly, the government is simply outmatched."[31] When top government tax staffers decide to leave government, they often turn to Price Waterhouse. Two former staff directors of the Joint Tax Committee, Congress's repository of tax information and analysis, started the trend when they joined the accounting firms, which by 1990 employed 123 professionals, compared with 45 at the Joint Tax Committee.[32]

DIRECT LOBBYING RESOURCES AND SKILLS

Direct lobbying requires three resources: access, information, and a mutually beneficial relationship. A lobbyist must also possess the persuasive skills of being an excellent listener, communicator, and negotiator.

Access

Personal access to legislative and regulatory decision makers is a prerequisite for lobbying. As stated by Edwin Epstein, "the chance to get a hearing and the opportunity to make one's case at crucial times and places" is a key political resource.[33] For this reason, former senators, representatives, legislative aides, White House cabinet members, press secretaries, and anyone else in a high position who has contacts are eagerly sought out as lobbyists. Being a member of a politician's family presumably enhances access. Linda Daschle, a powerful lobbyist for American Airlines, is the wife of Tom Daschle. According to Arianna Huffington, author of *Pigs at the Trough*, she was instrumental in the passage of the $15 billion bailout of the airline industry after 9/11. Chet Lott, Trent Lott's son, went from running a pizza joint to being a powerful Washington lobbyist. Huffington asks, "How can these things be legal? Why should they be allowed to be lobbyists and members of the families of politicians who make these key decisions?"[34]

Staff Directories.   Several available directories enable individuals and groups without preexisting personal contacts to least easily identify members of the legislative and executive branches of government.

- *Congressional Staff Directory* lists members of the Senate and House, as well as officers and staffs and their legislative specialties.[35] Every member page contains addresses, telephone and fax numbers, e-mail and web addresses; expanded member biographies, photographs; a state map with district highlighted; staff members with titles and legislative responsibilities; all district offices with address, phone fax, staff; and leadership positions, committees, subcommittees and caucuses.

- *Federal Staff Directory* lists 44,000 decision makers in the executive branch of the federal government and contains more than 2,600 biographies.[36] The directory provides information on the Executive Office of the President—which pinpoints senior officials and top aides working directly with the President and Vice President—cabinet departments, and independent and quasi-official agencies.
- *Leadership Directories* comprise 14 yellow books. Those most useful for lobbying purposes include the *Congressional Yellow Book* (members of Congress, including committees and key staff), the *Federal Yellow Book* (key personnel in federal departments and agencies), the *State Yellow Book* (elected and appointed officials in the executive branch, as well as state legislators and their committees), the *Judicial Yellow Book* (covers federal and higher state courts), the *Municipal Yellow Book* (leading city and county governments and local authorities, and *Foreign Representatives in the U.S.* (information on thousands of business and government decision makers in the United States). The Internet provides daily changes in the Leadership Library.[37]

Michael K. Deaver, a lobbyist with a long history of lobbying in the nation's capital, shows how he exploited his former employment in the White House by obtaining access to it for personal gain (see Box 9.5). Former Senator Bob Packwood (R–Oreg.) is another public official who used the "revolving door" to become a lobbyist. In November 1996, he filed papers to incorporate his new lobbying firm, just 11 days after the legal 1-year moratorium on lobbying expired. He will benefit from the knowledge acquired in government services because he will be lobbying for a business coalition on estate tax issues, a subject he oversaw as chairman of the Senate Finance Committee.[38] When their terms were up in January 2005, well-connected Senators John Breaux and Don Nickles planned to join the private sector as lobbyists. According to Political-MoneyLine.com, 272 former members of Congress have registered to lobby since 1995, a trend abhored by critics. "Many lawmakers stay in office only until they can cash in on their positions," says Larry Noble, executive director of the Center for Responsive Politics. "Then they use their special contacts on the Hill to benefit paying clients."[39]

The revolving door also applies to some civilian administrators. The case of the Air Force's Darleen Druyun, who for three decades had negotiated billion-dollar weapons contracts, received national notoriety when in January 2003 she accepted a job with Boeing. For about a year it was known that she was talking about job opportunities with three of the nation's largest defense contractors: Boeing, Lockheed Martin, and Raytheon. Both Michael Sears, Boeing's chief financial officer, and Druyun were fired a year later for "unethical conduct." Pentagon inves-

---

Box 9.5   Michael K. Deaver: The White House Insider

Michael K. Deaver is a prime illustration of the value of personal access. In May 1985, 2 weeks after he left the White House, where he was deputy chief of staff and an intimate of President and Mrs. Reagan, he and Canadian officials held formal discussions that led to a $105,000 lobbying contract. Among the clients he represented were Rockwell International (in its attempt to persuade the administration to build more B-1 bombers), a group of Caribbean nations (interested in the administration's initiative to help Caribbean Basin countries), and a South Korean manufacturer, Daewoo (accused of violating U.S. import restrictions).

Deaver was severely criticized because he was seen as blatantly taking advantage of his special access to the White House. As reported by *Newsweek,* Deaver, the "ultimate lobbyist," was allowed to keep his pass to the White House and access to its tennis court after resigning from his position. Also, on instructions from Nancy Reagan, he still received the president's detailed daily schedule. His purchase of a mobile-phone-equipped Jaguar XJ6 also received considerable publicity and added to the perception he was flaunting his position as an influence peddler.

---

tigators and the Justice Department were probing into whether she shared a rival company's information with Boeing and pushed a controversial $21-billion plan to have the government lease and later buy 100 Boeing-made airplanes while she worked as a government acquisition officer.[40]

Officers of major corporations have easy access to government decision makers because they and their companies possess the following political resources:

- Corporate managers have continual contact with government officials in their performance of important public functions.
- Businesses make political contributions, and public officials wish not to offend them. They at least give them an audience.
- Government agencies are sometimes required by law to consult groups affected by their regulations.
- Dinners between business leaders and top officials in the federal government are sometimes arranged for purposes of dialogue.
- As industrial statesmen and "leaders of industry," CEOs of the largest corporations are accorded the status of semiofficial spokespersons for the business community. This is one of the strengths of the Business Roundtable, mentioned earlier.
- As managers of the most important economic enterprises in the country, whose cooperation and assistance are critical to the na-

tional interest, business leaders have served in official capacities, for example, on top-level presidential public-service commissions and as consultants.

- On an informal basis, top executives rank high in social status. As social elites, they are thrown into contact with other notables, including leaders in politics and government.
- Also informally, the similarity of their socioeconomic background to that of a significant number of independently wealthy senators facilitates contact between them and contributes to understanding.[41]

Access Through Travel Gifts. Industry leaders and their professional and trade associations pay for the travel of regulators to conventions and conferences where they not only speak on panels but have a chance for cocktail conversations about policy matters. Cable companies, radio and television broadcasters, high-tech businesses, and the telephone industry, for example, have paid for scores of trips by FCC members and staff. Over the past 3 years, FCC members accepted more than $725,000 worth of airfare, hotel rooms, meals, and expenses from the industries they regulate, with smaller amounts provided by international agencies and few public groups and universities.

The National Association of Broadcasters, the largest trade group for the radio and TV broadcasters, spent more than $75,000 flying commissioners and more than a dozen staff members to its yearly convention in Las Vegas. Another group, the National Cable & Telecommunications Association, which represents about 200 member companies, also invites FCC members to its annual convention, attended by about 90,000 people. "That's probably the best opportunity to help people, both the FCC and staff, really understand how our business works," said Rob Stoddard, spokesman for the association. Individual companies, such as Viacom, owner of CBS, Infinity Broadcasting, Paramount Pictures, and Showtime, have also funded trips.[42]

Coincidence of Personal and Legislative Interests. The need for access to a member of Congress is diminished when a legislator's personal interests coincide with a corporation's because of stock ownership (see Box 9.6). There is no law or congressional rule that requires members of Congress to excuse themselves from legislation or subcommittees that could directly affect their major stock holdings.

Information and Knowledge

Although "nailing the right Congressman and influencing the right vote" is the essence of lobbying, such contact must be backed up with "superior information—at the right time," says Philip Lesly, a veteran public relations consultant.[43] Access alone, therefore, is insufficient for political influence; a lobbyist must be credible and knowledgeable. He or

---

Box 9.6   Two Cases of Overlapping Interests

Bristol-Myers Squibb   Bristol-Myers Squibb had an automatic ally in Congress through Senator Judd Gregg (R-N.H.), who owned between $100,000 and $250,000 of stock in the company, according to his 1995 financial disclosure statement. Accordingly, legislation that benefitted the company also benefitted Gregg. House consideration of the FDA Export Reform and Enhancement Act of 1995 was a case in point. It would enable pharmaceutical firms, such as Bristol-Myers, to sell non-FDA-approved drugs in other countries. Gregg was an outspoken advocate for the pharmaceutical industry in the 104th Congress. On one occasion, as the Senate's chief deputy whip, he tried to bring the measure to the Senate floor for a vote. Having failed in that endeavor, he used his seat on an appropriations subcommittee to attach an amendment onto an appropriations bill. When that amendment carried without debate and became law in April 1996, Bristol-Myers stock rose 65%, from $82 a share to $136 a share over the next 10 months. Gregg was enriched as the value of his stock holdings in Bristol-Myers Squibb increased by between $60,000 and $150,000.

Columbia/HCA   Another example of automatic access to Congress is Senator Bill Frist (R-Tenn.), whose father, Dr. Thomas Frist, Sr., was a founder of Columbia/HCA, the country's biggest chain of for-profit hospitals. Senator Frist's personal investment in the company was $13 million, representing 65% of his personal fortune of $20 million, according to his 1994 financial disclosure. Not surprisingly, Frist was an outspoken advocate to give Medicare recipients more "options" and to allow hospitals and doctors to join together as private entities that could contract with Medicare. Both measures would help Columbia/HCA. Defending his stand, Frist said, "Everybody knows my background, where I come from and the hats that I wear.... There is a stone wall that comes between any money that I get or interests that I have, and what I do here."

---

she must be able to assemble expert information and present a credible analysis of the pros and cons of specific issues.

Providing the best researched and best developed factual report on a legislative subject is an important and neglected means of assuring favorable legislation and regulation, says Lesly. Such information must be unimpeachably objective. It must also enter the pipeline of consideration at the right time; namely, when bills are still in the formative stage and officials are looking into the subject. Often the best studies made by business, think tanks, and other groups arrive after the sifting process has gone too far to undo many hours of work by many people.

When Michael Deaver was accused of flaunting his access to the White House for his client, the Canadian government, he defended himself by defining his function in knowledge terms: "working in the advisory field."[44] His role, he said, was to advise the Canadian government on how to deal with the United States. The reason foreign governments buy his services, he said, is that he helps them develop strategies about what their objectives should be and how to achieve them.[45]

Think Tanks.   The formation of think tanks by business interests has greatly facilitated the formulation of free-market policy proposals and the creation of data and knowledge to support lobbying activities, including material for news releases. From fewer than 70 in 1969, the number of think tanks grew to more than 300 by the late 1990s, with further growth expected.[46] The original purpose of think tanks, as envisioned by political scientists such as Charles Merriam, Harold Lasswell, and John Kingdon, was to "provide important background voices that bring rational, reasoned analysis to long-term policy discourse based on the best evidence available."[47] However, as the political environment became increasingly dominated by antigovernment conservatives who posed an effective challenge to the status quo, conservative think tanks found an increasingly engaged, attentive, and receptive audience among policymakers. These conservative think tanks outnumbered liberal ones by a ratio of two to one.[48]

Consistently the most helpful to the most conservative groups has been the Heritage Foundation, according to Andrew Rich, author of *Think Tanks, Public Policy, and the Politics of Expertise.*[49] Unlike earlier think tanks, like the centrist Brookings Institution, the Heritage Foundation aggressively markets its policy views by formatting and promoting its expertise—through short and accessible products, such as *Backgrounders.*[50] By the late 1990s, the Heritage Foundation became the largest and best known of the new generation of ideologically conservative think tanks and rated as most influential among think tanks generally.[51] It was ahead of two other influential conservative think tanks, the American Enterprise Institute and the Cato Institute.[52] In 1997 it was also ahead of the centrist Brookings Institution, which was the most influential think tank in 1993. (Andrew Rich measured influence by the frequency of providing congressional testimony and newspaper citations.)

The future influence of think tanks is likely to diminish, says Rich, based on his analysis of 135 in-depth interviews with officials at think tanks and those in the policymaking and funding organizations that draw on and support their work. The reason is that instead of providing scholarly analysis of issues, think tanks now tend to produce research "that is little more than polemical commentary."[53] Experts have been turned into advocates as the once-real boundaries between experts and advocates in American policymaking have become blurred. Between the mid-1960s and the mid-1990s, the proportion of think tanks with identifiable ideologies grew from less than one quarter to more than half.

A Mutually Beneficial Relationship

The power of access and information is strengthened when a lobbyist operates on the sound foundation of a mutually beneficial relationship with a legislator or other decision maker. Some ways of establishing such a relationship are the following:

- Find out which members of Congress have a particular interest in your company. For example, after finding out in what congressional districts and states company employees live, start calling on senators and members of the House who represent them.
- Find out which congressional committees can be important to the company. Then get to know the chairperson, ranking majority and minority members, and staff aides. Find out all you can about their jobs, how they view their tasks, and them personally. Discover what is on their political agenda.
- Help senators and House members make a good impression on their constituents by keeping them informed about what is going on in their own districts. Never cause embarrassment by giving them incorrect information.
- Do not hesitate to provide personal and professional service, for politics operates by exchange and mutuality of service. Within reason and the boundaries of ethics, help members of Congress and their families attend sports and theater events and provide summer job leads for their children. Help them to obtain local publicity when something important happens, such as a new factory opening in their district.
- When asking for favors, distinguish between issues that are really important to your company and those that are peripheral. Remember that the trick in Washington is to keep as unobligated as you can while piling up as many IOUs as possible.
- If you are a constituent of the legislator you are approaching, try to encourage folks back home, who are his or her constituents, to express their opinions and attempt to mobilize them into an effective grassroots network.
- Ask whether you or company constituents helped the legislator get elected by volunteering services and making personal or PAC contributions.[54]

SOME HELPFUL SKILLS

Besides possessing political resources, a lobbyist must acquire special lobbying skills. Among the most important are working with, and testifying before, congressional committees and arranging for media coverage.

Working With Congressional Committees

Lobbyists and citizens may arrange to be invited to appear before congressional committees. Anyone who learns how Congress works—which in itself is a must for any lobbyist—knows that these committees are key to the legislative process. Members of committees formulate drafts of legislation that, if approved by a committee, are then voted on by the entire Senate and House of Representatives.

Key personnel within a committee are the chairperson, who is almost always a member of the majority party of Congress, the ranking minority members, and the professional staff. (Lists of members of all committees and subcommittees are available from the Clerk of the House, U.S. Capitol, Washington, DC 20515, and the Secretary of the Senate, U.S. Capitol, Washington, DC 20510. Another source is the *Congressional Staff Directory* mentioned earlier.)

A businessperson who is from a committee member's home district and is already favorably known to the senator or House committee member is in the best position to make contact. He or she should do the following: (a) write a letter that spells out how an issue will affect the constituency of the member of Congress; (b) meet with members of Congress in their home districts rather than on the Hill; (c) cultivate congressional committee staff because they are knowledgeable and have influence on congressional members.

When meeting with congressional committee members or staff, a Washington expert who knows these persons should accompany a home district visitor. As stated earlier, this is one of the functions that can be performed by someone in the corporate Washington office, a trade association, or a law or public relations firm.[55]

Testifying Before a Congressional Committee

Thousands of citizens testify before congressional committees each year. Among them are business executives who wish to influence the outcome of a bill. When invited to testify before a committee, an executive should heed the advice of John Bartels, Rexnord's director of public affairs:

- Treat your testimony as an opportunity—not an ordeal. However, also remember that the experience can be unnerving: "Those 36-foot ceilings and marble walls, plus media, plus questions from congressmen are not duplicated in the business world."
- Put across some positive points of your own. You know more about the subject than they do, but stay in your ballpark.
- Congressional staff people do the work for a hearing, so contact them before you get there. Get an idea of what the audience will be, who will run the show, when you should be there, and who else will be appearing.

- Have a detailed statement, plus copies for distribution well (48 hours) before your appearance.
- Have a summary ready to read aloud. Read slowly and clearly.
- Answer questions straightaway. If you don't know, say so. Maintaining credibility during questioning is very important.
- You may defer a question by saying that if allowed, you'd like to answer that in writing. Remember, most hearings are to gain public notice and support for the committees' stands. They can use your statements in any way they see fit, so make them correct.
- Listen to questions carefully. Wait 2 to 3 seconds, then answer. Be cool. You may need a "drill" before you go.[56]

A committee appearance contains features of both a speech and a media interview. The spoken and written statement is the speech, and the questioning is the interview. However, these interviews can exceed the dangers of a media interview because congressional members are more interested in advancing their own cause than in even being as fair as some reporters. Caution, therefore, must be exercised in gauging the direction of questioning and in preparing for the "zinger," the ultimate question (see Box 9.7).

Box 9.7   Senator Kennedy's "Zinger"

Senator Edward Kennedy illustrated how to use the zinger when he was chairman of a subcommittee that investigated deregulation of the airline industry. He provoked witnesses, punched holes in opposing arguments, and stimulated controversy. He thereby managed to generate publicity out of the "obscure, tedious, and incomprehensible" subject of regulatory practice. His culminating question would be the zinger that, as explained from Kennedy's perspective, "makes an important point for your side ... is unanswerable, and ... shows that the person who is unable to answer the question satisfactorily can do so only because he's totally wrong and you're totally right. And it has to be obvious, clear, and easy for anybody who knows nothing about the subject, hearing the question, to understand those three things."

The dynamic behind hearings, says a popular Harvard Business School case study, is to "provide useful lessons to both the industry spokesmen and regulatory commissions. The deft handling of information, the well-timed release of reports, the prudent scheduling of witnesses: all of these can be used to present a fair representation of the facts while subtly influencing the perception of these facts." Hearings should be viewed as part theater, said Stephen Breyer, the same subcommittee's special counsel. They have to be carefully planned and directed in advance. They have to "make the intellectual point," and they have to be interesting in terms of conflict, revelation, and drama.

Arranging for Media Coverage at Hearings

Using congressional hearings to obtain publicity should not be forfeited to members of Congress. Increasingly, corporations and other organizations view the appearance of one of their witnesses as an opportunity to distribute VNRs as well as regular printed releases. An example is the appearance of Ken Mason, CEO of Quaker Oats, before an FTC hearing in Washington (see Box 9.8).

Other Advice for Effective Government Presentations

Lawyers and other lobbyists offer a potpourri of advice on how to present one's case to government more effectively. Some advice is about attitudes: a realization that many of the "legal things" are really "people things"; for example, don't assume that bureaucrats are dumb, lazy or rigid. Other advice is about contacts; for example, find someone who knows a legislator personally, set up a legislative network whether you represent an association or a corporation, and develop allies whenever possible. And some advice is about campaign tactics; for example, whenever possible, reduce issues to case studies, and make sure copies of your testimony are available to the media.[57]

Box 9.8   Testimony of Ken Mason, CEO of Quaker Oats

The aim of Ken Mason, CEO of Quaker Oats, was to personally enunciate the company's point of view about children's ready-to-eat cereals, child nutrition, Saturday morning television, and related interests. He wanted to make sure his views went beyond the hearing to the general public.

A Washington, DC, public relations firm, John Adams and Associates, arranged publicity. It invited radio and television network news as well as other opinion-leading Washington-based media to the FTC hearings. As insurance, the public relations firm went one step further and arranged for audio and television taping of Mason's testimony. An audiotape, made during the afternoon hearings, was immediately edited into a brief news report (called an *actuality*) and transmitted to the radio networks and local station news departments around the nation, in time for the evening news.

John Adams and Associates also had two different kinds of videotapes made. One was an interview with Mason, about a minute-and-a-half in length, based on his FTC testimony. The second, a shorter tape, was his statement about the company's position. Fifty television stations around the United States used the second tape; a larger number used the longer tape.

CONCLUSIONS

Direct lobbying conforms to the traditional meaning that allows persons to petition government. All interest groups, and especially corporations, do so. Corporations have special advantages of access because of the dominance of economic institutions and the high status of business executives in our society. Lobbying is no longer a folksy affair, however; it has become a highly skilled business run chiefly by professionals, many of whom are for hire by those who can afford them. They have considerable knowledge and other political resources. Direct lobbying is fortified with grassroots and fund-raising activities, as discussed in the following two chapters.

ENDNOTES

1. Charles Pope, "Media Groups Spent Millions Lobbying the FCC," *Seattle Post-Intelligencer,* June 3, 2003, p. C2.
2. V. O. Key, Jr., *Politics, Parties, and Pressure Groups,* 3rd edition (New York: Thomas Y. Crowell, 1953), p. 24.
3. Sharon Theimer, "Spending on 2003 D.C. Lobbying Near $2B," Associated Press, June 1, 2004. For details on the communications industry, see *Paying to Play: $100 Million to Influence Communications Policy, January–June 2003* by *Communication Daily.* Press release, March 10, 2004.
4. *Impact,* op. cit., p. 1.
5. "Masters of Access: How the Best Lobbyists Line Up," *The Hill,* March 24, 2004, p. 16.
6. "Influence, Inc.: Summary; Lobbyists Spending in Washington" (1999 edition), Center for Responsive Politics.
7. Susan Watkins Greenfield, "Interest Groups and Lobbyists: Sources of Information," *CRS Report for Congress* (Washington, D.C.: Congressional Research Service, July 18, 2002 update), p. CRS-1.
8. Francesca Contiguglia, "GAO Finds That Lobbyist Registration Has Soared," *Roll Call,* May 14, 1998. Internet.
9. Ken Silverstein, *Washington on $10 Million a Day* (Monroe, Me.: Common Courage Press, 1998), p. 18.
10. Michael Kilian and Arnold Sawislak, *Who Runs Washington?* (New York: St. Martin's, 1982), p. 142.
11. "Lobbyists Database," op. cit.
12. Ibid.
13. "Money in Politics Alert: Microsoft Antitrust Case: An Update on the Company's Lobbying and Campaign Contributions," Center for Responsive Politics; based on FEC data downloaded June 1, 2000.
14. Jim VandeHei and Juliet Eilperin, "Targeting Lobbyists Pays off for GOP; Party Earns More Funds, Influence," *Washington Post,* June 26, 2003, p. A01.
15. "Influence, Inc.: Lobbyists Spending in Washington" (1999 edition), Center for Responsive Politics.
16. Neil A. Lewis, "Spheres of Influence Grow in Washington: Once the Enclave of a Few Old Hands, Lobbying Is Corporate and Fast-Merging," *New York Times,* November 16, 1999, p. C-1.

17. Brody Mullins, "A Record Year for K St. in '02," *Roll Call*, April 21, 2003. Internet.
18. Murray L. Weidenbaum, *Business, Government, and the Public* (Englewood Cliffs, N. J.: Prentice-Hall, 1977), pp. 244–252.
19. "For Trade Association, Politics Is the New Focus," *BusinessWeek*, April 17, 1978, p. 107.
20. Figures provided by the ASAE, October 24, 2003.
21. Jeffrey H. Birnbaum, *The Lobbyists: How Influence Peddlers Get Their Way in Washington* (New York: Times Books, 1992), p. 7.
22. See Joseph F. Bradley, *The Role of Trade Associations and Professional Societies in America* (University Park: Pennsylvania State University Press, 1965).
23. Kim McQuaid, "The Roundtable: Getting Results in Washington," *Harvard Business Review*, Vol. 59, May–June, 1981, p. 115.
24. Jeffrey H. Birnbaum, "The Fallen Giant," *Fortune*, December 8, 1997, pp. 156–158.
25. Glenn R. Simpson, "Lobbying for 'Net Firms Gets Boost From 'Adhocracy,'" *Wall Street Journal*, December 21, 1999, p. A24.
26. Kilian and Sawislak, op. cit., p. 195.
27. Ibid., pp. 188–189.
28. Lewis, op. cit. The source of information is O'Dwyer's *Directory of Public Relations Firms*.
29. Ibid.
30. Jeffrey H. Birnbaum, "Big Firms Gobble up Lobbying Interest: Consolidation Is the Trend in Influence Industry," *Washington Post*, April 27, 2004, p. E1.
31. "Accounting Concerns Assume Burgeoning Role as Lobbyists; Often Outshoot Federal `Bureaucrats," *Wall Street Journal*, March 7, 1989, p. A26.
32. Birnbaum, op. cit., p. 217.
33. Epstein, op. cit., p. 197.
34. Tavis Smiley, "Arianna Huffington Discusses How Corporate Greed and Political Corruption Are Undermining America," National Public Radio, February 19, 2003.
35. Published by CQ Staff Directories, Inc., 815 Slaters Lane, Alexandria, VA 22314. It is published three times each year, in the spring, summer, and fall.
36. Published by CQ Staff Directories, Inc.; see previous note.
37. See www.leadershipdirectories.com.
38. Associated Press, "Packwood, the Lobbyist, Among Many Ex-Colleagues," *Boston Sunday Globe*, November 17, 1996, p. A9.
39. Jeffrey H. Birnbaum, "More Lawmakers See Lobbying as Next Job," *Boston Globe*, June 28, 2004, p. A8.
40. Anne Marie Squeo and J. Lynn Lunsford, "Missed Connections: How Two Officials Got Caught by Pentagon's Revolving Door," *Wall Street Journal*, December 18, 2003, p. A1.
41. Epstein, op. cit., pp. 197–203.
42. Anne C. Mulkern, "Industry-Paid Junkets Raise Ethics Issues for the FCC, *The Denver Post*, March 9, 2003, p. A-01.
43. *Managing the Human Climate*, no. 512, September/October, 1978, p. 2. Also see Margery Kraus, "Government Relations in the 90s and Beyond," in *Practical Public Affairs in an Era of Change: A Communications Guide for Business, Government, and College*, ed. Lloyd B. Dennis (Lanham, Md.: University Press of America, 1996), p. 95.
44. Martin Tolchin, "Aide Said Canada 'Could Use' Deaver," *New York Times*, May 11, 1986, p. 1.

45. Burt Solomon, "Hawking Access," *National Journal*, Vol. 18, May 3, 1986, pp. 1048–1053.

46. Andrew Rich, *Think Tanks, Public Policy, and the Politics of Expertise* (Cambridge, Mass.: Cambridge University Press, 2004), p. 204.

47. Ibid., p. 2.

48. Ibid., pp. 205–206.

49. Ibid., p. 216.

50. Ibid., p. 206.

51. Ibid., p. 53.

52. Ibid., p. 81.

53. Ibid., p. 220.

54. Dan H. Fenn Jr., Donald Grunewald, and Robert N. Katz, *Business Decision Making and Government Policy: Cases in Business and Government* (Englewood Cliffs, N.J.: Prentice-Hall, 1966).

55. See "How to Work With Congressional Committees," *Iron Age*, April 11, 1977, p. 154.

56. Rexnord/Public Affairs, "Governmental Contact—Testifying Before Congressional Committees," supplementary materials to Fraser/Associates, *Getting the Most From Grassroots Programs in the 1980s* (Washington, D.C.: Public Affairs Council, 1980).

57. *Tips & Tactics*, supplement of *pr reporter*, Vol. 17, August 6, 1979.

Chapter 10

Grassroots Lobbying

Grassroots lobbying is pressure from the bottom up. "The folks back home" tell a legislator what is on their minds, and these voices are important because more than anything else legislators want to get reelected. Because grassroots pressure seldom arises spontaneously, it must be organized by those seeking to become lawmakers. Thus grassroots advocacy has become an essential strategic tool in lobbying Congress and the state legislatures. Over the past 20 years, grassroots programs have grown in number and many corporations and associations have established positions and sometimes entire units devoted to grassroots.[1] Between 1993 and 1994, organizations spent $790 million on it at the federal, state, and local levels.[2]

A 1997 *Fortune* magazine survey that lists "the Power 25"—Washington's most important and powerful interest groups, labor unions, and trade associations—further demonstrates the importance of grassroots lobbying. Leading the list were the American Association of Retired Persons, the American Israel Public Affairs Committee, the AFL-CIO, the National Federation of Independent Business, and the Association of Trial Lawyers of America. The Power 25 wield enormous political clout, not only because they have money but also because they are able to mobilize support from actual voters back home. They can point to large numbers of geographically dispersed, politically active members with narrow interests. This, said *Fortune*, is the "New Lobbying."[3]

Focusing on the issue of health policy, researcher Michael T. Heaney found that grassroots strength mainly accounts for the high ranking in the newest list of the 25 organizations with the most influence on Capitol Hill. Based on interviews with 95 congressional staffers, these were the American Medical Association, AARP (formerly the American

Association of Retired persons), the American Hospital Association (AHA), and the United States Chamber of Commerce. Local presence is important: The AARP "upholds the gold standard for citizen lobbying, with 67% of congressional staffers reporting a strong local AARP presence"; and the AHA stands out for maintaining the best geographic coverage of any organization, with 83% reporting that it is politically organized in their areas.[4]

WHY GRASSROOTS ACTIVITIES HAVE BECOME IMPORTANT

Although direct lobbying is an excellent way of conveying information to lawmakers, it is usually an insufficient means of applying political pressure. Direct lobbying by itself is usually effective when an issue is highly technical or involves only selected constituencies. However, when an issue attracts public attention and concern, grassroots public opinion and pressure count. Lawmakers know that if they ignore the voice of their own constituents on issues that concern them, their reelection is at risk.

The American Bankers Association (ABA) has recognized the value of grassroots lobbying and organized a "Team 21" to help execute campaigns. In this way, calls and e-mails and faxes "come from real bankers running real banks across America. With more than 1.5 million people making their living at a bank, it shouldn't be impossible to mobilize big numbers when important legislation is on the line in Congress," says the *ABA Banking Journal*.[5] The Team 21 model is a highly structured, coordinated approach by ABA, the state executives, and bankers from institutions of all sizes. Federal legislative "captains," appointed by the ABA and each state executive, are responsible for setting up and running the program in each state. The captains, in turn, appoint team "leaders" for every U.S. representative and senator in each state. These leaders, in turn, organize volunteer teams of between 5 and 10 banks that work to build ongoing relationships and regular communications with their assigned members of Congress.

Two other factors, besides the nature and complexity of a policy issue, affect the appropriateness of various grassroots activities: (a) the issue's stage in the legislative process, and (b) the legislative chamber and legislator targeted.[6] Compared with direct lobbying by executives or professional lobbyists, legislators pay more attention to grassroots activities during that part of the legislative stage when an issue is voted on in committee or when it comes to the floor of the House or Senate. Legislators rely more on professional lobbyists, however, for detailed content of legislation.[7] The target of grassroots activity is more likely to be the House than the Senate because it is more likely to be influenced. House members represent a narrower constituency and are subject to reelection every 2 years instead of the Senate's 6 years.

Changes in Political Structure

Because of changes in the political structure and the availability of technology, one of the strongest trends in politics today is the movement toward the "golden age of grassroots lobbying." This "unstoppable force" is transforming U.S. culture and politics. Three changes in the political environment have increased the effectiveness of grassroots lobbying and provided enormous incentives and opportunities for corporations and others to engage in it:[8]

1. Political parties have been weakened and their control over members of Congress has loosened.

2. The reorganization of Congress in the 1970s decreased the power of committee chairpersons, which had the effect of more widely distributing power to individual legislators. They subsequently became political entrepreneurs who sought financial and other support directly from constituents. Corporations, with their rich political resources, are an important source of campaign support. They can provide PAC funds and soft money (see chap. 11), volunteers to help in campaign work, and feedback on issues and the political climate.

3. The decline in voter participation. Only about 40% of registered voters vote in off-year elections, and about 50% during presidential elections. As little as 20% of the population can determine who wins or loses in an off-year election, and 25% during presidential elections. For example, in 1994 freshman Republican Andrea Seastrand won in California's 22nd district with less than 2,000 votes to spare; her fellow California representative, Democrat Jane Harman, was returned to Congress by a vote margin of 812. In a closer race, Sam Gejdenson (D-Conn.) won an eighth term in Congress in 1994 with only 21 votes to spare.[9] When a small block of votes can determine the outcome of an election, a member of Congress is especially sensitive to grassroots pressure.

Effective Technology

The technology of the Internet is another reason grassroots lobbying has become more important and effective. As stated by Pete Engardio in *BusinessWeek*:

> By mastering the weaponry of the Web, everyone from clandestine Beijing dissidents to high-powered Washington lobbyists are finding that the Internet is an extraordinary tool for mobilizing support, raising money, and exerting influence. In the Internet Age, it's possible for a handful of Web-savvy activists to exert pressure on policymakers working out of their homes. The result may be a fundamental transformation of the nature of politics.[10]

The Internet, says Engardio, has ushered in the new social phenomenon of virtual organizations: "unstructured ad hoc clusters of people who perhaps never met" but who share a common passion—"a concern for environmental issues, an ethnic identity, or simply a sense of struggle. But they can be rapidly mobilized for political action."[11]

The Internet is changing the rules of the game, states a Foundation for Public Affairs report on the impact of the Internet on public policy-making.[12] It "lowers the barriers to entering the game."[13] Former Christian Coalition executive director Ralph Reed says the Internet is the latest in "a series of technologies that are democratizing the political process, making it possible [for activist groups] to bypass gatekeepers and the traditional print and broadcast media to communicate directly with their constituents."[14] The importance of the Internet will grow as more people use it, as more than half (55%) of U.S. adults were doing by mid-1999.[15]

Corporations, however, have lagged behind activist groups in their use of the Internet. Concern about security has made corporations shy about posting information on the Web, says Faye Gorman-Graul, director of Dow Corning's government relations office in Washington. "Look at company websites and you rarely see public policy positions." Even if companies are gun shy, they can use the Internet to monitor activists, says Matthew Benson, senior director at the Bivings Woodell public affairs consulting firm: It has the potential to be "a great place for early warning on emerging issues."[16] Ronald Budzik, vice president for government affairs at Mead, adds, "You can easily get the data that flows across the environmental groups. Go to a website and get any information that comes off of it. All it takes is an e-mail address to sign up" for many activist groups' e-mail alerts.[17]

ELEMENTS OF GRASSROOTS LOBBYING

From a public affairs viewpoint, grassroots lobbying is the mobilization of constituents to demonstrate public support for an organization's position. Raymond Hoewing, former president of the Public Affairs Council, defines grassroots programs as "organized efforts by a company or organization to recruit and deploy political power from constituencies in and out of the organization."[18] Edward A. Grefe, chief political consultant to Legislative Demographic Services, emphasizes, "Grassroots is one-on-one communications ... reaching out to individuals to seek their support and to recruit their participation."[19] It is also a two-way process that is based on the assumption that those most affected by an issue will respond to an invitation to become involved in any deliberation over its future.

Corporations, trade associations, and many other organizations recognize the opportunity as well as the necessity "to look beyond traditional political structures to the people."[20] As stated by Jack Bonner, a prominent grassroots specialist, grassroots works best when you "acti-vate politically important home district constituents who can demon-strate they understand both sides of an issue and can explain in their own words how this issue will impact their district."[21]

Grassroots lobbying consists of three essential steps: (a) constitu-ency building, (b) constituency communication, and (c) constituency activation.

Constituency Building

Constituency building is the process of identifying and recruiting people who are willing to become politically active on behalf of an organiza-tion. It is the attempt to harness the self-interest of individuals who have some kind of a relationship or common interest with an organiza-tion. The aim is to motivate them to join the company in its political programs and campaigns.

For organizations with sound existing public relations programs, constituency building is already well on its way. Established relation-ships with such stakeholders as employees, stockholders, and commu-nity citizens can be directed toward political support. If relationships are weak, however, support from these stakeholders is less likely and pre-liminary efforts have to be made to win their confidence.

Constituency building begins when an organization identifies those individuals or groups among its stakeholders who are most likely to be-come politically active. The composition of this collection of persons and groups is not constant but varies with different types of issues. Stock-holders, for example, are more likely to be interested in issues dealing with corporate governance and taxation; employees in the automotive industry are interested in the issue of protective tariffs and quotas.

Volunteers are an important segment of an organization's constitu-ents because they do much of the work of grassroots lobbying. The Na-tional Rifle Association (NRA) has one of the most effective groups of volunteers. It expends a significant amount of time and resources in re-cruiting, training, maintaining, and mobilizing volunteers for legisla-tive and political campaigns. For this purpose the NRA has a Grassroots Division with a full-time staff of 12. Box 10.1 describes these activities and how they were applied to a political campaign.[22]

Strategies for Selecting Constituents.   Wes Pedersen describes five methods for selecting constituents:

- *Ad hoc:* Changing with circumstances and each issue. Circum-stances, such as having to respond to an immediate legislative need or threat, may dictate this approach, in which the choice of constituents varies with each issue. For example, stockholders are an appropriate constituent group for issues dealing with corporate governance and

---

Box 10.1   NRA's Way of Recruiting and Managing Volunteers

The NRA recruits by making use of its "natural resources"—its base of support in guns shops, gun and hunting clubs, shooting ranges, and gun shows. Each volunteer is asked to recruit additional volunteers among family members, friends, business associates, Christmas card lists, alumni associations, and so on.

These volunteers are entered into a sortable database where their profile characteristics are recorded; for example, has a pickup truck (ideal for sign distribution), or owns a business with multiphone capacity. Their interests are noted so that assignments can be delegated that dovetail. Also, assignments make use of any previous volunteer experience.

Training is taken seriously. In the past two election cycles, the NRA conducted more than 110 grassroots-election workshops in 41 states. Volunteers are made to feel comfortable using a phone bank script, walk sheets, or precinct map. Their egos are also lifted by giving them titles commensurate with the jobs they are doing (e.g., phone bank coordinator, a neighborhood captain, or a literature drop coordinator).

At meetings everyone wears a name badge so people can get to know one another. During a campaign every effort is made to make the working environment enjoyable and—very important—to make sure each one is given something to do.

At the end of a campaign make sure volunteers are recognized A candidate might send a letter, a commemorative pin, or an autographed bumper sticker. Other forms of appreciation are a low-budget party or a pat on the back and a hearty "thank you."

---

taxation; employees in the automotive industry would be appropriate for the issue of protective tariffs and quotas.

• *Broad-based:* Targeting employees, shareholders, customers, distributors, suppliers, and other constituencies. The ABA used this approach when it appealed to the general public to oppose the inclusion of a 10% tax on interest and dividends in a tax reform package by Congress. Bankers feared the public would blame bankers once the withholding began. The ABA placed an ad titled "Congress Wants a Piece of Your Savings. What They Need Is a Piece of Your Mind" in many U.S. newspapers. More important, the ABA prepared a media and support kit that was sent to its 14,000 member banks. For media relations purposes, the kit contained two sample letters to the editor, one by a banker and one by a citizen. To reach other specific audiences, the kits included a Q&A sheet with specific answers to questions by employees, customers, and the media. The kit also provided a sample postcard/ballot that customers could fill out and drop into a "ballot box" in the bank lobby, which the bank would then mail to Congress. To further encourage grassroots activity, the kits contained three sample letters to Congress—from a banker, a consumer, and a senior citizen.[23]

• *Key-contact:* Using a cadre of line managers who are able and willing to meet one-on-one with senators and representatives on issues important to the company. It is a more formalized approach favored by several companies, such as Merck and Scott Paper.

• *Third-party advocacy:* Soliciting support from outsiders who are credible sources. Because they are outsiders, they generally have weaker interest in and commitment to the issue, a fact that lawmakers often recognize by according them higher credibility.

• *"God Bless America" approach:* Bringing people into the political process because it's the "right thing to do."[24]

Two additional approaches have been added: grasstops and astroturf. In the *grasstops* approach, persons are sought who are likely to gain access to, or have influence with, a member of Congress, perhaps because they were once close to him or her. They are "prominent, influential people in the area who agree to 'weigh in' with a lawmaker on behalf of your issue."[25] They are higher up the political food chain, so more lawmakers want to interact directly with them. Such persons may also enjoy clout because of their expertise on an issue or assistance they have provided during political campaigns. They include elected officials, opinion leaders, party leaders, campaign advisers, local association officers, community leaders, academics, and other policy analysts.[26] Used in key influential or key influencer campaigns, the grasstops strategy is best used as a supplement to a broader program.

The *astroturf* approach has been made possible by the help of modern information technology, which easily allows the creation of databases of potential constituents, which appear as apparent grassroots supporters. For example, when Bonner sought to identify groups that would be predisposed to oppose an amendment that would require the Big Three auto makers to build smaller, more fuel-efficient cars, he chose the elderly and the physically handicapped; they, he reasoned, would have a hard time getting into smaller cars with walkers, wheelchairs, and other special equipment.[27] As recognized by Ron Faucheux, such lists of potential supporters can be used for the "instant manufacturing of public support for a point of view in which either uninformed activists are recruited or means of deception are used to recruit them."[28]

Such manufactured support is a artificial and temporary—not to be confused with solid, lasting grassroots support from established relationships. The real difference between grassroots and astroturf, says Elizabeth J. Welsh, president of Executive Communications, is in the "level of understanding, belief, commitment and personal stake that advocates demonstrate during their communications with legislators."[29] Lawmakers have a growing suspicion of astroturf campaigns, causing them to "question their constituents to ascertain how knowledgeable they are on the issue and what prompted them to call the legislator."[30]

Newspaper publishers are also becoming more vigilant in screening astroturf letters to the editor. The *Boston Globe* is one such publisher, after unwittingly publishing letters that were written not by the local folks who signed them, but by the Republican National Committee. In response to greater media scrutiny of letter writers, public relations people are giving this advice: (a) Even when form letters are required, engage in "creative personalization"; (b) make an effort to tailor letters to each publication; (c) try to get letters signed by someone who will be recognized as a leader in a particular community; and (d) allude to the author's knowledge of an issue; for example, start out with "As a former patient of Local Hospital...."[31]

Categories of Key Constituency Groups.   Many campaigns find it helpful to refer to the following categories of constituents:

1. *Natural constituencies*. The most likely source of grassroots support for a company comes from those groups whose economic fate is linked with it. Employees and stockholders are therefore called natural constituencies because employees' jobs and stockholders' dividends are dependent on company profitability and survival. They share a commonality of interest with the company. An illustration is the campaign by several corporate giants—including GM, Citigroup, Southern Company, ChevronTexaco, and Verizon—to send letters to shareholders asking them to contact members of Congress to support President Bush's dividend tax cut. The letter from GM's president and CEO Rick Wagoner read, in part, "We think this proposal makes good economic sense, and is good for our stockholders and General Motors.... We've shared our enthusiasm for it with members of Congress, and we urge you to do the same promptly."[32]

2. *Extended constituencies*. Extended constituencies also have a link with a company, but the connection is weaker and more remote. Examples are retirees, royalty recipients, dealers, suppliers, merchants in communities where companies are located, and a miscellany of people, such as outside legal counsel and insurance companies with whom the company is insured. Sun Oil also recruits leasers who own property on which Sun drills.

The classic $1-billion bailout of Chrysler illustrates the use of extended constituencies. The company's carefully orchestrated lobbying effort included 4,700 dealers and 19,000 suppliers, who were asked to make an "all-out effort" to contact senators and representatives to "let them know how important 'Chrysler's business was to the local economies.'"[33]

Although customers are sometimes considered a natural constituency, they are for practical purposes best considered as either an extended constituency or outside constituency, depending on the nature of the industry. Companies in the tobacco industry use catalogs not only to market directly to customers but also to mobilize customers as a political force. For example, when Philip Morris's Benson & Hedges catalog offers customers a Mikasa crystal set in exchange for 300 proofs of purchase, the responses enable the company to build a database of its smokers, which can be used to drum up support for its legislative and other political goals. It also publishes a magazine, *Unlimited*, to reach its Marlboro smokers.[34]

3. *Outside constituencies.* Outside constituencies, drawn from the general public, do not have an economic link with a company; they may, however, identify with its issue and causes. Such groups, often considered third-party advocates, are important when a corporation or association has no constituent presence in key legislative districts.[35] The challenge is to find a way to identify these potential supporters.

The Health Insurance Industry of America (HIAA) identified and recruited outside constituencies by using paid ads to fight the Clinton administration's health care reform proposal. Its much publicized and highly successful Harry and Louise spots demonstrated the value of this approach. A vital feature of the $15-million spots was a toll-free telephone number. It generated more than 350,000 phone calls, which enabled the HIAA to send information packets to callers. The HIAA recruited 40,000 activist volunteers from the respondents, who are credited with producing 200,000 contacts with members of Congress.[36]

Constituency Communication

When time permits, recruitment of constituents can be followed up by regular communication about pertinent political issues and stressing the importance of constituent involvement in the political process. As stated by Pamela Jones-Lee, president of National Grassroots & Communications, "Clients need to take time to educate their constituencies so the constituency is still there after they leave."[37] The New York Power Authority has done this with its Ambassador Program, which is intended to establish two-way communications with more than 4,000 contacts statewide who appear on its computerized mailing list. One aspect of the program is a questionnaire asking these people about their involvement in the community, the level at which they would participate (e.g., letter writing, making phone calls), and the issues in which they would be interested.[38]

Communicating with and educating a company's natural constituencies of employees and stockholders is essentially an extension of existing public relations, employee communication, and investor relations programs—assuming they exist. For example, a company provides employees not only with company news and social activities, but also information about economic and political issues facing the company and, indirectly, themselves. Similarly, communication vehicles can be created with extended constituents, such as dealers.

When a vote on an issue is imminent, public affairs managers can instantly provide newly identified constituencies, as well as existing ones, with political and public policy information through some of the new media: cable television, online electronic services (e-mail, websites), and fax machines. For example, the Independent Insurance Agents of America (IIAA) supplemented its existing newsletters with satellite communications when it transmitted three live shows in one day to 200 sites around the country, reaching more than 5,000 people.[39]

Constituency communication is facilitated by the Internet, which is easy and cheap to use. For example, when people call up and ask for information, they can be told to get it on the organization's website. It saves time and the expense of mass mailings. Ken Deutsch and Mark Reilly of Issue Dynamics, Inc., take this strong view: "Any grassroots campaign organization without a website is missing the boat."[40] Any use of the Internet, however, should be integrated into the overall grassroots campaign strategy and not used by itself. Although serious grassroots efforts are now being conducted on the Internet, there has not yet been a single campaign conducted solely via the Internet that has had any major results.[41]

Constituency Activation and Methods of Pressuring Lawmakers

Although constituency activation is not always distinct from constituency communication, its goal is to alert and mobilize supporters on issues of importance to the company. Alerts have traditionally been announced through direct mail, such as action alert letters or newsletters, and telephone calls. Now phone calls are mostly automated voice messages, and faxes and e-mail are increasingly employed. Cyberlobby firm e-advocates, cofounded by Pam Fielding, used e-mail to help lead a National Education Association drive to save a federal requirement that Internet service providers give schools a discount rate after congressional Republicans moved to end it. Lawmakers and the FCC were swamped with 22,000 messages from moms, dads, business persons, teachers, or school administrators.[42] Such an avalanche of messages is losing its effectiveness, however, and consultants are advising a move from high quantity to high quality.[43]

Furthermore, the "contact tree" technique is frequently applied, whereby selected members use phone and fax communications to keep other members informed of legislative happenings. A more organized method, used by the HIAA, is to hire field directors in critical states to organize direct-mail and telephone contacts.[44]

Organizations send alerts to encourage constituents to communicate with their congressional members' offices through phone calls, letters, faxes, and e-mail, and also to have face-to-face meetings by visiting them on Capitol Hill or at their district offices.

Patch-Through Techniques.   When they mobilize the citizenry to take part in the political process (which is the way they like to define their work), grassroots lobbying-for-hire organizations such as Bonner & Associates depend heavily on phone calls by their hundreds of operators. During a call, operators present receivers with a programmed script, and, if receivers agree, the opportunity to send a postcard, letter, or fax. If receivers agree, operators arrange a preprinted, postage-paid mailing.

More typically, constituents are asked if they would like to talk to their congressperson. If so, they are immediately connected to the congressperson's office. This contact technique is called a *telephone patch-through*, which Ron Faucheux defines as "direct-connects or third party calling, in which a phone bank for a lobbying organization gets an agreeable activist on the line and directly connects him or her to the targeted public official or staff member so that the activist can deliver a personal message."[45] Consultants warn that it is becoming more and more important to provide more detailed information to those talking to legislators because resulting conversations sometimes enable lawmakers to turn callers around because of their lack of information.[46] Especially under such circumstances, patch-throughs are more likely perceived as astroturf efforts rather than having the appearance of a genuine grassroots call.

One of the newest trends is the *intercept*, which appears spontaneous. It occurs when a selected constituent with great influence walks up to an elected official unexpectedly. After some small talk, he or she leaves the lawmaker expressing how he or she feels about a selected issue.[47]

Computer scanners are sometimes used, especially with a grasstops campaign aimed at leaders in a community. Bonner sends fax letters to people won over during a phone conversation, asking them to sign their name inside a black box on the page and fax it back to Bonner's office. After scanning the signature into a computer, it can be transposed to petitions and, from a set of geographic locations, sent to lawmakers. The signature might also be affixed to a petition in an advertisement.[48]

In one of the most massive campaigns, the 1991 and 1992 B-2 Stealth bomber campaign, Bonner and Associates trained 200 phone bank operators to place calls to members of 5,000 groups—including farm, senior citizen, minority, and religious groups in more than 100 "politically responsive" congressional districts. Citizens were asked to send postcards or phone their representative in support of the bomber.[49]

Which Communications Are Most Effective.   A 1992 Gallup Poll survey of 150 new and returning members of the U.S. House and Senate indicates which forms and messages of communication they pay most attention to:

- More than 70% said they pay a great deal of attention to personally written letters from constituents, meetings with heads of groups, visits from CEOs representing companies with a job presence in the district, personally written letters from heads of groups in the district or from company officials with a job presence in the district, and phone calls from constituents.[50]

- Between 60% and 69% of the members of Congress pay attention to phone calls from heads of groups in their district; 20% to 25% to postcards and mailgrams from the district; and 19% or less to issue papers, form letters from constituents and company officials, editorials, CEO visits from a company without a district job presence, and advertisements.[51]

Other studies also show that letters or telephone calls from constituents, if they are perceived as personal and spontaneous rather than orchestrated, are given the most weight. The most effective method is to allow constituents to communicate in their own words to their elected officials, a method frequently used on the state and local level. Special events can be used to facilitate constituent contact with legislators; the IIAA, for example, established an interactive kiosk at a trade gathering.

A 1999 study of the effectiveness of constituent communications ranks fax and e-mail below the personal media previously mentioned, but ahead of a petition or mass mailing. "When members of Congress see there's an unorchestrated, honest grassroots interest in an issue, they tend to pay attention."[52] However, overzealousness in grassroots lobbying must be watched. Congressional staffers have become disconcerting interpreters of grassroots communications. As one said, "When it comes in bunches you can recognize it as Astroturf.... It's not taken very seriously."[53]

What also gets little or no attention from members of Congress are issue papers; editorials; visits from CEOs and officials of firms affected by an issue but without significant job presence in the home district; and newspaper, radio, or TV issue ads in Washington, DC, or in the home district.

TOOLS OF GRASSROOTS LOBBYING

Interpersonal communication dominates grassroots lobbying, and letters and personal conversations with members of Congress through visits or phones calls are supplemented with e-mail, faxes, and other electronic communication. Furthermore, such communications are stimulated and manipulated through organized efforts by corporations and interest groups.

The tools already mentioned merge with a broader list of services public affairs consulting firms provide for grassroots lobbying. The following list by Leslie J. Gianelli, vice president at Powell Tate, shows the overlap with direct lobbying and traditional public relations and marketing:

- Coalition building and grassroots outreach.
- Grasstops recruitment and mobilization.
- Database development and maintenance.

- Direct-mail preparation and distribution.
- Phone banking and telemarketing.
- Presentation and media training.
- website design.
- Polling and focus groups.
- Earned media outreach.
- Paid advertising.
- Fund raising.[54]

A Services Buyer's Guide published by *Campaigns & Elections* shows how these activities—and some additional ones—are categorized:

- Telephone contact and mobilization.
- Telephone patch-throughs, direct connects.
- Grasstops organizing and field operations.
- Targeting and demographic planning.
- Lists/labels/district matches/database.
- Lobbying direct-mail printing and processing.
- Lobby direct-mail creative, strategy, and planning.
- Electronic media buying: local markets.
- Electronic media buying: regional and national markets.
- Newspaper ad placement: local markets.
- Newspaper ad placement: regional and national markets.
- Public relations and event planning.
- Litigation support services.
- Media training and speech preparation services.
- Polling and focus groups.
- Satellite broadcasting services.
- Broadcast fax services.[55]

Coalition building pertains to both direct and grassroots lobbying, as does the use of the research tools of polling and focus groups. Many direct marketing tools—use of databases, direct mailings, and telemarketing—apply to grassroots lobbying. Public relations skills are especially important for broad-based third-party advocacy programs because they involve media relations efforts and the use of websites to influence general public opinion.

It is clear, however, that interpersonal communications prevail in the execution of grassroots lobbying. Personal conversations with members of Congress through visits or phone calls are supplemented with letters, e-mail, faxes, and other electronic communication. Furthermore, computer technology has greatly enhanced grassroots effectiveness. It has also enabled organizations to use astroturf techniques.

Telephones Are Still Useful

Phones are one of the most effective and essential tools of modern campaigns. Aside from door-to-door visits, the phone is the other chief medium of personal two-way communication. Only persons with phone numbers, however, can be reached, and of these, only about 70% answer.[56]

The phone allows a dialogue with voters to determine which issues they deem most important and what they think about them. When this feedback is used in subsequent conversations, a relationship is established, which cannot be accomplished through any broadcast medium, says Wally Clinton, president of the Clinton Group, a Democratic firm based in Washington, DC. Because the telephone is a medium of dialogue, not monologue, Clinton shuns making prerecorded calls, "which disallow the most powerful function of the telephone—the ability to communicate persuasively, delivering a message and capturing feedback."[57]

Although volunteers can handle a few hundred or up to a few thousand calls, paid telephone banks are needed for larger numbers. For example, the 1994 campaign of New York governor George Pataki started with 100,000 calls, followed by 1.1 million turnout calls 4 days before the election.[58]

Budget, of course, must be available. Thanks to deregulation of the communications industry, however, costs have dropped by more than 50% in the last 7 years, says Mac Hansbrough, president of National Telecommunications Services, a Democratic firm based in Washington, DC.[59] (See Box 10.2 for benefits and costs of phone banks.)

Use Phones in Combination With Other Media.   Phone calls work best in combination with toll-free numbers, direct mail, and the Internet, as the following campaigns illustrate.

- TeleMark, a telephone contact firm based in Portland, Oregon, was hired to take inbound toll-free calls from radio ads produced by the Public Response Group in Chicago on behalf of the Consumer Alliance for Electric Choice. After capturing the name and address of the respondents, the operators used their ZIP code to patch them through to their legislators to express their opposition to a bill.[60]
- National Telecommunications Services was hired by the Southern Utah Wilderness Alliance, the Sierra Club, and the National Wildlife Federation to persuade the president to veto the pave-the-parks legislation. Patch-through calls were made not to a single destination but to the president, key White House advisers, and members of Congress. This wider audience avoided a negative backlash that sometimes occurs when one target is overwhelmed.[61]

Modern technology helps in telemarketing as well as in other applications. For example, predictive-dialing technology allows computers to do the time-consuming work of dialing numbers, listening to busy signals, and getting wrong numbers. Automated digital recording technology enables the capture of fund-raising pledges, petition-signing commitments, and other conversations that benefit from a permanent audio recording. Furthermore, high-end computer systems and high-

Box 10.2 Benefits and Costs of Phone Banks

Consultants and vendors who specialize in telemarketing services categorize paid telephone calls used in campaigns into four categories:

1. An ID call, which identifies the political leaning of the voter.
2. A persuasion call, which seeks to influence the voter and encourage a patch-through call.
3. An attack "push poll" call.
4. A GOTV—"get out to vote"—call.

Push poll calls—distinguished from negative persuasion calls—are highly controversial and should never be used, says Hansbrough. On the other hand, Peck Young of Austin, Texas-based Emory, Young & Associates, says phone banks are now applied to persuasion calls.

To contact 40,000 voters with a persuasive ID call and a GOTV call may cost $50,000 says Tony Feather. Bob Corn, vice president of Alexandria, Virginia-based Landmark Strategies, estimates that the typical budget allocates 40% to 45% to ID calls, 30% to 35% to GOTV calls, and 20% to 25% to persuasion. Phone banks are highly cost-effective, as suggested in fund-raising applications, especially when used in combination with direct mail, television, radio, print, and other fund-raising media. Each medium reinforces the other, creating a powerful message, says Ellinger. Because phone calls increase donor awareness and motivation, he states response rates with current donors are three to five times that of direct mail, and with lapsed and nondonor audiences, response rates of 10 times or more are common.

Using paid telephone banks has several advantages besides the ability to reach a high volume of voters in a short period of time. Because professional operators are used, they can get reliable identification because they are unbiased. The enthusiasm of volunteers is likely to create a bias, although this motivation would not be harmful in persuasion or GOTV calls. It is essential, however, that phone bank operators be "well-trained, prepared to handle questions and are accent neutral with acceptable diction," says Linda Cherry, president of Cherry Communications, a Republican firm based in Tallahassee, Florida. She says that there is a wide range of quality, accuracy, and reliability within the industry.

Professionally trained operators can also take greater advantage of the targeting of calls to desired voters, who can be identified by improved voter lists, polling information, and demographic data. Data collected from previous phone conversations are also useful. In persuasion calls, operators can present tailored scripts to different segments of voters in a single advocacy program.

speed modems provide the capacity to track data in almost real time. Better desktop analysis allows for more detailed statistical information so that trends can quickly be spotted and adjustments made to messages where necessary.[62]

Computer Technology Enhances Grassroots Effectiveness

Modern information technology that combines such hardware as fast computers with vast storage capacity, software, and databases has greatly facilitated and enhanced the effectiveness of grassroots lobbying. State-of-the-art information systems support all of the elements of grassroots lobbying: constituency building, constituency communication, and constituency activation. The latter capability is particularly important because sudden legislative developments place a premium on capacity and speed.

Computer technology is used for the following purposes:.

1. *Maintain membership lists in databases.* One of the oldest uses of information technology is the creation and maintenance of membership lists, such as files of employees, stockholders, community leaders, and other company stakeholders. Computer databases allow easy updating and immediate access. An example of strategic use of databases is the National Association of Life Underwriters, which built a network of more than 10,000 members who serve as contacts in 521 of the nation's 538 congressional districts. Local coordinators routinely meet with each member of Congress three or four times a year.[63]

2. *Classify and sort constituents.* The computer can sort a constituent database into categories relevant to a specific campaign, provide cross-tabulations with other databases, and allow instant communication through connections with laser printers, telephones, and "broadcast" faxes. Through the use of available software, it is now easy to sort and mobilize constituents in a variety of ways:

   • *By congressional or legislative districts.* One specialized software is the Congressional District and State District Identifier System. Another is a program by Rocliff Associates of Delavan, Wisconsin, that enables an organization to identify the legislative districts where employees, stockholders, retirees, and other constituencies reside. If grassroots action is needed in particular districts, an organization can target those constituents, inform them, and ask them to take action. Anheuser-Busch used this software system in an effort to oppose an additional federal excise tax on beer. Using its file of 40,000 employees, 40,000 stockholders, 200 major suppliers, and 960 wholesalers, the company was able to target constituents in the districts of 22 key members of the House Ways and Means Committee. Anheuser-Busch also sent its 200 major suppliers information packages "consisting of a letter explaining the tax issue and the company's position, a background information sheet, talking points, and details of how the issue would affect the company, the industry, and the supplier."[64]

• *By activism and political connection.* For example, the National Federation of Independent Businesses (NFIB) maintains a database that includes names, addresses, phone and fax numbers, geographic regions, legislative districts, number of employees, types of business, issue positions, and political backgrounds. The NFIB has divided this membership list of 617,000 persons into target groups based on the degree of activism: an A list of 400,000 members who responded at least once to a direct-mail activation; an AA list of 200,000 members who responded to more than one direct-mail activation; a guardian list of 40,000 most active members; and a key contact list of 3,000 members who have close relationships with public officials.[65]

• *By ZIP codes.* Software used in marketing has been adapted for grassroots lobbying needs. For example, the Prizm Cluster System, provided by Claritas of Alexandria, Virginia, helps to reach consumers for public affairs purposes. According to ZIP code, every U.S. neighborhood is assigned to one of 40 clusters, each of which represents people with similar backgrounds, means, and consumer behavior. The Ford Motor Company used this system in 1985 when it, together with GM, successfully convinced the Department of Transportation (DOT) to reduce its miles-per-gallon fuel average for passenger cars. From an initial list of 1 million customers, Ford targeted 25,000 of them in a direct-mail campaign. The response rate, measuring those who communicated with DOT, was 12.6%.[66]

3. *Inform citizens and provide interactivity.* The Internet and other online networks can inform citizens and provide feedback and interactivity through specialized websites and online debates. Web home pages allow organizations to inform current and potential constituents who own computers and are likely highly educated with high incomes. For example, the American Crop Protection Association, a lobbying arm of the farm chemical industry, sought to enlist member support for the Republicans' version of the Safe Drinking Water Act when it was held back by Democrats. It posted a message on its website saying, "We have been meeting with committee staff and others to put back pressure on the GOP to not give away so much in their push for consensus that they produce a bill that our industry can't support."[67] Meanwhile the opposing group, the Environmental Working Group, used the Web to inform Internet users that Representative Greg Ganske received $17,750 from groups interested in changing pesticide standards, implying that the chemical industry intended this money to influence his stand.[68]

A website was at the center of Washington-based Edison Electric Institute's grassroots lobbying efforts to support the White House's

"Clear Skies" plan. Members of the association were urged to participate in the "industry outreach effort to mobilize employees, retirees
and shareholders" to counter controversy surrounding it, namely,
that it would roll back deadlines for meeting public health standards
and leave carbon dioxide emissions unregulated. The website features "a general advocacy page, talking points that members of each
group can use to write their Congressional representatives, and letters for members of each group to send to Congress."[69] The campaign also asked industry executives to travel to Capitol Hill in
support of the plan.

A deficiency of many websites is that they provide little opportunity
for interaction and therefore can't capitalize on the motivation that is
built when relationships are established with constituents. Although
focusing on social responsibility issues, this failing was noted in a
study of 100 websites of *Fortune* 500 companies by S. L. Esrock and G.
B. Leichty.[70] On the one hand, they found that 88% had websites, and
80% of them dealt with at least one social responsibility issue. For example, Olin described environmental and conservation issues and
Avon its Breast Cancer Awareness crusade. What the sites lacked, however, were sufficient "dialogic features"—features that encourage an
exchange of information and views between a company and its
publics. (The websites in the Esrock and Leichty study were aimed at
three major audiences: shareholders/investors [68%], prospective employees [68%], and customers and customer service [51%].)

Interaction is encouraged with such features as explicitly inviting
users to return to the site, including links to other websites, providing
a constantly updated calendar of events, and inviting users to voice
their opinions on issues. (See chap. 2 for how interest groups are
learning to incorporate these features.) The Esrock and Leichty study
showed that companies were at least making their sites more inviting. For example, three out of four prominently displayed icons or
links for site maps or search engines on the front page.

Some websites already permit a highly interactive way of disseminating information through a kind of coffee-shop exchange that can
"provide dialog, give-and-take, a depth of background and kinds of
information that are impossible, or at least rarely seen, in traditional
media."[71] One format allows each candidate to pose a tough policy
question to the other; by the next day, each would have responded to
that question at length and posed another. The process, which would
then be repeated, has two advantages: Relatively long written responses would be provided and appeals to emotion would be limited.
The written responses could also be retained in an archive.[72]

4. *Mobilize immediate support*. Grassroots lobbying technology,
such as e-mail advocacy, telephone patch-throughs, and grassroots
databases enable companies to mobilize immediate support for specific legislative events. For example, Bonner & Associates sent farm-
ers, senior citizens, and small-business owners predrafted e-mail

messages that, when forwarded to congressional representatives, appear self-composed.[73] Similarly, the Pesticide Action Network and the NRA have mobilized up to 200,000 members at a time.[74]

In applying the telephone patch-through technique, computers can sort and redirect a call to the office of a particular member of Congress. Databases can also be used to generate letters to Congress, as Citicorp did to reach its employee volunteers and generate 38,000 letters to Congress and to newspapers on the banking reform law. By using its computer-driven phone banks, the U.S. Chamber of Commerce can call 215,000 members about issues of concern to the organization. When a key vote looms, "a computer will start dialing their numbers with a recorded message with three options: Press 1 to have a mailgram or letter sent in their name to their representative; press 2 to record a voice-mail message for the lawmaker; press 3 to have a computer connect them immediately with the lawmaker's office."[75]

ORGANIZING AN INTEGRATED LOBBYING CAMPAIGN: HOW CSE DOES IT

Public affairs managers face the challenge of integrating all the elements of a grassroots lobbying campaign with its overall public affairs goals and activities. Citizens for a Sound Economy (CSE) has done this successfully. It transformed itself into an integrated lobbying organization in 1993 when the administration proposed an energy tax. Since then it has been interested in several other issues. In 1994 it spent close to $5 million on advertising and grassroots efforts to oppose the administration's health care reform proposal, and in March 1995 it became involved in the House debate on overhauling the nation's civil litigation system. It has also pushed for a balanced budget amendment and sought reform of the FDA.[76]

CSE is a 250,000-member conservative advocacy group that receives its financial support from such bastions of free enterprise economics as the David H. Koch Charitable Foundation, the John M. Olin Foundation, and the Sarah Scaife Foundation; from trade associations such as the American Petroleum Institute and Pharmaceutical Research and Manufacturers of America; and from companies such as CIGNA and R. J. Reynolds Tobacco. Its fight for legal reforms is supported by the American Council of Life Insurance, Americans for Lawsuit Reform, the NFIB, and the U.S. Chamber of Commerce.

To bolster its power base, CSE maintains a research-and-education foundation. It commissioned a poll by Luntz Research of Arlington, Virginia, showing that many Americans had serious doubts about the FDA. CSE's grassroots efforts are helped by its chapters in six states: Louisiana, New Jersey, New York, Oklahoma, Texas, and Virginia.

CSE recognizes the value of a professional staff and outside experts. Among the persons and organizations it hired are (a) well-connected field operatives to help organize campaigns in key states; (b) the San Diego-based firm Direct Communications Corporation, which "places calls to its members and allows them to patch calls through to their Members of Congress"; and (c) Elizabeth Sauer, a grassroots specialist who formerly worked for the public relations firm of Fleishman Hillard.

CSE uses a variety of tactics to achieve its political goals, including advertising, bumper stickers, and demonstrations. To help sway key senators on the balanced budget amendment, it took out ads in several states. It spent about $50,000 in Delaware, where Democrat Joseph R. Biden, Jr. was a late convert to the bill; and about $15,000 in North Dakota in an unsuccessful effort to persuade Democrats Kent Conrad and Byron L. Dorgan. Its spending on negative ads in the 1994 campaign approached $1 billion. It was the season of sleaze, as judged by a Ketchum newspaper ad deploring the excesses of negative advertising.[77]

In fighting the Clinton administration's health care reform proposals, CSE distributed bumper stickers and buttons to its members. It also coordinated a series of demonstrations to counter the bus tour the administration organized to promote its health care proposal.

CONCLUSIONS

Grassroots lobbying achieves its true purpose when it withdraws from astroturf techniques and draws on the true opinions, feelings, and goals of the electorate. It is unrealistic, however, to expect average persons to take the initiative in advancing even their own goals. Leadership is needed. Sometimes a spontaneous leader emerges, and often enough, a public interest group provides a leadership role.

Businesses can also legitimately provide leadership if their goals are consonant with those of the public; this public opinion surveys can determine. If public opinion is not yet sufficiently advanced, a company can choose to influence it. Part of the strategy of Glaxo Wellcome's Civic Action Network, for example, is to educate the public with such messages as that it takes 15 years to fund and develop a new life-saving drug.[78] This effort is part of constituency communication, discussed earlier. Furthermore, the instruments of opinion leader communication and strategic media relations should be used both before and during grassroots lobbying efforts. As stated by Margery Kraus, president and CEO of APCO Associates, "Popularizing your cause through talk radio and engaging the public through a variety of media actions have never been more useful tools for the government relations professional."[79]

ENDNOTES

1. Edward A. Grefe, "An Introduction to Grassroots," in *Winning at the Grassroots: A Comprehensive Manual for Corporations and Associations,* by Tony Kramer with Wes Pedersen (Washington, D.C.: Public Affairs Council, 2000), p. 8.

2. Ron Faucheux, "The Grassroots Explosion," *Campaigns & Elections*, Vol. 16, No. 1, December 1994–January 1995, p. 20.
3. Jeffrey H. Birnbaum, "Washington's Power 25," *Fortune*, December 8, 1997, pp. 144–158.
4. Wes Pedersen, "The Power of Grassroots Is Demonstrated Via a Study of Its Impact on Congressional Staffers," *Impact*, October 2003, pp. 1, 3.
5. Hjalma Johnson, "Team 21: Future of Grassroots Lobbying," *ABA Banking Journal*, Vol. 92, May 2000, p. 17.
6. Michael D. Lord, "Grassroots Strategy and Tactics: What Works, What Doesn't, and Why," in Kramer, op. cit., pp. 238–239.
7. Ibid., p. 239.
8. See Gerry Keim, "Corporate Grassroots Programs in the 1980s," *California Management Review*, Vol. 28, Fall 1985, pp. 110–123.
9. Chris Casey, *The Hill on the Net: Congress Enters the Information Age* (Boston: AP Professional, 1996), p. 223.
10. Pete Engardio, "Activists Without Borders," *BusinessWeek*, October 4, 1999, p. 144.
11. Ibid., pp. 144–145.
12. Tom Price, "Creating a Digital Democracy: The Impact of the Internet on Public Policy-Making" (Washington, D.C.: Foundation for Public Affairs, 1999), p. 2.
13. Ibid., p. 15.
14. Ibid., p. 9.
15. Ibid., p. 5.
16. Ibid., pp. 12–13.
17. Ibid., p. 13.
18. Wesley Pedersen, *Winning at the Grassroots* (Washington, D.C.: Public Affairs Council, 1989).
19. Grefe, op. cit., p. 4.
20. Fraser/Associates, *Getting the Most From Grassroots Programs in the 1980s* (Washington, D.C.: Public Affairs Council, 1980), p. 15.
21. Faucheux, op. cit., p. 24.
22. Glen Caroline, "Maximizing Campaign Volunteers: The NRA Way," *Campaigns & Elections*, Vol. 24 , April 2003, pp. 26–29.
23. See Jerry A. Hendrix, *Public Relations Cases* (Belmont, Calif.: Wadsworth, 1988), pp. 236–243.
24. See Michael E. Dunn, "Developing an Effective Grassroots Program: Templates for Success," in Kramer, op. cit., pp. 17–19; also see Pedersen, op. cit.
25. Dunn, op. cit., p. 13.
26. Dunn, "The Future of Grassroots," op. cit., p. 226.
27. Ken Silverstein, *Washington on $10 Million a Day* (Monroe, Me.: Common Courage Press, 1998), p. 94.
28. Faucheux, op. cit., p. 22.
29. Elizabeth J. Welsh, "Grassroots Activation and Mobilization: Tools and Technologies," in Kramer, op. cit., p. 119.
30. Michael E. Dunn, "The Future of Grassroots," in Kramer, op. cit., p. 279.
31. "Digging up the AstroTurf," *Ragan's Media Relations Report*, February 17, 2003, p. 3.
32. Paul Cordasco, "Corporate Giants Call on Shareholders in Support of Bush Tax Plan," *PR Week (US)*, April 7, 2003, p. 1.
33. "Bailout Lobby—How Chrysler Corp. Orchestrates Support of Bid for Federal Aid," *Wall Street Journal*, September 6, 1979, p. 1.

34. Sally Goll Beatty, "Philip Morris Boosts Marketing via Catalog," *Wall Street Journal*, November 4, 1996, p. 5.
35. Dunn, op. cit., p. 13.
36. Faucheux, op. cit., pp. 25, 53.
37. Ibid., p. 24.
38. Rick Chase and Stephen M. Ramsey, "Second Chances: Lessons Learned and Mid-Course Corrections," in Kramer, op. cit., p. 43.
39. Ibid.
40. Ken Deutsch and Mark Reilly, "Using the Internet for Grassroots Effectiveness," in Kramer, op. cit., p. 143.
41. Ibid., p. 140.
42. Engardio, op. cit., p. 148.
43. Interview by Mary Clare Jalonick, "Grassroots Lobbying: Trends and Techniques; Consultant Q&A," *Campaigns & Elections*, February 2003, p. 45.
44. Ibid., p. 22.
45. Ibid., p. 22.
46. Jalonick, op. cit.
47. Ibid.
48. Silverstein, op. cit.
49. Richard Alan Nelson, "Activist Groups and New Technologies: Influencing the Public Affairs Agenda," in *Practical Public Affairs in an Era of Change: A Communications Guide for Business, Government, and College*, ed. Lloyd B. Dennis (Lanham, Md.: University Press of America, 1996), p. 416. Also see Silverstein, op. cit., pp. 212–220.
50. Faucheux, op. cit., pp. 53–54.
51. Ibid.
52. Price, op. cit, pp. 15, 19. The author of the study is P. Michael Lord, Babcock Graduate School of Management.
53. Silverstein, op. cit., p. 95.
54. Leslie J. Gianelli, "Maximizing Consultant Relationships: Hiring, Managing and Assessing Your Consultants," in Kramer, op. cit., p. 51.
55. "Grassroots Lobbying & Issue Advocacy Services Buyer's Guide," *Campaigns & Elections*, February 2003, p. 44.
56. Ibid., p. 20.
57. Wally Clinton was one of eight consultants and vendors specializing in telemarketing services whose answers to questions were solicited for an article, "Telephones as Strategic Tools," *Campaigns & Elections*, Vol. 18, August 1997, p. 22.
58. "Telephones as Strategic Tools," ibid. p. 23. Stated by Tony Feather of New York-based Campaign Tel, Inc.
59. Ibid., p. 22. Stated by Clinton.
60. Ibid., p. 23. Stated by Powell.
61. Ibid., p. 23. Stated by Hansbrough.
62. Ibid., pp. 21–22. Stated by Feather.
63. Faucheux, op. cit., p. 23.
64. Pedersen, op. cit., p. 107.
65. Faucheux, op. cit., p. 21.
66. Pederson, op. cit., p. 107.
67. However, in retrospect, the association didn't want this message to be public, so it pulled the description of its lobbying efforts from public access.

68. Kenneth Pins, "Foes Make Pitches on World Wide Web," *Des Moines Register,* June 10, 1996, p. 5.

69. Sarah Bouchard, "Electric Utilities Power up Push for 'Clear Skies' Bill," *Roll Call*, July 9, 2003. Internet.

70. S. L. Esrock and G. B. Leichty, "Corporate World Wide Web Pages: Serving the News Media and Other Publics," *Journalism and Mass Communication Quarterly*, Vol. 76, No. 3, 1999, pp. 456–467; also their "Organization of Corporate Web Pages: Publics and Functions," *Public Relations Review*, Vol. 26, Fall 2001, pp. 327–344.

71. Ibid.

72. Ibid.

73. Birnbaum, op. cit., p. 152.

74. Ibid., p. 13.

75. Nelson, op. cit., p. 416.

76. Peter H. Stone, "Grass-Roots Group Rakes in the Green," *The National Journal*, Vol. 27, March 11, 1995, p. 621.

77. See "Can It Be Controlled? Ad Men Decry 'Sleaze' in Political Promos, but See Even More in '96," *Impact*, December 1994, pp. 1–2. *Impact* is a monthly newsletter of the Public Affairs Council.

78. Mike Morris, "Glaxo Wellcome's Civic Action Network: Case Study of a Broad-Based Grassroots Program," in Kramer, op. cit., p. 34.

79. Margery Kraus, "Government Relations in the 90s and Beyond," in Dennis, op. cit., p. 97.

Chapter 11

Electoral Activities

Electoral activities are political actions intended to influence election outcomes and agendas of political parties, legislative bodies (particularly the House and Senate), and presidential and gubernatorial contests. Indirectly, electoral activities support lobbying activities by enhancing access to, and influence on, lawmakers.[1] As stated by Charles S. Mack, president and CEO of the Business-Industry Political Action Committee, "Political action tries to affect the outcome of elections to produce political decision makers favorably inclined to the views of particular interest groups—either by involving their members directly in the political process or by providing financial support to friendly candidates."[2]

The common denominator of most electoral activities is money: PAC money, independent expenditures, soft money, and other money used for issue advertising. Money is so important that, as Republican political leader Mark Hanna once quipped, there "are two things important in politics. The first is money and I can't remember the second."[3] Money is provided by private financing of congressional campaigns, which is consistent with Americans' belief in capitalism. Consequently, wealthy individuals and well-organized segments of society, such as corporations and labor unions, have disproportionate political access.

Candidates recognize that more and more money is needed to run for office. In the costliest campaign in history, the 2004 presidential and congressional elections cost nearly $4 billion, compared with $3 billion in 2000, $2.2 billion in 1996, and $1.8 billion in 1992.[4] The five most expensive Senate races in the 2004 elections cost more than $20 million each, headed by the South Dakota Senate race costing slightly over $33 million. The most expensive House race was in Texas District 32, costing over $8.4 million.[5] Because of the precipitous rise in political campaign costs, elected officials increasingly depend on financial contributions and other resources to run for, or remain in, office.

It is no wonder members of Congress spend so much of their time on fund-raising activities. They must, in effect, contend with two campaigns: one for the vote and one for resources.[6] A snapshot of a day in the life of representative Gerald Solomon (R–N.Y.) shows him rushing to a $500-a-head breakfast meeting for the reelection of fellow Republican Rep. Deborah Pryce and leaving 25 minutes later saying, "Take a look at this. I've got three this morning—I've already been to two—and seven this evening. They're time-consuming."[7] Sometimes, however, collecting money is fast and simple. In the 2002 election, it took Thomas Siebel, a Silicon Valley money man, just a few weeks to collect more than $2 million from his top executives to form a PAC.[8]

Corporations, as well as other political participants, find an opportunity in the politicians' need for campaign funds. Contributors can ingratiate themselves with politicians to gain access and influence.

POLITICAL CAMPAIGN CONTRIBUTIONS

Providing candidates and political parties with money—and in-kind resources—is the most important corporate and business electoral activity. Money helps get the "right people" elected and adds clout to lobbying efforts. Justin Dart, CEO of Dart Industries, got to the core of the matter when, referring to lobbying, he said, "With a little money they hear you just a little better."[9] A member of Congress expects that anyone who wants to get a point across will have already contributed to his or her office. Conservative political analyst Kevin Phillips said of the system, "If you don't pay, you don't play."[10]

Public relations professionals must know how to respond to requests for political contributions and when to take the initiative in making political contributions a part of a public affairs program or campaign. The various ways politicians and political groups finance their campaigns are summarized next in the "big picture" and each source is then further described. Because political contributions can either promote or undermine the political process, Congress has passed laws that spell out procedures and limits. A summary of the provisions of the McCain-Feingold Campaign Reform bill serves as a guide to allowable actions and contributions.

Sources of Campaign Financing

The sources of political campaign funds are individual contributions—both large individual donors and small donations—candidates' self-financing, PAC money, soft money (now channeled primarily to 527 groups), and other forms. The relative importance of each is shown in the breakdown of projected spending in the 2004 elections as shown in Box 11.1.

Box 11.1 Sources of Projected Spending in the 2004 Elections[11]

	(In Millions)
Individual contributions to candidates and parties	$2,500
PAC contributions to candidates and parties	384
Candidate self-financing	144
527 spending (related to a federal election)	386
Public funds to presidential candidates and party conventions	207
Convention host committee spending	139
Other (loans, interest to candidates, Levin funds, independent expenditures)	102
Total	$3.9 billion

Specific Sources of Funding

Individual Contributions. The biggest single source of campaign cash in the 2004 elections was individuals. They donated an estimated $2.5 billion to federal candidates and political parties—an increase of $1 billion over the 2000 elections. Despite the McCain-Feingold reform law's intent to reduce contributions from large individual donors, they gave a disproportionate amount. Billionaires such as George Soros gave seven-figure checks to the 527s. On the positive side, however, more small-money donors—giving $200 or less—contributed in the 2004 elections than before.[12]

Giving by small-money donors was accelerated by the Internet. As demonstrated during the 2000 election cycle, leading political contenders used this tool effectively. Bill Bradley raised $650,000 as of September 30, 1999, followed by John McCain with $260,000, and George W. Bush with $90,000. Internet giving reached a new high in the prelude to the 2004 campaign. Vermont Governor Howard Dean shattered all records and entered the *Guinness Book of World Records* when in the 3 months prior to October 1, 2003, he raised more than $14 million online, and during his entire campaign raised $19 million in online contributions.[13] Some see this method of campaign financing as the least corrupting because the contributions are mostly small, thus reducing the danger of a quid pro quo relationship between givers and recipients.[14] Furthermore, the Internet will cause more people to give, says Jay Friesel of the advertising firm 24/7 Media, because of "the ease of execution, the ability to contact immediately."[15]

PACs. PACs have become a staple of national politics, with nearly every major issue group and federal candidate forming a PAC. Corporations, labor unions, trade associations, and others may legally solicit money from individual members of their organizations and disburse these funds to chosen candidates for federal office.[16] Campaign finance laws set limits on the amount individuals may contribute.[17] Called *hard money*, these funds are particularly valuable to a candidate because they can use them directly for personal advertising and other purposes.

The growth of PACs was spurred by the passage of the 1974 amendments to the Federal Election Campaign Practices Act that clarified what PACs could and could not do. From about 1,600 PACs in 1978, their number grew to more than 4,000 6 years later, with total contributions rising from $92.6 million to $228.7 million.[18] According to Political Money Line, there were 201 corporate PACs in September 2004, which collected $111 million in 2003.[19] In the 2004 elections, PAC contributions from all sources totaled $384 million, an increase of 33% over the 2000 elections.[20]

As shown in Box 11.2, trade and professional associations account for 6 of the 10 top PAC contributors to federal candidates in 2003–2004, followed by 3 labor unions and only 1 corporation. Membership organizations can aggregate the donations of many people while corporations are limited to their own employees and stockholders. The geographically spread United Parcel Service is an exception—and some predict that far-flung Wal-Mart, with its mounting legal problems, will join the list.[21] The three labor unions and the Association of Trial Lawyers of America consistently give the lion's share to Democrats, whereas most associations give more to Republicans.

Corporate PACs give more money to Republicans than Democrats, with about 9 out of 10 doing so from January 1, 2003, through October 13, 2004, according to a study by PoliticalMoneyLine. This preference

---

Box 11.2   Top 10 PAC Contributors to Federal Candidates, 2003–2004[22]

PAC Nam	Total (in Millions)	Dem %	Repbl %
National Association of Realtors	$ 3.7	48	52
Laborers Union	2.6	86	14
National Auto Dealers Association	2.5	27	73
National Beer Wholesalers Association	2.2	23	77
Association of Trial Lawyers of America	2.0	93	7
United Parcel Service	1.9	27	73
International Brotherhood of Electrical Workers	2.0	95	5
American Medical Association	1.9	20	80
United Auto Workers	1.9	98	1
National Association of Home Builders	1.8	35	65

reflects the "growing allegiance of the business community to the GOP, driven by ideological compatibility, respect for majority power and the concerted pressure exerted by Republican congressional leaders and conservative activities," says the *Washington Post*.[23] A study by the Federal Election Commission (FEC) of PAC giving for all of 2003 and the first half of 2004 showed that all corporate PACs gave $14.1 million to Republicans running for the Senate versus $8.3 million to Democrats. In the House, Republican candidates received $38 million versus $18.1 million for Democrats. Republican leaders have sought to accelerate the shift to the GOP through the K Street Project (named for the street where many lobbyists have their offices). House Majority Leader Tom DeLay (Tex.) and conservative advocate Grover Norquist have strongly suggested that companies favoring the Republican party will have better access than those that do not.[24]

The prevalence of corporate PACs, however, should not be exaggerated. According to a study by M.I.T. professor James M. Snyder, Jr., 40% of *Fortune* 500 companies did not even have a PAC in 2002, and the average corporate PAC gave only around $1,400 to legislators, well below the then legal limit.[25] Because of the soft money restrictions imposed by the new campaign finance reform law, PACs were expected to be more attractive in the 2004 elections. Furthermore, the appeal of PACs was recognized for other reasons as well. Greg Casey, president of the Business-Industry Political Action Committee, told business groups: "There is a growing realization that hard dollars raised through PACs will be the coin of the realm."[26] Also supporting this view is Ken Phelps, a fundraiser for Lockheed Martin's PAC, who stated, "We've got to grow the PAC. It's a political environment and we need to be a political company."[27] PACs have also become more appealing because e-mail and the Internet have made solicitation for donations cheaper and easier. New computer software has eased the formidable task of running PACs and reporting transactions to Washington.[28]

Candidate Self-Financing.   Few candidates finance their own campaigns, but rich candidates can. The Center for Responsive Politics reported that federal candidates were expected to have poured $144 million in personal funds into their campaigns in the 2004 elections.[29] Among House candidates, Benjamin Earl Streusand (R-Tex.) and Jeanne L. Patterson (R-Mo.) spent $2.8 million, and Michael McCaul (R-Tex.) spent $1.9 million. Among Senate candidates, Blair Hull (D-Ill.) spent $28.7 million, Douglas Gallagher (R-Fla.) spent $6.6 million, and Jack Ryan (R-Ill.) spent $4.6 million.[30]

In 2000 self-funders spent even more ($205 million), including the astounding $63 million laid out by Jon Corzine, co-chairman of the investment firm Goldman Sachs, when he decided to run in the New Jersey senatorial race. This huge outlay "brought the street-tough political order of New Jersey to its knees."[31] The size of his self-financing overshadowed the $37.4 million of self-financing by publishing magnate

Steve Forbes in the 1995–1996 election cycle, followed by Ross Perot with $8.2 million. As Scott Fitzgerald said, "The super-rich are different from you and me. They can become U.S. Senators."[32]

Soft Money and 527s. 527s, the new outlet for soft money, accounted for a slightly higher source of spending in the 2004 elections, $386 million, than PACs with $384 million, as shown in Box 11.1.[33] Soft money refers to unregulated donations to political parties by individuals, corporations, and unions. The use of soft money in federal campaigns has been a highly controversial issue because its rising use circumvented the goals of campaign finance laws, one of which was to remove the influence of "big money." However, as soft money contributions to national parties in the 2002 election cycle shows, 724 organizations gave $100,000 or more. Thirteen gave $3 million or more, with Saban Capital Group leading the list with $9.3 million. Eight gave $2 million or more, with government-sensitive companies Philip Morris giving $2.9 million and Microsoft giving $2.7 million.[34]

Soft money was intended to be used for supposedly generic party-building activities, such as get-out-the-vote drives, bumper stickers, yard signs, and generic TV ads that say "Vote Democratic" or "Vote Republican." Such donations, which the Supreme Court in its 1976 *Buckley v. Valeo* ruling declared legal,[35] had no limit, in contrast to hard money. The only conditions that had to be met were those of not coordinating efforts with a candidate and not constructing a political message that refers to a particular candidate. The Republican and Democratic national party committees, however, learned to circumvent these restrictions. They financed television ad campaigns that attacked or promoted congressional candidates by name, rationalizing that the law was not broken because the ads were "issue ads" that did not explicitly say "vote for" or "vote against" a particular candidate. In practice, therefore, soft money was often used to benefit specific federal candidates, thus becoming a major vehicle for skirting the limitations and restrictions of federal law, says the Center for Responsive Politics.[36]

In the 1996 elections, the record growth of soft money contributions became the big story and led to sharp criticism from several sources:

• Fred Wertheimer, former president of Common Cause, said, "This past election will go down as the worst in modern times, if not in our history as a nation."[37] He asserted that a record-shattering $200 million in contributions were made outside the federal law. Although saying most of it came from business interests, he also attacked the AFL-CIO for running its $20-million-plus television and radio ad campaign with the stated purpose of defeating Republicans in selected House districts.[38] Donald J. Simon, executive vice-president of Common Cause, said, "There's complete lawlessness out there."[39] "A new country club has taken root: a club of wealthy, high

powered donors who help set the political agenda, impact the outcomes and, in many ways, run the country."[40]

• Paul S. Herrnson, professor of government and politics at the
University of Maryland and author of many books on politics and
campaigning, concluded that most soft money contributions were
"little more than subterfuges that enable wealthy individuals, organizations, and party committees to skirt federal campaign finance statutes."[41] The result, he said, is that there is no public
accountability.

• Reporter Beth Ragan called soft money contributions the
"black market" economy of campaign finance.[42] (Soft money contributions were sought and made in many ways. As highly publicized
in the press, the president and members of Congress offered to meet
large contributors, whose gifts were unregulated. For example,
$50,000 brought an invitation to coffee with President Bill Clinton.
Further disclosures, such as the easy access to the White House and
Congress by Enron officers and lobbyists during the Bush administration helped create the momentum for reform. The media portrayed Kenneth Lay, Enron's former chairman, as having benefitted
from writing big checks to political parties—and aggressively urging other top officers and employees to make contributions.)

• Darrell M. West titled his book about our system of government
Checkbook Democracy, describing it as a form of government in which
money has hijacked the campaign process.[43]

Some corporations also joined the backlash to soft money, saying
that executives were "tired of endless appeals for funds that may not
serve their interests."[44] Two thirds (68%) of the 400 top executives who
responded to a *BusinessWeek*/Harris Poll conducted in mid-March 1997
favored "ending unlimited 'soft money' contributions to political parties by corporations and other interests."[45] Said General Motors vice-
chairman Harry J. Pearce, "There's no way to tell how the money is really being used."[46] The argument for campaign finance reform was
growing. Even some companies in heavily regulated industries—telecommunications, pharmaceuticals, finance, and tobacco—that used
to give soft money because they felt they had to were let off the hook
after the reform bill was passed.[47] At the urging of the Committee for
Economic Development, corporations mostly avoided 527 groups trying to pick up soft money in the 2004 elections.[48] Not a single top corporate political donor in 2000 gave to them in the 2004 elections,
partly because they felt they had even less control over them.[49]

After the McCain-Feingold reform bill outlawed old-fashioned soft
money contributions to national parties, the fast-proliferating 527
groups quickly became the new recipients of soft money contributions. From January 2003 through March 2004, they raised $146.4
million for federal elections compared to the $212.4 million in soft

money the national political parties raised over the same period during the 2002 election cycle.[50] They have not yet caught up with previous soft money donations to national party committees.

Named after section 527 of the Internal Revenue Code, 527 groups are tax-exempt and allowed to raise money for political activities, including voter mobilization efforts, issue advocacy advertising, and the like. They are supposed to be independent from the parties and the candidates. In reality, however, the groups overlap in many ways and the campaigns often swap consultants and lawyers. Bush campaign consultant Tom Synhorst, for example, was also founder of Progress for America, the largest pro-Bush 527.[51]

As with previous soft money contributors, the circle of major donors to 527 groups is small. Of the more than $290 million raised by those groups in the 2004 elections, 44% came from just 25 people. As of September 2004, billionaire investor George Soros gave $13 million to Democratic groups, insurance man Peter Lewis gave $15 million, and Hollywood producer Stephen Bing nearly $7 million.[52] Among the recipients, seven organizations spent two thirds of the money: Three groups ran television ads for Republicans, and four ran ads and assisted with voter turnout for Democrats. The most prominent recipients were America Coming Togther (ACT)—largely the brainchild of Steve Rosenthal, former political director of the AFL-CIO—which spent $72 million; The Media Fund, $51 million; MoveOn.org, $12 million; and New Democratic Network, $11 million. They were doing the advertising and voter mobilization work traditionally done by the Democratic National Committee.[53]

The Republicans got a late start with 527s in the 2004 elections because they sought to pressure the FEC to rein in Democratic operations. However, when the FEC failed to act, Republican-leaning 527s received funding and ended up having the greatest impact, said Fred Wertheimer, a veteran of campaign finance overhaul.[54] Texas developer Bob J. Perry led Republican donors with his $8 million to pro-Bush groups. Other major donors were Texas energy magnate T. Boone Pickens; $5 million from Alex Spanos, owner of the National Football League's San Diego Chargers; and $4.2 million from Jerry Perenchio, chairman of the Hispanic television network Univision. The major recipients were Progress for America, receiving $38 million; Swift Boat Veterans and POWs for Truth, $12 million; and Club for Growth, $8 million.[55]

Understandably, Senator John McCain, one of the reform bill's sponsors, feared that "with their billionaire backers and nasty, negative television ads" the 527 groups "threaten to bring politics to a new low."[56] He sees nothing wrong with 527s when used to fund get-out-the-vote efforts and educate voters about issues. However, he considers their activities "illegal, plain and simple" when used by "unscrupulous operatives on both sides … to run political smear campaigns against George Bush and John Kerry."[57] He vows to correct this abuse in future campaign finance reform legislation.

An unintended consequence of 527s is that the stabilizing role of political parties will be further weakened. Large donors will write checks to state parties instead, and these are likely to be more ideologically extreme, resulting in more partisanship in Washington. National parties will also have to spend more time and money eliciting small donations from individuals.[58] Although candidates and political parties can use PAC money for issue advocacy advertising, most ad campaigns are paid for by "money raised by nonprofit groups that claim no connection to candidates or political parties, and use their funds to run 'issue' ads."[59]

Financing Conventions and Inaugurals. At least 29 companies donated to the conventions of both parties in 2004. Big corporations and their lobbyists host receptions, dinners, and baseball outings and help to underwrite the costs of the convention itself, allowed by a loophole in the campaign finance law. The FEC concluded that such donors are civic-minded, not politically motivated.[60] Likewise, companies and individuals have been contributing to Bush's Presidential Inaugural Committee. According to *BusinessWeek's* analysis, at least 28 defense contractors, energy giants, financial firms, Big Tobacco, technology, and health care companies have contributed $100,000 or more. Among those giving the maximum of a quarter-million dollars were Exxon-Mobil, ChevronTexaco, Occidental Petroleum, Southern Co., United Technologies, Sallie Mae, and Altria.[61]

Campaign Finance Laws

After the Watergate scandal, which revealed large contributions to Nixon's reelection campaign, Congress passed the Federal Election Campaign Practices Act of 1971 to prevent candidates and their committees from soliciting large donations from individuals and organizations that might corrupt the political process. Only money from PACs raised and spent according to the requirements and restrictions of this law could be used in connection with an election for federal office. The law prohibited corporations and labor unions from making direct contributions from their treasuries to political candidates. In its place, the 1974 amendments to the Act authorized the establishment of PACs for corporations and labor unions, as well as for trade and professional associations.

McCain-Feingold Bill. The reform bill that was on the political agenda the longest is the McCain-Feingold bill. It seeks a ban on soft money to the national parties, restricts corporate and union spending on campaign advertising, and provides for greater disclosure of contributions.[62] Senator John McCain made a drastic overhaul of the campaign finance system the centerpiece of his campaign for the presidential candidacy of the Republican party in 1999 and he vowed to keep the issue alive. His stated aim was "to give the government of this country back to its citizens and take it back from the big money and special interests."[63] The bill was repeatedly introduced in Congress but killed in 1997 and again in 1998 and 1999.[64] Finally, his perseverence was rewarded on March 27, 2002, after the consequences of "checkbook democracy" were exposed by the Enron scandal. Congress had to bow to public pressure and pass the McCain-Feingold bill, formally known as the Bipartisan Campaign Reform Act of 2002, and President Bush signed it. The law went into effect on November 6, 2002.

The laws main provisions are as follows:

• *Soft money.* Bars unlimited donations to national party committees by individuals, companies, and labor unions. Donations to state and local party committees are permitted but are limited to $10,000 per year and money cannot be spent on federal elections. (State parties' donations are capped at $10,000 if used to impact federal elections.)

• *Hard money (PACs).* Doubles cap on regulated donations, allowing individuals to give up to $2,000 per primary and general election for both House and Senate candidates. Individual contributions to state party committees are limited to $10,000 a year and those to national party committees to $25,000. The maximum aggregate amounts that an individual donor may give per 2-year election cycle are $37,500 to candidates; $57,500 for all other contributions, of which not more than $37,500 may be to committees other than national party committees (i.e., federal PACs and federal accounts of state party committees). The limit to federal candidates and national parties over the 2-year election cycle is $95,000.

PACs may give up to $5,000 per candidate per election. A multi-candidate PAC may contribute up to $5,000 to a candidate, per election; $5,000 to another PAC, per calendar year; and $15,000 to a national party committee, per calendar year. No annual aggregate limit applies.

• *Advocacy advertising and other public communications.* Bars corporations and labor unions from financing radio or TV ads for a federal candidate within 60 days of a general, special, or runoff election or within 30 days of a primary, unless ads are entirely paid for with hard money (i.e., PACs). Any person who spends $10,000 for such electioneering communication must file a disclosure statement with the FEC within 24 hours and again for each subsequent $10,000 of expenditures.

A public communication that supports or opposes a clearly identified federal candidate must be paid entirely (100%) out of hard money, regardless of whether it contains express advocacy. State candidates and officeholders may not spend soft money on public communications that promote or attack a clearly identified candidate for federal office.[65]

- *Disclosure and penalties*. Toughens reporting requirements for those who pay for political advertising, requires faster public notices by the FEC, and extends the statute of limitations for criminal violations to 2 years for violations less than $25,000 and 5 years for violations involving $25,000 or more.[66]

Senator Mitch McConnell (R-Ky.) strenuously objected to the McCain-Feingold bill and filed a lawsuit that questioned its constitutionality on the basis that political fund raising and spending are protected by the free-speech clauses of the First Amendment. However, in December 2003, the Supreme Court, in a close 5–4 decision, rejected this claim, thereby leaving intact the restrictions on soft money. In a jointly authored opinion, Justices Stevens and O'Connor stated that previous rulings "have made clear that the prevention of corruption or its appearance constitutes a sufficiently important interest to justify political contribution limits."[67] (See chap. 14 for further information.)

Have Campaign Finance Reforms Worked?   Views vary widely about the success of the reform bill. *Newsday* called the law a "qualified success," noting that the candidates were forced to "swear off unregulated soft money."[68] Taking an opposite view, Larry Sabato, director of the Center for Politics at the University of Virginia, called the law "an utter failure." He blames 527s for undermining the reform legislation and laments that "Those who wrote (the law) promised that the system will be more open and there will be less money spent on elections. Of course, we have never seen an election with so much money."[69]

The McCain-Feingold bill was intended to reduce the excesses of soft money, which was largely used by national parties for issue advocacy advertising, and the undue influence of big contributions by corporations, unions, and wealthy individuals. The soft money goal was not achieved in that soft money contributions were simply diverted from national parties to 527 groups. Wealthy individuals accounted for a large share of these 527 contributions. The amount of soft money contributions, however, was lower than previous donations to national party committees.[70] The use of issue advocacy advertising was thus largely kept intact. What the reform bill bans is the financing of radio or television advertising by corporations and labor unions within 60 days of a general election or 30 days of a primary. The reform bill confirms what cynics have said: "Plug one loophole, and a dozen others will open up."

ISSUE ADVOCACY ADVERTISING

Attacks on soft money and 527s have largely centered on the use of funds for issue advocacy advertising. Its use in political campaigns represents an increasingly prominent source of communication in the U.S. political system.[71] It refers to ad campaigns paid for by "money raised by nonprofit groups that claim no connection to candidates or political parties, and use their funds to run 'issue' ads."[72] These ads are supposed to deal with matters that arise during a campaign; for example, plans for a Medicare prescription benefit, changing environmental regulations, the trading status of China, and various tax reforms. However, the millions spent by interest groups on single-issue ad campaigns have actually often been "thinly veiled plugs for candidates."[73] No wonder New York University's Brennan Center for Justice and researchers at Brigham Young University have concluded that these issue ads are in reality campaign ads and perceived as such by their audiences.[74] Campaign ads that urge citizens to vote for him or her and against the rival candidate are legal when candidates pay for their own ads, usually with PAC money.

The largest chunk of political advertising goes to television, but newspapers are vying for a larger share. During the 2000 presidential campaign, $807 million went to TV, whereas newspapers got about $30 million. The Newspaper Association of America points to a survey, conducted in the summer of 2003 by the Cromer Group, that found that voters surveyed said they trusted political ads in newspapers more than political ads on television or radio, and ranked newspapers second behind TV for providing the information most helpful when trying to make up their minds about how to vote in state and local elections. Newspapers also say that it's increasingly difficult for TV to gets its message out.[75]

Ads Financing by 527s and Other Nonprofit Groups

Several nonprofits, besides 527 groups, have been major sponsors of issue advertising. The Sierra Club exploited the 527 group loophole in 1996 when it began running its environmental issue advocacy ads. Another group, Citizens for Better Medicare, a drug industry group, used this device to fight White House efforts to create a Medicare prescription drug benefit.[76] More than $2 million was spent on television advertising in just 3 weeks before the House vote. Since its inception in July 2001, Citizens for Better Medicare has spent more than $30 million on television advertising alone and unknown amounts on radio, print, and Internet advertising, according to an analysis conducted by Democrats.[77] These examples demonstrate the overlap between campaign issue advertising and advocacy advertising discussed in chapter 8.

Other types of groups, such as 501(c) groups, may also engage in issue advocacy advertising and in varying amounts of political activity, depending on the specific type of group. For example, 502(c)(4) groups, commonly called social welfare organizations, may engage in political activities as long as these activities do not become their primary purpose.[78] A notable example are ads run in 20 congressional districts by the United Seniors Association, a conservative group that acknowledges it receives some financing from the drug industry's major trade group, the Pharmaceutical Research and Manufacturers of America. (It was previously known as the Pharmaceutical Manufacturers Association but the new name, which adds the word "research," improves its image.) The ad praises lawmakers for supporting legislation to provide prescription drug benefits to the elderly. Charles W. Jarvis, chairman of the group, says the ad is simply trying to spur "a civil debate in the public square" on an important issue, asserting it has no campaign considerations in mind, given its 501(c)(4) tax status. The Wisconsin Advertising Project at the University of Wisconsin said a conservative estimate of the ads' cost was $9 million at the time.[79]

On the state level, advertisements by Citizens for a Strong Senate, one of only a few 527 committees that focused on Congressional races in 2004, raised almost $11 million and unleashed more than 7,000 commercials to help Democrats in six states, including Colorado, where Peter Coors, chairman of the beer company that bears his family's name, was defeated. Three quarters of the money came from Herbert and Marion Sandler, large Democratic donors who run a California financial services company. Another group, Americans for Job Security, a business trade association, formed a 501(c) group that ran more than 5,000 television ads in at least five states before the election, all without having to disclose the source of its money.[80]

Secrecy. One advantage of 501(c) groups is secrecy. Whereas beginning late in the 2000 cycle, 527s were required to file detailed financial reports with the Internal Revenue Service, 501(c) groups were not required to disclose their contributions or expenditures. For example, when at the behest of Representative J. C. Watt (R-Okla.), a nonprofit group was created that planned to raise and spend as much as $1.5 million to help Republicans keep control of Congress, neither the expenditures nor the donors were disclosed.[81] This feature is troublesome. Karl Sandstrom, a member of the FEC, explained, "When office holders can maintain secret accounts, the opportunity for corruption is immense."[82] Another critic of the practice, Fred Wertheimer of proreform group Democracy 21, asserts, "The most dangerous money in American politics is the unlimited, secret contribution.... That's the door opened here."[83]

Occasionally, however, givers of issue advertising money do appear on "media radar screens." For example, the media revealed that Vance Opperman, whose company, West Publishing, was involved in a high-stakes merger and had sensitive dealings with the Justice Department, gave $100,000 to Democracy 21. Opperman and his family also gave $300,000 to Democratic state parties. The merger subsequently went through. Furthermore, West Publishing won a $14-million contract with the Justice Department for online legal research. Because of such media revelations, some groups, such as Citizens for Reform and Citizens for the Republic Education Fund, have switched their tax status away from "social welfare" to a tax status that clearly allows political participation.[84]

In a study of ads appearing in the 2000 election cycle, nonprofit advocacy organizations accounted for 85% of the ads. The other ads were sponsored by Democrats (9%) and Republicans (6%). Ad sponsors include Citizens for Better Medicare, the AFL-CIO, Planned Parenthood, the Chamber of Commerce, the Business Roundtable, the League of Conservation Voters, Americans for Job Security, Emily's List, and the Coalition to Protect America's Healthcare.[85] Prior to 2000, conservative Republicans benefitted most from tax-exempt social welfare organization support.[86]

Environmental groups, for example, have sometimes decided to channel their political spending away from traditional PAC contributions into attack ads of their own devising, a shift they consider more cost-effective. Accordingly, the League of Conservation Voters reduced its PAC contributions to congressional candidates from $1.1 million in 1994 to about $150,000 in 1996. The League then launched a $1.5-million "Dirty Dozen" campaign in July 1996 to fund radio and television ads aimed at ousting 12 House members. President Deb Callahan reasoned, "Giving PAC contributions to a candidate wasn't really saving our environmental heroes from defeat." Now, she says, "we're making a fundamental shift in the kind of political power we're exerting."[87]

The clever way in which these ads avoid the restriction of not advocating that viewers vote or not vote for a particular candidate is demonstrated in the ad by the Christian Action Network on "Clinton's Vision for a Better America." Innuendos, subtle associations, and various visual and auditory techniques are used, some bordering on subliminal perception techniques. Box 11.3 describes the campaign and the techniques used.

The number of issue ads typically grows with the approach of an election day. A week before the end of Campaign 2000, the Annenberg Center logged 861 such ads compared to only 104 earlier ads. The number of groups and party committees paying for them had similarly jumped—from 27 to 150.[88] Most of the ads were sponsored by organizations other than the two major parties. In a study of ads appearing in the 2000 election cycle, advocacy organizations—nonprofit organizations, some of which are tax-exempt—accounted for 85% of the ads, whereas Democrats sponsored only 9% and Republicans only 6%. Aside from the two political parties, the ad sponsors include such nonprofits as Citizens for Better Medicare, the AFL-CIO, Planned Parenthood, the Chamber of Commerce, the Business Roundtable, the League of Conservation Voters, Americans for Job Security, Emily's List, and the Coalition to Protect America's Healthcare.[89]

Following the example of the Christian Coalition, which pioneered issue ads, a small number of tax-exempt groups (supported by several conservative multibillionaires) poured hundreds of thousands of dollars into last-minute advertising blitzes to offset labor union advertising campaigns at the end of the 1996 campaign.[90] Corporations and business associations also engaged in last-minute preelection advertising.

For example, the pharmaceutical industry poured at least $16 million into an advertising blitz in 2002 in an effort to tip the balance of power in Congress toward Republicans who back the drug makers' legislative interests.[91] Also wishing to tilt the election outcome, the U.S. Chamber of Commerce financed a $13-million ad campaign and spent additional sums under the name Americans Working for Real Change.[92] The re-

---

Box 11.3 Christian Action Network's Television Commercials

In 1992, the Christian Action Network (CAN) aired the television commercial "Clinton's Vision for a Better America" 250 times in 24 major cities, along with newspaper advertisements, columns, and direct mail. None of CAN's $2 million in expenditures that year was publicly disclosed because the group called the activity public education rather than electioneering. The distinction was justified because the commercials did not urge the electorate to vote for or against specific persons. The Supreme Court's decision in *Buckley v. Valeo* in 1976 said that groups are considered to be engaged in electioneering only if they run ads or produce material including words like "Vote for (or against) Representative Jones." But as West points out, there are many ways to urge voting for or against a candidate by making use of nonverbal communication and techniques of video production, such as audio voice-overs, music, visual text, visual images, color, editing, and code words.

The ads used the following techniques:

1. Visual degrading of Clinton's picture into a poor-quality, grayish negative so that he looks bad.

2. Use of unfavorable colors (contrast between a bright color image of the American flag and a grayish, unflattering image of Clinton).

3. Ominous music; for example, halfway through the commercial, the pitch drops down into a deep bass, suggesting something bad will happen if Clinton is elected president.

4. Abrupt sequencing of images; for example, a color image of Clinton accompanied by an American flag quickly shifts "to a parade sequence of yelling, disagreeable-looking gay men clothed in chains, leather, and rope," thus creating a feeling that these individuals are threatening traditional American heterosexual values.

5. Use of "quota" and "vision" as code words unfavorable to Clinton; for example, one spot refers to "Job quotas for homosexuals" and asks, "Is this your vision for a better America?" (Quotas are viewed unfavorably by most Americans and the "vision thing" was much related to President Bush.)

6. Visual disappearance of Clinton in the presence of the flag at the end of the ad, strongly suggesting to voters to defeat him.

form bill's restrictions on advertising 30 or 60 days prior to an election are intended to limit such last-minute advertising.

Effectiveness of Campaign Ads

Like corporate advocacy advertising discussed in chapter 6, the effectiveness of political issue ads and other campaign ads cannot be assumed. According to Joshua Green, a senior editor of *The Atlantic*, campaign commercials are "Dumb and Dumber." Most people, he says, would agree that "televised political ads, almost without exception, are remorselessly bad."[93] They lag in quality and imagination. They still mainly follow the formats originated in the 1950s, such as the biographical ad, the negative attack, and the practice of using an opponent's words against him. Green not surprisingly concludes that political advertising is becoming less effective. Viewers need about 20 exposures before they can remember an ad—in contrast to around five or six viewings for consumer ads, which in contrast, prize originality.[94]

People tend to avoid ads with which they disagree, but because political ads fill the airwaves, it's almost impossible to shut them out completely, says Lynda Lee Kaid of the University of Florida.[95] In 2002, 1,497,386 spots aired in the nation's top 100 markets, according to the Campaign Media Analysis Group, a private firm that tracks televised political ads. Besides the number of ads, more information is crowded into them. For example, William Benoit found that from 1952 to 1996 the average number of issues covered in Republican ads rose by 115%, and in Democratic ads by 519%.[96]

Citizens who are unaffiliated with political parties—nonpartisans— are most likely to be influenced by campaign ads. Other factors count, too. Ads sponsored by a candidate serve to bolster the viewers' perception of the candidate's character. There is also broad agreement that negative ads are more persuasive than positive ones, despite widespread public distaste for them. Their incidence grew from around 11% to 43% between the 1960 and 1996 elections.[97] They are more likely to be noticed and actively processed; they contribute to more learning and provide superior recall; and they produce a larger effect on opinion formation than positive ads. There is also some evidence that they suppress voter turnout. Whether negative or positive, however, issue ads are inferior to candidate-sponsored ads in producing awareness or knowledge.[98]

As with advocacy ads in general, quality and creativity count. Green is optimistic that as the Internet becomes the hot new medium for political ads, more imagination will be fostered. For example, when the liberal organization MoveOn.org held a contest to design the best anti-Bush ad, more than 1,000 submissions were made and the best ones aired on television.[99]

HOW EFFECTIVE ARE POLITICAL CONTRIBUTIONS?

When asked why they make political contributions, corporate spokespersons typically reply that they like a particular candidate and party and want to support the democratic process. However, the companies and industries that have been the most generous in their giving are those that expect to benefit the most from government subsidies, tax benefits, and regulatory relief. The effectiveness of political contributions, therefore, is measured by two results: (a) getting favored candidates elected, and (b) obtaining favorable legislation and favorable treatment from the executive branch of government.

Helping a Candidate Win

Campaigns matter a great deal in the outcome of congressional elections, and how well a campaign is financed is expected to influence whether one's favored candidate wins. Joseph J. Fanelli, president of the Business–Industry PAC, wants candidates with his views to win. His aim in making contributions is to make races more competitive by "improving the philosophical balance of Congress—through the support of 'pro-private enterprise' challengers with reasonable chances to win and in assisting similarly-oriented incumbents who are in danger of losing their seats."[100]

Money Advantage of Incumbents.   The ability to outspend one's rival gives a candidate an important advantage. This advantage accrues mainly to incumbents because contributions mainly flow to them. In particular, federally registered lobbyists inordinately contribute to incumbents because they want to reach influential decision makers. Incumbents from both parties in congressional elections also enjoy disproportionate contributions from corporate PACs. Corporations are more interested in buttressing their lobbying clout in support of vital company interests than in the outside chance a challenger favorable to them might win an election.

The money advantage of incumbency was shown in the 2002 elections. A House incumbent raised, on average, nearly $900,000 to keep a seat (up from $650,000 in 1998); the typical House challenger raised only $197,000. As races grow more costly, the money gap between incumbents and challengers is expected to widen.[101] In the 2004 elections, incumbent senators raised a total of $223.6 million compared to $70.7 million by challengers; house incumbents raised $427.6 million versus $100.8 by challengers.[102]

The biggest spender in the 2000 Senate races was Jon S. Corzine, the Wall Street multimillionaire. He spent $63 million on his campaign, with $35 million in the primary election alone, most of it ($23.5 million) on advertising.[103] As Jeff Pilletts of the *Bergen Record* stated,

"Money supplies everything in politics—access, friends, even credibility.... He not only purchased commercials, he purchased the party machinery and the people who run it."[104] Corzine could make a virtue of his self-financed effort. "I won't owe anything to anyone but you," he declared to voters. In his primary campaign he bombarded the airwaves with 12 weeks of unrelenting audiovisual persuasion and financed at least 5,000 workers in an unprecedented get-out-the-vote (GOTV) operation. He spent $15 million on television time aired over a 2-month period leading up to the general election.

In roughly 9 out of 10 House races and three quarters of all Senate races in which incumbents seek reelection, the incumbent wins.[105] In the 2002 elections, 98% of House incumbents were reelected, as were 85% of incumbent senators.[106] Challengers have a fighting chance mainly when the incumbent is implicated in a scandal, has roll call votes that are out of sync with voters, or possesses other liabilities.

Money alone, however, does not buy elections for incumbents and certainly not for challengers, against whom the odds are so heavily stacked. An attractive candidate who has a coherent message and comes from a district whose voters are ideologically not too far from the candidate is needed. Among the losers have been some candidates who spent their own money in the 1998 election. Mark Warner, a Virginia Democrat, lost after spending more than $10 million; Guy Millner, a Georgia Republican, lost after spending $6.4 million.[107] In California's June 1998 primary, Republican candidate Al Checchi spent at least $37 million of his own money, and candidate Harmon spent $11.6 million. Both lost to Democratic candidate Lieutenant Governor Gray Davis.[108] In the 1998 election, the top Senate spender, Senator Alfonse M. D'Amato (R-N.Y.) lost to the Democratic challenger, Representative Charles E. Schumer (D-N.Y.).

More detailed analyses of election results demonstrate money is chiefly important in open-seat races. The amount of money a candidate spends on campaign communications significantly affects the outcome. The impact of spending is especially important because elections for open seats are usually won by far smaller margins than incumbent–challenger races.[109] A strong challenger, however, may be able to win if he or she can obtain campaign financing and assemble an effective campaign organization. Certain additional factors help: a contested primary, media support, campaigning on position issues, and group-based targeting.[110] Party support is also important.

Supporting Lobbying Efforts

Lobbyists want to reach the most influential decision makers. This contention is supported by a study by the Center for Public Integrity of the personal campaign contributions of more than 1,000 federally registered lobbyists from 1999 through September 2004. The study shows that they gave $2.9 million to Senate incumbents and their challengers in 2004 and a mere 5.4%, or $257,000 to challengers. Senate Minority Leader Thomas A. Daschle (D-S.D.) received the largest amount.[111]

Business people and lobbyists don't like to admit publicly that their reason for making political contributions is to obtain favors. Roger Tamraz, an oil executive, was an exception. When testifying at the 1996 Senate hearings on campaign finance abuses and asked why he gave $300,000 to the Democratic party, he bluntly replied: to win access to the White House and the Clinton administration.[112] A *BusinessWeek/Harris* survey of 400 top executives of major companies found a similar reason behind political contributions: 50% said, "My company and I hope to gain access to politicians so we can gain fair consideration on issues affecting our business."[113] The top reason, however, was, "I have strong political views and want to support a political party and candidates who share my convictions" (65%), and the second was "Making political contributions is my way of supporting the democratic process" (59%).

Robert J. Wager, president of the American Bakers Association, describes more graphically the aim of political contributions supporting lobbying efforts. He says, "The key to success for any PAC is to take a pragmatic approach which emphasizes effective action on behalf of the economic interests of the association."[114] He further explains that his BreadPAC makes bipartisan contributions on the basis of "merit." Reinforcing his belief that PAC funds should reinforce lobbying efforts, he says, "Whenever possible, the check, or a copy of it, should be personally delivered by the treasurer, or an association member, to the candidate. This is even more effective if the PAC treasurer is the association's chief lobbyist."[115]

After George W. Bush's election victory in 2000, businesses that invested in his campaign made no secret about expecting favors, as suggested in the *Wall Street Journal* headline, "Influence Market: Industries That Backed Bush Are Now Seeking Return on Investment."[116] Some of the expectations were as follows:

- MBNA, which gave $1.25 million to Bush, the Republican party, and the Inaugural Fund during the 1999–2000 election cycle—the second highest corporate donor after Enron—was pleased to hear that the president would sign a tough bankruptcy bill.
- Drug companies gave $14 million to Republican campaigns over the past 2 years and spent an additional $60 million to fund their own independent political advertising campaign. They are lobbying for an overhaul of the Medicare program that would include a prescription drug benefit for senior citizens, provided such a benefit doesn't lead to drug price controls.
- Some businesses are looking forward to repeal of the ergonomic regulations imposed by the Clinton administration, much to the annoyance of organized labor, which had fought for their enactment for 10 years.

The value of contributions in support of lobbying objectives is illustrated by Enron and Arthur Andersen, described in the Appendix. Among the many other examples is Archer Daniels Midland (ADM), which continues to received tax breaks for producing ethanol, a subsidy that was intended to serve as a friendly incentive to reduce America's dependence on foreign oil. However, this tax break is often cited as an egregious example of "corporate welfare."[117] Another example is Glaxo Wellcome, which benefitted by winning a patent extension on two drug patents for 19 months, which some analysts believe earned it at least an extra $1 billion in sales.[118] The Glaxo Wellcome PAC received contributions from 1,537 employees. Through its Civic Action Network, consisting of 1,800 employees across the country, Glaxo motivates rank-and-file employees to telephone members of Congress and asks them to support the company.

Helpful Conditions

PAC money "buys" congressional votes but only under certain conditions, which should assuage the fear that PACs are creating a "special interest state." As clarified by Larry J. Sabato, PAC contributions do, on some occasions, make a difference, but those occasions are not nearly as frequent as critics charge. His evidence is based on more than 60 interviews with PAC and party leaders, a mail survey of 399 PACs, and a review of available studies.[119]

Sabato concludes that PACs work best in influencing congressional votes under these conditions:

1. *Visibility.* When issues lack headline status, they do not draw the attention of constituencies. The Senate vote on deregulation of the trucking industry in 1980 illustrates this principle. There was a strong linkage between congressional votes and PAC money, much stronger than the relationship between votes and party, ideology, and constituency. The linkage was even stronger for the senators nearest to an election.
2. *Specialization and lack of opposition.* PAC gifts are not likely to be decisive on broad national issues, such as policy on El Salvador or the MX missile systems, where opposition is weak and unorganized.
3. *Alliance.* When large PACs or groups of PACs (e.g., business and labor PACs) are allied, they garner more attention. A congressman might dismiss $5,000 from a single PAC (the maximum gift), but $20,000 or more from a group fills a significant part of reelection campaign needs.
4. *Strong lobbies.* When PAC gifts are coordinated with direct or grassroots lobbying, they are more likely to influence congressional votes. Members of Congress are rewarded not for their political philosophy but for how they vote on an issue of concern to a PAC.[120]

Although it is "ludicrously naive to contend that PAC money never influences Congress member decisions," Sabato believes that merit matters most—merit as defined by ideological beliefs, party loyalty, and the interests of district constituents.[121] His optimistic view, however, is not shared by all.

OTHER POLITICAL ASSISTANCE AND CYBERPOLITICS

Large corporations have been seeking a more direct role in the electoral process and becoming "more creative as far as how they are going to be political."[122] In the 2002 elections, pro-Republican businesses were using such novel ways as stuffing voter guides into pay envelopes, e-mailing workers with candidate report cards, and mounting GOTV drives.[123] Many have merged political assistance programs with regular public affairs activities and strengthened programs on employee voter education. The Internet is playing an increasing role in fund raising and political action, achieving the designation of cyberpolitics.

Merging Political Assistance With Public Affairs

Political assistance takes many forms. For example, a study by the Public Affairs Foundation showed that in addition to supporting PACs, which 80% of them do, leading corporations engaged in such additional political activities as:

- Scheduling facility visits for elected officials (84%).
- Conducting voter registration programs (58%).
- Communicating on issues with "third parties" (43%).[124]

Added to this list of political activities is the granting of leaves of absence to allow or encourage a company's employees (usually on the managerial level) to run for political office or assist in a campaign. Because laws prohibit the use of company funds and other resources for such purposes, leaves of absence are without pay.

In the 2004 elections, corporations shifted some of their efforts from financing issue advertising by others to such direct activities as encouraging employees to support individual candidates and to lobby Congress on particular issues. For example, Dow Chemical reached out to its 37,000 retirees for extra lobbying clout. International Paper allowed employees to use special software to track political issues, which resulted in e-mails from 2,500 workers to the Senate encouraging postal reform (because many of the company's customers suffer when postal rates rise).[125]

Other activities and programs have also been undertaken. Peter Kennerdell, editor of *Managing the Business–Employee PAC*, refers to political assistance in the form of in-kind contributions, partisan communications, conduit/trustee accounts for employees making personal

political contributions, direct campaign involvement, and such miscel-
lanea as honoraria for speeches.[126]

Making Full Use of PACs.   Kennerdell reminds public affairs professionals that raising funds for politicians is not the only function of PACs.
More important, they are "vehicles for educating, motivating and mobilizing employees in politics."[127] His handbook stresses that PACs should
be part of an overall public affairs program and that broad-based grassroots efforts should be integrated with employee political education.

One way business and other interest groups can help candidates on
the local level is by printing stories about a candidate in PAC newsletters
and other publications. Professional journalists who are engaged in so-
called PAC communications turn out highly professional products that
play an important part in building employee involvement, says A. John
Adams, president of a Washington public affairs consulting firm bearing his name. He describes one oil company that set up a series of area
committees, which report on their activities in their own quarterly
newsletters. These area newsletters supplement the regular PAC
monthly newsletter (see Box 11.4) on the writing of a PAC newsletter),
which deals with political developments affecting the company. The
area committees also organize local events, such as backyard barbecues,
to which candidates for public office are invited.[128]

Box 11.4 Writing a PAC Newsletter

PAC communications should be objective and professionally written.
Adams says it is important to "de-Washingtonize" PAC communications, which are written in quite different language from that used
elsewhere in the company. In explaining company concerns to employees, companies must get on the same wavelength as the employees. It is not enough to make an ideological statement that an
opponent is "liberal" or "anti-business."[129] The purpose of *Washington
Window,* a professionally written PAC newsletter distributed by the
Corning Employees Political Action Committee (COREPAC), as explained by John R. Blizard, government affairs manager of the Corning Glass Works, is to "educate people who are eligible to participate
in COREPAC and to correct preconceived notions of what's happening
in Washington, D.C." The newsletter was published quarterly and distributed to approximately 1,800 exempt salaried employees.[130]

The company followed two simple guidelines in deciding what issues
to cover: Corning must have taken a stand on them, and they must
have a bearing on the company. Qualifying issues have been energy
problems, clean air, toxic substances, foreign trade, and labor reform.
The topics should also easily evoke employee interest; for example, the
Clean Air Act affects jobs in Corning's New York automotive plant,
where ceramic substrates are produced for catalytic converters.

Getting Out the Vote Programs

Corporations have stepped up grassroots efforts, an activity where unions dominated. In its 1998 political campaign, the AFL-CIO planned to focus on grassroots activity instead of issue advertising, which it did in the 1996 campaign. It spent at least $18 million in a GOTV drive, with some 300 paid activists leading the effort. In California it supplemented the door-to-door and phone bank campaigns with mass mailings to 1.4 million adults in union households.[131] According to exit polls, labor's GOTV efforts paid off in key congressional and gubernatorial races in November 1998. Among its goals for the November 1999 election, the AFL-CIO wanted to register at least 4 million new voters, focusing heavily on Blacks, Asians, and Hispanics.[132] Labor intensified its registration and GOTV efforts in 2004.

In the 2004 elections business groups and corporations gave much greater emphasis in employee GOTV campaigns. BIPAC, a business advocacy group, set a goal for local businesses in Ohio to encourage 80,000 employees who didn't vote in 2000 to go to the polls. Caterpillar made it possible for its 37,000 expatriate workers to vote by using absentee ballots that could be downloaded . Although it doesn't endorse candidates, its website does provide candidates' voting history on critical issues such as trade.[133]

Voter Education Programs

As companies slashed their political donations in the 2004 election campaign, many made an unprecedented effort to seek a more direct role in the electoral process by influencing the votes of their employees, says *Wall Street Journal* columnist Alan Murray.[134] Greg Casey of BIPAC, which is dedicated to electing business-friendly candidates, has been successfully convincing corporate executives they can play a big role in "educating" employees and getting them out to vote. Of the 150 members of the Business Roundtable, he has signed up 90 for voter-education programs, up from just a dozen or so 4 years ago.[135]

Such programs are not new. The Headquarters Unit Employees PAC at Dow Chemical distributed a booklet, *How to Evaluate a Candidate*, to its employees and taught them how to use it. The booklet explains that voting criteria should encompass three core values: belief in the American free enterprise system, fiscal responsibility, and reasonable government regulation. To these are added 10 quantifiable criteria, such as electability and whether Dow employees are in one's election district. A similar approach was used by the former LTV Corporation, which "sponsored a Leadership Series consisting of a wide range of information, analysis, news and insights on the major presidential candidates, the primaries, and the national conventions."[136] The articles, which were summarized in a booklet, were on issues developed through the cooperation of the Baruch College of Business and Public Administration of the City University of New York. Seven issues were covered: the federal budget deficit, the defense of the United States, foreign trade, employment, industrial policy, education in America, and the environment. The company did not, however, endorse a particular candidate.

Programs on the Free Enterprise System. Many companies believe teaching employees the fundamentals of the free enterprise system is an important way to influence how they make political judgments. When economic education flourished in the late 1970s, Dart Industries initiated a 20-week program at its West Bend Division. The first 10 weeks dealt with general economics, and the second 10 weeks with information relating the principles to the West Bend Division. It used a variety of media and techniques: posters, payroll stuffers, articles in the house organ, discussions between managers and line employees, and economic quizzes with prizes of $10 each awarded to outstanding employees.

However, when the Dart program was evaluated at the end of the 20 weeks, the results were declared unsatisfactory. Although employees' knowledge of facts improved, the key result, a change in their attitudes, was not apparent. Their attitudes were described as "still not fully favorable to 'big business.'" Hoping to improve results, the company subsequently worked on another program covering the six major theme areas of profits, inflation, government and taxation, productivity, general business information, and social responsibility.[137]

Public relations counselor Philip Lesly succinctly explains why formal programs such as Dart's are doomed to fail. He cites the following key faulty assumptions and practices: (a) the assumption that education will "take" if facts alone are exposed to the public, (b) continued insistence of business on formulating a gospel and projecting it at the audience to be swallowed whole, (c) failure to recognize the drastic change in the way influence is disseminated, (d) the assumption that the audience has the same interests and aspirations as the company, (e) use of the wrong semantics, such as the reference to "the free enterprise system," and (f) lack of clear objectives.[138]

To avoid the error of developing programs that are too abstract or ideological, Standard Oil of California's overall philosophy was "to address specific economic questions as they arise, relating them to the individual as much as possible."[139] The ingredients of such programs are several: Make economics an integral part of the regular flow of information in the employee communication system. Use employee publications, videotaped company newscasts, employee "jobholder" meetings, employee annual reports, and other media. Relate economics to daily business operations, and tap the experiences and interests of employees. When discussing public issues, demonstrate a "unity of interest" between the company and employees. A further way to make economic education effective is to combine it with political action programs.

Although formal economic education programs have fallen into disuse, the subject matter of economics is integrated into a variety of stories that appear in employee publications and videos. During the recession of the early 1980s, when auto and other manufacturing companies faced economic hardships, employees were told about the realities of global competition, to convince them of the need for givebacks and higher productivity. Company publications contained articles about sales won or lost, the need for restructuring, the reasons for acquisitions or mergers, plans for capital improvements, and reasons for plant closings. Some companies also informed employees about political issues affecting them and their industries, for example, the need for free trade or the need for a cap on insurance liability.

Whether to Engage in Partisan Communications

Companies normally avoid partisan communications and other activities. Legally, however, a company may engage in partisan activities if they do not go beyond the "restricted class" of high-level executives and administrative officers and their families, and stockholders and their families. Thus companies are allowed to sponsor a candidate or party appearances, invite a candidate to address the restricted class, produce and distribute printed materials of a very partisan nature, endorse candidates, and conduct very partisan voter registration and GOTV drives.[140]

A company may have a special reason for engaging in partisan communications. Duquesne Light Company, serving two counties in southwestern Pennsylvania, including the city of Pittsburgh, decided to do so because the utility became an issue in several elections. After deciding to support one of the three candidates, "we wrote letters to all our employees and shareholders who live in the state senatorial district, telling them what was being said, explaining when they make their decision on voting day, they keep in mind the facts about our relationship with the state house member," explained Jean F. Grogan, director of public service programs.[141] Grogan realizes the risks of offending some PAC members who support the other side. Thus she recommends caution in using partisan communications: Be very selective about the races in which to get involved and be extremely careful about language used in letters to employees.[142]

Cyberpolitics

The Internet has become a new method of political campaigning, as well as fund raising, proliferating more rapidly that anyone anticipated. A new term, *cyberpolitics*, now recognizes the Internet as "a mainstream, multipurpose political tool."[143] It has unleashed a new cadre of campaign workers who normally don't have time to man a phone bank and it is a marvelous tool for building networks, mobilizing supporters, and raising campaign funds.[144] Howard Dean's success as a Democratic presidential candidate in the early months of the 2004 election cycle showed what a mighty political tool the Web has become. He adopted the newly formed Internet service Meetup.com—which facilitates the gathering of people who share common interests—as his primary grassroots organization tool. By the end of May 2003 his campaign claimed to have 25,000 supporters on Meetup and twice that number of contributors or volunteers.[145]

Dean also paid attention to blogs—personal online journals—and treated relatively unknown bloggers as a critical opinion-making constituency. By some estimates, 750,000 people blogged in 2003, with the number growing daily.[146] Dean took advantage of the blog craze after 9/11 when people wanted to know what other Americans were thinking and feeling about the terrorist act. It gave each person his or her own voice. Journalists, too, became bloggers as they commented on the news, often in "rudely clever tones." Some of the most popular blogs come from big-name journalists and former editors.[147] Dean's impact on political campaigning is enduring. As *BusinessWeek* noted, "Dean has nudged American politics further into the Internet Age. Campaign Blogs and supporter 'meet-ups' have joined the political lexicon, online fundraising has become ever more important, and the Internet has become a vital organizing tool."[148]

The success of Dean's Internet campaign encouraged savvy politicians in both parties to revamp their tech operations. Consequently, Senator John F. Kerry raised an average of $1 million a day online in the 10 days following the Super Tuesday primaries.[149] The Bush team used GeorgeWBush.com as a political organizing tool, using the advantage that the Republicans had a head start because of their 3-to-1 edge in e-mail addresses. Also using the Internet as an organizing tool, the liberal advocacy group MoveOn.org organized one of the largest antiwar rallies in history in 2003, with some 10 million protesters around the globe. It had 2 million e-mail members and in early 2004 ran a $10-million TV ad campaign against President George W. Bush. Besides raising money from small donors, MoveOn.org obtained a $10 million to $75 million pledge for a GOTV campaign called Americans Coming Together from George Soros, the billionaire financier and avowed Bush critic. He is also providing $1 million a year for 3 years to the Center for American Progress, a new think tank headed by John Podesta, White House chief of staff during the Clinton administration.[150]

CONCLUSIONS

Electoral activities, especially political contributions, enhance a company's lobbying objectives and overall public affairs goals. At stake is who gets elected and what issues the candidates will support. Donors generally expect that PAC, soft money, issue advocacy advertising, and other contributions will provide them with access and influence in the political system. Business has a special advantage over other interest groups because it has more economic resources. Proving a connection between money and voting results, however, is not an exact science.

The role of money in politics is itself a political issue resulting in regulations—most recently by the McCain-Feingold reform bill. However, even as contribution restrictions are observed, political actors constantly explore ways of circumventing them. Contributions to 527 groups by a variety of special interest groups have particularly been questioned and efforts are contemplated further to tighten campaign finance rules.

Many corporations are engaging in other forms of electoral involvement besides making financial contributions. These include voter registration drives, voter education programs, and more basic economic and political education programs. In the future, corporations may be building stronger political communities that threaten the traditional nonpartisan policy of business.

APPENDIX
CASE STUDIES DEMONSTRATING HOW POLITICAL CONTRIBUTIONS SUPPORT LOBBYING

Case 1: Enron Corporation

Enron has become the textbook example of the blatant and widespread use of political contributions in support of lobbying efforts to obtain political favors. The company's rapid growth into the nation's seventh largest corporation proves the value of political contributions. Enron could not have become a trading company giant without succeeding in its strategy of establishing a deregulated energy market. "The objective was to break up monopoly control of energy markets by local utilities and change the rules so energy would be deregulated."[151]

To do this it spent lavishly to replace local utility monopolies. Since 1997, it gave more than 700 candidates in 28 states $1.9 million, according to the National Institute on Money in State Policies. In California, a major target, Enron gave Governor Gray Davis $97,500 of its $438,155 total contributions to politicians in the state. Jeffrey Skilling, Enron's president and chief operating officer since 1997, testified to utility commissioners that deregulation could save the state $8.9 billion. In the 2000 election cycle, Enron gave $1.1 million to local candidates. It became the leader of an emerging power-trading industry that shaped electricity deregulation plans affecting millions of household. Enron also stood to earn big profits for the company's trading of electricity and natural gas.[152]

Money, however, was not Enron's only advantage. As Mary Kenkel, former manager for federal affairs at the Edison Electric Institute said, "They were smart—they went after people who [they] knew would make a difference." They lobbied cleverly. In Texas, Enron hired 83 lobbyists, bought advertisements in local papers, and gave to local charities, including Laura Bush's book fair.[153]

Enron also targeted Congress and the White House to change the rules governing the energy industry. The corporation and its executives contributed almost $5.88 million to political war chests since 1989, including $1.9 million in soft money to both parties. Republicans received 73%.[154] Kenneth Lay, Enron's chairman and former CEO, and other executives contributed more than $500,000 to Bush's presidential campaign and donated more money to the inaugural and the campaign's legal effort in Florida during the disputed 2000 election vote count.[155] Enron was the top corporate donor in the 1999–2000 election cycle, having given $1.3 million to Bush, the Republican National Committee, and the Inaugural Fund.[156]

Money was used for other purposes too. Nationally, Enron "collected visible people": pundits, journalists, and politicians were given lucrative retainers in return for chatting about current events with executives at Enron's Houston headquarters. Lay called them his advisory council, saying to them in December 2000, "These are exciting times, and we need all the ideas we can get." One of the group, William Kristol, editor of the *Weekly Standard*, received a $50,000 annual retainer. He said he saw no conflict in collecting such money from Enron, simply likening it to a "regular and generous" honorarium for speaking before a trade association.[157]

The main strategic goal behind all of these efforts was to keep regulators away. Enron was highly successful. As summarized by Albert R. Hunt of the *Wall Street Journal*, "Few special interests got more access or results than Enron: legislative favors, a lax oversight of its risky financial derivatives, tax breaks, unsurpassed input into the Cheney energy legislation drafting process and most of what it wanted, and reportedly even veto authority over regulatory appointees."[158]

Case 2: Arthur Andersen

Enron's auditing firm, Arthur Andersen, and the other Big Five accounting firms were also major players in the political arena that expected to influence political decisions. Like Enron, these firms sought independence from government regulation and oversight, and they didn't hesitate to use their formidable political clout, largely gained by being a major contributor of PAC money to politicians and soft money to political parties. Senator Christopher Dodd, the influential Connecticut Democrat, had accepted nearly $500,000 in contributions from the accounting industry between 1989 and 2001.[159] The industry's major objectives were: (a) to stop Security and Exchange Commission (SEC) regulations and possible new legislation prohibiting accounting firms from also performing consulting services to their auditing clients; (b) to prevent the Financial Accounting Standards Board (FASB), an independent, private-sector body, from imposing their standards on accounting firms; and (c) to stop moves that would require stock options to be shown as an expense in company earnings statements.

Since 1989 Andersen had contributed more than $5 million in soft money, PAC, and individual contributions to federal candidates and parties, more than two thirds to Republicans. In the 2000 election cycle alone, the firm and its employees made contributions totaling $1.4 million, which was 10% of the overall donations from the accounting industry. The firm was the fifth biggest donor to Bush's White House run, contributing nearly $146,000 via its employees and PAC. The managing partner of Andersen's Houston office was one of the "pioneers"—an individual who raised at least $100,000 for the Bush campaign during 1999–2000.[160]

The Big Five, with a leadership role played by Joseph Berardino, Andersen's CEO, succeeded in achieving all three objectives until the Enron scandal unfolded. Their efforts demonstrate how electoral activities supported their lobbying activities. In his book, *Take on the Street: What Wall Street and Corporate American Don't Want You to Know. What You Can Do to Fight Back*, Arthur Levitt Jr., former SEC chairman, describes how the accounting industry and corporate lobbyists successfully applied their political clout (see Box 11.5).

After the Enron debacle revealed Andersen's complicity, the Justice Department indicted the company for its alleged shredding and destruction of documents. The limits of political contributions and lobbying were now obvious. When things were going well, their political clout worked, but when an embarrassing crisis occurred, political friends evaporated. As the *Economist* summarized Enron's treatment, Kenneth Lay, Enron's chairman, who was very close to President Bush and known as "Kenny Boy," now was accorded the response, "Ken Who?"[161] Political contributions could not stem the tide of the government's suit against the company and win support from politicians who had received contributions. Said Peter Deutsch, the senior Democrat on the panel's investigations subcommittee, "It doesn't matter if they gave us a million bucks. We are not going to cut them any slack." Andersen, like Enron, had become a political liability.

ENDNOTES

1. Edwin M. Epstein, *The Corporation in American Politics* (Englewood Cliffs, N.J.: Prentice-Hall, 1969), p. 11. He defines electoral politics as "activities related directly to the selection and support (financial and otherwise) of candidates or issues to be decided upon by the public."
2. Charles S. Mack, "Lobbying and Political Action," in *Practical Public Affairs in an Era of Change: A Communications Guide for Business, Government, and College*, ed. Lloyd B. Dennis (Lanham, Md.: University Press of America), p. 106.
3. Albert R. Hunt, "The Lessons of the 1996 Scandals: Do It Again, and More," *Wall Street Journal*, June 3, 1999, p. A27.
4. "'04 Elections Expected to Cost Nearly $4 Billion," press release dated October 21, 2004, opensecrets.org; "Campaign Finance Reform," www.opensecrets.org; Greg Gordon, "At What Price?," *Star Tribune* (Minneapolis, MN), November 8, 2000, p. 23A.

Box 11.5 Lobbying Tactics Used by Accounting Industry[162]

When Levitt said that "the SEC would insist on auditor independence and, through enforcement actions if necessary, require that companies adhere to the letter and spirit of the GAAP [generally agreed upon accounting practices], the accounting industry questioned the need for national standards.

It persuaded Congress to hold hearings on a proposed ruling by the FASB to expense stock options. Silicon Valley, also large campaign contributors, were especially opposed, pointing out that weak profits made cash compensation difficult. Senator Joe Lieberman, the Connecticut Democrat, introduced legislation to bar the SEC from enforcing the rule. He also sponsored a Senate resolution that declared the FASB proposal would have "grave consequences for America's entrepreneurs." The bill failed to pass, but the resolution did, by an overwhelming 88–9. Levitt consequently urged FASB members to back down in favor of a current, weaker rule that requires companies to disclose stock options grants in the footnotes to income statements.

The industry was able to block an attempt by the SEC and the American Institute of Certified Public Accountants to pass a rule banning auditors from doing most kinds of consulting work for the same companies they audited. Some 46 members of Congress sent letters to Levitt opposing the measure. Furthermore, Senate Banking Committee chairman Phil Gramm warned Levitt that Congress was preparing an "appropriations rider" that would bar the agency from spending taxpayer funds to enforce the rule. Faced with such threat to SEC independence, Levitt gave in and compromised. The final rules, adopted on November 15, 2000, allowed auditors to perform up to 40% of a company's internal audit work and an unlimited amount of consulting—as long as all this was disclosed. (It turned out that in 2000, S&P 500 companies paid their auditors $1.2 billion in audit fees and triple that amount, $3.7 billion, for nonaudit services.)

---

5. "2004 Election Overview: Most Expensive Races," opensecrets.org.
6. This is the reason for the subtitle in Herrnson's book: *Congressional Elections: Campaigning at Home and in Washington*, 2nd edition (Washington, D.C.: CQ Press, 1998), p. xii.
7. Phil Kuntz, "The Money Chase: A Day in Washington Is Just Another Day to Raise More Dollars," *Wall Street Journal*, October 23, 1995, p. A1.
8. Ellen Miller and Nick Penniman, "The Road to Nowhere: Thirty Years of Campaign-Finance Reform Yield Precious Little," *The American Prospect*, August 12, 2002, p. 14.
9. David Cohen, "PAC Power: An Abuse of Power," in *Political Action for Business: The PAC Handbook*, ed. Ken Clair (Washington, D.C.: Fraser/Associates, 1981), p. 313.
10. Ibid., p. 19.

11. "'04 Elections Expected to Cost Nearly $4 Billion," op. cit.
12. Lawrence Noble and Steven Weiss, "Op-Ed: Plenty of Individual Contributions," *Miami Herald*, November 25, 2004, as reprinted at www.open secrets.org.
13. *Good Morning America* show, September 30, 2003; Jeanne Cummings, "Cash Influx Tilts Campaign Calculus," *Wall Street Journal*, October 1, 2003, p. A12; Stephen Baker, "Click the Vote," *BusinessWeek*, March 29, 2004, p. 102.
14. Thoms B. Edsall and Juliet Eilperin, "PAC Attack II; Why Some Groups Are Learning to Love Campaign Finance Reform," *Washington Post*, August 18, 2002, p. B2.
15. Glenn R. Simpson, "The Internet Begins to Click as a Political Money Web," *Wall Street Journal*, October 19, 1999, p. A28.
16. Coercion, however, may not be used to force a political contribution. This does not mean that company executives may not be chided for failing to contribute, which Richard J. Lane did when he was president of Bristol-Myers's worldwide medicines division and co-chairman of its employee PAC. Concerned about "the politically motivated attacks against our industry ... to shackle our industry with price controls," his aggressive solicitation resulted in a $2 million contribution to the party and its candidates during the 2000 campaign, second only to Pfizer. Sheryl Gay Stolberg and Gardiner Harris, "Industry Fights to Put Imprint on Drug Bill," *New York Times*, September 5, 2003, p. A1.
17. PACs could exceed legal giving limits, however, when making "independent expenditures," defined as "disbursements made to pay for a communication expressly advocating the election or defeat of a clearly identified candidate without the candidate's cooperation." Clair, op. cit., p. 186. Also see "The Big Picture - Issue Ads/Expenditure & Communication Costs," www.opensecrets.org.
18. Jeffrey Milyo, David Primo, and Timothy Groseclose, "Corporate PAC Campaign Contributions in Perspective," *Business and Politics*, Vol. 2, No. 1, 2000, p. 77.
19. Jeanne Cummings, "Closing the Spigot: In New Law's Wake, Companies Slash Their Political Donations," *Wall Street Journal*, September 3, 2004, p. A4.
20. "'04 Elections Expected to Cost Nearly $4 Billion," op. cit.
21. "Top PACs," www.opensecrets.org/pads/toppacs.asp.
22. "Top 20 PAC Contributors to Federal Candidates, 2003–2004," based on data released by the FEC on October 25, 2004, www.opensecrets.org.
23. Thomas B. Edsall, "Study: Corporate PACs Favor GOP; Decisive Shift From Bipartisan Giving Began in 1995–97," *Washington Post*, November 25, 2004, p. A06.
24. Ibid.
25. Alan B. Krueger, "Economic Scene; Lobbying by Businesses Overwhelms Their Campaign Contributions," *New York Times*, September 19, 2002, p. C2.
26. Greg Hitt and Tom Hamburger, "New Campaign Law Restores PACs' Appeal," *Wall Street Journal*, July 29, 2002, p. A4.
27. Ibid.
28. Ibid.
29. Ibid.
30. "2004 Election Overview; Top Self Funders," www.opensecrets.org.
31. David Beiler, "Jon Corzine and the Power of Money," *Campaigns & Elections*, Vol. 22, April 2001, pp. 22–36.

32. Ibid.
33. An update on December 8, 2004, showed that 527 groups raised a higher amount, $409 million. See Political MoneyLine, www.tray.com.
34. "Soft Money to National Parties," www.opensecrets.org.
35. Mary Beth Regan, "Campaign Finance '96: It Doesn't Get Much Sleazier Than This," *BusinessWeek*, October 28, 1996, p. 59.
36. "Coming to Terms: A Money-in-Politics Glossary," Center for Responsive Politics, www.crp.org/pubs/glossary/contents.htm.
37. Fred Wertheimer, "The Dirtiest Election Ever; The Spending Abuses of 1996 Should Shame Us Into Reform," *The Washington Post*, November 3, 1996, p. 1.
38. Ibid.
39. Regan, op. cit. A notorious example is the acceptance by the Democratic National Committee of an illegal $250,000 donation from Cheong Am America, a South Korean company. The committee returned the donation after the *Los Angeles Times* exposed it as a violation of laws barring contributions from foreign firms. See Glenn R. Simpson and Jill Abramson, "Foreign Exchange: Legal Loopholes Let Overseas Contributors Fill Democrats' Coffers," *Wall Street Journal*, October 8, 1996, p. A1.
40. Vicki Kemper, Deborah Lutterbeck, and Christin Davilas, "The Country Club," *Common Cause*, Vol. 22, Spring/Summer 1996, pp. 16–17.
41. Ibid., p. 238.
42. Ibid., p. 236.
43. Darrell M. West, *Checkbook Democracy: How Money Corrupts Political Campaigns* (Boston: Northeastern University Press, 2000), p. 7.
44. Amy Borrus and Mary Beth Regan, "The Backlash Against Soft Money," *BusinessWeek*, March 31, 1997, p. 33.
45. Ibid., p. 36.
46. Lisa Zagaroli, "GM Puts Brakes on 'Soft Money' contributions," *Detroit News*, June 1, 1997, p. A1.
47. Alan Murray, "Corporate America Sits Mostly on Side During This Election," *Wall Street Journal*, July 27, 2004, p. A6.
48. Ibid.
49. Jeanne Cummings, op. cit., p. A1.
50. "527s Not Filling Soft Money Gap," June 25, 2004 press release, www.opensecrets.org.
51. Mark Hosenball, Michael Isikoff, and Holly Baily, "The Secret Money War," *Newsweek*, September 20, 2004, pp. 24, 26.
52. Hosenball, et al., op. cit., p. 25.
53. Jeanne Cummings, "Political Money Flows Faster in '04," *Wall Street Journal*, April 5, 2004, p. A6. They budgeted $95 million for the 2004 campaign to hire thousands of canvassers to sign up voters in 17 swing states. The Media Fund plans to use its $50 million budget to run issue ads in the same 17 states.
54. Jeanne Cummings, "Those 527 Fund-Raisers Prove Resilient," *Wall Street Journal*, December 6, 2004, p. A4.
55. Ibid.
56. John McCain, "Plugging the Loophole," *Newsweek*, September 20, 2004, p. 24.
57. Ibid.
58. Lorraine Woellert and Lee Walczak, "Campaign Reform's Dangerous Aftershocks," *BusinessWeek*, April 8, 2002, p. 42.

59. Glenn R. Simpson, "Democrats to Swivel Spotlight to 'Mush' Money Issue," *Wall Street Journal*, September 19, 1997, p. A16. However, the argument is made that Section 501(c)(4) or 527 tax-exempt organization may pay for issue ads if they are unincorporated and they pay from funds donated by individuals.

60. Jeanne Cummings, "Political Contributors Step up to the Plate," *Wall Street Journal*, July 29, 2004, p. A4.

61. Richard S. Dunham, "Hail to the Chief: Big Business Gets Behind Bush's Bash," *BusinessWeek*, January 10, 2005, p. 13.

62. Jill Zuckman, "McCain Takes Aim at System of Campaign Financing," *Boston Globe*, July 1, 1999, p. A6.

63. Phil Kuntz, "McCain's Financing Stance Recalls Keating-Five Role," *Wall Street Journal*, December 17, 1999, p. A16. He mentioned this theme on ABC's *Nightline*.

64. Ron Unz, "McCain-Feingold Loses. There Is an Alternative," *Wall Street Journal*, October 20, 1999, p. A26.

65. From a Public Affairs Council PowerPoint presentation on "Campaign Finance Laws," SASM&FLLP, December 2, 2003.

66. David Rogers, "Senate Approves Measure to Curb Big Donations," *Wall Street Journal*, March 21, 2002, p. A24. Also Trevor Potter and Kirk L. Jowers, "Summary Analysis of Bipartisan Campaign Finance Reform Act Passed by House and Senate and Sent to President," www.brook.edu.

67. Cummings, Greenberger, and Hamburger, op. cit., p. A8.

68. "Campaign Law Actually Works, But Reformers Still Have a Job to Do," *Newsday*, November 9, 2004, p. A36.

69. Joanna Chung, "Battle Over Funding Continues After History's Costliest Presidential Race," *Financial Times*, November 20, 2004, p. 9.

70. "527s Not Filling Soft Money Gap" June 25, 2004, press release, www.opensecrets.org.

71. Richard Tedesco, "Issue Ads to Boost Political Spending," *Broadcasting & Cable*, Vol. 128, September 7, 1998, pp. 11–14.

72. Glenn R. Simpson, "Democrats to Swivel Spotlight to 'Mush' Money Issue," *Wall Street Journal*, September 19, 1997, p. A16.

73. Mary Beth Regan, Stan Crock, and Paul Magnusson, "Campaign Finance: A Deepening Cesspool of Politics and Cash," *BusinessWeek*, July 22, 1996, p. 96.

74. See www.citizen.org.

75. Jack Brady, "Stumping for Ad Dollars; Newspapers Push for More Political Advertising Revenue," Newspaper Association of America, Inc., July–August 2004, Special Report, p. 28.

76. Greg Hitt, "'527 Groups' Use Tax Loopholes to Promote Politicians," *Wall Street Journal*, May 25, 2000, p. A28.

77. John M. Broder, "Clinton's Drug Plan Attacked by Industry," *New York Times*, June 27, 2000, p. A22.

78. For a description of these various types of advocacy groups see www.opensecrets.org/527s/types.asp.

79. Robin Toner, "The 2002 Campaign; The Drug industry; Democrats See a Stealthy Drive by Drug Industry to Help Republicans," *New York Times*, October 20, 2002, p. 20. Also involved in the ad campaign was the 60 Plus Association. Both were called "front organizations" by Merrill Goozner, a New York University professor of business journalism who is writing a book about the pharmaceutical industry. At least two groups were bankrolling

opposing campaigns: the senior citizens' lobby AARP's $4 million issue ads and the AFL-CIO's $1.5 million campaign. Greg Hitt, "Drug Makers Pour Ad Money Into Final Days of Campaign," *Wall Street Journal*, November 4, 2002, pp. A1, A4.

80. Glen Justice, "Concerns Grow About Role in Interest Groups in Elections," *New York Times*, March 9, 2005, p. A20.

81. Greg Hitt, "Political Groups Swarm to Campaign-Finance Loophole," *Wall Street Journal*, March 20, 2000, p. A36.

82. Hitt, "'527 Groups' Use Tax Loopholes … ," op. cit.

83. Dwyer, op. cit., p. 154.

84. Ibid.

85. These organizations were identified in the Annenberg Center's examination of television ad spending after Super Tuesday (from March 8–November 7, 2000). See Annenberg press release.

86. A review by the *Wall Street Journal* indicates that Democrats and moderate Republicans are receiving support from newly approved tax-exempt organizations. Among the new groups approved by the IRS in 1997 are the American Civil Rights Coalition, the Foundation for Responsible Government, Americans for Clean Energy, the American Small Business Alliance, and Americans for Job Security. The last is a trade association backed mainly by the insurance industry; its founder is Robert Vagley, president of the American Insurance Association. Cummings, op. cit. These groups and individuals were sometimes helped by Triad Management Services, a private consulting firm that helps conservative Republicans funnel money to tax-exempt groups and advises wealthy GOP clients on where to donate money. ("Triad" stands for Tactical Resources in American Democracy.) The firm used two affiliated nonprofits to take in $3 million in unpublished donations, and it helped Citizens for the Republic and another nonprofit organization spend millions of dollars in 1996 to influence congressional races.

87. Timothy Noah, "Environmentalists Take Leaf From Book of Right and Target Enemies, Allies in Issue Campaigns," *Wall Street Journal*, July 19, 1996, p. A14.

88. "Editorial: The Rise of the Non-Candidate," *Washington Post*, November 5, 2000, p. B06.

89. These organizations were identified in the Annenberg Center's examination of television ad spending after Super Tuesday (from March 8–November 7, 2000). See Annenberg press release.

90. Jeanne Cummings, "Issue-Advocacy Groups to Play Bigger Role," *Wall Street Journal*, March 6, 1998, p. A16.

91. Greg Hitt, "Drug Makers Pour Ad Money Into Final Days of Campaign," *Wall Street Journal*, November 4, 2002, p. A1.

92. Jeanne Cummings, Robert S. Greenberger and Tom Hamburger, "Supreme Court Upholds Key Parts of New Campaign-Finance Law," *Wall Street Journal*, December 11, 2003, p. A1.

93. Joshua Green, "Dumb and Dumber," *Atlantic Monthly*, Vol. 294, July–August 2004, pp. 83–86.

94. Ibid., p. 86.

95. Green, op. cit., p. 86.

96. Based on paper by William Benoit in *Advertising & Society*; ibid., pp. 84–85.

97. Based on documentation by Roderick P. Hart, a professor at the University of Texas; Green, ibid., p. 85.

98. Michael Pfau, R. Lance Holbert, Erin Alison Szabo, and Kelly Kaminski, "Issue-Advocacy Versus Candidate Advertising: Effects on Candidate Prefer-

ence and Democratic Process," *Journal of Communication*, Vol. 52, June 2002, p. 301.

99. Green, op. cit., p. 86.

100. Joseph J. Fanelli, "PAC Overview," in Clair, op. cit., p. 27.

101. "Campaign Finance: How to Fix a Rigged System," *BusinessWeek*, June 14, 2004, p. 74.

102. "2004 Election Overview: Incumbent Advantage—All Candidates," www.opensecrets.org.

103. David M. Halbfinger, "Deep Pockets: How Corzine Spent $35 Million in a Primary," *New York Times*, September 17, 2000, p. WK5.

104. David Beiler, "Jon Corzine and the Power of Money," *Campaigns & Elections*, Vol. 22, April 2001, pp. 22–36.

105. Ibid., p. 201.

106. See "2004 Election Overview: Incumbent Advantage—All Candidates," www.opensecrets.org.

107. Center for Responsive Politics.

108. Janet Hook, "Decision '98: Big Spenders Can Be Losers in Campaigns; Despite Wealth, Checchi, Harman, Issa and Others Came up Short in Political Wars," *Los Angeles Times*, June 5, 1998, p. A1.

109. Herrnson, op. cit., pp. 210–211. The first $100,000 spent adds 16.37% to the candidate's vote share; $200,000 adds 18.83%; $500,000 adds 22.09%. Spending by the opponent, however, decreases vote shares by only slightly less than the benefits cited for candidate spending.

110. Ibid., pp. 108, 206–208.

111. Jeffrey H. Birnbaum, "Lobbyists Rain Largess on Senate Incumbents," *Washington Post*, November 2, 2004, p. A05.

112. Jill Abramson, "Political Memo: 1996 Campaign Left Finance Laws in Shreds," *New York Times*, November 2, 1997, p. 1.

113. "BusinessWeek/Harris Executive Poll: Look Who Wants to Change the System," *BusinessWeek*, March 31, 1997, p. 36.

114. Robert J. Wager, "Toward an Effective PAC: What to Do and How to Do It," in Clair, op. cit., p. 160.

115. Ibid., p. 164.

116. Tom Hamburger, Laurie McGinley, and David S. Cloud, "Influence Market: Industries That Backed Bush Are Now Seeking Return on Investment," *Wall Street Journal*, March 6, 2001, p. A1.

117. Zachery Coile, "Senators Rap Ethanol Mandate; Energy Bill Provisions Called 'Corporate Welfare' for Midwest Producers," *San Francisco Chronicle*, April 12, 2002, p. A4.

118. Chris O'Brien, "How Glaxo Sells Itself to Congress," *The News and Observer*, February 23, 1997, p. A1.

119. Larry J. Sabato, "PAC-Man Goes to Washington," *Across the Board*, Vol. 21, October 1984, p. 18. Also see his *PAC Power: Inside the World of Political Action Committees* (New York: Norton, 1984). The strength of Sabato's assessment is his contention that findings associating PAC money with desired congressional votes are based on "correlational studies" that, although suggestive, are not conclusive. He cites the fallacy of the Common Cause argument that the defeat of President Carter's Hospital Cost Containment Act of 1977 illustrates the effectiveness of the American Medical Association's AMPAC. It gave $1.65 million during the 1976 and 1978 campaigns to 202 of the 234 House members who voted for a crippling amendment. But the correlation that those favoring the AMA amendment received more

than $8,100 on average compared with the $2,300 received by the 122 members who voted against the amendment is not sufficient proof the PAC payments influenced the vote. In proving that a correlation does not prove causation, Sabato examines studies based on more sophisticated statistical techniques that "hold steady" such variables as the party, ideology, and past voting record of a congressman. He gives the historical example of the 1975 congressional vote for milk price supports, which, he argues, was only slightly influenced by 1974 dairy PAC contributions. More relevant was how important dairy production was in each legislator's home district as well as his or her ideology and party affiliation. Ibid., p. 22.

120. Ibid., p. 23.
121. Ibid., p. 25.
122. Jeanne Cummings, "Closing the Spigot: In New Law's Wake, Companies Slash Their Political Donations," op. cit., p. A4.
123. Jonathan Weisman, "Adopting Union Tactics, Firms Dive More Deeply Into Politics; Employees Targeted With Voter Guides, Turnout Efforts," *Washington Post*, October 24, 2002, p. A8.
124. Raymond L. Hoewing, "The State of Public Affairs: A Profession Reinventing Itself," in Dennis, op. cit., p. 37.
125. Jeanne Cummings, "Political Contributors Step Up to the Plate," *Wall Street Journal*, July 29, 2004, p. A4.
126. Peter B. Kennerdell, *Managing the Business–Employee PAC* (Washington, D.C.: Public Affairs Council, 1992), pp. 8–9.
127. Kennerdell, op. cit., p. 14.
128. A. John Adams, "Communications and Political Action Committees," in Clair, op. cit., p. 178.
129. Baker, op. cit., p. 279.
130. "Case Study: Corning's PAC Publishes Newsletter; Potent but Possibly Divisive Public Affairs Tool," *pr reporter*, Vol. 21, June 26, 1978, p. 3.
131. Owen Ullmann, "Unions: Laboring Mightily to Avert a Nightmare in November," *BusinessWeek*, October 19, 1998, p. 53.
132. Glenn Burkins, "AFL-CIO to Raise at Least $26 Million to Support Democrats, GOP Moderates," *Wall Street Journal*, February 18, 1999, p. A24.
133. Ibid.
134. Jeanne Cummings, "Closing the Spigot: In New Law's Wake, Companies Slash Their Political Donations,"op. cit., p. A1.
135. Murray, op. cit. Also see Cummings, ibid.
136. Raymond A. Hay in preface to *The Candidates (Reagan vs. Mondale) Where They Stand* (Dallas: The LTV Corp., 1985). The booklet was provided by H. J. (Jerry) Dalton, Jr., manager of corporate communications.
137. Phyllis S. McGrath, *Action Plans for Public Affairs* (New York: The Conference Board, 1977), p. 43. The outcome of the new approach was not reported.
138. Philip Lesly, "Why Economic Education Is Failing," *Management Review*, Vol. 65, October 1976, pp. 17–23.
139. Myron Emanuel, Curtis L. Snodgrass, Joyce Gildea, and Karn Rosenberg, *Corporate Economic Education Programs: An Evaluation and Appraisal* (Financial Executives Research Foundation, 1979), p. 303. This is the most complete source of information on economic education programs used in the 1970s.
140. Lee Ann Elliott, "The Do's and Don'ts of Corporate Political Activity," in Kennerdell, op. cit.

141. Jean F. Grogan, "Using Partisan Communications to Aid a Candidate," in Kennerdell, op. cit., p. 165.
142. Ibid., p. 166.
143. Amy Borrus, "On the Stump, Online," *BusinessWeek*, April 12, 1999, p. 123.
144. Ibid.
145. Ryan Lizza, "Campaign Journal: Dean.com," *The New Republic*, June 2, 2003, pp. 10–12.
146. "Web Logs: Golden Blogs," *Economist*, August 16, 2003, p. 55.
147. Catherine Seipp, "Online Uprising," *American Journalism Review*, Vol. 24, June 2002, pp. 42–47.
148. Richard S. Dunham, "Commentary: Why the Dean Bubble Popped," *BusinessWeek*, February 16, 2004, p. 38.
149. Stephen Baker, "Click the Vote," *BusinessWeek*, March 29, 2004, p. 104.
150. David Bank, "Billionaires Back Online Activists' Anti-Bush Ads," *Wall Street Journal*, November 11, 2003, p. A3. Also see Jeanne Cummings and Julia Angwin, "Donors Look for the Loopholes to Campaign-Finance Limits," *Wall Street Journal*, December 12, 2003, p. A5. Also see Jeanne Cummings, "A Hard Sell on Soft Money," *Wall Street Journal*, December 2, 2003, p. A4.
151. Leslie Wayne, "Enron's Many Strands: The Politics; Enron, Preaching Deregulation, Worked the State House Circuit," *New York Times*, February 9, 2002, p. C-1.
152. Kevin McCoy, "Enron's Contributions Trail Reads Like a U.S. Road Map," *USA Today*, January 28, 2002, p. B1.
153. Wayne, op. cit.
154. McCoy, op. cit., p. 42.
155. Carla Marinucci, "Group Tallies Enron's Contributions, Lobbying," *San Francisco Chronicle*, January 30, 2002, p. A10.
156. Tom Hamburger et al., op. cit., p. A1.
157. Joe Stephens, "Hard Money, Strong Arms and 'Matrix'; How Enron Dealt With Congress, Bureaucracy," *Washington Post*, February 10, 2002, p. A1.
158. Albert R. Hunt, "Enron's One Good Return: Political Investments," *Wall Street Journal*, January 31, 2002, p. A19.
159. Michael Schroeder and Greg Hitt, "Accounting Industry Is Taken to Task," *Wall Street Journal*, March 8, 2002, p. A12.
160. "Arthur Andersen: The Enron Scandal's Other Big Donor," The Center for Responsive Politics; Greg Hitt, "Andersen Lobbyists Work to Ease Pressure of Probes, *Wall Street Journal*, January 17, 2002, p. A16.
161. "Lexington: Beware the K-Street Conservatives," *The Economist*, December 7, 2002, p. 36.
162. Arthur Levitt, "Arthur Levitt's Crusade," *BusinessWeek*, September 30, 2002, pp. 74–80.

Chapter 12

Litigation Communication

Since the 1960s and 1970s, American society has continuously become more litigious. Those were the decades when consumer and environmental movements gained momentum and government responded with an avalanche of regulations. Books and films such as *A Civil Action*, *Erin Brockovich*, and *The Rainmaker* have popularized the role of lawyers in society and reinforced the culture of a litigious society. Litigation became one of the favorite tactics used against corporations by consumer, environmental, and other public interest groups. For example, seven environmental and public health groups filed a lawsuit in the D.C. Circuit Court of Appeals to block industry-backed rules from the U.S. EPA that would weaken pollution monitoring standards and lead to increased emissions of mercury.[1] One of the groups, the Natural Resources Defense Council, has become known as one of the most effective litigating groups on U.S. environmental issues. Almost a quarter of the staff are lawyers.[2]

In the context of issues management, litigation communication is the fourth stage in the life cycle of an issue.[3] After laws are passed, relevant government agencies promulgate and enforce regulations. Laws are seldom, if ever, sufficiently complete and clear on such matters as enforcement standards and timetables for meeting legal requirements. If a business disagrees with a government regulation, it may file a challenging lawsuit. More likely, government, a public interest group, or an aggrieved party will sue when its interpretation of a law or regulation suggests lack of compliance. Business has seen the need, therefore, to extend its activities beyond legislation and into the judicial branch of government in the form of litigation communication.

JUDGESHIPS ARE OFTEN ELECTIVE OFFICES

The judicial system is no longer an isolated part of the government, immune to political pressures. In some jurisdictions, judges are no different from other elective officials. Fortunately, most judges keep themselves reasonably aloof from politics. Nonetheless, as members of society, they, too, are influenced by the news media and other activities that affect public opinion. The power of the judicial system is too immense to escape attention by corporate communication strategists.

In 38 states judges are elected, not appointed, so it is not surprising that the judicial candidates act like other political candidates. They "run attack ads, fill out questionnaires detailing their beliefs, and hit up big donors on the phone"—activities that were once considered beneath the dignity of the office.[4] The danger is that the image of an impartial judicial system is destroyed, as the core ideals of the American judiciary— "that judges are fair, objective, principled, and nonpartisan"—are compromised.[5] Lawyers and other special interests with a stake in court decisions attend fundraisers and contribute in other ways. When Pennzoil sued Texaco, Pennzoil gave $10,000 to the judge assigned to hear the case. Texaco struck back by making $72,700 in campaign contributions to five Texas Supreme Court judges expected to make a final ruling in the case. However, Texaco was outbid when Pennzoil ultimately contributed more than $315,000 to Texas Supreme Court justices, including donations to three justices who weren't running. The integrity of the court system is obviously in question when, in states such as Texas, California, and Ohio, where tort reform was an issue, some judicial candidates were known as the defense or plaintiff's candidate. Trial lawyers and defense attorneys who made contributions did so in the belief that the side with the most judges wins.[6]

Almost half (48%) of 894 elected judges surveyed in 2001 and 2002 by the Justice at Stake Campaign, a nonpartisan watchdog group in Washington, DC, said they felt a "great deal" of pressure to raise money during election years. When asked how much influence these contributions had on their decisions, 4% said "a great deal of influence," 22% said "some influence," and 20% said "just a little influence." The right answer is supposed to be "no influence at all," the response given by only 36%.[7] The Brennan Center for Justice, a judicial watchdog group based at the New York University School of Law, reports that candidates for the highest courts in 20 states raised $45.6 million in 2000, a 61% increase from 2 years earlier. The trend is expected to continue.[8]

Even when the judiciary is independent, parties to a lawsuit, recognizing the power of the courts, apply some of the same lobbying techniques to the judicial branch that are used with the legislative and executive branches of government. For example, an item in a 1995 *Columbia Jour-*

nalism Review article revealed that, over the previous 12 years, seven Supreme Court Justices had enjoyed first-class, all-expense-paid winter trips to luxury resorts where they gathered to select the winner of a $15,000 prize awarded annually by West Publishing for "Distinguished Service to Justice." Cases involving the company were heard by the justices during those years; all of the cases were decided in favor of West.[9]

Other approaches are also used to influence the judicial system. Koch Industries, an oil, natural gas, minerals and agribusiness giant, is the largest contributor, among approximately 90 other major corporations, law firms, and foundations, to a University of Kansas foundation that offers small groups of hand-picked state judges a two-part "Economics Institutes for State Judges" seminar, usually at resort hotels. They are taught hard-nosed, market-based economics. For example, one course talks about "the costs of overdeterrence" by judges who punish companies for harming people or the environment. The institute's syllabus for this session states, "Many potentially hazardous activities offer great benefits to society." At another session, judges were told that they "let too much 'junk sciences' into cases involving damage claims against companies and that the rules of the federal Environmental Protection Agency and the Labor Department's Occupational Safety and Health Administration are enormously expensive and often ineffective." Since 1995, 550 judges have attended these seminars. Koch has also launched a rating system for judges that "grades them on how their decisions affect the business community."[10]

POWER OF THE JUDICIAL BRANCH OF GOVERNMENT

The enormous power of the judicial branch of government is increasingly recognized. A book review of Kenneth W. Starr's *First Among Equals: The Supreme Court in American Life*, reflects this fact. Starr's view is, "The judiciary is not merely first among three equal branches of government. There's nothing equal about it: The Supreme Court reigns supreme."[11] A major reason why issues management extends to a fourth stage is that the courts have not restricted themselves to their traditional role of ruling on legislative matters; too often the courts appear intent on usurping the rights of the legislative branch of government. In recent Supreme Court cases, justices have repeatedly reversed judges "who had read new rights into the Constitution or expanded their own authority to resolve disputes."[12]

As a sign of business concern about the power of the Supreme Court, business is now focusing on replacements for the three soon-to-retire Supreme Court justices: Justice John Paul Stevens, Chief Justice William H. Rehnquist, and Justice Sandra Day O'Connor. More than ideological conservatism is sought because, as Robin S. Conrad, senior vice-president of the U.S. Chamber of Commerce's National Litigation Center, observed, "Being a conservative is not the same as being pro-business." For example, conservative justices Antonin Scalia and Clarence Thomas have consistently voted against efforts to restrain punitive damages, a top business priority. Judicial conservatives defend federalism by being generally unwilling to preempt state laws that place higher standards on companies than overlapping federal statutes.[13]

GROWTH OF LITIGATION PUBLIC RELATIONS

Lawsuits concern corporations because they have a dual impact: on reputation and the bottom line. When plaintiffs—government, other businesses, individuals, and public interest groups—file a lawsuit, corporations face the prospect that the case will receive widespread publicity. In fact, public interest groups file lawsuits as a way to raise public consciousness about an issue and to demonstrate the interest group's activity and effectiveness. In this process, however, corporate reputations may be tarnished. "Media coverage of a court battle can damage a company's reputation, destroy a product market, and shake up the confidence and morale of shareholders, managers, and other employees," wrote Christopher P. A. Komisarjevsky in 1983, then a senior vice president of the public relations firm Hill & Knowlton and recently the president and CEO of Burson-Marsteller Worldwide.[14]

As for their bottom lines, the tobacco companies have been most affected by litigation. A recent verdict against Philip Morris USA, the largest tobacco company, was for $10.1 billion. Plaintiffs accused the company of deceiving smokers that "low tar," "light," "ultralight," and "mild" cigarettes were less risky than other cigarettes. Altria, the parent company, faced a court order to post a $12 billion bond to appeal the Illinois verdict, and the cigarette division faced the possibility of being forced to file for bankruptcy-court protection.[15]

Companies that previously shunned the political arena have sometimes scrambled to catch up after facing judicial problems. When Judge Thomas Penfield Jackson ruled on April 3, 2000, that Microsoft was stifling innovation and on April 30 proposed a breakup of the company into two entities, Microsoft's chief lobbyist, Jack Krumholtz, launched a vigorous campaign with the aim to "convince official Washington that Justice's attempt to split the company up is misguided." Audiences included members of Congress, federal judges, and a future president.[16] Microsoft used its "apparently bottomless store of money" to convert it into virtually all the political resources available to a corporation (see Box 1.1).

This expensive, high-powered campaign, intended to influence the court system, possibly including the Supreme Court, did not go unchallenged. Microsoft's enormous presence in the capital, according to Ed Black, president of the Computer Communication Industry Association, amounted to intimidation: "It is an outrageously blatant attempt to try to nullify a judicial and law enforcement proceeding by leveraging their political muscle and money."[17] Another voice against "the unseemly campaign of Mr. Microsoft" was Mike France, who covered the Microsoft trial from New York. While acknowledging that Microsoft has the "constitutional right to make political contributions, fill the airwaves with ads, and lobbying Congress," he found something "quite disturbing about watching the world's richest man trying to buy his way out of trouble with Uncle Sam." He adds, "One of the most deepseated principles in American jurisprudence is that nobody should be above the law. Another is that judicial decisions should be free from political interference."[18] However, harsh political realities require bold action. On November 2, 2001, the Justice Department and Microsoft announced that they had reached a settlement.[19] It was very much in Microsoft's favor.[20]

Total War Against Corporations

Reflecting on trends in lawsuits against their corporations, general counsels from several large companies drew the disturbing conclusion that some forces in the United States have declared a "total war" against corporate America. As described by Coleman S. Hicks, a senior vice president of Oak Industries and former partner at Covington & Burling, this is a new form of litigation, where the aim is not only to seek damages from a company but also to "destroy the company, to question its moral ethic, to question the values of its officers and its board." He and other current or former corporate general counsels from Monsant, Exxon, Philips Petroleum, Kerr-McGee, and Browning–Ferris Industries met to discuss what most called "bet-your-company litigation."[21]

One conclusion drawn by this group, as stated by Rufus Wallingford of Browing-Ferris, is that "external forces are now part of the game.... It's wishful thinking for anyone to believe we can keep this [litigation] confined to the four walls of the courthouse, and the press or community will not get involved."[22] Even within the four walls of a courtroom, the group felt, the system of litigation leaves *Fortune* 500 companies at a competitive disadvantage. "Things like successor liability, joint and several liability, unlimited punitive damages and the inability to get to a resolution in the court system hang a bull's eye around American business," said Wallingford.[23] Unlimited punitive damages are the main problem, as demonstrated by the astonishing jury award of $4.9 billion against GM in a lawsuit involving burns on three passengers, caused by a fuel tank that exploded because it was too close to the bumper. Of this amount, compensatory damages amounted to only $107 million.[24]

"You can't just rely on a strategy within the courthouse. It has to be much broader than that," said R. William Ide, III, senior vice president and general counsel at Monsanto.[25] Furthermore, when external sources are involved, "you do not have rules and it's a free-for-all loaded with misinformation," added Charles W. Matthews, Jr. of Exxon.[26] Apparently agreeing with corporate general counsels, Acting Justice Harold J. Rothwax of the New York State Supreme Court commented, "Lawyers now feel it is the essence of their function to try their case in the public media.... It's no longer courtroom based ... it's a whole new ethic that has to be looked at carefully."[27] Ways must be found to deal with publicity surrounding a case.

Corporate Scandals Increase Vulnerability

The Enron and ensuing scandals of 2002 have made matters worse. A first-of-its-kind survey of potential jurors released in October 2002 by DecisionQuest, a Los Angeles trial consultancy, showed that 75% or more distrust corporations on a variety of counts; the historical level was 50%. The survey consisted of telephone interviews of 1,000 people eligible for jury service. Large majorities of those surveyed cited greedy executives, crooked accountants, and shredded documents. They were also critical of corporations in other areas; for example, 85% answered that they believe companies hide dangers associated with their products and their waste until the government or a lawsuit forces them to tell the truth. Attitudes toward managers and executives were particularly critical, with 71% of the respondents believing that those at the top are more likely to lie than lower level employees or expert witnesses. Placing top officials on the stand could thus prove risky. Moreover, says Stephen L. Hill, Jr., who delivered the news in a speech to a group of financial officers, pat, legalistic-sounding defenses that lack explanations for a company's actions just aren't going to cut it anymore. The survey supposedly sent shivers through boardrooms and executive offices.[28]

Antibusiness biases are also likely to affect jurors, according to defense lawyers who asked 50 prospective jurors about their reaction to this statement: "Corporate executives will lie to increase their profits." More than half agreed. When asked about the statement, "A representative of a company will say whatever it takes to keep the company out of trouble," 72% agreed, with 22% of these agreeing "strongly."

When companies are silent or evasive in the face of litigation, the public is inclined to find them guilty, according to a Hill & Knowlton/Opinion Research survey about public attitudes of corporate defendants. Unfortunately, this finding is likely to be reinforced because corporations are still mainly guided by a bunker mentality. Harlan Loeb, U.S. director of Hill & Knowlton's litigation services practice, advises that the "same savvy thinking and strategic fiber that sets apart a company in a spirited marketplace must be cut and pasted to the litigation communications domain."[29]

Thus the need for litigation public relations services is recognized. "Companies need an action plan that provides an organizational mandate to anticipate and control the public dimensions of litigation, "says Loeb. The corporate brand must be protected by devising an integrated strategy to preempt audience attitudes before a complaint is in the field. The opportunity aspect of litigation should also be recognized. When the spotlight is on the company, brand building is possible (e.g., by reaching out to tuned-in customers and other audiences).[30] Komisarjevsky advises the public relations staff and legal staff of companies to develop a close-working, mutually respectful, and trusting relationship.[31]

Litigation Public Relations Gains Recognition[32]

Within the last decade, the importance of litigation public relations has been recognized by books and articles on the subject and the addition of this service in law and public relations firms. An early book (1995) is Susanne A. Roschwalb and Richard A. Stack's *Litigation Public Relations: Courting Public Opinion*; a later one (2003) is James F. Haggerty's *In the Court of Public Opinion: Winning Your Case With Public Relations*. A typical law journal article is Deborah A. Lillanthal's "Litigation Public Relations: The Provisional Remedy of the Communications World."[33] One of the main points made by this literature is exemplified by Haggerty's statement, "Communication is now central to the management of modern litigation. It can mean communicating to external audiences such as the media, or to internal audiences like employees, investors, shareholders, and others with a vested interest in the organization."[34] Confirming the acceptance of litigation public relations, a recent survey of the top 200 corporate law departments in the United States found that nearly 50% regularly use public relations techniques in litigation and 23% said they do so "often" or "always."[35]

Companies fighting costly legal battles now recognize the need to sway public opinion as well as the courts, and accordingly, they turn to public relations. "Whether it's cameras in the courtroom or reporters on the courthouse steps, a media strategy to protect, enhance and bolster your litigation strategy is almost always a necessity," says Sheila Tate, president of Powell Tate.[36]

Martha Stewart, the high-profile celebrity and founder of Martha Stewart Living Omnimedia, accused of lying about an insider trading deal of Imclone stock, illustrates the complexity of litigation public relations. In the pretrial period, her defense team chose media appearances wisely and well, according to Judy Leon of DecisionQuest. She appeared on both the Barbara Walters and Larry King shows, which were "safe media 'venues' in which Stewart could remind the public that she is, after all, a human being, not a punch line, a person who has suffered intense public humiliation and immense financial loss months before the first day of her trial, and an American citizen facing a fundamental threat to her personal liberty."[37] Her courtroom performance apparently lacked public relations sensitivity. She and her defense team decided not to have Martha Stewart testify on her own behalf, which ran counter to jury and public expectations formed by TV law-and-order shows. Parading an array of celebrities through the courtroom to show support for Stewart was a bad idea, according to Alan M. Dershowitz, a well-known and outspoken professor of law at Harvard: "It made almost no impression. If anything, we may have taken it as a little bit of an insult."[38] Stewart lost the case.

Another person who turned to public relations is Richard M. Scrushy, who was ousted in March 2003 as HealthSouth's chairman and CEO after being charged for his alleged role in a $2.7 billion accounting fraud at the company. When relations between federal prosecutors and Scrushy's lawyers boiled over, the latter held a news conference on the courthouse steps alleging that prosecutors concealed evidence that proved Scrushy's innocence. Furthermore, one of Scrushy's attorneys appeared on a local radio shows on which he accused the government of witness tampering and manufacturing evidence.[39] The attorneys as well as Scrushy and his wife also appeared on their own television show. Scrushy and federal prosecutors agreed to a court order restricting public comments about his upcoming fraud trial, scheduled for September 2004.[40] Known to curry favor with the local community, Scrushy was recasting his persona from someone known for partying in Hollywood with his girl band 3rd Faze to that of a "humble man from the south whose faith will help him weather the current storm."[41]

Recognizing the role played by public opinion, the general counsels from the large corporations realized that they needed to involve their communications or public affairs people. William G. Paul, former general counsel of Phillips Petroleum, referred to the company's "really fine communications team ... who are skilled at dealing with the press— much more skilled than I or any of the lawyers internally and much more skilled than outside counsel." He added, "Those people work closely with lawyers. They know the case; they know the issues; they don't talk to the press until they are fully informed."[42]

Exxon also relies on specialists in the public affairs group to handle the news media. Charles W. Matthews, Jr., the company's general counsel, added that on occasion the lead trial attorney might become an integral part of the process "as long as the outside counsel understands the business, the problems, the needs, whatever concerns we have." Wallingford cautioned that trial lawyers "tend to pop off too much and they're not trained."[43] Referring to a south Texas situation, he said he prefers to let a community affairs specialist develop strategy and serve as company spokesperson in dealing with external matters.

What these corporate general counsels alluded to was the emergence of litigation public relations: the attempt to control the publicity surrounding a lawsuit, with the intention of influencing public opinion as well as the dispositions of juries and judges. The judicial branch of government, which traditionally has been treated as off limits to parties wanting to influence it beyond the courtroom, was now to be treated as another important audience by lawyers and public affairs professionals. As stated by Mary Gottschall, a legal affairs correspondent for *The*

New York Times: "This [litigation public relations] has emerged as an increasing trend, especially where major litigation is involved. The idea is that the case might be tried in the court of public opinion as well as before a jury."[44]

Growth as a Professional Service.

Many public relations and legal firms are now offering litigation public relations services, often in the context of crisis management.[45] Among the major players are public relations giants Burson-Marsteller and Hill & Knowlton, as well as others, such as Ketchum, the seventh largest global public relations firm. Based in Washington, DC, Ketchum's Litigation Communications practice confirmed the importance of litigation public relations by hiring a leading figure in the field in 2003, Rose Marshall. She had run her own firm, Legal PR, for 10 years and represented such clients as Monsanto, the American Trucking Association, and the Product Liability Advisory Council. Another prominent player in the field is The Lukaszewski Group, whose flyer, describing members as "management advisors in litigation communications," states, "When critical legal, regulatory, and ethical situations arise that threaten organizational reputation and credibility.... It's not a game!" Its principal, James E. Lukaszewski, favors active public relations participation in litigation matters on the premise that news media treatment of a case may affect legal judgments and undoubtedly affects corporate reputation, both in the short and in the long term.[46]

Public relations and other communications counselors have been hampered in giving advice to clients because they don't enjoy the same attorney–client privilege protection as lawyers. Richard E. Nicolazzo, president of Nicolazzo & Associates, has strongly stated that communications counsel must be accorded the same protection. He states that clients must "be ably represented in the court of public opinion *and* the court of law."[47] For example, in a case involving secret grand jury testimony about possible crimes committed by a well-known businessperson, identified in the lawsuit only as Target, prosecutors subpoenaed a public relations consultant hired by the client's attorney. When the consultant refused to appear or to supply records, the prosecutors moved to compel compliance. The judge in the case, Lewis A. Kaplan, sided with the consultant, saying,

> This court is persuaded that the ability of lawyers to perform some of their most fundamental client functions ... would be undermined seriously if lawyers were not able to engage in frank discussion of facts and strategies with the lawyers' public relations consultants. For example, lawyers may need skilled advice as to whether and how possible statements to the press—ranging from "no comment" to detailed factual presentations—would likely be reported in order to advise a client as to whether the making of particular statements would be in the client's legal interest.

Describing litigation public relations activities, Carole Gorney, a professor of public relations at Lehigh University, says, "In today's litigious society, generating publicity favorable to plaintiffs has become a well-planned, often-used legal strategy."[48] It has become common for plaintiffs, and sometimes their attorney, Gorney reports, to appear on televised talk shows or give interviews for highly personalized articles in newspapers and magazines with the purpose of shifting public opinion in their favor.

Among the lessons learned from litigation communication is that the news media typically consider an accusation by a plaintiff more newsworthy than a company's denial. A DuPont ad put it more bluntly: The media take "the perspective of a plaintiff's lawyer."[49] Often without any courtroom evidence, the media take up the plaintiff's cause, granting hours of unchallenged coverage. Meanwhile the company under attack is often restricted, from legal and public relations standpoints, in its own response. Not only might a corporate attorney advise the dubious "no comment" reply for his client; a judge might even curb the firm's public defense, forbidding the use of image advertising and publicity as "undue influence on the jury."

Another lesson is that caution must be exercised in attempting to improve a company's image prior to a trial. Image ads used by Northrop were ill advised and raised objections from the trial's judge (see Box 12.1).

Box 12.1 Image Ads by Northrop

Federal judge Pamela Rymer objected to Northrop's use of image ads a week before jury selection in the government's suit against the company. She ordered the ads to be pulled from local airwaves in Los Angeles, the site of the trial. One of the ads described the way people at Northrop think: "We try to get things to be as good as possible. This can take years and years ... so that we can get it just right before it goes into the aircraft." The spot appeared during such heavily watched programs as *Good Morning America*, *The Cosby Show*, the evening and late-night news, and Los Angeles Lakers basketball games.[50]

Because Northrop was indicted for allegedly falsifying tests on parts for the Harrier jet and the air-launched cruise missile, the judge thought this ad might prejudice jurists against the government's case, even without their realizing it. Judge Rymer's ruling for prior restraint exemplifies the "classic struggle between the First Amendment's protection of free speech and the court's interest in ensuring the integrity of the judicial process," according to an article in the *Wall Street Journal*.[51]

PRODUCT LIABILITY

The courts have increasingly become outlets for individuals who feel they have been victimized. Suits dealing with defective products, racial or sexual discrimination, sexual harassment, environmental pollution, and other matters have become commonplace. Of these, product liability cases have loomed largest in both number and cost.

Growth in Product Liability Cases

The Rand Corporation's Institute for Civil Justice reported that 17,000 U.S. companies were lead defendants in product liability lawsuits between 1974 and 1986.[52] Between 1974 and 1990, product liability case filings in U.S. federal courts increased by over 1,100%.[53] More recent records show that between 1985 and 1991, 107,000 personal injury suits, 48,000 asbestos liability suits, and almost 3,000 other product liability suits were filed in the United States. In 1991 alone, 1,500 product liability suits were brought in federal district courts against *Fortune* 1000 companies, 95% of which were personal injury cases.[54] The cost of liability suits, says business, displaces funding for research and development, increases insurance costs, and ultimately raises the price of consumer products and services.[55] The costs of some notable lawsuits are shown in Box 12.2.

Ominously, more class-action lawsuits are forecast. An insurance publication writes, "the next wave of mass tort cases threatens to engulf the nation's businesses and, in turn, their insurance carriers."[56] The number of plaintiffs will grow and the legal issues will be complex and wide in scope. Besides manufacturers and sellers, those affected will be building owners, landlords, contractors, and public housing authorities. Other battles include construction products defects, intellectual

---

Box 12.2 Notable Lawsuits

Lawsuits brought against some of the biggest U.S. corporations have resulted in billion-dollar judgments against them. Manville Corporation (formerly Johns-Manville) faced product liability suits stemming from asbestos-related deaths and illnesses estimated to cost over $2.5 billion; A. H. Robins, maker of the Dalkon Shield, was ordered to set aside $2.48 billion to pay claimants; Exxon was ordered to pay $5 billion to 34,000 fishermen and other Alaskans who said they were harmed by the Exxon *Valdez* oil spill; and Dow Corning and other silicone breast implant makers proposed a $4.75 billion settlement to handle the claims of thousands of lawsuits. A feature of these lawsuits is that they started with individual claims but ended up as class actions, which some companies agree are the most efficient way to deal with the thousands of suits.

property rights, and tobacco. In what could amount to "Asbestos II," building owners of about 14 million housing units face claims for injury or damage caused not only by asbestos and lead but also by chemicals in office furnishings and harmful vapors and gases in ventilation and air-conditioning systems.[57]

Cost of Litigation

Lawsuits cost Americans $80 billion a year plus another $300 billion in indirect costs, declares Peter Huber, an academician whose research is used by some to buttress a claim that the U.S. legal system is making the nation less competitive.[58] Other estimates are as low as $29 billion to $36 billion and as high as $117 billion.[59] A more recent study by Tillinghast-Towers Perrin says that the overall tort system cost the country $205 billion in 2001.[60]

Litigation costs to the nation, which already account for 2.3% of the gross domestic product (up from 1.76% in 1984, 1.5% in 1970, and 0.6% in 1950), will mount.[61] Furthermore, in studying the relationship between the prevalence of lawyers and economic growth in 28 countries, a University of Texas economist, Stephen Magee, found that having more lawyers is associated with less growth. Lawyers are engaged in "transfer seeking," says one theory; that is, getting richer by acquiring someone else's wealth rather than producing more wealth themselves. The number of lawyers over the past three decades has tripled, from 260,000 in 1960 to about 760,000 in 1992.[62]

U.S. businesses incur the highest liability costs in the world, said former vice president Dan Quayle when he announced the findings of the President's Council on Competitiveness; they are 15 times higher than Japan's and 20 times higher than Europe's.[63] In a speech about tort reform, William S. Stavroupoulos, CEO of Dow Chemical, said that in the United States Dow spends a dollar on litigation expenses for roughly every $100,000 in sales, whereas in Europe it spends a dollar for every $40 million in sales.[64]

The "I'll sue" culture is spreading to Europe. Cases in Britain's county courts have risen by almost two thirds in the past 10 years and totaled almost 114,000 in 1996. Several large class-action product liability suits have been moving through the courts, including one against two British tobacco companies.[65] Lawsuits by the middle class are facilitated by a "no-win, no-fee" system, a conditional fee system whereby the lawyer's cut, should he or she win, is limited to double the basic fee and to 25% of the award for the total bill.[66]

Class Action Suits Feed Lawyer Frenzy.   Lawyers motivated by self-gain are promoting class-action suits; this is one reason for the high cost of product liability cases. Newspaper headlines, such as the *Wall Street Journal's* "Widening Horizons: Lawyers Lead Hunt for New

Groups of Asbestos Victims," reveal the new aggressiveness of law-yers.[67] The Internet has made it easier for lawyers to broaden the base of class-action suits, largely because it allows lawyers to establish a web-site and recruit additional litigants. Furthermore, the Internet makes much more information and many more documents available, enabling lawyers to press claims. It allows people to look for manufacturers' vul-nerabilities instead of reactively waiting for something to happen.[68]

A *BusinessWeek* article, "The Litigation Machine," outlines how the Internet is giving plaintiffs' lawyers a field day.[69] It outlines five steps:

1. Find a victim. Don't wait for customers to come to you. Advertise on television or use a national referral network, such as USinjurylawyer.com. (See Box 12.3 for how one lawyer runs his law business.)
2. Get a litigation packet. Generally costing less that $200, these packets provide how-to guides for suits against a variety of indus-tries: the Firestone tire tread separation, Lambert diabetes drug Rezulin, and others such as handgun maker and tobacco compa-nies.
3. Find an expert. They can be found on websites such as DepoConnect.com, at attorneys' conventions where professional experts rent booths, or in advertisements in legal trade journals. Chicago's Defense Research Institute, which is also used by corpo-rate attorneys, offers an online library containing files on 50,000 expert witnesses.
4. Get money. Although cash advances—often required because courts move slowly—come at a high price, they are available from litigation-finance specialists such as Expert Funding.com in ex-change for a stake in litigation. In a 12-month period it made about 500 advances, ranging in size from a few thousand dollars to more than $500,000.
5. Obtain hot documents. To get the internal corporate documents they need to win over a judge and jury, plaintiff lawyers can access the Attorneys Information Exchange Group (AIEG) in Birming-ham, Alabama) and ATLA Exchange, which serve as warehouses of information. In 2001, the AIEG, a nonprofit group, which is an arm of the American Trial Lawyers Association, served 600 mem-bers who paid a $1,000 initiation fee, plus annual dues of $500. The AIEG had accumulated 400,000 pages of materials on the Ford–Firestone suits.

Ever since the June 1977 U.S. Supreme Court decision permitting lawyers to advertise, some lawyers have used their free-speech rights to pitch their services in newspapers, on television and radio, and by direct mail and other means.[70] In 1982 an ad with the headline "Did you use this IUD?" ran in Ohio newspapers. It was sponsored by Philip Q. Zauderer and other lawyers who were offering to represent women troubled by A. H. Robins's Dalkon Shield. Thus, as Chief Justice Warren E. Burger derisively commented, lawyers sell their services "in much the way that automobiles, dog food, cosmetics, and hair tonic are touted."[71] Reflecting on the trend, George Beall, chairman of an American Bar Association committee on professional responsibility, concluded, "Lawyers are hucksters today."[72] In hearing the Zauderer case in 1985, Associate Justice Sandra Day O'Connor opined that stricter limits on lawyer ads should be upheld, saying that lawyers should live up to "standards beyond those prevailing in the marketplace."[73] How one lawyer uses ads and publicity to run his law business is described in Box 12.3.

The courts appear to be rethinking the whole idea of allowing big class-action injury cases to go forward. A sign of this changed attitude is the U.S. Supreme Court's rejection of a supposedly model asbestos deal in the Amchem case, saying it ran roughshod over the rights of thousands of alleged victims.[74]

Box 12.3 How One Lawyer Runs His Law Business

Lawyer self-gain is evident in the standard contingency fee arrangement, whereby a lawyer typically gets at least one third of an award. The impact of this kind of incentive is revealed by a seasoned plaintiffs' lawyer, Paul Rheingold, in one of the diet pill lawsuits; he admitted, "This just reflects the fact that we are in a business and this is just another opportunity that comes along."[75] To help the opportunity come along, Rheingold scans medical journals for bad news. As observed by Richard B. Schmitt, "Over the years, Mr. Rheingold has shown a nose for emerging disasters, combining intellectual curiosity with the hustle of a carnival barker."[76]

Rheingold uses advertising and networking to attract clients. He ran ads in *TV Guide, Newsday,* and *USA Today* (paying $24,000 for a quarter-page ad in that newspaper) and appeared on a cable television segment hosted by O. J. Simpson lawyer Johnnie Cochran; his son tends his law firm's website, which features a diet pill litigation pitch. He also activated a network of trial bar colleagues to share documents and refer potential plaintiffs to one another. At a convention of the Association of Trial Lawyers of America, he printed signs calling for a meeting on the diet pill situation, which resulted in the formation of The Fen-Phen Litigation Group. Through the publicity that ensues when he wins a case, and by writing scholarly legal articles, Rheingold adds to his list of plaintiffs.

Rheingold, who prefers to handle each case separately, faces competition from large class-action law firms who have joined the feeding frenzy. By October 1997, more than 20 diet pill suits had been filed by class-action law firms. They hope that by playing a lead role they will win a seat on a future court-appointed legal steering committee, whose members are handsomely rewarded at settlement time.[77]

Tort Reform

Incensed by the number and cost, as well as the outrageousness, of some product liability lawsuits, business has lobbied for a national tort reform law that would limit liability and preempt state product liability laws. Business formed a Product Liability Coordinating Committee (PLCC) with a membership of 700,000 small and large companies and organizations to support a reform movement. PLCC advocated the following:

> Raise the standard of evidence used for punitive damage awards to "clear and convincing"; confine punitive damages to cases where the manufacturers showed "conscious, flagrant indifference" to public safety; have each defendant in a multiple suit pay noneconomic damages (e.g., pain and suffering) only in proportion to his or her responsibility; do not award punitive damages if the manufacturer gained premarketing approval from the FDA or FAA in good faith; waive litigation for injuries involving capital goods more than 25 years old; reduce damage awards when product misuse or alteration causes the injury; and exempt manufacturers from paying damages for injuries resulting from a person's intoxication or use of illegal drugs.[78]

Over the past few years, tort reform efforts have been stepped up. Tens of millions of dollars have poured into efforts by the Institute for Legal Reform, an arm of the U.S. Chamber of Commerce, launched in 1997. In 2003 it planned to raise upward of $40 million from a broad list of companies and trade groups, including Aetna, the American Council of Life Insurers, the Business Roundtable, Ford, General Electric, Johnson & Johnson, the National Association of Manufacturers (NAM), and other members of the institute's class-action coalition. At least a dozen companies gave a $1 million each. In 2002 it spent more than $23 million on its inside-the-Beltway lobbying and state political efforts to elect business-friendly attorneys general in state elections and state Supreme Court justices. With the backing of senior presidential adviser Karl Rove, chances were greatly improved for passage of a bill.[79]

Outrageous Punitive Damages.   Limits to punitive damages have been a major target of tort reform legislation, as some outrageous lawsuits have illustrated. One is an award of $4 million to a doctor in Birmingham, Alabama, who charged that BMW did not tell him it had partly repainted his purchased sedan to touch up damage. The Supreme Court, however, ultimately sent the case back to an Alabama court, which reduced the award to $50,000.[80]

Another high-profile case was the jury award against McDonald's of $2.7 million in punitive damages (and $160,000 in compensatory damages) to an 81-year-old woman from Albuquerque, New Mexico, who was scalded by a cup of carry-out coffee she spilled on her lap. She suffered third-degree burns of the groin, inner thighs, and buttocks. The coffee was 180 to 190 degrees when it was poured. The McDonald's training manual does state that its coffee must be brewed at 195 to 205 degrees and held at 180 to 190 degrees for optimal taste. A National Coffee Association spokesperson said McDonald's coffee conforms to industry temperature standards. A state court later reduced the punitive award to $480,000, which, together with the $160,000 award for compensatory damages, reduced the total award to $640,000.[81] During the previous decade, McDonald's had received at least 700 reports of coffee burns and had settled other claims arising from scalding injuries for more than $500,000.[82]

Another case is the suit against the CSX Corporation (see Box 12.4), which shows that plaintiff lawyers target those companies with deep pockets rather than those most responsible for injuries and damage.

Reform Campaigns.   According to Ken Silverstein, two Washington groups have been particularly active in waging lobbying campaigns in support of product liability legislation. The leading group is the American Tort Reform Association (ATRA), which is supported by insurance companies, drug manufacturers, tobacco companies, and pharmaceutical firms.[83] Another is Citizens for a Sound Economy (CSE), described in chapter 10. CSE used its resources to run television and radio advertisements supporting tort reform legislation in about 60 congressional districts.[84] Its efforts have been supported by the Pharmaceutical Research and Manufacturers of America, oil interests such as the American Petroleum Institute and Exxon, pesticide makers such as Dow, chemical companies such as Union Carbide, and insurers such as Allstate, all of which have been at the forefront of the tort reform movement.[85]

In 1996, Congress passed, but President Clinton vetoed, a product liability bill that was broadly supported by practically all of the nation's business establishment, the insurance industry, the medical profession (concerned about malpractice judgments), and various groups of educators and public officials. Those opposed were personal injury lawyers, labor unions, and consumer and environmental groups. Both sides lobbied strenuously and spent heavily on public relations and advertising. The Insurance Information Institute wanted the bill framed as a "lawsuit crisis" because it was sensitive to the bill's reference to an "insurance crisis."[86] The law would have capped damages at $250,000, even in cases where a company had lied about the dangers posed by its product; included a "loser pays" provision that would discourage plaintiffs from initiating a case; and contained a "statute of repose" that would bar lawsuits 15 years after "the date of delivery of the product involved to its first purchaser."[87]

Congress again attempted a limited product liability reform in 1998. Among the provisions were a $250,000 cap on punitive damages, but just for companies with less than $5 million in revenue and fewer than 25 employees; other provisions were a limited liability exposure for

Box 12.4 Deep Pockets: The CSX Case

That limits need to be place on punitive damages is illustrated by the suit against CSX, a company targeted by plaintiff lawyers because it has deep pockets. In a case that stemmed from a railroad car fire in New Orleans 10 years ago, a jury awarded $2.5 billion in punitive damages against CSX, and $1 million against other companies. A tank car containing butadiene, a volatile compound used in making synthetic rubber, leaked in a railyard and then burst into flames. Thousands of residents near the yard were evacuated as the fire, which lasted about 36 hours, burned itself out. The National Transportation Safety Board, which investigated the accident, found that CSX had not caused the accident and no serious injuries had resulted. Nonetheless, a group of law firms brought a class-action suit—eventually involving about 8,000 people who filed claims—against CSX and other companies, contending nearby residents had suffered various kinds of physical and mental anguish as a result of the fire and evacuation. (They claimed to have been nervous since the fire and in one instance, to have been bereaved over the inability to find two dogs.) CSX was the chief target of lawsuits, ostensibly because of its ownership of the interchange track where the fire occurred. However, it is suspected that penalties were based on the depth of each company's pockets rather than on its share of responsibility for the accident, according to Marshall S. Shapo, a professor at the Northwestern University School of Law. CSX was considered to have "deep pockets" because of its $5 billion in annual revenue.

A spokesman for CSX Transportation said, "We are very disappointed with a legal process that offers rewards where there has been little harm." Advocates of tort reform said the case is a prime example of the need to limit or abolish punitive damages and to discourage the filing of class-action claims. A lawyer defending the accused companies called the verdict outrageous and said it was the result of a jury's riding a "runaway train." The jury had indeed used the companies' financial statements to determine how much each defendant could afford. Ron Gomez, who heads Louisiana Citizens Against Lawsuit Abuse, said the civil-law system was "totally out of control." Victor E. Schwartz, a Washington liability lawyer, said, "This case shows that our system has turned into the world's richest roulette wheel."

Public opinion was a major factor in this case, suggesting that CSX failed to properly manage the crisis and neglected community relations. When the evacuation was ordered, CSX did nothing to help those evacuated, and the mayor's frantic request for help was initially declined. In contrast, when 13,000 gallons of gasoline from an underground pipeline owned by Calnev Pipeline ignited and killed two residents and injured 31 others in a neighborhood in San Bernardino, California, the company assumed responsibility. Calnev and Southern

Pacific immediately housed and fed the more than 200 families who were evacuated. Company representatives met with the families and participated in community meetings where safety concerns were vented. The company placed an ad in the *San Bernardino Sun* head-lined "Our Deepest Sympathy to the People of San Bernardino." CSX's community relations failure and previous unwillingness to listen to community grievances led a juror to say, "We just wanted to send them a message that you just can't ignore people.... We felt if we hit them a good, big chop, they'll do something—they'll stop parking those toxic chemical cars in the residential areas."

those who market defective goods and the barring of some product defect suits altogether. However, the bill was formally opposed by *Fortune* 100 companies and many considered the bill unnecessary and unhelpful.[88] In 2002, the House passed a tort reform bill that would, among other things, allow federal courts to hear more class-action suits. Federal courts are generally friendlier to business than state courts and would hinder plaintiffs' lawyers from shopping for state courts that have track records of ruling against business.[89] The plaintiffs' favorite court is in Jefferson County, Mississippi, with a population of less than 10,000, but where from 1995 to 2000 more than 21,000 people filed suit.[90] This problem was remedied in February 2005 when Congress passed the Class Action Fairness Act (CAFA) containing a key provision that shifts most large, class-action suits from state courts to federal courts. Other aspects of tort reform, however, have yet to be completed: Asbestos litigation, medical malpractice, and fast-food liability, such as obesity claims.[91]

As an alternative to major reconstruction of the civil justice system, business lobbyists are now trying a new strategy of incremental successes. Among them are: (a) making political contributions, where state laws allows, to business-friendly judges; (b) slipping targeted measures into larger bills, as attempted with the controversial Eli Lilly rider on the Homeland Security Act that would shield the company from liability for a vaccine ingredient; (c) lobbying for restricted access to e-mail, which has incriminated some companies; and (d) pushing to make jury duty mandatory, so that well-heeled citizens more likely to be sympathetic to business don't get out of serving.[92]

The Bush White House has placed a high priority on tort reform and it has been receiving support from the NAM, the U.S. Chamber of Commerce, and others. The new chairman of the NAM, Archie Dunham, stressed the problem: "We have the most expensive tort system in the world—more than double the average cost of other industrialized nations. It drains billions of dollars from our productive capacity and does not make us appreciably safer. It's time to do something about it."[93]

Pointing to asbestos litigation, he stated, "To date, over 2,000 companies have been dragged into asbestos litigation. More than 60 of these companies have been driven into bankruptcy. Over 138,000 jobs have been lost as a consequence."

The U.S. Chamber of Commerce's contribution to tort reform was the launching of a multimillion-dollar television advertising campaign against liability lawsuits, aimed at speeding a Senate vote on the Class Action Fairness Act, passed by the House in 2001 but stalled in the Senate. Two 30-second spots, which ran in five states (Texas, Michigan, Alabama, South Carolina, and New Mexico), focused on hidden costs a typical family pays to cover product lawsuits: $500 for a new car, $3.12 per week for groceries, and 70 cents on an average pair of blue jeans.[94]

Although success on the national level is still lacking, the ATRA has scored victories in more than a dozen states. Along with its allies, which include several tobacco companies such as Philip Morris, Brown & Williamson, and Universal Leaf & Tobacco, ATRA succeeded in pushing through the Civil Liability Reform Act in California in 1987. The law immunizes products customers know to be unsafe. Tobacco companies, whose product is deliberately not mentioned in the law, are major beneficiaries. As stated by Jim Fyock, a spokesman for R. J. Reynolds Co., When "there are risks associated with the products and they are well-known to the community, people who freely use these products should not be able to collect money damages."[95]

Consumer and several other advocacy groups oppose reform legislation, contending lawsuits are the most effective system of checks and balances for safeguarding consumer welfare in an open market system. They point out that some of the most infamous injuries have been "exposed and remedied mainly through lawsuits, not regulatory action."[96] Some conservative voices believe that the right for consumers to sue ultimately helps business because it removes the need for much consumer regulation.

SOME PRINCIPLES AND TECHNIQUES OF LITIGATION PUBLIC RELATIONS

The principles and techniques of litigation public relations combine those of issues management and crisis management with those of law, as summarized here:

> 1. Recognize the legitimate function of our system of justice as administered by courts. A trial by jury is a constitutional right of citizens. Consisting of a group of laypersons, a jury hears witnesses and decides the facts. The choice of jury members is obviously an important determinant of the verdict. In exercising their right to reject jurors for cause and the right to a number of peremptory challenges that do not require a reason, lawyers for the plaintiff and defendant increasingly use social science insights to select the most favorable ju-

rors. Some consultants help in searching jury background by examining occupations, other demographic information, psychographics, and opinion surveys.

Jurors are ordered to decide only on the evidence and arguments presented in court. However, news media reports about a case and its participants may contaminate jury judgment. In criminal cases, the First Amendment rights of the news media may be subordinated to the Sixth Amendment rights of an individual to a fair trial. The Sixth Amendment reads, "In all criminal prosecutions, the accused shall enjoy the right to a speedy and public trial, by an impartial jury of the State and district wherein the crime shall have been committed."[97] To assure such fairness, judges sometimes apply gag orders (which are, however, typically overturned) and restrictions on media presence in the courtroom.

Much of the controversy over pretrial publicity revolves around the goal of assuring justice, not only in criminal cases, but also in civil cases dealing with various rights. For this reason, Gorney "worries that trial lawyers and plaintiffs are pre-empting the role of the courts and seriously undermining due process."[98] A counterargument, however, is that media and public "viewing" of the courts is necessary to preserve public acceptance of the legal system.

2. Synchronize your strategy with lawyers and become an equal partner.[99] At all times, maintain an overview of legal cases before your organization or industry. Take initiative with legal counsel in discussing those you believe may have major public relations implications (e.g., AIDS, OSHA, equal pay, toxic waste). Do your homework on legal language and procedures. Knowledge of law, lawyer behavior, and legal institutions is important.

A study involving charges of sexual harassment indicates that although a legal strategy dominates the organizational decision-making process, public implications of statements made during such a crisis are of critical importance. A collaborative approach between legal and public relations professionals is recommended.[100]

3. Recognize the differences in values, disclosure policies, and ways of thinking between lawyers and public relations counselors.[101] Lawyers value winning a case in court. Although winning may not be everything, it is especially important to outside law firms that are trained in the adversarial mode and whose fees may depend on the size of an award. To legal counsel, stakes may also include a "winning" reputation, which helps secure future cases.

Public relations is concerned with company reputation and relationships. As stated by Lloyd Newman, public relations counsel brings long-term perspective to strategy decisions: What counts is maintaining successful relationships with customers, employees, investors, and other important publics—and not only winning in court. Senior public relations counselor John Budd states, "PR has a legitimate role in assessing the long-term impact of perceived guilt on the company's—or the CEO's—credibility and reputation and a responsibility for adding this pivotal consideration to the decision-making process..... [For this reason,] PR must be the architect of the communications—in both content and context."[102]

The difference in values is revealed in cases such as Sears Automotive's dispute with state attorneys general. When the latter accused Sears of charging customers for unnecessary work, the company hired a San Francisco law firm noted for its trial work. Aiming to win in court, the firm accused the attorneys general of being politically motivated. A better approach, which was later used, was to examine consumer complaints and to change the system in the repair shops.[103] Similarly, with GM's threatened suit against NBC for its rigged pickup truck explosion on television, GM lawyers were more interested in retaliation than they were in settling the dispute with their customers.

With respect to disclosure policies, lawyers prefer secrecy and have a proprietary attitude toward information. They fear the legal vulnerability of their clients, and recognizing the adversarial nature of their craft, they do not want to show their hand to the opponent. One reason that corporate attorneys often recommend the settlement of a lawsuit is to have the opportunity to ask a judge to seal the record.

Public relations counselors, on the other hand, prefer openness even though they are aware of the need for confidentiality on some matters. They know that, in major cases, concealed information eventually sees the light of day and such delayed disclosure harms the client's credibility. The media, when serving as public watchdog and protector of the public interest (as well as their own interests), like to disclose the risks to which the public is exposed; for example, the risks to women using silicone breast implants.

In their way of thinking, lawyers have a highly focused, systematic approach to a problem, says Lukaszewski. They ask sharp questions (many of them worded in a negative fashion; e.g., "Tell us how this won't work?"), are more concerned about the client than about various outside stakeholders and the media, and help the client select the correct option from among alternatives. Being rooted in the realities of the law, lawyers "are very slow to buy into any belief or strategy that seems to have as its basis emotional, intuitive, or unprovable approaches."[104] Moreover, they have "a high degree of information possessiveness" and only reluctantly share information outside the legal circle.[105]

Another characteristic is that lawyers prepare themselves for the known and not, as public relations people do, for a wide variety of scenarios. Lawyers believe a quick, competent response in the public arena may be the most effective technique available to reduce or eliminate reputational and other kinds of damage to the organization.[106]

Public relations counselors tend to be more intuitive; they prefer to deal with the court of public opinion, and focus on image—to present an honest, unambiguous face, and build for tomorrow. They want to "make the transition from a faceless corporate response to a personalized human rebuttal."[107] While sensitizing their CEOs and top executives to the reality of litigation journalism and the central role played by the media, they must also introduce them to the "nuances of perceptions and the megaton impact they have versus facts."[108] Public relations counselors are trained to consider such broad consequences as the "higher order impact" of actions, and not only legal victories or, as in the Ford Pinto case, cost–benefit calculations.[109]

4. Be ready to respond immediately when an accusatory media story or indictment looms. Philadelphia attorney Ralph G. Wellington urged his colleagues: As in all crisis situations, be prepared "immediately to say something" without engaging in speculation. Try to nullify, as much as possible, the initial charges. Learn how to deal with the press and use the media to neutralize harmful coverage.[110] Among the suggestions of John Budd are to "challenge the premise of the charges, challenge the source, suggest a hidden agenda."[111] By all means, avoid the "no comment" response. Examine cases in which an organization has publicly discussed issues without damaging its case or reputation. Also, remember that the media are most likely to cover an event when it is sensational or shocking, involves a prominent person or well-known corporation, and affects many people.

This advice is basically an application of media relations and crisis communication principles, including such important reminders as these:

- A spokesperson must be available and authorized to be interviewed.
- Third-party support of the company's position should be sought, especially with health or scientific issues.
- The effects of all communications on key stakeholders should be anticipated, including those on regulators and legislators.
- Communications should also be sent to a corporation's overseas offices in case developments affect their businesses.[112]

5. Manage the public perception of an issue by establishing a favorable image and frame of reference. Better yet, instead of waiting for the obligatory "ambush phone call soliciting comment," take the initiative. Once a story is written, harm is already done to the accused; reputations and careers may be harmed or made.

Some suggest that the public relations counselor consult with the CEO and legal staff on the advisability of making a statement before becoming the target of a district attorney's crusade. Sometimes it is possible to negotiate with the prosecutor's office over the timing and wording of a news release, as Dow did with the U.S. Attorney's office over the Agent Orange crisis. Dow subsequently prepared a 20-page document for press briefings.

The presence of cameras in the courtroom heightens the need to use public relations, as several high-profile criminal cases have demonstrated. Unlike most lawyers who have no training in public relations, O. J. Simpson's attorneys appeared to be well-schooled in its use. In dealing with television, "not only is the content critical, but how it's said, where it's said, and your appearance are equally important," said defense attorney Robert Shapiro at a meeting of the National Association of Criminal Defense Lawyers. Further revealing his sensitivity to public relations, he elaborated:

> There is no way to avoid having your client's picture on television. Therefore, do everything you can to have yourself and your client appear in the most favorable light. I always instruct my clients upon arrival at the courthouse to get out in a normal manner; to walk next to me in a slow and deliberate way; to have a look of confidence and acknowledge with a nod those who are familiar and supportive. Although the reporters will be shouting questions from all directions, answer no questions at this time. I simply tell the press a statement will be given at the end of the court day.[113]

In another criminal case, that of Amy Grossberg, who was accused of killing her newborn baby, her attorney was suspected of encouraging his client to appear in a nationally televised interview on the ABC program *20/20*. The motive for her appearance was presumably to capture the public relations high ground by humanizing the defendant and allowing her to assert her innocence. Her attorney considered the need for publicity so important he was apparently willing to risk being taken off the case by the presiding judge, who then did remove him because the attorney had violated a court-imposed gag order.[114]

6. Insist on First Amendment rights. A California consumer activist named Marc Kasky contends that Nike engaged in misleading speech when responding to public criticism of its treatment of workers in third-world countries. Nike had issued press releases, written letters to newspapers, and bought full-page ads in major newspapers to defend its reputation. Referring to a California law designed to prevent deceptive advertising, Kasky contends that Nike made inaccuracies and misstatements that violated the law.

The U.S. Supreme Court has taken on the issue of whether Nike's statements is political speech, which falls under the protection of the First Amendment, or is commercial speech, which is unprotected by the First Amendment and must comply with false-advertising criteria. The California Supreme Court ruled that Nike's campaign defending its reputation was commercial speech, not political speech. The California court contended that the underlying purpose of Nike's ads was to sell products. Kenneth A. Paulson, executive director of the First Amendment Center, argues: "In a society in which the marketplace of ideas and the marketplace are so often intermingled, the distinction between commercial and political speech may no longer be so meaningful."[115]

7. Work from a timeline. As stated by Lukaszewski, "Trials, litigation, events happen over time. Develop a timeline or 'calendar' ap-

proach beginning with today and working through the various milestone events and circumstances that can be forecast through the resolution of the problem"[116] He says it is 6 or 7 years for civil litigation; shorter for criminal cases (grand jury deliberations, development of evidence, trial conclusions, and appeal). Box 12.5 lists the typical stages in the legal process. Media interest varies with different stages of the legal process. In a product liability trial, interest is highest in the presentation of opening arguments and when the jury verdict is announced.[117]

OTHER CORPORATION STRATEGIES

In addition to seeking tort reform, corporations are using the strategies of waging a campaign against restricting public information (e.g., by gagging the media), and seeking legal sanctions against defendant lawyers.

Junk Science Campaign

Junk science is akin to a junk bond: It is not assigned high value. Junk science lacks clear thinking and objective truth. In the court of law, judges are debunking some expert testimony and dubbing it junk science.

Since the 1960s, experts have increasingly appeared in injury lawsuits and given them impetus. For a fee, they have identified flaws in gas barbecue grills, diagnosed toxic side effects from industrial accidents, and given opinions on tire defects. Until recently, "it was very rare for a judge to rule an expert's testimony to be inadmissible," said Joseph Sanders, a law professor at the University of Houston. Now federal judges are moving away from relying on juries to evaluate the credibility of experts and asking lower court judges to serve as gatekeepers.

Box 12.5 Stages in the Legal Process

1. Pre-event: Troublesome reports, for example, of product deficiencies.
2. Event reported in the media: An accident, an announcement by a government official that action is being considered.
3. Filing of lawsuit or criminal complaint.
4. Pretrial period, including discovery.
5. Jury selection.
6. Trial: Opening arguments, special witnesses, initial rebuttal/arguments, motions, summations, jury deliberation, the verdict, postverdict commentary.
7. Appeal.
8. Other posttrial matters.[118]

Business rejoices at this tough new attitude and considers it "a kind of quiet overhaul of the justice system."[119] "There was a kind of scandal of junk science in the courts.... It was tainting our system of justice, and we needed to find an intelligent way of purging it," said John L. McGoldrick, general counsel of Bristol-Myers Squibb, probably reflecting the views of most corporate general counsels.[120] This view is supported by Robin S. Conrad, an attorney for the U.S. Chamber of Commerce, who, in connection with *General Electric Co. v Joiner* (discussed later), said, "The problem has been that these so-called experts can march into court and testify to just about anything.... Often, these people have degrees that might impress a jury, but their conclusions are not based on scientific evidence."[121] This another case is further described in Box 12.6.

Box 12.6 GE v. Joiner *Decision Helps Dow Chemical*

The court's ruling in the Daubert case was further fortified in December 1997, in *General Electric Co. v. Joiner*, by extending the power of federal trial judges to exclude expert scientific testimony that the judges believe to be faulty. An electrician, Robert K. Joiner, filed a lawsuit, asserting he had been repeatedly exposed to highly toxic PCBs on the job—not only at GE but also at Westinghouse and Monsanto, companies that were also included in the suit.

Two medical experts were ready to testify that "research involving infant mice and studies involving workers in Italy and Norway convinced them that the electrician's cancer was linked to his exposure to PCBs." Writing for the court, Chief Justice William H. Rehnquist denied the appearance of the medical experts, saying that "there is simply too great an analytical gap between these seemingly far-removed animal studies and the conclusion that PCBs cause lung cancer in humans."

The eight-to-one decision was widely seen as tilting the law in favor of corporate defendants and against plaintiffs who are suing them. "This is very good news," said the Chicago attorney for Dow Chemical, fending off thousands of lawsuits filed on behalf of women who claim illnesses after having a silicone breast implant. Several dozen silicone breast implant suits were thrown out by Federal Judge Robert E. Jones in Portland, Oregon, in December 1996 after he determined that the testimony from plaintiffs' experts was not reliable. Since then state and federal judges in six states have excluded scientific expert testimony in breast implant cases. Furthermore, to examine the connection between silicone implants and disease, Federal Judge Sam C. Pointer of the Northern District of Alabama formed a panel of scientific experts in June.

Jeffrey White of the Association of Trial Lawyers of America said, "It is not great news for plaintiffs. The court appears to be imposing an additional requirement, that there must be a direct link that connects the studies to the injury of the plaintiff in the case."

As Fen-Phen and Redux diet class-action suits mount against American Home Products and its Wyeth-Ayerst division, the company is also invoking junk science arguments. The company is claiming that allegations the drugs are linked to heart-valve damage and a rare, but fatal, lung disease are unsupported by scientific proof. It is launching its own studies and standing by its warnings to consumers of the risks of these pills.[122] Furthermore, American Home Products is resisting massive class-action deals.

Suppression of Public Information

The discovery process in judicial proceedings obliges plaintiffs and defendants to provide information to each other. Because some of the information provided by a corporation might damage its reputation and make it more vulnerable to future lawsuits, a company is often willing to settle a case out of court, provided the court records are sealed. As some corporate lawyers have said, "Opening up evidence discovered in one case to everyone would allow plaintiffs' lawyers to piggy-back lawsuit after lawsuit against corporations."[123]

Secrecy Clauses in Settlements.   Dow Corning, one of the silicone gel manufacturers, agreed to a settlement in a 1984 case in which part of a secrecy clause that sealed court files was a significant condition. This occurred after the company appealed a San Francisco federal court jury award of $1.7 million to Maria Stern ($1.5 million of which was in punitive damages) for having committed fraud by marketing breast implants as safe. Not even the FDA could examine the evidence, and medical experts who had studied the company's data were prohibited from discussing them publicly. Robert T. Rylee, Dow Corning's health care general manager, defended his company's action, saying, "Secrecy is crucial to guard proprietary data that could benefit competitors.... We do not want to be overeducating plaintiffs' lawyers."[124]

How much information courts should keep secret has become a controversial public policy issue. In 1990 Florida and Texas enacted laws barring secrecy in settlements that involve possible threats to public health and safety. The New Jersey legislature also considered bills that would bar confidentiality agreements that have "the purpose or effect of concealing a public hazard," defined as "any device, instrument, procedure or product" that has caused or is likely to cause injury.[125] On the basis of this kind of thinking, federal district court judge H. Lee Sarokin, who once routinely signed orders sealing documents when requested to do so by both sides in a dispute, no longer does. He refused to seal information obtained through the discovery process in a case brought against the tobacco industry accusing it of producing a cancer-causing product. An appeals court subsequently modified his ruling, allowing access to lawyers but not the press.[126]

As might be expected, trial lawyers generally disagree with secrecy clauses. A lawyer who represents plaintiffs in civil suits against corporations said that corporations' payment of settlements "in return for secrecy is tantamount to hush money."[127]

Gagging the Media. Another litigation strategy is to obtain a court gag order against the media, forbidding a newspaper, magazine, or broadcaster to disseminate specified information. A judge issues a gag order to prevent privileged information attorneys obtained during the pretrial discovery period from being publicly disclosed. Gag orders protect litigants' privacy rights to trade secrets, proprietary information, or other information that might be damaging to them (see Box 12.7 for two examples).

Box 12.7 Examples of Gag Orders

In the DuPont Benlate DF case, ornamental-plant growers blamed DuPont's fungicide for killing or damaging their plants. DuPont extended the protective policy to keep internal documents from surfacing and, when they were revealed in a lawsuit, to ask the judge to cover them by a protective order to protect possible trade and other secrets. The plaintiff's legal counsel accused DuPont of seeking privacy rights for more than 1 million documents, including research journals, diaries, lab notebooks, and computer tapes. Information was withheld from customers and the government, namely, that its fungicide Benlate allegedly causes crop damage, particularly in ornamental plants.

After ornamental-plant growers filed more than 400 damage suits against DuPont, a judge issued a gag order prohibiting both the plaintiff and defendant from discussing matters publicly. When a gag order occurs, companies that eventually speak out often find the media's presentation of their views truncated, distorted, or weakly positioned. Furthermore, scientific documentation by a faceless firm can hardly compete with the emotional, sentimental story of a plaintiff. Thus, truthful or not, negative portrayals are used by juries to justify punitive damages or aid the plaintiffs in forcing lucrative out-of-court settlements

In another case, GM sought to extend information protection by seeking to prevent a former disgruntled employee from helping plaintiffs. The employee, Ronald E. Elwell, spent 15 of his 30 years at GM studying cars that were involved in product liability cases. As part of an employment dispute settlement, he had agreed not to help plaintiffs without GM's consent. The Supreme Court, however, decreed Elwell could testify in courts other than those in Michigan. As a result, Elwell served as a witness in a Missouri product liability lawsuit against GM in which the jury returned an $11.3 million verdict. The federal appeals court later, however, reversed the decision and ordered a new trial without Elwell's testimony.

Sometimes information that is prohibited by the court is deliberately leaked to the media—which occurred when *The New York Times* received and printed the Pentagon papers—or inadvertently becomes available, as happened when *BusinessWeek* obtained and printed information about the *Procter & Gamble v. Bankers Trust* lawsuit. This case is instructive because it explains the rationale behind court gag orders that limit public communications and because it explains why *BusinessWeek* sought exemption from the order.

In this case Procter & Gamble (P&G) alleged that Bankers Trust deliberately misled and deceived it about a financial instrument called derivatives and caused its finance costs to be $195.5 million higher than they should have been. P&G asserted that the bank sold it "speculative derivatives securities without explaining their risks," and blamed the bank's "culture of greed and duplicity" for the behavior. Unfortunately for Bankers Trust, one of its own lawyers unknowingly provided the file to an editor at *BusinessWeek*. Representatives for the publication, defending its First Amendment right to publish an article about the case, argued that a protective order entered between two parties should not be binding on it.

When the employee is an attorney of a company he or she wishes to blow the whistle on, various state laws vary widely on whether attorney–client confidentiality applies.[128] Some states allow disclosure only to prevent wrongdoing that will lead to death or serious injury; other states require disclosure to prevent crime or fraud.[129]

Controlling Research.   A Canadian research team found that many scientists who had publicly supported calcium channel blockers, a class of drugs that treats hypertension and angina, "have undisclosed financial ties to the companies that make them."[130] The research team studied 70 published articles on the risks and benefits of the drugs and found that 96% of the authors who supported them had financial relationships with the drugs' makers. Among other benefits provided were money to attend symposiums (67%), speaking honoraria (71%), money for educational programs (46%), funding for research (79%), and employment or consulting fees (21%).[131] It is not known whether their financial interests corrupted their research. Companies that control research are also able to control the disclosure of research results.

Destroying Records.   The ultimate suppression of information is its destruction. Harry W. O'Neill, vice chairman of the Roper Organization, reassures clients that once a survey is completed and validated by his organization, all respondent-identifiable information is removed and destroyed immediately. O'Neill advises others to keep lawyer–client written documents and correspondence to an absolute minimum. He quotes a lawyer as saying, "The more that is in writing—drafts, correspondence, written documents, whatever—the more there is documentation for the other side to pick up and pick upon, the more you will have to explain."[132]

Seeking Sanctions Against Opponents

Corporations are fighting back in the courts against plaintiff lawyers who file spurious class-action lawsuits. "We want to send a message so that lawyers will give pause before filing baseless claims," said Lewis Goldfarb, Chrysler's assistant general counsel.[133] Accordingly, Chrysler sought sanctions and other relief against five lawyers who brought class actions against the company. In one instance a group headed by Seattle attorney Steve Berman, who won more than $1 billion in class-action settlements over the past decade, was accused of "inventing the lawsuit" because Berman filed a case without obtaining the consent of the named plaintiff in the case. Similarly, John Hancock Mutual Life Insurance sued two class-action lawyers who had filed a suit alleging deceptive sales practices and then withdrew it. John Hancock said its purpose was to generate publicity for a future action.[134]

Chrysler was successful in at least one case against lawyers. Two lawyers, John Carey and Joseph Danis (who operate as Carey & Danis), owe Chrysler more than $850,000 because of a jury award that accused them of legal malpractice for filing class-action suits against the automaker. Chrysler had sought that amount as damages for what it spent defending class-action suits—alleging defects in Chrysler's antilock brake system—filed against them by Carey and Danis. However, Chrysler won the case on legal technicalities: Carey and Danis had confidential information about the automaker's defense strategy that they failed to disclose. U.S. District Judge Catherine D. Perry sided with the company by throwing out the lawyers' defense in Chrysler's suit against them.[135]

CONCLUSIONS

Public relations' involvement in court deliberations is likely to intensify as the news media expand their coverage of big cases that involve public health and safety or otherwise have emotional appeal. Many of the techniques of proactive media relations are applicable, but their use must be carefully coordinated with a corporation's legal team and tempered by judicial gag orders.

Lawyers can learn some lessons from public relations practice. One is that winning or losing in the courtroom is not everything. This short-term result must be placed in the context of what happens to a company's reputation in the long run. General public opinion counts, especially when government considers actions against a corporation. More important, the opinions of a company's various stakeholders—especially those of its customers, stockholders, employees, and community citizens—must be taken into account.

A second public relations lesson is that corporate social responsibility must prevail and its lack cannot be concealed for long by obtaining protective court orders. The public must demand that corporate actions threatening public health and safety be revealed. The best current example is the disturbing behavior of the tobacco industry, which had still denied that smoking is addictive and that it deliberately seeks to recruit youth smokers. Judges have begun to respond to public opinion.

As for trial lawyers, they have gone too far, and corporations should seek modest tort reform, such as curbing the size of contingency fees. However, tort reform should not go to the extreme of drastically weakening a powerful weapon that helps customers and others hold companies accountable. Many products have been withdrawn from the market only after litigation; these products include asbestos, the Dalkon Shield, Rely tampons, the Ford Pinto, phenylbutazone, and the Bjork–Shiley heart valve.

Class-action suits are likely to increase as the Internet makes it easier for aggrieved individuals and lawyers to identify problems and to organize. Just as people will look for manufacturers' vulnerabilities instead of reactively waiting for something to happen, companies, too, can monitor the Internet and take corrective action before a problem escalates into a lawsuit. Among the possible preventive steps is to create a dialogue with critics and, when feasible, collaborate in problem solving.

ENDNOTES

1. "Environmental and Public Health Groups Ask Court to Block EPA's Weakened 'Don't Ask, Don't Tell' Air Pollution Monitoring Rules," *PR Newswire*, March 18, 2004. The groups are the Environmental Integrity Project, Sierra Club, Natural Resources Defense Council, Physicians for Social Responsibility, Clean Air Council, Our Children's Earth Foundation, and the Northwest Environmental Defense Center.
2. For a description of the Natural Resources Defense Council, see *Public Interest Profiles, 1988–1989* (Washington, D.C.: Foundation for Public Affairs, 1988), pp. 313, 402.
3. Raymond P. Ewing recognizes this stage in "Issues Management: Managing Trends Through the Issues Life Cycle," in *The Handbook of Strategic Public Relations & Integrated Communications*, ed. Carke L. Caywood (New York: McGraw-ill, 1997), p. 183.
4. Mike France and Lorraine Woellert, "The Battle Over the Courts: How Politics, Ideology, and Special Interests Are Compromising the U.S. Justice System," *BusinessWeek*, September 27, 2004, p. 38.
5. Ibid.
6. Sheil Kaplan, "Justice for Sale," *Common Cause Magazine*, No. 13, May–June 1987, pp. 29–32.
7. France and Woellert, op. cit., pp. 39–40.
8. Ibid., p. 41.
9. Mentioned in Gary C. Woodward, *Perspectives on American Political Media* (Boston: Allyn & Bacon, 1997), p. 35. Reference is to "Darts and Laurels," *Columbia Journalism Review*, May–June 1995, pp. 23–24.

10. John J. Fialka, "How Koch Industries Tries to Influence Judicial System," *Wall Street Journal*, August 9, 1999, p. 20.
11. Dan Carney, "Is the High Court Too High and Mighty? *BusinessWeek*, October 21, 2002, p. 26.
12. Edward Felsenthal, "Legal Beat: In Blockbuster Cases, Justices Rule for Restraint," *Wall Street Journal*, June 30, 1997, p. B1.
13. Mike France, "High Court Anxiety," *BusinessWeek*, July 7, 2003, pp. 28–31.
14. Christopher P. A. Komisarjevsky, "Trial by Media," *Business Horizons*, Vol. 26, January–February 1983, pp. 36–43.
15. Vanessa O'Connell and Gregory Zuckerman, "Altria Verdict Unleashes Worries," *Wall Street Journal*, April 1, 2003, pp. C1, C3.
16. Dan Carney, with Amy Borrus and Jay Greene, "Microsoft's All-Out Counterattack," *BusinessWeek*, May 15, 2000, p. 103.
17. Stanley Holmes, "New Ads to Bolster Microsoft Image: Software Giant Tries to Make Up for Lost Time on Lobbying Front," *Ottawa Citizen*, April 29, 2000, p. D3.
18. France, op. cit.
19. "An Unsettling Settlement," *Economist*, November 10, 2001, p. 57.
20. John Wilke, "Hard Drive: Negotiating All Night, Tenacious Microsoft Won Many Loopholes," *Wall Street Journal*, November 9, 2001, p. A-1.
21. "A Total War Against the Corporation," *Corporate Legal Times*, October 1997, pp. 1ff.
22. Ibid.
23. Ibid.
24. "GM and the Law," *Economist*, July 17, 1999, p. 16.
25. Ibid.
26. Ibid.
27. John F. Budd, Jr., "Guilty—Until Proven Innocent: Litigation Journalism Tests Public Relations Acumen," *Public Relations Quarterly*, Vol. 39, Summer 1994, p. 12.
28. John Gibeaut, "Fear and Loathing in Corporate America: Big Business's Public Tribulations Have Led to Skeptical Juries, New Laws and In-House Lawyers Working to Tighten Compliance," *ABA Journal*, Vol. 89, January 2003, pp. 50–56.
29. Harlan Loeb, "Branding Possibilities Abound in the Litigation Process," *PR Week*, January 20, 2003, p. 8.
30. Ibid.
31. Komisarjevsky, op. cit.
32. A book devoted to this subject is Susanne A. Roschwalb and Richard A. Stack, editors, *Litigation Public Relations: Courting Public Opinion* (Littleton, Co.: Fred B. Rothman, 1995).
33. This literature is listed in Melvin L. Schweitzer, "In-House Counsel: A Matter of Judgment; A Working Framework for making Judgments," *New York Law Journal*, October 27, 2003, p. 26. Haggerty is published by Wiley, 2003.
34. Christine O'Dwyer, "In The Court of Public Opinion; Winning Your Case With Public Relations," *O'Dwyer's PR Services Reporter*, September 2003, p. 31.
35. Schweitzer, op. cit.
36. W. John Moore, "The Court of Public Opinion," *National Journal*, May 23, 1998, p. 1199.
37. "Judy Leon of the Nation's Leading Trial Consulting Firm, DecisionQuest, Comments on the Media' Influence in the Martha Stewart Case," *Business Wire*, January 16, 2004.

38. Alan M. Dershowitz, "With Lawyers Like These …," *Wall Street Journal*, March 8, 2004, p. A16.
39. Carrick Mollenkamp, "Scrushy Team to Argue Against Gag Order in HealthSouth Case," *Wall Street Journal*, April 9, 2004, p. C3.
40. Bloomberg News, "Scrushy, U.S. Will Restrict Comments About Trial," *Los Angeles Trial*, April 10, 2004, p. C3.
41. Betty Liu, "From High-Flier to Humble Churchgoer …," *Financial Times*, May 18, 2004, p. 26.
42. "A Total War Against the Corporation," op. cit.
43. Ibid.
44. Dirk C. Gibson, "Litigation Public Relations: Fundamental Assumptions," *Public Relations Quarterly*, Vol. 43, Spring 1998, p. 19.
45. In Washington, DC, some legal firms are expanding into the field. One example is Weber/Ryan McGinn of Arlington, Virginia, which recently recruited Regina Blakely, a former CBS News correspondent and a lawyer, to head up its litigation PR efforts. Another is Cassidy Cos., Inc., which acquired Bork & Associates Litigation Communications. Moore, op. cit. Also see Jodie Morse, "Media People," *National Journal*, Vol. 30, February 14, 1998, p. 360.
46. See James E. Lukaszewski's comprehensive chapter, "The Newest Discipline: Managing Legally-Driven Issues," in *Practical Public Affairs in an Era of Change—A Communications Guide for Business, Government, and College*, ed. Lloyd Dennis (Lanham, Md.; University Press of America, 1996), pp. 371–393.
47. From a letter, dated July 16, 2003, to the author, which also presents the opinion of Judge Lewis A. Kaplan. Nicolazzo & Associates is a strategic communications management firm located in Boston, Massachusetts.
48. Carole Gorney, "Fatal Attraction: Journalists and Lawyers; Litigation Journalism," *Current*, July 1994, and *MediaCritic*, Vol. 1, No. 2, 1994. Also see her "The New Rules of Litigation Public Relations," *The Public Relations Strategist*, Vol. 1, Spring 1995, pp. 23–29.
49. See *Wall Street Journal*, May 5, 1995, p. A5.
50. Rick Wartzman and Kathleen A. Hughes, "Northrop's Image Ads, Televised on Trial's Eve, Spark U.S. Objection, But Appeals Court Lifts Ban," *Wall Street Journal*, February 20, 1990, p. A26.
51. Ibid.
52. Cited in David W. Stewart and Ingrid M. Martin, "Intended and Unintended Consequences of Warning Messages: A Review and Synthesis of Empirical Research," *Journal of Public Policy and Marketing*, Vol. 13, Spring 1994, pp. 1, 19.
53. William Fay, "The Case for Products Liability Reform," *Risk Management*, Vol. 39, July 1992, p. 26.
54. Mentioned in Lawrence Susskind and Patrick Field, *Dealing With an Angry Public: The Mutual Gains Approach to Resolving Disputes* (New York: Free Press, 1996), p. 3.
55. See Fay, op. cit.; also Robert Kuttner, "Don't Make It Harder to Sue," *Washington Post*, June 24, 1994, p. A27.
56. Barbara Bowers, "The Next Big Risks," *Best's Review—P/C*, Vol. 99, May 1998, p. 36.
57. Ibid., pp. 37–40. For latex glove cases, also see Joseph Weber and Mike France, "The Gloves Come off Over Latex," *BusinessWeek*, June 16, 1997, pp. 85–86.

58. Mil Geyelin, "Tort Bar's Scourge: Star of Legal Reform Kindles Controversy But Collects Critics," *Wall Street Journal*, October 16, 1992, p. A1. Peter Huber has written two influential books on the subject: *Liability: The Legal Revolution and Its Consequences*, and *Galileo's Revenge: Junk Science in the Courtroom*.

59. Estimates by the Rand Institute for Civil Justice and Tillinghast, an insurance industry and business consulting firm. Ibid., p. A6.

60. Peter H. Stone, "Trial Lawyers on Trial," *National Journal*, July 12, 2003, p. 2250.

61. Ibid. Also see Stephen Wermiel, "Courting Disaster: The Costs of Lawsuits, Growing Ever Larger, Disrupt the Economy," *Wall Street Journal*, May 16, 1986, p. 1.

62. Jonathan Rauch, "The Parasite Economy," *National Journal*, Vol. 24, April 25, 1992, pp. 980–985.

63. Fay, op. cit.

64. William S. Stavroupoulos, "Tort Reform: Excessive Litigation by Trial Lawyers," *Vital Speeches*, Vol. 64, April 1, 1998, pp. 362–365.

65. In another industry, three English law firms, in the aftermath of the U.S. McDonald's hot coffee suit, are readying lawsuits against McDonald's for "bloodcurdling burns" suffered by around half a dozen customers. See "Dissent Under the Golden Arches," *Lawyer*, February 24, 1998, p. 15.

66. Heidi Dawley, "And Now, Mad Plaintiff Disease," *BusinessWeek*, November 10, 1997, pp. 66, E16.

67. Bill Richards and Barry Meier, "Widening Horizons: Lawyers Lead Hunt for New Groups of Asbestos Victims," *Wall Street Journal*, February 18, 1987, p. 1.

68. Bowers, op. cit.

69. Mike France, "The Litigation Machine," *BusinessWeek*, January 29, 2001, pp. 115–123.

70. See Stuart Auerbach, "Views of Lawyer Advertising Argued Before Md. High Court," *Washington Post*, December 2, 1977, p. C1.

71. Daniel B. Moskowitz, "Lawyers Learn the Hard Sell—and Companies Shudder," *BusinessWeek*, June 10, 1985, p. 70.

72. Ibid.

73. Ibid., p. 71.

74. Richard B. Schmitt, "Thinning the Ranks: Diet-Pill Litigation Finds Courts Frowning on Mass Settlements," *Wall Street Journal*, January 8, 1998, p. A1.

75. Richard B. Schmitt, "Feeding Frenzy: Trial Lawyers Rush to Turn Diet-Pill Ills Into Money in the Bank," *Wall Street Journal*, October 24, 1997, p. A6.

76. Ibid.

77. Ibid.

78. Fay, op. cit.

79. Stone, op. cit., pp. 2250–2252.

80. Mentioned in Carol Marie Cropper, "Jury in CSX Case Sent Angry Message with a $3.4 Billion Stamp," *New York Times*, September 15, 1997, p. D1.

81. John M. Broder, "Stares of Lawyerly Disbelief at a Huge Civil Award," *New York Times*, September 10, 1997, p. 1.

82. See Andrea Gerlin, "A Matter of Degree: How a Jury Decided That a Coffee Spill Is Worth $2.9 Million," *Wall Street Journal*, September 1, 1994, p. A1. Also, "McDonald's Coffee Award Reduced 75% by Judge," *Wall Street Journal*, September 15, 1994, p. A4.

83. Ken Silverstein, *Washington on $10 Million a Day* (Monroe, Me: Common Courage Press, 1998), p. 103.
84. Peter H. Stone, "Grass-Roots Group Rakes in the Green," *National Journal*, Vol. 27, March 11, 1995, p. 621.
85. Stone, op. cit. Also Silverstein, op. cit., pp. 103–126.
86. Brooks Jackson, "Proposals to Curb Damage Awards in Lawsuits Lead to Flood of Lobbying Efforts on Both Sides," *Wall Street Journal*, April 9, 1986, p. 64.
87. Ibid., p. 113.
88. Thomas B. Edwsull, "Unwise Product Liability Reform," *Los Angeles Times*, July 7, 1998, p. B6.
89. Jim VandeHei, "Bush's Cherished Tort-Reform Plans Survive Enron—Barely," *Wall Street Journal*, March 14, 2002, p. A20.
90. "Tort Reform: A Little Here, A Little There," *BusinessWeek*, January 20, 2003, p. 60.
91. Mike France, "How to Fix the Tort System," *BusinessWeek*, March 14, 2005, pp. 70–78.
92. Ibid.
93. "Tort Reform," *Impact*, the newsletter of the Public Affairs Council, January 2003, p. 2.
94. Christine B. Whelan, "U.S. Chamber of Commerce Takes Tort-Overhaul Campaign to TV," *Wall Street Journal*, August 27, 2002, p. A4.
95. Gregory L. Burden, "Up in Smoke," *ABA Journal*, June 1989, News Section, n.p. Also see Silverstein, op. cit., p. 113.
96. Robert Kuttner, "Phony Litigation 'Crisis'" *Washington Post*, June 24, 1994, p. A27. Also see Robert Kuttner, "Don't Make It Harder to Sue," *Washington Post*, June 24, 1994, p. A27. Nexis. The $4 billion figure includes all insurance premiums paid by business to cover possible damages and actual damages collected by injured consumers and all legal fees.
97. See "Press Coverage of the Administration of Justice" in chapter 10, *The First Amendment and the Fourth Estate*, 6th edition, by T. Barton Carter, Marc A. Franklin, and Jay B. Wright (Westbury, N.Y.: The Foundation Press, 1994), pp. 474–516.
98. Budd, op. cit.
99. This principle is emphatically stated by John Budd who says, "There has to be recognition of the absolute need for intimate synchronization with the lawyers heretofore considered adversaries."
100. See Kathy R. Fitzpatrick and Maureen Shubow Rubin, "Public Relations vs. Legal Strategies in Organizational Crisis Decisions," *Public Relations Review*, Vol. 21, Spring 1995, pp. 21–33.
101. Discussed in Lukaszewski, op. cit., pp. 371–393.
102. Budd, op. cit.
103. Lerbinger, op. cit., pp. 188–190.
104. Lukaszewski, op. cit., p. 381.
105. Ibid., p. 383.
106. Ibid., op. cit., pp. 380–384.
107. Budd, op. cit.
108. Ibid.
109. See Lerbinger, op. cit., p. 277.
110. "A Total War Against the Corporation," op. cit.
111. Budd, op. cit.
112. These reminders are mentioned by Komisarjevsky, op. cit., pp. 38–39.

113. Susanne Roschalb, "Does Television Belong in the Courtroom?" *USA Today Magazine*, November 1994, p. 69.

114. Pat Dawson, "Amy Grossberg, Woman Accused of Killing Newborn, Loses Lawyer Because He Broke Court's Gag Order With Interviews," NBC News Transcripts, July 4, 1997.

115. "Free Speech Inc.: When Companies Defend Themselves," *Impact*, the newsletter of the Public Affairs Council, February 2003, p. 4.

116. Lukaszewski, op. cit., p. 389.

117. Komisarjevsky, op. cit., p. 41.

118. Ibid., p. 390.

119. Richard B. Schmitt, "Witness Stand: Who Is an Expert? In Some Courtrooms, the Answer is 'Nobody,'" *Wall Street Journal*, June 17, 1997, p. A1.

120. Bruce Rubenstein, "Trend Toward Pre-trial Rejection of Evidence Emerges; The Junk Science Debate Sharpens," *Corporate Legal Times*, June 1998, p. 34.

121. David G. Savage, "High Court Limits 'Junk Science' Claims," *Los Angeles Times*, December 16, 1997, p. A29.

122. Ibid.

123. Joseph F. Sullivan, "In Lawsuits, How Much Should the Courts Keep Secret?," *New York Times*, March 3, 1991, p. E6.

124. Lerbinger, op. cit., pp. 219–220.

125. Sullivan, op. cit., p. E6.

126. Ibid.

127. Ibid.

128. Paul M. Barrett, "Silent Partners: When Lawyers See Fraud at a Company, What Must They Do?" *Wall Street Journal*, August 22, 1997, p. A1.

129. Ibid., p. A8.

130. Elyse Tanoute, "Does Corporate Funding Influence Research?" *Wall Street Journal*, January 8, 1998, p. B1.

131. Ibid.

132. Harry W. O'Neill, "They Can't Subpoena What You Ain't Got," *AAPOR News*, Vol. 19, Winter 1992, p. 4.

133. Richard B. Schmitt, "Chrysler Bites Back at Class Action Lawyers," *Wall Street Journal*, March 27, 1996, p. B1.

134. Ibid.

135. Tim Bryant, "Chrysler Wins Case Against 2 Lawyers; Clayton Pair Must Pay Company $850,000, *St. Louis Post-Dispatch*, September 15, 1998, p. B2.

V

Dominance Versus Competition

All the public affairs strategies to produce a favorable sociopolitical environment for business must be assessed from two perspectives: (a) Has corporate power relative to government, interest groups, and the media given corporations the upper hand? (b) Are there long-term unintended consequences in the amassing of this power corporate power?

Chapter 13 examines corporate power strategies from the first perspective and asks such questions as these: Are corporations gaining dominance over government? How much vitality do countervailing interest groups possess? Are the media still able to serve as society's watchdog? The model of the economic marketplace is applied to the political arena by asking to what extent competition exists and whether significant information is available to allow citizens to make rational and wise decisions.

The inherent danger in the exercise of corporate public affairs campaigns is that victory is always sought. Every effort is made to win a battle. Winning becomes an addiction, and, like all addictions, there is blindness to long-term consequences—over whether the war is also won. Grand strategies may be talked about, such as reducing the role of government in the economy and society. However, the real war should be to preserve a market economy and democratic society. People must feel that their standard of living is rising and that freedom is promoted. Talking about maximizing profits, increasing the rate of return on investments, and improving the price–earnings ratio is fine for investors but doesn't inspire public support for our free enterprise system.

A survey of crises over the two decades shows an alarming rise in "crises of management failure." The number has risen so rapidly that a book, *The Crisis Manager,* found it necessary to divide these crises into three subcategories: crises of skewed values, crises of deception, and crises of misconduct.[1] Enron and other corporate scandals illustrate each of these types of scandals. They also demonstrate the need to distinguish between a free market economy and laissez-faire. There must be a role for government, as well as professional societies and the institutions of society. The excesses of "unbridled capitalism" must be avoided

Chapter 14 ventures into the controversial question of how corporate behavior can be modified to increase the chances for "sustainable capitalism" and the long-term viability of our economic and political system. Some answers are found by applying the economic model of competition to the political marketplace. For example, it is argued that the very interest groups that so often represent the "opposition" should, with few exceptions, be kept alive.

Chapter 15 examines ways in which corporations can help to advance the public interest. By accepting corporate social responsibility and moving up in the pyramid of social responsibility the new expectations of Americans and citizens all over the world can better be satisfied. Making reforms in corporate governance structure and practices is another way to address the public interest; for example, by adding a concern for more stakeholders beyond the often singular concern with investors. Finally, establishing and maintaining healthy stakeholder relationships can further promote the formation of socially conscious organizations. Adopting these changes may restore public confidence in business and enhance the reputation of business.

Renewed corporate concern for their reputations is a healthy trend that shows promise. It extends thinking beyond the narrow bottom line and considers the larger force of public opinion, which summarizes the feelings and thoughts of corporate stakeholders and society at large. Much of the focus is on the behavior of CEOs because their reputation accounts for 50% of their corporation's public standing.

ENDNOTE

1. Otto Lerbinger, *The Crisis Manager: Facing Risk and Responsibility* (Mahwah, NJ: Lawrence Erlbaum Associates, 1997).

Chapter 13

Ascendancy of Corporate Power

The grand strategy of business has been to curb the growth in power of three challenging forces: interest groups, media, and government. Foremost, business has sought "to get government off our backs." To accomplish that paramount goal, business has also had to arrest the growth of consumer, environmental, and other interest groups, which had successfully achieved legislative gains, as the steep rise in regulations in the 1960s and 1970s shows. Because of the pervasive influence of the media on public opinion and political decision makers, business has endeavored to tame the news media.

Corporate executives seek stability in their sociopolitical environment so they can pursue their mission of producing products and services at a profit. They invoke the economist's *caterus paribus*—"let all other things remain constant"—when they want to concentrate on business problems and opportunities. However, during the turbulent 1960s and 1970s, these "other things" have moved dynamically, upsetting comfortable assumptions and routines. Some semblance of equilibrium had to be reestablished.

To accomplish this goal, top management assigned public affairs managers the responsibility to regain control over the sociopolitical environment. To this end, public affairs managers designed new methodologies to scan and monitor the external environment. They formulated the process of issues management that extended environmental monitoring into issue analysis, strategy formulation, and issue implementation. They developed new ways of dealing with interest groups, the media, and all three branches of government, especially legislative. This book has catalogued the resultant strategies and tactics. However, the impact of corporate success in achieving power must be assessed—whether public opinion is becoming more anxious about corporate power and whether anger will lead to pressures for extreme reforms.

347

CORPORATE GAINS IN POLITICAL POWER: THE BIG PICTURE

The results of the corporate public affairs counteroffensive have been impressive. "Big business, in league with small business, roundly defeated the public-interest coalition and organized labor in a series of confrontations in the late 1970s," said Scott R. Bowman, author of *The Modern Corporation and American Political Thought*.[1] Another scholar, David Vogel, reported in his book *Fluctuating Fortunes* that by 1978 business had "clearly regained the political initiative and defeated many of the regulatory measures hard won by public interest activists."[2] Referring to corporate dealings with environmentalists, Sharon Beder in *Global Spin* wrote that corporations, "alarmed by the gains environmentalists made in the 1960s and 70s, are fighting back and winning the public relations and policy wars."[3] She elaborated on how "corporations have used their financial resources and power to counter gains made by environmentalists, to reshape public opinion and to persuade politicians against increased environmental regulation."[4]

Business further advanced its grand design during the Reagan and Bush administrations, both of which were lax in enforcing existing laws. Furthermore, they discouraged new legislation by requiring proposals to pass rigorous economic tests. Even when Republicans lost the presidency to the Democrats in 1992, their message was soon echoed by the new president, Bill Clinton. Although during his first term of office Clinton attempted to increase the role of government through his health care reform proposals, he changed his tune at the beginning of his second term in 1996 when he grudgingly declared in his State of the Union address that the "era of big government" was over.

With George W. Bush's victory in the 2000 presidential election, corporate influence in government reached its zenith. His vice president, Dick Cheney, was the former CEO of the major energy corporation Haliburton, and his appointment of many former corporate or probusiness executives indicated that marketplace economics would prevail and the role of government would further be reduced. One indication of heightened corporate influence was Cheney's invitation to energy companies to help shape the administration's energy policy. Their executives met more than 30 times with top officials. In contrast, environmental organizations were relegated to hasty phone calls and two low-level meetings in 2001. Neither Cheney nor Energy Secretary Spencer Abraham granted the request of the head of New York–based Environmental Defense, Fred Krupp, to meet with the so-called Green Group, which represents 30 of the nation's largest environmental organizations.[5] Cheney's meetings with the energy task force have become controversial. Both Judicial Watch, a public interest law firm, and the Sierra Club have sued the energy task force, officially called the National Energy Policy Development Group, saying it is obliged to disclose the role of energy corporations and lobbyists in developing its recommendations.[6] However, the Court of Appeals for the District of Columbia Circuit unanimously rejected the suit and ordered a lower court to dismiss the case.

The theme of excessive corporate power is increasingly reflected in recent literature. *Atlantic Monthly* senior editor Jack Beatty contends in his *Colossus: How the Corporation Changed America*, that the corporation has evolved into the dominant institution in the United States, arguing that most scholars have vastly understated its role in shaping the economy and society.[7] Another book, Kevin Danaher and Jason Mark's *Citizen Challenges to Corporate Power*, ominously states: "A new rebelliousness haunts the world. With each day, more and more people are challenging the institutions that exert control over our lives. The new rebels have set their sights on that force which during the last generation has nearly supplanted the nation-state as the possessor of true power: the transnational corporation."[8]

SCANDALS REVEAL EXTENT OF CORPORATE DOMINANCE

That corporate influence had gone too far was brought to public attention in December 2001 when the bankruptcy of Enron implicated the Bush administration. Jonathan Chait wrote in *The New Republic*, "Put simply, the administration is subservient to economic pressure groups to an extent that surpasses any administration in modern history."[9] Another critic of corporate power, Kevin Phillips, accused Republicans as being "too friendly to corporations, too inclined to give them a regulatory pass, too likely to be permissive to their misdeeds."[10]

Four Dangers of Corporate Dominance Exposed by Scandals

Public disclosures about Enron's false financial reporting and executive misdeeds were soon followed by a torrent of reports about other corporate scandals, all of which added to the impression that corporate dominance was becoming a reality. *USA Today* published a "rogues gallery" of "The 5 Biggest" companies whose executives were facing or had settled charges in financial scandals in 2001. Besides Enron, it listed Imclone's Samuel Waksal, Adelphia Communications' John Rigas, Tyco International's Dennis Kozlowski, and WorldCom's Scott Sullivan.[11] The list grew. In 2002, some 250 American public companies restated their earnings, compared with only 92 in 1997 and 3 in 1981.[12]

The growing number of corporations that were emboldened to engage in unethical and often illegal conduct, exemplified by Enron, demonstrated the symptoms and dangers of corporate dominance: (a) enormous political influence, (b) economic power to manipulate some energy markets, and (c) control over financial disclosure, and (d) self-enrichment by a small group of company insiders.

Political Influence.   "Enron is a story about big dollars that influence public decisions," said Representative Christopher Shays (R–Conn.).[13] Its tremendous growth depended heavily on political influence. Its primary objective was to break up monopoly control of energy markets by local utilities and to change the rules so energy would be deregulated. The company sought these changes on both the national and state levels. Enron's former chief executives Kenneth L. Lay and Jeffrey Skilling frequently met with utilities commissions, testified before statehouse committees, and called on local politicians. To facilitate access and influence on the national level, the corporation and its executives contributed almost $5.88 million to political war chests since 1989.[14]

Enron's return on its political expenditures was highly favorable. As stated by Albert R. Hunt in the *Wall Street Journal*, "Few special interests got more access or results than Enron: legislative favors, a lax oversight of its risky financial derivatives, tax breaks, unsurpassed input into the Cheney energy legislation drafting process and most of what it wanted, and reportedly even veto authority over regulatory appointees."[15] It also escaped enforcement of existing laws, as demonstrated in its manipulation of energy prices in California.

Market Power.   In one of the most brazen violations of social responsibility and blindness to inevitable public outrage, Enron, Duke, El Paso, and other energy traders have been accused of blatantly manipulating the market for electricity and natural gas in California and other western states. Power prices in California rose tenfold in late 2000. During a 4-month period ending in February 2001, electricity sold on California's wholesale electric market cost $16.68 billion—more than double the cost of electricity for all of 1999. The state spent nearly $20 billion to keep the lights on before the Federal Energy Regulatory Commission (FERC) intervened to impose price caps on western power markets.[16]

FERC was slow, however, in the early days of the energy crisis. When complaints of manipulation were made in July 2000, 2 months after the crisis began, it began a tepid investigation. Its staff report in November 2000, according to the *Wall Street Journal*, said "investigators were unconvinced that sellers purposely were withholding supply and pursuing bidding strategies designed to exploit weaknesses in market rules." Without actually analyzing power-plant outage data or bids, the FERC blamed insufficient power supplies, poor market rules and weak infrastructure for the peak prices. Later, however, it reported that it found "epidemic" efforts by big power suppliers to manipulate electricity and natural gas markets (natural gas is an important fuel for power plants) during California's 18-month-long energy crisis in 2000–2001.

Corruption of Financial Information Infrastructure.   Blatant deception and fraud by corporate officers in Enron and other scandal-ridden corporations exposed how the exercise of corporate power both internally and externally corrupted the financial information infrastructure on which the efficient and ethical functioning of the economic system depends. Enron used all the tools of "creative accounting" to inflate earnings and to conceal debt (e.g., the notorious off-books partnerships). Its exercise of internal authority was so strong that it was able to muzzle its own employees, who were afraid of losing their jobs. All seven of the components of this supposedly failsafe system were compromised: corporate accountants, auditors (e.g., Enron's Arthur Andersen), lawyers, boards of directors, security analysts and investment banks, the New York Stock Exchange, and the SEC (see chap. 14 for discussion of the seven components).

Enron was aided by a mystique hyped by the business media. It was portrayed as what a modern company should look like, stressing innovation, risk management, and intangibles. Smart employees were its key assets. Its highly admired top executives, Kenneth Lay, Andrew Fastow, and Jeffrey Skilling were filled with "weening ambition." They created a "cowboy culture" in which everything was pushed to the limits: business practices, laws, and personal behavior. They "lived large," drove fast cars, and spent big money at clubs.[17] The resulting portrayal of its financial condition satisfied Wall Street and investors.

Self-Enrichment.   Instead of serving in their fiduciary responsibility of benefitting stockholders, the new goal of Enron's top managers—the CEO, CFO, and other insiders—was to enrich themselves through high salaries, generous benefits, and, most of all, stock options. Kenneth Lay received $152.7 million in payments and stock in the year leading up to the company's collapse. His take in 2001 was more than 11,000 times the maximum amount of severance paid to laid-off workers.[18] The ratio of the pay of corporate CEOs to the hourly wages of production workers rose to 419 in 1999 from 93 times in 1988.[19] Some top executives added to their riches by accepting tempting initial public offerings from their investment bankers in return for cooperation. Others continued to reap rich rewards even after they were dismissed by their boards. After pleading guilty to criminal charges in connection with Enron's special-purpose entities, CFO Andrew Fastow admitted as part of his plea, "I also engaged in schemes to enrich myself and others at the expense of Enron's shareholders and in violation of my duty of honest services to those shareholders."[20]

Impact of Scandals

The steady flow of news about corporate and executive abuses resulted in a major loss of public confidence in business and consequent passage of the Sarbanes-Oxley corporate reform legislation to correct the failures of the system. Even though the Bush administration and Republican-controlled Congress were ideologically opposed to more government intervention, they had no choice because the public demanded action.

Public Opinion Sours.   Public opinion survey findings conducted in July 2002, after disclosures of Enron and other corporate scandals, show how seriously public confidence in business was shaken:

- One third of Americans said they had "hardly any confidence" in big-company executives—the highest proportion in more than three decades.[21] This finding shows a decline from a June 1999 Gallup survey, which reported 74% of respondents as having confidence in business.[22]
- 57% said they don't trust corporate executives or brokerage firms to give them honest information.[23]
- 71% of Americans believe that profit-hungry businesses cut corners on service and overcharge customers, a finding that also affects faith in the marketplace.[24] An earlier November1997 survey showed the more positive view that 45% of Americans believed "business tries to strike a fair balance between profits and the interests of the public."[25] At the time, this finding was a triumph for business because in 1977 only 15% held this view—down from a high of 70% in 1968.
- Two thirds think that big business has too much influence on the Bush administration.[26] In a further blow, pluralities of Americans now disapproved of the presence of prominent former executives in the administration.[27]
- 42% feel things are generally going in the wrong direction in this country.[28]

These post-Enron surveys give credence to the significant and disturbing *BusinessWeek*/Harris poll finding, released in August 2000, that 74% of Americans believe big companies have too much political influence over government policy, politicians, and policymakers in Washington. Furthermore, 72% of Americans say business has too much power over too many aspects of American life.[29] Rarely, said *BusinessWeek*, have business and its leaders been held in such low esteem.[30] In answer to its cover story title "Too Much Corporate Power?" in the September 11, 2000 issue, *BusinessWeek* appeared to answer yes. It is well to heed its editorial comment—that although there has been the "triumph of the market over the state," there is an uneasiness with the powerful institution of the corporation.

President Bush attempted to downplay the significance of the scandals by arguing that only a "few bad apples" were responsible for the corporate crises. To dramatize this contention, the Justice Department made a few high-profile arrests of top corporate executives. Television viewers could see the 78-year-old former Adelphia CEO John Rigas escorted from his home in handcuffs at 6 a.m. A *Wall Street Journal* editorial called such scenes "useful public theater."[31] However, Americans were not necessarily buying the President Bush's "few bad apples" argument and instead were agreeing more with economist Paul Krugman of Princeton University, who believes the problems in business were systemic: "Executives seemed to have lost the sense that there are rules ... that there are things you don't do." SEC settlements with offenders haven't even required an admission of guilt, a practice the SEC is reconsidering because it wants its settlements to include a degree of punishment serious enough to serve as a deterrent against future violations.[32]

Public Tolerance.   Americans' confidence in business has eroded, but despite this attitude, Americans have been amazingly tolerant of corporate abuses. One likely reason is that they, too, were caught in the wave of get-rich mentality that pervaded the 1990s. Over 50 million Americans were shareholders who saw the value of their securities, including 401(k) retirement funds, soar. High executive salaries were tolerated, if not condoned, because millions of people shared in high stock values and someone was always known who "became a millionaire." The media seemed to cheer as the stock market reached new heights, and they gave CEOs due credit, elevating some into celebrity status, which seemingly entitled executives to high rewards similar to those accorded to Hollywood stars and sports stars.

Another reason for public tolerance is that Americans are generally satisfied with business's economic performance: 68% of Americans rate large U.S. companies favorably in "making good products and competing in a global economy,"[33] and the same percentage agree that "American business should be given most of the credit for the prosperity that has prevailed during most of the 1990s."[34] When the economy performs well, positive attitudes dominate over the negative ones.

One critical test of whether the corporate scandals would affect the course of political and economic events came in the November 2002 elections when Republicans won majorities in both houses of Congress. Similarly, little reference to corporate scandals was made by the candidates in the Democratic primaries in 2004. Corporations must not become too sanguine, however, for a souring of the economy could erase public tolerance and crystallize latent negative attitudes against them. Big business must remind itself of *BusinessWeek*'s conclusion that it lacks deep public support and is vulnerable on a number of specific issues, as reflected in responses to a question about how well corporations do in caring about their stakeholders.

When business overreaches in its quest to increase its political power—and, perhaps, even achieve dominance—it generates opposing forces. Corporate power is balanced or contained by government, as well as by the countervailing power of interest groups and the watchdog function of the news media.

GROWING CORPORATE INFLUENCE OVER GOVERNMENT

The campaign to get government off the backs of people created the political climate that enabled business to whittle away at the role of government. Reinforcing this mood was a December 1998 Gallup poll showing that big government, not big business, was seen as "the biggest threat to the country in the future"—64% of U.S. adults named big government versus 24% for big business.[35] However, as strongly suggested by a front-page *Wall Street Journal* story "Rising Anxiety: What Could Bring 1930s-Style Reform of U.S. Businesses?," public support for corporate America has seriously suffered because of corporate scandals and the accompanying meltdown of stock values.[36] By more than two to one, the poll's respondents said the administration was more interested in protecting the interests of large companies than those of ordinary Americans.[37]

Nevertheless, business has been succeeding in two areas that could move it closer to marketplace dominance of economic affairs: (a) deregulating more industries and relaxing antitrust laws to allow greater concentration of business, and (b) pushing for greater privatization of government enterprises and activities. Although there has been a pause after the corporate scandals, business has succeeded in both areas.

More Deregulation and Lax Antitrust Laws

The move toward greater deregulation of business has been a major corporate objective, as demonstrated by Enron's successful deregulation of the energy industry. However, the publicized excesses of Enron and others in causing the California energy crisis has convinced, if not forced, Congress and the White House to support more regulation. Reform legislation was the answer to these doubts. First, the long awaited campaign finance reform bill (discussed in chap. 11) was passed, largely because of disclosures of Enron's reckless wielding of political influence. Evidence had mounted that corporate campaign contributions led to excessive deregulation in the energy and telecom industries. Second, the Sarbanes-Oxley bill was passed to correct the systemic weaknesses exposed by the scandals. President Bush had no choice but to sign both bills. At stake was public confidence in the American business system and his administration. (Chapter 14 discusses the scope of these bills and what business must do to reach a better balance of power with government so that public confidence in business will revive.) The big question is whether this reform legislation will satisfy the public or whether a fourth wave of antibusiness legislation is beginning, similar to several previous waves since the end of the 19th century.

Lenient antitrust action has led to greater concentration of business. With greater size, large corporations have been able to increase their political as well as economic power. As commented on by Robert Reich, former Labor Secretary in the Clinton administration, the real danger of the new corporate giants is not their power to raise prices but to raise political money.[38] This power adds to the triple advantage of corporations of "extraordinary sources of funds, organization at the ready, and special access to government," said Scott Bowman. "Corporate executives regularly exploit their privileged status and connections.... They out-organize, they out-spend, they out-lobby, and they out-maneuver their opposition."[39]

The pace of economic concentration has been quickening. In 1998, mergers and acquisitions in the United States reached a high of $1.613 trillion, a 78% increase from the previous year. Blockbuster mergers punctuated 1998: Travelers Group and Citicorp ($70 billion), Daimler-Benz AG and Chrysler ($38.3 billion) , and Exxon and Mobil ($80 billion).[40] The year 2000 started with the announcement of the biggest merger of all: AOL's acquisition of Time Warner for $156.14 billion.[41] Government lawyers and economists at the FTC and the Justice Department's Antitrust Division were overwhelmed. Although between 1991 and 1999 the number of merger proposals to be reviewed tripled—from 1,529 applications to 4,642—the number of FTC staffers barely increased, from 313 to 347.[42]

As pointed out in chapter 1, the significance of rising economic concentration of business is that it enables corporations to increase their political power. The income and wealth resulting from economic concentration has helped big business enormously by enabling it to convert economic power into political power. Money allows corporations to buy the best lobbyist available; to make large political campaign contributions; to aid philanthropic organizations and their causes; to hire the most talented public relations and public affairs professional to implement their proactive media relations strategies and other means, such as advocacy advertising, to win public support; and to hire organizations that mobilize public support and thereby compensate for its relative lack of people power.

Creeping Privatization—Including the Military

The privatization movement—the selling of government assets and the transfer of some traditionally government services to business—is a wholesale change that restructures the relative strength of the public and private sectors of society. It is a long-term means of shrinking government and growing the private sector. Privatization is a barometer of corporate success in strengthening marketplace economics and, indirectly, a measure of growth in corporate power.

In Britain, where a mixed economic system of free enterprise and socialistic industries existed after World War II, privatization led to the growth of marketplace economics and strengthening of the private sector, especially after Margaret Thatcher became prime minister in 1979.

In the United States, there have been fewer government assets to transfer. One of the most prominent public corporations, created in 1933, is the Tennessee Valley Authority (TVA). It was authorized to develop and control the Tennessee River and its tributaries for several purposes: flood control, the improvement of navigation, the generation of electric power, and the creation of recreational opportunities.[43] Some members of Congress would now like to see the TVA privatized. A more recent candidate for privatization is the government's uranium-enrichment operations. To facilitate this possibility, Congress turned the agency that ran the operation into an independent government-owned corporation, called U.S. Enrichment Corporation.[44]

Another form of privatization is when government subcontracts government services to private companies. For example, in the United States 73% of local governments use private janitorial services and 54% use private garbage collectors. Prisons have been built and run by private companies; for example, in 1998 roughly 1 in 20 federal inmates was in a for-profit prison.[45] The Internal Revenue Service has also started to outsource debt collection to private firms, which it is authorized to do under the American Jobs Creation Act passed in October 2004. When fully running, private collectors will handle an estimated 2.6 million cases a year. Critics foresee two problems: that call-center workers will not know the law as well as IRS personnel and that they might overstep their bounds by suggesting they have enforcement powers.[46]

The subcontracting that has recently received the most attention is the Pentagon policy of freeing troops for purely military missions, which has triggered a boom in the outsourcing of work to private contractors. Defense Secretary Donald Rumsfeld argues that the Army should focus on what it does best and contract out the rest. Private contractors have become a permanent part of the military machine, doing everything from providing food services to guarding top U.S., Iraqi, and Afghan officials.[47]

P. W. Singer, a fellow at the Brookings Institution and author of *Corporate Warriors: The Rise of the Privatized Military Industry*, estimates that privatized military services constitute a $100 billion industry with several hundred companies operating in more than 100 countries. In the United States, the big five private military contractors are Kellogg Brown & Root (Haliburton), Fluor, Parsons, WashingtonGroup International, and Perini. The extent of privatization is difficult to assess because no central registry of contracts exists.[48]

Singer estimates that private military contractors provide as much as 30% of the military's services in Iraq—including reconstruction. Besides feeding and housing troops, to which there is little objection, they employ about 20,000 security workers; they train American troops; they restore Iraqi policing; and they recruit police, pilots, and bodyguards for overseas work funded by the U.S. government, including the guarding of Afghan president Hamid Karzai. DynCorp International, a Texas company with a $1 billion contract, is the largest security provider. The contractors also maintain sophisticated weapons systems, because military technology is changing so quickly that the armed forces have to call in technical support from civilians.

Furthermore, the sensitive task of interrogating prisoners at Abu Ghraib prison was shared by military personnel and two private contractors: CACI International and Titan. Former Rear Admiral John D. Hutson, now dean of the Franklin Pierce Law Center, expressed opposition, saying, "I have a problem with people carrying weapons in an offensive way. And I have a serious problem with people in sensitive positions, like interrogators."[49] A special problem is that U.S. law and international law have yet to catch up with the pervasive use of civilian contracts supporting the military on the battlefield.[50] They aren't subject to court martial under the Uniform Code of Military Justice because they aren't members of the uniform military. Furthermore, contractors appear to be operating with little or no supervision.

Even as many military functions are being outsourced, there will be continuing debate over which activities associated with national defense, considered a core government function in the U.S. Constitution, are suitable for privatization. In the case of airport security, duties previously performed by the private sector were nationalized because of national security considerations. The private sector had lost the confidence of Congress because the 9/11 terrorists managed to pass through security gates without any difficulty. Apparently, one side effect of 9/11 is that government was again in favor with the public as it dealt with terrorism.

Nevertheless, a special privatized feature may be added to airport security: a Registered Traveler program that gives select preregistered air passengers access to special security lines. Although the Homeland Security Department's Transportation Security Administration initiated the idea, private interests such as Verified Identity Pass in partnership with Lockheed Martin are interested in running and marketing the program. The select passengers would pay between $50 and $100 for membership. Privacy advocates fear that passenger privacy would be further invaded and that although the program is voluntary, more harassed passengers might feel compelled to join the program.[51]

POWER OF INTEREST GROUPS FLUCTUATES BUT ENDURES

Activists and noncorporate groups in society typically fret about their relative political weakness in comparison with corporations, but their power remains formidable. Taking the dark view, Beder argues that big business has taken control of the democratic process so that it is now dominated by corporate power rather than public opinion. She describes how a unified business coalition defeated the Clinton administration's health care reform efforts and succeeded in the passage of the North American Free Trade Agreement (NAFTA). An important factor in both of these achievements was the high degree of cooperation among different firms and industries, in small business as well as by *Fortune* 500 companies.[52] Business spent between $100 million and $300 million opposing the health care reforms—more than total spending by all the presidential candidates in 1992.[53] Obtaining approval for NAFTA cost business over $25 million in one of the largest concerted PR and lobbying campaigns conducted by the Mexican government and U.S. business.[54]

Beder's assessment, however, is overstated. Public membership in various groups fluctuates, but they remain viable. Many public interest organizations have faced a gradual decline in membership in the past 10 to 15 years. Common Cause, for example, shows a 7% drop in total revenue between 2000 and 2001, from $9 million to $8.4 million. However, the group intends to continue to wage battles on such issues as whistle-blower protection and a push for free airtime for candidates.[55] Major public interest groups are far from being powerless, as illustrated by two groups: environmental and labor unions.

Environmental Groups

Major environmental groups have maintained their power and have been able to influence both public policy and industry practices. At a minimum they have been able to call public attention to attacks by both government and corporations on existing environmental laws; more ambitiously they have been able to make incremental improvements in public policies when political conditions are favorable. Also important is that environmentalists are slowly convincing corporations that acceptance of sound policies like sustainable growth is good for both the environment and business. Collaborative efforts are producing results. Those who had hoped the environmental movement would reach some kind of maturity point and the end of its life cycle have been proven wrong. Environmental disasters rekindle public interest in the environment and strengthen the movement.

Political Arena.   In the political arena, corporate successes have largely depended on which political party is in power. Lobbying, along with campaign contributions, play an important role—as they do for environmental groups. Even when a Republican president, George Bush, was in office, the auto industry suffered a resounding defeat when the Clean Air Act Amendments were passed in 1990. These amendments imposed strict deadlines on states and industry for compliance with national air quality standards.[56] Another failure was the inability of supporters of the Republican initiative, Contract With America, to rewrite environmental laws. The continuing policy dispute over global warming shows although the business view has thus far prevailed, environmentalists are winning some arguments, even among some business executives.[57] Environmentalists have also prevailed thus far in preventing drilling in the Arctic National Wildlife Preserve.

Under George W. Bush's administration, environmental policies became considerably more favorable to business. The aim has been to find ways to ease what the administration considers excessive regulatory burdens on business. Utilities, and their allies the coal producers, fared exceedingly well. A *Wall Street Journal* article, "Mercury Issue Takes Wing," describes how the Clinton administration's costly directive to sharply reduce mercury emissions by requiring expensive equipment at each of the nation's 1,100 largest power plants was replaced by a more modest plan. Mercury would no longer be regulated as a hazardous pollutant. The plan would require smaller reductions in emissions over a longer period of time. It would also call for a market-based system that would allow dirtier utilities to buy pollution credits from cleaner ones. New appointees, all of whom worked in cases defending business against EPA regulations, helped produce this change. Jeffrey Holmstead, who represented GE in its legal battle with the EPA on the cleanup of the Hudson River, became the top official in the EPA's air-policy office. One of his aides was James Connaughton, who headed the White House Council on Environmental Quality under the first president Bush and was on the legal staff of Latham & Watkins, a firm that represents corporations in environmental disputes.[58]

Environmentalists also lost out to other industries during the Bush administration. In 2002, the automobile industry successfully fought off the environmentalists' objective of raising the Corporate Average Fuel Economy standards (CAFÉ). The timber industry also gained a victory when the Bush administration decided to widen its planned overhaul of a Clinton-era timber plan protecting millions of acres of Pacific Northwest forests. No longer would federal land managers have to take into account certain impacts on threatened fish habitat when they considered timber sales.[59]

In November 2003, *BusinessWeek* gave this scoreboard on the Bush administration's environmental record:

- Air quality: "The Bush plan will result in cleaner air—but not as clean as the greens would like."
- Water: "A big chunk of the nation's wetlands, streams, and rivers could be threatened. But little has happened yet."
- Public lands: "The cumulative impact will be much less land.... It could literally change the landscape."
- Climate: Fred Krupp, president of Environmental Defense, is quoted: "Looking forward, whether or not the President remains in denial on global warming will have a dramatic impact on health of the planet, on how the world views America, and on how environmentalists view Bush."[60]

Environmental groups, especially large ones like Greenpeace and the Natural Resources Defense Council, remain viable contestants in determining public policy in political arena. Along with corporations, they remain active in lobbying and electoral activities.

Corporate Practices. Equally important to political successes and failures has been the growing influence of environmental groups on business practices. One of the most remarkable changes in company attitude is by the country's top coal-burning utility, American Electric Power. Whereas it once fought the idea of combating climate change, in the late 1990s, the then-CEO E. Linn Draper, Jr. convinced the company that instead of denying that global warming existed, it would prepare for limits. Besides trying to accumulate credits for cutting CO_2, it has been exploring ways to burn coal more cleanly, investing in renewable energy projects in Chile and retrofitting school buildings in Bulgaria for greater efficiency. Scores of other companies have also been taking action and seeing big benefits. Among them are DuPont, which has cut its greenhouse-gas emissions by 65% since the 1990s; Alcoa, which is aiming at a 25% cut by 2010; and GE, which is spending millions to develop hydrogen-powered cars that don't emit.[61] GE's strategy is to dominate the market for renewable-energy technologies. Its new $52 million research center near Munich, Germany, will work on hydrogen fuel cells, wind turbines, biomass fuels, and photovoltaics based on polymers.[62]

A PricewaterhouseCoopers survey of 140 large U.S. companies finds that the vast majority are moving to adopt environmentally cleaner and "sustainable" business practices. Box 13.1 describes some of them, even though 72% of the respondents say intentions are not yet followed through in a "systematic manner."[63]

These business initiatives show that the environmental message is getting through. However, collaboration has its limits. GM, which cooperated with CERES in reducing pollution at some of its factories—and saved on energy costs and precluded expensive government-mandated cleanups—nevertheless opposed environmentalists on the CAFÉ standards that a Senate proposal sought to raise. Gas-guzzling SUVs and pickups were simply too profitable to give up because of environmental concerns. As Elizabeth Lowery, the company's vice president for environment and energy stated, "We make cars and trucks, and we ... run a business."[64] Despite disagreements when economics and environment clash, some companies are "talking," and environmentalists are increasingly working directly with big corporations.

Conflicts between environmental groups and corporations will undoubtedly continue in both the political arena and in confrontations or collaboration between specific groups and specific industries and corporations. Some corporations may seek dominance over environmental groups but there is a rising realization that the consequences of environmental decisions are too great to be left to any notion of "victory" over opponents. Consensus is growing among scientists, government, and

Box 13.1 Examples of Improved Corporate Environmental Practices

1. ForestEthics, a San Francisco environmental group, was active in a campaign to turn Home Depot and Lowe's into supporters for so-called green forest practices. These lumber retailers had been carrying wood from ecologically rich ancient forest.

Home Depot, the nation's largest wood retailer, which sells more than $5 billion of lumber, plywood, doors, and windows a year, vowed to stop selling wood from environmentally sensitive forests by the end of 2002. On January 2, 2003, it delivered a report to more than 20 environmental and government entities detailing its efforts. Rainforest Action, a San Francisco-based group that led protests at Home Depot stores 3 years previously, gave the company a solid B. The group wants Home Depot to push their top suppliers out of the old-growth wood trade.

ForestEthics next targeted paper retailers like Staples. One accomplishment: Staples distributed a letter to store customers that states, "We work closely with our vendors to insure they do not sell Staples any products made from old-growth forest." The company, however, admits, "we have to take on good faith from our suppliers that they've responded accurately." ForestEthics contends that Staples will carry papers that include wood fiber from three "old-growth forest regions": the Canadian boreal forest, the interior of British Columbia, and Indonesia. Paper firms are gearing up for a public relations battle as activists continue to exert pressure to place certain areas off-limits to logging.

2. Business has warmed up to the idea that factory waste water can be reduced and made clean enough to drink and that toxic-free products can be manufactured. Ford CEO William Clay Ford, Jr. hired a leading guru of green growth, Bill McDonough, to lead a $2 billion renovation of its Ford Rouge plant outside Detroit. Ford looked at it as "sound business" rather than "environmental philanthropy." Another company, Steelcase, hired McDonough and his partner Michael Braungart, a top European chemist and a founder of Germany's Green Party, to make an ecologically safe fabric for its subsidiary Designtex. They managed to create a fabric that is so free of toxins that you can eat it! (But showing business reluctance to deviate from past practices, the only chemical company out of 60 invited to join the project was Ciba-Geigy.) Nike is another convert. "It makes sneakers virtually free of PVCs and is developing one that can biodegrade safely into soil," reports *BusinessWeek*. McDonough believes companies can in such ways innovate their way out of regulation. In their book, *Cradle to Cradle*, McDonough and Braungart say that their eco-effective strategies can take the sting out of such new regulations as the European Union's "end-of-life" legislation, which requires auto makers to recycle or reuse at least 80% of their old cars by 2006.

business that action to combat climate change must be hastened.[65] The basic emerging idea is to place mandatory reductions or taxes on carbon emissions together with a worldwide emissions-trading program. Another favorable sign that business attitudes are reflecting the environmental values is that the tide of collaborative efforts is rising and environmental groups can be expected to play a large role. In sum, environmental groups continue to hold sway in the political arena and are affecting business practices.

Labor Union Power Eroding But Still to Be Reckoned With

The power of big labor has been on the decline. Society's power structure no longer shows labor unions rivaling the power of big business, as it did in the 1950s when labor unions represented 40% of the work force.[66] Only about 13% of the U.S. workforce were union members in 2004, marking a steady decline from 24% in 1973, 20% in 1983, and 16% in 1993.[67] If only private-sector employees are counted, the percentage is even lower. Only 8.2% of them belonged to a union in 2001, a decline from about 13% a decade earlier and 9% in 2001.[68] Even in the historical stronghold of manufacturing, union membership declined from 21% in 1992 to less than 16% in 2001. Labor experts conclude that the balance of power has continued to shift toward management's favor. Some say that the very future of collective bargaining is in question—which is reflected in the scant media coverage of collective bargaining outcomes and events.[69]

Nevertheless, labor unions are still exerting power in collective bargaining in some sectors of industry. A prime example is the United Auto Workers (UAW), one of the most powerful unions in the United States, followed perhaps by the airline unions and the professional baseball and football unions. However, the UAW's power is not secure because it now needs new members to keep its strength. Over half of the 80,000 members who have joined since 1998 aren't in the auto industry; for example, it represented about 20% of all parts workers. Assembly plants run by foreign car makers remain mainly nonunion.[70]

Membership Decline. Union membership has been declining for a number of reasons. One is the increasing use of antiunion strategies by employers, as discussed in chapter 2, along with improved corporate human resources management, following the assumption that satisfied workers don't join unions. Other reasons for declining union power are increased competition from foreign labor because of globalization, emerging technologies, the decline of the manufacturing sector, high job turnover, disqualifying employees from the right to organize because they have a managerial component in their job description, and the lack of appeal of labor unions (e.g., for favoring seniority rights over merit). Unions also have themselves to blame for their diminishing numbers because of their shortcomings: internal union corruption and autocracy by top leaders, lack of a compelling social agenda, perception that unions are a monopolistic special interest group, outmoded methods and philosophies for today's new workforce and economy, and profound image problems.[71]

Some labor experts says that unless the labor movement is able to transform itself, it will have to contend with a smaller role in society. As stated by Thomas A. Kochan, codirector of the Institute for Work and Employment Research at M.I.T.'s Sloan School of Management, there is a mismatch between today's workforce and workplace and the institutions and policies that support and govern them.[72] This view is endorsed by Peter Hoier, a labor counselor at the Royal Danish Embassy, Washington, DC, who states, "the national trade unions have not yet adapted to the new global economy." He suggests that "with the globalization of the economy and still bigger and more powerful corporations there is an increasing demand for an international labor movement." Furthermore, he believes that the way the unions are run today probably needs re-examination; for example, fostering education, cooperating with co-workers, providing access to computer facilities, and introducing insurance schemes.[73] By providing a wider range of services, unions hope to attract more members.

Efforts to Revitalize Unions.   When the current president of the AFL–CIO John J. Sweeney took office in 1995 he sought to revitalize a fossilized bureaucracy with the aim of making the labor movement more unified and focused. He filled key posts with reformers with a history of activism and he established several new offices: a department of corporate affairs, a center for strategic research, and a center for worker ownership and governance.[74] Henceforth, the national office would play a greater role in setting an agenda for all its state and local affiliates.[75] Sweeney also opened the Organizing Institute with the aim of training some 1,000 fresh union organizers in 2 years.[76] However, his reorganization and rejuvenation efforts over 9 years largely failed, with union membership falling 2% under his tenure, the same rate of decline that occurred under the previous president, Lane Kirkland.[77]

New union leadership offers some hope and a few unions have been able to increase membership. Sweeney is being challenged by Andrew L. Stern, president of the 1.6-million-member Service Employees International Union (SEIU). Stern charges that the AFL–CIO has become an antiquated structure that "divides workers' strength." He says that the federation's 60 unions are too many and proposes to replace them with 15 or 20 powerful mega-unions that would focus on building membership density, or share of the labor market, in specific industries. This would give unions more clout to match heightened corporate power. Stern, along with the heads of the carpenters, the laborers, the needle-trades, and the hotel workers' union merged in the summer of 2004 to form the New Unity Partnership (NUP).[78] Another merger was announced in January 2005: the United Steelworkers and the Paper, Allied Industrial, Chemical and Energy Workers International Union (PACE). These two of North America's largest industrial unions will comprise an 850,000-member union. It will be the largest in the manufacturing sector and the sixth largest within the AFL-CIO.[79]

The SEIU and a few other labor unions are among the few that have succeeded in increasing membership. During Sweeney's tenure, SEIU doubled its membership. Another union, the Union of Needletrades, Industrial, and Textile Employees (UNITE), which had lost more than 200,000 members through the late 1990s, largely because of offshore competition, also increased its membership. J. Bruce Raynor, who became UNITE's president in 2001, concentrated his efforts on low-wage industries such as retail distribution. Workers there are mostly nonwhite immigrants who earn $8 an hour. Raynor launched a major drive in commercial laundry, knowing that it couldn't be moved offshore.[80]

The UAW showed that even basic U.S. industries could be targets for membership drives. It started to reunionize the U.S. auto parts industry so that by mid-2004, 25% of the industry's 570,000 workers were union members, up from 23% in 1999. It achieved this result by using new "wholesale" organizing methods. Instead of trying to organize workers from the bottom up, which was costly and achieved poor results, it organized from the top down by organizing employers, not employees.[81] The union leaned on their Detroit car makers to persuade their parts suppliers to remain neutral when UAW recruiters arrived. When a majority of a plant's workers signed union-recognition cards—a process known as *card check*—the company voluntarily recognized the union. The big three car makers—GM, Ford, and DaimlerChrysler—benefitted from labor peace and the parts makers benefitted by getting more work from the car makers.[82]

Beyond the collective bargaining arena, unions are learning to exert power over corporations through their huge $3-trillion-plus pension assets. The key instrument is the right of stockholders meeting minimum ownership requirements to file shareholder proxies on a wide range of issues, as long as they do not deal with ordinary business matters. Although they exclude all collective bargaining issues, certain social policy issues may be raised. These have included compliance with CERES principles and other environmental initiatives, equal opportunity, human rights, and *maquiladoras*.[83] By getting together and saying no to a particular company, unions have had a great impact on individual stock prices.[84] In the 2002 proxy season, labor submitted 28% of all shareholder resolutions versus 18% in 2001, which is more than any other institutional investor.[85] Even before the Enron debacle, big labor led the charge for corporate governance reforms, such as auditor independence.

In the political arena, Sweeney plunged the labor movement into politics as never before. He pledged to spend $35 million educating voters and getting out the vote in the 2000 election. Changing its vocabulary and broadening its appeal, the AFL-CIO speaks about job safety and raising wages for all working families, not just union members.[86] Steve Rosenthal became the union's new political director and architect of the federation's return to politics, which at times was highly successful. One of his most effective efforts was to switch from leaflets endorsing candidates to voter guides that compare the candidates' positions without endorsing anyone.[87] Together with Stern, Rosenthal helped found the Democratic party's most successful 527 political committee (see chap. 11), America Coming Together. In 2004, Stern was building separate political muscle by allocating $65 million to elect John Kerry with the aim of making the political atmosphere more receptive to a labor comeback.[88]

The success of the labor movement depends heavily on which political party is in power. Democrats generally favor labor and Republicans oppose labor. A watershed event was when President Ronald Reagan fired more than 11,000 air traffic controllers who belonged to the Professional Air Traffic Controllers Organization (PATCO) and blacklisted them from future federal employment. PATCO leadership had assumed that no political authority could stand up to its power to call a strike. Reagan's bold move, although it slowed air traffic, heralded a new era that seriously compromised labor's main weapon of the strike.[89]

Similarly, Bush's election in 2000 has been bad news for labor unions. A minor incident reflected the tenor of the new relationship. When AFL-CIO president John J. Sweeney left a message congratulating George W. Bush on winning the presidency, he didn't get a return call, because he was confused with another Sweeney of upstate New York. In other words, the labor leader was barely recognized. Most of the bad news, however, came during the first 2 months of the Bush administration, through a "series of executive orders and legislative blitzkriegs," all of which were aimed at defanging unions. In seeking a compromise on campaign finance reform, it sought to force unions to get members' permission before spending dues on political activities.[90] Among other actions, Bush signed legislation that repealed workplace ergonomics standards aimed at preventing repetitive motion injury and took a tough line against labor amid contentious contract negotiations between several major airlines and their unions.[91] In the summer of 2004, the administration announced new rules for overtime payment. The Republican dominated National Labor Relations Board is also reviewing the legality of the card check system for union recognition, which would severely hamper union organizing drives.

Although union membership has seriously eroded over several decades and unions are facing fierce resistance in organizing drives, business cannot dismiss the power of labor unions. New leadership and new strategies may belatedly help unions to overcome their weaknesses and convert themselves into a more viable force in society.

GROWING CORPORATE MEDIA POWER

In his June 1999 PBS special, "Free Speech for Sale," Bill Moyers presented the view that never before have so few owners controlled so much media and exercised such extensive control over news and information. He said "government can't keep you from getting your two cents worth into the public debate. But what the framers of our government didn't reckon with is that two cents don't buy much free speech these days.... If you really want to be heard today, we're talking big money. The framers didn't reckon with the mass media."[92] A widespread contention among critics of corporate and media behavior is that the mass media allow only a very narrow band of dissenting opinions to enter political debates while allowing "the rich and powerful" to launch propaganda campaigns in support of their objectives.[93]

Dangers of Media Concentration

Media concentration translates into huge power of media corporations, with attendant dangers. An extreme one is the media's power to influence political elections, as illustrated by the ability of Italy's media mogul Berlusconi to win the election to become prime minister. In the U.S., Sinclair Broadcasting's overt attempt to influence the 2004 election is a sign that our media may become excessively politicized. A second danger is that the big media companies have the potential to influence the course of political debate on specific issues, such as the debate over the Telecommunications Act of 1996. A third, direct danger to society is the loss of community-based journalism and diversity of views.

Italy's Berlusconi. Italy provides a scenario of what can happen when a media mogul enters politics and becomes the country's prime minister. Silvio Berlusconi, Italy's richest man, owns three major private TV networks, two national newspapers, 50 magazines, the country's biggest advertising agency, the biggest publishing company, the biggest film distributor, and is an Internet service provider.[94] As prime minister he has indirect control over the country's three state-run channels. As summarized by the *Financial Times*, Berlusconi family's media group, Mediaset, and Rai, the Italian state broadcaster, attract about 90% of the national TV audience as well almost all TV advertising.[95]

Since he came to power, several journalists and talk-show hosts have been kicked off the airwaves, seen by critics as a strategy of intimidation. As another indication of his power, the Italian senate approved a decree allowing one of Berlusconi's TV channels to continue terrestrial broadcasting, contrary to a ruling by the constitutional court. Italy's president, Carolo Azeglio Ciampi, refused to sign the bill, and Reporters Without Borders has accused the prime minister of taking a step that was "a flagrant and shocking example of conflict of interest in the media." The group relegated Italy to 53rd on world press freedom ranking in 2003. The so-called "Gasparri law's" purpose was also to lift a ban on cross-ownership of media and would allow one person to own more than two national broadcasting stations, thus enabling Berlusconi to retain ownership of his three national channels.[96] On nonmedia issues, Berlusconi has pushed laws through Parliament that are specifically designed to shield the prime minister from charges of corruption and to favor his business interests. He had been indicted numerous times for fraud and corruption, but most charges were dropped due to the statue of limitations.[97]

The example of Italy raises the specter that excessive media concentration gives the media inordinate power, especially when used by powerful individuals or institutions. No media owner in the United States has yet succeeded becoming president, but some have succeeded in running for state offices, or, like William Randolph Hearst, becoming a House representative. However, there is a potential danger that as the media become more politicized, they may unfairly seek to influence the outcome of elections.

Sinclair Broadcasting Episode.   The danger of politicized media was illustrated by partisan actions by Sinclair Broadcasting Group, the nation's largest owner of television stations. It ordered its 62 television stations nationwide to preempt regular programming days before the November 2, 2004, election day to air "Stolen Honor: Wounds That Never Heal," a highly charged documentary critical of Senator John Kerry, the democratic candidate. Six months previously, the right-wing broadcaster took the extraordinary step of banning its ABC affiliates from showing a special edition of *Nightline* in which anchor Ted Koppel read the names of U.S. soldiers kill in Iraq. Its partisanship had already been evidenced by its daily running of right-wing commentaries dubbed "The Point" and delivered by Sinclair's vice president of corporate relations Mark Hyman.[98]

Fortunately for the preservation of a free press, the backlash to the proposed showing of the Kerry documentary was intense. Michael Copps, a Democratic FCC commission, blasted Sinclair, saying, "This is an abuse of the public trust, and it is proof positive of media consolidation run amok."[99] Former Federal Communications Commission chairman Reed Hundt called it "ordering stations to carry propaganda" and said it was "absolutely off the charts." He said, "Sinclair's acting more like a cable channel.... Broadcasters are given spectrum for free with a quid pro quo to serve the public interest." Bob Zelnick, chairman of the Department of Journalism at Boston University, calls Sinclair's decision "an unfortunate precedent" that runs counter to "good journalism" and "is not what network news ought to be about." He added, "Whether you're liberal or conservative, if you have roots in the journalism profession, there are core values that transcend and need to survive election to election. You avoid airing, very close to elec-

tion, highly charged, partisan material that takes the guise of a documentary."[100] Angry democrats contacted Sinclair's advertisers urging
them to pull their business or face consumer boycotts. And most important for Sinclair's commercial interests, its stock, already
underperforming (it had fallen 53% in 2004), declined even further.[101]
Bowing to pressure, Sinclair later announced that it would not broadcast the entire film and planned to use segments in a special news program, "A POW Story,"on 40 of its 62 stations.[102]

Telecommunications Act of 1996

The ability of the media to control public debate was illustrated in the
television coverage of the Telecommunications Act of 1996, which deregulated many parts of broadcasting. The stated purpose of this legislation was to enhance market competition among rival communication
firms which, in turn, would stimulate technological innovation and improve services and public access. One aspect of the bill was the handing
out of new channels for digital television, which was worth an estimated fair market auction price of $70 billion. Some observers consider
this act, which gave each existing broadcaster an additional six mega-
hertz of spectrum, "one of the greatest gifts of public property in history."[103] Strenuous lobbying by the industry is credited for the act's
provision that the new channels—a piece of the "digital spectrum"—be
given to existing broadcasters. The decision-making process involved no
input from consumers, labor, or community groups. According to Patricia Aufderheide's *Communications Policy and the Public Interest*, "It
makes the American public, and public life itself, a derivative of the vigor
and appetites of large business."[104]

Particularly significant is that "the media did not want to discuss
what it was doing," according to Charles Lewis, director of the Center
for Public Integrity, who appeared in the Moyers program. The major
networks devoted a combined 19 minutes of coverage to 9 months of
congressional debate, suggesting the media conglomerates do indeed
control TV news concerning their own conduct. Moyers warned that
the treatment of the Telecommunications Act by the networks is only
the beginning when six corporations control everything on U.S. network television.[105]

The FCC's attempt at further deregulation of media-ownership rules
was restricted by Congress in December 2003 and then halted entirely
by the courts in June 2004. Despite his media-rules upset, Powell maintained that he was right but "too early."[106] As new types of media, e.g.,
satellite radio and digital technology, proliferate, existing rules are
likely to be challenged in the future, increasing the prospects of further
media concentration.

Loss of News about Local Issues.   A study released by the Project
of Excellence in Journalism in February 2003 concluded that larger TV

station-owning companies used their market power to reduce their commitment to local journalism.[107] Local broadcasters complain that raising the cap would give the networks too much power over what news and programs are broadcast locally. These "absentee corporations" don't show much personal concern for the community. Affiliated stations argue that independent stations are better able than network-owned stations to preempt the network's prime-time programs when a major news story of local importance breaks. One example is that in September 2002, CBS strong-armed a Florida affiliate into airing the season premier of *48 Hours* instead of an important gubernatorial debate (some affiliates refused).[108] "Local issues like school board and road-building decisions won't get covered," warns Mark Cooper of the Consumer Federation of America. "And if election coverage isn't balanced, fewer people will vote. This is about citizens and civic discourse, not consumers and profits."[109]

Communities can actually be harmed when they lack local media. An example is when in the small North Dakota city of Minot a 1 a.m. train derailment released a toxic cloud of anhydrous ammonia. The local police tried to broadcast an alert by contacting the six local commercial radio stations, but they couldn't reach anyone fast enough. All the stations were owned by radio giant Clear Channel Communications, which was piping in music and newstalk from a remote location. Three hundred people were hospitalized and some residents were left partially blind.[110]

"The concentration of power—political, corporate, media, cultural—should be anathema to conservatives," said William Safire in an editorial, "The Great Media Gulp." He argues that the diffusion of power through local control, thereby encouraging individual participation, is the essence of federalism and the greatest expression of democracy.[111] *BusinessWeek* agrees, saying, "One of the central pillars of America's democracy and market economy is an independent media with multiple voices.[112]

Media Concentration Grows

The six giant media conglomerates—Time Warner, News Corporation (Fox), Viacom (CBS), Disney, Vivendi, and Bertelsmann—exert enormous influence over film production, cable, television, radio, book publishing, and other forms of print journalism. For example, Rupert Murdoch's News Corporation owns, among other properties, Fox News, the FX cable channel, Fox Sports, National Geographic, and the Speed Channel, Sky News, 20th Century Fox, HarperCollins Publishers, and several U.K., Australian, and Asian media. Some fear that "their capacity to maintain ideological hegemony in and through the public sphere has reached qualitatively new heights" and results in a corporate stranglehold over political dialogue.[113] This view, however, is held by only a few critics of corporations and is unlikely to take hold in the public mind precisely because few programs like Moyers's are publicly disseminated.

Media Ownership Rule Changes. Media concentration is likely to grow in the future because Michael K. Powell, chairman of the FCC, is seeking to remove restrictions on media ownership.[114] He has proposed to:

- Raise cap on market share of TV stations any one company can own to 45% of U.S. households, from the current 35%.
- Ease rule to allow ownership of two stations in markets with five or more, as long as only one is in top four in ratings.
- Make it easier for companies to own both a newspaper and a TV station in large and midsize markets.[115]

Chairman Powell argues that technological advances, such as the Internet, cable TV, and direct broadcast satellites have made existing limits on ownership less essential. It is often assumed by policymakers that the Internet, radio and newspapers are substitutes for TV. Others, like Philip Meyer, journalism professor at University of North Carolina, disagree, arguing that the Internet is not an information solution. "It's just a vast distribution system, with too much information, much of questionable quality."

A *BusinessWeek* editorial agrees, saying, "Despite all the innovations of recent years, the vast majority of Americans do not get their news from 132 cable channels or news.bbc on the Web."[116] Furthermore, the major Internet sites that people use for news are owned by big media; their editorial content is indistinguishable from what those broadcasters and newspapers put out.[117] Some of the debate centers around the question of whether the Internet is a mass medium. As computer ownership grows, the answer will increasingly be yes, but the *Columbia Journalism Review's* editor-at-large states "the Internet is not a mass medium, no matter what you may have heard: little more than half of U.S. households have Internet connections, and among the poor people the figure is lot lower."[118]

Rule changes in media ownership are opposed by defenders of the public interest, such as Consumers Union, Consumer Federation of America, and the Center for Digital Democracy, who are concerned about diversity of content and media consolidation.[119] This concern is also shared by a few voices among newspaper proprietors and writers. Frank Blethen, publisher of *The Seattle Times*, whose family has controlled the paper for generations, fears that the citizens of Seattle would not benefit from greater concentration of ownership. Henry Holcomb, a business writer at Knight Ridder's *Philadelphia Inquirer* worries about a corporate mentality that may try to "squeeze as many dollars as possible" out of a newspaper–TV combination and "blur all the distinctive ways we try to stimulate and inform the public."[120]

Corporate Advertising and Public Relations.   Corporate money spent on advertising and public relations also indirectly helps maximize corporate power because, over time, all the impressions made on the public mind confirm the authority and legitimacy of a company and the entire business system. As stated by Scott R. Bauman, "Corporations also have access to the hearts and minds of Americans through mass media, especially television commercials that aim to shape public opinion on issues of corporation social responsibility. A systematic public-relations campaign waged by leading corporations since the early 1970s has gone a long way toward transforming a negative public image of the large corporation."[121]

Part of the public relations campaign, says Bauman, is that power is institutionalized by "the ideological construct of the corporate citizen," which serves to legitimize, but also to disguise, the power wielded by large corporations. This ideological view is "communicated daily to a wider audience, through the artful use of mass media in various forms and forums, including political advertising, commercial advertising, and the incessant reproduction of popular culture."[122] Another type of advertising, advocacy (or issue) advertising, permits corporations to engage in agenda setting—influencing what people talk about and what issues politicians may consider.[123]

The role played by public relations in the corporate quest to humanize the corporation and transform it into a venerable social institution is reviewed by historian Roland Marchand in his recent book *Creating the Corporate Soul: The Rise of Public Relations and Corporate Imagery in American Big Business.*[124] When faced with a hostile New Deal government in the 1930s, corporate executive after executive "confessed that he and his peers had unwisely ignored the need to explain and defend the greater mission of his own company and of the capitalist system."[125] Business leaders are portrayed as wanting their enterprises to be seen as "something higher than money profits," even though GM CEO Alfred P. Sloan, Jr., averred that the primary object of his company was "not to make cars but to make money."[126]

Through a variety of public relations programs—institutional advertising, radio programs (e.g., Du Pont's *The Cavalcade of America*), company exhibits (including the World's Fair of 1939), employee magazines—corporations "trumpeted their contributions as patrons of the arts, beneficent providers of welfare for their employees, builders of progress through civic leadership and creators of the inspirational 'cathedrals of commerce.'"[127] Public relations became an accepted and essential function of business, so much so that Paul Garrett, GM public relations director, confidently said, "the time will come … when the big jobs in industry will be bossed not by the technicians of production, engineering or merchandising but by the generalissimo of public relations."[128]

Possible Backlash to Business Control and Influence Over the Media. The danger facing business is that public fear of business control and influence over the media may lead to a backlash. The public is already leery about big business influence. In answer to the Roper Center question "How much of the time do you think news reporting on television, newspapers and radio is improperly influenced by big business," 49% said "often" and an additional 38% said "sometimes." (Only 10% said "rarely" and 2% said "never.") One of the experts presented in the Moyers program thought that the relationship between big money and free speech would be the top issue of the 21st century.[129]

Such attitudes could lead to future congressional action. A little over 20 years ago, two congressmen sought legislative action against business on grounds their communications threatened to deprive citizens of full and accurate information about social and political issues. In 1978, Representative Benjamin Rosenthal (D-N.Y.) and Senator James Aborezk (D-S.D.) proposed an investigation into corporate advertising practices, charging big business was brainwashing the American public. The Association of National Advertisers took this charge so seriously it responded by conducting a major study of corporate communications on public issues. Its findings contradicted the charge.[130] This historical attention by legislators to the perceived dangers of excessive business control over the media should serve as a warning of possible future legislative action.

In contrast to business, interest groups, except for large ones like the Natural Resources Defense Council and AARP, receive little media coverage. AARP's position on an issue like Medicare drug benefits are reported upon but receive considerably less attention compared to the Pharmaceutical Research & Manufacturers of America and its key members. The media generally ignore labor union views on issues beyond strikes and specifics like minimum wages.

The government is a major news source and enjoys more coverage than business. However, it does not own media outlets, as is true in several European countries (e.g., Italy as described earlier). The press in the United States enjoys the protection of the First Amendment free speech rights. Broadcasters must conform to the ownership restrictions imposed by the FCC but these may be further loosened. Content is not regulated except for decency standards, as illustrated by the Janet Jackson exposure. The Fairness Doctrine that required broadcasters to air opposing views was rescinded in 1987 by the FCC. Furthermore, the government's use of advertising has been highly limited and its use of other payments to the media and reporters has not been a significant problem.

A recent exception was the payment of $240,000 by the U.S. Department of Education to conservative columnist Armstrong Williams to promote the administration's "No Child Left Behind" law. The Government Accountability Office criticized the administration for an illegal "covert propaganda" campaign and congressional Democrats leapt on the Williams incident as an abuse of White House power.[131] In some other countries, such as Brazil, government advertising expenditures are huge and the resulting media dependency on the government can be construed as indirect government control.[132] A free press must guard against influence based on government financial support.

Business Constraint Needed.   Since the muckraking period in the late 19th century, corporations have complained about media bias against them and hired public relations people, most of whom were ex-journalists, to balance media treatment of them. As the chapters in Part III indicated, the tools of proactive media relations, along with getting greater control over the media through broadcast appearances, have enabled business to seize the initiative. Furthermore, by buying media space in the form of advocacy advertising, business could use the pages and broadcast time of the media to promote its agenda and views. Advances have also been made in making the media more accountable and, in extreme cases, to intimidate the media by suing objectionable newspapers and broadcasters. As a final tool, business is increasingly able to bypass the mass media and reach target audiences directly through direct mail and a variety of private media, especially the Internet.

Although tamed, and sometimes manipulated by business, the mass media can act independently when it suits their own corporate interests. Hence they remain a potential menace to the general corporate community. As *PR Watch* comments, the media have become so ratings-conscious and sensationalistic they are literally "out of control" and willing to run stories with popular appeal, even when they present big business interests in an unfavorable light.[133] This happens especially when crises occur, as Exxon, Dow-Corning, Prudential, and Metropolitan Life Insurance can attest. Furthermore, business is not a monolithic entity. When media conglomerates find it in their business self-interest to disclose questionable corporate behavior—namely, those of nonmedia corporations—they often do so. The media still have a penchant for sensationalizing scandals and seeking entertainment value at the expense of business. There is no unbreakable bond between media corporations and nonmedia corporations, except when they are one and the same.

For this reason, the greatest potential danger of corporate dominance of the media is the outright ownership of the news media by nonmedia companies. GE and Disney have crossed that line, leading to accusations of interference with editorial judgments. As an example given in the Moyers program "Free Speech for Sale," NBC's *Saturday Night Live* once presented a cartoon sketch about the wide corporate interests of big media owners, including GE, and mentioned the increasing partnerships between companies that ostensibly are competitors. The latter mention, however, was missing in a repeat of the NBC program.[134] The increasing concentration of ownership of newspapers and broadcasting stations and their emphasis on profits over public service makes the media more vulnerable to public criticism.

Part II presented and explained the strategies that corporations can use to gain fair treatment by the media. Many of the same strategies are also used to win people over to their viewpoints. Richard Vigueri, co-author of *America's Right Turn: How Conservatives Use New and Alternative Media to Take Power*, boasts "we won" and sees nothing wrong when his political view dominates the news media. He believes, "journalism is all opinion" anyway, disagreeing with objective journalists who believe that too many views masquerade as news. The liberal media had their day and now the conservative media will have theirs. But concentration of opinions is a serious threat to democracy and, potentially to business and other interest groups. When a big media chain like Sinclair can determine that its viewers will be exposed to one particular political view, those who agree with that viewpoint can feel victorious. But they have to consider that at some future time an antithetical viewpoint may be presented. Rather than play the win-lose game, all groups in society must have confidence that the public will be exposed to a wide spectrum of views, with none predominating.

Media concentration aggravates the danger of dominance by one group in society. Those in control can exercise too much power, especially when the FCC is lax in demanding that broadcasters observe the public interest in exchange for their license to broadcast. Journalists are under increasing pressure to conform to the wishes of their managers. When these wishes reflect commercial interest and promote a particular point of view, this pressure undermines the concept of a free press that serves as society's watchdog. Journalists cannot march lockstep with whatever political view dominates at a particular time. They have become careless in checking out facts and asking tough questions at press conferences, as *The New York Times* acknowledged when it admitted that it let the Pentagon dominate its view about the Iraq war.

CONCLUSIONS

Corporations have had to enter politics and build up their power to achieve a balance with government and opposing interest groups. However, by continuing to seek and exercise more power, some leading corporations engaged in unethical and illegal actions that fomented public opposition. As a result, public attitudes toward corporate America have worsened, causing a new round of government regulation. The *BusinessWeek*/Harris survey reinforces the need for business to change its beliefs and behavior. A *BusinessWeek* editorial, recognizing the "triumph of the market over the state," warns that there is an uneasiness with the powerful institution of the corporation. Its advice to corporate America is threefold: Get out of politics by embracing the McCain-Feingold campaign finance reform legislation; take responsibility for overseas factories; and spread the wealth.[135] Depending on public satisfaction with corporate reform and such other factors as economic recovery, corporations can either continue to become more powerful or face growing opposition from government, interest groups, and the media.

ENDNOTES

1. Scott R. Bowman, *The Modern Corporation and American Political Thought* (University Park, Penna.: The Pennsylvania State University Press, 1996), p. 276.
2. David Vogel, *Fluctuating Fortunes* (New York: Basic Books, 1989), p. 237.
3. "Global Spin: The Corporate Assault on Environmentalism," *Publishers Weekly*, January 26, 1998, Vol. 245, No. 4, p. 82.
4. Sharon Beder, *Global Spin: The Corporate Assault on Environmentalism* (White River Junction, Vt.: Green Books & Chelsea Green Publishing Company, 1997), p. 15.
5. John J. Fialka and Jeanne Cummings, "Energy Documents Show Different Levels of Access," *Wall Street Journal*, March 27, 2002, p. A4.
6. Robert S. Greenberger, "Court to Rule on Energy Task Force," *Wall Street Journal*, December 16, 2003, p. A2. "Cheney Energy Panel Wins Court Ruling," *Wall Street Journal*, May 11, 2005, p. A4.
7. See book review by Christopher Farrell, "A Nation Shaped in the Image of Big Business," *BusinessWeek*, April 30, 2001, p. 20.
8. Robert Weissman, "Insurrection: Taking on Corporate Power," a book review. *Multinational Monitor*, Vol. 25, January–February 2004, pp. 40–41.
9. "Special K: Why the Bush Administration Is Worse Than DiIulio Said," *The New Republic*, December 30, 2002, p. 16.
10. Anthony Mason (anchor), "Corporate Wrongdoing Can Have Widespread Effect," *Sunday Morning* show, July 7, 2002, CBS News Transcript.
11. "Funny Numbers," *USA Today*, October 21, 2002, p. 3B.
12. "Corporate America's Woes, Continued," *Economist*, November 30, 2002, p. 59.
13. Richard S. Dunham, et al., "The Fallout for Bush and Congress," *BusinessWeek*, January 28, 2002, p. 43.
14. Carla Marinucci, "Group Tallies Enron's Contributions, Lobbying," *San Francisco Chronicle*, January 30, 2002, p. A10.
15. Albert R. Hunt, "Enron's One Good Return: Political Investments," *Wall Street Journal*, January 31, 2002, p. A19.
16. Rebecca Smith and Alexei Barrionuevo, "Dynergy Ex-Trader Is Indicted on Criminal-Fraud Charges," *Wall Street Journal*, January 28, 2003, p. A6.
17. Anita Raghavan, Kathryn Kranhold, and Alexei Barrionuevo, "Full Speed Ahead: How Enron Bosses Created a Culture of Pushing Limits," *Wall Street Journal*, August 26, 2002, p. A1.
18. Brad Foss, "The Year of the Corporate Scandal," *Toronto Star*, December 26, 2002, p. J02.
19. Kevin Phillips, *Wealth and Democracy* (New York: Broadway Books, 2002), p. 153.
20. Editorial: "Enron Justice," *Wall Street Journal*, January 15, 2004, p. A14.
21. Gerald F. Seib and John Harwood, "Rising Anxiety: What Could Bring 1930s-Style Reform of U.S. Business?" *Wall Street Journal*, July 24, 2002, pp. A1, A8.
22. Accession No. 0331489, Question No. 014, June 1999. Roper Center at University of Connecticut, Public Opinion Online.
23. John Harwood, "Americans Distrust Institutions in Poll," *Wall Street Journal*, June 13, 2002, p. A4.
24. Seib and Harwood, op. cit., p. 8.
25. Roper Center at University of Connecticut, Public Opinion Online, Accession No. 0335858, Question No. 010, November 1997.

26. Seib and Harwood, op. cit., p. A1.
27. Tom Hamburger and Jeanne Cummings, "Business Ties Now Bind Bush," *Wall Street Journal*, July 24, 2002, p. A4.
28. Seib and Harwood, op. cit.
29. Ibid., pp. 145, 149.
30. John A. Byrne, "Restoring Trust in Corporate America," *BusinessWeek*, June 24, 2002, p. 32.
31. "CEOs in Handcuffs," *Wall Street Journal*, July 26, 2002, p. A10.
32. Deborah Solomon, "SEC Considers Stronger Sanctions," *Wall Street Journal*, June 16, 2003, p. A2.
33. Ibid., p. 149.
34. Ibid., p. 148.
35. Ibid. The Gallup survey was conducted between June 24 and June 27.
36. Seib and Harwood, op. cit.
37. Richard W. Stevenson and Janet Elder, "Poll Finds Concerns That Bush Is Overly Influenced by Business," *New York Times*, July 18, 2002, p. A1.
38. Robert B. Reich, "Commentary; Perspective on Business; Democracy and Megacorporations May Be Mutually Exclusive." *Los Angeles Times*, May 13, 1998, p. B-9.
39. Bowman, op. cit., p. 255.
40. Paul M. Sherer, "The Lesson From Chrysler, Citicorp and Mobil: No Companies Nowadays Are Too Big to Merge," *Wall Street Journal*, January 4, 1999, p. R8.
41. Martin Peers, Nick Wingfield, and Laura Landro, "Media Blitz: AOL, Time Warner Leap Borders to Plan a Mammoth Merger," *Wall Street Journal*, January 11, 2000, p. A1.
42. Kirk Victor and Michael Posner, "Merger Mania: Federal Regulators and Lawmakers Are Struggling to Stay on Top of the Surge in Mergers," *National Journal*, Vol. 32, July 15, 2000, pp. 2280–2289.
43. Vernon A. Mund, *Government and Business* (New York: Harper & Brothers, 1950), p. 553.
44. David Wessel and John Harwood, "Selling Entire Stock!: Capitalism Is Giddy With Triumph; Is It Possible to Overdo It?" *Wall Street Journal*, May 14, 1998, p. A10.
45. Ibid.
46. Rob Wells, "IRS to Begin Outsourcing Debt Collection," *Wall Street Journal*, November 24, 2004, p. D1.
47. "Private Security Firms in Iraq: Dangerous Work," *Economist*, April 10, 2004, pp. 22–23.
48. Spencer E. Ante and Stan Crock, "The Other U.S. Military," *BusinessWeek*, May 31, 2004, pp. 76–78.
49. *Economist*, op. cit.
50. Greg Jaffe, David S. Cloud, and Gary Fields, "Iraq Contractors Pose Problem," *Wall Street Journal*, May 4, 2004, p. A4.
51. Amy Schatz, "Effort to Speed Airport Security Is Going Private," *Wall Street Journal*, January 12, 2005, pp. D1, D3.
52. Vogel, op. cit., p. 12.
53. Beder, op. cit., p. 120.
54. Ibid.
55. Amy Keller, "After Victory, Reformers Start to Face Hard Times," *Roll Call*, January 27, 2003, Section: Welcome Congress.
56. Beder, op. cit., p. 144.

57. See John J. Gialka, "Global Warming Treaty Is Sparking Differing Views From 2 Business Groups," *Wall Street Journal*, May 14, 1998, p. A8.

58. Greg Hitt, "Mercury Issue Takes Wing," *Wall Street Journal*, June 9, 2004, p. A4.

59. Jim Carlton, "Bush Administration Proposes Wider Overhaul of Forest Plan," *Wall Street Journal*, November 26, 2002, p. A6.

60. John Carey, "How Green Is the White House?" *BusinessWeek*, November 3, 2003, pp. 96–98.

61. John Carey, "Special Report: Global Warming," *BusinessWeek*, August 16, 2004, p. 62.

62. Tobias Huerter, "GE: Green and European," *Technology Review*, Vol. 107, September 2004, p. 24.

63. Jim Carlton, "U.S. Firms Are Getting 'Greener' But They Fail to Codify Practices," *Wall Street Journal*, August 19, 2002, p. B2.

64. Jeffrey Ball, "Rocky Road: After Long Detente, GM, Green Group Are at Odds Again," *Wall Street Journal*, July 30, 2002, p. A1.

65. John Carey, "Global Warming," *BusinessWeek*, August 16, 2004, pp. 60–69.

66. See a diagram of "The Power Structuring of American Institutions in 1950" in Delbert C. Miller and William H. Form, *Industrial Sociology* (New York: Harper & Brothers, 1951), p. 854.

67. Aaron Bernstein, "Can This Man Save Labor?," *BusinessWeek*, September 13, 2004, p. 84.

68. Stated in a *Wall Street Journal* editorial, "State of the Unions," January 23, 2004, p. A14.

69. Paul F. Clark, John T. Delaney, and Ann C. Frost, "Private-Sector Collective Bargaining: Is This the End or a New Beginning?" *Collective Bargaining in the Private Sector*, Industrial Relations Research Association Series (Champaign, IL: Industrial Relations Research Association, 2002), pp. 2–5.

70. Joann Muller and David Welch, "Can the UAW Stay in the Game?" *BusinessWeek*, June 10, 2002, p. 78.

71. Bruce E. Kaufman and David Lewin, "Is the NLRA Still Relevant to Today's Economy and Workplace?," in Paula B. Voos, ed., *Labor Law Journal: Proceedings of the 50th Annual Meeting*, Vol. 2 (Industrial Relations Research Association, 1998), p. 1124.

72. Thomas A. Kochan, "Building a New Social Contract at Work: A Call to Action," *Perspectives on Work*, Vol. 4, No.1, p. 3.

73. Peter Hoier, "The Obsolesence of Organized Labor?" *Perspectives on Work*, Vol. 5, No. 1, p. 9.

74. Robert L. Rose, "New AFL-CIO President Seeks to Revitalize Old Federation, *Wall Street Journal*, October 29, 1996, p. B1.

75. Glenn Burkins, "AFL-CIO Plans First Restructuring in 44 Years," *Wall Street Journal*, October 6, 1999, p. A2.

76. Robert L. Rose, "Love of Labor: Training the Newest Generation of AFL-CIO Organizers," *Wall Street Journal*, October 26, 1995, p. B1.

77. Aaron Bernstein, "Labor's New Organization Man," *BusinessWeek*, April 7, 2003, p. 86.

78. Ibid., p. 82.

79. Paul Glader and Kris Maher, "Two Large Unions in Industrial Sector to Merge," *Wall Street Journal*, January 12, 2005, p. A4.

80. Ibid., p. 80.

81. Jarol B. Manheim, *The Death of a Thousand Cuts: Corporate Campaigns and the Attack on the Corporation* (Mahwah, N.J.: Lawrence Erlbaum Associates, 2001), pp. 37–38.

82. David Welch, "A Breakthrough for Labor," *BusinessWeek*, August 2, 2004, pp. 76–86.
83. Manheim, op. cit., p. 224.
84. Amy Borrus and Paul Dwyer, "Governance: Getting the Boss to Behave," *BusinessWeek*, July 15, 2002, p. 110.
85. Ibid.
86. Steven Greenhouse, "Labor's Labors Not Lost," *New York Times*, May 12, 1996, p. E4.
87. Aaron Bernstein and Richard S. Dunham, "He's Got Washington Listening to Labor Again," *BusinessWeek*, November 4, 1996, p. 89.
88. Bernstein, "Can This Man Save Labor?," op. cit., p. 83.
89. Manheim, op. cit., pp. 34–36.
90. Paula Dwyer, "Big Labor: So Out It's 'Off the Radar Screen,'" *BusinessWeek*, March 26, 2001, p. 55.
91. Kathy Chen, "Bush Halts Union-Friendly Rules; Carpenters Sever AFL-CIO Link," *Wall Street Journal*, April 2, 2001, p. A24.
92. Tom Feran, "Big Business Raises the Price of Free Speech; PBS Looks at Effects of Consolidating Media Ownership," *The Plain Dealer*, June 8, 1999, p. 1E.
93. Charlotte Ryan, *Prime Time Activism: Media Strategies for Grassroots Organizing* (Boston, Mass.: South End Press, 1991), p. 14. A stronger view is voiced by Edward Herman and Noam Chomsky in what they call the "propaganda model"; it " focuses on this inequality of wealth and power and its multilevel effects on mass-media interests and choices. It traces the routes by which money and power are able to filter out the news fit to print, marginalize dissent, and allow the government and dominant private interests to get their message across to the public." See their *Manufacturing Consent: The Political Economy of the Mass Media* (New York: Pantheon, 1988), p. 2.
94. Sylvia Poggoli, "Italian Prime Minister Silvio Berlusconi Celebrates 10th Anniversary in Politics as Critics Decry His Control of the Media," National Public Radio, January 27, 2004.
95. Tony Barber, "Berlusconi Under Attack for Media Power," *Financial Times*, April 23, 2004, Edition 2, p. 8.
96. "Reporters Without Borders—ITALY—Silvio Berlusconi Saves One of His TV Channels by Decree in Flagrant Example of Conflict of Interest," Canada NewsWire, January 30, 2004.
97. Poggoli, op. cit.
98. Eric Boehlert, "Sinclair's Disgrace," Salon.com, October 14, 2004, feature.
99. Joe Flint, "Sinclair Draws Partisan Scrutiny With Plans for Kerry Broadcast," *Wall Street Journal*, October 2, 2004, p. B13.
100. Boehlert, op. cit.
101. Bill Carter et al., "Risks Seen for TV Chain Showing Film About Kerry," *New York Times*, October 18, 2004, p. C-1.
102. Bill Carter, "Broadcaster's Stock Picks up After Change on Kerry Film," *New York Times*, October 21, 2004, p. A-27; Joe Flint, "Political Shows Prove Costly to Sinclair CEO," *Wall Street Journal*, October 22, 2004, p. B1.
103. Kevin Phillips, *Wealth and Democracy* (New York: Broadway Books, 2002), p. 248.
104. Patricia Aufderheide, *Communications Policy and the Public Interest* (New York: Guilford, 1999), p. 62.
105. Ibid., Tom Feran, "Media Access Examined [by] Bill Moyers Special," *Columbus Dispatch*, June 8, 1999, p. 7F. The number will be reduced to five if Viacom succeeds in acquiring CBS.

106. "Face Value: Beyond Janet Jackson's Breast," *Economist*, January 22, 2005, p. 64.

107. Robert W. McChesney, *The Problem of the Media: U.S. Communication Politics in the 21st Century* (New York: Monthly Review Press, 2004), pp. 276–277. He refers to Catherine Yang, "The News Biz: Is Bigger Better?" *BusinessWeek*, March 3, 2003, p. 97.

108. Ibid.

109. David Lieberman, "TV's New Look: All Business, All the Time," *USA Today*, January 14, 2000, pp. 1A, 2A.

110. Will Harper, "Rethinking the Media Monopoly," *East Bay Express (California)*, July 7, 2004, in news and features section.

111. William Safire, "The Great Media Gulp," *New York Times*, May 22, 2003, p. A-33.

112. Editorial: "Media: The Dangers of Concentration," *BusinessWeek*, July 8, 2002, p. 118.

113. Carl Boggs, *The End of Politics: Corporate Power and the Decline of the Public Sphere* (New York: Guilford, 2000), p. 9.

114. "Relaxing Rules Raises Concerns About Diverse Media Voices," *USA Today*, January 16, 2003, p. 1B.

115. As summarized in Yochi J. Dreazen and Joe Flint, "FCC Eases Media-Ownership Caps, Clearing Way for New Mergers," *Wall Street Journal*, June 3, 2002, p. A1.

116. "Beware Media Consolidation," *BusinessWeek*, May 26, 2003, p. 126.

117. William Safire, "Merged Media Giants Have Us at Their Mercy," *The International Herald Tribune*, January 22, 2003, p. 9.

118. Neil Hickey, "Power Shift: As the FCC Prepares to Alter the Media Map, Battle Lines Are Drawn," *Columbia Journalism Review*, March/April 2003, p. 26.

119. Yochi J. Dreazen and Joe Flint, "Court Rejects Curbs on Media Ownership," *Wall Street Journal*, February 20, 2002, p. A3.

120. Hickey, op. cit.

121. Bauman states that positive corporation images can also be conveyed effectively on television through product endorsements. "Smiling faces, high production values, and a corporate logo can also shape attitudes, especially those of a new generation." p. 150 Also: Bauman: "Corporate individualism continues to be the most important ideological weapon in the arsenal of corporate power. Through modern methods of advertising—especially television commercials—the corporate persona regularly advises, entertains, and indoctrinates a captive audience." Bauman contends that "The selling of corporate America takes many forms in which commercial and political advertising often become indistinguishable." This is witnessed when "the sales pitch fades into the background in what appears to be public-service announcements or self-congratulatory 'commercials' lauding corporate good deeds and praising the American way.... Public responsibility becomes increasingly important as corporate power transforms social relationships. To succeed in the long term, corporate leaders must take into account social and political realities." See Bauman, op. cit., pp. 182–183.

122. Ibid., p. 33.

123. This criticism is similar to discussions about advertising as an unfair method of competition. Vernon A. Mund states that this occurs when advertising is false and when used excessively. He states, "The very fact of being able to employ large-scale advertising gives an advantage to a few producers which is not equally available to smaller but perhaps just as effi-

cient firms." See his *Government and Business* (New York: Harper & Brothers, 1950), p. 305.

124. Roland Marchand, *Creating the Corporate Soul: The Rise of Public Relations and Corporate Imagery in American Big Business* (Berkeley, Calif.: University of California Press, 1998).

125. Ibid., p. 204.

126. Ibid., p. 161.

127. See book review by Susan G. Davis, "Corporate Affairs; Big Business Uses PR as a Tool and a Club," *The San Diego Union-Tribune*, January 31, 1999, p. Books-1.

128. Marchand, op. cit., p. 357.

129. Ibid.

130. Press release dated October 27, 1978, from ANA, "Public Issues & Corporate Constituents: Highlight of A.N.A.–Business Week Survey on Business's Understanding of Public Issues."

131. Christopher Cooper and Brian Steinberg, "Bush Draws Fire Over Fee Paid to Columnist to Promote Policy," *Wall Street Journal*, January 10, 2005, p. B3.

132. Melvin L. Sharpe and Roberto P. Simoes, "Public Relations Performance in South and Central America," in Hugh M. Culbertson and Ni Chen, editors, *International Public Relations: A Comparative Analysis* (Mahwah, N.J.: Lawrence Erlbaum Associates, 1996), p. 287.

133. "They're Rich, They're Powerful and They're Running Scared," *PR Watch*, Vol. 4, First Quarter 1997, pp. 1–3.

134. Feran, op. cit.

135. "Editorials: New Economy, New Social Contract," *BusinessWeek*, September 11, 2000, p. 182.

Chapter 14

Constructing a Competitive Political Marketplace

Corporations can mitigate fears of excessive corporate power, if not out-right dominance, by accepting the model of a political marketplace and constructing ways to implement it. Its fundamental requirement is the maintenance of competition among society's myriad of interests. Just as the economic marketplace requires vigorous competition to work properly and protect the public interest, so does the political market-place.[1] When competition exists everybody can pursue their economic interests and express their personal viewpoints because, as Adam Smith stated, the "invisible hand" of the marketplace allows people to work for their own self-interest and still produce a desirable social outcome.[2] In the economic marketplace, the existence of competition with many buyers and sellers prevents the domination by any one of them because the price is set by the market. Similarly, in the political marketplace competition among a diversity of interest groups enables people to pro-mote their position on issues and compete in influencing public policy.

Competition in the economic marketplace is protected by "rules of the game" established by business and supplemented by laws that seek to preserve a competitive structure. The most important laws are the Sherman Antitrust Act of 1890 and the Clayton Act of 1914. Just as the Sherman Act forbade the combination of economic entities that would restrain commerce, the rules of the political marketplace would prevent the excessive building up of power blocs. These understandings about the requirements of competition are required in both marketplaces to avoid, in the words of the Sherman Act, a "ruthless, savage war to the death, waged without rules of fairness or reasonableness, and legiti-mate as long as it promotes the interest of the person practicing it."[3] Just as the Clayton Act curbed the use of unfair methods of competition, the

381

political marketplace needs prohibitions against the use of "unfair" techniques.[4]

The economic and political marketplaces are basically communication networks that bring together selected information from groups of people. Consumers are said to have "purchasing power" and citizens "voting power." Businesses sell products and services in the economic marketplace to buyers, the consumers. In the political marketplace, legislative regulatory bodies are the sellers of preferred public policies and a variety of favors, such as subsidies, tax benefits, and tariff protection, to a variety of buyers. This demand side of the market comprises citizens, businesses, associations, and the many interest groups in our society. They react to the political products proposed by lawmakers and regulators. They have the right to express their demands through the right to petition government, sometimes backing up their demands with campaign contributions, which to some is tantamount to "buying" legislative votes. This analogy between the economic and political marketplaces has one notable difference: Government can impose its products on corporate and other citizens. However, if buyers are dissatisfied, they may engage in political campaigning to change the composition of the sellers; that is, the lawmakers and the president.

In economics, full and accurate information from both sellers and buyers is an essential condition for a market to function efficiently. In the simple world of the general store, a customer possesses what economists call "full knowledge"—of what products are available, what their essential characteristics are, and what their prices are. Similarly, the local merchant is aware of his or her customers' needs and the prices suppliers charge for their products. Price is the core information required in the market.[5] It is an incredibly efficient way to reflect the strength of demand for a product and the willingness of sellers to provide the product.

Nothing comparable to price exists in the political marketplace.[6] The closest type of information is public opinion, which reports on the number of people and the intensity with which they support a particular public policy—the equivalent of "quantity demanded" in the economic arena.[7] Constant reference by lawmakers, public officials, and politicians to "market research" findings to determine what citizens want and, therefore, what "products" they should provide, shows the importance politicians place on public opinion. Candidates running for office play the game of "product differentiation"; that is, identifying themselves with selecting issues that resonate with voters.

In applying the economics model to the political marketplace, therefore, two features are essential: maintaining competition and ensuring truthful and timely disclosure of information.

MAINTAIN COMPETITION IN THE POLITICAL MARKETPLACE

Just as the public interest in the economic marketplace is preserved by competition among large numbers of sellers and among buyers, so is the public interest in the political marketplace safeguarded by competition among citizens and a variety of interest groups. The model of a pluralistic society represents this state of affairs where "citizens are all well informed, all share and treasure core public values, all care about what their government does, and all participate in their collective governance through advocacy, voting, and the other avenues of the democratic process."[8]

However, population growth and the formation of a myriad of interest groups have required that this "town hall" model be replaced by a more complex one: the pluralist democratic elite theory in which a diverse and competing group of elite leaders replace ordinary citizens. Democratic ideals are thereby sacrificed because this system of elites functions more like a "protected market with high entry barriers than a system of free and open competition."[9] Furthermore, it is likely that "some groups—larger, richer, with better access—will have disproportionate power." Andrew Hacker's metaphor is often cited: "When General Electric, American Telephone and Telegraph, and Standard Oil of New Jersey enter the pluralist arena we have elephants dancing among the chickens."[10] To avoid gross inequality of power and maintain a competitive political marketplace, attempts should be undertaken to provide equivalent opportunities for all political participants.[11]

Encourage Diversity of Interest Groups

To build and maintain competition in the political marketplace, the existence of a large number and wide assortment of interest groups to represent various businesses and social institutions is desirable. This feature provides a large source and reservoir of political and social ideas. Some of these ideas gradually work their way through the issues management process and result in changes in the political agendas of Democrats, Republicans, and, possibly, politicians of other parties. Corporate policymakers also have the option of acting on some issues independently or resolving them with others in the private sector instead of waiting for ideas to percolate through government.

To maintain competition in the political marketplace it is important that the voices of interest groups not be eliminated or muted, tempting as this strategy is in short-term campaigns. Some controversial examples are as follows:

> 1. SLAPP suits, which intimidate individuals and small groups from speaking out against some business interests. Speaking for consumer groups, Ralph Nader attacked these suits as "blatant attempts by corporations to bully citizens into silence."[12]
> 2. Questionable and sometimes outright illegal antiunion tactics by employers. The Taft-Hartley Act corrected the prolabor bias of the 1935 Wagner Act by giving employers the right to tell their employ-

ees why they should not join a union. However, when employers threaten to close facilities if a union wins, that is a violation. Firing union supporters during elections is also illegal, which, however, a third of companies in an NLRB study admitted doing (up from 8% in the 1960s). Requiring workers to meet one-on-one with supervisors on a union issue is, at best, questionable.[13] George Schultz, the former secretary of state who was also once an industrial relations expert, believes a system of collective bargaining should survive. He fears we are now looking at megacorporations and microlabor as we enter the 21st century.[14]

3. Seeking restrictions on political spending by unions. On this highly partisan issue, business supported California Proposition 226, which would require unions to obtain permission from individual members to use dues in political campaigns. (As some legal experts believe, such a prohibition might also require employers who take deductions on employees' behalf to get annual permission from each worker.)[15] Serious consideration has to be given to the argument that unions should be treated the same as other voluntary associations. Members have the right to participate in the governance of that association, but the majority rules.[16]

4. Depriving legitimate groups of financial support when they speak out against corporations. A distinction should be made between the so-called Packard Doctrine, which advises companies not to give financial support to their critics, and efforts to disqualify 501(c) nonprofit groups from exercising their advocacy role.

5. Asking the courts to treat corporate free speech as commercial speech is equally repressive to the expression of viewpoints, as argued in the *Nike v. Kasky* case.

It may appear unrealistic and self-defeating from a short-term viewpoint to ask corporations to mitigate or abandon these strategies, because doing so conflicts with the public affairs spirit of "fighting to win." However, in the long run the preservation of viable opposing interest groups is part of the system of checks and balances needed to preserve the democratic foundations of marketplace economics.

Recognize the Legitimate Function of Government

Ideological faith in free enterprise does not rule out a legitimate role of government in making sure that at least the "rules of the game" in the marketplace are observed. This requirement was the minimum prescription of Adam Smith, the ideological godfather of the free enterprise system. The basic economic function of government is to create and operate a system of institutions that allows for the conduct of business activity. These include the right to private property, freedom of contract, money and credit, weights and measures, and a system of civil law for adjudicating the private disputes of individuals.[17]

Other functions of government have been added that, to various degrees, are controversial: (a) to promote the maximum production of goods and services in the conduct of business activity—which would be assured where freedom of competition exists—and (b) to provide for a determination of prices and incomes that are in harmony with the public welfare. Few would disagree that government must regulate prices where monopoly exists, as has been done with public utilities. Greater disagreement exists over government interference with income, such as the setting of minimum wages or limiting executive salaries.

The underlying political issue in the United States is whether people want more or less government. President Reagan believed that government is the root of social and economic evil, so that once government is "off the people's backs," problems can more easily be solved through the automatic functioning of the marketplace. Some measures, however, like deregulation, have gone too far. If the Enron and other corporate scandals have taught any lesson, it is that the unbridled pursuit of profit results in periodical excesses that trigger public outrage and greater government regulation.

Few would argue against the idea that government has a basic regulatory function to perform. This lesson was reinforced by the widespread U.S. power outage in the summer of 2003. Secretary of Energy Spencer Abraham said that voluntary compliance with standards that ensure reliability are inadequate and that enforceable standards are required to lessen the risk of further power failures.[18] A U.S.–Canadian task force report warned that there was little reason to believe the electric system was hardier at the beginning of 2004 than it was in 2003.[19]

A few conservatives have warned against demonizing government. William J. Bennett and John J. Dilulio, Jr. note that some of their fellow conservatives believe so strongly in antigovernment ideology, they come perilously close to delegitimating the idea of government itself.[20] Furthermore, says Bennett, "Unbridled capitalism ... is a problem for that whole dimension of things we call the realm of values and human relationships."[21] If there are limits to capitalism, government must play a role. Whether social justice and democratic ideals are thereby achieved is a question that the competitive system can only partly answer.

Political parties provide voters with some choices about social ideals in that they differ among themselves on the principles that guide their interpretation of the national interest. As defined by Joseph A. Schumpeter, members of political parties "propose to act in concert in the competitive struggle for political power."[22] When considering the wide range of political ideologies that have existed—ranging from communism and socialism to conservatism—the Democratic and Republican political parties are distinctly procorporate, believing in free markets, free trade, deregulation, and welfare reform. Nevertheless, they differ on some major issues of concern to environmental and labor groups; for example, the extent to which oil and gas development should be allowed in western wildlands, and whether to allow the card check system for recognizing a union. Other differences, however, revolve around such narrow issues as the size of tax cuts, the degree of privatization of Social Security, whether patient rights should include the right to sue, and new prescription drug benefits.

Avoid Gross Disparities in Political "Purchasing Power"

Laws governing the political marketplace barely exist. The Constitution of the United States says nothing about political parties. Laws prohibit only a few "unfair practices" by political parties. The most specific but limited law is the Hatch Act (referring to two federal statutes, the 1939 act and the 1940 act), which restricts the permissible political activity of most federal employees. More general and of broader impact are laws about campaign fund raising that specify the size and type of contributions interest groups and citizens may make and how this money may be used. Campaign financing thus essentially determines the existence and manner of competition in the political marketplace.

As in the economic marketplace, money largely determines how much "purchasing power" each group on the demand side of the political marketplace has. Obviously, corporations, trade organizations, labor unions, and wealthy individuals have much more influence in the political marketplace than do most other groups. To preserve democratic values, however, the gap between those with large political funds and those with few or no funds must not become analogous to the well-publicized inequality between the top 10% and bottom 10% of people's income and wealth.

Campaign Finance Laws.   The purpose of the Federal Election Campaign Act amendments of 1974, as discussed in chapter 11, was to curb the influence of big money by setting limits to allowable campaign contributions by individuals, labor unions, and corporations. The overall objective of the act is congruent with the goal of increasing political competitiveness, namely, to increase the competitiveness of congressional elections so a greater number and variety of candidates can run for office.[23] However, by taking advantage of unlimited soft money contributions, campaign contributors thwarted the act's intention, with the result that money continued to play a much too significant role in elections.

Passage of the McCain-Feingold bill severely restricted soft money contributions to national political parties, but it has not stemmed the flow of money from the usual sources. A *BusinessWeek* article, "The New Fat Cats," reports "record fund-raising and record-shattering influence by the same special interests that the reforms sought to stifle."[24] It particularly refers to "super fat cats" like Peter B. Lewis and George Soros, who write megamillion-dollar checks to liberal 527 groups like America Coming Together and the Media Fund. Equally important are the "bundlers," who are high-powered executives and lobbyists who open up the taps at Wall Street firms, health care companies, manufacturers, and oil and gas companies. President Bush, for example, has 188 "Rangers" who have brought in upwards of $200,000 each, followed by 270 "Pioneers" who have raised at least $100,000.[25] Thus the impact of the law is limited because some of the new special interest groups, especially 527 groups, are new vehicles for political contributions and have simply become surrogates for political parties.

As campaigning in the 2004 elections confirms, controversy over political money will continue and new campaign finance proposals will be made, especially the controversial proposal to provide candidates with broadcast opportunities. For example, Paul S. Herrnson proposed that broadcasters be required to make free or discounted television time available, using the argument that airwaves are a public resource.[26] Even the conservative magazine *The Economist* recommended reducing "the cost of television time—the most burdensome component of campaigns—by requiring broadcasters to offer free time as a condition of getting a license."[27] Agreeing with these views, Senator John McCain, speaking before the National Press Club in November 2002, said he "would require radio and television broadcasters to provide candidate-centered programs before elections, provide vouchers for free political advertising for political candidates, and ensure that air time is available to candidates at a reasonable rate."[28] The powerful National Association of Broadcasters, however, would never stand for it and, even if passed, it is believed candidates would go on spending the same amount of time raising the same amount of money they did before.[29]

A more radical proposal is public financing of congressional candidates.[30] In addition to broadcasting time, Herrnson proposes that government provide vouchers and free postage for candidates, or at least for political parties. These measures would lessen the advantage incumbents now enjoy of using franking privileges. Incumbents already have the other advantages of inertia, seniority, name recognition, pork, perks, and patronage.

Unless there are further major scandals or political upheavals, these more radical campaign finance proposals are unlikely to gain acceptance. Differences in financial resources among political participants will continue to give some voices advantage over others. However, competition can still flourish when interest groups mobilize people power and use the power of the Internet to communicate with others and mobilize for action.

TRANSPARENCY: REPAIR THE FINANCIAL INFORMATION INFRASTRUCTURE

A competitive marketplace—whether economic or political—depends on the availability and accuracy of relevant information, known as "material facts" in the world of finance. The availability and disclosure of "full and timely" information establishes the trust needed in our economic transactions. That trust was undermined by the corporate scandals and continuing news reports of manipulation of accounting records to hide losses and inflate earnings.

Scandals Expose Fractures in the Financial Information Infrastructure

Cries for transparency have been loud and clear. Support has grown for the SEC's requirements for full and timely disclosure. On one level this involves improved communications between a corporation and its investors. However, in today's complex financial marketplace, many professional groups and institutions process, interpret, and judge information. Their role is reflected in what can be called the financial information infrastructure. It comprises seven components: (a) corporate accountants, (b) auditors, (c) lawyers, (d) boards of directors, (e) security analysts and investment bankers, (f) stock exchanges, and (g) the SEC. An examination of recent corporate scandals reveals how the failures of each component of the financial information infrastructure contributed to the corruption of information.

Corporate Accountants. They record business transactions in corporate journals and ledgers and prepare periodic and annual financial statements showing the health of the business. These accountants generally report to the chief financial officer (CFO). Together they start the supply chain of financial information. Unfortunately, the CFOs in the scandalized companies were more interested in strategic maneuvers to give the impression of profitable operations and growth than in the accuracy of information. In fact, most CFOs have backgrounds in strategic management rather than accountancy.

When accountants discover questionable entries, they are supposed to bring them to the attention of higher management. However, out of concern for keeping their jobs and being loyal to their employer, most accountants often fail to follow up on discrepancies. Some have been co-opted, as Enron demonstrated. Although Sherron Watkins, an Enron accountant, was chosen by *Time Magazine* as the "Person of The Year," as one of a trio of whistle-blowers—along with Coleen Rowley, an FBI staff attorney, and Cynthia Cooper, an accountant at WorldCom—her actual behavior was less heroic.[31] Long before she wrote her now-famous letter to Enron Chairman Kenneth Lay in 2001 warning him of the impending scandal, she had observed questionable accounting and business ethics but remained silent.[32]

Auditors. Businesses are required by law to hire certified public accountants to *certify* that the information provided by company accountants is correct. The "big five" accounting firms—now four with the demise of Arthur Andersen—represent most large corporations. The practice of auditing was started by U.S. Steel in 1903 when it hired Price, Waterhouse and has since become standard. However, over the past two decades, the truthfulness of the audited reports has deteriorated. During the 1990s bubble, the incentives for corporate managers to distort the information they provided investors grew. One incentive is the benefit that accrues from the close tie of compensation to stock prices; another is that the rewards through initial public offerings, stock options, and takeovers are huge. As a result, "Too many companies treat accounting rules the way they treat tax laws: If it isn't expressly forbidden, it's OK."[33]

Arthur Andersen, which employed 85,000 people in 84 countries, was Enron's auditing firm until its collapse. However, this auditor safeguard failed because, like many other auditing firms, Andersen became more interested in making money by offering consulting services than in performing its primary duty of checking and certifying the books. In 2001 it earned $27 million from Enron in consulting fees and other work, more than the $25 million in audit fees. Arthur Andersen, among others, allowed itself to be coopted by the companies it audited. Andersen even proposed using its own employees to serve as regular Enron accountants, seemingly oblivious to the basic idea of outside audits. The 340,000 member American Institute of Certified Public Accountants (AICPA), the purpose of which is to provide oversight and discipline auditors, failed to defend the integrity of audits and financial statements, the very underpinning of the profession, and has steadfastly opposed reform.[34]

Certified public accountants, and its professional association, the 340-member American Institute of Certified Public Accountants who had steadfastly opposed reform, lost heavily with passage of the Sarbanes–Oxley Act. By favoring consulting and other profitable services, the AICPA failed to defend the integrity of audits and financial statements, the very underpinning of the profession. Stubbornly, accountants seem not to have caught the spirit of reforms of their profession. For example, they still wanted to use off-balance-sheet entities to hide some assets and liabilities by exploiting a loophole in the rules laid down by the FASB, a practice that would obviously hinder transparency.[35]

Some auditing firms have taken the high road and engaged in advertising campaigns to announce corrective moves. The outstanding example is PriceWaterhouseCoopers, which inaugurated a "stand and be counted" advertising campaign on "how to rebuild investor confidence in America's public companies. Some of its themes are the use of audits to better detect fraud and misrepresentation, ways to improve internal controls, and the Board of Directors' role. Integrity was addressed in one ad carrying the headline, "Integrity 101, Education for the Public Trust," which then discussed the "importance of attracting new talent to the accounting and tax professions."[36] Another auditing firm, KPMG, which was accused by the SEC of accounting fraud in connection with Xerox, started an "KPMG Discussion Series. In its Issue Five, it educates companies about Section 404 of the Sarbanes-Oxley Act which adds the responsibility to corporate managements to assess and report "on the effectiveness of their internal control processes and their procedures for financial reporting."[37]

Lawyers.   At Enron, the CFO obtained advice from outside attorneys to approve of a particular accounting practice, such as "special-purpose entities," which keep liabilities off the balance sheet. An Andersen memo noted that two high-ranking partners from Vinson & Elkins LLP concluded that "the client's position" on the Raptor (a special-purpose entity used to dress up the company's earnings) restructuring was acceptable.[38] The order to the Houston office to shred thousand of records and delete tens of thousands of e-mail messages originated from Arthur Andersen's professional standards group at the firm's Chicago headquarters, but was supported by Nancy Temple, a lawyer with the firm's legal department.[39]

Law firms implicated in the Enron and other financial manipulations have generally denied wrongdoing. In contrast, after passage of the Sarbanes-Oxley Act, corporate lawyers have seized the opportunity to dwell on compliance. It was the buzz at the American Corporate Counsel Association's October 2002 annual meeting, attended by a record 2,000 in-house lawyers. It released a survey of its 12,000 members (1,200 responded) showing that 57% believed in-house counsel should play just as important a role as a company's top officers in preventing fraud and other illegal or unethical behavior. Yet, 49% complained that they were kept out of the loop on some important financial and accounting developments. In contrast, 85% said their companies' general counsel had a great deal of access to the CEO and slightly more thought they had access to the board of directors as well.[40]

Board of Directors.   The function and responsibilities of boards of directors is to hold management accountable. As Charles Elson, director of the Weinberg Center for Corporate Governance at the University of Delaware, observed: "Go back to all those corporate scandals, and it all comes down to a board that missed warning signals."[41] There is no quick fix. The relationship among a corporation, its stakeholders, and society requires rethinking.

Boards of directors neglected their fiduciary responsibility through negligence, or knowing connivance, as Arthur Andersen's former CEO Joe Berardino observed. He blamed board members for not serving as watchdogs. He said they were too disengaged and failed to ask the right questions. After making nearly 300 presentations to audit committees, he got this impression: "Nobody fell asleep, but many of them didn't understand the business. They just sat there and received reports....

Some directors just don't want to know. They might have to do something about it."[42] Corporate governance has become a major subject in the post-Enron era. It is discussed in chapter 15.

Security Analysts and Investment Bankers.   Working for brokerage firms and other buyers and sellers of stocks and bonds, security analysts are supposed to provide investors with impartial, objective advice about a company. Instead, they misled small investors by hyping research on companies that were also investment banking clients. By becoming allies of investment banks and promoters of securities, they subverted their role in the financial infrastructure.

Jack Grubman, telecom expert at Salomon Smith Barney's, a unit of Citibank, became Exhibit A. He gave the seal of approval to WorldCom and, later, AT&T, whose stocks and bonds were being sold by the investment bank unit of Citibank. The fiction of firewalls—that analysts would not talk to the investment bankers whose stock they were evaluating—was exposed when Grubman became part of the team that touted stocks. His "boosterism" statements were sometimes inconsistent with his true views, as exposed by his e-mails.[43] He became an adjunct to marketing and by so doing allowed the investment bank to make a mint while sacrificing the interests of ordinary investors. In response to this conflict of interest, Citibank proposed splitting research and investment banking.[44]

Some investment banks share the blame for the corporate scandals. For example, Citibank helped Enron disguise financing as trades to avoid booking it as debt. This unusual financing technique enabled the company to appear rich in cash rather than saddled with debt.[45] Another abuse associated with the investment companies, where many security analysts work, has been the improper doling out of coveted shares in initial public offerings to corporate executives to win their banking business, a practice of Citigroup's Salomon Smith Barney and Credit Suisse Group's Credit Suisse First Boston. William Donaldson, chairman of the SEC, commented, "I am profoundly saddened—and angry— about the conduct that's alleged in our complaints. There is absolutely no place for it in our marketplace and it cannot be tolerated."[46] He also said, "These cases reflect a sad chapter in the history of American business—a chapter in which those who reaped enormous benefits from the trust of investors profoundly betrayed that trust." Reflecting this sentiment, Paul Sarbanes (D–Md.) wondered, "How is it possible that the regulators could have missed for so long the supervisory problems at all ten of the nation's top investment firms?"

Accordingly, it was not the SEC but New York Attorney General Eliot Spitzer who has been the prime mover in exposing deception and other abuses of investors by Wall Street firms. In May 2002, he obtained a $100 million settlement from Merrill Lynch over conflicts of interest that affected its research analysts. Without acknowledging guilt, Merrill settled to place its operations above suspicion.[47] The following year, the SEC and several Wall Street firms agreed on a broader settlement which the SEC called "a pact that could change the face of Wall Street." In it 10 of the nation's largest securities firms agreed to pay a record $1.4 billion to settle government charges involving abuse of investors during the stock market boom of the 1990s.

The agreement sets new rules regarding the handling of research. Some security analysts at investment banks had presented positive reports about certain companies to the public while privately thinking otherwise. The purpose of issuing routine overly optimistic, if not deceptive, stock research to investors was to win investment bank business. The settlement now requires securities firms to have separate reporting and supervisory structure for their research and banking operations. Analysts' compensation is to be tied to the quality and accuracy of their research. Furthermore, analysts will no longer be allowed to accompany investment bankers during their "road-show" sales pitches to clients.[48]

Stock Exchanges.   Attention focused on the New York Stock Exchange (NYSE) which handles the daily purchases and sales of major companies' securities. It is essentially a private club of members who hold a seat on the exchange, but the SEC also allows it to regulate the behavior of its floor traders and member firms, such as the specialists who manage the trading of the exchange's listed stocks. Its board failed in the latter duty, as the scandal of the exorbitant pay ($140 million) of its chairman Richard A. Grasso and cozy relations with directors revealed.[49]

The NYSE was insufficiently transparent and failed to act on phony research. Its insensitivity to its public responsibility was evidenced when it invited discredited Sanford I. "Sandy" Weill, chairman and CEO of Citigroup, to represent the public on its board.[50] Its chairman, John S. Reed, also a former Citigroup chairman, is undertaking a drastic overhaul of the governing structure, but critics, including the SEC, say more is needed.[51] His plan doesn't separate the Exchange's regulatory and commercial functions, and it doesn't include a public pension fund (major users of the Exchange) representative on the board, nor does it consider replacing the specialist system in favor of an electronic trading model embraced by most other exchanges.[52] Specialists are accused of routinely placing their own trades ahead of those of customers.[53] A member of CALpers, the country's largest pension fund, says that the Reed proposal merely reorganizes rather than truly reforms, the Big Board.[54]

Securities & Exchange Commission.   The nation's rule maker and enforcer of securities and exchange regulations failed in its oversight function. Even as corporate scandals unfolded, former SEC chairman Harvey Pitt seemed more interested in protecting the interests of his former law clients in the accounting field than regulating them. For example, he held a private meeting with KPMG, his former law client, which was under SEC investigation.[55] His insensitivity to the requirements of the SEC was further revealed when he proposed William Webster, former FBI director, to head the new Public Company Accounting Oversight Board. Pitt failed to reveal that Webster had served on the audit committee of a firm, U.S. Technologies, facing fraud charges.[56] *Take on the Street*, written by Arthur Levitt, Jr., former SEC chairman, and Paula Dwyer describe how the accounting profession's power in Congress stymied his efforts at enforcement and reform.[57] Robert Kuttner, who writes a column for *BusinessWeek*, observed that in the past two decades, "free-market ideologues and self-interested Wall Street insiders" had dismantled securities regulations. "The nub of the problem," he says, "is that Wall Street and its regulators remain far too clubby."[58] Fortunately, new SEC chairman, William H. Donaldson, although a former Wall Streeter, has been getting high marks for reforming the SEC.

The Sarbanes-Oxley Act Seeks to Repair the Information Infrastructure

The main effort to rid the financial system of unethical practices and repair the badly battered financial information infrastructure is the wide-sweeping corporate oversight bill, the Sarbanes-Oxley Act, officially called the Public Company Accounting Reform Investor Protection Act of 2002. Recognizing that an economic system cannot survive when people no longer trust basic information, Congress passed this reform legislation on July 25, 2002, by an overwhelming majority (423–3 in the House and 99–0 in the Senate). Although initially opposed by most Republicans, fear of voter backlash in the coming November election left no alternative. There was a rising tide of opinion that free markets and property rights require the rule of law to function.

The act gets to the heart of the accuracy of financial reporting by establishing new accounting regulations. A newly established independent five-member Public Company Accounting Oversight Board under the jurisdiction of the SEC has the power to set auditing standards and to investigate and discipline auditors. The act also addresses the conflict of interest by an auditing firm that often makes more money providing consulting than auditing services. CEOs and CFOs are given the responsibility of certifying the authenticity of financial statements. Adding to safeguards, lawyers are required to report serious violations of securities laws. Box 14.1 outlines these and other provisions of the act.

Certified public accountants and their professional association, the AICPA, both of whom had steadfastly opposed reform, lost heavily with passage of the Sarbanes-Oxley Act. By favoring consulting and other services, the AICPA failed to defend the integrity of audits and financial statements, the very underpinning of the profession.[59]

Box 14.1 Main Provisions of the Sarbanes-Oxley Act

1. Establishes new accounting regulations. For example, it establishes an independent five-member oversight board under the jurisdiction of the SEC with investigative and disciplinary powers. The board has the power to set auditing standards and to investigate and fine auditors.

2. Places limitations on the types of consulting an auditing firm can do for a specific client so as to remove a major conflict of interest. Auditors will not be inhibited from honest reporting out of fear that the client will severe more lucrative consulting services. The law prohibits accounting firms from offering nine types of consulting services to corporate clients, including building financial-information systems. It also requires accounting firms to rotate lead or reviewing partners from client assignments every 5 years and requires auditors to be hired by and report to the audit committee of the board (not by the company managers).

3. Stiffens criminal penalties. For example, it raises the maximum penalty for securities fraud to 25 years and increases CEO and CFO penalties for false statements to the SEC or failing to certify financial reports; and establishes penalties of up to 10 years in jail for fraud and obstruction of justice involving shredding of documents.

4. Increases corporate responsibility by requiring corporate CEOs and CFOs to certify the authenticity of financial statements—or face criminal sanctions (prison terms of up to 20 years for "willingly and knowingly" permitting seriously misleading material into reports); corporate chieftains must forfeit profits and bonuses when earnings are restated due to securities fraud; prohibits executives from selling company stock during blackout periods and requires insiders to report all company stock trades within 2 days; prevents executives from receiving company loans unavailable to outsiders; requires companies to immediately disclose "in plain English" material changes in their financial conditions.

5. Creates new protections. For example, in a first-ever protection that applies to employees of all public companies, it broadens ability of whistle-blowers to sue and prohibits investment firms from retaliating against analysts who criticize clients of the firm.

6. Extends the amount of time investors have to file suits to 2 years from 1 after they have discovered an alleged fraud, and to 5 years from 3 after it occurs.

7. Sets up a restitution fund for wronged shareholders, financed by fines from any ill-gotten gains that securities regulators squeeze from wayward executives.

8. Requires lawyers for publicly traded companies to report material violations of securities laws up the chain of command, all the way to

the board if necessary. A threat of financial harm or material violation of SEC rules requires lawyers to report such matters to the SEC. Only 35% of lawyers in a survey support changing such client confidentiality rules.

9. Requires auditing firms to rotate partners who manage audits for a company every 5 years.

10. Boosts SEC budget.

THE CULTURE OF WALL STREET CHANGES SLOWLY

"What Wall Street really needs is a change in culture, starting at the very top," says *BusinessWeek*.[60] Real change may depend on taking action against senior managers, including CEOs. As stated by New York State's Attorney General Eliot Spitzer, who has spearheaded the investigation of Wall Street, "If the responsibility for these improprieties is not directly laid at the feet of senior management, then we will have failed to send a message to the right people." Corporate leaders as well as Wall Street players must be held accountable for corrupting the accuracy and availability of vital financial information and blocking reform efforts.

Corporate Leaders

The response of corporate leaders to the recent corporate scandals has mostly been silence and, sometimes, opposition. "Sadly, business lagged for years in its understanding of the political effects of corporate governance despite the pleas of savvy CEOs and public affairs professionals for corporate transparency and ethical orthodoxy," wrote Wes Pedersen, editor of *Public Affairs Review*.[61] One exception was billionaire Warren Buffett, who advised corporate chieftains to reform. In his opening address to 120 executives attending The Forum for Corporate Conscience in March 2003, he said that the need to restore corporate integrity was "vital to this country." He specifically criticized the high pay CEOs are collecting, regardless of company performance, which, he said, was undermining corporate America's image. "What really gets to the public is when CEOs get rich, really rich, and they get poorer," he said. "I think the acid test is going to be CEO compensation."[62]

Some business leaders who voiced opinions were either opposed to reforms or offered weaker remedies. For example, even before the NYSE released its far-reaching proposals to upgrade corporate governance standards, letters of protest started to pour in from at least a dozen members of the Business Roundtable, including General Mills Chairman Stephen W. Sanger.[63] When the Business Roundtable as a body took a stand, it issued a narrowly focused statement in a full-page ad that essentially said it supported: (a) "totally open" corporate financial statements—"What you see is what you get"; (b) independent corporate boards of directors, especially in audit, compensation, or governance committees; and (c) "fairness"; for example, shareholders must approve all stock option plans.[64] It didn't talk about greater responsibility of the accounting profession or a government role in achieving greater transparency of financial information. In short, it really didn't support the Sarbanes-Oxley reform bill. The Business Roundtable seems to believe that corrections made by the free market would make regulation unnecessary.

More candor by business executives would be a good place to start regaining public confidence and lessen the need for more legislative solutions. "For their own sake, it's time to break radio silence and declare their positions on what practices are proper and how the improper ones should be fixed," says Jerry Useem, a scholar of corporate governance. He quotes Jeffrey Garten, dean of the Yale School of Management and author of *The Politics of Fortune: A New Agenda for Business Leaders*, "It would take only a dozen major CEOs to give the business community a good chance of rebuilding its reputation.."[65] Seymour Trachimovsky, general counsel and corporate secretary of DuPont Canada, extends this argument in support of free market capitalism. Speaking of the CEOs role, he said, "It will take the leadership and sound judgment of senior corporate managements willing to accept accountability and willing to confront their own narcissism and hubris. This is not a job for the legislature but for business leaders with maturity and intestinal fortitude."[66]

When executives violate the law, "they have to be held individually accountable for specific crimes," argues a *Wall Street Journal* editorial.[67] The deterrent effect on executive behavior of seeing their counterparts punished is likely to be more powerful than prescriptions coming from Congress or the SEC. However, few top-echelon executives have landed in jail. It took 2 years before the prosecutors of Enron's CFO Andrew Fastow collected enough evidence to persuade him to plead guilty. He faces a 10-year prison term and forfeiture of more than $29 million, which is unusual for a white-collar crime. Enron's former treasurer Ben Glisan was also imprisoned after pleading guilty to criminal activity in doctoring Enron's financial statements to make the company look far healthier than it was.[68] Although U.S. prosecutors filed an indictment against Enron's former president and CEO Jeffrey Skilling, who arrived at a Houston courthouse in handcuffs, he pleaded "not guilty to all counts."[69] His lawyers are expected to argue that the charges are really "a general indictment of corporate business" and an attempt to "demonize some normal procedures of corporate activity."[70]

It took over two-and-a-half years before Kenneth Lay, Enron's former chairman and CEO was indicted for massive conspiracy to deceive and defraud investors. When he was led handcuffed into a Houston courthouse in July 2004, he pleaded not guilty.[71] His defense was that his CFO, Andrew Fastow, was to blame. After having previously said "I and the board are also sure that Andy has operated in the most ethical and appropriate manner possible," he changed his mind and said that Fastow had "betrayed" his trust. He added that "to the extent that I did not know what he was doing ... then indeed, I cannot take responsibility."[72] As John Budd, a veteran public relations counselor, noted, "If an executive hailed as a brilliant leader, with a PhD in economics can be so easily duped what does it portend for mere mortal CEOs?"[73] The "plausible deniability" defense has become routine among CEOs. Also calling this legal tactic the "30,000 foot" defense, "the notion is that a chief executive can't possibly be held responsible for all the goings on so far below him."[74]

In other big scandal cases, indictments and imprisonments are moving slowly. In March 2004, the federal government indited Bernard J. Ebbers, WorldCom's CEO, after Scott Sullivan, the company's former CFO, pleaded guilty; Tyco's former CFO Mark Swartz and CEO Dennis Kozlowski were on trial in a New York state court on charges of looting the company of $600 million in unauthorized compensation and illicit stock sales; and two HealthSouth executives agreed to plead guilty and former CEO Richard Scrushy went on trial in August 2004.[75] In March 2004, a jury found Martha Stewart guilty on all counts facing her, but after appealing the verdict, she decided to report to prison as soon as possible to reclaim her life.[76] Remorse by corporate leaders appears to be absent or rare, which doesn't bode well for a change in corporate culture.

Wall Street

Lawmakers examining the settlement by the SEC and several Wall Street firms alleged that the high-profile agreement with the SEC doesn't go far enough to punish wrongdoers. They said the pact hasn't done anything to change the culture of Wall Street and prevent future abuses. "Without holding executives and CEOs personally accountable for the wrongdoing that occurred under their watch, I do not believe that Wall Street will change its ways or that investors' confidence will be restored," said Richard Shelby (R-Ala.), chairman of the Senate Banking Committee. Doubt was also expressed about the adequacy of the present self-regulatory system to police the industry and enforce the new rules of the settlement. The SEC's regulatory commitment was weak, as was Donaldson's statement that his agency was committed to "vigilance" in enforcing the terms of the settlement and issuing new rules to prevent a recurrence of the problems.[77]

The SEC, however, has been reluctant to regulate Wall Street. It was only after an investigation by Spitzer that the SEC (along with the New York Stock Exchange and the NASD) took action. As former SEC chairman Arthur Levitt reported in his memoir, *Take the Street*, the SEC was often stymied by Wall Street's allies in Congress. Robert Kuttner, who writes a column for *Business Week*, observed that in the past two decades, "free-market ideologues and self-interested Wall Street insiders" had dismantled securities regulations. "The nub of the problem," he says, "is that Wall Street and its regulators remain far too clubby."[78]

Showing how difficult it is to change organizational cultures, the lessons of the settlement were initially ignored by some Wall Street firms. Chairman Philip Purcell of Morgan Stanley, one of the 10 companies in the $1.4 billion settlement, told a group of institutional investors that he didn't see anything in the settlement that would concern the retail investor about Morgan Stanley. In response, Donaldson, in a strongly worded letter, said, "Your reported comments evidence a troubling lack of contrition and lead me to wonder about Morgan Stanley's commitment to compliance with the letter and spirit of the law." He also cautioned Purcell not to deny the SEC's allegations. Purcell subsequently replied, "I deeply regret any public impression that the commission's complaint was not a matter of concern to retail investors"—a statement that falls far short of an apology.[79]

Another firm, Bear Stearns, reverted to the practice of using an analyst to promote a new stock offering when one of the firm's analysts, James Kissane, appeared in one of its promotional webcasts. SEC enforcement chief Stephen Cutler said, "It's just astonishing to me that a firm could allow an analyst to participate in a roadshow—and the fact that the prohibition on such conduct isn't literally in effect yet doesn't make me any less disappointed."[80]

Wall Street epitomizes the core ideology of capitalism, which is to maximize profits for the benefit of shareholders. However, it is also obliged to follow the rules of the marketplace as established by stock exchanges and the SEC. Wall Street is also expected to act ethically and be aware that violations of public trust inevitably lead to undesirable consequences: greater government regulation and, especially important in the financial world, a loss of public confidence in financial institutions and business in general. In his speech on the outlook of the economy in the late 1990s, Federal Reserve Chairman Alan Greenspan recognized the seriousness of the crisis of confidence, saying that an "infectious greed" had gripped business. He warned that breakdowns in corporate governance could undermine the trust necessary for efficient markets.[81]

CONCLUSIONS

Corporations must voluntarily curb their short-term drive for dominance in society and be willing to accept competition in the political marketplace. In the long run the survival of marketplace economics and the free enterprise system is at stake. Pushing back the extent of corporate influence is a never-ending effort, says the *Economist* in its 160-year anniversary article "A Survey of Capitalism and Democracy." This publication, which since its founding in 1843 by a Scottish businessman named James Wilson, has stood for liberty—especially economic liberty—states one antidote to corporate dominance: "In democracies, governments have to be the arbitrators, the counterweights to powerful private groups. But if they allow, or even encourage, companies and wealthy individuals to manipulate them, they risk stretching public faith in democracy to the breaking point."[82]

Business is urged to support a competitive political marketplace in which political parties and interest groups, by competing with one another, seek to promote their individual interests in a way that does not jeopardize the public interest. This model of competition, borrowed from economics, requires a free flow of "full and timely" information so that everyone can make efficient decisions. In addition to the news media, the entire financial information infrastructure must help produce and distribute needed information. The failures exposed by the Enron-era scandals can be corrected by improving on the rules of the game, changing organizational structures and cultures, and recognizing the needed function of government in enforcing the rules.

To mitigate public fears that corporations have too much power, corporations must show that they are willing to change their organizational cultures and comply with the rules of the financial marketplace. However, as the experience of the almost-forgotten savings-and-loan scandal in the early 1980s demonstrated, business sometimes seems incapable of reforming itself unless prodded by the government. This experience should convince businesspeople as well as the public that laissez faire has its limitations. The self-correcting mechanisms of the marketplace need prodding; market excesses don't necessarily correct themselves. Government has the responsibility to assure the public that companies do not take advantage of their market power.

ENDNOTES

1. Some theorists envision an organizational chart with two senior vice presidents: one in charge of operations (representing the economic marketplace), and the other in charge of public policy. See chart in W. Howard Chase, *Issue Management: Origins of the Future* (Stamford, Conn.: Issue Action Publications, Inc., 1984), pp. 36–37.
2. Robert D. McTeer, Jr., "The Dismal Science? Hardly!" *Wall Street Journal*, June 4, 2003, p. A16.
3. The Sherman Act is designed to preserve competition by declaring illegal "any contract, combination in the form of trust or otherwise, or conspiracy, in restraint of trade or commerce among the several states, or with foreign nations." Without this safeguard, profit maximization would inevitably lead to cutthroat competition, defined by one economist as a "ruthless, savage war to the death, waged without rules of fairness or reasonableness, and legitimate as long as it promotes the interest of the person practicing it." When a competitor is too successful in the economic marketplace and comes close to achieving a monopoly, the government intervenes, sometimes by imposing draconian solutions, as illustrated by the breakup of Standard Oil of New Jersey in 1911.

4. The Clayton Act reinforces the Sherman Act by curbing the use of unfair methods of competition: "Competition must be made an orderly, regulated process, conducted according to rules of fair play, for otherwise it will not perform its social purpose of providing more and better goods at lower prices."

5. Alfred Marshall, the well-known classical economist, gives this definition of a market: "the whole of any region in which buyers and sellers are in such free intercourse with one another that the price of the same goods tend to equality easily and quickly." See his *Principles of Economics*, 8th edition (London: Macmillan, 1947), p. 324.

6. Unless one takes the cynical view that lawmakers extract a "price" for choosing and processing a public policy demanded by some voters and their interest groups, in which case those who propose a law would have to decide how much they are willing to bid to obtain legislative action. The rise in soft money contributions supports this view.

7. The intensity of public opinion can be seen as the equivalent of the elasticity of demand; for example, people who feel strongly about an issue would be more fervent supporters of a public policy.

8. Barry M. Mitnick, editor, *Corporate Political Agency: The Construction of Competition in Public Affairs* (Newbury Park, Calif.: Sage, 1993), p. 24.

9. Ibid., p. 25.

10. Ibid., p. 32. Quoted by Mitnick as appearing in Andrew Hacker, "Introduction: Corporate America," in Andrew Hacker, editor, *The Corporation Take-Over* (New York: Harper & Row, 1964), pp. 7–8.

11. Mitnick calls such a system one of "contestable competition"—whereby all participants have the resources that enable them to compete effectively in the political process; op. cit., pp. 12, 24.

12. Stephanie Simon, "Nader Suits up to Strike Back Against 'Slapps,'" *Wall Street Journal*, July 9, 1991, p. B1.

13. Aaron Bernstein, "All's Not Fair in Labor War," *BusinessWeek*, July 19, 1999, p. 43.

14. Harley Shaiken, "Labor's Decline Has Meant Wages' Decline," *Los Angles Times*, March 8, 1998, p. M5.

15. Aaron Bernstein, "A Shot in the Foot?," *BusinessWeek*, May 4, 1998, p. 52.

16. An argument made by Orrin Baird, "Labor's Right to Speak Under Attack," *Legal Times*, May 18, 1998, p. S34.

17. Vernon A. Mund, *Government and Business* (New York: Harper, 1950), p. 7.

18. Stated on *Lehrer Newshour*, November 19, 2003.

19. Rebecca Smith, "Blackout Could Have Been Avoided," *Wall Street Journal*, April 6, 2004, p. A6.

20. Arthur Schlesinger, Jr., "Government Isn't the Root of All Evil," *Wall Street Journal*, January 30, 1998, p. A14.

21. Paul Starobin, "Rethinking Capitalism," *National Journal*, Vol. 29, January 18, 1997, p. 106.

22. Jay M. Shafritz, *The Dorsey Dictionary of American Government and Politics* (Chicago: The Dorsey Press, 1988), p. 417.

23. Herrnson includes the further objectives of improving the accountability of the electoral process, enhancing representation in Congress, and endeavoring to increase the legitimacy of the election system in the eyes of citizens; op. cit., p. 234.

24. Paula Dwyer, Robert D. Hof, Jim Kerstetter, and Ronald Grover, "The New Fat Cats," *BusinessWeek*, April 12, 2004, p. 32.

25. Ibid., p. 34.

26. Paul S. Herrnson, *Congressional Elections: Campaigning at Home and in Washington*, 2nd edition (Washington, D.C.: Congressional Quarterly Press, 1998), pp. 190–195.

27. "Goodbye, Soft Money," *Economist*, April 7, 2001, p. 22.

28. "Campaign Finance Reform," Federal News Service, November 14, 2002.

29. Ellen Miller and Nick Penniman, "The Road to Nowhere; Thirty Years of Campaign-Finance Reform Yield Precious Little," *The American Prospect*, August 12, 2002, p. 14.

30. Eliza Newlin Carney, "The Soft-Money Battle Turns Bitter," *National Journal*, Vol. 34, July 6, 2002, pp. 2028–2029.

31. Dan Ackman, "Whistleblower?" *Wall Street Journal*, December 24, 2002, p. A10.

32. Wendy Zellner, "An Insider's Tale of Enron's Toxic Culture," *BusinessWeek*, March 31, 2003, p. 16.

33. David Wessel, "Capital: When Standards Are Unacceptable," *Wall Street Journal*, February 7, 2002, p. A1.

34. David Henry and Mike McNamee, "Bloodied and Bowed," *BusinessWeek*, January 20, 2003, pp. 56–57.

35. David Henry, "Commentary: An End Run Around Accounting Reform," *BusinessWeek*, April 28, 2003, p. 85.

36. *Wall Street Journal*, April 2, 2003, p. A5.

37. See ad, "A mandate or a smart business practice," in *Wall Street Journal*, February 24, 2003, p. A15.

38. "Enron: The Case Against Skilling," *BusinessWeek*, March 1, 2004, p. 35.

39. Kurt Eichenwald, "Andersen Guilty in Effort to Block Inquiry on Enron," *New York Times*, June 16, 2002, p. YNE-1; Michael Schroeder and Tom Hamburger, "Congressional Panel Investigates Andersen's," *Wall Street Journal*, January 14, 2002, p. 3.

40. John Gibeaut, "Fear and Loathing in Corporation America," *ABA Journal*, January 2003.

41. Kurt Eichenwald, "In String of Corporate Troubles, Critics Focus on Boards' Failings," *New York Times*, September 21, 2003, p. 1.

42. John A. Byrne, "Fall from Grace," BusinessWeek, August 12, 2002, pp. 50–56.

43. Charles Gasparino, "Analyst Pack Is Held up by Words," *Wall Street Journal*, January 16, 2003, p. C1.

44. Charles Gasparino, Susan Pulliam and Randall Smith, "Citigroup Proposes Pact Splitting Research and Investment Banking," *Wall Street Journal*, September 27, 2002, p. A1.

45. Jathon Sapsford and Paul Beckett, "Citigroup Deals Helped Enron Disguise Its Debts as Trades," *Wall Street Journal*, July 22, 2002, p. A1.

46. Randall Smith, Susanne Craig, and Deborah Solomon, "Wall Street Firms to Pay $1.4 Billion to End Inquiry," *Wall Street Journal*, April 29, 2003, p. A1.

47. "Wall Street: Merrill Settles," *Economist*, May 25, 2002, p. 72.

48. Smith, Craig, and Solomon, op. cit., p. A6.

49. See Gary Weiss, "The $140,000,000 Man," *BusinessWeek*, September 15, 2003, p. 84.

50. Paula Dwyer, "Commentary: Why the Market Can't Police Itself," *BusinessWeek*, June 2, 2003, p. 84.

51. Gary Weiss, "NYSE: How Deep Will Reform Run? BusinessWeek, November 10, 2003, p. 48. Also see Deborah Solomon and Susanne Craig, "Market Discipline: SEC Blasts Big Board Oversight of 'Specialist' Trading Firms," *Wall Street Journal*, November 3, 2003, p. A1.

52. Paula Dwyer, et al., "The Big Board's Blueprint: Done Deal?" *BusinessWeek*, November 24, 2003, pp. 45–46.

53. Solomon and Craig, op. cit.

54. Susanne Craig and Ianthe Jeanne Dugan, "NYSE Begins Its Huge Overhaul," *Wall Street Journal*, November 9, 2003, p. C11.

55. Scot J. Paltrow, "Concerns About SEC Chairman Mount," *Wall Street Journal*, May 6, 2002, p. C1.

56. Michael Schroeder, "Regulator Under Fire: As Pitt Launches SEC Probe of Himself, Criticism Mounts," *Wall Street Journal*, November 1, 2002, p. A1.

57. See a book excerpt, "Arthur Levitt's Crusade," *BusinessWeek*, September 30, 2002, p. 74.

58. Robert Kuttner, "Wake Up, Wall Street: Eliot Spitzer Is a Hero," *BusinessWeek*, May 19, 2003, p. 24.

59. Henry and McNamee, op. cit.

60. Paul Dwyer, with Mike McNamee, Emily Thornton and Nanette Byrnes, "Will It Matter?" *Business Week*, May 12, 2003, p. 31.

61. Wes Pedersen, "As Election '04 Nears, New Calls for an Examination of the Corporate Soul," *Public Affairs Review*, annual report, 2004, p. 4.

62. Paul Nowell, "Execs Talk Corporate Integrity at Forum," Associated Press Online, March 2003.

63. John A. Byrne, "Restoring Trust in Corporate America," *BusinessWeek*, June 24, 2002, p. 31.

64. Ads in *Wall Street Journal*, July 8, 2002, p. A5, and July 9, 2002, p. A11.

65. Jerry Useem, "From Heroes to Goats and Back Again? How Corporate Leaders Lost Our Trust," *Fortune*, November 18, 2002, p. 48.

66. Seymour Trachimovsky, "Sarbanes Oxley and Canadian Counterparts: Any Prospects for Improved Corporate Ethics," *Management Ethics*, Fall 2003, pp. 1–3.

67. Editorial, "Enron Justice," *Wall Street Journal*, January 15, 2004, p. A14.

68. John R. Emshwiller, "Ex-Treasurer Is First Enron Officer to Go to Prison," *Wall Street Journal*, September 11, 2003, p. A3.

69. John R. Emshwiller and Alexei Barrionnevo, "U.S. Prosecutors File Indictment Against Skilling," *Wall Street Journal*, February 20, 2004, p. A1.

70. Ibid., p. A13.

71. John R. Rmshwiller et al., "Lay Strikes Back as Indictment Cites Narrow Role in Enron Fraud," *Wall Street Journal*, July 9, 2004, p. A1.

72. Alan Murray, "CEO Responsibility Might Be Right Cure for Corporate World," *Wall Street Journal*, July 13, 2004, p. A4.

73. "Lay Pleads Ignorance: CEOs Shudder," *Observations*, a news

74. Susan Pulliam, "The 'It Wasn't Me' Defense," *Wall Street Journal*, July 9, 2004, p. B1.

75. Susan Pulliam, Almar Latour and Ken Brown, "Reaching the Top: U.S. Indicts WorldCom Chief Ebbers," *Wall Street Journal*, March 3, 2004, p. A1.

76. Keith Naughton and Barney Gimbel, "Martha's Fall," *Newsweek*, March 15, 2004, pp. 28–37. James Bandler, Kara Scannell, and Suzanne Vranica, "Martha Opts for Jail Now," *Wall Street Journal*, September 16, 2004, p. B6.

77. Deborah Solomon and Randall Smith, "Wall Street's Deal Comes Under Fire," *Wall Street Journal*, May 8, 2003, p. C1.

78. Robert Kuttner, "Wake up, Wall Street: Eliot Spitzer Is a Hero," *BusinessWeek*, May 19, 2003, p. 24.

79. Deborah Solomon, "Morgan Stanley Remarks Draw Criticism by SEC," *Wall Street Journal*, May 2, 2003, p. C8; Amy Borrus and Mike McNamee,

"Commentary: Go Ahead, Make the SEC's Day," *BusinessWeek*, June 2, 2003, p. 27.

80. Ann Davis, "Bear Stearns Used Analyst to Tout IPO Despite Pact With Regulators," *Wall Street Journal*, May 12, 2003, p. A1.

81. Greg Ip, "Greenspan Issues Hopeful Outlook as Stocks Sink," *Wall Street Journal*, July 17, 2002, p. A1.

82. "A Survey of Capitalism and Democracy," *Economist*, June 28, 2003, p. 16.

Chapter 15

Heed the Public Interest

The political marketplace is where public policy decisions are made. These decisions provide the framework within which individual businesses operate and determine in what activities government should or should not engage. Government protects the liberty of its citizens, sets the rules of the game that businesses must follow, and operates a system of economic institutions, such as private property. It is also generally agreed that so-called public goods and services—such as police protection and national security, city streets, roads, and other facilities that can't be sold as individual units—should be provided by government.[1]

Public policy decisions are guided by the criterion of what is in the public interest. All participants in the public policy process, including corporations and interest groups and not only government, claim that what they seek is in the public interest. But what does that mean? Henry Mintzberg in *Power in and Around Organizations* rightfully recognizes that even regulatory agencies typically lack an adequate definition of the public interest and are therefore unsure of what to do.[2] The public interest is simply defined as what is good for the public as a whole. The ostensible concern is with broad societal interests rather than private interests. Those representing the latter will, of course, argue that what they seek is in the public interest. The distinguishing feature of the public interest from a corporate viewpoint is that the frame of reference is not the individual organization but what is external to it: the physical environment, the local community, and the welfare of society as a whole.

A generation ago the leading CEOs were public-minded statesmen who were comfortable addressing big public policy questions about business's role in society. Reginald Jones, former chairman and CEO of GE, was one of them, as his belief indicates:

Public policy and social issues are no longer adjuncts to business planning and management. They are in the mainstream of it. The concern must be pervasive in companies today, from boardroom to factory floor. Management must be measured for performance in noneconomic and economic areas alike. And top management must lead.

This statement was part of the Business Roundtable's October 1981 *Statement on Corporate Responsibility,* which said: "The Business Roundtable issues this statement out of a strong conviction that the future of this nation depends upon the existence of strong and responsive business enterprises and that, in turn, the long-term viability of the business sector is linked to its responsibility to the society of which it is a part."[3] Reginald Jones was not blind to Wall Street pressures. Shortly after retiring in 1981, he told *U.S. News & World Report,* "Too many managers feel under pressure to concentrate on the short term in order to satisfy the financial community and the owners of the enterprise—the stockholders.... Boards of directors have to understand that they must shelter management from these pressures." And he added, "They should do it in the interest of the nation."[4]

Before the 1980s, CEOs seemed to listen more closely to their public relations advisors, many of whom held vice presidential status and had the confidence of the CEO. These advisors paid close attention to public opinion and subscribed to Abraham Lincoln's famous statement: "Public sentiment is everything. With public sentiment, nothing can fail; without it, nothing can succeed." Public relations people spoke about the importance of the intangible asset called goodwill,[5] which would provide some respite from a bad press or a crisis. However, as Wall Street pressures mounted, often accelerated by hostile takeovers of companies that didn't maximize profits sufficiently, public relations was challenged by marketing people and others whose focus was almost entirely on the singular bottom line. It took at least another two decades for companies to recognize the double bottom line, which added social responsibility.

Helping to raise corporate awareness of the importance of the public interest is the Public Affairs Council, an outstanding professional organization that has recognized the necessity for greater corporate social responsibility and ethical behavior. Its 45th Anniversary Report concludes with a section on "Ethical Guidelines" and ends with this admonition: "The public affairs professional ... understands the interrelation of business interests with the larger public interests, and therefore:

- Endeavors to ensure that responsible and diverse external interests and views concerning the need of society are considered within the corporate decision-making process.
- Bears the responsibility for management review of public policies which may bring corporate interests into conflict with other interests.

- Acknowledges dual obligations—to advocate the interests of his or her employer, and to preserve the openness and integrity of the democratic process.
- Presents to his or her employer an accurate assessment of the political and social realities that may affect corporate operations."[6]

In sum, the corporate attitude toward greater public responsibility has changed. As stated by Lord John Browne, group chief of British Petroleum, "Companies can't thrive in isolation. We are part of society and we are dependent on its success. We have to invest in the development of society if we want to ensure that we can do business successfully over 30 years or more."[7]

As such statements suggest, management is increasingly under pressure to heed the public interest. This chapter discusses three major strategies to achieve that goal: (a) embracing corporate social responsibility, (b) engaging in stakeholder relationships, and (c) incorporating the public interest in corporate governance.

EMBRACING CORPORATE SOCIAL RESPONSIBILITY

Definitions of corporate social responsibility (CSR) are often similar to the concept of the public interest. Writing about business and society, Keith Davis and Robert L. Blomstrom said, "The idea of social responsibility is that decision-makers are obligated to take actions which protect and improve the welfare of society as a whole along with their own interests."[8] In one way or another, most definitions state that the objectives and values of society must be considered in conducting a company's business.[9] Unfortunately, however, CSR has largely been viewed as an autonomous activity unrelated to business operations that was associated with "do good" programs and philanthropy; for example, writing checks to worthy charitable organizations and their causes. At best such gestures served to improve a company's and CEO's image, which in turn was said to help sell products, recruit workers, and aid lobbying.

During the 1980s, this mainly altruistic type of philanthropy was replaced by the new concept of strategic philanthropy. Every contribution was measured against the test of whether it advanced corporate goals. Mutual benefit—not only helping various beneficiaries but also the company—became the chief justification of social expenditures. Whenever possible, a company would also seek to reap "private benefits" rather than benefitting all companies, especially the "free loaders."

However, to some managers and academics even this version of strategic philanthropy inadequately addressed corporate self-interest because its connection to a company's business was vague or tenuous. Instead of talking about generating goodwill and positive publicity and boosting employee morale, the goal of strategic philanthropy should instead be to enhance a company's ability to compete, declared Michael

Porter of the Harvard Business School. He says that true strategic giving "addresses important social and economic goals simultaneously, targeting areas of competitive context where the company and society both benefit because the firm brings unique assets and expertise."[10] Even cause-related marketing lacks strategic intent, he says, because it is essentially a form of strategic philanthropy used to improve the reputation of a company by "linking its identity with the admired qualities of a chosen non-profit partner or a popular cause."[11] Porter's more focused approach acknowledges the importance of CSR and anticipates some of the criteria a company should use in applying it. The larger significance of modern strategic philanthropy is that CSR has been reconnected to overall management decision making.

Climbing the Pyramid of CSR

Many approaches have been taken to describe the specifics of CSR. For example, in his *Corporate Social Responsibility*, Chris Marsden lists these imperatives: (a) running business activity safely, legally, and effectively; (b) minimizing adverse impact on community and society (i.e., do no harm); and (c) do good by addressing those social issues that impact the corporation's activity, are within the corporation's competence to influence, and offer opportunities for mutual benefit.[12] Expanding on this scheme, the pyramid of CSR, as shown in Box 15.1, places the meanings of CSR on five levels of corporate involvement, ranging from a minimum level of simply performing its basic economic function to heeding the public interest in the fullest sense.

Each step up the pyramid represents an advance in corporate social responsiveness to the surrounding environment. As Robert W. Ackerman and Raymond A. Bauer recognized, it takes many years for management to recognize a problem, formulate new policies, engage in specialized and administrative learning, and, finally, change the organization.[13]

Level 1: Perform Basic Economic Function.   Forty years ago, widely respected conservative economist Milton Friedman stated, "There is one and only one social responsibility of business—to use its resources and engage in activities designed to increase its profits so long as it stays within the rules of the game, which is to say, engages in open and free competition, without deception or fraud."[14] Making as much money for their stockholders was the sole objective of business; doing more was a fundamental subversive doctrine. This exceedingly limited view of social responsibility does not even recognize society's expectations of business, namely, to provide goods and services.

Perhaps his ideal model of a CEO would be Albert J. Dunlap, a former parachuter, who symbolized the benefits and perils of a fixation on the bottom line and stockholder value (see Box 15.2).

The 1980s mistakenly extended Friedman's singular corporate goal of making money for stockholders into a "greed is good" ideology. For-

Box 15.1 The Pyramid of CSR

5. Support
public policies that
are in the public interest.

4. Make social investments to
strengthen society's infrastructure.

3. Help solve social problems.

2. Minimize the social costs imposed on society.

1. Perform basic economic function of producing goods
and services for society, and, thereby, also provide jobs.

Box 15.2 "Chainsaw Al": A Narrow View of Social Responsibility

Albert Dunlap was known as "Chainsaw Al" because his prescription for achieving results was to apply what *The Economist* called "the patented two-pronged strategy" of firing half the workforce then berating the other half. After taking over Scott Paper in 1994, he fired 11,200 employees, about a third of the workforce. But benefits abounded for stockholders: In only 20 months, Dunlap sold Scott Paper to Kimberly-Clark at a price that gave stockholders a 225% increase in the value of their stock. His disdain of corporate responsibility was symbolized by his cancellation of a charitable gift to the Philadelphia Museum. As Dunlap said, "If you want a friend, get a dog." His view is reflected in the title of his book, *Mean Business*. His approach was so highly regarded on Wall Street that when it was announced that Al Dunlap had been hired as CEO of Sunbeam, the company's share rose by half.

Although some of this downsizing was necessary to make companies more competitive in the global marketplace, it can be argued that managers were relying too heavily on the time-tested remedy of cost cutting rather than inventing new remedies and attempting to transform their companies. Even Wall Street retreated from the chainsaw approach as it saw its limitations. At first Wall Streeters like billionaire financier Ronald O. Perelman and influential mutual-fund manager Michael Price cheered him on and placed him in charge of the underperforming Sunbeam. Here Dunlap repeated the old pattern. Stock prices immediately jumped nearly 50%, from $12 ½ to $18 5/8, and in about 8 months reached a high of $52. After 2 years in office, the board fired him. Although he succeeded in slashing cost—eliminating about half of 12,000 jobs—he wasn't able to deliver on his promise to transform the company into a high-growth profit machine. Stock prices had tumbled to $8 13/16 about a week after his departure, below the level when Dunlap took over.

gotten was Friedman's condition that the rules of the game be followed, without deception or fraud. Freedom from moral constraints led to a national scandal of the savings-and-loan industry in the mid-1980s, causing the biggest financial mess in U.S. history.[15] Loose morality also led to deceptive practices by some well-known companies, such as Prudential Insurance of America, the nation's biggest insurer, and Metropolitan Life Insurance, the nation's second biggest life insurer. These insurance company scandals revealed how agents allegedly defrauded their policyholders through a practice called *churning*, whereby agents persuade customers who have old policies with built-up cash value to take out new, bigger policies on the false promise that the added coverage will cost little, if anything.[16] One of the basic meanings of social responsibility was violated: not doing harm to others.

Level 2: Minimize Social Costs.   Business can usually make higher profits by ignoring the harm done to others and to the environment as it obtains resources and engages in manufacturing. The concept of social costs considers the social consequences of corporate products and actions, such as the impact of a product on the health of people or the impact of excessive sex and violence in movies and television on social morality and stability. Mostly, however, the emphasis has been on environmental damage.

In the early days of the Industrial Revolution, plant location was often decided on the basis of cheap ways of disposing of the wastes of production and little if any thought was given to the depletion of natural resources. As the authors of *Natural Capitalism* point out, "Humankind has inherited a 3.8-billion-year store of natural capital. At the present rates of use and degradation, there will be little left by the end of the next century."[17] Their concept of natural capitalism states that "the environment is not a minor factor of production but rather is 'an envelope containing, provisioning, and sustaining the entire economy.'"[18]

A company's responsibility to address environmental damage was recognized by British Petroleum group chief executive Lord John Browne in a speech given at Stanford University on May 19, 1997. In addressing the global warming issue, he remarked, "It is a moment for change and a rethinking of corporation responsibility." Although acknowledging that the scientific evidence about the link between greenhouse gas emissions and an increase in temperature is inconclusive, he said the risk was great enough to "take precautionary action" and that under his watch, British Petroleum would help take "responsibility for the future of the planet."[19]

Level 3: Help Solve Social Problems.   Society's social problems are numerous and tenacious. They include such problems as drug and alcohol abuse, illiteracy, poverty, unemployment, employment discrimination, inadequate housing, crime, poor transportation, and deficiencies in the educational system. One use of issues management is to identify urgent social problems. Under the old division of labor in society, these problems were assigned to government and nonprofit organizations. However, this approach is inadequate for three reasons: (a) business is sometimes the cause of some social problems, (b) it is affected by some of them, and (c) it can help address some of them.

A particular company must determine which problems to address alone and which require a partnership with other companies and with government and nonprofits. Companies have developed guidelines to help them choose the social problems that are most relevant to them and that—by virtue of their line of business, resources, and competencies—they are best equipped to handle.

Level 4: Make Social Investments.   Social investments refer to programs that replenish and strengthen the community's and society's infrastructure; that is, the external resources that business depends on to conduct business. Included are physical resources like roads and other transportation facilities, water and other utilities, a sound educational system that provides a pool of labor, housing, medical facilities, and social services. The meaning of infrastructure has expanded over the years, so that it includes such assets as cultural amenities that improve the quality of life.

Responsibility for major infrastructure, such as roads, falls mainly on government because of the huge funds required and the nature of "public goods"; that is, they are available to all and would be difficult to charge for. Oil and mining companies know, however, that when they must locate in remote regions where resources are found, the responsibility for all infrastructure is theirs. In underdeveloped areas, companies may also bear some costs for infrastructure they need. After discovering oil in the sub-Saharan country of Chad, an ExxonMobil-led consortium spent $3.5 billion to build an entire community and a 663-mile pipeline from Kome, Chad, to a port in neighboring Cameroon.[20] In China, a high-tech company agreed with a local mayor to pave roads and build bridges because the community could not afford these projects.[21]

Business can help build society's infrastructure. The life and health insurance industry, for example, has for many years followed the social policy of setting aside some funds to be used for what they explicitly call social investments. These were defined as "those which would not otherwise be made under the company's customary lending standards, or those in which social considerations played a substantial part in the investment decisions." These funds were made available at lower than market rates. Projects included an inner-city health center that provides 24-hour emergency service; rehabilitation of several hundred vandalized homes, providing housing for inflation-squeezed middle-income families; and preservation and restoration of a historic marketplace.[22] Other examples of social investments are described in Box 15.3.

Box 15.3 Examples of Company Social Investments

Cisco Systems invested in the Cisco Networking Academy, with the objective of training computer network administrators. Michael Porter says it exemplifies the powerful link between a company's philanthropic strategy, its competitive context, and social benefits. The program is relevant because Cisco, as the leading producer of networking equipment and routers used to connect computers to the Internet, was able to address a limiting factor to its growth, namely, the problem of a chronic shortage of qualified network administrators. After working with a high school near its headquarters it developed a Web-based distance-learning curriculum to train and certify secondary and postsecondary school students in network administration. It also worked with the United Nations to expand the effort to developing countries, adding to their infrastructure. With its obvious specialized expertise, Cisco was able to create a high-quality curriculum rapidly and cost-effectively. Several leading technology companies joined the effort by donating or discounting products and services of their own, such as Internet access and computer hardware and software. After 5 years, it operated 9,900 academies in secondary schools, community colleges, and community-based organizations in all 50 states and in 147 countries.

Pfizer donated its cost-effective treatment for the prevention of trachoma, the leading cause of preventable blindness in developing countries. Working with the Edna McConnell Clark Foundation and world health organizations, it created the infrastructure needed to prescribe and distribute the treatment to previously relatively inaccessible populations. The program was expanded when the Bill and Melinda Gates Foundation and the British government joined as partners.

FleetBoston Financial launched its Community Renaissance Initiative to help in the inner-city economic revitalization, especially in its major markets in older East Coast cities. It combined its philanthropic contributions with its expertise in financial services, such as small business services, inner-city lending, home mortgages, and venture capital. The bank's foundation chose six communities where the bank had a presence and committed $725,000 to each and built a coalition of local community, business, and government organizations to work on issues identified by the community as central to its revitalization. The foundation amplified its own $4.5 million investment by attracting $6 million from private and municipal sources.

Level 5: Support Policies That Are in the Public Interest.   A company can support policies that are in the public interest and generally agreed on in society, such as energy conservation and human rights. Manufacturers of appliances, for example, would strive to achieve maximum efficiency standards. In making building loans, insurance companies would mandate certain insulation requirements and nondiscrimination in choosing tenants. When business doesn't strive to reach such standards, these requirements are sometimes imposed by states and localities. Some are passing stringent energy codes for new commercial buildings, which is causing designers to consider natural light as a way to save electricity.[23]

Most nations of the world would include human rights as a high-priority public policy issue. Yet many business executives believe they have no particular responsibility for human rights. When DuPont chairman Edgar S. Woolard met with the Chinese president in the summer of 1994, he commented that it "is inappropriate for business people to be involved when governments are involved on this issue."[24] Deciding what behaviors touch on human rights is itself a thorny issue. With reference to China, the American Chamber of Commerce in Hong Kong (AmCham) believes in a strong and direct pledge to "refuse to do business with firms which employ forced labor, or treat their workers in inhumane or unsafe ways." AmCham, Human Rights Watch, and others propose that a corporation is responsible to:

• Maintain acceptable working conditions in its own operations and uphold the rights of its employees to freedom of expression.
• Take responsibility for the actions of its business partners in such matters as employment practices, wages and benefits, working hours, use of child labor, use of prison labor or forced labor, discrimination and disciplinary practices.
• Resist pressure from the Chinese government to use the multinational corporation as a vehicle to abuse human rights, for example, by not hiring (or rehiring) employees who are punished by withholding jobs from them.[25]

The loftiest and most controversial view of this fifth level of social responsibility is that corporations should aspire to build a just society. It is the societal equivalent of the highest level on Maslow's hierarchy of needs, namely, self-achievement. This view was expressed by well-known public relations counselor David Finn in his *The Corporate Oligarch:*

> But there is no reason why the primary goal of management cannot eventually be defined as the utilization of corporate resources for the service of public interests in every way possible. This will require putting the old maxims of profit, growth and corporate benefit where they truly belong, in the junkyard of outmoded symbols, and in their place, raising a new standard which will make it clear that the corporate oligarch's mission is to build a just society capable of fulfilling the potentialities of its citizens.[26]

This noble and visionary statement should inspire business to climb as far as they can on the pyramid of social responsibility. How far a corporation can climb will depend not only on a corporation's philosophy but on the sociopolitical, as well as economic, pressures that surround it.

Growing Support for CSR and Ethics Programs

Some major public relations agencies and ethics centers are advising corporate clients on CSR and the related subject of ethics. One of them is Burson-Marsteller, which created a CSR unit in its London office with a full-time managing director of corporate responsibility, Bennett Freeman.[27] Another public relations counselor is Robert L. Dilenschneider, head of the Dilenschneider group and former head of the giant public relations firm of Hill & Knowlton. In writing about the challenges facing business in the new millennium, he stated, "But the bigger challenge will be mustering the courage to insist that all organizations adopt a broader, more socially conscious view of their company's responsibilities to their employees, their customers, and the communities in which they operate."[28]

Ethics programs in business are also enjoying a boom. The subject is suddenly all the rage, reports the *Economist*.[29] Aside from restoring public confidence, companies are motivated to act ethically for many reasons: ethical investors demand it; employees feel better working for socially responsible companies; bad behavior might stir up a public fuss and lead to unwanted legislation; and, finally, companies need to command a reputation for trust in dealing with customers and partners. These pressures help explain why the Ethics Officer Association, formed in the United States in 1992, today has 650 members and why more books are being written about ethics.[30] One is Lynn W. Paine's new book, *Value Shift*, which argues that companies can't consider themselves amoral or apart from society any more and that the relationship between companies and society at large necessitates bringing a moral dimension to decision making.[31]

Michael Hoffman, executive director of the Center for Business Ethics at Bentley College, saw Enron's collapse as a "success story for the importance of business ethics." He observed that Enron's four stated company values—communication, integrity, respect, and excellence—and code of ethics, were "words, with no substance."[32] Nevertheless, business has crafted more words. In December 2002, leaders from about two dozen U.S. companies announced the formation of a group to set ethical guidelines for the American business world. Called The Open Compliance and Ethics Group, the group will create a suggested "blueprint" for financial employees and environmental standards.[33] Hopefully, plans will be translated into action.

ENGAGING IN STAKEHOLDER RELATIONSHIPS

The need to develop and strengthen relationships with an organization's primary stakeholders—investors, employees, community citizens, and customers—is widely recognized. Excellent stakeholder relationships contribute to goodwill, that accounting term included under intangible assets in a firm's balance sheet. In the new economy, these assets are often more important than physical assets in determining a company's market value. A 1997 study by Ernst & Young titled *Measures That Matter* found that up to 65% of the investment decisions made by mutual fund managers were based on these intangible assets as compared to company financial information.

Corporations that build relationships are more likely to succeed. Samuel B. Graves and Sandra A. Waddock call them "visionary companies" and "built-to-last companies" and say that they focus on more than profits by treating their multiple stakeholders generously. They refer to a study that shows that these companies outperform others both financially and in the ways they treat other primary stakeholders—employees, customers, and community members—as well as showing a concern for the environment.[34] Graves and Waddock say that having an immutable core ideology, while also stimulating progress with audacious goals that change over time, is the essence of a visionary company. This core ideology consists of "end values," such as integrity, service, helping humanity, meritocracy, valuing people, improving the quality of life, making contributions, and alleviating pain and disease. Additional core values are reflected in the description of 18 visionary companies listed in the study (e.g, 3M's innovation and integrity, Johnson and Johnson's hierarchy of responsibilities to a range of stakeholders, and Merck's preserving and improving human life.

The claim that stakeholder relations results in better financial performance in terms of return on equity, return on assets, and return on sales can be extended to include an increase in the intangible asset of goodwill. A firm's public standing—its reputation—is enhanced when it is perceived as operating in the interests of multiple stakeholders, and not only its investors.

Subscribing to the Managerial Creed

The idea of balancing the interests of a wide range of stakeholders is a business ideology called the managerial creed, which asks that management serve as a trustee for all of a corporation's stakeholders. This creed differs from the opposing classical creed, which states that management's responsibility is solely to investors; that is, to maximize shareholder value. This was the prevailing creed during the ebullient 1990s. Although supporters of the classical creed conveniently assume that the interests of other stakeholders are automatically satisfied by the marketplace, this has not happened. The extreme example is "Chainsaw Al," previously described in Box 15.2.

Acceptance of the managerial creed is likely to grow because public opinion surveys show that Americans do not support the classical creed.

They reject the notion that "U.S. corporations should have only one purpose—to make the most profit for their shareholders—and their pursuit of that goal will be best for America in the long run." Only 4% of Americans subscribe to this ideology. What the overwhelming 95% say is: "U.S. corporations should have more than one purpose. They also owe something to their workers and the communities in which they operate, and they should sometimes sacrifice some profit for the sake of making things better for their workers and communities."[35]

The deluge of corporate scandals has shown that CEOs and other corporate insiders didn't even subscribe to the classical creed of raising shareholder value; their concern was self-enrichment. The public interest was in no way heeded. Support for the free enterprise system cannot endure if the public sees corporate leaders as selfish and exploitive in their relationship with others in society. The lesson learned from corporate scandals is that trust in the political as well as economic marketplace will erode unless corporate managers consciously incorporate concern for the public interest in their decision making.

When an organization applies the managerial creed and achieves mutually satisfying relationships with its stakeholders, it is likely advancing the public interest. Thus employees feel they are paid fair wages and benefits and that other personal needs are cared for; investors feel that the dividends or interest received is satisfactory; the community is satisfied with the jobs provided, taxes paid, and other benefits received from an organization; and customers are pleased with the variety, quality, and price of products and services purchased. The aggregate of these satisfied stakeholders can be summed up by saying that the public interest has been served. As suggested by the managerial creed, however, a balancing of different stakeholder interests is needed because their interests are not necessarily compatible. For example, paying high wages to employees may lead to higher prices, and satisfying investors' desire for higher returns may lead to smaller philanthropic contributions to the community or recklessness with environmental goals. The concept of the public interest requires that all stakeholders recognize the need for compromises among them.

An expression of the managerial creed is the willingness of corporations to collaborate with opposing groups. For example, Jerry D. Choate, recently retired chairman and CEO of Allstate Insurance,[36] said the need to engage employees has become more important in light of the recent increase in mergers and acquisitions. Business has gone too far in absolving itself of social responsibility. It should at least attempt to provide employment security. To this end, the Collective Bargaining Forum, a group of key U.S. business and labor leaders, agreed on this principle: acceptance by corporations of employment security, the continuity of employment for its workforce, as a major policy objective that will figure as importantly in the planning process as product development, marketing, and capital requirements.[37] Labor was also assigned responsibilities. In a related statement, the Forum states, "All parties to an enterprise should support strategies and practices necessary to secure and maintain a competitive market position while enhancing the employment security and marketability of the workforce."[38]

Identifying Stakeholders

A corporation is more than what appears on a formal organizational chart, with the board of directors on the top and its chain of command headed by the CEO. As Chester Barnard observed in his classic *Functions of the Executive*, outside groups like customers are essential parts of an organization and form the extended organizational chart. The field of public relations is based on the recognition that an organization must identify all of the publics that can affect an organization's welfare. This requirement is well-stated by James E. Grunig, a professor at the University of Maryland and editor of the influential book *Excellence in Public Relations and Communication Management:* "The first step in strategic management of public relations, therefore, is to make a list of the people who are linked to or have a stake in the organization."[39] These people are called publics, stakeholders, or constituents, terms that are often used interchangeably. Several authors classify and describe an organization's strategic stakeholders. In their *Managing Public Relations*, Grunig and co-author Todd Hunt, list and describe some of them in the context of four key linkages that are critical for an organization to survive:

- Functional linkages: Inputs from employees, unions, and suppliers, and outputs to consumers, industrial purchasers, users of services, and employers of graduates.
- Enabling linkages: Stockholders, Congress, state legislators, government regulators, boards of directors, and community leaders.
- Normative linkages: Associations, political groups, and professional societies.
- Diffused linkages: Environmentalists, community residents, students, voters, minorities, women, media, and other publics.[40]

The same idea of identifying and categorizing an organization's strategic publics appears in the management literature. James E. Post, Lee E. Preston, and Sybille Sachs list three components of what they call the *extended enterprise* in the framework of three dimensions:

1. Resources (investors, shareowners, and lenders; employees; customers, and users).
2. Industry structure (supply chain associates, regulatory authorities, unions, and joint venture partners and alliances).
3. Social-political setting (governments, private organizations, local communities, and citizens).[41]

Another contribution to stakeholder management is described by James R. Emshoff and R. Edward Freeman.[42] Its two basic principles are that (a) the central goal is to achieve maximum overall cooperation between the entire system of stakeholder groups and the objectives of the corporation, and (b) the most efficient and effective strategies for managing stakeholder relations involve efforts to deal simultaneously with issues affecting several stakeholders. These are the same principles followed by public relations, although initially Freeman relegated public relations to serving as a buffer between an organization and society, whereas stakeholder management was credited with focus on negotiations. As chapter 3 indicates, negotiations are used in public affairs and public relations in dealing with interest groups.

A Relationship Model

Public relations scholars have added important ideas to the concept of stakeholder relationships. The basic contention is that the primary goal of public relations is to build effective relationships with various constituencies. Reflecting the managerial creed, another principle is that "effective organizations are able to achieve their goals because they choose goals that are valued both by management and by strategic constituencies, both inside and outside the organizations."[43] The joint endeavor of management and its constituencies is to cultivate and maintain long-term relationships. It is important to measure the outcome of relationship-building activities. Four measures have been proposed: (a) mutual satisfaction, (b) trust, (c) commitment, and (d) control mutuality.[44]

When an organization and a stakeholder group fulfill the expectations of the other, mutual satisfaction results. The aggregate of all the mutual satisfactions is one way of assessing whether an organization is advancing the public interest. When mutual satisfaction is achieved, trust, a second dimension of a relationship, is more likely to be achieved. The trust of stakeholders is won when they believe that the corporation is acting in their interests as well as its own. This state of affairs is more likely when some degree of control mutuality—"the degree to which parties agree on who has the rightful power to influence one another—is achieved."[45] In the context of the public interest, the most relevant aspect of control mutuality is whether management recognizes the value of inputs from its stakeholders and listens to them.[46] A popular name for this kind of decision making is participatory management. This form of management, along with mutual satisfaction and trust, is likely to lead both parties to want to continue the relationships (i.e., commitment is achieved).

Betrayal of Trust. One outcome of a relationship, trust, has been severely damaged during the last decade.[47] Since the Enron and other corporate scandals, Wall Street has recognized that it faces a crisis of confidence. Trust is a component of public confidence in business, which, in turn, is affected by the presence or absence of transparency. Transparency, a topic discussed in chapter 14, is one of the prerequisites for establishing trust and a solid, long-term relationship. When people do not trust the information they are given, they lose confidence. Corporations and financial institutions are consequently engaging in confidence-building campaigns in the hope that trust will be restored.

Former American Airlines CEO Donald J. Carty provides a glaring example of how trust can be betrayed. After the union membership had narrowly voted to accept $1.62 billion worth of annual concessions in the name of "shared sacrifice" to avoid bankruptcy, Carty admitted that he and six other executives still benefitted from executive-retention bonuses and pension protections. *BusinessWeek* called this lack of timely disclosure a megablunder.[48] Carty was seen as trying to pull a fast one on the unions. Later he and the other executives agreed to give up their retention bonuses, which would have paid them twice their base salary.[49]

Restoring trust was the theme of the Public Relations Coalition, a partnership of 19 major U.S.-based organizations representing corporate public relations, investor relations, public affairs, and related communications disciplines. They have challenged corporate America to do three things: adopt ethical principles, pursue transparency and disclosure in everything they do, and make trust a fundamental precept of corporate governance. Its first report, "Restoring Trust in Business: Models for Action," contains several worthy ideas.[50] A basic one, credited to Arthur W. Page, who is recognized as the first corporate public relations vice president in the history of public relations, is the view that "real success, both for big business and the public, lies in a large enterprise conducting itself in the public interest and in such a way that the public will give it sufficient freedom to serve effectively."[51] To this end ethical behavior must be encouraged and promoted.

In discussing disclosure and transparency, the report emphasizes the importance of creating an open company and lists nine steps, among which are these:

- Be willing to disclose all of your business, social, and political activities, as long as doing so does not raise legal issues or jeopardize your competitive position in the marketplace.
- When addressing issues of public concern, localize the message by involving company employees in affected communities and enlisting the help of independent, objective third parties.
- Proactively engage your stakeholders in dialogue, with particular emphasis on employees and middle management.[52]

The report reflects the application of the relationship model, especially the importance of making trust a board-level precept. This is in keeping with new corporate governance guidelines.

INCORPORATING THE PUBLIC INTEREST
IN CORPORATE GOVERNANCE

A potent way to incorporate the public interest into corporate policymaking and decision making is to link it to corporate governance. Even before recent developments in corporate governance reforms, Peter Drucker, the management guru, wrote in a well-known *Wall Street Journal* editorial, "The Real Duties of a Director": "The board is responsible for making sure that a company has adequate policies for its key outside relationships—with government, with the labor union, with the public in general; and that it have adequate policies with respect to its legal and regulatory responsibilities."[53]

Drucker's ideas were reflected at the 54th American Assembly on Corporate Governance in America held in the late 1970s when business leaders recognized that "Boards of directors have a primary role in interpreting society's expectations and standards for management."[54] These leaders recognized that boards of directors were indeed the key organ by which the corporation interfaces with society—and not only with the economic marketplace. This was a major theme in the 1970s in response to consumer, environmental, and other social movements. They concluded that corporations "can and should improve their responsiveness to emerging social and ethical questions." One suggestion was to hold open regional meetings with public groups to discuss social issues and related corporate actions. The assembly stressed the importance of disclosure, recognizing the value of a well-informed public. For this reason they recommended giving the press access to "responsible and well-informed corporate officers." These and other policies and procedures pertaining to corporate governance deserve to be revisited in the wake of today's loss of public confidence in corporations.

Signs are appearing that corporations are reforming their corporate governance structures, not only in the traditional operational and financial areas but also in the social and public responsibility areas. Responding to this interest, management consultants, law firms, and public relations firms offer a variety of services in advising on corporate governance.[55] Moreover, some companies and professional groups are making efforts to comply with the spirit of reform. GE, for example, made the following changes, some of which exceed Sarbanes-Oxley and the NYSE proposals:

- Two-thirds of GE's board members must be independent—a matter not addressed by the Sarbanes-Oxley Act, and the NYSE requires only a majority to be independent. All members of the audit committee are independent.
- Directors not employed by GE must meet at least three times a year without management present, a requirement only in the NYSE proposals.

- Each director must visit two GE businesses a year without representatives of corporate management, which is not required by federal law or the NYSE.
- GE senior managers must hold a specified amount of company stock as part of their salaries and hold for at least a year any GE shares they acquire through stock options, neither of which is required by federal law or the NYSE.[56]

Most of the post-Enron discussions about corporate governance have focused on the need for greater transparency, greater responsibility by boards, and their restructuring (e.g., more independent directors). With all the attention going to financial reforms, little has been said about the broader issue of improving corporate responsibility to society and acting in the public interest. These are concerns of public affairs and public relations. As stated by Douglas A. Pinkham, president of the Public Affairs Council, "Many business leaders claim to understand how their business environment affects long-term profitability, but remarkably few embrace all of the public relations and public affairs tools available to them."[57] Wes Pederson, editor of the *Public Affairs Review*, reinforces this view by reminding business executives, "Sadly, business lagged for years in its understanding of the political effects of corporate governance despite the pleas of savvy CEOs and public affairs professionals for corporate transparency and ethical orthodoxy."[58]

To integrate public interest considerations in corporate governance, three promising approaches have been discussed: (a) forming a public interest committee, (b) expanding the composition of the board, and (c) conducting social audits and publishing social reports

Form a Public Interest Committee

The formation of a public interest committee—also labeled public policy, corporate responsibility, or social responsibility committee—is a useful structural addition to corporate governance. Such a group could educate board members on significant happenings in the larger society and introduce new ideas on how to relate to this larger world. An excellent example is Dow Chemical, whose corporate governance structure includes a Public Interest Committee:

> The Public Interest Committee shall have oversight responsibility and shall advise the Board on matters impacting corporate social responsibility and the Company's public reputation. The Committee's focus includes the Company's public policy management, philanthropic contributions, international codes of business conduct, and corporate reputation management. Recognizing that positive perceptions of the Company's policies and practices are valuable assets, the Committee will monitor these perceptions and will make recommendations to the Board and management to continually enhance the Company's public standing.[59]

Such board committees are reminiscent of the 1970s when they were seen as a response to the social issues and concurrent public pressures that arose in the 1960s. Top management recognized that a full board often cannot devote enough time and consideration to social issues. Nor do board members feel they have sufficient specialization in this area, a fact recognized by Milton Friedman. One of the first companies to establish a public policy committee was GM in 1970 as a response to Ralph Nader's proxy resolution, "Campaign GM." The then GM chairman, Richard C. Gerstenberg, described its purpose as follows:

> The purpose of the Committee is to give matters of broad national concern a permanent and prominent place at the highest level of management—and I emphasize "at the highest level of management"—on the board of directors which ought to be the first to perceive change and the first to grasp the opportunity of responding to it.
>
> The Committee's mandate is to inquire into every phase of the corporation's business activities that relates to matters of public policy, and to recommend any changes it feels appropriate to management or the full board of directors. The Public Policy Committee assures us that broad national concerns are considered in the major policy decisions of the corporation.[60]

As of early 1979, the Conference Board identified 103 companies with public policy committees. A notable one was GE, whose function corporate strategist Ian Wilson described as providing "an independent checkpoint on the issues—present or potential—that affect General Electric; and to appraise the effectiveness of management's response."[61] A *Harvard Business Review* article listed 35 companies with public responsibility committees, including Aetna Life and Casualty Company, AT&T, Citicorp, International Paper, Philip Morris, and Sears, Roebuck.[62]

Members of a public interest committee should represent diverse backgrounds, including experience outside the world of business. A survey showed that their number was somewhat larger than that of most other board committees, ranging from 3 to 14 members, with the median size of 5 to 6. Most of them were outsiders, although 55% of the committees included some insider directors (e.g., retired CEOs). Most committees included more women, minorities, and academics than are typically on corporate boards of directors. As a university president on one committee reported, managing conflicting interest groups can be a challenge.[63]

The charter of a public interest committee might include the following activities:

- Identify major constituencies, both internal and external, and examine what each expects of the corporation's performance socially and environmentally.

- Recommend specific issues for board and management consideration.
- Recommend corporate policy to respond to the priority issues.
- Consider and recommend potential new areas of social responsibility and involvement.
- Examine and report to the full board on corporate attitudes toward the needs and concerns of the major constituencies of the corporation.[64]

These are typical concerns of public affairs and public relations specialists who can provide staff support to public interest committees. Every large public corporation should have an office that represents the interests and concerns of its extended organization, which includes all of its stakeholders. Public affairs and public relations professionals can identify issues and trends affecting the corporation, analyze them, and recommend appropriate management responses. This broader function exceeds the stereotypical PR function of "serving as unthinking conduit to the media, and of being responsible for 'polishing the corporate image.'"[65]

Some senior public relations counselors recommend that corporations consider such broad-scope executive vice president titles as public diplomacy, corporate public policy, or advisor to the CEO on public policy.[66] In revamping its corporate governance, Tyco, which suffered through a scandal, created another kind of position: that of a corporate ombudsman. This person, along with the company's senior vice president of corporate governance and the vice president, corporate audit, reports directly to the board of directors. At least some of the information a public interest committee would normally report directly to the board could be conveyed by the ombudsman.[67]

Expand Composition of Board Membership

Another way to introduce social and political considerations into board deliberations is to expand the composition of board membership. More is required than including more women on the board. Catalyst, the organization that advances women in business, reported in its 2003 annual census that women held 13.6% of all board seats in the *Fortune* 500 companies, an increase from 12.4% in 2001. The top 100 companies have at least one woman director and have the highest percentage of women directors, at 16.0%. Women of color hold 3.0% of board seats in 415 companies for which Catalyst has data.[68] From the perspective of reflecting the public interest, however, consideration must be given to special interest directors beyond the question of gender or race.

The proposal that boards should include public directors is highly controversial and presents practical problems of implementation.[69] One problem is knowing where to draw the line on what interests should be represented and whether their loyalty would be to the corporation or their interest group. The dominant view is that the basic legal responsibility of the board is to manage the company in the interests of the stockholders.[70]

Special interest directors, therefore, have appeared only under special conditions. A *BusinessWeek* editorial in 1987 stated that it would be "a good idea for unions—and employees generally—to be represented on boards of directors, particularly where workers own a significant amount of stock."[71] When employees represent a major cost factor or their unions are deemed to have significant political influence, boards may be motivated to include labor representatives. A notable past example is Chrysler, which during its effort to obtain a government bailout invited the president of the United Auto Workers to join the board.[72] Other examples of a labor voice on boards are United Steel Workers retired chief economist at CF&I Steel, retired president of Flight Engineers at Pan American Airlines, a Massachusetts Institute of Technology professor of industrial relations at PIE Nationwide, and former NLRB chairman and former director of the Federal Mediation Service at Transcon.[73]

In Germany the concept of "worker representative democracy" has a long history and has taken the form of codetermination. A 1951 law gave workers and union leaders in the larger mining and steel companies almost equal representation (5 of 11 members) with shareholders on corporate boards. A law passed in 1976 applies codetermination to most large German corporations.[74] In practice, a study by A. E. Bergmann concludes that in general workers' representatives have really been interested only in decisions that affect workers directly, such as personnel and welfare.[75]

Some corporations have nominated special interest directors in response to proxy resolutions. An early example is GM's appointment in 1971 of Reverend Leon Sullivan, a black urban affairs leader, in response to Ralph Nader's Campaign GM proxy resolution. The resolution demanded the inclusion of three "public directors." Illustrating the problem of conflict of interest, Sullivan claimed he represented the interests of blacks, not stockholders. He was able to increase advertising in black publications and increase the purchase of parts and supplies from black manufacturers.[76] Another example, is Exxon's appointment of Dr. John M. Steel, a scientist from the Woodshole Oceanographic Institute, to represent environmental interests.

The idea of public directors was pursued by Robert Townsend, former head of Avis Corporation, who in 1973 made the extreme proposal that all manufacturing companies with more than $1 billion in assets should be required to have public directors. This idea raises many basic questions. The major one is how such an individual would be selected and to what extent government would become involved. The meaning of the free enterprise system would be undermined. Would this be a role of members of corporate accountability groups, such as the Committee for Economic Development, Council on Economic Priorities, the Independent Sector, or the Interfaith Center on Corporate Responsibility? One of the duties of such a director would be to call at least two press conferences a year to report on the company's progress or lack thereof on issues of public relevance.[77]

There is no indication that corporations will institute public directorships, but their purpose can to at least a small degree be achieved through social audits and social reports.

Conduct Social Audit and Publish Social Report

In 1953, Howard R. Bowen, an economist, made a bold proposal that "Just as businesses subject themselves to audits of their accounts by independent public account firms, they might also subject themselves to periodic examination by independent outside experts who would evaluate the performance of the business from the social point of view."[78] The resulting social audit can thus be seen as performing part of the function of a public director. Although one consulting firm, Abt Associates, experimented with the idea of a social audit, and even publishing a social balance sheet, corporations rejected the idea. As one vice president of public relations of a large firm said, there are two problems with the concept: The word *social* connotes socialism and the word *audit* conjures up government intrusion.

The stated purpose of a social report—also called public report, sustainability report, and corporate citizenship report—is to inform stakeholders and the general public about a company's social performance in selected areas, such as its handling of environmental issues, health and safety, community investment and philanthropy, governance, workplace issues, and ethics. The need to regain public confidence after disclosures of corporate deception and wrongdoing have made an increasing number of corporations eager to provide "greater transparency" in the social as well as financial arena, according to a study by the Public Relations Society of America and Business for Social Responsibility.[79] Supporting this finding, the Public Affairs Council reports that more than 200 CSR practitioners and communication professionals signed in to express their opinions when an online discussion of CSR reports was held by the London-based Institute of Public Relations and the British version of *PR Week*.[80]

These discussions recommended that social reports should go beyond journalistic efforts to describe laudable corporate programs in a seeming effort to demonstrate compliance with the increasing public demands and government regulations. Because the "gap between what companies do and what they say remains wide," the opportunity should be seized for corporations "to be open and honest with themselves, their employees, their customers, and the community about what they are doing."[81] Some suggestions:

- A company should state its social objectives and how it plans to achieve them.

- A two-way dialogue should be developed with stakeholders, giving them an opportunity to influence corporate decisions.
- Standards—such as ISO 14000, CERES, or the Sullivan Principles—should be employed.
- Ultimately reports should be verified by an external reviewer, which 35% of the companies in the PRSA study did (30% used an NGO, 30% a consultant, and 20% a for-profit accounting or auditing firm).

These aspects of social reports suggest that they should primarily be associated with business strategy rather than communications. Business strategy increasingly recognizes the value investors and others place on a company's intangible assets, including human capital and social capital. To be recognized as the other part of the double bottom line, social responsibility must be integrated into a company's policies and actions. Social reports can help communicate this information.

UPHOLDING A CORPORATION'S REPUTATION: THE CEO'S ROLE

Corporate governance changes that incorporate public interest considerations in deliberations will go a long way to reestablish public confidence in business. This will be reflected in improved corporate reputations, which is a major concern of corporate CEOs. They know that it matters whenever people can punish a company by buying products elsewhere, working elsewhere, and filing lawsuits. Whenever the option of not dealing with a company exists, or just the opposite, attacking a company through social activism or lobbying government for regulations, company reputation counts. The *PRWeek*/Burson-Marsteller CEO Survey 2003 shows that 81% of CEOs are concerned about their company's reputation, with 34% "very concerned" and 47% "somewhat concerned."[82]

Views differ, however, about what constitutes s company's reputation and how it is measured. The *Concise Oxford Dictionary of Current English* provides a good beginning by defining reputation as "what is generally said or believed about a person's or thing's character." When Harris Interactive and the Reputation Institute, a New York-based research firm, report the reputation of many of the best known companies, they ask people to name the companies they currently believe have the best and the worst reputations. This is followed up by a second survey of 22,000 online respondents that asks them about 20 attributes of the most nominated companies. An overall rating of each company is then made.[83] *Fortune*'s "America's Most Admired Companies" is probably the longest running and most highly visible of all reputation studies. Its typical sample of about 5,000 comprises "industry insiders": financial analysts, senior executives, and outside directors of the industries being evaluated. Each company is rated on eight attributes: quality of management; quality of products and services offered; innovativeness; value as a long-term investment; soundness of financial position; ability to attract, develop, and keep talented people; responsibility to community and/or environment; and wise use of corporate assets. To obtain the overall reputation score, ratings on the eight attributes are simply averaged.[84]

When overall measures of a company's reputation are based on what the general public thinks and says about an organization, they are of limited value. Such public opinion may be important in an antitrust decision involving a well-known company like Microsoft. More important and relevant are the impressions and attitudes of specific constituent groups, like investors, customers, or employees, because these stakeholders affect investment, purchasing, or employment decisions pertaining to a company. These are groups that likely have direct experience in dealing with a company and therefore have formed attitudes that represent their evaluation of the quality of relationships established. Perceptions among these groups may greatly differ, influenced by the segment of the company to which they are exposed. People with no connection with a company would at best have an impression, not an evaluation, of a company based on media reports or hearsay.

Judgments about the CEO play an important role in determining the quality of management. According to Leslie Gaines-Ross, chief knowledge and research officer at Burson-Marsteller, 50% of a company's reputation is determined by the CEO. She builds on this fact in her aptly titled book, *CEO Capital: A Guide to Building CEO Reputation and Company Success*. She defines CEO capital as:

> the asset created by a CEO's reputation (not mere public acclaim) when it is harnessed to advance a company's success. It is the collective esteem that significant others, inside and outside a company, hold for the company's chief executive officer and, as a consequence, for the company. CEO capital is the composite of perceptions about a CEO that a company's stakeholders hold, whether these constituents are employees, Wall Street analysts or investors, customers, the media, government regulators, community leaders, or other business influentials.[85]

When corporations face serious crises of management deception or misconduct, CEOs are the ones who are blamed and replaced by new CEOs with untarnished reputations. An example is the replacement of WorldCom's defamed Bernard J. Ebbers with Michael D. Capellas, former CEO of Compaq and a recent president of Hewlett-Packard.[86] The turnover rate of CEOs reflects their vulnerability as well as a judgment of corporate performance. Half of all current CEOs have held their jobs for less than 3 years, according to a survey of 476 global corporations in 2000 by the outplacement firm Drake Beam Morin.[87] Leslie Gaines-Ross found that "Close to two-thirds of all major companies replaced their CEOs in the past five years."[88] As the fallout from corporate scandals continued, *USA Today* reported on June 10, 2002, that CEO job losses were running two a day in 2002 thus far.[89] In May 2002 alone there were 80 CEO departures, according to outplacement firm Challenger Gray & Christmas. Apparently boards of directors agree with the admonition of Warren Buffet: "If you lose dollars for the firm by bad decisions, I will be understanding. If you lose reputation for the firm, I will be ruthless."[90]

This concern about corporate reputation has elevated the role of public relations counsel. Compared to other professionals, they are at the forefront of managing a company's reputation. Julia Hood, editor-in-chief of *PRWeek*, comments, "It is clear that public relations has grown in stature among America's CEOs as they begin to understand its role in shaping their companies' reputations." In fact, the survey reports that 75% of CEOs mention the contribution of internal PR counsel and 35% mention external PR counsel. CEOs also turn to their board of directors 29% of the time and their internal legal staff or attorney 25% of the time (which is up from 9% last year). Chris Komisarjevsky, former president and CEO of Burson–Marsteller Worldwide, notes that reputation and litigation threats are considered in tandem far more often: "Now the lawyers and PR professionals sit at the same table."[91]

Whether a company's reputation can be managed, however, is questionable.[92] Publicity efforts that put a positive spin on all that a company does may result in improving a company's image, as would various forms of image advertising. Although such efforts might influence a general public that has little or no direct experience with a company, they are unlikely to affect a company's important stakeholders. Customers, investors, and employees in particular would base their impressions and attitudes on their experience with a company's actual behavior; that is, on their relationship with the company. The fundamental purpose of public relations is to help an organization improve these relationships. Communication contributes because better two-way communications, combined with efforts to collaborate with stakeholders, help to achieve this goal. Communications are also needed to assure that a company's positive performance is known by its constituents.

The CEO, as the chief communicator and ultimate spokesperson for a company, plays a vital communication role and, therefore, affects the company's reputation. Ideally, the CEO possesses good communication skills. Public relations assistance in speech writing and dealing with the media, as well as media training sessions, can help. Modern public relations practice, however, goes far beyond media relations and communications. It includes monitoring the sociopolitical environment and analyzing issues, preparing crisis contingency plans, planning and executing public affairs campaigns, and, in general, engaging in problem-solving about matters involving public opinion and the public interest.

As recognized by Komisarjevsky: "We are the ones who devote our careers to studying human behavior, anticipating reactions and, in some cases, knowing better than anyone else what the implications will be."[93]

Komisarjevsky also believes that public relations managers are the guardians of integrity "by identifying issues during their earliest stages and before they grow into a crisis. We play a very important role in shaping organizational values and behavior." One of these is in the establishment and expression of CSR as described earlier in this chapter. He says, "The covenants between the individual and the community, the employee and company, and the company and its unions are unalterably changed." He quotes Harold Burson, chairman of Burson-Marsteller, on the relationship between public relations and CSR: "I do not believe there is a relationship between the two. They are not cousins or even siblings. They are even closer than identical twins. They are one and the same."[94]

CSR in the broad sense of managing a company for the benefit of all of its stakeholders is one way to sustain a company's reputation and public confidence in business. Improving transparency and reforming corporate governance are other essential measures.

CONCLUSIONS

The growing disquietude of the public with corporate behavior reflects the need to place economic activity in the framework of society. From this perspective, the basic purpose of the economic system is to provide the goods and services wanted by consumers and the public goods required by society. A chart of this relationship would show these major outputs of the economy balanced by society's inputs of capital, labor, and other factors of production. The implication is that the economic system does not exist for the sole purpose of allowing managers and entrepreneurs to make money, even though profit maximization is the guiding motivator of every business.

Corporations must stay attuned to changing public standards of CSR. By achieving the double bottom line of profits and social responsibility, corporations have less to fear from government and social action groups.[95] Corporations have learned that they can reduce the extent of government involvement by looking beyond the bottom line and considering their relationship to society. To reflect the added corporate goal, some corporations have examined and even practiced the changes in corporate governance discussed earlier.

By adopting the broader managerial creed in preference to the narrowly focused classical creed and by accepting the goal of a double bottom line, corporations become better integrated with society. Changing the composition of boards of directors and adding the public interest to their concerns helps to institutionalize the enlightened approach to societal expectations. Furthermore, new approaches in stakeholder management are likely to improve relationships with an organization's strategic stakeholders and advance the public interest. These efforts, together with the major theme of this book of promoting a pluralistic society in the political marketplace, enable corporations to maintain public confidence. By demonstrating that they use their power not only for self-gain but also to address larger societal issues, corporations allay public fears of corporate power and assure a system of sustainable capitalism.

ENDNOTES

1. This concept is explained by Rogene A. Buchholz, *Business Environment and Public Policy: Implications for Management* (Englewood Cliffs, N.J.: Prentice-Hall, 1982), p. 20.
2. Henry Mintzberg, *Power in and Around Organizations* (Englewood Cliffs, N.J.: Prentice-Hall, 1983), p. 577.
3. The Business Roundtable, *Statement of Corporate Responsibility*, October 1981, p. 1.
4. Jerry Useem, "From Heroes to Goats ... and Back Again?" *Fortune*, November 18, 2002, p. 43.
5. Accountants use one word for goodwill; public relations people usually use two words: good will.
6. *Public Affairs Council 45! Sapphire Anniversary Report* (Washington, D.C.: Public Affairs Council, 1999), p. 31.
7. Leslie Gaines-Ross, *CEO Capital: A Guide to Building CEO Reputation and Company Success* (New York: Wiley, 2003), p. 220.
8. Keith Davis and Robert L. Blomstrom, *Business and Society*, 3rd edition (New York: McGraw-Hill, 1975), pp. 6–7.
9. Howard Bowen, *Social Responsibilities of the Businessman* (New York: Harper & Row, 1953), p. 155.
10. Michael E. Porter and Mark R. Kramer, "The Competitive Advantage of Corporate Philanthropy," *Harvard Business Review*, Vol. 80, December 2002, p. 58.
11. Ibid.
12. Archie B. Carroll used this term but listed different tiers. See his "The Pyramid of Corporate Social Responsibility: Toward the Moral Management of Organizational Stakeholders," *Business Horizons*, Vol. 34, July–August 1991, pp. 39–48. These levels agree with a host of descriptions of CSR.
13. Robert W. Ackerman and Raymond A. Bauer, *Corporate Social Responsiveness: The Modern Dilemma* (Reston, Va.: Reston, 1976).
14. "Business Ethics: Doing Well by Doing Good," *Economist*, April 22, 2000, p. 65. Friedman did, however, acknowledge, "It is entirely appropriate ethat men make sacrifices to advocate causes in which they deeply believe. Indeed, it is important to preserve freedom only for people who are willing to practice self-denial, for otherwise freedom degenerates into license and irresponsibility." Arthur Sharplin, "A Challenge to Shareholder Supremacy in the Public Firm," *Business and Society Review*, Vol. 108, Summer 2000, No. 2, p. 232.
15. See Otto Lerbinger, *The Crisis Manager: Facing Risk and Responsibility* (Mahwah, N.J.: Lawrence Erlbaum Associates, 1997), p. 252.
16. Leslie Scism, "Florida Regulators Investigate Met Life," *Wall Street Journal*, November 6, 1997, p. A3.

17. Paul Hawken, Amory Lovins, and L. Hunter Lovins, *Natural Capitalism: Creating the Next Industrial Revolution* (Boston: Little, Brown, 1999), p. 3.

18. Ibid., p. 9.

19. Gaines-Ross, op. cit., p. 180.

20. Roger Thurow and Susan Warren, "Pump Priming: In War on Poverty, Chad's Pipeline Plays Unusual Role," *Wall Street Journal*, June 24, 2003, p. A1.

21. Chun-ju Flora Hung, *The Interplays of Relationship Types, Relationship Cultivation, and Relationship Outcomes* (Doctoral dissertation, University of Maryland, 2002).

22. See *Response*, a publication of the Center for Corporate Public Involvement, for examples.

23. Alex Frangos, "Here Comes the Sun," *Wall Street Journal*, November 12, 2003, p. B1.

24. Michael A. Santoro, "Engagement With Integrity: What We Should Expect Multinational Firms to Do About Human Rights in China," *Business & the Contemporary World*, Vol. X, No. 1, 1998, p. 30.

25. Ibid., pp. 34–45.

26. David Finn, *The Corporate Oligarch* (New York: Simon & Schuster, 1969), p. 250.

27. Erin White, "PR Firms Advise Corporations on Social-Responsibility Issues," *Wall Street Journal*, November 13, 2002, p. B10.

28. Robert L. Dilenschneider, "Public Relations for the New Millennium: Back to Social Responsibility," *Public Relations Strategist*, Vol. 5, Spring 1999, p. 12.

29. Ibid.

30. Ibid.

31. Lynn W. Paine, *Value Shift: Why Companies Must Merge Social and Financial Imperatives to Achieve Superior Performance* (New York: McGraw Hill, 2002).

32. "Company's Collapse Shows System Works," *CBS News*, Vol. 10, Issue 1, 2002, p. 6.

33. *USA Today*, December 10, 2002, p. 1B.

34. B. Graves and Sandra A. Waddock, "Beyond Built to Last ... Stakeholder Relations in 'Built-to-Last' Companies," *Business and Society Review*, Vol. 105, No. 4, 2001, pp. 393–418.

35. Aaron Bernstein, "Too Much Corporate Power?" *BusinessWeek*, September 11, 2000, p. 149.

36. Melissa Berman, "Research Roundup: Boss Issues," *Across the Board*, Vol. 36, July–August 1999, pp. 55–56.

37. "Principles for New Employment Relationships: The Collective Bargaining Forum," *Perspectives on Work*, Vol. 3, No. 1, 1999, p. 33.

38. Ibid., p. 34.

39. James E. Grunig and Fred C. Repper, "Strategic Management, Publics, and Issues," in James E. Grunig, editor, *Excellence in Public Relations and Communication Management* (Hillsdale, N.J.: Lawrence Erlbaum Associates, 1992), p. 126.

40. James E. Grunig and Todd Hunt, *Managing Public Relations* (New York: Holt, Rinehart & Winston, l984); see chart on p. 141.

41. James E. Post, Lee E. Preston, and Sybille Sachs, "Managing the Extended Enterprise: The New Stakeholder View," *California Management Review*, Vol. 45, Fall 2002, p. 10.

42. A brief summary is James R. Emshoff and R. Edward Freeman, "Who's Butting Into Your Business?" *Wharton Magazine*, Vol. 4, Fall 1979, pp. 44–59.

Also see R. E. Freeman, *Strategic Management: A Stakeholder Approach* (Marshfield, Mass.: Pitman, 1984).

43. Linda Childers Hon and James E. Grunig, *Guidelines for Measuring Relationships in Public Relations* (Gainesville, Fla.: University of Florida, The Institute for Public Relations, 1999), p. 6.

44. Ibid., pp. 16–17, for a definitions of these outcomes.

45. Ibid., p. 1.

46. Control mutuality is expressed by sentiments like "the management of this organization gives people like me enough say in the decision-making process" and that "generally speaking, the organization and we are both satisfied with the decision-making process." Ibid., p. 2.

47. Trust consists of three components: (a) integrity—the belief that an organization is fair and just; (b) dependability—an organization will do what it says it will do; and (c) competence—the ability to do what it says it will do. Some typical expressions of trust or the lack of it in research on trust are: "Generally speaking, I don't trust the organization," "Members of the organization are truthful with us," and "The organization treats me fairly and justly, compared to other organizations." Ibid., pp. 1–2.

48. Wendy Zellner, "Commentary: What Was Don Carty Thinking?" *BusinessWeek*, May 5, 2003, p. 32.

49. Scott McCartney, "Unions Weigh Options at American," *Wall Street Journal*, April 21, 2003, p. A3; "AMR's Decision to Keep Quiet About Perks Could Undo Pacts," *Wall Street Journal*, April 22, 2003, p. A3.

50. John Elsasser, "From the Editor: The Public Relations Coalition Addresses the Crisis of Trust," *The Public Relations Strategist*, Vol. 9, Fall 2003, p. 1.

51. Ibid., p. 4.

52. PR Coalition, "Restoring Trust in Business: Models for Action," Supplement to *The Public Relations Strategist*, Vol. 9, Fall 2003.

53. Peter Drucker, "The Real Duties of a Director," *Wall Street Journal*, June 1, 1978, p. 20.

54. Leonard Silk, "American Assembly Consensus About 'Corporate governance,'" *New York Times*, April 18, 1978, p. 66.

55. Vanessa O'Connell and Stephanie Paterik, "PR Firms Get Into Advising on Governance," *Wall Street Journal*, July 22, 2002, p. B1.

56. Ibid.

57. Douglas G. Pinkham, "Reforming the Corporation: What Role for Public Affairs" *Public Affairs Review*, Annual Report 2003, p. 7.

58. Wes Pederson, "As Election '04 Nears, New Calls for an Examination of the Corporate Soul," *Public Affairs Review*, Annual Report 2003, p. 4.

59. See http://www.dow.com/corpgov/bylaws/comm.htm.

60. Phyllis S. McGrath, *Corporate Directorship Practices, Report No. 775* (New York: The Conference Board), 1980, pp. 1–2.

61. Ian Wilson, "One Company's Experience With Restructuring the Governing Board," *Journal of Contemporary Business*, Vol. 8, First Quarter, 1979, pp. 71–81.

62. Michael L. Lovdal, Raymond A. Bauer, and Nancy H. Treverton, "Public Responsibility Committees of the Board, *Harvard Business Review*, Vol. 55, May–June 1977, p. 60.

63. Ibid., p. 42.

64. Michael L. Lovdal, Raymond A. Bauer, and Nancy H. Treverton, "From the Boardroom: New Standing Committee Plays Active Policy Role in Initiating

Corporate Responses to Public and Social Pressures," *Harvard Business Review*, Vol. 55, May–June 1977, pp. 40–41.

65. James Lichtenberg, "Corporate Governance: Can the Firm Reach Its Public?" *Journal of Contemporary Business*, Vol. 8, No. 1, 1979, p. 119.

66. John F. Budd, Jr., "Public Relations Is the Architect of Its Future: Counsel or Courtier? Pros Offer Opinions," *Public Relations Review*, Vol. 29, November 2003, p. 382.

67. Eric M. Pillmore, "How We're Fixing Up Tyco," *Harvard Business Review*, Vol. 81, December 2003, p. 101.

68. Catalyst, *Perspective*, January 2004. See www.catalystwomen.org.

69. Buchholz, op. cit., pp. 116–117.

70. Mintzberg, op cit., p. 68.

71. Editorial, "Why Workers Belong in the Boardroom," *BusinessWeek*, December 14, 1987, p. 146.

72. The bailout is described in Buchholz, op. cit., pp. 134–137.

73. "Move Over Boone, Carl, and Irv—Here Comes Labor," *BusinessWeek*, December 14, 1987, p. 128.

74. Mintzberg, op. cit., p. 553.

75. A. E. Bergmann, "Industrial Democracy in Germany—The Battle for Power," *Journal of General Management*, Summer 1975, pp. 20–29.

76. Buchholz, op. cit., p. 116.

77. Robert Townsend, "A Modest Proposal: The Public Direct," in *Corporate Power in America*, Ralph Nader and Mark J. Greens, editors (New York: Grossman Publishers, 1973), pp. 157–259. Mentioned and discussed in Buchwald, op. cit., and Mintzberg, op. cit., p. 550.

78. Bowen, op cit., p. 155.

79. *pr reporter*, Vol. 47, January 5, 2004, p. 1.

80. Alastair Ray, "CSR: Altruistic Policy or Cover for Corporate Gaffes? Join the Debate," *Impact*, January 2004, p. 1.

81. Ibid., p. 4.

82. PRWeek/Burson-Marsteller CEO Survey 2003, "Wrestling With Rules and Reputations," *PR Week*, November 10, 2003, p. 17. The survey was based on a national study of nearly 200 American CEOs, conducted in October 2003 by Impulse Research. Written questionnaire were sent to CEOs at *Fortune* 1000 companies and their subsidiaries. See www.prweek.com for complete survey results.

83. Ronald Alsop, "Corporate Scandals Hit Home," *Wall Street Journal*, February 19, 2004, p. B1.

84. Jeffries-Fox Associates, *Toward a Shared Understanding of Corporate Reputation and Related Concepts; Phase II: Measurement Systems Analysis*, prepared for The Council of Public Relations Firms, March 24, 2000, Appendix B, pp. 25–30.

85. Gaines-Ross, op. cit., pp. 11–12.

86. Announced in WorldCom's full-page ad, *Wall Street Journal*, December 6, 2002, p. A7.

87. Shane McLaughlin, "A New Era: Managing CEO Successions in Tumultuous Times," *The Strategist*, Vol. 7, 2001, p. 9.

88. Leslie Gaines-Ross, "CEOs Stranded in Wonderland," *Journal of Business Strategy*, Vol. 23, March–April 2002, p. 18.

89. Del Jones and Gary Strauss, "CEOs Are Going, Going, Gone," *USA Today*, June 10, 2002, p. 1B.

90. Quoted in "CEO Reputation 2003," a brochure published by Burson-Marsteller.
91. Julia Hood, "Wrestling With Rules and Reputations," *PR Week*, November 10, 2003, p. 17.
92. James G. Hutton, Michael B. Goodman, Jill B. Alexander, and Christina M. Genest, "Reputation Management: The New Face of Corporate Public Relations?," *Public Relations Review*, Vol. 27, Fall 2001, p. 256.
93. Chris Komisarjevsky, "A Perspective on the Role of the Public Relations Professional," Remarks before the ICCO International Summit, Berlin, October 15–17, 2003.
94. Ibid.
95. This view is in accord with Bowman who says, "In the decades to come, one can expect that corporate power, as a socially comprehensive force, will be exercised with broad social objectives in mind, objectives that have traditionally been associated with the political governance of nations and empires, objectives that transcend mere economic interest." Scott R. Bowman, *The Modern Corporation and American Political Thought* (University Park, Penn.: The Pennsylvania State University Press, 1996), p. 282.

Author Index

435

Subject Index

Mercury News, 183
Mergers and acquisitions, 355
Merriam, Charles, 242
Merrill Lynch, 210, 391
Metabolife, 102
Metropolitan Life, 182l, 409
Metzger, Sidney M., 39
Meyerhoff, Al, 44
Michigan Journalism Fellows program, 200
Microsoft
    big soft money contributor, 278
    campaign contributions, 231
    entry into Beltway, 232
    importance of public opinion in
        antitrust suit, 426
    political resources, 12
    settles with Justice Dept., 314
Middleberg Interactive Communications, 104
Middleberg/Ross Survey of Media in
    the Wired World, 90, 125
Migid, Larry, 126
Military, 356
Millner, Guy loses election, 290
Milyo, Jeff, 202
Minnesota News Council, 177
Minot, N. D., 370
Mobil, 143, 156–157, 355
    imposes news boycott on Wall
        Street Journal, 113
Mobilize support with computers,
    267
Modes in strategic decision making,
    21
Mondale, Walter, 139, 208
Money, 273, 289
Monsanto
    general counsel speaks on litigation, 314
    represented by legal PR, 318
    targeted by Greenpeace, 40
Morgan Stanley, 399
Moskowitz, Laurence, 121
Mother Jones, 175
Motorola, 141, 210
MoveOn.org 527 group, 280
    held contest on best anti-Bush
        ads, 288
    used to organize rally, 298
Moyers, Bill, 366, 370
MSNBC, 127

Municipal Yellow Book, 238
Murdoch, Rupert, 370
Muris, Timothy, 205
Mutual gains approach, 78
Mutual satisfaction
    outcome of relationship building,
        417
Mutually beneficial relationship, 16,
    406

N

New York Times, 110
Nader, Ralph, 28, 32, 232
    "Campaign GM," 421
    SLAPP suits, 383
NADIA, 213
National Association of Broadcasters
    opposes free political advertising,
        387
    provide travel gifts to gov't officials, 240
National Association of Criminal Defense Lawyers, 332
National Association of Life Underwriters, 265
National Association of Manufacturers (NAM), 324
National Association of Radio Talk
    Show Hosts, 129
National business groups, 234
National Cable & Telecommunications Association, 240
National Cattlemen's Association, 115
National Education Association, 259
National Federation of Independent
    Business, 234, 250, 268
    identifies audiences by activism
        and political connection,
        266
National Grassroots & Communications, 266
National Highway Traffic Safety Administration, 192
National Institute on Money in State
    Policies, 299
National Journal, 161
National Labor Relations Act, 199
National Labor Relations Board, 368
National News Council, 113, 176
    sides with Shell and Exxon, 194
    The Day files complaint, 113

9 780805 856439